DATE DUE

MAR 0 3 2001	
DEC 1 1 2002	
FEB 2 8 2004	
4/24/04	
May 9-09	
11/3/2016	

1. Tehuantepec
2. Nicaragua
3. Panama

Prize Possession is a comprehensive history of U.S. policy towards the Panama Canal between 1903 and 1979, focussing on five salient themes: the canal's defence and its place in American strategy; the Zone's regimental system of government; its strictly segregated labour force; its commercial development at the expense of Panama; and the equally controversial issue of U.S. intervention in Panamanian politics. The book is based for the most part on hitherto largely untapped sources of U.S. government agencies, namely, the State, War, and Navy departments and the Canal Zone administration, as well as on the papers of such key figures as Philippe Bunau-Varilla, General George Goethals, and Theodore and Franklin Roosevelt.

Prize Possession

Prize Possession
The United States and the Panama Canal
1903–1979

JOHN MAJOR

CAMBRIDGE
UNIVERSITY PRESS

Published by the Press Syndicate of the University of Cambridge
The Pitt Building, Trumpington Street, Cambridge CB2 IRP
40 West 20th Street, New York, NY 10011–4211, USA
10 Stamford Road, Oakleigh, Melbourne 3166, Australia

First published 1993

Printed in the United States of America

Library of Congress Cataloging-in-Publication Data
Major, John, 1936–
Prize Possession: the United States and the Panama Canal,
1903–1979 / John Major.
p. cm.
Includes bibliographical references.
ISBN 0–521–43306–1
1. United States – Foreign relations – Panama.   2. Panama – Foreign
relations – United States.   3. Panama Canal (Panama)   I. Title.
E183.8.P2M24 1993   92–32406
327.7307287 – dc20   CIP

A catalog record for this book is available from the British Library.

ISBN 0–521–43306–1 hardback

To my family

This canal, with the exception of our home territory, is the most valuable possession we have.

(Senator Claude Swanson, 14 July 1919)

In all the range of our international relations, I do not hesitate to affirm that there is nothing of greater or more pressing importance than the construction of an inter-oceanic canal. Long acknowledged to be essential to our commercial development, it has become, as the result of the recent extension of our territorial dominion, more than ever essential to our national self-defense.

(President Theodore Roosevelt, 4 January 1904)

Contents

vii

Contents

Part IV. Recessional: 1956–1979

Part V. Epilogue

Preface and acknowledgements

'What's a fucking bloody guy like you doing down here?' The question came from the Panama Canal Commission pilot who escorted me aboard the tanker *Achilles* at the Balboa terminal on 4 April 1981. He already had his own answer. As he turned away to pour himself a cup of coffee, I heard him mutter the single word 'Subversive!'

I was not in fact the agent of an international Yankeephobe conspiracy. I was in Panama to explore the canal administration's archives as part of my work on a history of the United States and the canal. When the project first took shape, I had planned to use Panamanian as well as American sources, but when I made enquiries at Panama's Washington embassy, I was told that their records were 'in the process of organisation' for the foreseeable future. So I was compelled to base the study exclusively on American material, and here again I had to reduce its original scope. I had wanted to develop a picture not only of U.S. government policy but also of the American community in the Canal Zone. Regrettably, the sheer volume of official documentation took so much time to absorb that I abandoned the idea of investigating the Zonians. As a result, an important dimension of the Zone's experience is missing from my survey, and the gap must be left for someone else to fill.

What I have attempted, then, is an historical analysis of the way in which the United States operated and defended the Panama Canal and of the impact the canal made on its relations with the tiny republic whose heartland that waterway cut in two. The view is thus the view from Washington – from the White House, the Congress, and the State, War, and Navy departments – and from the U.S. agencies on the isthmus – the canal régime and the military and naval commands in the Zone, and the American diplomatic mission in Panama City.

The examination of American policy in the seventy-five-year lifetime of the Zone follows on two introductory chapters. The first covers Washington's

pursuit of an isthmian canal in the nineteenth century; the second, its controversial acquisition of treaty rights to build and control a canal in Panama.
Thereafter I have defined the subject in terms of five topics: the administrative
structure of the Zone; the Zone's repercussions on the politics of Panama; the
influence of the Zone on the Panamanian economy; the management of the
canal's tri-national labour force; and the problems of canal defence in a period
dominated by war and the threat of war. The penultimate chapter charts the process whereby Washington eventually decided to transfer authority over the
canal to Panama via the treaties signed in 1977. The last chapter brings out the
significance of the canal to the United States as an expression of its national
might.

My thanks are due to numerous institutions and to a host of individuals, many
of whom became friends in the course of the enterprise. I gratefully acknowledge the generous grants-in-aid given me by the British Academy, the Economic
and Social Research Council, and the Sir Philip Reckitt Educational Trust. I
was greatly encouraged by successive heads of my department, namely John
Kenyon, Richard Vaughan, Ken Andrews, Bill Speck, David Palliser, Howell
Lloyd, and above all that penetrating anatomist of inter-American affairs Gordon
Connell-Smith.
   The staffs of the following libraries provided me with every facility I could
have wished: American Federation of Labor – Congress of Industrial Organiza-
tions; the British Library's Newspaper Division at Colindale and its Document
Supply Centre at Boston Spa; the Brynmor Jones Library, University of Hull;
Cambridge University Library; the Center for Air Force History, Washington,
D.C.; the Franklin D. Roosevelt Library, Hyde Park, New York; the Library of
George Washington University; the Library of Congress Reading Room and
Manuscript Division; the Nimitz Library of the U.S. Naval Academy; Princeton
University Library; Stanford University Libraries; and the Sterling Memorial
Library, Yale University.
   I also owe a personal word of thanks to Roger Anders, archivist at the U.S.
Department of Energy; David Herschler, of the Office of the Historian, U.S.
State Department; Allan Lodge of Rhodes House Library, Oxford; John Pinfold
of the British Library of Political and Economic Science; Donald Ritchie of
the Historical Office, U.S. Senate; Celso Rodríguez of the Department of Cul-
tural Affairs, Organization of American States; Jack Shulimson of the Marine
Corps Historical Center, Washington Navy Yard; Peter Snow of the Bodleian
Library, Oxford; and Hannah Zeidlik of the Center for Military History,
Washington, D.C.
   The following gave me indispensable help in my work on the records of the
Panama Canal: U.S. Army historian Carol Rodrigues; Pandora Alemán, Chief
Archivist of the Panama Canal Commission; Harold Carroll, Keeper of the

Commission's Diablo Heights archive; Nan Chong, Librarian of the Commission's Panama Canal Collection; Beverly Williams and Irene de González, also of the Collection's staff; Melvin Kennedy, Chief of the Graphic Branch; Hazel Murdock of the Washington Secretariat; and two indefatigable custodians at the Washington National Records Center at Suitland, Maryland: Patrice Brown and Fred Pernell.

For their introduction to the material on the U.S. Navy in the 1940s, my gratitude goes to the staff of the Naval Historical Center, Washington Navy Yard, notably Dean Allard and his team at the Operational Archives; John Reilly, head of the Ships' History Branch; and the personnel of the Navy Department Library.

My debts to the staff of the U.S. National Archives are manifold, and I wish to pay particular tribute to all who helped me in the Central Research Room and the Microfilm Reading Room.

My thanks, too, to the Audiovisual Division, which houses the incomparable collection of canal photographs, and to R. Michael McReynolds of the Judicial, Fiscal, and Social Branch of the Civil Archives Division.

Members of the Modern Military Branch supplied me with invaluable guidance to the records of the U.S. Army in the 1940s: Robert Wolfe and his dedicated staff, notably Marilla Guptil, Wilbert Mahoney (who also greatly assisted me at Suitland), Gibson Bell Smith, and John Taylor.

In the Navy and Old Army Branch I wish particularly to thank Timothy Nenninger, Dale Floyd, Michael Musick, and Cary Conn for their exemplary professionalism, which made it possible for me to come to terms with the awesome mass of material in their charge.

The Diplomatic Branch was likewise a patient and assiduous pathfinder, and here I should like to thank Milton Gustafson and his staff, especially Gerald Hains, Sally Marks, Cathy Nicastro, and Ronald Swerczek, who kept me furnished with the equally voluminous output of the State Department.

I should also like to single out a number of individuals who, in their several ways, made my workload easier to bear: Karl Bendetsen, William Braisted, Ernesto Castillero Pimentel, Jorge Conte Porras, Elliott Converse, Margot and Cabot Coville, Robert Eldridge, Karl Habermann, Charles Hadfield, Thomas Leonard, Alice McClintic, Anthony Moncrieff, Ambler Moss, Antony Preston, Hatsue Shinohara, Robert Sprague, Roger Squires, Philip Taylor, Haruo Tohmatsu, and George Westerman. Thanks besides to my indefatigable typist Mrs Gill Fincham, who made immaculate sense of my less than perfect manuscript, and to Frank Smith, Herbert Gilbert, and Jane Van Tassel of Cambridge University Press, who carefully shepherded it through to publication.

I am especially indebted to Jane Brooks, who gave me a second home in Washington throughout almost the whole span of my research. The sprightly companionship of Sergei Tolstoi provided welcome light relief from the pressures of work. That doyen of Panama Canal historians the late Captain Miles DuVal, USN, was an unfailing source of advice and new documentation. My good friends Alger and Isabel Hiss provided me with a highly agreeable respite from my labours, in New York City and East Hampton. Bob Love, of the U.S. Naval Academy, helped the project along in numerous ways, not least through the hospitality offered in a series of pleasant Annapolis weekends, together with his wife Rose and his children, Robert and Kirstie. Michael Conniff, the leading authority on the West Indians in Panama, was everything a colleague should be and quite remarkably generous in sharing his material with me.

Finally, my family. My late and greatly missed father-in-law, Eric Waggott, scrutinised several articles and chapters in draft, always with something pertinent and useful to say. My daughter, Jenny, copied the typescript with breathtaking speed and efficiency. My son, Patrick, turned up recherché matter from the shelves of various Oxonian libraries. My wife, Rosemary, worked for six weeks in the U.S. National Archives and produced a record output of flawless notes. I cannot thank her enough for this and for many other reasons.

Without the aid of all those listed, the finished product would undoubtedly have been even longer in the making. The responsibility for it is, of course, entirely mine, and I hope it will be of more than passing interest, in particular to the American reading public. One Saturday lunchtime I was engaged in conversation by an elderly fellow researcher in the snack bar of the National Archives. Echoing the jibe repeatedly tossed out by Reagan in 1976, he asked me what I thought of 'that tin-horn dictator they've got down there'. When I replied that General Torrijos seemed to be voicing the same nationalism as the Egyptian Colonel Nasser when he took the Suez Canal from Britain in 1956, he clearly found the parallel outrageous. And, like the paranoid pilot, he did not take kindly to alien intruders moving into the sensitive area of a vital American interest. 'Well, professor,' he grated as he took his leave, 'I'm sure we all look forward with impatience to the enlightenment you're going to provide.' I sincerely trust he won't be disappointed.

Cottingham   J. M.
February 1993

Abbreviations used in the notes

AAF: AAG	Army Air Forces: Air Adjutant General, Bulky Files 1942–4 (U.S. National Archives, Washington, D.C., Record Group 18)
AAF: CDF	Army Air Forces: Central Decimal Files, 1939–42 (U.S. National Archives, Washington, D.C., Record Group 18)
AG	Adjutant General of the U.S. Army:
	1784–1917 (U.S. National Archives, Washington, D.C., Record Group 94)
	post-1917 (U.S. National Archives, Washington, D.C., Record Group 407)
BB	Bureau of the Budget, Executive Office of the President (Series 39–37) (U.S. National Archives, Washington, D.C., Record Group 51)
BB Report	U.S. Congress, House of Representatives, *Communication from the President of the United States transmitting the report and recommendations of the Bureau of the Budget with respect to the organization and operations of the Panama Canal and Panama Railroad Company* . . . (1950)
BD	Library of Congress, Congressional Research Service, *Background documents relating to the Panama Canal* (Washington, D.C., 1977)
B-V Papers	Papers of Philippe Bunau-Varilla (Library of Congress, Manuscript Division)
CDC	Caribbean Defense Command, U.S. Army
CINCUS	Commander-in-Chief, U.S. Fleet, U.S. Navy
CIT	Confederación Interamericana de Trabajadores
CNO	Chief of Naval Operations, U.S. Navy

CR	*Congressional Record*
CS	Chief of Staff, U.S. Army
CZ	Canal Zone
DDRS	*Declassified Documents Reference System*, various years (Arlington, Va., 1976–81; Woodbridge, Conn., 1982–)
Drafts	Drafts of Treaties, vol. 4, Department of State, 1903–6 (U.S. National Archives, Washington, D.C., Record Group 59)
Executive Orders	U.S. President, *Executive orders relating to the Panama Canal (March 8, 1904, to December 31, 1921)* (Mount Hope, CZ, 1922)
FBI	Federal Bureau of Investigation
FDR	Franklin D. Roosevelt
FRUS	U.S. Department of State, *Papers relating to the foreign relations of the United States*, various years (1866–1946); *Foreign relations of the United States: Diplomatic papers*, various years (1948–69); *Foreign relations of the United States*, various years (1969–91)
GAO	General Accounting Office
GB	General Board of the U.S. Navy (Operational Archives, Naval Historical Center, Washington Navy Yard, Washington, D.C.)
Goethals Papers	Papers of George Washington Goethals (Library of Congress, Manuscript Division)
GSR	General Staff Reports, U.S. Army, 1903–17 (U.S. National Archives, Washington, D.C., Record Group 165)
Hay Papers	Papers of John Hay (microfilm edn) (Library of Congress, Manuscript Division)
HCMMF	House Committee on Merchant Marine and Fisheries, U.S. Congress
Hiss Papers	Papers of Alger Hiss (U.S. National Archives, Washington, D.C., Record Group 59)
HPCD	U.S. Army, Caribbean Defense Command, Historical Section, *History of the Panama Canal Department*, 4 vols. (Quarry Heights, CZ, 1947)
ICC	Isthmian Canal Commissions, 1904–14 (Washington National Records Center, Suitland, Md., Record Group 185)
ICC Report	U.S. Isthmian Canal Commission, *Annual report* [for the years ending 1 December 1904, 1905, and 1906, and for the fiscal years 1907 to 1914] (Washington, D.C., 1904–14)

JAG	Judge Advocate General, U.S. Army
JB	Joint Board of the U.S. Army and Navy, 1903–38 (U.S. National Archives, Washington, D.C., Record Group 225)
JCS	Joint Chiefs of Staff, U.S. Armed Forces (U.S. National Archives, Washington, D.C., Record Group 218)
JPC	Joint Planning Committee, U.S. Army and Navy
Libro azul	Colombia, Ministerio de relaciones exteriores, *Libro azul: Documentos diplomáticos sobre el canal y la rebelión del Istmo de Panamá* (Bogotá, 1904)
Loomis Papers	Papers of Francis D. Loomis (Stanford University Libraries, Stanford, Calif.)
MID	Military Intelligence Division, U.S. Army (pre–August 1941) (U.S. National Archives, Washington, D.C., Record Group 165)
MID-D	Military Intelligence Division, U.S. Army (post–August 1941), Decimal File 1941–5 (U.S. National Archives, Washington, D.C., Record Group 165)
MID-G	Military Intelligence Division, U.S. Army (post–August 1941), G-2 Geographic Subject File 1940–6, Latin American Branch (U.S. National Archives, Washington, D.C., Record Group 165)
MID-R	Military Intelligence Division, U.S. Army, Regional File 1933–44 (Washington National Records Center, Suitland, Md., Record Group 165)
MS	Microform supplement (to *Foreign relations of the United States*)
MTC	Metal Trades Council
NAACP	National Association for the Advancement of Colored People
NFL	Notes from Foreign Legations to the U.S. Department of State, 1863–1903 (U.S. National Archives, Washington, D.C., Record Group 59)
1911 Hearings	U.S. Congress, Senate, Committee on Interoceanic Canals, *Hearings . . . on . . . a bill to provide for the opening, maintenance, protection and operation of the Panama Canal, and the sanitation and government of the Canal Zone* (1912)
1950 Hearings	U.S. Congress, House of Representatives, Committee on Merchant Marine and Fisheries, Subcommittee on the Panama Canal, *Hearings on authorization and provision for the maintenance and operation of the Panama Canal*

	by the present corporate adjunct of the Panama Canal, as renamed (1950)
1906 Hearings	U.S. Congress, Senate, Committee on Interoceanic Canals, *Investigation of Panama Canal matters: Hearings . . .* (1907)
1960 Hearings	U.S. Congress, House of Representatives, Committee on Foreign Affairs, Subcommittee on Inter-American Affairs, *Hearings on United States relations with Panama* and *Report on United States relations with Panama* (1960)
NLP	Notes from the Legation of Panama to the U.S. Department of State, 1903–6 (U.S. National Archives, Washington, D.C., Record Group 59)
NSAM	National Security Action Memorandum
NSC	National Security Council
NYT	*New York Times*
OA, NHC	Operational Archives, Naval Historical Center, Washington Navy Yard, Washington, D.C.
OF	Official File, Franklin D. Roosevelt Library, Hyde Park, N.Y.
ONI	Office of Naval Intelligence, U.S. Navy (U.S. National Archives, Washington, D.C., Record Group 38)
ONRL	Office of Naval Records and Library, U.S. Navy (U.S. National Archives, Washington, D.C., Record Group 45)
OpD	Operations Division, U.S. Army, 1942–6 (U.S. National Archives, Washington, D.C., Record Group 165)
OSA	Office of the Secretary of the Army
OSS	Office of Strategic Services (U.S. National Archives, Washington, D.C., Record Group 226)
OSW	Office of the Secretary of War
PC	The Panama Canal, 1914–51 (Washington National Records Center, Suitland, Md., Record Group 185)
PCC	The Panama Canal Company, 1951–60 (Washington National Records Center, Suitland, Md., Record Group 185)
POD	Plans and Operations Division, U.S. Army, 1946–50 (U.S. National Archives, Washington, D.C., Record Group 319)
RG	Record Group
Roosevelt Papers	Papers of Theodore Roosevelt (microfilm edn) (Library of Congress, Manuscript Division)

Root Papers	Papers of Elihu Root (Library of Congress, Manuscript Division)
SAPF	Secretary of the Army Project File, 1946–7 (U.S. National Archives, Washington, D.C., Record Group 107)
SASF	Secretary of the Army Subject File, 1940–2 (U.S. National Archives, Washington, D.C., Record Group 107)
SCFR, *Hearings*	U.S. Congress, Senate, Committee on Foreign Relations, *Hearings on [the Panama Canal treaties of 1977]*, 4 vols. (1978)
SD	State Department (U.S. National Archives, Washington, D.C., Record Group 59)
Sen. Deb.	U.S. Congress, Senate, Committee on the Judiciary, Subcommittee on Separation of Powers, *Panama Canal treaties [U.S. Senate debate] 1977–78*, 3 vols. (1978)
Skilled Labor	U.S. Congress, Senate and House of Representatives, Committees on Appropriations, *Extracts from hearings . . . relative to . . . conditions of employment of skilled labor on the Panama Canal . . . 1907–1915* (1914)
SLC	Standing Liaison Committee of the State, War, and Navy Departments, Minutes, 1938–41 (U.S. National Archives, Washington, D.C., Record Group 165: General Staff, Secretary, Series 30)
SN	Secretary of the Navy
SNGC	Secretary of the Navy General Correspondence, 1897–1926 (U.S. National Archives, Washington, D.C., Record Group 80)
SNSCC	Secretary of the Navy Secret and Confidential Correspondence (U.S. National Archives, Washington, D.C., Record Group 80)
SPD	Strategic Plans Division, U.S. Navy
Stimson Diary	Diary of Henry L. Stimson (Sterling Memorial Library, Yale University, New Haven, Conn.)
Stimson Papers	Papers of Henry L. Stimson (Sterling Memorial Library, Yale University, New Haven, Conn.)
SWCF	Secretary of War Classified File (U.S. National Archives, Washington, D.C., Record Group 107)
SWS–OC	Secretary of War Semi-Official Correspondence
Taft Papers	Papers of William Howard Taft (Library of Congress, Manuscript Division)

3 CFRC   United States, President, *Title 3 (The President) Code of Federal Regulations Compilation, 1936–65* (1968)

TR letters   Elting Morison (ed.), *The letters of Theodore Roosevelt*, vols. 1–7 (Cambridge, Mass., 1951–4)

TS   Top Secret

USD   Dispatches from U.S. Ministers in Panama to the U.S. Department of State, 1903–6 (U.S. National Archives, Washington, D.C., Record Group 59)

USNA   United States National Archives, Washington, D.C.

USSPCC   United States Special Panama Canal Commission

WCD   War College Division, U.S. Army, 1903–17 (U.S. National Archives, Washington, D.C., Record Group 165)

WNRC   Washington National Records Center, Suitland, Md.

WPD   War Plans Division, U.S. Army, 1917–42 (U.S. National Archives, Washington, D.C., Record Group 165)

YBUN   *Yearbook of the United Nations*, various years (New York, 1947–)

Dates in the notes and appendices are given in British style throughout: '1.8.14' means '1 August 1914'.

Prize Possession

Introduction

On 10 July 1992 the erstwhile *caudillo* of Panama, General Manuel Antonio Noriega, was sentenced by the U.S. District Court in Miami to forty years in jail for conspiring to smuggle cocaine into the United States. So ended a five-year campaign against Noriega waged by the U.S. government, beginning with the suspension of economic and military aid to Panama in July 1987. In February 1988 he was indicted by two federal grand juries for drug trafficking, and following his dismissal of the Panamanian president shortly afterwards the Reagan administration imposed a drastic set of financial sanctions. Noriega's access to Panama's dollar accounts in New York was blocked, revenues from the Panama Canal Commission were withheld, and all payments to Panama by American citizens were prohibited. At the same time, the U.S. garrison in the Canal Area was reinforced, a coup by the Panamanian army was encouraged, and an attempt was made to persuade Noriega to step down in return for dropping the drug indictments.[1]

None of it worked. After more than a year of pressure, the resourceful Noriega had still not been destabilised, even though the sanctions inflicted more economic damage, in the view of a former U.S. ambassador, 'than . . . since Henry Morgan, the pirate, sacked Panama City in 1671'. In May 1989 he prevented the winner of the presidential election, Guillermo Endara, from taking office. In October a second army putsch failed, and in November Noriega again refused a deal which would have sent him into early retirement. So President George Bush decided to mount Operation JUST CAUSE, a large-scale military intervention involving 24,000 U.S. troops launched on 20 December. In the process, 26

---

[1] *Guardian Weekly*, 19.7.92, 17/3–5. Andrew Zimbalist and John Weeks, *Panama at the crossroads: Economic development and political change in the twentieth century* (Berkeley, Calif., 1991), 146–9. Bruce Watson and Peter Tsouras (eds.), *Operation JUST CAUSE: The U.S. intervention in Panama* (Boulder, Colo., 1991), 201–4.

I

Americans lost their lives, along with at least 700 Panamanians. Some 18,000 Panamanians were reportedly made homeless, and estimates of the losses caused by the invasion ranged between $1 and $2 billion. All this was the price paid for the installation of Endara and the capture of Noriega, who surrendered on 3 January, to be taken to Florida for his eventual court appearance.[2]

The objectives of the intervention, as Bush outlined them, were fourfold: 'to protect American lives, to defend democracy in Panama, to apprehend Noriega and bring him to trial . . . , and to ensure the integrity of the Panama Canal Treaties [of 1977]'. In the opinion of most of the international lawyers who have given their verdict on the operation, none of these justifications was valid. JUST CAUSE, in their view, was a grossly disproportionate response to the threat posed to the American community in Panama by the Noriega régime and went far beyond the administration's claim to have acted in self-defence. Despite Noriega's atrocious record on human rights, intervention to change a country's political system had always been deemed an infringement of national sovereignty. The seizure of Noriega was likewise a violation of Panamanian sovereignty, since U.S. law enforcement had no right to trespass on a foreign jurisdiction, even though Noriega was charged with an international crime. And although the canal treaties gave Washington the authority to safeguard the waterway, Noriega had made no move against it during the entire period of the pre-invasion crisis, and riders to both accords expressly excluded intervention in Panama's politics from the scope of U.S. military action.[3]

If all these arguments held good, then other forces underlay the American strike. It could simply be that the chief executive of the most powerful state in the world would no longer endure the humiliation of being outfaced by such a petty challenger as Noriega. Some years earlier, Reagan's UN ambassador, Jeane

[2] Statement by Ambler Moss of 4.5.88 in U.S. Congress, House of Representatives, Committee on Foreign Affairs, Subcommittee on Western Hemisphere Affairs, *The Political situation in Panama and options for U.S. policy: Hearing*, 100th Cong., 2d ses. (1988), 37. Zimbalist and Weeks, *Panama*, 152–5. Watson and Tsouras, *JUST CAUSE*, 207–20.

[3] *Public papers of the presidents of the United States: George Bush: 1989*, vol.2 (Washington, D.C., 1990), 1734. Hostile commentaries on the invasion include Charles Maechling, 'Washington's illegal invasion', *Foreign Policy*, no. 79 (Summer 1990), 113–31; Louis Henkin, 'The invasion of Panama under international law: A gross violation', *Columbia Journal of Transnational Law*, 29 (1991), 293–317; Jennifer Miller, 'International intervention – The United States invasion of Panama', *Harvard International Law Journal*, 31 (1990), 633–46; Ved Nanda, 'The validity of United States intervention in Panama', *American Journal of International Law*, 84 (1990), 494–503; and John Quigley, 'The legality of the United States invasion of Panama', *Yale Journal of International Law*, 15 (1990), 276–315. For papers sympathetic to the action, see that by the former legal adviser to the State Department, Abraham Sofaer, 'The legality of the United States action in Panama', *Columbia Journal of Transnational Law*, 29 (1991), 281–92, and Anthony D'Amato, 'The invasion of Panama was a lawful response to tyranny', *American Journal of International Law*, 84 (1990), 516–24.

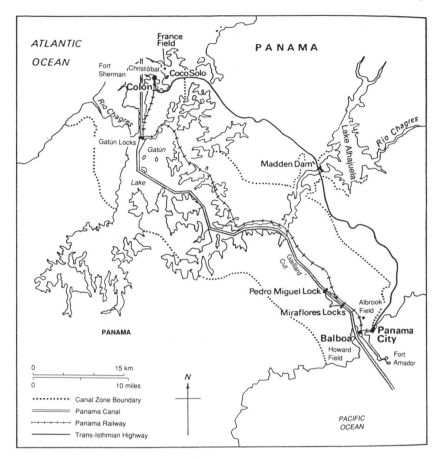

The Panama Canal Zone

Kirkpatrick, had drawn a distinction between communist and non-communist dictatorships, the totalitarians and the authoritarians. The latter, she claimed, were 'less repressive' than their Marxist counterparts, 'more susceptible to democratic change' and 'less likely to be hostile to the interests of the USA'. Noriega's whole performance since taking over in 1983 had effectively shifted him into the totalitarian category. Once the ally of Washington in its vendetta against the revolutionary Sandinista government of Nicaragua, he had begun to run out of control, and his time was up. Other equally baleful satraps who had outlived their usefulness, Diem in South Vietnam and Marcos in the Philippines, had been taken care of by their internal opposition, but that had not happened in Panama. The stage was thus set for the death-blow administered to such

errant figures as Mossadeq in Iran, Arbenz in Guatemala, Bosch in the Dominican Republic, Sukarno in Indonesia, Allende in Chile.[4]

Or, as a pair of recent analysts have suggested, the long-term history of
relations between the United States and Panama may help explain the climacteric
of 1989, though not quite in the way they and others seem to think. Washington
had been closely involved with Panama from 1848 on, by virtue of a treaty
which allowed it a right of way across the isthmus, soon given body in the shape
of the American-owned Panama Railroad. But the U.S. Navy detachments
landed periodically over the next half-century were under orders to protect the
railway, not to sort out the often factious politics of the province, and the same
priority governed the policy of Theodore Roosevelt in 1903. He sent in the
Marines to fulfil the ambition of 'a canal under American control', and abetting
Panama's secession from Colombia, as he did, was only a means to that end.
The canal treaty he then secured established a Canal Zone straddling the line of
the waterway, where the United States was sovereign and from which Panama
was entirely excluded. Britain was master of the Suez Canal via its occupation
of Egypt as a whole, but the United States had no need to colonise Panama,
thanks to possession of a private enclave. With the dissolution of the Zone in
1979, this immunity was lost overnight, and the Americans on the isthmus were
at once exposed to the Panamanian nationalism they had hitherto kept at a very
safe distance. And with the collapse of Noriega they found themselves drawn
into Panamanian affairs to a degree never required in the Zone's lifetime.[5]

This is not to say that the impact of the Zone on Panama was not extensive
and profound. The Roosevelt corollary of 1904, whereby the United States
asserted its right to be the policeman of the Americas, was not applied so
seriously in Panama as it was elsewhere, in Cuba, Nicaragua, Haiti, and the
Dominican Republic. Direct intervention on the isthmus ended in the mid
1920s, and the protectorate set up in 1903 was formally relinquished in 1936.
Yet no Panamanian government could ignore the bearing of the American
presence on its electoral politics or its public order and its national budget. The
Zone administration, by contrast, was well able to keep to a minimum the
interference of Panama – and Washington – in its own business. Its labour

---

[4] *Encounter*, 61 (November 1983), 31. Professor Kirkpatrick's thesis was first published in her
book *Dictatorships and double standards* (New York, 1982).

[5] John Weeks and Phil Gunson, *Panama: Made in the USA* (London, 1991), 18. Colby
Chester, 'Diplomacy of the quarterdeck', *American Journal of International Law*, 8 (1914),
443–76. John Major, 'Who wrote the Hay–Bunau-Varilla convention?' *Diplomatic History*,
8 (1984), 115–23. The point about the impact of the Zone's disappearance is made by Ruth
Wedgwood, 'The use of armed force in international affairs: Self-defense and the Panama
invasion', *Columbia Journal of Transnational Law*, 29 (1991), 610, and by Richard Millett,
'Looking beyond Noriega', *Foreign Policy*, no. 71 (Summer 1988), 58. Watson and Tsouras,
JUST CAUSE, 127–32.

policy largely cut Panamanians out of a canal work force made up of Americans
and West Indians, and its provision of Commissary stores for the Zonians
denied Panamanian suppliers entry to a lucrative market. Panama was also
expected to place itself at U.S. disposal whenever the defence of the canal
demanded it, subjecting its railroads, its highways, its radio broadcasting, and
its air traffic to American regulation and handing over whatever land outside
the Zone might be earmarked for canal purposes, operational or strategic.[6]

The Panamanian struggle against these manifold restrictions made comparatively little headway for decades but finally triumphed in the treaties of 1977
abrogating the 1903 convention and promising the withdrawal of American
troops and the transfer of the canal to Panama at the close of 1999. But, as the
crisis of the late 1980s proved, the instinct to hegemony in Washington still ran
deep in a State Department determined to pursue what Bush's admirers called
a 'muscular' foreign policy and in a Pentagon reportedly set on having a Panamanian government agreeable to a permanent U.S. military base on its territory.[7]

As one commentator put it soon after the swoop on Panama and the simul-
taneous end of the Cold War with the Soviet Union, 'military intervention by
the United States in Central America antedated the East–West contention, and
the Panama invasion demonstrated that it has outlived it'. In November 1915
Secretary of State Robert Lansing wrote with brutal candour that the Monroe
Doctrine was 'founded . . . upon a fact, namely the superior power of the United
States to compel submission to its will. . . . In its advocacy of the Monroe
Doctrine, the United States considers its own interests. The integrity of other
American nations is an incident, not an end.' Lansing was speaking of the need
to protect the canal as a vital national asset and to keep alien influence well away
from its approaches. Neither of these requirements was of much consequence
at the dawn of the new world order: The canal had long since lost the status of
a prize possession, and Japanese participation in studies of a replacement raised
few American qualms. But Panama remained a significant U.S. concern as a
vantage-point at the heart of the hemisphere from which to keep close tabs on
developments in the region as long as it continued to be politically cyclonic.
Judging by past experience, that would be for some considerable time to come.
If Washington has climbed down from its isthmian watchtower when General

[6] On the various repercussions of the Zone on Panama, see John Major, 'The Panama Canal
Zone, 1904–1979', in Leslie Bethell (ed.), *The Cambridge History of Latin America*, vol. 7
(New York, 1990), 645–61.

[7] Ibid., 665–7. Robert Love, *History of the U.S. Navy 1942–1991* (Pittsburgh, Pa., 1992),
808. Zimbalist and Weeks, *Panama*, 142–3, 165. Joseph Lombard, 'The survival of Noriega:
Lessons from the U.S. sanctions against Panama', *Stanford Journal of International Law*, 26
(1986), 317 n. 234, cites a Pentagon spokesman's description of Elliot Abrams, the most
prominent State Department interventionist, as 'extremely arrogant and a zealot in the
Oliver North mode'.

Noriega applies for parole in January 2000, it will be remarkable, to say the least. President Arnulfo Arias once described Panama and the United States as 'Siamese twins'. In the century to come, as in the century gone by, their destinies are almost certain to stay interlocked.[8]

[8] Quigley in *Yale Journal*, 315. Arthur Link (ed.), *The Papers of Woodrow Wilson*, vol. 35 (Princeton, N.J., 1980), 249, 252. Ambler Moss, 'A policy dilemma: The future of United States interests in Panama' (typescript of lecture delivered in October, 1988 at Bridgewater College), 9–10. For Arias's remark, see Chapter 11 at n. 34.

Part I

Prelude: 1826–1904

The Government of New Granada guarantees to the Government of the United States . . . the right of way or transit across the Isthmus of Panama . . . and the United States . . . guarantee . . . the rights of sovereignty and property which New Granada has and possesses over the said territory.

(Treaty between the United States and
New Granada, 12 December 1846)

The Republic of Panama grants to the United States all the rights, power and authority within the zone . . . which the United States would exercise if it were the sovereign of the territory . . . to the entire exclusion of the exercise by the Republic of Panama of any such sovereign rights, power or authority.

(Convention between the United States and
Panama, 18 November 1903)

1

The quest for an American canal,
1826–1903

In 1904 the United States gained treaty rights to build and control a canal across the isthmus of Panama. It was the fulfilment of a long-standing ambition. Washington had fixed on the transit as one of the country's key requirements, and it was to be seen as a critical element in American national security for generations to come. This book is mainly a study of the way in which successive governments handled their prize acquisition, but the roots of U.S. canal policy lie deep in the nineteenth century. The course of events then foreshadows many of the underlying features of the subsequent American approach to the waterway and adds an important dimension to our understanding of what Panama meant to the United States during its long tenure of this major interoceanic thoroughfare.

The idea of a canal across Central America dates from early in the sixteenth century, soon after the territory was absorbed into the burgeoning Spanish empire. Though Spain had access to the newly discovered Pacific Ocean by way of the Magellan Strait at the southernmost tip of the continent, the shortest approach to the Pacific lay via the Caribbean and the isthmus. When the search for a sea passage proved fruitless in the 1520s, plans for a canal were put forward. But these projects were bound to be visionary, given the limited technology of the period, and the only practical possibility was an overland crossing. Such a route already existed in Panama, where the ports of Panama City and Nombre de Dios had been linked by a paved track grandiloquently styled a royal highway. After Spain's conquest of the Peruvian Inca empire in 1532, it took on pivotal importance in the Spanish imperial economy. Silver from Peru was transshipped over Panama before being convoyed to Seville, and during the rainy season from May to November the trail was supplemented by the lower reaches of the Chagres River, which flowed into the Atlantic. The journey was slow – the fifty miles from coast to coast took four taxing days –

9

but travel by mule and river-craft was to be the best means of traversing Panama for more than three centuries to come.[1]

Interest in an isthmian canal revived in the 1780s, but it was given its biggest stimulus by the publication in 1811 of a work by the German explorer Alexander von Humboldt. Von Humboldt's verdict that the most suitable locations were Tehuantepec, Nicaragua, and Panama had already been reached in the mid sixteenth century. None the less, his book began an intense wave of canal speculation, and a host of blueprints flooded off the drawing board.[2]

The United States government became caught up in this movement in the 1820s, a favourable juncture on two counts. Technically, the prospects for a canal seemed good, and Americans were in the forefront of canal development. In 1822 the interoceanic Caledonian Canal was opened in Scotland, and in 1825 American engineers matched the achievement with the inauguration of the Erie Canal connecting the Hudson River and the Great Lakes. Politically, the collapse of the Spanish empire had removed Spain as an obstacle to American policy on the continent. Spain was replaced by half a dozen weak successor states, and in 1823 President James Monroe claimed that Washington was their sole defence against European reconquest. Before long his declaration was enshrined as a guiding principle of U.S. foreign relations: the Monroe Doctrine. Both in terms of technological prowess and national interest, therefore, the United States considered itself entitled to construct and to dominate a trans-isthmian canal.[3]

There were, however, several tremendous barriers in the way. First, a choice had to be made among the three possible routes, and even then the scheme's feasibility was doubtful. No canal had yet been built in the tropics, and the isthmus presented immense difficulties of climate and terrain, not to mention the steep tidal differential between the Caribbean and the Pacific. In the second place, it would be uphill work reaching agreement with any of the isthmian republics – Mexico, Central America, and New Granada. All were poor, backward, and unstable, incapable of engineering and defending a transit themselves, and dependent on foreign money, expertise, and protection to do it for them. Jealous of their newly won sovereignty, they were fearful of losing it to a domineering canal administration, and this made them deeply mistrustful negotiators. Finally, the United States faced a formidable rival in Britain, the

[1] Gerstle Mack, *The land divided: A history of the Panama Canal and other isthmian canal projects* (New York, 1944), 30–5, 40–2, 48–60.

[2] Ibid., 98–101, 111–19, 224. David McCullough, *The path between the seas: The creation of the Panama Canal, 1870–1914* (New York, 1977), 27–31.

[3] McCullough, *Path between the seas*, 31. Gordon Connell-Smith, *The United States and Latin America: An historical analysis of inter-American relations* (London, 1974), 54–5, 2–3, 61–3. See also, with reference to the whole of this chapter, Richard Collin, *Theodore Roosevelt's Caribbean: The Panama Canal, the Monroe Doctrine, and the Latin American context* (Baton Rouge, La., 1990), 127–236.

greatest naval and commercial power in the world, with every reason to be interested in the strategic and mercantile potential of an isthmian seaway. Britain also saw itself as the leading influence in post-colonial Latin America, and it possessed both the will and the resources to obstruct U.S. ambitions in the hemisphere.[4]

For the moment, therefore, the reach of the United States exceeded its grasp, and for some time to come every administration displayed realistic awareness of the republic's inferiority vis-à-vis Britain. Thus in 1826 when the government of Central America asked Washington to give its backing to a canal through Nicaragua, Secretary of State Henry Clay replied that no one country should have a monopoly over the project. While this appeared to be an act of self-denial, it was in fact aimed at preventing British control, and the readiness to accept a multilateral solution reflected inability to overlord canal development, not an idealistic devotion to internationalism.[5]

Washington's gingerly approach was again revealed a decade later. In 1836 the U.S. government agent, Charles Biddle, signed an exclusive contract with New Granada for modernising the 300-year-old *camino real* across Panama by building a new road or a railway from the Pacific coast to the Chagres and linking it up with a steamboat service on the river. He was disowned by an administration which had sent him on a purely exploratory mission. Similarly, after Panama seceded from New Granada in 1840 there was no attempt to exploit the situation and secure special privileges for the United States. When the New York canal promoter William Radcliff asked for American diplomatic recognition of Panama as the prelude to U.S. entry into a multinational canal consortium, his overtures were turned down. Radcliff pointed out that British interests were active in Panama: In 1841 the Royal Mail Steam Packet Company had secured a right of way over the isthmus from the secessionist régime. At the same time, Britain had occupied the port earmarked as the Atlantic terminal of a future Nicaraguan canal. But the most the State Department was ready to aim for was a commercial treaty with New Granada to block a British monopoly over the Panama transit. It was certainly not prepared to become involved in a treaty arrangement to build a canal and guarantee its neutrality, commitments far beyond anything yet undertaken by a state dedicated since its foundation to the avoidance of 'entangling alliances'.[6]

This unwillingness to make a practical reality of its professed wish to see a canal built and operated on a collaborative basis was highlighted in 1843 when

[4] Connell-Smith, *United States and Latin America*, 56–7, 67–8.
[5] Mack, *Land divided*, 172–3. *BD*, 3. Connell-Smith, *United States and Latin America*, 44.
[6] *BD*, 4. Mack, *Land divided*, 105, 125–6, 131, 181–2. William Manning (ed.), *Diplomatic correspondence of the United States: Inter-American affairs 1831–1860*, vol. 5, *Chile, Colombia* (Washington, D.C., 1935), 342, 526, 350–1, 547, 574–5, 579–81, 352–3. Connell-Smith, *United States and Latin American*, 69, 85. Manning, *Diplomatic correspondence*, 5: 353–4.

New Granada offered a canal treaty to the United States, Britain, and France. The administration did not even trouble to take a position on the proposal and left Britain to make the running. When London turned the treaty down in 1845, it came to nothing.[7]

Yet while Britain appeared indifferent to a Panama canal, it was much more assertive in Nicaragua. In 1844 London established a protectorate over the Mosquito coast, at the Atlantic end of the projected canal. British patronage of Mosquitia thus meant control of any Nicaraguan venture and domination of the Caribbean approaches to a Panama waterway. Therefore when Benjamin Bidlack was sent as U.S. minister to New Granada in the summer of 1845, he carried instructions to stop Britain from getting exclusive advantages in relation to the Panama route, by means of the commercial treaty which his predecessor had failed to clinch.[8]

In December 1846 Bidlack did sign a commercial treaty, but it went well beyond the limited agreement his masters had envisaged. U.S. benefits were twofold: the abolition of discriminatory tariffs against American trade, and a guarantee by New Granada 'that the right of way or transit across the Isthmus of Panama, upon any modes of communication that now exist, or that may be, hereafter, constructed, shall be open and free to the government and citizens of the United States'. In return Bidlack gave three things: a reciprocal cancellation of tariffs on New Granada's exports, and two far-reaching political guarantees. The first pledged 'the perfect neutrality of the . . . Isthmus, with the view that the free transit from the one to the other sea, may not be interrupted or embarrassed'. The other, deriving from the first, affirmed 'the rights of sovereignty and property which New Granada has and possesses over the said territory'.[9]

It remained to be seen whether Bidlack's engagements would be approved by the U.S. Senate. American protection for New Granada was objectionable for two reasons: Not only did it open up the risk of a clash with Britain, but since it came close to an alliance, it also ran counter to the abiding principle of diplomatic autonomy. President James Polk therefore had to justify the guarantee at some length, arguing that support for New Granada was better than risking a British monopoly. Bogotá – unlike London – was too weak to make control of the isthmus an international weapon, yet it was strong enough to provide the framework of civil government within which a modern transit could be built.[10]

After lengthy hesitation the Senate sanctioned the treaty, and it went into

---

[7] Manning, *Diplomatic correspondence*, 5: 598; vol. 7, *Great Britain* (Washington, D.C., 1936), 254–5 n. 1. E. Taylor Parks, *Colombia and the United States, 1765–1934* (Durham, N.C., 1935), 195–8.

[8] Manning, *Diplomatic correspondence*, 5: 622 n. 1, 605–6, 357. Eduardo Lemaitre, *Panamá y su separación de Colombia* (Bogotá, 1971), 58, 60–1.

[9] *BD*, 7–10.   [10] *BD*, 11–13.

force in June 1848. Passage of the accord was almost certainly clinched by its relevance to the mood of the country in the late 1840s. This was the moment when U.S. territorial expansion reached a climax under the banner of 'Manifest Destiny', the conviction that the United States had a mission to rule the entire North American continent. In 1845 Texas was annexed to the Union. In 1846 Britain agreed to divide the disputed Oregon Territory in the Pacific North-West, and the same year the country entered a war with Mexico which ended with the cession of New Mexico and Upper California. The urge to absorb the continent from coast to coast was accompanied by two other long-standing drives, to the west and south. In the early 1840s other powers had been warned off Hawaii, and a trade treaty had been signed with China; and the march to the Pacific seaboard was acclaimed as the prelude to a further westward advance across the ocean to Asia. The thrust south towards Latin America was marked by Polk's revival of the Monroe Doctrine in 1845, by the Mexican war, and by mounting pressure for acquisition of the island of Cuba from Spain as the centre-piece of a bid to make the Caribbean 'an American Mediterranean'.[11]

The Panama isthmus had a key rôle to play in all three movements. It was the hinge of the shortest sea route between Washington and its new possessions in the West. It offered much quicker access to Asia and the Pacific for the products of the industrial North-East. And it had high potential value as a local base for watching over American interests in the Caribbean and Central America. Bidlack's treaty was thus an outstanding token of the efflorescence of U.S. power. Though it did not grant the United States rights to a Panama canal, it gave Americans a privileged position on the isthmus which was consolidated well before the agreement went into force. In 1847 government contracts were made with steamship companies for services connecting Panama with New York, New Orleans, Seattle, and San Francisco. They came into operation in October 1848, just in time to reap huge profits from transporting prospectors via the isthmus to the Californian gold rush. Simultaneously the New York promoters of the Pacific shipping line formed the Panama Railroad Company and in December 1848 contracted with New Granada to build a trans-isthmian rail-way, work on which began in 1850. So an intercoastal route took shape which, in the absence of a transcontinental railway, was to be an American national asset of the first importance.[12]

The United States was also closely interested in the two other principal isthmian crossings, in Mexico and Nicaragua. In April 1847 the negotiators of

[11] Frederick Merk, *Manifest destiny and mission in American history: A reinterpretation* (New York, 1963), 24–60. Richard Van Alstyne, *The United States and East Asia* (London, 1973), 22–23. Connell-Smith, *United States and Latin America*, 71–2, 77–81.

[12] Manning, *Diplomatic correspondence*, 5: 585–7. John Kemble, 'The Panama route to the Pacific coast, 1848–1869', *Pacific Historical Review*, 7 (1938), 2–4, 11–12. Mack, *Land divided*, 138–9, 149–53. *BD*, 31.

the peace treaty with Mexico were authorised to double the proposed indemnity to get perpetual transit rights over Tehuantepec, and though they did not succeed, control of the route remained a high American priority. U.S. ambitions in Nicaragua were more restrained, given the British presence on the Mosquito coast, and it was not surprising that the government did not countenance a canal treaty negotiated independently by its minister, Elijah Hise. Signed in June 1849, this agreement represented the summit of American nationalist aspirations. It gave the United States a monopoly to build and operate a canal, and jurisdiction over its terminal cities. Washington was also given rights to fortify the transit, to put its warships through, and to ban the passage of enemy vessels in wartime. Nicaragua enjoyed no share in canal revenues and no reversionary rights in the waterway, but its sovereignty and neutrality were to be guaranteed by an American military alliance. All this was far beyond what Britain could be expected to tolerate, and Hise's successor, Ephraim Squier, was told to scale down both American concessions and American demands.[13]

Yet even Squier's treaty was too much for Washington to accept. A further compromise with Britain was considered necessary, in the form of the Clayton–Bulwer convention, signed in April 1850. Both states thereby renounced the right to exclusive control over a Nicaraguan canal and agreed not to fortify it. They would jointly guarantee its security and its neutrality, and extend their protection to any canal or railway built across Tehuantepec or Panama. All this was a bitter pill for ultra-nationalists to swallow, even though the treaty recognised the new weight which the United States carried as a result of the enormous territorial acquisitions it had made between 1845 and 1848.[14]

This made for a great deal of frustration over Nicaragua. The Pierce administration which came to office in 1853 was hostile to the Clayton–Bulwer compromise and felt itself entitled to negotiate a Nicaraguan canal treaty without reference to Britain. A succession of drafts fell through, however. The last, in March 1859, failed when Nicaraguan misgivings about American intentions made ratification impossible. In 1860 the United States still had no canal treaty with Nicaragua.[15]

Nor did Washington fare better with Mexico. Here too agreement on a canal was prevented by local suspicions of American policy, understandable in a country which had recently been forced to cede half its territory to the United

---

[13] Manning, *Diplomatic correspondence*, vol. 8, *Mexico, 1831 – June 1848* (Washington, D.C., 1937), 203–5. *BD*, 16–21. Manning, *Diplomatic correspondence*, vol. 3, *Central America, 1831–1850* (Washington, D.C., 1933), 383–6, 38–9, 40–1, 50–1, 360–1 n. 2, 367–9.

[14] *BD*, 27–30. Connell-Smith, *United States and Latin Ametica*, 86 n. 24.

[15] Connell-Smith, *United States and Latin America*, 86. Manning, *Diplomatic correspondence*, vol. 4, *Central America, 1851–1860.* (Washington, D.C., 1934), 343, 360, 385–6, 63; 7: 152–3; 4: 629 n. 2, 730 n. 1, 740–1, 143, 761–2, 172, 938, 945–53. Connell-Smith, *United States and Latin America*, 86–7.

States. When negotiations began in 1849, Mexico insisted on a series of safe-guards being built into the treaty draft. In the treaty eventually signed in 1853 the Mexicans conceded only a right of way over Tehuantepec, and it was not until 1859 that a settlement was reached granting the United States the right to transit troops. Yet the accord was defeated in the U.S. Senate as part of an alleged programme to extend slavery below the Rio Grande. So by the eve of the American Civil War, the possibilities of Tehuantepec had also come to nothing.[16]

There remained Panama. Here Britain did not wish to bring Clayton–Bulwer into play: Its stake in Panama was unimportant, and London was content for Washington to take the lead. So the British did not assert a claim to protect the railway across the isthmus which went into operation in 1855, and the sole guarantee of the line came from the United States under the treaty of 1846. Its first test arrived in April 1856, when traffic was interrupted by a riot in Panama City in which at least fifteen Americans were killed. The incident immediately exposed the fallacy of Polk's assumption that Bogotá could be relied on to provide an orderly environment within which rail services could function smoothly. In the official American view, the initial responsibility for keeping the track open fell on New Granada, but the U.S. minister, James Bowlin, urged Washington that if American lives and property were to be protected on the isthmus 'it must be by the strong arm of our own power'. The question would then be 'when they drive us to the necessity of governing it, whether we ought to govern it under the shadow of their power, or seize it and protect it as it should be protected for the uses of mankind'.[17]

Pierce was certainly prepared to take a strong stand. Warships were stationed at the terminal ports of the railway, Panama City on the Pacific and Colón on the Atlantic, and in September 1856, in the first of several such interventions, U.S. sailors and Marines were landed to occupy the railway station in Panama City for three days. This touch of gunboat diplomacy was followed by the presentation of a draft claims convention which set out a list of extravagant American demands. The first was for a zone twenty miles wide spanning the

---

[16] Manning, *Diplomatic correspondence*, vol. 9, *Mexico, June 1848–1860* (Washington, D.C., 1937), 40, 364 n. 4, 108, 119, 512–17. William Malloy, *Treaties, conventions, international acts, protocols and agreements between the United States and other powers, 1776–1909*, vol. 1 (Washington, D.C., 1910), 1124. Manning, *Diplomatic correspondence*, 9: 1138–40. Connell-Smith, *United States and Latin America*, 88–90. J. Fred Rippy, 'Diplomacy of the United States and Mexico regarding the isthmus of Tehuantepec, 1848–1860', *Mississippi Valley Historical Review*, 6 (1919–20), 503–31.

[17] Mary Williams, *Anglo-American isthmian diplomacy, 1815–1915* (Washington, D.C., 1916), 273. Joseph Smith, *Illusions of conflict: Anglo-American diplomacy toward Latin America, 1865–1889* (Pittsburgh, Pa., 1979), 88–92. Parks, *Colombia*, 221–3. Manning *Diplomatic correspondence*, 5: 746, 747.

railway and including the terminals. Order in the zone was to be maintained by United States consuls empowered to summon American naval and military forces in emergencies. Washington was also to be granted the franchise to have 'any other railroad or passageway' built across the isthmus.[18]

If accepted, these conditions would have given the United States absolute control over the Panama route, but this was not yet to be. There was fierce opposition from New Granada, which saw the American demands as a diktat to surrender Panama. This Bowlin denied: The nation, he affirmed, was 'averse to Colonies, and would not have it as a gift'. Bowlin was technically correct: The United States did not plan to make a colony of Panama, but American dominance of the railway zone would certainly have cut a deep gash in New Granada's sovereignty. More important, Washington had to reckon with Britain, the co-guarantor of the isthmus under the Clayton–Bulwer treaty. The British minister in Washington, Lord Napier, feared that the incoming Buchanan régime was on the brink of annexing Panama and in the spring of 1857 invoked Clayton–Bulwer. Soon afterwards, Secretary of State Lewis Cass signed a claims convention which contained none of the original American demands. Though Cass had told Napier that it was inadmissible 'that these Governments should exercise over [international highways] an arbitrary and unlimited control, or close them or embarrass them without reference to the wants of commerce or the intercourse of the world', the convention acknowledged New Granada's title to keep the peace along the railway.[19]

This was a complete climb-down by the United States, and the convention marked the return to a highly unsatisfactory status quo from the American point of view. The maintenance of order continued to depend on ad hoc interventions by the Navy, and the United States still lacked a firmer legal base for the protection of its interests in the Panama transit than the extremely general phraseology of the 1846 treaty. Its position was made even more unsure by the current political chaos in New Granada. In 1859 Panama broke away from Bogotá once more, and though it returned to the fold, under the new constitution of 1863 it was quasi-autonomous as part of the restyled United States of Colombia, a highly volatile confederation.[20]

One possible solution was to appropriate Panama. Amos Corwine, the official U.S. investigator of the 1856 riots, was to predict that the isthmus must sooner

---

[18] Parks, *Colombia*, 224. Manning, *Diplomatic correspondence*, 5: 399–403 n. 1. The model for this arrangement may well have been the Land Regulations of 1854 establishing municipal government for the British, French, and American communities in Shanghai.

[19] Manning, *Diplomatic correspondence*, 5: 835–7, 843, 856, 403, 859, 848. Richard Van Alstyne, 'British diplomacy and the Clayton–Bulwer treaty, 1850–1860', *Journal of Modern History*, 11 (1939), 180. Manning, *Diplomatic correspondence*, 7: 701–2, 709–10, 172–3. Malloy *Treaties*, 1: 319–21.

[20] Parks, *Colombia*, 299, 274, 224. Manning, *Diplomatic correspondence*, 5: 417 n. 4. Lemaitre, *Panamá*, 28–33.

or later fall into U.S. hands: The fruit was ripe and 'we need only come and take it'. His view was shared by no less a personage than the British prime minister. Writing on the very same day as Corwine, Lord Palmerston forecast that Washington would some time use adventurers to set up 'some independent North American state' on its behalf in Central America 'in alliance with the United States if not in Union with them, in short Texas all over again'.[21]

Colombia for its part was naturally anxious that Washington should stand by its promise to uphold Bogotá's sovereignty over the isthmus. In yet another flurry over Panamanian secession in 1866, Colombia took the view that the guarantee would come into play if there were a movement in Panama 'with a view to making that section of the republic independent and attaching it to any other foreign nation or power, that is to say, in order to transfer by any means whatever the sovereignty which Colombia justly possesses over that territory to any foreign nation or power whatsoever'.[22]

Secretary of State William Seward, however, was concerned only to safeguard the railway. He had already made this clear when he construed the U.S. pledge of neutrality in 1865. 'The purpose of the stipulation', Seward had said, 'was to guarantee the Isthmus against seizure or invasion by a foreign power only.' This he repeated a year later. 'The United States have always abstained from any connection with questions of internal revolution in the State of Panama . . . and will continue to maintain a perfect neutrality in such domestic controversies. In the case, however, that the transit trade across the isthmus should suffer from an invasion from either domestic or foreign disturbances of the peace in the State of Panama, the United States will hold themselves ready to protect the same.'[23]

In other words, the United States interpreted the treaty to serve its own interests in the protection of the transit route, not those of Colombia in the preservation of its national sovereignty. Yet the question was not nearly so simple. The railway could not be divorced from the politics of Panama, because it was the only rapid means of travel between its two chief political centres, Panama City and Colón. If by 'perfect neutrality' the United States meant excluding both sides in a civil conflict from using it, the stronger of the two would automatically be favoured, and neutrality would become a mockery. And if the use of the railway were denied to the Colombian government as well as to a rebel movement, that would be a violation of the 1846 treaty. Though it tried to escape the logic of its commitments to Colombia as regards the railway, Washington could not do so as long as the 1846 treaty remained in force.

---

[21] Parks, *Colombia*, 225–6. Kenneth Bourne, 'The Clayton–Bulwer treaty and the decline of British opposition to the territorial expansion of the United States, 1857–60', *Journal of Modern History*, 33 (1961), 290.

[22] *FRUS*, 1866, 579, 574–5.

[23] U.S. Congress, Senate, *Use by the United States of a military force in the internal affairs of Colombia*, 58th Cong. 2d sess., S. Doc. 143 (1904), 27. *FRUS 1866*, 572.

Seward - Railway

In 1868 the treaty was due to lapse unless renewed or renegotiated, and Washington wanted a new agreement, to get terms which would ensure the building of a Panama canal unequivocally under American control. The trans-continental railway across the United States, first mooted in 1845, was at last nearing completion, and once it was in business the Panama Railroad would lose its previous importance. But the railway had been seen from the start as the prelude to a canal. Bowlin in 1855 had declared 'as a fixed fact, that a Ship Canal will follow the Rail Road'. And pressure for a canal was intensified by the forthcoming opening of Suez. So the Johnson administration staked the American claim by negotiating treaties to cover the routes through Nicaragua and Panama.[24]

The Nicaraguan treaty of 1867 tried, like its predecessors, to reconcile the American preoccupation with the security of the transit and the junior partner's concern not to let the American watchdog become a menace to its own inde-pendence. Thus, though U.S. forces could be used to protect American lives and property without reference to Nicaragua, they could be sent in to defend the canal only with Nicaragua's agreement or at its request, and had to be withdrawn whenever the Nicaraguan government decided.[25]

The same tension underlay the canal treaty signed with Colombia in January 1869. For Washington the crucial issue in the negotiations was the defence of the transit, where it demanded complete responsibility, including the right to reserve the passage of troops to itself and Colombia at all times and to close the canal to enemy shipping during war. Yet if a naval power such as Britain contested that right, the canal area would become a theatre of war, and Colombian territory would be laid open to an attack against which the negligible U.S. Navy could afford virtually no security. Bogotá therefore conceded the right merely for American troops to pass through the canal in peacetime; in wartime the canal was to be closed to all belligerents, including the United States.[26]

In other ways too the treaty revealed Colombia's determination to protect its position. Though U.S. forces were to defend the canal, they were not to set up a permanent garrison, nor were they to act except under joint command. The canal was to be built and operated for one hundred years by the United States or its contractor, within a twenty-mile zone under American management but under Colombian sovereignty and jurisdiction. If the contractor encouraged secession in Panama, its grant would be forfeit. The 1846 American guarantee of the neutrality of the isthmus was reduced to a guarantee of the neutrality of the

[24] Manning, *Diplomatic correspondence*, 5: 700. See also Miles DuVal, *And the mountains will move: the story of the building of the Panama Canal* (Stanford, Calif., 1947), 3.

[25] Malloy, *Treaties*, vol. 2, 1279–87.

[26] U.S. Congress, Senate, *Correspondence in relation to an Interoceanic canal between the Atlantic and Pacific oceans, the Clayton–Bulwer treaty and the Monroe Doctrine, and the treaty between the United States and New Granada of December 12, 1846*, 56th Cong., 1st sess., S. Doc. 237 (1900), 37, 39–40, 48.

canal only, but the guarantee of Bogotá's sovereignty over the isthmus remained as before, and other powers were invited to subscribe to both pledges. Colombia was compensated first with 10 per cent and ultimately with 25 per cent of canal receipts, and the project was to revert to Colombia after the concession expired.[27]

The 1869 treaty was turned down by the Colombian Senate in the hope of still better things from the new administration of President Ulysses S. Grant. Grant, however, had committed himself to a canal that would be 'an American enterprise . . . to be undertaken under American auspices', and the terms of his treaty, signed in 1870, were much more favourable to the United States, giving it a huge land grant, sites for naval dockyards at both terminals, the right – shared only by Colombia – to send troops through in war as well as in peace, and authority to close the route to an enemy during hostilities. The quid pro quo for Colombia was a military alliance, but this was restricted to the canal zone and did not apply beyond it.[28]

This second attempt at a treaty also came to grief, however. When Colombia persisted in denying passage to all belligerent combat vessels in wartime, negotiations lapsed, and Secretary of State Hamilton Fish showed little interest in renewing them. In 1873 when Colombia submitted a fresh draft, Fish's reply was designed to ensure rejection. He refused to pledge the United States unconditionally to construct the canal; demanded that it be closed to enemy ships but withdrew the commitment to ally with Colombia in defending it; repudiated the guarantee of Colombia's sovereignty over the isthmus; doubled the size of the land grant; and reduced the Colombian share of the proceeds to 7 per cent. Understandably, the talks did not progress beyond this point.[29]

Fish's rebuff to Colombia partly reflected his own indifference. In conversation with the Colombian envoy in Washington he remarked that the United States had lost interest in the waterway now that the transcontinental railroad was in operation. But the unwillingness to come to terms with Colombia also stemmed from the fact that the administration was engaged in a long survey to decide which of the three main routes to choose should a canal be built. In 1876 the investigators opted for Nicaragua. This was the death-blow for Tehuantepec, and Panama too seemed knocked out of the running. Fish, however, did not press Nicaragua for a treaty, and Grant left the White House without inaugurating his all-American venture. Little more than a year after his retirement the foreign interests which the United States had contested for the past half-century moved in to take up where Washington had apparently left off.[30]

[27] Ibid., 45–51.   [28] Ibid., 51–61.

[29] Ibid., 75–6, 79, 103, 104, 110–11. Parks, *Colombia*, 351–4. Smith, *Illusions* 98. NFL, Colombia, vol. 6, Martín to Fish, 11.7.73; Despatches from Ministers, Colombia, vol. 29, Scruggs to Fish, 17.11.74.

[30] *FRUS 1874*, 363, 356. Parks, *Colombia*, 355. Jackson Crowell, 'The United States and a Central American canal, 1869–1877', *Hispanic American Historical Review*, 49 (1969), 45–9.

In March 1878 the French lieutenant Lucien Napoléon-Bonaparte Wyse secured a concession from Colombia for a canal in Panama. It was to be built and operated by a private company for ninety-nine years, after which time it would revert to Colombia; transfer of the grant to a foreign government was forbidden. The company would also be given a canal zone 400 metres wide, as well as whatever public lands might be needed to serve its purposes. Colombia was to be awarded up to 8 per cent of the tolls, and the payment was never to be less than $250,000 a year. In May 1879 the arrangement was approved by an international congress meeting in Paris, and the concession was bought by Ferdinand de Lesseps, the architect of the Suez Canal. De Lesseps went on to promote the Compagnie Universelle du Canal Interocéanique de Panama, with a view to starting work as soon as possible.[31]

This turn of events came as a severe shock to Washington. In the summer of 1879 the U.S. minister to Bogotá, Ernest Dichman, forecast that the Wyse contract would put American interests in serious jeopardy. Neither the company nor Colombia could police the canal against internal disorder or defend it against external attack. Since the canal's security would eventually have to be guaranteed by the United States, Dichman argued, Washington should have control over the management and use of the transit. As it was, the agreement allowed foreign troops to pass through the canal only with the permission of the Colombian Congress, and it ordained that the waterway should be closed in wartime to all but Colombian naval vessels. The first stipulation collided head-on with American rights of way under the 1846 treaty, and the second denied the United States a vital strategic advantage. At the same time, the formation of de Lesseps's company raised the spectre of a French colony on the isthmus, in clear defiance of the Monroe Doctrine and its stand against new European enclaves in the hemisphere.[32]

The immediate American response was guarded. One possible option would have been to detach Panama from Colombia. But Washington did not need to go to the extreme of backing a breakaway movement so long as it could get what it wanted from Colombia. Instead President Rutherford B. Hayes voiced the U.S. concern over Panama through a major policy speech in March 1880 in which he called for 'a canal under American control'. Washington, Hayes declared, could not consent to 'the surrender of this control to any European power or to any combination of European powers', since the isthmus was 'virtually a part of the coast line of the United States'. The future canal, Secretary of State William Evarts asserted, would be dependent on the U.S. guarantee of 1846. This had so far been confined to the relatively minor task of protecting the

---

[31] *BD*, 40–5. McCullough, *Path between the seas*, 63–6, 85–6, 101–3.
[32] McCullough, *Path between the seas*, 67. Mack, *Land divided*, 286. Parks, *Colombia*, 360–1. *BD*, 42. *FRUS 1879*, 290–7.

railway, but once the isthmus became a busy international thoroughfare, the commitment would take on critical proportions. Washington, he told Dichman, could therefore not consider itself excluded by the Wyse concession from a direct interest in the canal or, if need be, from 'a positive supervision and inter-position' in the development of a project so vital to its national security.[33]

To give body to these pretensions, the Americans tried for a hard-and-fast agreement with Colombia. Existing American rights under the 1846 treaty were confirmed and were acknowledged as the basis of an alliance placing the defence of the future canal entirely in American hands. Under this arrangement the isthmus was to be fortified and given an infrastructure of naval and military installations. In the event of an emergency bringing into play U.S. obligations under the 1846 treaty, American forces were to land and operate in conjunction with the Colombian army. As an extra assurance to Bogotá, Washington took on a commitment more extensive than anything it had yet agreed to. If the two governments should decide to close the canal to foreign warships and any part of Colombia were threatened as a result, the United States was pledged to come to Colombia's aid.[34]

The alliance did not materialise, since it was immediately rejected by the Colombian Senate for fear that Colombia's sovereignty would be eroded, not sustained, by an American armed presence, however carefully controlled on paper. The move was distinctly unwelcome to Washington, and when it became known that Colombia was sounding out the European capitals over a multilateral guarantee of the canal, there was a furious American reaction.[35]

In June 1881 Secretary of State James Blaine circularised American diplomatic missions in Europe with a salvo against the Colombian overtures for European involvement. This, Blaine declared, besides flouting the Monroe Doctrine, would come close to 'an alliance against the United States', and the U.S. pledge of 1846 was perfectly adequate. European interests on the isthmus were slight, but for the United States it was 'a highway between its two coasts', and Washington could no more tolerate the passage through it of the warships of a hostile state than it could allow such a state to used its transcontinental railways.[36]

In November, Blaine went on to demand from London the revision of the Clayton–Bulwer convention, that is, cancellation of the article prohibiting fortification and exclusive control of an isthmian canal by either power. That

[33] Parks, *Colombia*, 288. Smith, *Illosions*, 105. Kenneth Hagan, *American gunboat diplomacy and the old Navy, 1877–1889* (Westport, Conn., 1973), 153. Parks, *Colombia*, 277. *BD*, 51, 47. Thomas Williams (ed.), *Hayes: The diary of a president, 1875–1881* (New York, 1964), 258, 261–4, 265. U.S. Congress, S. Doc. 237, 23–4, 471–3.

[34] Parks, *Colombia*, 364. *FRUS 1881*, 374–6.

[35] Parks, *Colombia*, 368–9, 362, 277. Mack, *Land divided*, 278. Smith, *Illusions*, 106.

[36] *FRUS 1881*, 537–40.

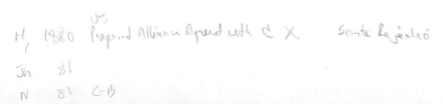

stipulation, Blaine argued, left the American stake in Panama wide open to attack by an enemy fleet. Yet Britain was free to protect its empire as it saw fit and to preserve the holding in the Suez Canal which Disraeli had acquired six years before. The United States sought to redress the balance by getting the same liberty of action that Britain enjoyed. So it must insist that in wartime the canal be closed to its enemies, and only American supervision of the waterway could ensure its neutrality, since it would be 'under the control of that government least likely to be engaged in war'.[37]

The importance of Blaine's initiative lay in the way it brought together three of the essentials of American canal policy: unilateral control; the right to fortify; and the power to close the canal to enemy shipping. But like all previous American attempts to assert dominance in Central America, it foundered on the lack of sea-power, which alone could make it good. It stood no chance whatever of being accepted in London, which saw straight through Blaine's bravado. His invocation of the Monroe Doctrine was received with the tart reminder that it had been dismissed by Lord Clarendon in 1854 as 'only . . . the dictum of the distinguished personage who announced it, and not . . . an international axiom which ought to regulate the conduct of European states'. As far as Britain was concerned, times had not changed, and in January 1882 the British suggested regulating the canal by an international convention – in other words, broadening the concept of Anglo-American responsibility for its protection by introducing the very multilateral guarantee the Americans had condemned.[38]

It is worth noting that the British proposed no such solution to the crisis then brewing in Egypt, which threatened to affect the Suez Canal. The day after giving their reply to Washington, they joined the French in an unmistakable assertion of their control over Suez by giving the ruling Khedive assurances 'against whatever might menace the order of things established in Egypt'. Six months later British forces intervened to crush the opposition to the Khedive and were soon occupying the country. Gladstone's justification of the policy he had reluctantly embarked on was different in one major respect from the American arguments for U.S. guardianship of the Panama route. Britain had gone into Egypt not only to ensure 'the safety and free use of that great maritime highway' but to convert Egypt as a whole 'from anarchy and conflict to a state of peace and order'. There was no comparable readiness on the United States's part to solve its own canal problem by seizing Panama. The U.S. minister in Bogotá, George Maney, told the Colombians that as long as the 1846 treaty remained in force it placed a ban on any such action. Washington could, of course, have paved the way for annexation by denouncing the

[37] Ibid., 554–9.
[38] Clive Parry (ed.), *A British digest of international law, compiled principally from the archives of the Foreign Office: Phase I, 1860–1914*, vol. 2B (London, 1967), 291, 292, 197, 198. U.K., Parliament, *Accounts and papers*, vol. 82, (1882), C. 3106, 5.

Am Canal Policy

treaty, but it accepted that Panama was out of reach and looked elsewhere for a canal.[39]

The obvious alternative was Nicaragua. In 1884 Blaine's successor, Frederick Frelinghuysen, signed an agreement which gave the United States sole rights to construct and manage a canal within a zone under Nicaraguan jurisdiction, in exchange for a defensive alliance which guaranteed Nicaragua's frontiers. It was not pursued by the new régime of President Grover Cleveland, however. For Cleveland, a treaty as exclusive as the U.S.–Nicaragua alliance was inconsistent with the principle of a canal neutral and open to all nations, and he would have nothing to do with it.[40]

It was therefore supremely ironical that Cleveland's first major act of foreign policy was to sanction a massive intervention in Panama – indeed, the largest overseas expedition to be mounted between the war with Mexico in 1846 and the war with Spain in 1898. The operation was triggered by the outbreak of full-scale civil war on the isthmus, starting with the burning of most of Colón by the insurgents at the end of March 1885. Its purpose was to keep the railway open in accordance with the 1846 treaty, and once the security of the transit had been reestablished, Cleveland ordered withdrawal. The Nicaraguan treaty had shown the danger of 'paramount privileges of ownership or right outside our own territory when coupled with absolute and unlimited engagements to defend the territorial integrity of the state where such interests lie'. Colombia was no different: Responsibility for the isthmus was a burden, not an opportunity, and Cleveland was not about to emulate Gladstone and become an imperialist in spite of himself.[41]

Unwillingness to take on Panama was reinforced by subsequent events. In 1889 de Lesseps's company collapsed, and calls in the American press for its purchase by the U.S. government went unheeded. The following year Wyse secured an extension of the company's contract, and in 1894 a successor was formed, the Compagnie Nouvelle du Canal de Panama (hereafter called the New Company), with a ten-year concession expiring in October 1904. Yet though desultory operations went on, canal construction had effectively ceased. So from being a potential hub of world trade and strategy, the isthmus sank to the level of a forlorn backwater with no apparent future. Moreover, the only remaining American interest, the Panama Railroad, had lost its earlier significance as the harbinger of the canal and was now merely the link between two provincial

---

[39] John Gallagher and Ronald Robinson with Alice Denny, *Africa and the Victorians* (London, 1961), 115–20. U.K., Parliament, *Parliamentary debates*, (Commons), 3rd ser. vol. 272 (1882), cols. 1586–90. U.S. Congress, S. Doc. 237, p. 433.

[40] *FRUS 1882*, 282. Hagan, *American gunboat diplomacy*, 147. *BD*, 59–63. James Richardson, *A compilation of the messages and papers of the presidents, 1789–1897*, vol. 8 (Washington, D.C., 1898), 539. U.S. Congress, S. Doc. 237, p. 434.

[41] Richardson, *Compilation*, 8: 326. Hagan, *American gunboat diplomacy*, 172–87.

towns in a minor Latin American state. By the 1890s, therefore, Panama had become a distinct liability to Washington. The exasperation felt in American circles was graphically expressed by Admiral Richard Meade in 1895. In the event of another upsurge on the isthmus, Meade felt, the terminal cities should be occupied by black American troops, advice which could not have conveyed more clearly the contempt felt for the partner in a now decidedly unhappy liaison.[42]

Depression over Panama, however, by no means reflected the general mood of the time, which witnessed a full-blooded revival of the Manifest Destiny movement of the 1840s. Once again the United States was possessed by an overwhelming sense of its natural right to mastery in the Americas and the Pacific, but this time there was an even fiercer impetus behind the chauvinism. The country, together with Germany and Japan, was one of a trio of thrusting new industrial states, and each believed that the moment had come for it to take its place in the sun in competition with the old establishment of Britain, France, and Russia. The badges of international status in this contest for supremacy were trade, empire, and sea-power, and in all three areas an isthmian canal held a pivotal place for the United States. It offered the prospect of a huge expansion of American mercantile potential through quicker access to the markets of Europe and Asia. It would abridge the enormous distances between American interests in the Caribbean and the Pacific, and it would significantly enhance the capacity of the U.S. Navy, by allowing it to concentrate rapidly, to meet a threat in one ocean or the other.[43]

Fortunately for Washington, there was still the alternative of Nicaragua, and in 1893 the influential pundit Captain Alfred Thayer Mahan called for an American-controlled canal there, secured by a powerful fleet and bases in its Caribbean approaches. Mahan saw an isthmian seaway as the justification for making the United States a naval power of the first rank. In 1880 he had written that the Navy must begin to lay down a battle-fleet 'as soon as the first spadeful of earth is turned at Panama', and ten years later he pointed out that only superior naval force would ensure control of the isthmus in wartime. Pressure for a canal was thus maintained by the naval expansionists, and it was stepped up by the lobbying for the annexation of Hawaii. But the most spectacular argument for the project was provided during the war with Spain in 1898 when

[42] Alfred Richard, *The Panama Canal in American national consciousness, 1870–1922* (New York, 1990), 45, 51–3. *BD*, 93–5, 97–100. U.S. Congress, S. Doc. 237, pp. 532–45. Smith *Illusions*, 114. McCullough, *Path between the seas*, 240–1. Parks, *Colombia*, 316. John Grenville and George Young, *Politics, strategy and American diplomacy: Studies in foreign policy, 1873–1917* (New Haven, Conn., 1966), 122.

[43] Charles Campbell, *The transformation of American foreign relations 1876–1900* (New York, 1976), 140–60.

the battleship *Oregon* had to make a long voyage round Cape Horn from its base in Seattle to join the blockading force off Cuba. At the end of the war Mahan added another consideration. A canal would have given the Navy an enormous advantage if reinforcements had been sent to Admiral Dewey's squadron in the Philippines; the most direct existing route was eastabout via Suez, whereas a passage via Nicaragua would have been some two thousand miles shorter. A third good reason was furnished by Britain. The Spanish flotilla despatched from Spain to the Philippines midway through the war was held up by the Suez Canal authorities for several days. Ten years earlier Britain had signed the Constantinople convention, declaring Suez open to ships of all nations in war or peace, but it had shown that a great power could bend such a promise if it chose, and the lesson was not lost on Washington.[44]

The war was to prove a watershed in the long campaign for an American canal. It made possible the seizure of Hawaii, and the peace settlement with Spain gave the United States much more: a stake in the Pacific through its acquisition of Guam and the Philippines, and dependencies in the Caribbean in the shape of Puerto Rico and Cuba. All these widely scattered holdings seemed to demand the linkage an isthmian transit could provide, and so the moment had arrived for cancelling the British veto of a U.S. canal monopoly, for reaching a final decision on the location of the route, and for getting a suitable treaty from either Nicaragua or Colombia.

The bid to remove the obstacle of the Clayton–Bulwer convention opened in December 1898 when the secretary of state, John Hay, approached the British ambassador in Washington, Lord Pauncefote. By February 1900 Hay and Pauncefote had agreed that the United States should have the exclusive rights to build and operate the waterway and to station military police in the vicinity to keep order. The canal was to be run in conformity with the Constantinople convention, which meant, among other things, that it would not be fortified, that it must be open to every kind of vessel at all times, and that other states could be parties to the agreement. Since these provisions nullified key objectives of previous American canal policy, the U.S. Senate in December 1900 made some drastic alterations. Multilateralisation of the treaty was disallowed, and the Constantinople regulations were not to apply to security measures. Though the reference to the Constantinople ban on fortification stood, the Senate had

1900
HAY-PAU

[44] Alfred Mahan, 'The isthmus and sea power', *Atlantic Monthly*, 72 (July–December 1893), 465, 471–2, and 'The United States looking outward', ibid., 66 (July–December, 1890), 819. French Chadwick, *The relations of the United States and Spain: War*, vol. 2 (New York, 1911), 388. Robert Seager, *Alfred Thayer Mahan: The man and his letters* (Annapolis, Md., 1977), 122, 395. Douglas Farnie, *East and west of Suez: The Suez Canal in history, 1854–1956* (Oxford, 1969), 458–61. Edward Hertslet (ed.), *A complete collection of the treaties and conventions and reciprocal regulations at present subsisting between Great Britain and foreign powers*, vol. 18 (London, 1893), 369–73.

1900 - Hay-Pauncefote
Britain agrees to exclusive
U.S. rights

also declared that Clayton–Bulwer was superseded. Since Clayton–Bulwer too had forbidden fortification, this could well leave the United States free to fortify if it wished.[45]

In February 1901 the British refused to accept the Senate's revisions. The central British objection was to the amendment whereby the United States could exempt itself from most of the Constantinople rules, even though the Senate had taken British policy as its model in doing this. Before signing the Constantinople convention, Britain had entered a reservation to it which preserved complete British freedom of action during the occupation of Egypt. In July 1898 the House of Commons was told that the reason why Spanish warships had been given a less than unobstructed passage through the canal was that the convention had not been brought into practical effect, and it was to remain in abeyance as long as Britain thought it expedient.[46]

Yet while Britain was able to have its way over Suez, it had lost the power to dictate to the United States over the terms of a Central American canal. In 1901 it faced challenges to its international position from several quarters: from the Boers of South Africa, where it was fighting its costliest war for half a century; from the Russians in the Far East after their occupation of Manchuria; and most importantly from the Germans in Europe, following the German decision to build a battle-fleet capable of threatening the Royal Navy in its home waters. This was no time to risk a confrontation with the United States over what to Britain were inessentials. So Pauncefote agreed to a second treaty which gave the United States practically everything the Senate had demanded.

Britain now accepted the abrogation of the Clayton–Bulwer convention, and the manifold restrictions it had placed on American power were removed. The silence of the revision on the key issues of multilateralism and fortification and its avoidance of a categorical commitment to unrestricted access to the canal meant that Britain had tacitly abandoned its objections on all three counts. The United States would have legal obligations only to Britain in operating the project, it would be free to construct whatever defence installations it thought necessary, and it would be entitled to protect its interests in wartime by closing the waterway to its enemies. On this basis the treaty was signed on 18 November 1901 and approved by the Senate four weeks later. The first hurdle between Washington and the consummation of its canal policy had been cleared.[47]

Now that a settlement with Britain had been reached, the time had come

[45] Dwight Miner, *The fight for the Panama route: The story of the Spooner Act and the Hay–Herrán treaty* (New York, 1940), 93, 105–6. *BD*, 116–17.

[46] *BD*, 119–20. Norman Padelford, 'American rights in the Panama Canal', *American Journal of International Law*, 34 (1940), 421 n. 12. Farnie, *Suez*, 341. U.K., Parliament, *Parliamentary debates* (Commons), 4th ser., vol. 60 (1898), col. 800, and vol. 61 (1898), col. 667.

[47] *BD*, 127–9. Miner, *Panama route*, 117–18. Richard Olney, 'Fortification of the Panama Canal', *American Journal of International Law*, 5 (1911), 298–301.

Hay–Pauncefote: ratified 1901

to choose between Nicaragua and Panama. Since the ruin of the de Lesseps scheme, Nicaragua had been the strong favourite, but in the aftermath of the war with Spain, Panama resurfaced, boosted energetically by the American legal adviser of the New Company, William Nelson Cromwell, and the 'battle of the routes' began. In March 1899 the Isthmian Canal Commission was appointed to survey the alternatives and advise on which to select. Its report opted for Nicaragua while making it clear that Panama would have been preferable in many ways. The stumbling block was the price. The New Company had valued its assets at $109 million, whereas the Commission put them at $40 million. In January 1902 the Company announced that it would accept $40 million, but when the House of Representatives soon afterwards voted over-whelmingly for a Nicaragua canal, the fate of Panama looked sealed.[48]

In fact Panama was about to draw ahead of its rival. President Theodore Roosevelt was convinced that Panama was a far better prospect than Nicaragua, especially now that the price was right, and the Commission was persuaded to change its recommendation. At the end of January, Senator John Spooner introduced a resolution authorising the president to buy out the New Company and have a canal cut across the Panama isthmus. For the next five months Spooner's amendment was promoted assiduously by Cromwell and Philippe Bunau-Varilla, a French engineer who had worked on the de Lesseps project in the 1880s and who was passionately committed to its completion. They did not labour in vain: In June 1902 the Spooner bill became law. The second barrier to a Panama canal had been removed, and the way stood open for a canal treaty with Colombia.[49]

The shape of such a treaty had, of course, already been outlined by the treaty with Britain. Hay–Pauncefote had envisaged exclusive American control of a canal, and this was at the core of the terms set out by the Canal Commission in May 1901. Its report insisted on perpetual tenure and would not consider giving Colombia either reversionary rights or a share in canal revenues. Washington was also to have sweeping administrative powers. The French had not been granted jurisdiction over the neighbourhood of the canal, and they had consequently been impotent to curb the anarchy that flared along the transit during the insurrection of 1885. Nor had they been authorised to enforce pub-lic health regulations, and malaria and yellow fever had played a key rôle in bringing the project to a standstill. The Hay–Pauncefote settlement had already admitted the American right to install military police along the line of the canal

[48] Miner *Panama route*, 79–90, 115–16, 118–20. *BD*, 133–9.
[49] Miner, *Panama route*, 120–1, 123–6, 137, 147–56. Charles Ameringer, 'The Panama Canal lobby of Philippe Bunau-Varilla and William Nelson Cromwell', *American Historical Review*, 68 (1962–3), 352–5. *BD*, 144–52. Gustave Anguizola, *Philippe Bunau-Varilla: The man behind the Panama Canal* (Chicago, 1980), 54–113, 209–19.

to protect the works from disorder, and the Commission demanded that U.S. officials be placed in charge of both police and sanitation within the zone which would gird the waterway. This would be ten miles wide, and it was to include the terminal cities of Panama and Colón, the main breeding grounds of lawlessness and infection. Colombia's rôle in the canal's affairs was to be purely symbolic: It would have titular sovereignty over the zone, and its judges would sit on mixed tribunals there, but the United States would be the real master.[50]

Passage of the Hay–Pauncefote treaty forced the Colombian legation in Washington to bow to these propositions. While aware that an agreement along the Commission's lines would make severe inroads into Colombia's sovereignty, the Colombian minister, Carlos Martínez Silva, believed it would be wiser to come to an accommodation than to hold out. It would also be shrewd tactics to outbid Nicaragua in any competition for American favour. In January 1902 he embodied his ideas in a draft which effectively accepted the American position and which was drawn up with the benefit of advice from both Cromwell and Bunau-Varilla.[51]

To soften the hard fact of the American take-over and to salvage the principle of Colombian sovereignty, the lease of the canal was not to be perpetual but for a one-hundred-year term, renewable at the sole option of the United States. This concession, however, was hugely outweighed by Colombian renunciation of future proceeds from the canal and of reversionary rights to it, and by the token part assigned to Colombia in canal administration. Washington was granted powers to police and defend a ten-kilometre-wide zone, and though a façade of Colombian authority was carefully erected, it was not difficult to see through it. Sanitary and police regulations in the zone were nominally to be a joint responsibility, as were the courts that would enforce them, but in reality jurisdiction would belong with the United States, and though Panama City and Colón would not formally be part of the zone, the regulations would none the less apply there. The duty of protecting the waterway against external attack would in theory rest first with Colombia, but in practice Colombia would have to call on American troops for 'assistance', and in emergencies the United States could defend the canal without being asked and without seeking Colombia's permission. All these provisions gave Colombia very little of substance, and it was even to lose the old American guarantee of Colombian sovereignty over the isthmus, which was narrowed down to cover only the zone and the terminal cities.[52]

Such a thinly disguised capitulation was not acceptable to Bogotá. Martínez was replaced by José Vicente Concha, who was instructed to work for a multilateral guarantee of the canal, and if that were feasible, to denounce the 1846

---

[50] Miner, *Panama route*, 111–13, 126–30. *BD*, 117. Anguizola, *Bunau-Varilla*, 194–5. Lemaitre, *Panamá*, 352–4.

[51] Drafts, 1–3. Lemaitre, *Panamá*, 344–5, 350, 373–4. Miner, *Panama route*, 129–30.

[52] Miner, *Panama route*, 129–30. *Libro azul*, 90–102.

treaty. In March 1902 he was sent terms for a new treaty which were all to
Colombia's advantage. The canal was, as under the Wyse concession, to revert
to Colombia after ninety-nine years; payment was to be through a share of
tolls higher than the percentage granted by Wyse; the zone was to be policed
by Colombia at American expense; and the United States was to continue to
guarantee Colombia's sovereignty over the entire isthmus. The stiffness of
these proposals reflected awareness of the need to take a stand on grounds of
national pride, but it also revealed the government's inability to appreciate the
weakness of its position. With the abrogation of the Clayton–Bulwer treaty,
Colombia had lost the protective shield of British involvement in Central America,
and it lay wide open to U.S. hegemony.[53]

Both Martínez and Concha had pointed all this out to Bogotá, and Concha
therefore drew up a treaty based essentially on Martínez's proposals and again
drafted in consultation with Cromwell and Bunau-Varilla. There were a number
of significant changes. The United States was to return to Colombia all the land
beyond the zone previously conceded to the Railroad and the New Company,
while Concha underlined Colombia's sovereignty by cutting out all reference to
the joint courts. Soon after these terms were submitted to Hay, he told Concha
he would sign the draft as soon as Congress authorised an agreement along the
suggested lines.[54]

Congress, however, wanted much more from Colombia. The Spooner Act,
passed in June, demanded perpetual control of a canal zone where the United
States would exercise exclusive jurisdiction. Moreover, not only did it not
envisage returning any existing land-holdings to Colombia, but it sanctioned
the acquisition of yet more outside the zone for canal purposes. Hay consequently
demanded a lease in perpetuity and the retention of Company land in Panama
City and Colón. He also vested command of its defence, policing, and sanitation
unreservedly in the United States. American legal authority over the zone
would be manifested in U.S. courts of justice, though the joint tribunals
were to be restored, and Colombia was to be allowed some zone courts of its
own.[55]

In presenting these conditions, Hay knew he held the whip-hand, and his
bargaining power was strengthened still further by a sudden reverse inflicted on
Bogotá in the civil war, which had been raging since 1899. This placed Panama
at the mercy of the rebels, and in September Washington tightened the screw
on Colombia by refusing to transport government troops on the railway. It had
done the same thing the previous November and on both occasions had contravened the 1846 treaty. But the Colombians were powerless to alter the

[53] Miner, *Panama route*, 131–2, 134, 138–9. *Libro azul*, 116–17.
[54] Miner, *Panama route*, 139–43, 216–20. *BD*, 159–67. Anguizola, *Bunau-Varilla*, 195–201.
   Lemaitre, *Panamá*, 376–80.
[55] *BD*, 178–80. Miner, *Panama route*, 160–2. *Libro azul*, 222–31.

situation, and in the event the insurrection failed. In November a peace settlement was thrashed out on board the U.S. flagship, and the thousand-day war came to a close without the loss of Panama.[56]

This outcome accelerated the progress towards a canal treaty. Hay reinserted Martínez's face-saving formula giving Colombia some ostensible responsibility for canal defence. He also dropped the insistence on a perpetual lease, reverting to the euphemism of a one-hundred-year concession renewable at Washington's option. On the other hand, he brushed aside Concha's belated call for a prior agreement between Colombia and the New Company on the sale of the Company's property to the United States whereby Colombia expected to take a share of the Company's $40 million asking price. This had been one of Colombia's central demands since the beginning of the negotiations, but it had not pressed the issue earlier, and Hay took the Company's view that it had the right to sell its assets to Washington without reference to Bogotá. He also denied Concha's contention that all land so far held outside the zone by the Railroad and the Company must revert to Colombia; the worthless tracts outside the terminal cities would be transferred, but the valuable areas in Panama City and Colón would remain in U.S. hands. Rather than sign a treaty on this basis, Concha resigned, but his replacement, Tomás Herrán, carried the negotiations through to completion after Roosevelt had decreed that he would pay Colombia no more than a $10 million lump sum and an annuity of $250,000 after nine years. On 22 January 1903 the Hay–Herrán treaty was signed.[57]

It came before the Senate for approval in March, where its arch-opponent was the venerable Senator John Tyler Morgan, for the past decade the doyen of the Nicaraguan canal lobby. During the debate Morgan introduced a batch of amendments designed to wreck the treaty's chances when it was scanned by the Colombian legislature. Among many other things, the cash payment was to be reduced to $7 million, the annuity was to be cut off in 1966, the joint tribunals were to be eliminated, Panama City and Colón were to be absorbed into the zone, and the United States was to have total discretion in defending the canal. All these revisions were voted down, however, and the treaty went through as signed.[58]

The result no doubt came as a great relief to Hay after the fate of the first treaty he had signed with Pauncefote. The settlement still had to be approved by the Colombian legislature, however, and Bogotá maintained that it would not go through before the question of a Colombian share in the New Company's $40 million had been decided. In January 1902 the Colombian foreign minister had suggested an equal division of the spoils, but Cromwell was adamant that Colombia should not have a cent. Once again Hay upheld the

---

[56] Miner, *Panama route*, 163–4, 169–81, 220–3, 234–7.

[57] Ibid., 182–95. *BD*, 188–200, 202–13.

[58] Miner, *Panama route*, 197–9. *CR* (Senate), 9 and 14.3.03, 14–16, 22, 92.

Company's view in a lengthy note sent to Bogotá at the end of April; as far as he was concerned, the matter was closed.[59]

The Roosevelt administration was thus not prepared to offer Colombia inducements to ratify the treaty; instead, it used threats. On 9 June, shortly after the Colombian Senate met to open its debate, Hay indicated that if the treaty were rejected or shelved, 'action might be taken by the Congress next winter which every friend of Colombia would regret'. Following a visit to the White House four days later, Cromwell added to the pressure by inspiring a newspaper prediction that Panama would secede in the event of a Colombian rejection and would make its own agreement with Washington. When the Colombian general Rafael Reyes intimated that $10 million from the New Company and another $5 million from the United States might make all the difference, Hay replied that 'any amendment whatever or unnecessary delay' would put the treaty at risk. 'They are mad to get hold of the forty million of the Frenchmen,' he told Roosevelt, 'and they want to make us a party to the gouge.' The president was equally outraged. 'Those contemptible little creatures in Bogotá', he wrote to Hay, 'ought to understand how much they are jeopardizing things and imperiling their own future.'[60]

The Colombians disregarded all the warnings. On 4 August a Senate committee reported against the treaty as it stood on six main counts. There was to be a preliminary deal with the New Company before the transfer of its concessions, and the Company's land-holdings outside the zone were all to revert to Colombia. The United States was to maintain its guarantee of Colombian sovereignty throughout the isthmus, and it was to have no jurisdiction in the zone. Such franchises as it would be granted there would be rights of tenancy, not ownership, and police and sanitary regulations for the zone would have to be determined by special agreement.[61]

Three weeks later Colombian hostility to the treaty was vented by another committee, which brought up the explosive subject of money. In his justification of Hay–Herrán the previous March, the chairman of the Senate Foreign Relations Committee, Senator Shelby Cullom, had pointed out what Colombia stood to lose financially: the reversionary title to both the railway and the canal; the $250,000 annuity from the Railroad; and the percentage share in canal receipts, amounting to an annuity of at least $250,000. Assuming that the $10 million indemnity could generate investment interest of $400,000 a year, Colombia would enjoy an annual return from the canal of $650,000. That is to say, its

[59] William Roscoe Thayer, *The life and letters of John Hay*, vol. 2 (Boston, 1915), 393. Miner, *Panama route*, 109, 111, 134, 138, 183, 207–16, 273–84. *BD*, 218–23.
[60] Miner, *Panama route*, 284–6, 293–5, 307–8. *BD*, 228, 233, 235. Miles DuVal, *Cadiz to Cathay: The story of the long diplomatic struggle for the Panama Canal* (Stanford, Calif. 1947 edn.) 261. Henry Pringle, *Theodore Roosevelt: A biography* (New York, 1956 edn), 219.
[61] Mack, *Land divided*, 477. Miner, *Panama route*, 314–20, 326. Lemaitre, *Panamá*, 445–63.

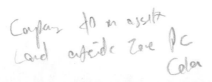

compensation for the losses Cullom had itemised would clearly be a good deal
less than what it had been promised under the Wyse concession and its 1867
contract with the Railroad.[62]

The Colombian committee felt that a much more generous settlement was
in order. The New Company should pay Colombia $10 million, and the U.S.
indemnity should be raised to $20 million. The canal annuity would be $150,000,
but Washington would also continue to pay the Railroad's annuity of $250,000
until the expiry of the Railroad's lease in 1966. The canal annuity would then
be stepped up to $400,000 to make good the loss of income from the Railroad,
and the Railroad would revert to Colombia in spite of having been sold to the
United States as part of the New Company's properties. In return, the U.S.
guarantee of Colombian sovereignty would be abridged to apply only to the
zone, and joint judicial tribunals would be allowed in the zone. Washington
would, however, have to acknowledge Colombia's responsibility for the defence
of the canal and for the policing and sanitation of the zone, and Colombia would
be entitled to call on the U.S. authorities to provide these services at their own
expense.[63]

Surveying the débris, Hay blamed everyone but himself, and he had no
sympathy for Cromwell, who, he snapped, 'must not whimper over the ruin of
the treaty through the greed of the Colombians and the disinclination of the
Canal Company to satisfy it'. The Company had apparently been 'willing to be
bled' to the tune of $8 million and, Hay believed, ought to have said so and
'closed the bargain'. Washington would have turned a blind eye; the arrangement would have been 'a thing we could not share in, nor even decently know'.
This was a curious comment from the man who had so unwaveringly backed
Cromwell's earlier refusal to divide the Company's quittance with Colombia,
but Hay, like Cromwell, was wise after the event, and the clock could not be
turned back.[64]

It was transparently clear that the Hay–Herrán treaty was so much waste
paper, but the point was finally rammed home in another complication, which
emerged in October. In April 1900 the cabinet of President Manuel Sanclemente
had ordained an extension of the New Company's grant, from October 1904 to
October 1910. The Senate committee now insinuated that the decree might
be unconstitutional, for it had not been approved by the legislature. This was
a gratuitous provocation to the United States, because it raised the possibility
that the assets of the New Company would revert to Colombia in a year's time.
In the event, the Colombian Senate did not pronounce on the idea, nor on the
treaty amendments. It adjourned on 31 October having thrown away the only
ace in Colombia's hand, the power to give the United States what it wanted by

[62] *CR* (Senate), 17.3.03, 110.   [63] Miner, *Panama route*, 327–8.
[64] Hay Papers, roll 4, Hay to Adee, 21.9.03. Loomis Papers, roll 2, Thayer to Loomis, 6.6.15.

agreement. In that agreement Colombia would certainly have got less than its financial due, and its sovereignty would have been badly damaged. These things were tolerable compared with the risk it ran of losing Panama itself and with it the canal, but Bogotá seemed unaware that it was courting disaster when it crossed the United States. For Washington did not accept the Colombian verdict on the treaty as a death sentence on the Panama canal. The Roosevelt administration had made the isthmian waterway a high national priority, and it had come too close to possessing it to give way now and abandon the project. It had in fact already decided to ignore Colombia and make the canal its own.[65]

[65] Alfred Dennis, *Adventures in American diplomacy, 1896–1906* (New York, 1928), 338–9 n. 20. Miner, *Panama route*, 331–4.

2

'I took the Isthmus', 1903–1904

Colombia's rejection of the Hay–Herrán treaty plunged the Roosevelt administration into a comprehensive reappraisal of its canal policy. Several options lay open. First, the president could persevere with Colombia in the hope it would endorse the treaty in 1904. Second, as the Spooner Act provided, he could go ahead with a Nicaragua canal. Third, he could leave the matter entirely for Congress to decide. Fourth, he could begin construction in Panama without reference to Colombia. Finally, he could negotiate a new treaty with a secessionist Panamanian state.

The first course was out of the question as far as Roosevelt was concerned, and he swore he would have no more to do with 'the foolish and homicidal corruptionists in Bogotá'. In retirement twelve years later he expressed his feelings even more pungently to his biographer William Roscoe Thayer. 'To talk of Colombia as a responsible power to be dealt with as we should deal with Holland or Belgium or Switzerland or Denmark is a mere absurdity. The analogy is with a group of Sicilian or Calabrian bandits; with Villa and Carranza at this moment. You could no more make an agreement with them than you could nail currant jelly to a wall.'[1]

The Nicaraguan solution was also turned down. In May 1902 Nicaragua had offered terms for a canal treaty in some ways more favourable than the concessions achieved under Hay–Herrán – including exclusive police authority over the canal zone and much lower compensation. But Roosevelt was convinced that to develop the Nicaragua route would be 'against the advice of the great majority of competent engineers – some of the most competent saying that we had better have no canal at this time rather than go there'.[2]

---

[1] *TR letters*, 3: 599; 8: 944–5. Roosevelt's policy is exhaustively dealt with in Richard Collin, *Theodore Roosevelt's Caribbean: The Panama Canal, the Monroe Doctrine, and the Latin American context* (Baton Rouge, La., 1990), 237–338.

[2] *BD*, 169–75. *TR letters*, 3: 628.

Handing the issue to Congress was ruled out for largely the same reasons. In a celebrated speech made in 1911 Roosevelt claimed that to have done this would have meant stagnation. 'If I had acted strictly according to precedent,' he told his Berkeley audience, 'I should have turned the whole matter over to Congress; in which case, Congress would be ably debating it at this moment, and the canal would be fifty years in the future.' His real motive for avoiding Congress, however, was to forestall a vote for the unacceptable alternative of Nicaragua.[3]

Roosevelt's choice was Panama, and for some time the president thought of taking possession by virtue of eminent domain. In August 1902 he had asked Hay why it should not be feasible to buy Panama instead of entering into a lease with Colombia, and after Colombia refused to ratify he told a correspondent that he would 'infinitely prefer to get title to the canal outright'. There were others who felt likewise. In December 1902 Senator Cullom had argued that if Colombia would not accept Washington's conditions, the government should deal direct with the New Company and appropriate the line of the canal under the justification of 'universal public utility'. In August 1903 much the same case was advanced by John Bassett Moore, professor of international law at Columbia University, but with the added refinement that a legal basis for a seizure existed in the shape of the 1846 treaty.[4]

This was an extraordinary proposition. One of the central features of the treaty, after all, was the American guarantee of Colombia's sovereignty over the isthmus, and it had always been seen as a curb on U.S. freedom of action in Panama. Denunciation of the treaty had been regarded as the only way for Washington to achieve that freedom, and in April 1902 Concha had warned Bogotá that Washington might take this drastic step. There were, however, strong reasons for keeping the treaty in effect and using it to underpin administration policy. Roosevelt therefore welcomed Moore's analysis enthusiastically when it was forwarded to him at his summer residence in Oyster Bay.[5]

Moore began with the assumption that the 1846 agreement had implicitly been a canal treaty: 'It looked . . . above all to the construction of a canal.' Indeed, he contended that the canal had been started by the French under the aegis of the American guarantee of Colombia's sovereignty over Panama. Because Colombia had enjoyed that guarantee, it was in no position to impede canal construction by the United States. Washington was therefore entitled to reap

---

[3] Roosevelt Papers, roll 421, speech of 23 March 1911. Howard Hill, *Roosevelt and the Caribbean* (Chicago, 1927), 67.

[4] *TR letters*, 3: 318, 595. The idea of buying Panama had been mooted by Frederic Penfield, a former U.S. minister-resident in Egypt, in his article 'Why not own the Panama isthmus?' *North American Review*, 174 (1902), 272. DuVal, *Cadiz to Cathay*, 196. Miner, *Panama route*, 341.

[5] Parks, *Colombia*, 340, 360. DuVal, *Cadiz to Cathay*, 181.

the full benefit of Colombia's reciprocal grant of a right of way across the
isthmus, which Moore freely elevated into a canal concession. All Roosevelt
needed from Colombia, Moore concluded, was its consent to the transfer of the
New Company's property and 'an unqualified license to construct and operate'.
The United States would not then be subject to Colombian jurisdiction, and its
rights would not be dependent on the 1846 accord. Once in possession, it would
have no difficulty in making Colombia bend to its will.[6]

Moore's readiness to flout Colombian sovereignty in the process of acquiring
the canal was based on the traditional justification of the Monroe Doctrine. As
we have seen, Blaine had invoked it in 1881 in his war of words with Britain
over Clayton–Bulwer, and in 1904 Elihu Root was to bring it into play to
vindicate sweeping Colombian sovereignty aside. The doctrine, said Root, was
'an assertion of a right under the universal rule that all sovereignty is held
subject to limitations in its exercise for the just interests of other nations' (above
all, without doubt, those of the United States).[7]

Moore was prone to the same arrogance, and it engrafted a basic flaw in his
thesis. As Hay was quick to point out, Moore's assumption that Colombia
would not resist an American swoop on the isthmus was doubtful. Roosevelt
saw Moore's proposal as a way of making sure that what he called 'the Bogotá
lot of jack rabbits' should not be allowed 'permanently to bar one of the future
highways of civilization'. Hay's reply was that if Washington decided to press
on with the canal regardless of Colombia, 'the fact that our position in that case
would be legal and just might not greatly impress the jack-rabbit mind. I do not
believe we could faire valoir our rights in that way without war', though that
would be 'brief and inexpensive'.[8]

Hay's caution was based on State Department disquiet over talk of dispossession. 'Such a scheme', his assistant secretary, Alvey Adee, had told him,
'could, of course, have no countenance from us – our policy before the world
should stand, like Mrs. Caesar, without suspicion.' Doubtless underlying this
unease was the awareness that the action would be an undisguisable breach of
the 1846 treaty. It was also likely that a war on these grounds would get a hostile
reception in Congress. A war with Colombia for the Panama Canal could not be
seen as anything but imperialistic, and the political repercussions for the government might be very damaging, especially with a presidential election
year imminent.[9]

Roosevelt eventually came round to this conclusion. On 3 October 1903 he
began to draft his annual message to Congress, in which he planned to say that
the administration 'should purchase all the rights of the French company, and,

[6] Miner, *Panama route*, 341–5, 427–32.
[7] Elihu Root, 'The ethics of the Panama question', *Addresses on international subjects* (Cambridge, Mass., 1916), 181:
[8] *TR letters*, 3: 567. Hay Papers, roll 4, Hay to Roosevelt, 22.8.03.
[9] DuVal, *Cadiz to Cathay*, 262.

without any further parley with Colombia, enter upon the completion of the canal which the French company has begun'. On 5 October he told the Senate Republican leader, Mark Hanna, that he felt 'we are certainly justified in morals, and . . . in law, under the treaty of 1846, in interfering summarily and saying that the canal is to be built and that they shall not stop it'. But just two days later he wrote to the ultra-imperialist Albert Shaw that 'as yet, the people of the United States are not willing to take the ground of building the canal by force. . . . To obtain . . . terms now by bribery or violence would be wrong.' So the option of an overt land-grab was discarded.[10]

Fortunately from Roosevelt's point of view, another instrument of policy lay to hand. In his letter to Shaw he spoke of the possibility of a Panamanian revolt which could bring about 'a condition of things that will warrant the action we desire being taken openly, honestly, and in good faith'. This scenario hardly tallied with the despoliation of Colombia which subsequently took place when the United States connived at Panama's secession in order to get the canal, but dispossession by proxy was preferable to a less than splendid little war with Bogotá, and as such it served the president's purposes admirably.[11]

The independence movement which became Roosevelt's co-conspirator was a vigorous force which had already given Bogotá a lot of trouble. Though Panama had chosen to become part of Colombia when it broke away from Spain in 1821, it seceded four times in the next forty years, and there had been continual secessionist rumblings from the mid 1860s to the 1880s, culminating in the rising of 1885. After its suppression, Panama was demoted to no more than a department in a highly centralised Colombia, but though the outcome of the thousand-day war in 1902 confirmed Bogotá's authority, Panamanians did not lose their appetite for independence. Indeed, it was immediately revived by signature of the Hay–Herrán treaty. The canal promised to regenerate Panama as the busy highway it had been in the heyday of the Spanish empire, and the prospect of a bonanza could only stimulate the Panamanian urge to nationhood.[12]

As long as Colombia had the power to grant a canal concession to the United States, Washington had no interest in sponsoring Panamanian separatism. During Colombia's debate over the treaty, this was still true. Predictions of American support for isthmian independence and of a subsequent treaty with Panama were made only as a means of increasing pressure on Colombia to ratify, and both Herrán and Cromwell made them for that reason. Colombia's dismissal of the treaty changed things completely. A canal agreement with a Panamanian state was now a serious option, though not one to the taste of Hay, who considered that Cromwell's refusal to split the Company's cash payment with Bogotá had made a coup in Panama 'the only alternative'. But leading Panamanians stood

[10] Theodore Roosevelt, *The works of Theodore Roosevelt, vol. 20, An autobiography* (New York, 1926), 549–50. *TR letters*, 3: 625, 626; 6: 897–8. See also *Times*, 14, 15, and 16.11.03.

[11] *TR letters*, 3: 626.

[12] Lemaitre, *Panamá*, 9–32, 154–7, 275–99.

ready and willing to come to terms with Roosevelt, and the stage was thus set for the making of a mutually satisfactory deal.[13]

Feelers had already been put out by the Panamanians after the arrival in New York on 2 September of the most senior figure in the secessionist junta, Manuel Amador. He began by seeing Cromwell, who apparently promised the New Company's aid, but from this point on Amador's mission ran into unexpected difficulty. One of his travelling companions had been José Gabriel Duque, owner of the Panama *Star and Herald*. On 3 September, Duque had an interview in Washington with Hay and then instantly told Herrán that if the treaty were not ratified, the isthmus would sever its ties with Bogotá. Convinced that Roosevelt was about to throw his weight behind Panama, Herrán warned Cromwell against becoming an accessory to the plot on pain of forfeiting the Company's franchise. Consequently, when Amador next came to call, Cromwell refused to receive him.[14]

This setback was coupled with the fact that Washington had not declared its intentions. In August, Adee had advised against recognising and protecting Panama as an independent state, 'like a second Texas'. When in mid September Hay asked Roosevelt to consider his reaction to an insurgency in Panama, he made his own preference clear enough in saying that if U.S. forces had to be sent in to secure the railway, their intervention 'should not be . . . to the profit, as heretofore, of Bogotá'. Roosevelt would only say he wanted 'in some shape or way to interfere when it becomes necessary' so as to get the Panama route without treating any further with Colombia. On this unspecific note, the matter was left for decision some time in October.[15]

Roosevelt's willingness to tread water was due partly to the fact that he had still to make up his mind on what to do. But it also stemmed from the failure of the Panamanians to inspire confidence. The elderly Amador was not the dynamic promoter the secessionists needed, and after his rebuff by Cromwell he had not dared to approach Washington. This deficiency in Panama's leadership was soon made up, however, by the arrival in the United States of Bunau-Varilla, who immediately set out to convince the administration that the dissidents had a coherent strategy which would work.[16]

Bunau-Varilla's first indirect contact with the government was through Moore, whose approach to Panama he approved whole-heartedly. In a recent newspaper article, Bunau-Varilla had compared Colombia to a landlord trying to stop a railway being built across his estate. Roosevelt, he believed, was entitled to

---

[13] DuVal, *Cadiz to Cathay*, 218. Miner, *Panama route*, 293–5. Loomis Papers, roll 2, Thayer to Loomis, 6.6.15.

[14] Miner, *Panama route*, 335–9, 347–50. DuVal, *Cadiz to Cathay*, 287.

[15] DuVal, *Cadiz to Cathay*, 262. Miner, *Panama route*, 350–1. *TR letters*, 3: 599.

[16] Miner, *Panama route*, 354, 356.

demand from Bogotá what it refused to concede and to resort to 'legal coercion exercised in virtue of a treaty'. Writing to Moore on 3 October, he told him that Washington could not let Colombia behave like an African tribe extorting tribute from passing caravans. What was needed was a 'Roosevelt Doctrine' to complement the Monroe Doctrine. The latter protected Latin American interests against Europe; the former would protect European and North American interests against Latin America's 'interference'. This was odd coming from a man who supposedly held a brief for Panama, but it was an indication of where Bunau-Varilla really stood. For him the canal was paramount, and both the French company and the American government had powerful reasons for wanting it completed. By contrast, the interests of the state in possession of the isthmus were ancillary, and it was immaterial whether that state were Colombia or Panama. He had taken up the Panamanian cause only because Colombia had failed to deliver a treaty, and though he was to act as the spokesman for Panama, he was determined to work for a canal settlement which reflected his basic priorities.[17]

Those priorities were, of course, fully shared by the Roosevelt administration. This is not to say that when Roosevelt received Bunau-Varilla on 10 October he gave support to his plan for the U.S. Navy to protect the infant Panamanian republic after it had declared its independence. Though Roosevelt privately wished for Panama's secession, he could not say so. However, as Root later pointed out, it would not have been difficult for Bunau-Varilla to see where the president's sympathies lay, since throughout the interview Roosevelt was pouring forth a stream of vituperation against the Colombians, and Roosevelt himself knew that Bunau-Varilla had picked up his signals.[18]

Rightly construing his audience as a green light to proceed with the revolution, Bunau-Varilla concerted plans with Amador in New York. Their discussions showed again that Bunau-Varilla's main concern was the canal, not Panama. As he saw it, the new republic would comprise 'the territory embraced only by the watersheds of the Chagres and Rio Grande rivers', that is, the belt of land on either side of the railway. The breakaway would have to take that form, since Washington's intervention would be justified as an operation to guarantee freedom of transit under the 1846 treaty, and that would cover a secession only 'from Colón to Panama'. His restrictive approach exactly matched the American distaste for the 1846 guarantee of Colombian sovereignty over the entire isthmus. As we have seen, Washington had successfully narrowed the commitment

---

[17] Philippe Bunau-Varilla, *Panama: The creation, destruction, and resurrection* (London, 1913), 295–6, 287, 308–9.

[18] McCullough, *Path between the seas*, 352. *TR letters*, 3: 628, 689. Philip Jessup, *Elihu Root*, vol. 1 (New York, 1938), 403–4. Margaret Clapp, *Forgotten first citizen: John Bigelow* (Boston, 1947), 313. See also Thomas Schoonover, 'Max Farrand's memorandum on the U.S. role in the Panamanian Revolution of 1903', *Diplomatic History*, 12 (1988), 504–6.

down to the canal zone and the terminal cities during its negotiations with Colombia, and when Amador left for Panama on 20 October he could by no means
be sure that the pledge of isthmian sovereignty would be transferred to Panama.[19]

He did know, however, that vessels of the U.S. Pacific Squadron had been
instructed to move south towards the isthmus. Hay had given Bunau-Varilla
this information during an interview on 16 October, a day after the commander
of the squadron, Admiral Henry Glass, had been told to take four ships from
San Francisco to Acapulco, Mexico, on 22 October, ostensibly on exercise.
Preparations were therefore already under way when Roosevelt interviewed
two junior Army officers recently returned from Colombia. The president later
claimed that it was their report of an imminent coup in Panama that prompted
him to order the Navy into position, but the orders that went out on 19 October
merely elaborated the decision taken some days earlier. These were to send the
USS *Boston* ahead of the remainder of the Pacific flotilla to reach San Juan del
Sur, Nicaragua, by 1 November, while in the Atlantic *Nashville* was directed to
Kingston, Jamaica, and *Atlanta* and *Dixie* to the new base at Guantánamo, Cuba,
the latter with 400 Marines aboard. The date of the Panamanian rising had not
yet been fixed, but the intention was clearly to have *Boston* and *Nashville* in place
at the terminal ports by the time the insurrection began, to block a Colombian
counter-stroke. The entire coastline would be closed off after the other vessels
joined them.[20]

This measured time-table was thrown out of phase by an unexpected development. On 28 October, the day after his return to Panama, Amador was told
that Colombian reinforcements would probably reach the isthmus in five days'
time. Bunau-Varilla immediately rushed to Washington to alert Francis Loomis,
his connection in the State Department. On 30 October, Loomis told Bunau-
Varilla that a warship could be expected at Colón within the next few days.
This was *Nashville*, which had just been ordered to leave Kingston and which
sailed for Colón in the forenoon of 1 November, arriving the next evening.[21]

Nashville's appearance on 2 November was rightly taken by the secessionists
as a pledge that the might of the United States was behind them. This was not,
of course, how American intervention was presented in two Navy Department
signals. The first, to *Nashville*, gave orders to prevent 'any armed force with
hostile intent' disembarking on the Atlantic coast. The second instructed

[19] Bunau-Varilla, *Panama*, 313–14, 316.
[20] Miner, *Panama route*, 356, 353–4. *TR letters*, 7: 944–5. Roosevelt message of 4 January
    1904 is in *BD*, 307. DuVal, *Cadiz to Cathay*, 304. John Nikol and Francis X. Holbrook,
    'Naval operations in the Panamanian revolution of 1903', *American Neptune*, 37 (1977), 254–
    6. Richard Turk, 'The United States Navy and the "taking" of Panama, 1901–1903',
    Military Affairs, 38 (1974), 93.
[21] Miner, *Panama route*, 360–1. Bunau-Varilla, *Panama*, 327–8, 330–1. Loomis Papers, roll 3,
    Loomis to Secretary, Central and South American Telegraph Company, 23.10.03.

Admiral Glass to forbid landings on the Pacific coast 'at any point within 50 miles of Panama'. The stated purpose was to maintain uninterrupted transit along the railway in accordance with the 1846 treaty obligation, and both messages stressed the importance of keeping a Colombian expedition out.[22]

These justifications bear a remarkable resemblance to Sir Anthony Eden's gloss on the Anglo-French intervention in Egypt in October 1956 after Israel had invaded Egypt and advanced on the Suez Canal. Britain and France, Eden professed, were mounting a police action 'to protect the Canal and separate the combatants' – 'to stop hostilities, prevent a resumption of them, and safeguard traffic through the Canal'. In truth, Britain and France were operating in collusion with Israel in order to repossess the canal after its seizure by the Egyptian government three months earlier. In 1903 the United States was likewise an accomplice of the Panamanians, with the object of taking Panama from Colombia.[23]

This judgement is amply borne out by the course of events after 2 November. Though a Colombian battalion did land at Colón the following morning, that was because the instructions to *Nashville* had not reached her, and Washington was insistent that 'in the interest of peace' the detachment should not be transported along the railway to Panama City. Its officers were taken there, but their men remained in Colón. When the coup took place in Panama City with the arrest of the Colombians early in the evening of 3 November, their troops were neutralised fifty miles from the scene of the rebellion.[24]

In September, Herrán had predicted this would happen if an independence movement took Panama City, and once the United States brought its power to bear, the result was certain. When the Colombians agreed to leave Colón on 5 November, and when *Dixie* with her complement of Marines arrived, the secession of Panama was irreversible. That this had been the real purpose of the American action was clearly suggested by the speed of the de facto recognition given to Panama in the afternoon of 6 November. Even before then, American officials on the isthmus did not bother to hide their sympathies. On 4 November the commander of the Panamanian army, General Esteban Huertas, was openly escorted in Panama City by the U.S. consul, Felix Ehrman, and on the morning of 6 November the Panamanian flag was hoisted over Colón by Major William Murray Black of the U.S. Army.[25]

The true nature of the administration's policy also came out in the response to the Colombian appeal for American support. Hay subsequently claimed that

[22] *BD*, 266.

[23] U.K., Parliament, *Parliamentary debates* (Commons), 5th ser., vol. 558 (1956), cols. 1448, 1649.

[24] Miner, *Panama route*, 362–3. McCullough, *Path between the seas*, 364–71. *BD*, 250, 254–6, 267, 268–9. Nikol and Holbrook, 'Naval operations', 257–8. Turk, 'U.S. Navy', 94.

[25] Miner, *Panama route*, 349, 364–7. Turk, 'U.S. Návy', 94. Nikol and Holbrook, 'Naval operations', 257–8. Miner, *Panama route*, 368–70. *BD*, 252. DuVal, *Cadiz to Cathay*, 332.

the rebellion faced the United States with a choice of nothing more than active or passive neutrality between the two sides. 'We had to decide on the instant', he wrote, 'whether we would take possession of the ends of the railroad and keep the traffic clear, or whether we would stand back and let those gentlemen cut each other's throats for an indefinite time, and destroy whatever remnant of our property and our interests we had there.' Yet the answer to the Colombian call for help was decidedly unneutral. On 7 November the U.S. legation in Bogotá was asked whether Washington would allow Colombia to land its troops on the isthmus and whether (on the basis of the 1846 treaty) it would itself act to suppress the revolt if Colombia could not. The reply came on 11 November that it was 'not thought desirable' for Colombian forces to enter Panama, for fear of 'civil war' and disruption of the railway. Roosevelt had spelled out the message more bluntly in a letter to his son Kermit a week earlier. 'I do not intend in the police work that I will have to do in connection with the new insurrection any longer to do for her [Colombia] work which is not merely profitless but brings no gratitude. Any interference I undertake now will be in the interest of the United States and of the people of the Isthmus.'[26]

The Colombian leadership had no reason to expect anything different from Washington, and its forebodings were confirmed when news of the U.S. recognition of Panama reached Bogotá on 11 November. Reyes had just left for talks with the Panamanian junta in Colón, but the announcement doomed the mission to failure. Though Reyes offered Panama complete autonomy plus all the revenue due to Colombia under the Hay–Herrán treaty, the Panamanians were not interested, and Reyes left to continue the uphill struggle in Washington. Meanwhile, anguished notes were delivered to U.S. Minister Beaupré. The first denounced the U.S. recognition – correctly – as a violation of the 1846 treaty and proposed submitting the issue to the Permanent Court of Arbitration at The Hague. The second held out the desperate hope that Washington would promote a settlement based on a renunciation of Panamanian independence. The Roosevelt administration had done with Colombia, however, and it turned its back decisively on Bogotá by signing a new canal treaty with Panama.[27]

The man it dealt with was Bunau-Varilla, who on 6 November was nominated envoy extraordinary and minister plenipotentiary to Washington, fully empowered to conduct diplomatic and financial negotiations. This was an extremely dangerous appointment from Panama's point of view, bearing in mind the disregard for Panamanian national interests Bunau-Varilla had already revealed to Amador, and the junta soon had second thoughts about its wisdom. On 9

---

[26] Thayer, *Hay*, 2: 326. *BD*, 260, 261, 262, 268. *TR letters*, 3: 644.

[27] Miner, *Panama route*, 372–4. Ernesto Castillero Pimentel, *Panamá y los Estados Unidos* (Panamá, 1953), 75–6. U.S. Department of State, *Diplomatic history of the Panama Canal . . .* (1914), 478–9.

November the new envoy was told to negotiate no agreement without consulting Amador and Federico Boyd, who were to join him in Washington. The two Panamanian delegates left for the United States the next day, armed with authority to supervise discussions closely and, if need be, to deal directly with Hay. Though Bunau-Varilla had their instructions countermanded while they were at sea, he knew they were likely to insist on having everything cleared with them. This could well produce a treaty unacceptable to the U.S. Senate and so prevent ratification. Bunau-Varilla was therefore determined to get an agreement signed before Amador and Boyd arrived in New York on 17 November.[28]

The junta's thinking on the shape of a new treaty was cabled to Bunau-Varilla on 9 November; it instructed him to work for six main concessions. Lands in Panama City and Colón leased to the canal and railway companies, and lands in Panama City unoccupied by them, should revert to Panama. The canal company should agree in advance to hand over the Panama a share of the proceeds from the sale of its assets. Panama should have the power to levy duty on imported tobacco, cigarettes, spirits, and opium. The projected U.S. courts for the zone should be replaced by joint tribunals, and the United States should be asked to make Panama a protectorate. Finally, $2 million of the canal indemnity should be given to Panama, leaving $8 million to be invested by the U.S. government so as to produce an annual income of $240,000 in addition to the $250,000 annuity.[29]

Much more in tune with Bunau-Varilla's approach was the treaty outline sent to Hay by Duque. Panamanians, Duque told Hay, wanted a treaty which granted the United States everything it required, in exchange for a protectorate and a guarantee of Panama's sovereignty. Washington should be given a wider canal zone where it would exercise absolute police and sanitary control; the police should be American-officered, since Panamanians would 'never be able to cope with a riot or a strike'. There must be no Panamanian army and no state gambling concession (Duque himself leased the highly profitable lottery franchise). The feeling in Panama, Duque concluded, was 'to do nothing and take no steps without the guidance of the United States'.[30]

But Hay needed no prompting from Duque on what served American interests best. On 10 November he produced a draft which amounted to a fundamental revision of the Hay–Herrán treaty. Although half the articles of Hay–Herrán were retained, the remainder were either deleted or reworded in order to maximise American authority over the canal and leave Panama no loophole for evasion. Thus, American tenure of the canal was to be in perpetuity, while U.S. rights over the canal were extended to include ownership and the power to

[28] BD, 258–9, 254. Miner, *Panama route*, 374–5. B-V Papers, De la Espriella to Bunau-Varilla, 9.11.03 and Junta Decree of 9.11.03.

[29] B-V Papers, De la Espriella to Bunau-Varilla, 14.11.03.

[30] Hay Papers, roll 18, Duque to Hay, 2 and 16.11.03.

develop the waterway as a commercial enterprise. The canal zone straddling the cut was to be widened from ten kilometres to ten miles, and the terminal cities, previously left out of the zone, were now to be brought into it. No land whatever, in or beyond the zone, would revert to Panama.[31]

Nor was Panamanian sovereignty over its territory anywhere recognised, and by the same token the draft cancelled the guarantees which Hay–Herrán had given of local sovereignty over the zone, the terminal cities, and coastal islands and harbours. Panama also suffered by being cut out of any share of jurisdiction in the zone, and by elimination of the indigenous courts and the joint tribunals hitherto provided for. Similarly, while Colombia had been allotted a nominal role in canal defence, the United States was now to enjoy complete discretion. Finally, though the draft proposed maintaining the annuity of $250,000, the figure for the canal indemnity was now left blank.[32]

In scrapping the Hay–Herrán convention, Hay had stripped away the window-dressing which it had draped over the reality of American power and left Panama with barely a shred of independence. In doing so, he modelled his draft on the amended version of Hay–Herrán put together the previous March by Senator Morgan. Morgan's amendments had been designed to make the treaty so overwhelmingly favourable to Washington that it would stand no chance of being ratified by Colombia. Hay, however, was well aware that Panama would have to swallow the amendments willy-nilly, and he followed them closely. Of the fifteen articles in the draft that departed from Hay–Herrán, no fewer than twelve were influenced by Morgan's revision, and several reproduced Morgan's wording verbatim. On three important issues – defence, the recognition of local sovereignty, and U.S. jurisdiction in the canal zone – Hay even went beyond Morgan, but there too it was Morgan who supplied the inspiration.[33]

By 15 November, when it was handed to Bunau-Varilla, the project had been added to in several respects. A new clause made Panama City and Colón responsible for paying off the capital cost of the water and sewerage systems the canal administration was to install. Fortifications for canal defence were explicitly authorised, and a stipulation inserted at the Navy Department's behest obliged Panama to sell or lease land on both its coasts for naval or coaling stations.[34]

Most important, a new first article proclaimed, 'The United States guaran-

[31] Jessup, *Root*, 1: 406. Root Papers, Hay to Root, 10.11.03, with enclosed treaty draft.
[32] The Hay draft articles referred to in this and the preceding paragraph are 2, 3, 11, 20, 21, and 22; the Hay–Herrán articles stricken were 4, 6, 19, and 24. The text of the Hay–Herrán convention may be found in *BD*, 202–13.
[33] The Hay–Herrán convention as revised by Morgan is printed in *CR*, 9.3.03, 14–16. In the debate on the new convention in February 1904, Morgan noted that though his amendments had been rejected the preceding year, they were now incorporated in the substitute agreement: *CR*, 20.2.04, 2127.
[34] Drafts, 95–110. Richard Challener, *Admirals, generals and American foreign policy, 1898–1914* (Princeton, N.J., 1973), 93–4.

tees and will maintain the independence of the Republic in Panama.' This appeared to mark a significant change in U.S. policy. Such a guarantee had not been offered to Colombia under the Hay–Herrán treaty, and it had not been featured in Hay's draft of 10 November. However, it was probably intended to do no more than serve notice that whoever questioned Panama's title to statehood would have to reckon with Washington. In other words, it ensured Panama's national survival against any threat from Colombia.[35]

Hay was certainly not prepared to offer the specific pledges which Panama had asked Bunau-Varilla to secure, namely, of Panama's sovereignty, its territorial integrity, and its public order. His deletion of the various Hay–Herrán acknowledgements of local sovereignty indicated that he saw any such recognition as a potential challenge to American rights, and the new article did nothing to contradict that stance. Nor did he guarantee Panama's frontiers as the 1846 treaty had guaranteed the isthmus 'from its southern extremity until the boundary of Costa Rica'. As we have seen, in the Hay–Herrán accord he had whittled the 1846 guarantee down to cover only the canal zone and the terminal cities, and the new article was entirely consistent with that restrictive approach. Finally, he was unwilling to underwrite law and order throughout the new republic. This was completely in line with Washington's refusal since 1846 to interpret its treaty commitment as an obligation to maintain internal security in Panama; the independence guarantee signified no change in that policy.[36]

The existence of the two American drafts was ignored for a remarkably long time, despite several pointers to them. In Thayer's biography of Hay, Hay is quoted as saying of the convention with Panama, 'Not only did I embody in it all [Morgan's] amendments to the Herran treaty, but I went further than he has ever done in getting the proper guaranties for jurisdiction over the Canal.' The Hay papers contain a letter to Senator Spooner of 14 November 1903 where Hay points out that in the altered version of the treaty Panama and Colón come inside the canal zone, entirely under American authority. In his biography of Root, Philip Jessup recounts that on 10 November 1903 Hay sent Root the first draft for his comments, and it can be found in Root's papers. Finally, in a survey of U.S.–Panamanian relations by the veteran Panamanian diplomat Ricardo Alfaro there is a summary of the American revision of 15 November which tallies closely with the text held in the U.S. National Archives.[37]

---

[35] Drafts, 95–6.

[36] B-V Papers, De la Espriella to Bunau-Varilla, 9.11.03. *BD*, 8. The American guarantee to Panama was notably more guarded than the French guarantee to the rebel United States of their 'liberty, sovereignty, and independance, absolute and unlimited' in the alliance treaty of 1778: See Malloy *Treaties*, 1: 481–2.

[37] John Major, 'Who wrote the Hay–Bunau-Varilla Convention?' *Diplomatic History*, 8 (1984), 115–23. Thayer, *Hay*, 2: 327. Hay Papers, roll 14, Hay to Spooner, 14.11.03. Jessup, *Root*, 1: 406. Ricardo Alfaro, *Medio siglo de relaciones entre Panamá y los Estados Unidos* (Panamá, 1959 edn), 18–20.

The failure to follow up these clues perpetuated the myth created by Bunau-Varilla that he had been the architect of the new treaty. In his memoirs he stated that he had written it 'from the first line to the last'. The draft he received from Hay on 15 November was 'the Hay–Herrán treaty with insignificant modifications', which he then proceeded to recast fundamentally.[38]

Bunau-Varilla's account of his treaty-making rôle was taken for gospel from then on. Thus William McCain, in his standard work on U.S.–Panamanian relations, affirms that 'the Frenchman drafted the convention, and Hay speedily accepted it without important alteration'. For Walter LaFeber, author of another influential book on the canal, the agreement was 'the Frenchman's treaty', and, in the words of Charles Ameringer in his detailed study of the treaty's composition, the United States 'accepted the windfall'.[39]

Only one man guessed the truth. In 1953 the American diplomat Roy Tasco Davis, Jr, suggested that 'Bunau-Varilla's compulsion to always depict himself as the mastermind of the negotiation and ratification of the treaty may have resulted in a distorted version of the facts and a picture of Bunau-Varilla's importance in the determination of the terms of the treaty that is out of proportion'. Mr Davis was right. Bunau-Varilla's claim to be the only begetter of the accord is an impudent misrepresentation, designed to keep the spotlight of history permanently fixed on his own achievement.[40]

This is not to say that Bunau-Varilla's tale was pure vainglory. He did indeed set his personal mark on the treaty in his response to Hay's draft, produced in less than forty-eight hours in collaboration with the New York lawyer Frank Pavey. His reply was twofold. First he presented a revision of the Hay project which accepted the bulk of Hay's changes to Hay–Herrán. However, he suggested some amendments, all of which restored the wording of Hay–Herrán. The proposed right to develop the canal commercially was seen as objectionable, as were the American refusal to allow any land to revert to Panama and American insistence that the terminal cities be included in the zone. Critics of the treaty would attack U.S. retention of the land outside the cities as a 'grab' by Washington, and the same stricture would be levelled at the absorption of the terminals into the zone. It would also be indefensible for Panama either to move its seat of government elsewhere or to maintain it in an area under U.S. jurisdiction.[41]

In the second place, Bunau-Varilla offered a counter-draft of his own. It

[38] SD, 1910–49, 711.1928/185. Bunau-Varilla, *Panama*, 384, 368.
[39] Ernesto Castillero Reyes, *El profeta de Panamá y su gran traición* (Panamá, 1936). William McCain, *The United States and the Republic of Panama* (Durham, N.C., 1937), 17. Walter LaFeber, *The Panama Canal: The crisis in historical perspective* (New York, 1977), 39. Charles Ameringer, 'Philippe Bunau-Varilla: New light on the Panama Canal treaty', *Hispanic American Historical Review*, 46 (1966), 52.
[40] SD, 1950–4, 811F.5301/8–1453, Davis memo of 13.8.53.
[41] Drafts, 136–9.

reinstated the $10 million indemnity which Hay had put in doubt and restored a highly important condition struck out by Hay, namely, that the canal should be operated in keeping with the terms of the Hay–Pauncefote treaty. It deleted the rights which the Hay draft had claimed to the ownership and control of the canal, besides an article safeguarding U.S. prerogatives if a sea-level canal were built and a clause which gave the United States exclusive control of immigration into the zone.[42]

At the same time, however, Bunau-Varilla conceded even more than Hay demanded. By the terms of Article 2 the United States was to have not only the perpetual lease of a canal zone but a lien in perpetuity over any lands and waters outside the zone which might be required for canal purposes. In Article 5 Washington was granted a permanent monopoly over any future isthmian canal or railroad. Article 7 reflected Bunau-Varilla's deep preoccupation with the danger of disease, understandable in a man who had nearly died of yellow fever during French project. He had already added sanitation to the list of American rights, and here he gave the United States the power to expropriate property in Panama and Colón on public health grounds, as well as the authority to enforce the sanitary regulations it prescribed for the two townships if the Panamanians failed to do so.[43]

Most important, in Article 3 Bunau-Varilla alienated Panamanian sovereignty to the United States. His counter-draft gave the United States, both within the zone and on land it might acquire beyond it, 'all the rights, power and authority . . . which [it] would possess and exercise if it were the sovereign of the territory . . . to the entire exclusion of the exercise by the Republic of Panama of any such sovereign rights, power or authority'. The formula stood as the centre-piece of Bunau-Varilla's counter-proposal, and its gift of the equivalent of sovereignty was clearly designed to make his project irresistible to the administration and to the Senate when the time came for ratification.[44]

The phraseology of the sovereignty article coincided closely with the thinking in some American circles. In 1896 Professor Theodore Woolsey of the Yale Law School had argued that control of an interoceanic canal might best be secured by 'the transfer of sovereignty over the region in which the canal lies'. In 1902 Admiral George Dewey had cited the foreign spheres of influence recently set up in China as a sound precedent for a canal zone. Russia had been given 'the absolute and exclusive right of administration' in the lands leased to it for a trans-Manchurian railway (soon to be known as 'the railway zone'). When it allowed Germany to occupy Jiaozhou, China had agreed to suspend its own sovereign rights in the area and left their exercise to the German authorities. These concessions were sharply criticised by Washington as infractions of China's

[42] Ibid., 111–31.
[43] Ibid. On Bunau-Varilla and the French project, see Anguizola, *Bunau-Varilla*, 88–114.
[44] Drafts, 111–31. *Times*, 10.11.03, 5/3. Bunau-Varilla, *Panama*, 368–9.

sovereignty, and Hay did not write a similar donation into his own draft. Yet he was not loath to take it when it was offered by Panama's ultra-generous envoy.[45]

In doing so, moreover, Hay knew that Article 3 gave the United States an unshakeable tenure not enjoyed by the foreign powers in China. Their enclaves were leaseholds of up to ninety-nine years, whereas the American zone was to be everlasting. It was true that, as the *New York Tribune* pointed out, the nation was not 'in a political sense acquiring territory or annexing new lands to its domain'. But the canal zone was to be decidedly more than what the *Tribune* called 'merely a commercial cession . . . of land for a specified purpose'. It was to become the exclusive preserve of the United States, and it was effectively lost to Panama, whose prerogatives over it had been emphatically suppressed. Both these momentous consequences were the legacy of Bunau-Varilla.[46]

Bunau-Varilla's counter-proposal was delivered to Hay's office early in the morning of 17 November, together with the amended version of Hay's draft. The counter-project, he felt, was the better of the two in that it had the advantage of 'conferring upon the United States in broad and general terms the rights she is entitled to have; rendering it thus unnecessary to enumerate in an infinity of *cas particuliers*, what right [*sic*] Colombia was generous enough to grant'. Moreover – a prediction that could scarcely have been more disingenuous – it offered 'infinitely less probability of eventual discussions between the two countries than the old form'.[47]

At a meeting with Bunau-Varilla in the evening of 17 November, Hay accepted that Bunau-Varilla's counter-draft was preferable to his own. At the same time, he raised the possibility of dividing the $10 million canal indemnity between Panama and Colombia as a gesture to the pro-Colombian element in the Senate, where the treaty would have to go for approval. Though Bunau-Varilla was all in favour of disarming Senate opposition, he drew the line at this. Splitting the indemnity would make it seem as though Washington were succumbing to blackmail 'on account of a concealed crime', that is, by abetting secession in a fellow American republic. In compensation he threw in two more concessions under Article 7: to apply the American right of expropriation to 'anything in reference to the canal' and to give the United States the additional right of

[45] Theodore Woolsey, 'An interoceanic canal from the standpoint of self-interest', *Yale Review*, 4 (1896), 357. GB, 414, s.284, Dewey to Moody, 7.10.02. John MacMurray (ed.), *Treaties and agreements with and concerning China, 1894–1919*, vol. 1 (New York, 1921), 76, 114. Richard Baxter, *The law of international waterways: With particular regard to interoceanic canals* (Cambridge, Mass., 1964), 72. Paul Varg, *The making of a myth: The United States and China, 1897–1912* (East Lansing, Mich., 1968), 20–6.
[46] *Times*, 23.11.03, 5/2, quoting the comments of the *Tribune*.
[47] Miner, *Panama route*, 375. Bunau-Varilla, *Panama*, 370. *CR* (Senate), 17.3.03, 107–10, gives Senator Cullom's convincing reasons why the United States had nothing to fear from Colombia under the Hay–Herrán treaty.

intervention to preserve public order in Panama City and Colón if, in Washington's judgement, the Panamanian authorities should be incapable of it.[48]

Bunau-Varilla's counter-draft and his proposed addenda were scrutinised over lunch next day by Hay; Root; the attorney general, Philander Chase Knox; and the secretary of the Treasury, Leslie Shaw. Both his text and the two additions to Article 7 were accepted, and only one significant change was made in the counter-draft. In Article 2 he had proposed the perpetual lease of a canal zone to the United States. Hay, however, preferred the phraseology of his own draft, which had followed Hay–Herrán in stipulating a grant in perpetuity of the use and control of the zone. Hay added 'occupation' for good measure, though this was a marginal alteration beside his insistence on a grant rather than a lease. Bunau-Varilla had tried to establish Panama and the United States in the relation of landlord and tenant. In 1938 he was to write that 'the concession [to] a lessee of the rights of the proprietor, within certain limits and for a certain purpose, never [was] held anywhere as an abandonment of the property itself'. By securing an outright grant of the zone, however, Hay was placing Panama in a much weaker position vis-à-vis the United States, and his amendment deprived the Panamanians of useful leverage in any future dispute over the treaty. On this basis the Hay–Bunau-Varilla Convention was signed early in the evening of 18 November.[49]

The accomplishment came not a moment too soon for Bunau-Varilla. Amador and Boyd were then on their way to Washington by train, and Bunau-Varilla was delighted to present them with a fait accompli. As he had expected, the news came to them as a very unwelcome surprise, and the aged Amador almost collapsed. Next day the two Panamanians refused to accept responsibility for ratifying the treaty and claimed it would have to go to Panama for consideration by the junta. Hay's response was twofold: the threat of 'grave consequences' if Panama did not ratify quickly and the promise of a supplementary agreement to cover points not in the convention.[50]

[48] Bunau-Varilla, *Panama*, 369, 374–5. NLP, Bunau-Varilla to Hay, 18.11.03. Auguizola, *Bunau-Varilla*, 59–65, gives Bunau-Varilla's reaction to the 1885 insurgency.

[49] Thayer, *Hay*, 2: 318. NLP, Bunau-Varilla counter-draft of 17.11.03, Article 2, as amended. Bunau-Varilla, *Panama*, 376. B-V Papers, De la Espriella to Bunau-Varilla, 7.12.03, with marginal note of 12.8.38. Bunau-Varilla, then nearly eighty years old, appears to have thought that the treaty ordained a lease, not a grant, on Panama's part. It is a common mistake, made by, among many others, John Foster Dulles in conversation with James Forrestal in 1946; see *FRUS 1946*, 1: 638. See also Hans Aufricht, 'On relative sovereignty', *Cornell Law Quarterly*, 30 (1944–5), 54–6: 'A State which acquires a lease on foreign territory for but a limited purpose is entitled to exercise the rights of territorial jurisdiction which are expressly conferred by the underlying agreement. In all other respects the lessor retains the rights of jurisdiction implied in "territorial sovereignty".' Aufricht contrasts this with the situation obtaining under the 1903 convention.

[50] Miner, *Panama route*, 378. Castillero, *Panamá y los EEUU*, 38.

The interview produced the intended effect when on 21 November the delegates cabled approval of the treaty, which they assured the junta was tantamount to Hay–Herrán 'with very slight modification'! This matched Bunau-Varilla's misleading description of the treaty as a settlement containing the same political and financial conditions as its predecessor but with 'necessary simplifications referring to jurisdiction and analogous stipulations'. Panama should respond with an immediate ratification. Thus it would ensure a favourable reception for the treaty in the U.S. Senate, whereas delay on Panama's part could only strengthen Roosevelt's enemies.[51]

At first the junta was unwilling to endorse a document it had not yet seen and insisted that the treaty be sent to the isthmus by the next steamer out of New York, due to reach Colón on 1 December. Bunau-Varilla was reluctantly compelled to agree, but on 25 November he warned that if Panama did not act as soon as the treaty got to Colón, Washington was likely to pull out its forces and come to terms with Colombia. The reply came instantly from Panama that the treaty would be sanctioned 'on receipt'. Even then Bunau-Varilla was nervous. General Reyes, on his arrival in Washington on 28 November, told the press that he was ready to grant a canal concession to the United States 'without the payment of a cent'. The slightest hesitation on Panama's part, Bunau-Varilla feared, could play directly into Reyes's hands. The junta rose to the occasion. At 11:30 in the morning of 2 December, less than twenty-four hours after being brought to Panama City, the convention was ratified. There cannot have been time to make a Spanish translation of the English text or to make copies for distribution to the nine men due to confirm the agreement. The likelihood is that the Hay–Bunau-Varilla treaty was not even read by the signatories of the ratification decree, though it was to reduce their country to little more than vassalage.[52]

The first sign of regret came in a plaintive letter to Bunau-Varilla from the Panamanian foreign minister on 7 December, in which he lamented 'the explicit renunciation' of Panamanian sovereignty. The new treaty differed from the old 'in a manner detrimental to the Republic', though he took comfort in saying that Washington had guaranteed not only the independence and sovereignty of the new state but also its public order – 'an inestimable benefit'. This was in fact a delusion. The United States had guaranteed Panama's independence but not its sovereignty. Indeed, Article 2 of the treaty could in principle have been interpreted to justify American acquisition of the whole of Panama for canal purposes, and the United States would then have possessed sovereign rights over the entire republic. As for the guarantee of public order, this by Article 7

[51] Castillero, *Panamá y los EEUU*, 42–4. B-V Papers, Bunau-Varilla to de la Espriella, 18 and 21.11.03.

[52] Ameringer, 'Bunau-Varilla', 45–8. Castillero, *Panamá y los EEUU*, 44–59. *NYT*, 29.11.03, 1/1.

was confined to Panama City and Colón, and the Panamanian leadership was
again giving way to wishful thinking brought on by the junta's deep sense of
insecurity. It felt exposed to an imminent Colombian onslaught, and recent
trouble in the army had raised the possibility that the revolution would run out
of control and turn against its creators. Panama was thus clinging to the United
States as its saviour from a military coup as well as from the nightmare of
Colombian retribution.[53]

Panamanian fears on both counts were wildly exaggerated, but to provide the
necessary reassurance some 1,500 more U.S. Marines were sent out to the
isthmus in December, bringing the total strength to close on 2,000. This would
have a chastening effect on any of the Panamanian military who might be 'luke
warm in their allegiance to the new government' and serve as a salutary show
of force for what the *New York Times* called 'the motley gang of boys and
roustabouts constituting the army of the Republic of Panama'. The threat from
Colombia was also well in hand. When General Reyes repeated the request that
Washington allow Colombian troops to land, Roosevelt fired back that in the
event of a landing 'they will be repelled and their ports blockaded'. Hay for his
part made it plain that the administration would not let Colombian forces in,
since the new treaty had created 'inchoate rights and duties' which committed
the United States and Panama to 'preserving peace and order on the Isthmus'.
There was, of course, no such commitment in the treaty, and Hay presumably
meant the unilateral American guarantee of Panamanian independence. If so,
this could be achieved by the U.S. Navy: As long as its warships dominated the
sea approaches to Panama, a Colombian invasion was out of the question. The
only alternative was a ground assault, but between the Colombian border and
the secessionist capital lay nearly two hundred miles of impassable mountain
and jungle terrain, and as Reyes himself was to admit, this ruled out an overland campaign. The revolution appeared impregnable against outside attack.[54]

Even so, the service departments were anxious to cover the contingency. On
11 December, Marines were ordered into the frontier province of Darién, and
Admiral Glass was told to make the outposts strong enough to resist a Colombian
thrust. On 18 December the naval commanders were instructed to confine the
defence of Panama to the vicinity of the railway, but this policy of minimum
commitment came up against considerable War Department opposition. An
Army report from the isthmus warned of the possibility that the Colombians
would wage 'a desultory and annoying irregular guerrilla warfare', and on 23
December the Joint Board of the Army and Navy recommended that Darién be

[53] B-V Papers, De la Espriella to Bunau-Varilla, 7.12.03.
[54] *NYT*, 9.12.03, 1/5; 15.12.03, 3/1; 29.12.03, 1/1; 10.12.03, 1/5. WCD, 7113B, Cloman and
Haan memo of 7.12.03. *BD*, 320. Loomis Papers, roll 3, Loomis to Hay, 10.12.03. *BD*, 320–
1. WCD, 7113B, Edie to O'Reilly, 28.11.03. *BD*, 330.

reinforced at once to forestall a Colombian occupation, which would be certain to bring on large-scale hostilities.[55]

The proposal was rejected by Roosevelt, partly because he wanted to avoid a clash with Colombia that could lead to war rather than prevent it. War would almost certainly have met with fierce resistance in Congress, and it would have been fought for no better reason than to cancel out the marginal disadvantages of a Colombian base at a spot still 130 miles from Panama City.[56]

Roosevelt also had strong diplomatic motives for avoiding hostilities. He was under some pressure from Senator Henry Cabot Lodge to try for a settlement on lines put forward by General Reyes, namely, Colombian acceptance of the new treaty in toto, the reunion of Colombia and Panama, and the division of the $10 million indemnity between them. Though averse to the scheme, Roosevelt was willing to prompt a Panama–Colombia rapprochement on the basis of their separate statehood, and he therefore chose not to provoke Colombia. For the same reason, Hay told Reyes that the administration would not regard a Colombian invasion of Panama as a casus belli in spite of the U.S. guarantee of Panama's independence. American caution was equalled by that of the Colombian leadership. On 13 December, Reyes had urged Bogotá not to move troops into Panamanian territory while his mission was still in progress, and the commander of the expeditionary force was given orders to remain where he was. So the military confrontation with Colombia failed to materialise.[57]

Holding back from the brink did not, however, improve the chances of an agreement over Panama, as Reyes well knew. When he saw Hay on 23 December to hand over a long note of protest, he confessed that Bogotá had expected him to achieve the impossible. Hay for his part underlined the hopelessness of the Colombian position by telling Reyes that Panama was 'an accomplished fact which we would neither undo ourselves nor permit any outside parties to overthrow'. Reyes's statement of grievances therefore had no chance from the moment of its presentation, even though its arguments were incontrovertible. Reyes contended that Washington had broken its 1846 guarantee of Colombia's rights of sovereignty and property over the isthmus, and to make the pledge good once again, it should 'return the property to its legitimate owner'. Meanwhile he proposed to take Colombia's case to the Permanent Court of Arbitration at The Hague.[58]

[55] DuVal, *Cadiz to Cathay*, 362–72. Lemaitre, *Panamá*, 603–5. Challener, *Admirals*, 156–8. JB, 326–1, Young to Root, 21.12.03. GSR, Report 818 of 23.12.03.

[56] GSR, Report 818 of 23.12.03. *TR letters*, 3: 678. Challener, *Admirals*, 158–9.

[57] Henry Cabot Lodge (ed.), *Selections from the correspondence of Theodore Roosevelt and Henry Cabot Lodge 1884–1918*, vol. 2, (New York, 1925), 72–3. *TR letters*, 3: 663. BD, 321–2. Lemaitre, *Panamá*, 605–10. Nikol and Holbrook, 'Naval operations', 259–60.

[58] Hay Papers, roll 4, Hay to Roosevelt, 24.12.03. BD, 330–1, 332, 333, 335. After handing the protest note over, Reyes was ready to deal with Washington only on the basis of Hay-

Hay's reply – drafted by Moore – was given within a fortnight. Washington, Hay argued, had met its commitment to protect the isthmus against outside attack and had no obligation to defend Bogotá against a Panamanian insurrection. When it recognised Panama, it acted in a double sense to fulfil the 1846 treaty, not to violate it. First, it elected to deal with a state that was ready to consummate the treaty's 'great design', an isthmian transit. Second, as the treaty intended, it simply carried over the guarantee of 'the sovereign of the Isthmus' from Bogotá to Panama City. Panama, 'as the successor in sovereignty of Colombia, became entitled to the rights and subject to the obligations of the treaty'. The rights were those of a protectorate; the obligations, to grant its protector control of a canal. In short, it was Colombia, not the United States, which had contravened the treaty, and Reyes's accusations had no force, since their grounds were political and so beyond the scope of international arbitration.[59]

Reyes was quick to point out the fallacies in Hay's reasoning. In the first place, whatever the merits of the American assertion that the 1846 guarantee did not apply in the case of a domestic insurgency, the United States had no treaty right to prevent Colombia from putting down a rebellion. In the second place, the guarantee of sovereignty and property was given specifically to Bogotá and was not transferrable. 'It is as untenable a proposition in law', wrote Reyes, 'to hold obligations toward a nation as fulfilled in one of its rebellious or separated provinces as, in mathematics, to insist that the part and the whole are equivalent.' These again were irrefutable arguments, but they were meaningless to Washington. In a cursory reply drafted by Bunau-Varilla, Hay suggested a plebiscite in Panama to choose between independence and reunion with Colombia and the submission to a special court of arbitration of the claims which the two governments could agree to bring against each other. Since both proposals assumed Colombian recognition of the new status quo, there was nothing here for Colombia's comfort. In any case, Reyes had already left Washington, and with his departure a mission that had been doomed from the beginning came to its foregone conclusion.[60]

The fate of the treaty in the Senate was still undecided, however. Reyes and Herrán had been working for its defeat since early December, and they had some important allies. On 9 December, Senator George Hoar introduced a resolution questioning the legality of the Panamanian junta and hence the validity of its ratification decree. Senatorial approval of the treaty, Hoar claimed, could not be given until Panama had a constitutional government. The next day Bunau-Varilla pressed the junta to arrange a speedy legitimation. On 27 December

Herrán, a sure sign that he had abandoned hope of winning over the Senate: See Drafts, 156–7.
[59] *BD*, 345–8.
[60] *BD*, 354, 355–6. Bunau-Varilla, *Panama*, 418–19.

voting for a constitutional assembly of thirty-three members took place, and it met on 15 January 1904.[61]

The administration's interest in a Panamanian constitution had been prompted solely by the need to get a favourable decision on the treaty in the Senate. The document which shortly emerged did a great deal more than this for the United States, however, endowing it with an extensive power neither offered nor sought in the treaty negotiations. It was bestowed thanks to the Conservative majority in the Assembly and the newly appointed U.S. minister to Panama, William Buchanan. On 4 January, Buchanan reported that many Panamanians wanted an article giving their protector a right and an obligation 'to intervene at all times to stop internal revolutions'. Some were even ready to see Panama annexed to the United States to forestall revolt. Buchanan's own alternative was to eliminate the only real danger, the Panamanian army, and set up a police force carrying only revolvers and dispersed around the country so as to avoid a concentration in Panama City and Colón. Tight gun control should be introduced and the government's arms and ammunition stored in the canal zone. Panamanians should forswear their long-standing 'disorder, inconsistencies and irrational procedure', and if 'a strong tactful capable man' were brought in as United States minister and governor of the zone, everything would be 'smooth sailing after the first year or two'. The immediate need, however, was for a clause in the constitution authorising U.S. intervention 'anywhere within the Republic to insure public safety and orderly government'.[62]

In saying these things, Buchanan was recalling the language of the so-called Platt Amendment on Cuba drawn up by Root and written into the Cuban constitution in 1901. Root's proviso gave the United States the right to intervene in Cuba 'for the preservation of Cuban independence and the maintenance of a stable government adequately protecting life, property, and individual liberty'. In the view of the editor of the *New York Tribune*, Whitelaw Reid, Panama was a parallel instance. It was 'a suzerainty somewhat similar to that which the inevitable application of the Monroe Doctrine . . . must ultimately compel us to assume with reference to the whole region of the Caribbean Sea and the Gulf of Mexico – as we have already assumed it with reference to Cuba'.[63]

[61] Ameringer, 'Bunau-Varilla', 50–1. B-V Papers, Bunau-Varilla to Loomis, 10.12.03, and Bunau-Varilla to de la Espriella, 10.12.03. *NYT*, 13.12.03, 1/7. Gustavo Mellander, *The United States in Panamanian politics: The intriguing formative years* (Danville, Ill., 1971), 46–8.

[62] USD, Buchanan to Hay, 4, 5, and 7.1.04. WCD, 7113A, Cloman to Young, 18.1.04. Hay Papers, roll 18, Duque to Hay, 16 and 30.11.03. See also Harold Peterson, *Diplomat of the Americas: A biography of William I. Buchanan (1852–1909)* (Albany, N.Y., 1977), 238–60.

[63] Malloy, *Treaties*, 1: 362. Royal Cortissoz, *The life of Whitelaw Reid*, vol. 2 (London, 1921), 293. On the Platt Amendment, see H. F. Guggenheim, *The United States and Cuba: A study in international relations* (New York, 1934), 52–3, 61–101. Root's original wording is quoted; it was later altered by Senator Platt to 'the maintenance of a government adequate for the protection of life, property, and individual liberty'. See also David Healy, *The United States*

Yet the position of the two protectorates was different – internationally, internally, and historically. Root had described Article 3 of the amendment as 'the Monroe Doctrine, but with international force', and as such it was designed to close the door on European involvement in Cuban affairs. In Panama, by contrast, now that the only serious foreign competitor, Britain, had chosen to withdraw from the scene, the United States was absolute, and there was no other external threat on the horizon.[64]

Domestically too, Panama presented fewer problems than Cuba. After the U.S. seizure of Cuba from Spain in 1898, the island was held under military occupation until it was considered safe to hand over to the Cubans. Washington imposed no such régime on Panama, because the country's capacity to challenge American power was negligible. It was smaller in area than the state of Maine, and Cincinnati had a bigger population. Its economy was pre-industrial, it had no navy, and its army totalled no more than a few hundred poorly armed troops, some of them barefoot juveniles. Such a puny ward was unlikely to trouble its guardian enough to warrant the kind of tutelage clamped on Cuba.[65]

American attitudes towards the two territories had also been quite dissimilar. Washington had coveted Cuba for at least a century. It was seen as a natural appendage of the U.S. mainland, it dominated the Caribbean strategically, and American citizens had built up substantial economic interests throughout the island. Panama, however, was geographically part of Central America, its strategic value was confined to the transit, and there were few American investments in the country at large. U.S. attention had consequently been fixed on the transit alone, and as long as that was safe, what went on elsewhere on the isthmus was at best peripheral in American eyes.[66]

This was certainly the view taken in the State Department, where Buchanan's advice was not welcome. Hay's assistant secretary, Alvey Adee, was strongly against the idea of U.S. political intervention. For Adee it was only the canal zone that counted, and the Panama constitution should contain nothing that would impede the 'free discretion' of the United States in protecting it. Hay fully agreed. He had, after all, denied Reyes's argument that Washington had a responsibility to keep the peace on the isthmus, and he told Buchanan that the suggested article would 'morally bind' the United States to intervene. The constitution should therefore include 'nothing in conflict with the widest liberty of action on our part.'[67]

    in Cuba, 1898–1902: Generals, politicians and the search for policy (Madison, Wisc., 1963), 159–78, 211–15.

[64] Jessup, *Root*, 1: 406–7, 309, 315, 319. John Campbell, 'Taft, Roosevelt and the arbitration treaties of 1911', *Journal of American History*, 53 (1966–7), 295. Healy, *Cuba*, 172, 213.

[65] See Healy, *Cuba*, 48–52, 86–7, 110–15, 121–2, 132–4, 150–78, 207–15.

[66] Connell-Smith, *United States and Latin America*, 45, 59–60, 66–8, 81–2, 100.

[67] USD, Adee to Hay, 18.1.04; Adee to Loomis, 20.1.04; Hay to Buchanan, 19.1.04.

Buchanan, however, ignored these instructions. On 28 January he reported that he had secured what became Article 136 of the constitution, which allowed the United States to intervene 'in any part of the Republic of Panama to re-establish public peace and constitutional order in the event of their being disturbed'. This wording threatened to raise a host of difficulties, though Buchanan managed to persuade himself that the provision need never be brought into play. Its deterrent effect would be everything: 'the mere fact of the article reading thus being sufficient of itself' to ensure domestic tranquillity in Panama. That remained to be seen.[68]

In view of its potential importance, it is surprising that the intervention clause produced no discernible repercussions in the Senate, where debate on the treaty was under way. On 18 January the Senate Foreign Relations Committee entered three amendments, formulated to deny Panama any leeway arising from ambiguities of phrasing. The first delimited the harbours of Panama City and Colón in such a way as to ensure that the deep-water terminals of La Boca and Cristóbal could not be brought within them and so be excluded from the zone. The second likewise defined the land areas of the two municipalities as narrowly as possible to give the utmost territory to the zone. The third sought maximum U.S. control of sanitation in the townships by giving the zone authorities permanent powers to regulate public health.[69]

As the administration saw it, the committee's amendments put the treaty in jeopardy, and Cullom and Spooner were urged to have them dropped. Hay told Spooner that he doubted whether the Panamanians would accept the revisions, and he wrote to Cullom that it needed only a glance to see 'what an infinite field of amendments there is from their point of view'. The convention was, he added to Spooner, 'we must confess, with what face we can muster, not so advantageous to Panama'. It gave the United States, Roosevelt told Spooner, 'practically everything . . . which we can possibly desire'. Fortunately – for Washington at least – Bunau-Varilla was on hand to supply a helpful exegesis. La Boca and Cristóbal, he asserted, were unequivocally inside the zone. The ground area of the two terminals was only the space covered by existing buildings; everything else was zone territory, and it was entirely up to the United States to decide whether it would hand any of it over for future municipal expansion. As for sanitation, the stricter the ordinances were, the happier Panama would be for the zone authorities to enforce them. With this comprehensively satisfactory gloss, the amendments were withdrawn and passage of the treaty virtually guaranteed.[70]

[68] Ibid., Buchanan to Hay, 28 and 30.1.04; Buchanan to Russell, 1.2.04. Mellander, *United States in Panamanian politics*, 52–3, 55. Peterson, *Diplomat of the Americas*, 246–8.

[69] *Times*, 14.1.04, 3/5, and 21.1.04, 6/1. *NYT*, 19.1.04, 8/1.

[70] Hay Papers, roll 4, Hay to Spooner, 19 and 20.1.04; Hay to Cullom, 20.1.04. TR letters, 3: 700–1. *BD*, 440–2.

The final debate in the Senate revealed a general collapse of the opposition. Morgan's erstwhile ally Senator Hernando DeSoto Money gasped at the magnitude of the concession. 'In fact,' he accurately surmised, 'it sounds very much as though we wrote it ourselves.' In the vote on 23 February, the treaty was approved by 66 to 14, and it entered into force three days later. Bunau-Varilla was exultant. 'I had safeguarded the work of the French genius', he wrote in his memoirs. 'I had avenged its honour; I had served France.' Amador, when the news came through, paid Bunau-Varilla a fulsome tribute: 'The inestimable services rendered by you to this nation will live always in the hearts of its citizens.' Neither cared to admit that the real beneficiary of the treaty was neither France nor Panama but the United States.[71]

Panama, however, could now claim its indemnity of $10 million. In November it had asked for $8 million to be deposited in the U.S. Treasury, but when the Treasury refused, an alternative had to be found, and the quicker it came the better. The government had already borrowed $200,000 from its financial agent, J.P. Morgan, and it needed ready money urgently. Buchanan reported on 28 December that if Morgan refused to send more, Washington would have to take 'some heroic measures . . . to avoid a crash of the whole structure'.[72]

Pavey's advice to Bunau-Varilla was to invest the indemnity in a trust fund run by Morgan, but Panama had other plans. Bunau-Varilla was told to use Morgan only as the channel for an initial payment of $1 million to settle outstanding debts, while the balance of $9 million was to be held in the U.S. Treasury pending legislation by the National Assembly. The $1 million was paid over on 2 May, and shortly afterwards a Panamanian decree named Ricardo Arias and Eusebio Morales as commissioners empowered to turn $6 million of the remainder into a constitutional fund – under Article 138 of the constitution – and to leave the final $3 million on deposit in the Treasury. This would have repudiated Morgan as financial agent and given direct control of the indemnity to Panama, an arrangement quite unacceptable to Washington. The entire $9 million was paid over to Morgan, and the Panamanians were expected to invest at least $8 million of it. It was eventually agreed that $6 million should be invested in uptown Manhattan properties and some $2.8 million placed in bank deposit accounts. This portfolio was calculated to bring in an aggregate income from interest of at least $340,000 a year. In a parallel settlement, the New Company in Paris received its $40 million after a vain court action by Reyes to block the sale of its concessions to the U.S. government.[73]

[71] *CR* (Senate), 20.2.04, 2133; 23.2.04, 2261. Bunau-Varilla, *Panama*, 428, 429. B-V Papers, Amador to Bunau-Varilla, 24.2.04.

[72] B-V Papers, De la Espriella to Bunau-Varilla, 14.11.03 and 28.12.03. USD, Buchanan to Hay, 28 December 1903.

[73] B-V Papers, Pavey to Bunau-Varilla, 26.1.04; Bunau-Varilla to Hay, 6.3.04. USD, Hay to Russell, 30.4.04. NLP, 16.5.04. *BD*, 408–10. USD, De la Espriella to Russell, 21.5.04.

These transactions gave the United States full title to its treaty rights. On 4 May a U.S. Army lieutenant took delivery of the New Company's property in Panama, and on 9 May Roosevelt issued an executive order setting up an administration for the Canal Zone. With the arrival in Colón on 17 May of the Zone governor, General George Davis, the United States entered into its isthmian kingdom.[74]

Years later the dubious methods used to get control of the Zone had become something of a national joke in the USA. 'We stole it fair and square,' quipped Professor Samuel Hayakawa as he campaigned for the Senate in 1976. Others were less flippant. To Samuel Flagg Bemis – an American historian not often censorious of his own country's international behaviour – Washington's handling of the affair was 'the one really black mark in the Latin American policy of the United States', 'a rash and lawless act'. The *New York Times*, editorialising at the close of 1903, was equally severe: The canal was 'stolen property', and the administration's 'partners in the theft' were 'a group of canal promoters and speculators and lobbyists who came into their money through the rebellion we encouraged, made safe, and effectuated'.[75]

The main target for attack was President Roosevelt, the intervention's commander-in-chief. In private Roosevelt dismissed his detractors as 'a small body of shrill eunuchs', but he was deeply offended by their charges, because he himself believed in the justice of what he had done. At one cabinet meeting he protested his innocence so strenuously as to provoke the comment from Root, 'You have shown that you were accused of seduction and you have conclusively proved that you were guilty of rape.'[76]

To try to persuade the country that the criticisms were unfounded, Roosevelt embarked on a remarkable exercise in self-exoneration whereby quantities of secret records were published, supposedly telling the whole truth. This may be compared with the massive effort by President Richard Nixon to conceal his real part in the Watergate episode by the issue of volumes of carefully edited documentation; like Nixon, Roosevelt suppressed evidence. For example, no correspondence was published between Hay and Loomis, the State Department's link with Bunau-Varilla, and the Loomis papers fail to repair the omission. Important items were also taken out of the copies of the Navy Department files

---

NYT, 22.5.04, 1/5. McCullough, *Path between the seas*, 400. Mack, *Land divided*, 479–80. Details of the disposition of the $10 million can be found in *BD*, 520–2.

[74] Loomis Papers, roll 2, Knox to Loomis, 21.5.04. *BD*, 411–16. McCullough, *Path between the seas*, 406–8.

[75] Samuel Bemis, *The Latin American policy of the United States: An historical interpretation* (New York, 1943), 151. *NYT*, 29.12.03, 1/1.

[76] *TR letters*, 3: 663, 699. Jessup, *Root*, 1: 405. See also Schoonover, 'Max Farrand's memorandum', 505–6.

for 1901 and 1902 which were transmitted to Congress, though these have survived in the archives. The administration also tampered with the original sources in small but tell-tale ways. Ehrman, for instance, had telegraphed to Hay in the late afternoon of 3 November 'No uprising yet reported. Will be in the night.' The published version of the cable read 'No uprising yet. Reported will be in the night.' On 6 November Ehrman sent to Hay 'The situation is good.' In the printed text this read 'The situation is peaceful.'[77]

Publication of the Panama papers was accompanied by a series of statements designed to justify administration policy. The first was put out by Hay on 6 November; the second formed part of Roosevelt's annual message to Congress on 7 December; the third was a special message sent to Congress by Roosevelt on 4 January which, like Hay's reply to Reyes the next day, was taken from a draft supplied by Moore; and the fourth was a speech given by Root on 22 February. Both Root and the president followed the points developed by Hay, who claimed that the government had acted with two objects in mind: 'to put a stop . . . to the incessant civil bickerings which have been for so many years a curse of Panama' and 'to preserve, for the benefit of all, free transit over the Isthmus'. The intervention had been based on U.S. rights and obligations under the 1846 treaty and on 'the interest of the Isthmus, the people of Colombia, the people of the United States, and the commerce of the world'.[78]

It was the last of these interests which provided the starting point for the official apologia. World trade, in Root's view, required easements which over-rode 'the formal rules of international law' and rights of passage which tran-scended the sovereignty of nation-states. Colombia, as one of those states, must accept that its sovereignty was qualified, because, as Roosevelt put it, 'the possession of a territory fraught with such peculiar capacities as the Isthmus . . . carries with it obligations to mankind'. But, Root argued, Colombia had shown it could not meet those obligations. It was as impotent to protect international interests as China had been during the Boxer Rising in 1900, and so it was bound to give way to a power with the ability to do so. As Mahan wrote some years later: 'India, Egypt, Persia, Tripoli, Tunis, Algiers, Morocco, all stand on the same general basis as Panama. The world has needed them; and technical possession by legal prescription has fallen, still falls, and should continue to fall, before the advance of the world, when the owners are unable or unwilling to improve or to confer security.'[79]

---

[77] Most of the documentation is available in *BD*, 214–45, 249–78. The remainder may be found in U.S. Department of State, *Diplomatic history*, 377–479. Turk, 'U.S. Navy', 95. *BD*, 250, 252. On the question of the 'sanitising' of the records, see also Dennis's comment on the dearth of Panama material in the Hay and Roosevelt papers in *Adventures*, 323.

[78] Texts in *NYT*, 7.11.03, 1/5, *BD*, 291–300 and 301–19, and Root, 'Ethics', 175–206.

[79] Root, 'Ethics', 179, 180, 189, 205. *BD*, 299. Alfred Mahan, 'Was Panama "a chapter of national dishonor"?' *North American Review*, 196 (1912), 567–8.

The reason for making Colombia submit was the Monroe Doctrine. By the Doctrine, Mahan asserted, the United States had claimed a monopoly over the canal, and 'such exclusion of other nations by force . . . necessarily entails an obligation to them that that which we forbade their undertaking for the general benefit should be by us accomplished without delay'. Roosevelt shouldered the burden gladly in his message of 4 January. 'If ever a Government could be said to have received a mandate from civilization to effect an object the accomplishment of which was demanded in the interest of mankind, the United States holds that position with regard to the interoceanic canal.' Washington had 'in effect, policed the Isthmus . . . for the good of the entire civilized world'. To his critics, taking Panama in the name of international eminent domain was no more than a moralistic brand of imperialism, but in Roosevelt's own eyes he was answering the call of destiny and in doing so fulfilling the purpose of the treaty of 1846.[80]

The treaty was the vehicle whereby Colombia was expected to perform its duty to offer the world an international thoroughfare, and the guarantee of Colombia's sovereignty was subordinate to 'the dedication of the Isthmus to . . . free and unobstructed interoceanic transit', as Roosevelt phrased it. Though the United States had not specifically been given a canal concession in 1846, it had been allowed rights of way over any subsequent crossing, and, Roosevelt claimed, 'the obvious intent of the treaty rendered it unnecessary, if not superfluous, in terms to stipulate that permission for the construction of such modes of communication should not be denied'.[81]

The assertion did not hold water. As the Colombian foreign minister later pointed out, it was stretching the 1846 agreement impossibly far to read into it an American right to build a canal and a corresponding Colombian duty to make the grant. But the line was taken in an attempt to place the legal onus for the failure to produce a canal treaty squarely on Colombia. In Root's opinion (shared by no single U.S. negotiator of a canal treaty), Washington had been outstandingly generous in not insisting on a free concession. 'We had yielded to the last point, beyond reason and justice, in agreeing to pay for a privilege to which we were already entitled.' Colombia, however, by failing to ratify the 1903 convention, had refused to repay the services rendered to it by the United States over the past half-century, and its refusal had triggered the Panamanian revolt. Since the Panamanians were willing to assume Colombia's obligations, Washington reciprocated by transferring to them the guarantees hitherto given to Colombia, and recognised them as 'the proper custodians of the sovereignty of the Isthmus'.[82]

Recognition was held to be legal by virtue of an argument concocted by a

---

[80] Mahan, 'Was Panama?' 555. *BD*, 316, 313.

[81] *BD*, 314.

[82] *BD*, 399 (Rico to Snyder, 12.4.04). Root, 'Ethics', 187–8. *BD*, 298, 315.

friend of Roosevelt's, Oscar Straus, and first used by Hay. The 1846 treaty, Hay claimed on 6 November, was 'a covenant . . . that runs with the land . . . not dependent for its efficacy on . . . the name of the territory it affects'. As long as the isthmus endured, Hay declared, the treaty bound 'the holders of the territory' to grant the United States unimpeded transit and the United States in return to maintain it. In the message of 4 January, Roosevelt took it as axiomatic that 'treaties relating to boundaries and to rights of navigation continue in force without regard to changes in government or in sovereignty'. But it was Root who took the most extreme stance. 'The people of Panama', in his view, 'owned that part of the earth's surface just as much as the state of New York owns the Erie Canal.' Panama had not surrendered its sovereignty when it confederated with Colombia in 1863; it had merely entrusted it to Bogotá, and the Colombians had broken their compact with 'the true owner' of the isthmus when they imposed centralised rule on Panama after the upsurge of 1885. The breakaway movement of 1903 was thus launched to restore to Panama the rights forcibly taken from it, among them, presumably, the right to make a canal treaty.[83]

Again the administration's position did not stand scrutiny, as Moore well knew. Writing to Straus, he merrily termed the 1846 treaty 'a covenant running (away!) with the land'. As the Colombians were to observe, it was spurious to claim that the treaty applied to Panama when it had been contracted with New Granada, whose lawful successor was Colombia. The Spooner Act, they could have added, authorised the president to make an agreement with 'the Republic of Colombia' and not, as Roosevelt stated on 7 December, 'the power in actual control of the Isthmus of Panama'. But it was Root's advocacy of the cause of Panama's statehood which bore least examination. One leading historian has written that had Root been in Washington during the canal crisis, 'his influence would undoubtedly have been cast on the side of restraint'. The extravagant rhetoric of Root's address makes this judgement hard to accept, and Root would certainly not have welcomed a British bid to seize the Erie Canal via patronage of a separatist New York State. He was, however, prepared to take the argument for states' rights to its logical conclusion when it came to Panama, while carefully steering clear of the fact that the federal government at the end of the American civil war in 1865 had pinioned the defeated Confederacy no less tightly than Colombia shackled Panama twenty years later.[84]

Little more than a generation after the rebellion of the southern states against the Union, secession was still very much a live issue in American politics, and as leader of the party of Lincoln, Roosevelt had powerful reasons to dissociate himself from the charge of conspiring to detach the isthmus from Bogotá. In his

[83] *TR letters*, 3: 648–9 n. *NYT*, 7.11.03, 2/1. *BD*, 291, 319. Root, 'Ethics', 196, 200. *BD*, 487–8 (Root to Mendoza, 10.2.06).

[84] David Patterson, *Toward a warless world: The travail of the American peace movement, 1887–1914* (Bloomington, Ind., 1976), 124–5. *BD*, 403, 178. Miner, *Panama route*, 390–1.

private correspondence he repeatedly denied that he had condoned secession, especially when the Daughters of the Confederacy hailed the recognition of Panama as a vindication of the South. In his January message he proclaimed that the United States had acted to prevent bloodshed and suffering by rescuing the Panamanians from Colombia's allegedly atrocious and degenerate régime. 'We gave the people of Panama self-government', Roosevelt wrote in his auto-biography, 'and freed them from subjugation to alien oppressors.' He was even to assert 'as much moral justification for what we did in Panama in 1903 as for what we did in our own country in 1776'. The opponents of U.S. intervention in Panama, he told Congress, would do well to remember what had been achieved for Cuba as a result of the war with Spain. 'The people of Cuba', Roosevelt declared, 'have been immeasurably benefited by our interference in their behalf, and our own gain has been great. So it will be with Panama.'[85]

The United States thus claimed to have acted in the interest of the Panamanians as well as in the interest of the world as a whole. But, as Roosevelt's last-quoted dictum indicates, it had also clearly had the national interest at stake. The point was not given great prominence, for understandable reasons, and attempts to justify the Panama affair on the ground of national security were rare. Loomis affirmed that Roosevelt had moved in to forestall a possible French intervention and snuff out 'the spark to set half the world in flames'. Roosevelt himself did not make much of this fantastic supposition, nor did he raise the spectre of a German foothold in the hemisphere, which has sometimes been seen as an important reason for the U.S. appropriation of Panama. After the outbreak of the First World War, Roosevelt asserted that in 1903 he had been determined to stop Germany from acquiring a naval base in Venezuela which it could have used to threaten the Caribbean approaches to the canal, but he did not say so at the time.[86]

There can, however, be no doubt that the strategic importance of the canal weighed more heavily than any other consideration in deciding the administration's course. Hay, in his 6 November statement, referred to the way in which the new U.S. dependencies in Hawaii and the Philippines had enhanced the advantages of a gateway to the Pacific first discerned by Polk and had made a canal an asset 'of transcendent import'. Root elevated the United States's protection of its right of way into 'a duty of the highest obligation' which, by definition, outstripped all duties to Colombia. For Mahan, an equally uncompromising devotee of *Machtpolitik*, the purpose of both U.S. treaty guarantees in 1846 had been the security of the transit. This was Washington's 'one

[85] *TR letters*, 3: 662, 675, 688. *NYT*, 10.12.03, 1/5. *BD*, 314, 315, 318. T. Roosevelt, *Works*, 20: 514. Theodore Roosevelt, 'How the United States acquired the right to dig the Panama Canal', *Outlook*, 99 (1911), 318. *BD*, 317–18.

[86] *NYT*, 16.12.03, 1/6. *BD*, 316. Turk, 'U.S. Navy' 95. *TR letters*, 8: 956, .1101–3. Challener, *Admirals*, 154. Dennis, *Adventures*, 338 n. 14.

specific interest in Colombian territory', and the United States possessed 'an unimpaired international right' to do whatever it considered necessary to defend that interest.[87]

Not even Bogotá had denied that Washington was entitled to intervene to keep the railroad open in an emergency, but as the Colombians had said, that did not mean it might intervene in a civil war to destroy Colombia's sovereignty and dismember its territory. It would scarcely be argued, wrote an American lawyer sympathetic to the government, that Colombia would 'stipulate with the United States ... to maintain free transit through Colombian territory at the price of excluding Colombia from sovereignty over her territory'. In the event of civil conflict, it would be like 'denying to the master of a house the right to resist robbers on the ground that it might disturb the business of a tenant'. As another commentator saw it, the treaty positively bound Washington not to take sides against the Colombian government when it faced an internal challenge. 'Otherwise, it were as if the guardian of a dependent child ... should himself expropriate his ward's possessions and assume dictatorial control.' In his February 1904 address Root had said, 'The trustee was faithless to its trust; it repudiated its obligations without the consent of the true owner; it seized by the strong hand of military power the rights which it was bound to protect.' He was referring to Colombia's treatment of Panama in 1885, but it could not have been a closer description of the American handling of Colombia in 1903.[88]

Roosevelt, however, in his exposition of the sovereignty issue to Congress, showed how little he cared about it. What mattered to him was that he had secured a crucial prize for the nation, and he was eager to take complete responsibility. 'The vital work, getting Panama as an independent Republic, on which all else hinged,' he told Lodge, 'was done by me without the aid or advice of anyone, save in so far as they carried out my instructions.' 'I have always felt', he confided to Taft, 'that the one thing for which I deserved most credit in my entire Administration was my action in seizing the psychological moment to get complete control of Panama.' 'If I had hesitated to act,' he later wrote, 'I would have esteemed myself as deserving a place in Dante's inferno beside the faint-hearted cleric who was guilty of *il gran rifiuto*.' Fortunately, 'the crisis came at a period when I could act unhampered. Accordingly I took the Isthmus, started the canal, and then left Congress – not to debate the canal, but to debate me.'[89]

[87] *NYT*, 7.11.03, 2/1. Root, 'Ethics', 205. Mahan, 'Was Panama?' 560, 559, 561.

[88] U.S. Department of State, *Diplomatic history*, 478–9. William Dennis, 'The Panama situation in the light of international law', *American Law Register and Review*, 52 (1904), 301, 300. Leader Chamberlain, 'A chapter of national dishonor', *North American Review*, 195 (1912), 164, 151–2. Root, 'Ethics', 200.

[89] *TR letters*, 6: 1491; 7: 179. T. Roosevelt, *Works*, 20: 513. Roosevelt Papers, roll 421, Speech at Berkeley, 23.3.11.

Part II

Beginnings: 1904–1929

The negroes, Italians and Spaniards toiled away at their tasks without appearing to take much interest in their work. . . . But on the faces of the 'gold-men,' as the engineers and Americans are termed, was the stern determination of men animated by a great purpose. . . . They seemed to be, in a way, instruments of a great destiny.

(Howard Payson, *The Boy Scouts at the Panama Canal*, 1913)

The people, as a rule, are untrustworthy, poorly educated, lazy and dirty. . . . They resent our marked superiority as to intelligence, ability, wealth, and, above all, our power; and the whole structure of ill feeling is based on the jealousy of a small, narrow minded and insignificant country for one which is greater in every way and which has lifted it to whatever slight degree of world's prominence it may have.

(Captain Montgomery Taylor, USN, 21 October 1921)

3

The Zone régime

The Canal Zone established in 1904 was the latest in a series of American acquisitions outside the continental United States: Alaska in 1867; Hawaii, Puerto Rico, the Philippines, and Guam in 1898; American Samoa in 1899. These outposts of empire were governed in three different ways. Alaska and Hawaii were 'incorporated territories' subject to all the provisions of the federal Constitution, endowed by Congress with organic laws, and administered by the Department of the Interior. The Philippines and Puerto Rico were classed as 'organised but unincorporated territories' and came under the War Department's Bureau of Insular Affairs. Though they too were given organic statutes, only the so-called fundamental provisions of the Constitution applied to them, in the shape of a modified version of the Bill of Rights.[1]

The third denomination, 'unorganised possessions', embraced the Pacific islands of Guam and American Samoa. Like the unincorporated territories, they were granted a truncated form of the Bill of Rights, but they were not chartered by Congress. Their structure of government was fixed by executive order, placing them directly under the jurisdiction of the president exercised via the secretary of the navy and U.S. Navy governors on the spot who ruled their tiny domains with all the authoritarianism of a naval command.[2]

The Canal Zone fell into this third category. It was differentiated from the unincorporated territories as early as December 1904, when the Interior Department held that it was not 'organised' and that consequently federal laws

---

[1] 'N.K.', 'Applicability of Federal statutes to noncontiguous areas', *University of Pennsylvania Law Review*, 97 (1949), 866–70. Julius Pratt, *America's colonial experiment: How the United States gained, governed, and in part gave away a colonial empire* (Gloucester, Mass., 1964), 154, 159–62. Jessup, *Root*, 1: 346–8.

[2] Pratt, *America's colonial experiment*, 221–4. Earl Pomeroy, 'The Navy and colonial government', *U.S. Naval Institute Proceedings*, 71 (1945), 291–7.

were not applicable to it. Testifying before a Senate hearing in 1911, one prominent Zone official judged that the closest parallel was the presidential fief of Guam.[3]

A régime on the pattern of Guam and Samoa was certainly the objective of Senator John Spooner when he offered his bill for the construction of a Panama canal in January 1902. The work was to be placed in the hands of the War Department and executed by the U.S. Army's Corps of Engineers. By this time, however, civilian governors had taken over from the military in both Puerto Rico and the Philippines, and the eventual Spooner Act came down in favour of running the canal through a seven-man Isthmian Canal Commission, which Roosevelt made answerable to Secretary of War William Howard Taft.[4]

This arrangement was incapable of producing quick decisions, and its irresolution was compounded by the absurdity of basing the Commission two thousand miles away from the isthmus, in Washington. The most important figure on the project, the chief engineer, John Wallace – not himself a commissioner – was thus forced to refer every major on-site problem back to the distant ICC head office. The result was paralysis and muddle on a grand scale: Requisitions piled up unopened at the receiving end, and medical supplies ordered in August 1904 had still not arrived on the isthmus six months later.[5]

Commissioner Davis, as a former military governor of Puerto Rico, believed there was only one way to bring order out of this chaos. Just as the Philippines Commission was centred in Manila, so the ICC should base its headquarters in the Canal Zone. At the same time, the Commission should be reduced to three: a new chairman, the chief engineer, and himself, acting both as governor and as diplomatic envoy to Panama. Taft was attracted to both propositions. As the first civilian governor of the Philippines, he knew the advantages of having a tight-knit proconsulate in situ, with a Washington bureau to 'do the errands'. He was also convinced that to fuse the posts of governor and minister would improve the situation at a time when morale was low over the confusion which had swamped the project and over widespread fear of a yellow fever epidemic.[6]

Roosevelt therefore asked Congress to revise the Spooner Act, but it adjourned without taking action. So the changes were put through by presidential order. The elderly Admiral John Walker was put out to grass and supplanted as chairman by Theodore Shonts, an experienced railway executive. Chief Engineer

[3] NYT, 28.12.04, 9/1. 1911 Hearings, 292.

[4] Henry Abbot, 'Present status of the Panama project', Annals of the American Academy of Political and Social Science, 31 (1908), 26. Pratt, America's colonial experiment, 183–7, 195–9. BD, 179–80, 411, 412–13.

[5] Alfred Chandler, 'Theodore Roosevelt and the Panama Canal: A study in administration', in TR letters, 6: 1548–9. DuVal, And the mountains, 147–8. McCullough, Path between the seas, 438–9. 1906 Hearings, 3: 2541.

[6] Taft Papers, ser. 3, Davis to Taft, 6.1.05. 1906 Hearings, 3: 2545. Taft Papers, ser. 4A, Taft to Roosevelt, 3.2.05.

Wallace joined the Commission, and its legal counsel Charles Magoon took on the twin responsibilities Davis had coveted. Both Davis and Minister John Barrett were dropped, Davis because he treated the Panamanians with open contempt, Barrett because he was thought too prone to take sides in local politics. Though the ICC of seven remained in being, it was now in practice a triumvirate and the other four commissioners no more than ciphers. On 1 April 1905 the reorganisation went into effect.[7]

Yet the travail of the Commission did not end there. The yellow fever scare persisted, and in June Wallace resigned to go to a private company at more than twice his current salary. For Magoon, like Spooner, the answer was to assign the work to the Corps of Engineers, with the head of the corps as Wallace's successor. Roosevelt, however, chose to appoint John Stevens, a prominent railway engineer, who took over in July.[8]

During the next eighteen months Roosevelt was besieged by crises over the canal. In December 1905 Senate confirmation of the Commission was recalled out of resentment at his allegedly excessive patronage in the project. The following month accusations of corruption in the Zone by the journalist Poultney Bigelow led to a full-dress inquiry by the Senate's Interoceanic Canals Committee, which picked over the shortcomings of the ICC in minute and painful detail.[9]

For at least two of the participants in the hearings, the lesson was clear. For Senator John Tyler Morgan the Zone needed placing 'under the same regimen with a military reservation in the United States'. It would not be properly administered 'until the Government of the United States had absolute charge of every foot of it in every respect' to deal with 'as uncontrollable and as mischievous a rabble as ever collected at any place in the world'. 'The only way you can do your work down there successfully', Wallace testified, 'is to put it in the hands of a pure, absolute despot, and hold his hands up, and keep the wolves off of his back.' Stevens drew much the same conclusion. The Commission 'must resolve itself into what will amount to a one-man proposition', with, of course, himself as that one man.[10]

To institutionalise the change, Stevens had drafted an executive order placing the headships of all the Commission's departments in the gift of the chairman and empowering the chief engineer to act on the chairman's behalf. Since Shonts was normally in Washington, this gave Stevens plenary power, and the order was duly issued by Roosevelt. When Shonts resigned as chairman in January 1907, it was generally believed that Stevens would succeed him.[11]

---

[7] *NYT*, 14.1.05, 1/3, and 7.3.05, 6/1. *Executive Orders*, 35–7. Taft Papers, SWS-OC, Taft to Roosevelt, 19.12.04 and 13.4.05.

[8] *NYT*, 30.6.05, 1/1, and 1.7.05, 4/2. ICC, 9-A-1, Magoon to Taft, 27.6.05.

[9] *NYT*, 15.12.05, 1/1; 21.12.05, 1/7; 5.1.06, 7/4; 9.1.06, 1/1; 10.1.06, 4/4. *1906 Hearings*, passim.

[10] *1906 Hearings*, 1: 350, 646. DuVal, *And the mountains*, 224–5.

[11] DuVal, *And the mountains*, 224–5. *Executive Orders*, 55–7. *NYT*, 24.1.07, 3/4.

At precisely this moment, however, Stevens burned his boats in a letter to Roosevelt asking to be relieved of his post. He had, he said in an extraordinary outburst, been continually attacked by people 'that I would not wipe my boots on in the United States'. Though he was made chairman on 4 March, it was no more than a formality. A few days earlier the ICC had followed Roosevelt's recommendation that the canal be finished by the government and designated Major George Washington Goethals of the Corps of Engineers as the next chief engineer. Joining him on the Commission were two other corpsmen, Majors David Gaillard and William Sibert. The new appointments were clearly intended to bring in the discipline and the continuity hitherto so conspicuously absent. The Army, commented the *New York Times*, would make 'no back talk, no complaint, and no criticism', and Roosevelt declared that he was putting the project in the hands of men 'who will stay on the job until I get tired of having them there or till I say they may abandon it'.[12]

The installation of Goethals was a watershed in the history of the canal's construction. The Walker Commission had lasted just over one year; the Shonts Commission, barely two. The Goethals Commission was to stay the distance until the waterway was set to open. At its apex the figure of Goethals was paramount. On 2 April 1907, the day after becoming both chairman and chief engineer, he was enabled to administer the Zone as well as build the canal, though even then he was unhappy. In August he told Roosevelt that he needed still more authority, and Roosevelt supplied it in the shape of a further executive order which, as Goethals interpreted it, vested him with 'dictatorial powers so far as consistent with existing law'.[13]

Yet Goethals was uneasy because his leadership had no legislative basis, and extensive though his prerogatives were, he lacked the right to remove any other commissioner. In 1909 a congressional sympathiser introduced a bill to give Goethals what he wanted, but it did not go beyond the House. Goethals remained no more than first among equals and brimming with suspicion of his fellow commissioners. Three he identified as the core of the opposition – Gorgas (the sanitary officer), Gaillard, and Sibert – and they were looking for a fourth to give them a majority 'to overthrow my authority'. 'There are times', he once admitted, 'when I have wished that I had the powers of a general officer in the field during actual hostilities.' There were also times when Goethals behaved as though he possessed such powers. The ICC met, he told a Senate hearing, 'whenever I conclude that I have business enough to occupy them for the afternoon'. In August 1911 he looked forward to phasing his colleagues out

[12] DuVal, *And the mountains*, 254–65. Taft Papers, ser. 4A, Stevens to Roosevelt, 30.1.07. *NYT*, 27.2.07, 1/3. McCullough, *Path between the Seas*, 504–5.

[13] *Executive Orders*, 65, 72–3. Joseph Bucklin Bishop and Farnham Bishop, *Goethals, genius of the Panama Canal: A biography* (New York, 1930), 182–5, 191–3. Goethals Papers, Goethals to Robins, 2.12.10.

by degrees as the project neared fruition. 'I do not see', he wrote, 'why we should be encumbered with high-salaried men after their services are no longer needed, it being my intention to drop each Commissioner as soon as the work assigned to him is finished.'[14]

By this time, with completion of the canal only three years away, the need for legislation was becoming urgent. The president's mandate to superintend the Zone was valid only for the construction period; before the canal went into operation Congress would have to pass a new act setting up the framework of an organisation for the long-term future. In the debate that followed, the nature of that organisation was to be decided by a hard-fought bureaucratic struggle for power.

Five styles of government were in contention: a civilian administration which would make the Zone a microcosm of the American commonwealth; a military régime headed by the commanding officer of the Zone garrison; a naval governorship like the Navy's Pacific island fiefdoms; the collective leadership of a canal commission; or a continuation of the absolutism perfected by Goethals, to be retained in the keeping of the Corps of Engineers.

Magoon had the first scenario in mind when he persuaded the ICC to parcel the Zone into five municipalities in September 1904. To one of his admirers, the structure was 'like a kindergarten of democracy and civics – something that must soon prepare the way for local home rule'. But when Magoon raised the idea of a model community with Shonts the following July, he was told to forget it, and the townships were subsequently abolished. In July 1911, however, the chief of the Department of Civil Administration, Maurice Thatcher, memorialised Goethals with a scheme for 'a permanent population on both sides of the canal, which would afford [it] both moral and police protection'. Testifying before the Senate, Thatcher envisaged his homesteaders 'under the dominion of an American government, under American laws, and under the security of American sanitation'. 'A well-administered civil government in the zone', he believed, would have far-reaching educational value 'as an example to Latin American nations'.[15]

Thatcher's vision was strangled at birth. 'Introduce the franchise,' said Goethals, 'and we'd go to pieces.' The Zone's natural order was despotism, 'and that's the best form of government'. His legislative adviser, Judge Frank Feuille, told the Senate that the Zone should be 'very much like a large corporate

---

[14] Goethals Papers, Goethals to Robins, 2.12.10. *NYT*, 12.12.09, 9/6. *1911 Hearings*, 75–6. Goethals Papers, Goethals to Flint, 8.12.09; to Edwards, 10.9.12; to Goodell, 11.8.11.

[15] Wayne Bray, *The common law zone in Panama: A case study in reception with some observations on the relevancy thereof to the Panama Canal Treaty controversy* (San Juan, P.R., 1977), 65–6. Walter Pepperman, *Who built the Panama Canal?* (New York, 1915), 130. John Foster Carr, 'Building a state', *Outlook*, 83 (1906), 440. DuVal, *Aad the mountains*, 186–7. ICC, 80-A-3, Thatcher memo of 20.7.11. *1911 Hearings*, 204, 207, 208, 224–6.

enterprise, and political questions . . . should be reduced to a minimum', as they were in what he took as the soundest precedent, the District of Columbia. In December, when President Taft asked Congress for legislation, he took the Goethals line in calling for 'the management of a great public work, and not the government of a local republic'. The Zone should be regulated 'by the orders of the President, issued through the War Department, as it is today'. The life, liberty, and property of individuals should be guaranteed, but beyond these basic provisions Canal Zone government should be 'that of a military reservation managed in connection with this great highway of trade'.[16]

This was not, however, the way the Navy saw it. In January 1912 the General Board concluded that the Zone should be governed by an Army officer 'who combines in his own person the functions of military command and civil control', since the Zone's war readiness depended on continuous military authority in peace as well as in war. In other words, the Zone should be ruled by the garrison commander, with a naval lieutenant–governor as his right-hand man.[17]

This finding was predicated on the belief that the canal's primary importance to the country was strategic, an assumption which Goethals adamantly refused to share. 'I look upon the operation and maintenance of the Canal as a distinctly civil and commercial function', he told the Senate. It should be placed under the Army only in time of war. The commander of the troops in the Zone, he later wrote, 'should not be hampered with duties for which he has no special training and has as a rule no fitness'.[18]

He was equally resistant to the project for a three-man commission prompted by Thatcher and Gorgas. A commission, he told his legislative aide Colonel William Judson, like a board, was 'long, narrow and wooden', and it could not cope with the demands of canal operation, which required 'subordination of everything – sanitation, civil administration, supplies and the military'. Judson wholeheartedly agreed. The commission system of government worked well enough in American cities wherever the commissioners were responsive to public opinion. In the Zone there would be no such thing as public opinion, and 'internal politics fostered by personal ambitions would distract the Commission from the very start'.[19]

[16] Bishop and Bishop, *Goethals*, 249. *1911 Hearings*, 278–9, 286, 288, 292. GB, 426–1 of 1.11.13, has the text of Taft's speech of 21.12.11. Two contemporary articles by supporters of Goethals are William Adamson, 'Needed Panama Canal legislation', *Independent*, 72 (1912), 610–14, and Emory Johnson, 'Necessary Panama Canal legislation', *North American Review*, 194 (June–December 1911), 714–22.

[17] WCD, 6178–49.

[18] DuVal, *And the mountains*, 321–2. George Washington Goethals, *Government of the Canal Zone* (Princeton, N.J., 1915), 82.

[19] Goethals Papers, Goethals to Adamson, 13.6.12; to Stimson, 21.6.12; to Judson, 21.6.12. *1911 Hearings*, 187–8. Goethals Papers, Goethals to Judson, 21.6.12; Judson to Goethals, 16.7.12.

The Panama Canal Act of August 1912 dealt a body-blow to the commission lobby. The ICC was to be abolished shortly before the waterway opened, and in its place the president would appoint a governor of the Panama Canal to serve for a four-year term. The governor was 'to complete, govern, and operate the Panama Canal and govern the Canal Zone'. Only when the United States was at war or when the president considered war imminent would he hand over control in both areas to an Army officer designated by the White House.[20]

The Act was a triumph for Goethals, but with Taft's election defeat in November his expectations drooped. He was undoubtedly anxious to be the first governor, and Taft was poised to nominate him. But Taft was obliged to leave the reorganisation to be consummated by the incoming Democratic president, Woodrow Wilson. Sibert was reportedly jubilant at the damage inflicted on Goethals by Taft's departure, and in June Wilson appointed Richard Metcalfe, a crony of William Jennings Bryan's, as successor to Thatcher. This was a sure sign that he would keep the Commission at full strength in the immediate future and not let it wither on the vine as Goethals had planned. Shortly afterwards, Goethals heard that Bryan was pushing for Metcalfe as governor, and in October Metcalfe revived the idea of a triumvirate of governor, sanitary officer, and chief engineer. The trio would comprise himself, Gorgas, and Sibert. 'The responsibilities that will fall upon the Canal Zone Government', Metcalfe told Goethals pointedly, 'are too great to be entrusted to a single individual.'[21]

The other claimants to leadership of the permanent organisation also began to renew their bids. In April 1913 the General Board told Secretary Josephus Daniels that the Navy Department should run the mechanism of the waterway, since the board regarded the canal 'in much the same light as it regards a ship. Both are built by skilled technicians, but for the use of others when completed.' The board was subsequently prepared to concede the governorship to the Army, in the person of the commanding general in the Zone, but the senior naval officer present should be in charge of both operation and maintenance and be authorised to take the governor's place in the event of his absence, disability, or death. Both these demands were unacceptable to the Army, which wanted no naval heir-apparent and which insisted on a monopoly of power through the garrison commander as governor and through the Corps of Engineers as the controller of operation and maintenance.[22]

Goethals struck back energetically. In 1912, he told the Army chief of staff, congressional feeling against military control had run very high, and the Panama Canal Act had implicitly recognised that there should be no military régime

---

[20] BD, 597, 600, 605–6.
[21] Goethals Papers, Goethals to O'Laughlin, 7.12.12; Showalter to Goethals, 7.8.13; Goethals to Rodman, 10.4.13; to Devol, 16.5.13. NYT, 14.12.12, 3/4; 26.12.12, 1/5; 3.6.13, 1/7. ICC, 2-C-124, Metcalfe to Goethals, 1.10.13.
[22] GB, 426–1, General Board to Secretary of the Navy, 12.4.13 and 1.11.13. WCD, 6178–62 of 13.1.14.

in peacetime by allowing for an Army take-over in time of war or threatened hostilities. As for government by commission, Zone administration was 'an executive one purely, and the conditions prevailing in the States or Territories, where local civil governments prevail independent of the executive authority of the United States, do not exist here. Everything on the Zone is within the control of the President.' And the *New York Times* was clearly speaking for Goethals when it reported that Army men on the isthmus were aghast at the 'endless opportunities for graft' inherent in the Metcalfe plan for a troika, which seemed designed to provide 'countless political jobs for hungry Democrats' and which would ruin the efficiency of the organisation raised up over the past seven years.[23]

Fortunately for Goethals, he had a powerful ally in the secretary of war, Lindley Garrison, who had been advised by Feuille that the canal could not be operated except under the terms of the 1912 Act. On 16 January 1914 Garrison recommended Goethals to Wilson as the first governor, though it took an adroit piece of leakage on Goethals's part to trigger a public announcement. On 23 January the mayor of New York told the *New York Times* that Goethals had said he would consider taking the job of police commissioner at the end of the year. Wilson and Garrison, Goethals was told, fell over themselves to pass on the assurance that he would be governor; 'no politician could have used his cards more effectively'.[24]

The executive order of 27 January 1914 which established the form of government for the operational era was a close reflection of Goethals's thinking. So too was the accompanying presidential memorandum of interpretation, which ordained that the organisation would come under the secretary of war and not the War Department. The secretary had been overlord of construction, and it was therefore logical that the governor of the Panama Canal should be his agent. He would be an officer of the Corps of Engineers, and he would also act as head of the Division of Operation and Maintenance. The engineer of maintenance, again from the corps, would be governor-designate. Operation of the canal was placed in charge of the marine superintendent, a navy billet. This arrangement kept the Navy decisively out of the topmost flights of the zonal hierarchy. Both Canal and Zone were to be the preserve of the Engineers, as Goethals had intended, and when the new régime came into effect in April there was no reason to suppose it would change in the foreseeable future.[25]

[23] JB, 326–1, s.10, Goethals to Wood, 15.11.13. ICC, 88-A-3, Goethals to Garrison, 28.11.13. *NYT*, 22.11.13, 3/3. WCD, 6178–49. Goethals, *Government of the CZ*, 50.

[24] WCD, 6178–62. ICC, 2-C-124, Garrison to Feuille, 1.11.13; Feuille to Garrison, 11.11.13; Garrison to Wilson, 4.12.13. Goethals Papers, Boggs to Goethals, 17.1.14. *NYT*, 17.1.14, 1/4; 24.1.14, 1/5. Goethals Papers, Goethals to Mitchel, 14.1.14; Mitchel to Goethals, 26.1.14; O'Laughlin to Goethals, 27.1.14.

[25] *Executive Orders*, 155–7. ICC, 2-C-124, Daniels to Rodman, 2.2.14; Goethals to ICC, 27.3.14; Rodman memo of 1.6.14.

In August 1914, however, the First World War broke out, just two weeks before the opening of the canal. Though the United States was not a belligerent, the growing possibility that it might be drawn in led to a venomous power struggle between Goethals and the recently appointed commander of the Army garrison, General Clarence Edwards. Through the Panama Canal Act of 1912, as we have seen, the governor was given responsibility for the canal's protection in peacetime, but in time of war or imminent hostilities he was to hand over control of the Zone to any Army officer designated by the president. By the beginning of 1916 Goethals saw Edwards as the likeliest choice but also as a usurper who tried every 'vicious and pernicious' trick he knew to sweep obstacles from his path. In May he insisted on the publication of a special executive order underlining his statutory authority in the realm of defence. The military and naval forces in the Zone were henceforth enjoined to furnish him with 'such assistance . . . as the respective commanding officers may be required by him to render'.[26]

But this only postponed the moment of truth. Goethals was scheduled to retire soon, and he was all too aware that Edwards was waiting expectantly in the wings. In his letter of resignation to Wilson in November he counselled against putting Edwards in charge of Zone administration as well as defence. 'Due to too much rambling, indiscreet, fault-finding and criticizing talk,' Goethals told the president, Edwards had 'succeeded in arousing an antagonism between the two interests which would result in an unfortunate and difficult situation should such a combination of the duties be made.' On Goethals's departure, Colonel Chester Harding was nominated in his place, but as Washington moved closer to war with Germany, Edwards stood ready to supersede him whenever Wilson gave the word.[27]

Edwards did become governor in April 1917 when the USA declared war. But he held the office for only forty-eight hours before leaving the isthmus for another posting. In January, Harding had urged the War Department not to keep him on, and the General Staff was in wholehearted agreement. Moreover, the preferment of the commanding general was for the duration only. General Leonard Wood had recommended the permanent combination of civil and military power in the hands of the Army commander on the ground that the Zone was simply 'a fortified garrisoned area with a canal running through it'. Secretary of War Newton Baker refused to pursue the idea, however, and Harding knew the status quo ante would be back in force once the war was over.[28]

---

[26] Goethals Papers, Goethals to Wigmore, 24.2.16. *Executive Orders*, 214–15. See also *BD*, 605–6, for the relevant clause of the Panama Canal Act.

[27] Goethals Papers, Goethals to Wilson, 11.11.16.

[28] PC, 47-H-17, Harding to Brown, 13.1.17. WCD, 6278–9, Scott to Edwards, 9.4.17. AG, 1784–1917, 2462429, Wood to Adjutant General, 4.1.17; Bliss to Scott, 23.1.17; Baker note of 25.1.17.

So it proved. In February 1919 Harding regained his full powers over the canal and the Zone, and things seemed back to normal. Yet almost immediately the canal hierarchy came under fire from a congressional visitation demanding a thorough shake-up in its inner workings. Two years later, in the spring of 1921, the assault was renewed by an incoming Republican régime which planned 'a reorganisation of the entire method of administration', which Secretary of War John Weeks charged with serious extravagance. Weeks went on to set up a commission of inquiry under General William Connor, with the task of finding economies in every area of Zone government and canal operations.[29]

When the Connor board reported in September, it recommended numerous alterations to the existing structure. The Panama Railroad should be taken out of the Canal's domain; the functions of the Civil Affairs Division should be hived off to a number of federal agencies; the auditor of the Canal should no longer be allowed to spend its funds as well as scrutinise its budget. At the same time, Connor maintained that the Canal's approach to Panama had often been abrasive, and he was uninhibited on the subject of its employees' moral standards. Venereal disease among them was 'far worse than it ought to be', and brothels were being run on Railroad property in Colón leased to Panamanian tenants.[30]

The reaction at Canal headquarters on Balboa Heights was explosive. Connor's report had been inspired by 'some secret animus inimical to the Canal organization' and designed to break it down 'so that it might be more readily swallowed by the military'. Governor Jay Morrow denied outright Connor's argument that the Zone was no more than a U.S. possession like Hawaii or Puerto Rico. It was a 'separate government entity with its own laws and system'. To assign any of its responsibilities to Washington would be to invite indecision, which could be highly damaging if ever U.S. intervention were needed in Panama.[31]

Faced with this unyielding stand, Weeks left the Canal apparatus very largely untouched, and in 1923 Morrow published a defiant counterblast to Connor, written to ward off any subsequent bid to bring in 'improper political influences' and 'unnecessary legal restriction'. *A Great People's Great Canal* portrayed the waterway as 'a model of sureness and efficiency, and an example to the world of the capacity of the American people' – in other words, a paragon of management which needed no lessons from interfering busybodies in the nation's capital.[32]

---

[29] PC, 88-A-21, Harding to Flint, 28.2.19. Michael Conniff, *Black labor on a white canal: Panama 1904–1981* (Pittsburgh, Pa., 1985), 55. *NYT*, 21.4.21, 17/6.

[30] U.S. President, Special Panama Canal Commission, *Report* . . . (1922), 13, 17, 14–15, 24–5, 20, 21.

[31] PC, 28-B-5, memo for Morrow, 1.2.22; Connor to Weeks, 4.1.22; 59-G-1, Morrow to Weeks, 31.3.22.

[32] Jay Morrow, *A great people's great canal* (Mount Hope, CZ, 1923), 16.

The same high pretensions were on display over the issue of the Zone's dealings with Panama, taken up in the treaty negotiations which began in 1924. When the State Department urged that all correspondence on the interpretation of the 1903 convention be handled by the minister and not the governor's executive secretary, the response of Morrow's successor, Meriwether Walker, was emphatic. Certainly the State Department should be responsible for 'all matters as between the United States and the Republic of Panama', but the Canal Zone was not part of the United States. It was quite exceptional, 'somewhat like a great corporation of which the President is the executive and the Congress the legislative body', and so it had to represent itself in any transactions with Panama.[33]

To Minister John Glover South, this was nonsense. The governor had put himself 'on a plane equal with the President of a sovereign state', when he was in fact no more entitled to do business with a foreign government than the governor general of the Philippines. The protest made no impression on Executive Secretary McIlvaine, whose office, he claimed, 'functions in a modest way as the State Department of the Canal Zone government in its relations with Panama'. Viewed from this perspective, the governor was entirely his own master, 'the regent of the President and Secretary of War, *the trustee of sovereignty rights within the Canal Zone*'.[34]

In the event, the State Department won the jurisdictional battle, and in 1928 the minister took over prerogatives the governor had exercised since 1904. The legation and not Balboa Heights was to handle the conveyance of land taken from Panama and to call U.S. troops into the terminal cities to keep order. These were palpable inroads into the Zone's status, and though Walker tried to put the best possible face on the demotion, it showed how much times had changed since the construction era. In form the canal organism remained just as Goethals had fashioned it, and the Canal still ruled the roost in other areas of policy. But while it had shrugged off the post-war onslaught of the military, it had lost significant ground to the diplomats, and in the next generation of American tenure on the isthmus it would have to meet a challenge more severe than anything it had yet experienced.[35]

[33] SD, 1910–49, 711.192/196, White memo of 23.12.24; 811F.812/982, Walker to Flint, 19.5.25.
[34] Ibid., 811F.812/985, South to Kellogg, 3.9.25. PC, 80-G-2, McIlvaine to Walker, 19.11.27 (emphasis in original).
[35] WPD, 1652–16, Davis to Walker, 19.3.28; Walker to Flint, 31.3.28. AG, post-1917, 336, Kellogg to Davis, 30.4.28.

4

The labour force

Construction decade, 1904–1914

The labour policy brought in by the canal régime during the construction decade spelled trouble throughout Washington's tenure of the Zone. Trouble brewed because from the outset the policy discriminated expressly between the two sections of the canal work force, the Gold and Silver Rolls, so called from their different styles of payment. In June 1904 the Isthmian Canal Commission chairman, Admiral Walker, told Secretary of War Taft that 'the people sent down from here we should pay once a month in gold or in United States currency, but the laborers and the people of the Isthmus would go on the silver roll and be paid every two weeks'.[1]

To one Zone official, the Gold and Silver system was best explained in military terms. 'Roughly,' wrote Colonel Robert Wood, 'the "Gold" force may be compared to the officers and non-commissioned officers of an army – the "Silver" force to the privates in its ranks.' But there was more to the labour hierarchy of the canal than regimentalism. The basis of the Gold–Silver duality was race, as Walker's remark implied. His successor, Theodore Shonts, openly stated as much when he told a Senate committee that 'the broad distinction is white and black'. The chief engineer, John Stevens, testified that 'the "gold" men there are the white men. . . . The "silver" men are the black men.' Franklin Roosevelt, visiting the isthmus in 1912, automatically equated gold workers with whites. A former constable in the Zone police considered that 'caste lines are as sharply drawn as in India. . . . The Brahmins are the "gold" employees.'[2]

---

[1] *1906 Hearings*, 3: 2591. Conniff, *Black labor*, 31–2.
[2] Robert Wood, 'The working force of the Panama Canal', in George Goethals (ed.), *The Panama Canal: An engineering treatise*, vol. 2 (New York, 1916), 189. *1906 Hearings*, 1: 374, 20. Elliott Roosevelt (ed.), *The Roosevelt letters*, vol. 2 (London, 1950), 162. Harry Franck, *Zone Policeman 88: A close range study of the Panama Canal and its workers* (New York, 1913), 219.

There were exceptions to the rule on either side of the colour line, but the Commission was anxious to keep these anomalies to a minimum. In 1906 Shonts was to say that while there were some Silver whites, 'we are getting them into the Gold rolls as fast as possible'. In November 1906 Stevens decreed that all non-American blacks in Gold positions be decanted on to the Silver Roll, the black U.S. citizens allowed to remain on Gold serving mainly as policemen, teachers, and postmasters. The following month the Commission could report that its 3,700 Gold employees were 'virtually all white Americans', while the 13,300 Silvers were 'mainly aliens'.[3]

The privileges that went with allocation to the Gold Roll were considerable. Its men were paid some 50 per cent more than their counterparts in the continental United States, and their income was untaxed. They also enjoyed free furnished quarters, light, fuel and water, health care, and schooling for their children, cut rates on Panama Railroad Company steamers, fifteen days' sick leave every six months, and for the salaried majority six weeks' vacation with pay every year. In the view of the Commission's secretary, Joseph Bucklin Bishop, white Americans could not have been persuaded to stay in the Zone without this range of inducements, and the administration resisted all efforts to curtail it until the canal was near completion. No less a figure than the Commission chairman, Colonel Goethals, told Congress in 1907 that he thought skilled labour was overpaid and gave the cue for a clause in the 1908 appropriation bill fixing the pay differential between the Zone and the United States at no more than 25 per cent. It was taken out at the insistence of Roosevelt and Taft on the grounds that it would lower morale and damage recruitment.[4]

In other respects the Gold Roll men were markedly worse off than their stateside equivalents. Since United States laws did not necessarily apply in the Canal Zone, American labour stationed there was denied the liberties held by workers at home. Thus from the very start of the project the Commission planned to ignore the 1892 statute prescribing an eight-hour day for U.S. government employees. In June 1905 Governor Charles Magoon did set an eight-hour day for the work force, but in January Civil Service regulations for U.S. employees in the Zone were rescinded. The following June the eight-hour provision was cancelled for unskilled alien labourers and their American foremen and superintendents. Though this left most of the Gold force on an eight-hour day, the arrangement satisfied neither the canal authorities nor the Golds,

[3] *1906 Hearings*, 1: 374. ICC, 2-F-14, Stevens to Williams, 30.11.06; Shannon to Williams, 10.4.07. *ICC Report*, 1906, 5.
[4] *Skilled Labor*, 103, 137, 286–7. Joseph Bucklin Bishop, 'A benevolent despotism', *Scribner's Monthly*, 53 (January–June 1913), 304–5, 309, 313. *Skilled Labor*, 57, 58. *NYT*, 30.4.08, 1/6. *TR letters*, 6:1019. WNRC, RG 335, OSA 004.06 Panama Canal (16–12–49). *Skilled Labor*, 10–11.

whose spokesman, Samuel Gompers, president of the American Federation of Labor, protested strenuously at the violation of the law.[5]

Roosevelt foresaw a big political storm. Gompers had good connections in House and Senate, and the president told Taft that while Shonts and Stevens were perfectly competent as canal executives, they could not grasp 'that a row with labor means a row with Congress'. Yet though he listened to grievances Roosevelt was not prepared to give American employees a voice in policy making, and labour representation on the Commission was dismissed as 'an absurdity'. The canal administration shared power with no one, and the American work force on the isthmus remained a body without basic trade union rights.[6]

Above all, it was deprived of the right to strike. Roosevelt's executive order of 9 May 1904 setting up the government of the Zone authorised the Commission to deport, among others, 'anarchists, those whose purpose it is to incite insurrection and others whose presence it is believed by the Commission would tend to create public disorder, endanger the public health, or in any manner impede the prosecution of the work of opening the canal'. In August 1904 Chief Engineer John Wallace urged that this be construed to authorise Governor George Davis to deport strike leaders, and in November 1907 Goethals did not hesitate to break a strike by steam-shovel operatives and locomotive men by bringing the threat of deportation into play.[7]

Goethals was equally uncompromising in his general attitude to the work force. When a congressional visitation called on him to place a secretary for labour affairs on the ICC, he refused point-blank. He already heard individual petitioners at his Sunday morning 'court', and he would merely give Bishop permission to receive delegations of workers in the capacity of complaint commissioner. This did not constitute recognition of any trade union, and the groups that met with Bishop had no organisational standing. In other words, labour relations were handled by what one contemporary observer rightly described as 'a military paternalism'. Justice in this area, wrote William Ghent, was 'not the sort that would be tolerated long in a democracy.... An Army régime must necessarily fail in many respects in interpreting the viewpoint of workingmen.'[8]

The Silver men functioned under many more disadvantages. They could not expect the backing of an American union, they were granted hardly any fringe

[5] See above, Chapter 3, n. 3. ICC, 9-A-1, Wallace to Parsons, 15.3.05. On the eight-hour-day law, see Philip Foner, *History of the labor movement in the United States*, vol. 2 (New York, 1955), 98–104, 178–84. PC, 5-D-25, Magoon to Taft, 29.5.05. *TR letters*, 4:1319 n. 1. *ICC Report, 1906*, 14. *1906 Hearings* 1: 641–6, 807–11; 4: 3227. *NYT.* 12.8.06, 4/5.

[6] *TR letters*, 5: 355–6, 508.   [7] *BD*, 414. ICC, 2-P-59, Wallace to Walker, 25.8.04.

[8] DuVal, *And the mountains*, 306–7. William Ghent, 'Labor and the Commissary at Panama', *Independent*, 66 (1909), 1132–3, and 'Work and welfare on the canal', ibid., 66 (1909), 909, 913, 908.

benefits, and their initial hourly wage was only half the minimum rate paid to common labour in the United States. As confirmation of their inferior grading, the currency they were paid in had only 50 per cent of the face value of the U.S. dollar reserved for the Gold force.

The vast contingent of Silver workers who shouldered the drudgery of the canal excavation were mostly imported from the West Indies and Southern Europe. Very few indeed were Panamanians. 'The native Isthmian', asserted Commissioner Peter Hains, 'will not work. He is naturally indolent; not over strong; has no ambitions; his wants are few in number and easily satisfied. He can live for a few cents a day, and he prefers to take it easy, swinging in a hammock and smoking cigarettes.' So the citizens of the republic that gave the canal its name were to be largely no more than spectators of its construction.[9]

Nor were many U.S. citizens, white or black, enlisted in the Silver cadres. Hains himself urged the use of American blacks, as did Theodore Roosevelt, but Governor Davis threw out the idea. The West Indians, he argued, were bound to clash with black Southern labourers, and the white Zone policeman Harry Franck expressed a widespread view when he wrote that 'the American negro is an untractable creature in large numbers'. The Commission did not plan to compound its difficulties by adding this seismic ingredient to a labour force already split along the fault line of Gold and Silver.[10]

White American labourers likewise were given no encouragement to join the project. In November 1904 Davis affirmed that it was 'useless to discuss the question of utilizing the white race for heavy out-of-door work with pick and shovel, in the mud and rain, on the Isthmus; no one has ever succeeded in obtaining such a force of the Caucasian race'. 'American working men have no call to Panama,' wrote Willis Johnson, 'any more than English working men have to the plains of India.' Given the stratification of canal workers by colour, it was unthinkable for the ICC to place white men in the lower depths alongside blacks and upset the racial balance.[11]

The chief source of unskilled labour was meant to be Jamaica, and in December 1904 Taft met the governor, Sir Alexander Swettenham, to negotiate an agreement. But the island's government had had to pay out $100,000 in gold to repatriate Jamaican labourers stranded in Panama after the collapse of the French project in the late 1880s, and Swettenham insisted that the ICC fund all future repatriation. When Taft refused, Swettenham forbade Jamaicans to sign contracts to go to work on the canal, and the Commission turned for its contract labour mainly to Barbados. Though contract labour was illegal under a U.S. law

[9] Peter Hains, 'The labor problem on the Panama Canal', *North American Review*, 179 (1904), 50.

[10] Ibid., 51. *TR letters*, 5:504. *1906 Hearings*, 3: 2498–9. Franck, *Zone Policeman 88*, 119.

[11] *1906 Hearings*, 3: 2498–9. Willis Johnson, *Four centuries of the Panama Canal* (New York, 1907), 357.

of 1885, union leaders in Washington were not disposed to resist the West Indian influx, since so few Americans were considered for Silver jobs. So contract labourers flooded in – 500 a month in the second half of 1904 and 1,000 a month throughout 1905. By November 1905 more than 14,000 men were carried on the Silver Roll of the Commission and the Railroad, almost all of them from the Caribbean.[12]

During the first two years of the project there were continual complaints about the quality of this West Indian labour. One American supervisor commented acidly that 'fifteen cents an hour [Silver] is about ten cents too much for the work they do', and Shonts rated the West Indian at only one-third the efficiency of his white American counterpart. The annual report of the ICC for 1906 bemoaned 'the impossibility of doing satisfactory work' with the Barbadians. 'Their disposition to labor', it concluded, 'seems to be as frail as their bodily strength. . . . Many of them settle in the jungle, building little shacks, raising enough to keep them alive, and working only a day or two occasionally, as they see fit.' Secretary Taft took a philosophical view of the problem. The West Indian, he believed, 'has his faults; he is lazy, and he does loaf about a good deal, but he is amenable to law, and it does not take a large police force to keep him in order'. But the Commission was already looking elsewhere, since it seemed as though the canal would never be finished otherwise.[13]

The preferred source of supply was China. As railroad engineers, both Wallace and Stevens knew the phenomenal capacity of Chinese coolies for toil. But one of the first acts of the Panamanian government in March 1904 was to ban the immigration of Chinese, and the United States itself had practised exclusion since 1882. Governor Davis believed it would be ill advised to bring in a 'deluge' of Chinese; they would want to open illicit gambling-houses, not to work, and their presence would be 'bad in every respect'. Moreover, the executive order of 9 May 1904 followed the language of the thirteenth amendment to the Constitution in forbidding 'involuntary servitude' in the Zone, and Taft told Shonts that 'peonage or coolieism, which shortly stated is slavery by debt', was 'as much in conflict with the thirteenth amendment . . . as the usual form of slavery'. At the same time, the Knights of Labor, who had not raised a

[12] Taft Papers, SWS-OC, Taft to Roosevelt, 19.12.04. SD, 1906–10, 243, Magoon memo of 3.9.06. On the anti-contract labor law of 1885, see Kitty Calavita, *U.S. immigration law and the control of labor* (New York, 1984), 39–72. *ICC Report, 1905*, 9, 10. PC, 2-E-1, McIlvaine memo of 1.8.28. *1906 Hearings*, 3: 2664.

[13] ICC, 5-D-25, Karner to Wallace, 1.10.04. *1906 Hearings*, 1: 486. *ICC Report, 1906*, 5. *1906 Hearings*, 3: 2766. Bishop, 'A benevolent despotism', 308. See also the comment of a Zonian doctor: 'As long as [the West Indian] has a roof over his head and a yam or two to eat he is content, and his idea of personal hygiene is on a par with his conception of marital fidelity': A. Grenfell Price, 'White settlement in the Canal Zone', *Geographical Review*, 25 (1935), 9.

murmur over hiring West Indians, kicked up an almighty clamour against using Orientals.[14]

Others saw Chinese labour as the only hope of making rapid progress on the canal. As early as June 1904 the ICC's legal counsel, Charles Magoon, had pressed hard for Chinese work gangs, and in May 1906, exasperated by the West Indians' lethargic performance, Stevens urged Shonts to advertise for Chinamen. In July the president himself took up the call. 'I shall permit nothing to stand in the way of getting this labor,' he wrote Taft, 'save the law of the land and the requirements of morality.' In August the *New York Times* reported that the ICC was looking for 'strong men from the rice fields of Southern China' via a circular sent out to U.S. consuls in the treaty ports.[15]

The bid for Chinese labour came to nothing, however. Chinese coolies had recently been abominably treated in the British-occupied Transvaal when they were brought in to substitute for black African workers, and Beijing was unwilling to risk repeating the experience. In November the Chinese minister in Washington refused to cooperate with the Commission, and the ICC was also the target of an angry barrage of protest in the Panamanian press. In the face of the opposition on both these fronts, Roosevelt gave way. In March 1907, soon after Stevens's resignation, it was officially stated that no Chinese labour would be engaged.[16]

So the Commission had to think again. Failing the Chinese as the spearhead of its labour battalions, it turned to Southern Europe. Early in 1906, 900 Spanish workers were shipped in and proved so satisfactory that they were paid twenty cents an hour, twice the West Indian rate. Over the next two years no fewer than 12,000 men from Spain, Italy, and Greece were imported to act as the corps d'élite of the Silver force. They were supported by a further huge batch of West Indians from Barbados, which was ultimately to furnish nearly 20,000 contract workers, and from Martinique and Guadeloupe, which sent in some 7,500. The great legion of West Indians made up two-thirds of the Silver work force – and it had an additional part to play. In 1906 the engineer William Burr remarked that a 'surplusage' of labour was needed to provide the

[14] ICC, 79-F-8, Panamanian law of 11.3.04. On the 1882 Chinese exclusion law, see Rose Lee, *The Chinese in the United States of America* (Hong Kong, 1960), 11–13. BD, 414. ICC, 79-F-8, Davis to Walker, 29.6.04; 2-E-1, Taft to Shonts, 13.4.05, and Moody to Taft, 5.6.05. *NYT*, 16.4.05, 2/1. On the anti-peonage statutes, see Charles Mangum, *The legal status of the Negro* (Chapel Hill, N.C., 1940), 164.

[15] ICC, 79-F-8, Magoon to Walker, 29.6.04. Taft Papers, ser. 3, Magoon to Taft, 15.7.04. ICC, 2-E-1, Stevens to Shonts, 5.5.06. *TR letters*, 5:337–8. William Howard Taft, 'The Panama Canal: Why the lock-system was chosen', *Century Magazine*, 73 (July–December 1906), 310–11. *NYT*, 12.8.06, 4/5. SD, 1906–10, 637, memo of 28.8.06.

[16] On the Chinese in the Transvaal, see Alfred Gollin, *Proconsul in politics: A study of Lord Milner in opposition and in power* (London, 1964), 61–73. SD, 1906–10, 637, U.S. Consul in Fuzhou to Bacon, 19.4.07. *NYT*, 8.3.07, 4/3.

Figure 1. The other ranks: West Indian recruits for the 'Army of Panama'
arrive to join the construction project. (Panama Canal Commission)

Commission with a ready pool of employables to inhibit any strike movement.
The black and what one high-ranking Zonian called the 'semi-white foreigner
(Dago)' sections of the Silver Roll thus complemented each other perfectly.
'Our Gallego and other white labor', wrote Wood to Stevens, 'would be our
dependable nucleus, and the negro our floating supply.' It was on this basis that

the Silver force went on to operate under the direction of Stevens's successor, Goethals.[17]

In February 1908 Goethals drew the line between Gold and Silver more sharply through an executive order which reserved all future appointments to the Gold Roll to American citizens. Existing non-American Golds were to remain in place, but whenever a reduction in force might come about, they would be the first to go. As Commissioner David Gaillard explained, it was policy 'to keep employees who are undoubtedly black or belong to mixed races on the Silver rolls', and as Goethals's deputy, Harry Hodges, saw it, the order 'put a stop to the employment of British West Indians on a Gold basis'. Americans would monopolise Gold assignments from this point on.[18]

To the Panamanians this came as a deep affront. During his visit to the isthmus in November 1906 Roosevelt had promised Panama 'a full and complete and generous equality' in the canal partnership. But Taft did not write equality into the executive order, which the Panamanians felt put them down on the same level as the black *antillanos* they so comprehensively despised. Soon afterwards, however, he relented. The administration could afford to admit the principle of equality, since in practice only 16 Panamanians were currently featured on a Gold payroll of some 5,400. In December 1908 the order was amended accordingly and Panama's hurt pride assuaged. Yet to the ICC this was a side issue. The basic purpose of the order had been to formalise American superiority within the work force, and in November 1908 Goethals confirmed this when he agreed that white American labourers should not be treated the same as 'the class of men engaged on this work'. Instead they were to be paid at Gold rates and given Gold quarters to distance them from their fellow Silvers off duty, if not in working hours.[19]

Not even this, it seemed, could satisfy some U.S. employees, who protested that Silver aliens were doing work which should have been designated as Gold and were thus denying jobs to Americans. This was to become a perennial complaint of the Gold corps, but the canal authorities' response, then and in future, was to point to the prohibitive expense of Americanising the Zone's entire labour force. The cost of replacing all foreign Silver workers was estimated at $500,000 a year, quite apart from the money that would have to be spent on Gold-standard housing and recreational amenities. Given Goethals's

[17] *ICC Report, 1906*, 5, 14. Wood, 'Working force', 196. PC, 2-E-1, memo of 25.3.31. *1906 Hearings*, 2:1573–4. ICC, 2-E-1, Wood to Stevens, 22.10.06.

[18] *Executive Orders*, 78. ICC, 2-F-14, Gaillard to Slifer, 15.2.08; 2-E-11, Hodges to Taft, 11.2.09, and Goethals memo of 14.8.08.

[19] *BD*, 711. *NYT*, 4.4.07, 1/5. SD, 1906–10, 637, Squiers to Root, 3.4.08. Taft Papers, sws-oc, Taft to Roosevelt, 16.5.08. PC, 2-E-12, Lansing to Baker, 19.7.19. ICC, 2-F-14, McIlvaine to Goethals, 27.11.08; Goethals to Sibert, 28.11.08. *Executive Orders*, 86.

conviction that the Gold Roll was already pampered enough, the idea was taken no further.[20]

Nor did Goethals care to pursue a proposal to frame hard-and-fast rules of membership for the Gold or Silver categories. That would have been to limit the wide discretion he enjoyed in this area and exercised freely. It was he, for example, who decided that a black American aspirant to Gold status would stay a Silver. He also determined that segregated Gold and Silver facilities be made a fixture in the Commissary stores. It is true that he also revoked an order requiring black Gold employees to take off their hats when dealing with white female Commissary clerks, but this was a minor concession to black feeling. On the big issues of race relations there can be no doubt where Goethals's sympathies lay.[21]

Goethals's solidarity with the Americans of the Gold Roll stopped short, however, at the question of their pay, and he stuck to his firm conviction that 25 per cent more than the salaries paid to American government employees in the Eastern United States was ample. In the Panama Canal Act of August 1912, Goethals's 25 per cent differential was accepted as the yardstick for Gold Roll wages once the canal began to go into service.[22]

Goethals recognised that the reduced pay scale would stir unrest, and in March 1914 the American Federation of Labor formed the Metal Trades Council to fight the cutback. To lower the temperature, he had issued a new executive order which put Americans on an immensely strong footing. It was, said Goethals, 'intended to make mandatory the employment of American citizens in higher grades' (that is, Gold), and besides this they were to be given preference for jobs in all grades (that is, Gold *and* Silver). As in 1908, Panamanians would be allowed token equality with Americans, but otherwise the effect would be 'to further restrict the percentage of positions at present open to aliens'. Foreign workers were to be granted Gold standing only if they had already been on the Gold strength for two years or in case of emergency, after which they were to be replaced as soon as practicable.[23]

With this fiat the canal directorate took into the operational era the latest refinement of the labour policy elaborated so purposefully over the construction decade. That policy had created an 'Army of Panama' whose two components were not only separate but most emphatically unequal and with a gulf fixed between them as unbridgeable as the racial chasm which divided American society itself. It had accomplished the pressing task of driving the canal through on

[20] ICC, 2-P-49/P, Rousseau to Goethals, 3.2.09.

[21] ICC, 2-F-14, 26.10.09 to 6.12.09, and Goethals to Smith, 22.7.10; 2-C-55, 6.1.10 to 20.1.10; 58-A-13, Whitlock to Goethals, 23.7.12, and Goethals to Whitlock, 2.8.12; Price to Goethals, 17.3.10; memo for Goethals, 18.3.10.

[22] *Skilled Labor*, 10–11. DuVal, *And the mountains*, 320. *BD*, 597.

[23] ICC, 2-D-4, Goethals to Boggs, 20.12.13. *NYT*, 23.3.14, 4/6. ICC, 2-E-11/P, Goethals memo of 8.11.13; 2-D-4, Goethals memo of 27.1.14. *Executive Orders*, 158–61.

schedule; it now remained to be seen how it would stand up to the less dramatic but equally demanding test of keeping it running for the foreseeable future.

First World War, 1914–1918

The employment structure erected during the construction decade, like the canal itself, was built to last. As we have seen, the work force was polarised between a skilled Gold Roll virtually monopolised by white Americans and a semi-skilled and unskilled Silver Roll almost entirely made up of black West Indians. The tensions in this carefully segregated community heightened still further in the first years of canal operation, thanks largely to the dreaded acronym RIF – reduction in force. Dismissals had started early in 1913, and the run-down went on steadily for four years after the canal opened. Between July 1914 and July 1918 the Gold Roll was slashed by nearly 36 per cent; Silver, by close on 43 per cent. Redundancy therefore provided the context for labour relations in the Zone as the canal began its working life.[24]

The Golds were vocal in their own defence, blue-collar workers via the Metal Trades Council (MTC) and white-collar personnel through the Central Labor Union. On one front they did succeed in pushing the Zone into retreat. In January 1915 Governor Goethals began billing all members of the force for housing, fuel, and electricity. After a mass outcry by Gold employees, the charges were first suspended and then revoked – at least for the Gold men. Silvers were not so fortunate.[25]

When it came to employment policy, however, Goethals could not be budged. In October 1914 the MTC asserted that many skilled jobs were currently held by aliens and demanded them all for U.S. citizens. Goethals was prepared to appease the clamour merely to the extent of having two or three blacks replaced. He was convinced that the union was trying to make him pay skilled rates for unskilled work, and this he refused to do. He was ready, he said, to replace all aliens by Americans, but only at Silver wages, and this he knew was an offer the MTC was bound to refuse. Quite apart from that, Goethals pointed out, it was 'not compatible with the white man's pride of race to do the work which it is traditional for the negroes to do in this country'. The MTC did not press its case.[26]

Goethals was also on the receiving end of protests from Panamanians likewise caught in the squeeze of contraction. In December 1914 they alleged that they were being dismissed exactly like West Indians in spite of their supposedly protected position. Goethals was quick to spell out a preference for Panamanians whenever the Silver Roll had to be trimmed. When it came to the Gold Roll,

---

[24] PC, 2-E-11/A, Paul memo of 23.9.32.

[25] *Executive Orders*, 213, 215–16. SD, 1910–49, 811F.504/36, Kagy to Bryan, 15.2.15.

[26] PC, 2-E-11/P, MTC memo of 11.10.14 and Goethals memo of 13.10.14; 2-E-11, Goethals memo of 5.3.15 and Goethals to Boggs, 20.3.15; 2-E-11/P, Garrison to Foster, 16.10.15.

his reaction was very different. The Panamanians claimed the same legal employment status as U.S. personnel, but this was a delusion, and Goethals decreed that they would be treated like any other aliens when it came to cutbacks.[27]

Black Americans in both employment categories were similarly kept in their place. One U.S. black on the Gold Roll who complained to Executive Secretary McIlvaine about racialism was given a decidedly unsympathetic answer. In reply to a suggestion that all black American Silvers be transferred to Gold, McIlvaine demurred: 'The color question raises trouble and I'm "agin it" for that reason.' The most that American blacks achieved at this time was a regulation stipulating that U.S. citizens, Gold or Silver, white or black, had preference over aliens for promotion to vacancies. But the concession was grudging in the extreme. 'I feel that we cannot "coddle" these American negroes without spoiling them', McIlvaine told Governor Chester Harding; 'they would forever after be intolerable nuisances.' Black Americans thus remained despicably neglected by the government they served. 'I am powerless', stated Harding, 'to correct a situation which results from centuries of habit and custom. . . . The reasons for racial antipathy are too deep-seated to be corrected or reached by rules and regulations, except such rules as recognize that antipathy and try to avoid pain and discomfort.'[28]

The West Indians on the Silver Roll were not so easily ignored. In October 1916 they staged a strike which brought out some 6,000 of the 21,000-strong Silver force. The root cause of the stoppage was the desperate poverty of a community whose basic wage had been cut from thirteen to ten cents an hour in 1914 and pegged there ever since – this in spite of the escalating cost of living in Panama, where most West Indians lived. There they faced high rents and extortionate food prices and bills for schooling and medical care, as well as the burden of their unemployed. Though the organisation behind the upsurge was rudimentary, it had spread like wildfire in the first twenty-four hours, and the potential for future disruption was incalculable.[29]

Harding's immediate reaction was to summon Panama to break the movement. If it failed to cooperate, he warned that he would invoke Article 7 of the canal treaty and send in U.S. troops, even in the absence of the necessary Panamanian request. The newly installed regime of President Ramón Valdés jumped to comply, closing saloons, banning parades, dispersing meetings, and arresting and deporting strike leaders. It was all over in five days.[30]

[27] PC, 2-E-12, Panamanian memo of 7.12.14, Circular 604–3 of 10.12.14, and Chief Clerk memo of 11.6.15; 2-E-11, Goethals to Sweeney, 5.3.15.

[28] PC, 28-B-233, McIlvaine to Eagleson, 2.9.14; 2-F-14, McIlvaine memo of 19.8.15; 2-E-11, Circular of 19.5.17; 2-D-6, Memo of 19.5.17; 28-B-233, Harding memo of 22.8.18.

[29] SD, 1910–49, 811F.504/45, Harding to Baker, 14.10.16; /44, Price to Lansing, 15.10.16. PC, 2-D-4, West Indian Progress for November 1916; 2-P-12, Gompers to Weeks, 28.10.24.

[30] SD, 1910–49, 811F.504/45, Harding to Baker, 17.10.16. PC, 2-P-59/16, Harding report of 21.10.16.

Looking beyond the episode, Harding recognised the central West Indian grievance by setting up a Silver Rates Board, which advised a wage level sufficient for labourers to live 'in reasonable comfort and decency'. The first step in this direction was an 11 per cent pay rise, utterly inadequate but the most Harding was prepared to concede. The Canal's funding calculations, he reminded Washington, were based on low rates of pay for Silvers, and low pay for Silvers and a large pool of West Indian unemployed were both essential if the Zone's cheap-labour policy were to be sustained.[31]

Harding also planned to house the entire Silver force in the Zone, partly as an answer to the problem of exorbitant Panamanian rents, partly to corral the Silvers within the Zone's own police jurisdiction and avoid reliance on Panama to bring a crisis under control. For this purpose an extra $1.5 million was added to the estimates for fiscal 1918. The idea came as bad news to the landlords of the West Indian tenants in the terminal cities, and the government leaped to their aid with a plaintive protest note. In the event, Congress rejected the housing scheme, but the notion continued to enthuse canal officialdom. Model townships would furnish all the amenities the West Indians could possibly want, including churches, recreation halls, and cricket fields. Happy as Southern blacks on the plantations, 'such laborers would have no desire to strike'.[32]

Pending fulfilment of that idyll, the Canal in March 1917 went through another short-lived bout of industrial action when a hundred West Indians downed tools on the dry-dock at Cristóbal. This, it transpired, was the work of the Colón Federal Labor Union, founded the year before under the leadership of a black Panamanian, Victor de Suze. Thereafter the CFLU was kept under close surveillance by a spy in the pay of the Canal Zone police. By the end of 1918 it had made no more than a minor nuisance of itself, but as the First World War drew to an end the United States stood on the edge of one of the most turbulent strike movements in its history, and the Panama Canal was not beyond its reach.[33]

The twenties, 1919–1929

The employment policy mapped out for the operational era was heavily influenced by a determination to minimise the Canal's wage bill, and with the massive lay-offs which came when construction ended, the authorities were in a commanding position. In the decade after the First World War an employer's

[31] Conniff, *Black Labor*, 49, 52. PC, 2-E-11/P, Harding to Brown, 28.10.16; Baker to Cummins, 25.1.17.
[32] PC, 2-P-59/16, Harding to Brown, 18.10.16; 13-Q-1, Harding to Brown, 20.10.16; Garay to Harding 6.11.16. SD, 1910–49, 811F.502/1, Panamanian note of 1.12.16;/3, Porras to Lansing, 15.1.17; /5, Panamanian note of 24.3.17. PC, 79-F-5, Wilson, to McIlvaine, 26.6.17.
[33] *NYT*, 14.3.17, 13/2. PC, 2-P-59/17, Memo of 29.3.17; 2-P-70, Marshall (alias Muschett) to Johannes, 19.10.17, 8.11.17, 14.4.18.

market continued to dominate the Zone's relations with its work force, though only after a powerful challenge from a number of quarters had momentarily thrown the canal establishment on the defensive.

The first shock to the system came in the spring of 1919, when the American Federation of Labor (AFL) began a membership drive among the West Indians on the Silver Roll, promising to get them the same pay as black American labourers and denouncing the Zonians as 'hogs'. The head of the Canal's Washington office was convinced that the campaign was really a ploy to eliminate the West Indians: If their wages were raised to U.S. levels, Americans would be taken on in preference. This was a subtlety that escaped Governor Harding and white union leaders in the Zone, who demanded the immediate recall of the AFL organisers or their deportation. Before Washington could react, Harding faced a walkout by more than a thousand West Indians on the docks at Cristóbal early in May. Though the AFL was not behind it, the strike revealed the potential for disruption once unionisation took hold in the West Indian community.[34]

For Harding the lessons of the stoppage were clear. To neutralise 'professional negro agitators', he advised the West Indians to elect leaders of their own background, 'not men who have a high education, for they will turn the deal on you'. And, as in 1916, he planned to immunise the Silvers from the unions by housing as many as possible in the Zone. Funds were released for the construction of quarters for the dockers at the Cristóbal terminal, and a settlement was founded at Las Cascadas as a ready reserve of labour for emergencies. At the same time the Silver base rate was upped from seventeen to nineteen cents an hour.[35]

There, however, the line was drawn. In the view of the inspector of Silver Labor, the West Indians seemed to feel that the Canal was 'a semi-philanthropic, non-dividend-paying commercial institution which is to be continued indefinitely, with a drawing account on the people of the United States'. The Zone was not about to slacken its purse-strings any further in respect of either the Silvers or the white Americans on the Gold Roll. Though a War Department investigator attacked the Gold unions for forcing the governor to provide a 'socialistic utopia', Harding stood out against renewed calls for the replacement of semi-skilled aliens by U.S. citizens.[36]

Perhaps for Harding the 1919 strike seemed as much a flash in the pan as the short-lived upsurge of 1916. In fact it was the prelude to a convulsion in the Zone which grew out of the flood-tide of syndicalism that raced across the

[34] PC, 2-P-70, Verner to Calhoun, 24.3.19; 2-P-59/20, Police memo of 28.3.19; 2-P-70, Flint memo of 3.4.19; Flint to Harding, 11.4.19; Harding to Flint, 31.3.19 and 5.5.19.
[35] PC, 2-P-59/19, Police memo of 13.5.19. MID, 10634-672, Harding to Flint, 21.8.19; Gilkey to Harding, 18.8.19. Conniff, Black labor, 55-6.
[36] MID, 10634-672, Gilkey to Harding, 18.8.19. Conniff Black labor, 55, quoting Williams report of 24.7.19 in PC, 2-C-129. PC, 2-E-11/P, Memo of 18.6.19.

United States in the autumn of 1919, closing down the steel industry on 22 September and bringing the bituminous coal fields to a standstill on 1 November. A railway strike was also in the wind, and the canal workers were bound to be drawn in, since recruitment into the AFL had taken place under the banner of a railroad union, the United Brotherhood of Maintenance of Way Employees and Railway Shop Laborers. Faced with the likelihood of trouble, Harding took no chances. At the end of September the revolutionary black leader Marcus Garvey was banned from entering the Zone. In November two Brotherhood organisers en route for the isthmus were refused permission to land after a police report that one of them had anarcho-syndicalist leanings. In February 1920 Army Intelligence eavesdropped on cable traffic between union headquarters in Detroit and the Panama local. Although the projected national stoppage was called off, labour relations in the Zone were so bad that an unofficial strike was inevitable. In spite of a warning from Harding that strikers would be evicted from Zone housing and stripped of Commissary privileges, no fewer than 11,000 of the 16,000 West Indians on the force came out on 24 February.[37]

Yet the 1920 strike collapsed after only eight days. One major cause of the failure was a critical shortage of funds. The sum of $30,000 had been lodged with the Brotherhood in 1919, but none of it was remitted to the West Indians when they called for aid from Detroit. They also faced a ruthless adversary in Governor Harding. After twenty-four hours Harding dismissed all men who had refused to go back to work and decanted more than three hundred families from the Zone into Panama. This put immediate pressure on the Panamanian government, and Harding added a threat to occupy the terminal cities unless Panama itself acted to break the strike. By this time the West Indian leadership was in deep difficulty, and it suffered a body-blow when the AFL suspended the Brotherhood as an affiliate. When Panama banned strike meetings on 2 March, it delivered the coup de grâce. The Silvers had been utterly defeated, and it was to be more than a quarter of a century before they regrouped as members of a trade union.[38]

In the aftermath of the débâcle, the West Indians had still more to endure. The average pay of a married labourer with two children in February 1920 lagged nearly 40 per cent behind his outgoings, and the union had been petitioning for an increase of that order. But the rise in the base rate to twenty-three cents an hour which came in July was an increment of only 20 per cent, and since Silver

---

[37] On the strike movement of 1919–20, see Selig Perlman and Philip Taft, *History of labor in the United States*, vol. 4 (New York, 1935), 435–72. MID, 10634–672, Flint to Baker, 4.9.19; Wilson to Pratt, 25.9.19. PC, 2-P-70, Flint to Harding, 30.9.19; 28-B-233, Harding memo of 27.9.19; 2-P-59/20, Johannes to Harding, 19.11.19; Harding to Baker, 26.2.20. MID, 10634–672, Randolph to MID, 16.2.20.

[38] MID, 10634–672, Report of 4.3.20; 2657-M-5, Report of 3.3.20. PC, 2-P-59/20, Harding to Baker, 26.2.20; 2-P-70, Marshall report of 7.7.19.

earnings were index-linked to Commissary prices, they were destined to fall during a recession. The strike leaders themselves tasted summary retribution: The Barbadian William Stoute was hunted down and deported and the American Nicholas Carter accused as a U.S. citizen of 'an act of disloyalty' to his government. Several dozen semi-skilled West Indians were dismissed in a systematic purge of the upper Silver echelons which had provided the strike movement with its spearhead. Strikers re-engaged were told they would be treated as new employees and paid at the bottom rate; if their quarters had been reassigned, they would be put on the waiting list. All told, as one commentator approvingly observed, the Zone administration had 'the bridle hand on the negroes', and no further difficulty with them was expected for a long time to come.[39]

As the West Indians fell back into thraldom, the Americans on the Gold Roll were sitting pretty. It was they who picked up the jobs of the Silver artisans Harding had fired, and shortly after the strike Harding decreed that in future enough posts should be filled by Americans to guarantee the Canal against a renewed Silver 'defection'. The AFL's interpretation of this directive was ambitious. In September its president, Samuel Gompers, demanded the replacement of all alien tradesmen by U.S. citizens, but the Canal refused to pay a Gold rate of forty cents an hour for work that could be done for nearly half the cost by a Silver man.[40]

Where the budget was not an issue, the canal administration was prepared to be accommodating. The Gold Salary Board included an American union member, and the president of the blue-collar Metal Trades Council sat on the Gold Wage Board set up in March 1919. The Grievance Board introduced in July 1920 confined labour representation to AFL affiliates, thus making it exclusive to the MTC and the white-collar Central Labor Union. By the end of the year the Golds were more snugly entrenched than ever.[41]

Their all-providing welfare system was admiringly described by an academic from progressive Wisconsin. The whites of the Canal Zone, wrote R. H. Whitbeck, 'live under a paternalistic socialism. The state does practically everything for them, [furnishing] not only ... water, light, schools, sanitation, etc., but ... homes to live in if they are married or lodgings if they are unmarried. It supplies the furniture, plants, trees and shrubs ... fills the coalbin and woodbox ... conducts restaurants and clubs, non-profit stores, ... buses and launches ... and other benefits.' This gave a substantially accurate picture of what for the

[39] SD, 1910–49, 811F.504/59, UK Embassy, Washington, to Hughes, 14.6.21. Darrell Smith, *The Panama Canal: Its history, activities, and organization* (Baltimore, 1927), 131–2. Conniff, *Black labor* 59. PC, 2-P-59/20, Hearing of 21.4.20; Harding memo of 16.3.20. MID, 10634–672, Memo of 4.3.20; 153–33, Report of 22.5.20.

[40] PC, 2-E-11/A, Memo of 13.3.20; 2-E-11/P, Gompers to Baker, 17.9.20, Baker to Gompers, 8.11.20.

[41] Smith, *The Panama Canal*, 129–30. Marshall Dimock, *Government-operated enterprises in the Panama Canal Zone* (Chicago, 1934), 172–3.

Golds had become another Eden, and they were understandably intent on keeping it that way.[42]

Not so the incoming Republican administration of Warren Harding. In April the *New York Times* revealed that his secretary of war, John Weeks, was planning to put a tighter rein on canal spending, and a commission of inquiry headed by General William Connor left for the isthmus. Senator William McKinley had recently told the Senate with heavy sarcasm that in 1920 it took no fewer than 17,500 men to transit fewer than eight ships a day. Though employment on the canal had fallen by 36 per cent in the current recession, the Harding régime appeared to think that an upturn in the business cycle would bring back overmanning. What was needed, in its view, was a radical change in the pattern of the work force, in the shape of 'silverisation', that is, the replacement of Golds by Silvers wherever possible in order to trim labour costs.[43]

This was the conclusion reached by Connor. Washington was 'forced to pay exorbitant wages and to bear many additional expenses such as bonuses . . . which would be unnecessary if local labour were employed'. Most of the positions on the canal could be filled almost entirely with 'tropical labour'. Casting a cold eye over the Gold Roll, he recommended charging Gold workers for housing, water, and electricity; reviewing their 25 per cent pay differential and their generous leave allowances; and adopting an open-shop policy to break the hegemony of the craft unions. In short, the Canal should model itself on U.S. business corporations whose overseas branches were run by a few high-salaried American managers in charge of a mainly foreign work force. As it was, the waterway had to carry too much skilled American labour, and its top executives did not get adequate financial rewards. The governor and his division heads should be paid 50 per cent more and the West Indians lifted above subsistence level. Americans would lose all but the most essential posts, and those who stayed on would see their handsome standard of living appreciably reduced.[44]

Governor Morrow and the AFL were both appalled at the Connor report. 'The adoption of these recommendations at once and in toto', Morrow advised Weeks, 'would ruin the canal. . . . We would soon have a halting, limping service, damage bills to an incalculable extent, a very considerable traffic loss, a wholesale desertion of highly expert employees, resulting in a disorganized service that could never be restored to even a small fraction of its present high efficiency; also a valuable strategic asset would be almost totally destroyed.' Gompers too denounced the report lock, stock, and barrel and in mid October took the issue direct to the White House.[45]

The silverisation plan was consequently abandoned. At his interview with the AFL, Harding promised that he 'would not sanction the employment of

[42] *NYT*, 27.8.20, 22/2.
[43] *NYT*, 21.4.21, 17/6. PC, 28-B-5, Weeks to Morrow, 6.6.21. *CR* (Senate), 14.5.21, 1456–7.
[44] USSPCC, *Report* [September 15, 1921] . . . (Washington, D.C., 1922), 9, 10–11, 12–13, 15.
[45] Ibid., 51–2. *NYT*, 7.10.21, 8/1.

alien negroes except for such classes of work as the white Americans did not care to handle'. As Morrow noted, this was tantamount to disapproval of silverisation and undoubtedly came as welcome news to those Zonians who had convinced themselves that blacks capable of doing the work of a first-class mechanic were 'as rare as a red ear of corn in a field'.[46]

Even so, the American unions were bitterly resentful, and when Harding accepted Connor's proposal to make charges for some of their amenities, they fought it through the courts. When their case was finally lost in April 1922, they aired their grievances before Congress. There the MTC's man in Washington, William Hushing, blamed Morrow for favouring silverisation and a week later told the *New York Times* that new economies had undermined the Zone's public health services and increased the chances of a malaria epidemic. For Morrow this was intolerable, a malicious lie designed 'to promote discord and to create a class feeling in the Canal organization'. The punishment was Hushing's dismissal without notice. Relations between the Canal and its U.S. personnel had never been so sour.[47]

Nor were they sweetened by Gompers's visit to the Zone in January 1924, when he called for the restoration of rent-free quarters or a 35 per cent pay differential. 'They want to take the hide out of the American employees on the Canal strip,' Gompers told reporters on his return to New York, and he pressed their case industriously in subsequent petitions to Weeks. Since the canal was so vital to national security, its staff should not be preponderantly foreign-born. Life in the Zone was 'not a bed of roses', and the expatriates there deserved maximum compensation for missing the comforts of home. Because Congress had excluded aliens from the United States, it should do the same on the isthmus. To keep the Zone up to U.S. standards, Americans should hold all grades above messenger and common labourer – in other words, take 3,300 Silver jobs. Once more, however, all AFL claims were denied, and the Golds gained no further ground at the Silvers' expense.[48]

There was some consolation for the Silvers, but not much. The West Indians were the first to feel the impact of the post-war recession which hit the canal in the summer of 1921. Nearly 7,000 West Indians were discharged, and they and their dependents joined a destitute community in the terminal cities numbering well over 20,000 by the end of the year.[49]

[46] PC, 2-E-11, MTC to Harding, 8.12.21; Morrow to MTC, 12.12.21; Evans memo of 18.11.21. USSPCC, *Report*, 53–5.

[47] *NYT*, 18.12.21, 4/1; 20.12.21, 3/6; 26.12.21, 25/5; 7.1.22 6/5; 5.4.22, 2/6; 12.4.22, 4/3.

[48] PC, 2-P-12, Conference minutes of 8.1.24. *NYT*, 18.1.24, 1/3, 5/3. PC, 2-P-12, Gompers to Weeks, 27.2.24 and 28.10.24. Samuel Gompers, 'Conditions of life and labor on the Panama Canal Zone', *American Federationist*, 31 (1924), 213 214, 216–17, 218. PC, 2-P-12, Morrow to Weeks, 7.6.24.

[49] PC, 46-D-8, Morrow to Mallet, 12.9.21. SD, 1910–49, 811F.504/60, UK Embassy, Washington, to Hughes, 20.10.21.

Solutions for their plight were hard to come by. Wholesale silverisation of the workforce was a political impossibility, and a recovery in canal business was thought capable of producing only 2,000 labouring jobs. Repatriation to the islands was an option hardly any West Indians were prepared to take. The settlement founded at Las Cascadas in 1919 had not so far attracted many takers. In December, Morrow implemented Connor's idea of leasing truck gardens in the Zone under revocable licence, where the unemployed could make a slender living by marketing their produce. But this was merely a stopgap, and the scale of the problem remained daunting.[50]

Things were made no easier by the canal authorities' abiding determination to keep the West Indians in their place. For Morrow they were undeserving poor, 'ignorant, unambitious, lazy, thriftless'. In the spring of 1924, when the Panama Canal West Indian Employees' Association was founded, he denied it official recognition. The following October the Canal rejected every item in a seven-point petition drafted by the PCWIEA organiser, Samuel Whyte. The demands were for an appreciable wage increase; a fixed Gold–Silver job ratio; technical training; secondary education; twenty-four days' leave a year; free accommodation and half-fares on the railway; and overtime after an eight-hour day. Higher wages were ruled out on the ground that they would bring in a flood of unemployables, and Morrow had already asserted that there was no need for West Indians to be educated beyond primary level, because they could never hope for skilled positions.[51]

The minority of Panamanians on the Silver Roll were given an equally dismissive reception. When Panamanian trade unionists pushed to replace the 'intellectually and racially inferior' West Indians after the 1920 stoppage, Morrow was decidedly unsympathetic. The Panamanian government met the same chilly reaction in the wake of the rent strike of October 1925. This explosion was touched off partly by widespread unemployment, and one of Panama's answers was a larger slice of the Silver cake. The reply from the Zone was that there was not even enough work to occupy West Indians who had given long service to the Canal. In other words, the Panamanians would no longer enjoy the preferential treatment they had been promised in 1914.[52]

Panama consequently took matters into its own hands by passing an immigration law aimed directly at the West Indians. It prohibited the entry into the

---

[50] PC, 46-D-8, Morrow memo of 25.11.21; Smith to McIlvaine, 20.9.21. SD, 1910–49, 811F.504/63, Morrow to British chargé d'affaires, 23.9.21. PC, 88-H-3, Connor to Morrow, 28.6.21. SD, 1910–49, 711.192/205½, Circular 713–1 of 2.12.21.

[51] PC, 28-B-233, Morrow to Denison, 3.4.22; 2-P-70, Whyte to Morrow, 8.5.24; Whyte to Burgess, 14.5.29; Silver Rates Board meeting of 3.10.24; 28-B-233, Morrow to Denison, 24.3.22 [not sent].

[52] PC, 2-E-12, Star and Herald, 30.11.19; 2-P-70, Victor to Smith, 6.4.21; 2-E-12, Alfaro to McIlvaine, 23.10.25; Gilkey to McIlvaine, 31.10.25; McIlvaine to Alfaro, 2.11.25.

republic of all blacks whose mother tongue was not Spanish and imposed a poll-tax on West Indians resident in Panama on pain of deportation for non-payment. Though Canal employees were exempt, the statute would prevent West Indians from bringing in their relatives and deny readmission to those visiting their home islands. In 1928 came a further assault in the shape of an act granting West Indians Panamanian citizenship only after the age of twenty-one.[53]

For the U.S. minister, John Glover South, the legislation was a necessary response to a severe economic and social problem which deserved American sympathy. The canal administration saw the Panamanians differently, however. In the summer of 1928 departmental chiefs met to discuss the practice of giving American teenagers casual employment on the Silver Roll. 'Nepotism', intoned Governor Meriwether Walker, 'must be guarded against.' But Executive Secretary McIlvaine was convinced that 'as a matter of policy, any of these young Americans employed at a Silver rate should be placed on the Gold Roll'. Not so the Panamanians on Silver. They, according to one Canal functionary, were 'inferior in every respect' and 'could not be expected to have the good of the service at heart the same as an American citizen'.[54]

The West Indian Silvers were dealt with no less arbitrarily. In 1927 the governor was authorised to take on up to one hundred at the basic Gold rate of $960 a year. By the end of the 1920s, however, only nine West Indians were inside that privileged circle. In 1928 Governor Harry Burgess proposed a Silver wage increase because he found it difficult to see 'how a number of these employees manage to exist and to provide for their families'. Yet soon afterwards he recanted on the ground that the canal deficit was a heavy burden on U.S. taxpayers. As for the PCWIEA call for some form of retirement benefit, old-age pensions were inadequate in the United States 'and all over the world'. Progress could only be achieved gradually, and it was damaging to the West Indian cause if they put up 'impossible proposals'.[55]

Burgess took this stand in May 1929, at a time when the canal was prospering as never before, with international maritime trade at an all-time peak. Within six months of that zenith, however, the United States crashed into the abyss of the worst depression in its history. For the American government and people it was to prove a catastrophic experience. The consequences for the canal's labour force were to be equally traumatic.

---

[53] SD, 1910–49, 819.55/85 to 92, 21.9.26 to 26.10.26.
[54] Conniff, *Black labor*, 66. SD, 1910–49, 819.55/103, South to Kellogg, 28.4.27. PC, 2-F-14, Meeting of 14.7.28; 94-A-3/1926, Collins to Walker 29.7.27; 2-E-12, Silver Association of the Panama Canal to Hurley, 31.10.29; Williams memo of 11.12.29.
[55] PC, 2-E-11, Ridley statement of 27.9.38. 2-P-70, Whyte to Burgess, 14.5.29. Conniff, *Black labor*, 63, quoting Burgess memo of 16.11.28 in PC, 2-D-40. PC, 2-P-70, Burgess to Whyte, 18.5.29.

5

The Commissary

Construction decade, 1904–1914

Panama's importance in modern history derives exclusively from its location at one of the great nodes of international maritime trade. Its livelihood has always hinged on its function as the narrowest land bridge between Atlantic and Pacific, first for the portage of Spanish bullion across the isthmus, then as the mid point of the shortest sea route between the coasts of the continental United States. Panamanian dependence on its transit traffic was absolute. When the Spanish treasure-fleets no longer sailed, the province relapsed into desolation – 'a profound solitude', as one American envoy remembered it in the 1830s. The revival set off by the Californian gold rush of 1849 was consequently acclaimed as a deliverance from the economic wilderness, and the construction of the trans-isthmian railway straight afterwards was seen as the prelude to an interoceanic canal which would once again make Panama one of the world's busiest commercial highways. These expectations were jarred by the crash of the French canal project in the 1880s, but when Washington chose Panama as its preferred route and went on to recognise the secessionist Panamanian state, the promised land seemed close over the horizon.[1]

One unmistakable thunder-cloud loomed on that horizon, however, in the shape of the Hay–Herrán treaty signed by the United States and Colombia. Article 8 ordained that the canal terminals were to be free ports and debarred Colombia from levying customs duties on goods brought in for canal purposes. Article 12 gave the United States the right to import into the Canal Zone whatever was 'necessary and convenient' for the canal or for U.S. government employees.[2]

[1] Manning, *Diplomatic correspondence*, 5: 746 (Bowlin to Marcy, 1.8.1856).
[2] *BD*, 206–8.

The new Panamanian régime justifiably feared the consequences if these conditions were retained in the treaty it now had to negotiate. If they were, Panama would lose most of its revenue from tariffs, which it counted on for close on one-third of public income. In particular the government would no longer collect its percentage from the highly profitable monopolies on alcohol, tobacco, and opium, which were farmed out to private licensees and reckoned to be worth over $1 million a year to the national treasury. In his instructions to the republic's envoy in Washington, Philippe Bunau-Varilla, the Panamanian foreign minister was especially anxious to protect the owners of these franchises, 'who cannot be deprived of the rights they have bought'.[3]

By then, however, Hay and Bunau-Varilla had already produced a canal convention which was to be a sharp disappointment to Panama in this respect, as in many others. It is true that Bunau-Varilla was able to strike from Article 2 a clause granting Washington the additional right to manage the Canal Zone 'for commercial uses and purposes'. But he did not contest Articles 9 and 13, copied almost verbatim from the damaging Articles 8 and 12 of Hay–Herrán, which took away tariff autonomy at a stroke. The milk and honey so blissfully anticipated was apparently not to flow.[4]

There remained the hope that the commercial clauses might be amended in the course of the U.S. Senate debate. The revolutionary junta was encouraged in this by the American minister, William Buchanan. Article 9, he claimed, seemed to envisage the establishment of a U.S. government store in the Zone, and if Panama City and Colón were to be free ports the country would face bankruptcy. One possible solution would be to allow Panama to impose tariffs on luxury imports until the canal was completed. On 1 February the junta followed up this suggestion with an offer to reduce its duties overall to 5 per cent but to keep higher rates on alcohol, tobacco, opium, and perfumery, which would be certified 'not necessary and convenient' for American employees and would therefore not be shipped in duty-free from the United States.[5]

Hay would not hear of it, and the convention went through the Senate unaltered. Worse still from Panama's point of view, the Canal Commission was given the power to place tariffs on goods entering the Zone from everywhere but the United States. The rates were set at the level of the highly protectionist Dingley Tariff of 1897, and they were designed to give the Commission its own source of revenue. Though it had a profound impact on the Panamanians, the arrangement was introduced without any reference to them. It did not feature in the convention, and it was sanctioned by executive orders which clearly treated the Zone's commercial status as a matter for Washington alone to decide – this in spite of the fact that, as Secretary of War Taft later put it, the ICC was

[3] B-V Papers, De la Espriella to Bunau-Varilla, 14.11.03. *1906 Hearings*, 3: 2349–50.
[4] Drafts, Bunau-Varilla comments on U.S. treaty draft of 15.11.03, 17.11.03.
[5] USD, Buchanan to Hay, 18.1.04, 28.12.03, 2.1.04. ICC, 94-A-3, Junta to Buchanan, 1.2.04.

'building a big wall around the Zone in such a way that the cities of Panama and Colon should be excluded from any business association with the Zone'.[6]

At first Panama seemed to resign itself to the inevitable. On 6 June, President Amador was authorised to make the necessary tariff convention with the Commission, and ten days later the foreign minister, Tomás Arias, signed a provisional boundary agreement with Governor Davis which put the ports of La Boca and Cristóbal inside the Zone. Early in July, therefore, when Arias protested at the Commission's clearance of a ship at La Boca on the ground that it lay outside the Zone, the complaint rang hollow. Davis's reply was terse: Switzerland had no ports; Canada, Russia, and Austria–Hungary relied on foreign outlets for their trade. Panama should think itself lucky. Hitherto a byword for 'the idea of disease and death', it now stood on the threshold of an era of unprecedented prosperity, and it could safely entrust its commercial destiny to the United States.[7]

Arias did not give up. In a further protest at the end of July he launched an argument which was to be brought up time and time again to justify Panama's contentions in the commercial field. According to Arias, the United States had waived its 'fiscal and economical sovereignty within and without the . . . Zone'. At the same time, Panama retained the right to levy and collect taxes in the Zone because it had not explicitly given it up and so 'clearly reserved what it did not expressly surrender'.[8]

This was a demonstrably tortured construction of the treaty. The language of Article 3 was unequivocal. The United States possessed 'all the rights, power and authority' of a sovereign, 'to the entire exclusion' of their exercise by Panama. This was a rock on which all Panamanian counter-claims were doomed to founder. Even so, Panama battled on, developing its case in a long state paper transmitted in the name of the Panamanian minister in Washington, José Domingo de Obaldía, but written by the secretary of the legation, Eusebio Morales.

Studiously ignoring the fact that canal rights had been granted, not leased, Obaldía depicted the relation between Panama and the United States as one between lessor and lessee. American prerogatives, it followed, were not absolute. Articles 6, 10, and 13 all derogated from the supposedly unconditional donation of Article 3, and the wording of Article 3 'implicitly convey[ed] the idea that

---

[6] USD, Adee to Loomis, 20.1.04. The executive orders of 9.5.04 and 24.6.04 are in *BD*, 414, 420–1. On the Dingley Tariff, see Tom Terrill, *The tariff, politics, and American foreign policy, 1874–1901* (Westport, Conn., 1973), 200–3. *1906 Hearings*, 3: 2764.

[7] ICC, 94-A-3, Decree of 6.6.04. Charles Bevans (ed.), *Treaties and other international agreements of the United States of America, 1776–1949*, vol. 10, *Nepal–Peru* (Washington, D.C., 1973), 678–80, has the text of the boundary agreement of 16.6.04. USD, Arias to Davis, 5.7.04 and 9.7.04. ICC, 94-A-3, Davis to Arias, 11.7.04.

[8] Arias to Davis, 27.7.04, in *BD*, 427–9.

[the United States was] not sovereign' – because Panama had made the grant of its own accord. The reality was that 'the two countries exercise conjointly the sovereignty over the territory of the Canal Zone', and wherever the treaty was silent, the rights of Panama remained 'unalterable and complete'. The Canal Commission thus had no authority to collect customs duties, and Panama was entitled to put tariffs on all imports not brought in for canal purposes.[9]

Hay's reply set out a detailed rebuttal of the Panamanian argument, and it was to remain the definitive exposition of the American view. Hay took his stand on the plenitude of power conceded by Article 3, which made Panamanian sovereignty in the Zone at best a 'barren scepter'. Articles 10, 12, and 13, indeed, demonstrated that Panama exercised sovereign powers only outside the Zone, and Article 3 of the Panamanian constitution recognised the loss of sovereignty in the Zone when it spoke of 'jurisdictional limitations stipulated or which may be stipulated in public treaties with the United States'. Panama should come to terms with its position, Hay concluded, and Washington was ready to make a supplementary tariff agreement to ease the admitted hardship to the republic of the duty-free entry of merchandise from the United States.[10]

Negotiations for such an agreement had already been decided on, and for political reasons. Trouble was stirring in Panama, and the army was soon to attempt a coup with the backing of the Liberal opposition. To strengthen Amador's Conservative régime, concessions were in order, and Roosevelt picked Taft as his envoy. He outlined his policy in an open letter to Taft which was to be acclaimed by Panama for generations to come as clear recognition of the justice of its cause. 'We have not the slightest intention of establishing an independent colony in the middle of the State of Panama,' Roosevelt declared. 'Least of all do we desire to interfere with the business and prosperity of the people of Panama' through 'a competing and independent community which shall injuriously affect their business, reduce their revenues, and diminish their prestige as a nation.'[11]

In conference with Amador, Taft developed the conciliatory approach Roosevelt had sketched out. Hay's note, he explained, did not insist on total sovereignty for Washington but only on the right to wield sovereign powers. He had come to Panama to see 'how far I can go in waiving the exercise of these powers', and he went on to propose a modus vivendi on that basis. American treaty rights, he accepted, had been granted 'solely for the purpose of enabling us to construct, maintain and operate the Canal'.[12]

Within a few days a deal was struck, embodied in the so-called Taft Agreement. This allowed Panama to collect tariffs on all but the imports described as

[9] Obaldía to Hay, in ibid., 430–9.
[10] Ibid., Hay to Obaldía, 24.10.04, 444, 445, 449, 451, 458, 459.
[11] Ibid., 511, for Taft statement of 18.4.06. Ibid., 460–1.
[12] Ibid., 515–17.

'necessary and convenient'. In return Panama was to lower the average rate of its duties from 15 per cent to 10 per cent. Imports of alcohol and opium would be liable to a higher rate, but Panama would lose the tobacco monopoly after it expired in 1906. At the same time, reciprocal free trade was established between the Canal Zone and Panama: The Dingley Tariff for the Zone was repealed, eliminating duties on goods coming in from Panama, while Panama gave up the right to tax merchandise brought in from the Zone. The whole arrangement would remain in force until the canal opened.[13]

Taft felt he had given away nothing of substance and had conserved everything Washington needed to control the canal, even though Article 3 of the convention seemed to confer 'titular sovereignty' over the Zone on Panama. Less than three months later Taft the lawyer took quite a different view of a Panamanian bid to retain juridical authority in the Zone, instructing Davis to give 'not the least countenance [to] any pretension adverse to unqualified right of United States to exclusive jurisdiction in the exercise of judicial power'. On the commercial issue he was altogether more relaxed. Looking back on the Taft Agreement, he agreed that 'to the Anglo-Saxon mind a titular sovereignty is . . . a "barren ideality", but to the Spanish or Latin mind, poetic and sentimental, enjoying the intellectual refinements, and dwelling much on names and forms it is by no means unimportant'. Here the United States could afford to be generous.[14]

The compromise achieved by the Taft Agreement left one problem outstanding. As early as August 1904 it was evident that Panamanian suppliers could not meet the consumer demand of the rapidly expanding canal work force. Taft's suggested answer was a Zone commissary for American employees, to be run by the Commission. It was an explosive proposal. In January, Buchanan had relayed Panama's objections to a Zone emporium undercutting its traders by the sale of duty-free goods. Taft therefore advised restricting access to Americans alone. Roosevelt agreed, and in January 1905 admission to the Commissary was forbidden to 'natives of tropical countries wherein prevail climatic conditions similar to those prevailing on the Isthmus of Panama', that is, the mass of foreign labourers on the Silver Roll. If, however, Panamanian merchants began overcharging, the thousands of Silver men would be granted Commissary privileges, and Panama would lose their custom.[15]

This was a necessary precaution. Within months there was surging unrest among the West Indians, who could not afford the 'Klondike prices' charged by Panamanian retailers. On a wage of seventy cents a day, they were being asked seventy-five cents for a dozen eggs and sixty cents for a chicken. In their

---

[13] Ibid., 468–72, 517.

[14] Taft Papers, SWS-OC, Taft to Roosevelt, 19.12.04. ICC, 94-A-78, Taft to Davis, 11.3.05. *BD*, 513.

[15] ICC, 58-A-6, Smith to Goethals, 26.11.07. Taft Papers, SWS-OC, Taft to Roosevelt, 19.12.04. USD, Buchanan to Hay, 18.1.04. *BD*, 474–5.

desperation, many were subsisting on a diet of sugar cane, and the resultant malnutrition was slowing down their already languid work rate still further. The proviso in the January order had to be brought into play.[16]

At the end of July the new governor, Charles Magoon, was instructed to tell Amador that Silver Roll employees must be allowed to buy at the Commissary for the time being. Shops were set up at the camps along the line of the canal, and each morning a train brought in replenishments. Under pressure from the chambers of commerce in Panama and Colón, the Commission agreed to furnish the shops with no more than basic necessities but refused to specify what goods should be held in stock.[17]

This was to give the Zone authorities more than enough latitude in their choice of provender, and the Commissary was soon importing an ever larger number of luxuries. Faced with such an inflow into the Zone and the ease with which Commissary goods could be smuggled across the unsupervised Zone boundary, Panama's merchants were at a huge disadvantage. They could, of course, have been made competitive if their government had been prepared to reduce or eliminate Panamanian customs duties, but that would have meant depriving the national exchequer of its greatest single source of revenue. Tapping the alternative source of higher income and property taxes was politically impossible, since it would hit the very people who ran the country. For the foreseeable future, Panama was therefore constrained to make what it could out of the Zone and plead for more of the apparent magnanimity displayed in Roosevelt's now venerated letter to Taft.[18]

It could expect little from Colonel George Washington Goethals, who became chairman of the Commission in April 1907. The following December Foreign Minister Ricardo Arias asked for a return to the exclusion of all labourers from the commissaries and for a ban on the sale of such exotic items as European silks and lace. At a session with the Panamanian merchants Goethals professed being ready to stop selling luxuries, but he was also quoted as saying that if once the merchants 'get their grip on us they will squeeze us dry'. Both Panama's main demands were turned down.[19]

Given his strong feelings on the subject, Goethals was incensed by the treaty signed with Panama in January 1909, the handiwork of the outgoing secretary of state, Elihu Root. Article 3 allowed for both the revision of the Taft Agreement and the submission of any differences to an arbitration tribunal. Goethals foresaw serious trouble with his 27,000 labourers if this led to their being thrown back on 'the tender mercies' of the Panamanian market, and his fears were not

---

[16] *1906 Hearings*, 1: 345, 469. *NYT*, 24.9.05, 14/6. ICC, 58-A-6, Magoon to Arias, 21.8.05.

[17] ICC, 58-A-1, Magoon to Amador, 28.7.05; de la Guardia to Magoon, 1.8.05; Magoon to de la Guardia, 11.8.05. *NYT*, 15.8.05, 7/5. ICC, 58-A-6, Magoon to Taft, 10.10.05.

[18] *NYT*, 29.1.06, 1/1. SD, 1906–10, 234, Arias to Magoon, 30.7.06.

[19] ICC, 58-A-6, Arias to Blackburn, 5.12.07; 58-A-20, Transcript of conference between Goethals and Panamanian merchants, 6.12.07; 58-A-6, Report of subcommittee, 29.1.08.

groundless. Root was reported as saying that the treaty was 'designed to restrict commissary privileges', and the secretary of the Commission, Joseph Bucklin Bishop, urged a rapid move 'to have it killed or withdrawn'. In March the Senate obliged, with the reservation that there should be no arbitration of any issue affecting American treaty rights in the canal. When told that the Panamanians objected that this would injure their trade, Root's successor, Philander Chase Knox, commented tersely, 'Let it injure them.' The Commission's hold on the business of the Zone remained unbroken.[20]

It was business on a sizeable scale. Commissary sales in 1908 came to over $4.5 million (as compared with Panamanian national revenues in 1907 of under $2.5 million). In 1909 the Commissary comprised wholesale dry-goods and grocery departments, mail-order and purchasing divisions, fourteen retail stores, seven cigar stands, a cold-storage and ice-making installation, a laundry, a bakery, a coffee-roasting plant, an ice-cream factory, a printing house, a clothes-mending and -pressing shop, seventeen hostels along the canal line, two hotels at the terminals, twenty-four messes for European labourers, and twenty-four kitchens for West Indian workers.[21]

In 1908 Goethals brought this money-spinner under his own control. The Commissary was operated by the Panama Railroad Company, which had passed into U.S. government ownership through the canal treaty and maintained an autonomous existence in parallel with the Commission. Its manager was responsible to the general manager of the Railroad, but Goethals saw to it that henceforth the manager reported to the subsistence officer of the Commission, who in turn reported to the Commission chairman.[22]

The Railroad itself, however, was not absorbed into the Commission and retained its independent status as a corporation, for a compelling reason. The Commission, as a federal agency, had to resort to Congress for its annual appropriation. Though, as one governor of the Canal, Jay Morrow, later acknowledged, the canal organisation was 'relieved from the blight of fiscal year limitation' and appropriations were available until spent, its books, like those of any other government department, were liable to scrutiny on Capitol Hill. The Railroad, on the other hand, as a corporation was not subject to congressional surveillance. This, in the words of Governor Julian Schley, was a useful device 'for carrying on necessary commercial and quasi-commercial activities of the Canal enterprise with the required amount of freedom from the usual departmental regulations relating to accounting and disbursement of funds which would have seriously impeded the conduct of such [activities]'. A governor thus

[20] *BD*, 566. ICC, 94-A-3, Goethals to Wright, 19.1.09. SD, 1906–10, 637, Bishop to Goethals, 8.2.09; 1502, Senate reservation of 3.3.09 and Bacon memo of conversation, 28.5.09.
[21] Ghent, 'Work and welfare on the canal', 914. SD, 1906–10, 11447, Squiers to Root, 18.1.08.
[22] *TR letters*, 6: 1009–10, 1029. *1911 Hearings*, 127–8. Ghent, 'Labor and the Commissary at Panama', 1129.

had, as Morrow put it, 'the legal authority to use over and over as a revolving fund the moneys received from the Canal's business operations'. It was a handy arrangement which Goethals and all his successors deployed to the Canal's considerable advantage.[23]

Goethals went on to make a number of moves to maximise the Commissary's business potential. In December 1910 he struck a deal with Panama whereby access to the Commissary by Silver Roll labourers was made permanent in exchange for acceptance of a Panamanian tariff rate of 15 per cent. He also had ambitious plans for the full-blown development of the Zone as a commercial centre. This Goethals aimed to have written into the organic law for the government of the Zone, and in his testimony on the legislation Goethals asked that the Commissary be authorised to make to ships using the canal sales of coal, fuel oil, water, and 'subsistence supplies'. This would bring in welcome revenue and help keep tolls down to a dollar a ton, making Panama that much more attractive as a transit route. Congress responded just as Goethals wished. Section 6 of the Panama Canal Act of August 1912 gave the Railroad the power to furnish 'coal and other materials, labor, repairs, and supplies for vessels of the Government of the United States and, incidentally, for supplying such at reasonable prices to passing vessels'.[24]

Goethals's legal adviser, Judge Frank Feuille, had a buoyant vision of where this all could lead. In October 1911 he told the Senate that he believed 'there will be industrial and commercial enterprises established at both ends of the canal, and that some of our manufacturers and merchants in the United States would like to come down here and establish their headquarters in the Zone to operate in the Latin Americas, and we ought to let them do so'. Goethals himself had publicly called for large warehouse complexes at the terminals, and in 1912 he tried to acquire Colón from Panama, presumably with this scheme in mind. The Railroad already owned all but a few acres of land in Colón, and Goethals proposed to obtain the handful of Panamanian holdings by exchanging them for Railroad property in Panama City. Nothing came of the idea before the canal was completed, but it showed how intent Goethals was on commercialisation.[25]

The biggest obstacle to Goethals's grand design was, of course, the Taft Agreement. In May 1913 the new secretary of commerce, William Redfield, proposed its replacement by a commercial treaty, and Feuille agreed whole-heartedly.

---

[23] Dimock, *Government-operated enterprises*, 31, 32–3, 149. Jay Morrow, *The maintenance and operation of the Panama Canal* (Mount Hope, CZ, 1923), 43. ICC, 65-J-3, Schley to Dern, 1.8.36.

[24] ICC, 94-A-3/T, Goethals to Boggs, 13.12.10; Feuille to Goethals, 19.12.10; 58-A-6, Goethals to Dickinson, 21.12.10. *1911 Hearings*, 72, 5, 7, 8, 168, 169. *BD*, 600.

[25] *1911 Hearings*, 294. SD, 1910–49, 811f.244/20, Secretary of Colón Board of Commerce to Knox, 29.8.11. ICC, 80-A-3, Goethals to Porras, 6.4.15.

Above all, the treaty should insist on 'the right of the United States to establish and maintain revenue and shipping systems in the Zone'. In other words, the Zone would become the entrepôt which Roosevelt had disclaimed in October 1904. Soon afterwards Goethals asserted that the Commissary's expansion would be essential to the canal's success as an ocean highway and that the moment had come for the U.S. commercial position to be settled 'for all time'. The Taft Agreement should lapse once the canal was built, and Washington should not 'pay annual tribute to Panama' by allowing it to collect duties in the Canal Zone. But no negotiations with Panama were broached before the canal opened to shipping in August 1914, and Taft's compromise of 1904 remained in force. The struggle for the commercial destiny of the isthmus entered its second decade undecided, and many more years of conflict stretched ahead.[26]

First World War, 1914–1918

The opening of the canal in August 1914 brought no resolution of the dispute over its commercial future. The Taft Agreement of 1904 had been intended only as a stop-gap, to tide things over until construction was finished. At the end of the First World War, however, it was still in force, more than four years after the transit began to operate.

For the canal authorities this was profoundly frustrating. When Panama sought to place a 20 per cent duty on Commissary purchases imported from the Zone, Goethals's legal counsel was quick to assert that the introduction of the new tariff would nullify that section of the agreement. The executive secretary of the Canal, Charles McIlvaine, for his part saw no reason why Panama should be allowed to collect duties on material coming into the Zone as the agreement stipulated. The treaty payments to Panama were quite enough, and Washington must be released from the extra subsidy Taft had given. Goethals could not have agreed more. 'I could never see why the canal should not be made a business proposition,' he told the *New York Times*. 'I do not think any should benefit from it at the expense of others.' The Zone, in other words, did not exist to make profits for Panama.[27]

The Panamanians took precisely the opposite view. Soon after Goethals's pointed comment, they published the draft of their 'dream treaty', framed by Panama's minister in Washington, Eusebio Morales. Among other things, this called for perpetuation of the Taft Agreement, closure of the main Commissary stores at Balboa and Cristóbal, cancellation of the Railroad's privileges under its

---

[26] ICC, 23-C-2, Bryan to Garrison, 22.5.13; Feuille to Goethals, 12.7.13. SD, 1910–49, 811F.812/421, Goethals to Garrison, 21.8.13; 711F.1914/32, Goethals to Boggs, 2.2.14. ICC, 80-A-3, Goethals to Boggs, 8.1.14.

[27] PC, 23-C-2, Feuille to Goethals, 14.11.14 and 4.12.14; 94-A-3/T, Bryan to Garrison, 11.1.15, and McIlvaine memo of 22.4.15. *NYT*, 9.9.15, 6/2.

1867 contract, and the transfer to Panama of all undeveloped Railroad land in the terminal cities. This was followed by demands that the Silver workers be once again forbidden to use the Commissary's outlets and that Panamanian merchants be allowed to sell to canal shipping. In February 1916 a formal protest was made against the Zone's sale to ships of goods other than coal and oil. At the same time, the Railroad came under assault for charging its Panamanian customers discriminatory freight rates and for wrongfully claiming wholesale exemption from Panamanian taxes.[28]

The American response to this onslaught disclosed a rift within the administration. The State Department felt the allegations on sales to ships were justified, while its Solicitor's Office admitted that the Taft Agreement had placed a curb on the Zone's treaty power to import whatever it wished. The Zone, on the other hand, argued that Taft had imposed no such restriction on U.S. treaty rights and that sales to ships had been authorised by the organic law of 1912. As for Panama's attack on the Railroad's prerogatives, 'whatever the Railroad Company may do in the Canal Zone is not subject to question on the part of the Republic of Panama'.[29]

On the issue of sales to ships, the outcome was victory for the Zone. The sales were upheld under the 'necessary and convenient' formula of Article 13, and the Panamanians were told they could not levy duties on them. The Zone's bid for repeal of the Taft Agreement was not sanctioned, however. Chester Harding, Goethals's successor as governor, envisaged the agreement being replaced by a commercial treaty which would grant Washington the right to import duty-free articles for sale to ships in transit and 'inhabitants of the Canal Zone' as well as to build warehouses to stockpile the duty-free goods. His draft of March 1917, while allowing Panama's right to tax merchandise brought in from the Zone, drained the concession of very much significance by excepting all purchases made by employees of the Canal and the Railroad or of American contractors.[30]

But negotiations for a new treaty could not be started until the Taft Agreement was revoked. With the United States poised to enter the war against Germany, the State Department thought it wisest to suspend the issue for the duration. The decision was upheld by the attorney general, and when the war ended in November 1918 the commercial fate of the canal still lay in the balance.[31]

---

[28] SD, 1910–49, 611.1931/12, Price to Bryan, 30.9.15 and 9.10.15; 811F.244/27, Morales to Lansing, 12.2.16; 819.77/232, Morales to Lansing, 28.2.16.

[29] SD, 1910–49, 811F.244/27 and 29, Solicitor's Office memo of 4.4.16 and Feuille to Harding, 10.3.16; 819.77/232, Feuille to Goethals, 14.4.16.

[30] SD, 1910–49, 811F.244/32 and 27, Johnson to Baker, 4.10.16, and Lansing to Porras, 22.11.16. PC, 94-A-3/T, Harding to Feuille, 15.11.16; Brown to Baker, 20.3.17.

[31] SD, 1910–49, 811F.812/861 and 835, Lansing to Baker, 31.3.17, and Davis to Baker, 25.9.17.

The twenties, 1919–1929

During the post-war decade the wrangle between the Zone and Panama over the commercial development of the canal fell tantalisingly short of a solution. The official opening of the canal in 1920 prompted abrogation of the Taft Agreement's modus vivendi and negotiations for a treaty to replace it. But the Panamanian refusal to ratify meant that on this crucial issue relations dropped back into a stalemate.

In the immediate aftermath of the war, the Canal hierarchy was straining at the leash to have its plans for an entrepôt in the Zone given the imprimatur of a treaty. In December 1919 it went back to its draft project framed just before U.S. entry into the war, whereby the New Cristóbal section of Colón was to become part of the Zone and the mutual free trade set up by Taft terminated. In theory the end of free trade would restore Panama's tariff autonomy, but in practice the republic was to be hamstrung. The draft denied it the right to charge duty on merchandise brought in from the Zone by American employees living in Panama or to tax goods entering the Zone via Panama. The second prohibition, in the view of Governor Chester Harding, 'by inference asserts the right of the United States to import anything at its pleasure directly into the Canal Zone'. In other words, commerce with Panama would once more be regulated by the 1903 convention, and, as Harding saw it, that would 'remove all claims and contests concerning the operation of the Commissaries within the Canal Zone'. The Zone would thus be rid of the incubus which had sat on its back for the past fifteen years.[32]

At the same time, Harding was ready to abstain from establishing bonded warehouses in the Zone. Opening bonded warehouses, he considered, would contravene a 1912 order limiting the auxiliary businesses in the Zone to those directly related to the canal's operations, such as cable, oil, and shipping firms. And he also agreed with the State Department that the warehouses would hurt Panama at no great profit to the Canal, so Panama was told that the Zone was willing to suspend its self-appointed right to hold goods in bond as long as Panama's wholesalers met American requirements.[33]

Panama showed little appreciation of the gesture and reiterated long-familiar complaints about the Commissary: its dealing in luxuries, its sales to ships, the smuggling of its wares across the Zone line. Like the Canal, Panama was looking to a new treaty to supplant the Taft Agreement. The objective, however, was to use Taft as the basis for 'an understanding that may once for all define the extent of the rights and obligations flowing from the treaty [of 1903]'.

[32] SD, 1910–49, 811F.812/874, State Department commentary on treaty draft, 30.12.19. PC, 94-A-3/T, Feuille to Harding, 18.3.20; Harding to Flint, 10.4.20.
[33] SD, 1910–49, 811F.244/42, Harding to Baker, 5.9.19, referring to executive order of 5.12.12; /88, Reed to White, 10.1.23.

This was wholly unacceptable to the new governor, Jay Morrow. Commenting on Panama's long bill of grievances, Morrow emphatically rejected the thesis that 'we are obligated to yield to Panama any revenue to which she is not entitled, or that we must agree that the commerce of the world be hampered and traffic through the Canal reduced through a senseless agreement to an indefensible attitude on the part of Panama'.[34]

Morrow was prepared to relent on one issue: prohibition. Though the Volstead Act of 1919 confirmed the Canal Zone as 'dry' territory, it did not apply to liquor in transit through the canal or on the railway, and this proviso had been broadly construed to allow alcohol to be transported via the Zone to and from Panama. In the summer of 1922 the U.S. Treasury proposed to interpret the Act so strictly as to stop liquor from being landed in the Zone for transfer to Panama, threatening to ruin a lucrative drink trade which furnished the republic with a sizeable slice of its revenue. Morrow's advice was to carry on as before, avowedly for Panama's sake but in fact to preserve the Zone's access to the beers, wines, and spirits so copiously on tap in Panama City and Colón.[35]

When it came to a new commercial treaty, Morrow was disposed to make concessions only if Panama were willing to cede the whole or part of Colón to the Zone. His redraft of the treaty envisaged the acquisition of the entire town in exchange for cancelling its debt to the Canal, building a highway across the isthmus, and restoring Portobelo as Panama's chief Atlantic port of entry. This package would cost Washington up to $11 million, but Morrow was ready to pay the price for the sake of establishing a U.S.-owned Colón as the site of the bonded warehouse project.[36]

The State Department, however, was still hostile to the warehouse scheme and to the Zone's bid to absorb the whole of Colón to give it room to grow. It had also recently clashed with Morrow over the so-called Bermúdez Claim entered by Panama in a dispute about compensation for land acquired by American developers. Whereas the department recommended payment of the claims umpire's award of $102,000, Morrow condemned a settlement as 'an illegal raid' on the U.S. Treasury. The department's attitude only deepened his conviction that the canal was much too serious a matter to be left to the diplomats. Hay, Root, and Knox had accepted this, but Bryan had not, 'and we have been in trouble ever since'. The one thing that could improve the situation

[34] PC, 80-A-3, Panama Note of 25.11.20. SD, 1910–49, 811F.244/50, Panama note of 2.4.21; /51, Morrow to Flint, 30.6.21.

[35] SD, 1910–49, 811F.114/920, Morrow to Flint, 28.6.22 and 14.7.22; 1150, Hughes to Mellon, 5.1.23. The relevant section of the Volstead Act may be found in *United States statutes at large*, 41/1 (Washington, D.C., 1921), 322.

[36] SD, 1910–49, 819.00/1459, Morrow to White, 4.1.22; 611.1931/37, Morrow to Weeks, 13.10.22; *La Estrella*, 11.9.22. Morrow, *Maintenance*, 11. SD, 1910–49, 711.192/196, Memo on meeting of 11.7.24; White to Kellogg, 17.7.25.

would be to cancel the Taft Agreement and so 'remove from our path this abominable handicap to efficient operation'.[37]

The Panamanians, on the other hand, sought a treaty which at the very least would continue the agreement and make it mutually binding instead of revocable at the will of either party. Best of all, they wanted a thorough-going revision of the 1903 convention in their favour, but the newly arrived minister to Washington, Ricardo Alfaro, was told that any forthcoming accord would only complement 1903, not take its place. Alfaro's subsequent assertion on Panama's behalf of 'jurisdiction over the foreign trade of the Canal Zone' thus stood no chance whatever of being accepted. In his commentary on Alfaro's argument, Assistant Secretary Francis White recognised that Panama would need help when the Taft Agreement was rescinded. On the basic item of jurisdiction, however, he was immovable. Article 3 of the 1903 treaty granted the United States sovereign rights in the Zone ad infinitum, and the Panamanian claim shattered on that granite wall.[38]

The American refusal to yield an inch on fundamentals was spelled out majestically by Secretary of State Charles Evans Hughes. While Alfaro had essentially repeated the case made by Obaldía in 1904, Hughes's answer was, as Alfaro rightly put it, 'an intensified restatement' of Hay's refutation of Obaldía. Article 3 of the canal convention, Alfaro was told, gave Washington the right 'to bring any goods which it desired into the Canal Zone', and when the Taft Agreement was revoked that right would come back fully into play. As for Panamanian jurisdiction over the Zone, this could 'no longer be considered as open to discussion'.[39]

Hughes later professed that he found it difficult to understand what Panama had to be aggrieved about: 'The Canal had made Panama. They had no complaint whatever.' And it was 'an absolute futility to expect any American Administration . . . ever to surrender any part of the rights which the United States had acquired under the Treaty of 1903'. That said, Hughes was ready to talk about practical ways of aiding Panama after the Taft Agreement was annulled, through a new treaty which did not touch on matters of principle. In order to concentrate the minds of the Panamanian negotiators, he gave notice that the agreement would be abrogated on 1 May 1924. With that club poised over their heads, they were confidently expected to sign on the dotted line within a matter of weeks.[40]

[37] SD, 1910–49, 711.192/196, White memo of 6.12.22; /22A, Hughes to Harding, 21.8.22. PC, 94-A-3/T, Morrow memo of 28.9.22; Morrow to Weeks, 29.12.22; Morrow to Flint, 7.4.23.

[38] Ricardo Alfaro, 'Historia documentada de las negociaciones para la celebración del tratado de 1926', Revista Lotería, 248–9 (October–November 1976), 51–3. SD, 1910–49, 611.1931/45, Panama note of 3.1.23; 711.192/196, White to Hughes, 5.1.23.

[39] Alfaro, 'Historia', 53. SD, 1910–49, 611.1931/57B, Hughes to Alfaro, 15.10.23.

[40] SD, 1910–49, 611.1931/63, Memo of conversation of 15.12.23; 711.192/7, Hughes to South, 18.10.23.

There was to be no instant treaty, however. In 1904 Taft and the Panamanians reached a compromise in six days because the Canal Commission was
not allowed to get in the way. Twenty years later the Canal was a force to be
reckoned with, and it proved well capable of delaying an agreement. Com-
pounding this difficulty was the fact that negotiations opened in an election
year, and while the outgoing régime of Belisario Porras had every incentive to
close a bargain before leaving office in October 1924, Porras's successor, Rodolfo
Chiari, was certain that more could be gained by holding out. In the event, it
was to be two and a half years before a treaty was signed, in July 1926.

Panama's priorities were established at the outset in a trio of general propositions which blithely ignored Hughes's warning to keep off the high ground of
principle. They echoed Roosevelt's letter to Taft of 18 October 1904 which for
Panama had practically attained the status of holy writ, and they were to remain
the basis of Panama's case for the next generation and more. They read as
follows:

> 1st.   That the Canal Zone be occupied and controlled exclusively for the
>   purpose of maintaining, operating and protecting the Canal already
>   built and sanitated and that, therefore, the Zone be not open to the
>   commerce of the world as an independent colony.
>
> 2nd.   That the Republic of Panama be enabled to secure for its own de-
>   velopment the commercial advantages inherent in the geographical
>   situation of its territory, without interfering in any way with the
>   operation and exploitation of the Canal by the United States, and
>   its complete judicial, police and administrative jurisdiction over the
>   Canal Zone.
>
> 3rd.   That the provisions of the new Treaty be inspired by these pur-
>   poses: not to injure the prosperity of Panama; not to reduce the
>   revenues of her government and not to diminish her prestige as a
>   nation.[41]

There was no chance at all that Washington would let itself be bound by such
a comprehensive set of commitments. Hughes was ready, however, to preface
the treaty with a preamble stating that the Zone 'shall not be open to the
commerce of the world as an independent colony'. This meant that sales to
ships would go on and bonded warehouses would start up. But no other private
businesses would be allowed in the Zone, and Commissary purchases would be
made only by U.S. government personnel, contractors, and the employees of
auxiliary companies sited alongside the canal. In other words, most of the self-
denying ordinances Taft had introduced would continue to hold good, though
only for a ten-year period.[42]

[41] SD, 1910–49, 611.1931/64, Panamanian propositions, of 4.1.24.
[42] SD, 1910–49, 711.192/196, Baker to Read, 21.1.24; /11A, Hughes to Weeks, 9.2.24; /196,
    Conference of Hughes, Weeks, and Morrow, 14.3.24.

Hughes first tried his package out on Governor Morrow, with foreseeable results. The preamble Morrow considered a serious curb on American rights, and he saw the ten-year waiver as a token that the United States would end by promising the Panamanian merchants 'to perpetually handle them like soft-shelled eggs'. Much better, in his view, to put the arrangement in the form of a verbal note, that is, as a unilateral affirmation of policy which, like the Taft Agreement, Washington could annul whenever it chose. Hughes disagreed, and the offer was presented as a treaty article when negotiations proper began in March 1924. Far from accepting it, however, Panama bore out Morrow's worst fears by demanding a permanent U.S. concession. The conditions of its relationship with the Zone were 'invariable and perpetual', and adjustments to them should be likewise. In June, Porras brought matters to a head by insisting on permanence as the price for the surrender of New Cristóbal to the Zone.[43]

Porras's move touched off a crisis because it linked the two issues of first importance to both Panama and the Zone and on which they were completely at odds. For the New Cristóbal area Morrow was ready to cancel Colón's entire debt to the Canal for street-laying, water supply, and sewerage, to the tune of $1.25 million. Panama, on the other hand, wanted a much bigger pay-off for a cession that was likely to be enormously controversial, and demanded instead all the Railroad land in Panama City and Colón not required for Canal purposes – which Morrow estimated as worth between $12 and $14 million.[44]

To the rock-ribbed Morrow this was unacceptable. Throughout his governorship he had despised what he saw as the State Department's 'currying favor' with the Panamanians at the Canal's expense, and he told White it was nonsense to think of Panama as a sister republic. Assistant Secretary White for his part identified the canal directorate as the root cause of recent bad relations with Panama, and Morrow as a man 'prone to take the position that the Panamanians are an inferior race who should be kicked about and told what to do'. This was no exaggeration. Faced with the impasse over New Cristóbal, Morrow argued that Panama would hand it over on American terms if given an ultimatum that otherwise there would be no treaty and therefore no commercial concessions, and his advice was taken. Early in August, Alfaro was notified that failing a new treaty Washington would resume the plenitude of power granted by the 1903 convention.[45]

Uncomfortably aware that he had run himself into a dead end, Porras recalled Alfaro and, without consulting him, made a last-minute bid for agreement

[43] SD, 1910–49, 711.192/18, Morrow to Weeks, 25.2.24; /196, Conference of 14.3.24; /205, Minutes of meetings of 24.3.24, 31.3.24, and 14.6.24; /75, White to Hughes, 26.6.24.

[44] SD, 1910–49, 711.192/7, Hughes to Coolidge, 9.1.24; /196, Conference of 14.3.24; White to Hughes, 2.4.24; /48A, Hughes to Weeks, 14.5.24.

[45] PC, 80-G-2, Morrow to Weeks, 6.5.24. SD, 1910–49, 711.192/30, Morrow to White, 3.4.24; /196, White to Hughes, 17.7.25; Morrow to Flint, 1.7.24; /77A, Hughes to South, 15.8.24.

before quitting the presidency on 1 October. Twenty years was accepted as the duration of the commercial article, extendable by periods of seven years. For New Cristóbal, Porras was now willing to take the remission of Colón's debt for civic infrastructure plus $1.25 million towards the cost of building a trans-isthmian highway. With a week to go before Porras's departure, the treaty seemed ready for signature.[46]

Not so. Hughes had deleted a Panamanian provision barring the Zone from making any further demands for territory in Colón. In his anxiety to seal the compact, Porras immediately agreed, but the incoming foreign minister, Eusebio Morales, reinserted the clause and added several more objectionable items for good measure. The motives behind his manoeuvre were unclear, but its effect was plain enough. Hughes broke off negotiations, and the treaty was lost for the time being.[47]

Governor Morrow greeted the rupture with loud hosannas. The treaty as it stood was 'an abominable instrument' which would 'hang over the Canal for all time'. In the summer of 1925, as a new round of treaty talks approached, Morrow's successor, Meriwether Walker, urged on White suppression of the commercial article. At the same time, he denounced a State Department pro-posal to let Panamanian customs officials into the Zone to inspect passengers and cargo bound for the republic: To have the 'dilatory and devious' Panamanians on 'our docks' would create an intolerable situation. But when White made it clear that there was no question of going back on the commercial concessions, Walker dropped his objections, and a final settlement appeared within reach.[48]

It still took a full year to clinch, and throughout this long concluding phase the State Department had less trouble coming to terms with Panama than persuading the Canal that Panama deserved some consideration. White took the view that 'if we demand our pound of flesh under the 1903 Treaty, Panama has the right to do the same', and he and his colleagues were utterly out of sympathy with the Zone's drive for commercialism. 'I do not see', wrote Acting Secretary Joseph Grew, 'how it will ever be necessary for us in maintaining, operating and protecting the Panama Canal . . . to sell a miscellaneous assortment of merchand-ise at a profit for a few thousand dollars a year to all comers.' That merchandise included Sèvres and Copenhagen porcelain, Chinese rugs, and French perfumes, and their availability inevitably bred corruption. When the Panamanian consul general in New York accused Canal employees of regularly selling duty-free

---

[46] SD, 1910–49, 711.192/89, South to Hughes, 15.9.24; /88, Hughes to South, 18.9.24; /92, South to Hughes, 20.9.24.

[47] SD, 1910–49, 711.192/88, Hughes to South, 18.9.24; /111, South to Hughes, 27.9.24; / 127, South to Kellogg, 22.4.25.

[48] SD, 1910–49, 711.192/136, Morrow to Weeks, 4.10.24. PC, 94-A-3/1926, Morrow to Weeks, 20.10.24. SD, 1910–49, 711.192/136, Flint to White, 14.5.25. PC, 94-A-3/1926, Walker to Flint, 12.5.25. SD, 1910–49, 711.192/137B, Kellogg to Acting Secretary of War, 2.6.25; / 136, White to Flint, 26.5.25. AG, post-1917, 388.1, Walker to Flint, 24.6.25.

goods in Panama, the U.S. minister reported that the allegation was well founded. High officials of the Zone repeatedly smuggled purchases through, and a deferential police force turned a blind eye.[49]

Change was thus long overdue, in the State Department's opinion, and the Canal was asked to make the commercial concessions to Panama in perpetuity, as Panama itself had urged. Once again the governor dug in his heels, and his inflexibility was shared by the Army General Staff. 'It is a fact, supported by history,' declared the War Plans Division, 'that as soon as a government surrenders a sovereign right, it is followed by further concessions . . . in relation to the right surrendered.' Unlimited freedom of action was essential in the commercial field as well as in the realm of canal security.[50]

Most of the next six months were taken up with meeting the War Department's objections, first by tightening the three treaty articles on defence to the Army's satisfaction, then by underscoring the fact of U.S. sovereign rights in a revised preamble. The Panamanians were thereby implicitly committed to acknowledging Washington's omnicompetence in the Zone, and the preamble thus served to counter the revival of their claim that American sovereignty fell short of running the canal as a business. On that understanding, the commercial concessions were made perpetual, while Panama agreed to cede New Cristóbal in exchange for an American-built trans-isthmian highway, of which the United States would bear roughly half the cost. This was the basis on which the treaty was finally signed on 28 July 1926.[51]

Its chances of ratification by the Panamanian National Assembly, however, were slender. In a last-minute bid to improve its prospects, Alfaro asked first for enhanced American funding for the trans-isthmian road, and when that was refused, for a $30 million loan. When this too was turned down, Chiari's government had nothing but the treaty to offer, and on 27 January 1927 the Assembly voted unanimously to suspend ratification until changes could be negotiated which would 'satisfy the aspirations of the nation'.[52]

The treaty failed for many reasons. Minister South may have been exagger-

---

[49] SD, 1910–49, 711.192/196, White to Kellogg, 17.7.25; /145A, Grew to Acting Secretary of War, 3.7.25; /195, Division of Latin American Affairs to Kellogg, 21.7.25. *NYT*, 29.4.26, 14/1. SD, 1910–49, 811F.244/87, South to Kellogg, 13.7.26.

[50] SD, 1910–49, 711.192/145B, Kellogg to Weeks, 24.7.25. PC, 94-A-3/1926, Flint to Walker, 16.7.25. SD, 1910–49, 711.192/196, White to Kellogg, 17.7.25. WPD, 1652–4, War Plans Division memo of 28.7.25. SD, 1910–49, 711.192/151, Acting Secretary of War to Kellogg, 24.8.25.

[51] PC, 94-A-3/1926, Office to Chief of Staff memo of 11.11.25. WPD, 1652–5, War Plans Division to Hines, 11.11.25. PC, 94-A-3/1926, Walker to Flint, 13.2.26 and 18.3.26. WPD, 1652–7, War Plans Division memo of 30.3.26. SD, 1910–49, 711.192/194, Meeting of 27 July 1926. See *BD*, 827, 829–31, for treaty text.

[52] SD, 1910–49, 711.192/253, Alfaro note of 14.10.26; /318, Stabler memo of conversation with Alfaro, 8.12.26; /263, Alfaro to Kellogg, 18.12.26 and Kellogg to Alfaro, 21.12.26; /294, South to Kellogg, undated.

ating when he concluded that 'nothing short of the complete surrender of essential rights enjoyed by the United States under the 1903 Treaty will ever satisfy the "national aspirations" of Panama'. There can be no doubt, however, that the accord came as a severe disappointment when its text was leaked to the press by Alfaro's political enemy, Harmodio Arias. Its language was seen, in Alfaro's view, as 'unnecessarily harsh' and in some instances 'practically insulting'. The transfer of New Cristóbal was branded as a capitulation, the commercial concessions denounced as inadequate, and the articles on defence condemned as an aggravation of Panama's satellite status. And when the hated Bunau-Varilla chipped in on the eve of the Assembly debate with a ringing endorsement of the American position, he brought resentments to flash-point. So more than two years of painstaking diplomacy went up in smoke, though the damage to Panama was limited in a way which surprisingly drew no comment. Instead of bringing the 1903 convention back into force, as threatened, Washington informally prolonged the Taft Agreement, and Panama continued to be shielded from the full impact of Zone competition for the time being.[53]

In January 1928 Chiari listed the modifications Panama required. The preamble should be altered to remove the impression that it recognised the United States's 'absolute and unrestricted sovereignty' in the Zone. The cession of New Cristóbal should be withdrawn and more restraints placed on commerce in the Zone, notably by the abolition of the bonded warehouses, which the Canal had put into operation without reference to Panama or Washington at least a year before the treaty was signed.[54]

As during the treaty negotiations, the American reaction was divided. While the State Department declined to reword the preamble, it was happy enough to abandon the acquisition of New Cristóbal. It also believed Washington could afford to be more generous on commercial matters. Governor Walker, on the other hand, disagreed outright and insisted that New Cristóbal must be taken into the Zone. A year later, when Panama's leading American creditor suggested the Zone lease sites to Panama for port installations under Panamanian jurisdiction, the response of Walker's successor, Harry Burgess, was unyielding. Panama, Burgess wrote, 'cannot and ought not to have anything to do with the operation of the Panama Canal as an international highway, or with the Canal's auxiliary facilities'.[55]

[53] Ibid. /302, South to Kellogg, 1.2.27, quoting *Le Figaro* of 23.1.27; /264, U.S. Minister, Havana, to Kellogg, 17.12.26; /309, Morgan memo of conversation with Alfaro, 1.3.27; / 395½, Wilson memo, undated; /288, South to Kellogg, 17.1.27; 811F.244/98, South to Stimson, 22.4.29; 711.19/210, Dern to Hull, 30.8.35.

[54] SD, 1910–49, 711.192/354, Alfaro to Kellogg, undated; /196, White to Kellogg, 17.7.25. WPD, 3550, Clarence Ridley, 'Commitments of the Republic of Panama with respect to the Canal Zone', 1.3.31, 12–13.

[55] SD, 1910–49, 711.192/343½, Morgan memo of 3.2.28. WPD, 1652–15, Davis to Kellogg, 28.5.28. PC, 80-A-4/B, Roberts to Good, 17.7.29; Burgess to Good, 16.8.29.

By the close of the 1920s, then, Panama's hopes for a bigger commercial dividend from the canal were unsatisfied and the canal administration's plans for the Zone as the mercantile hub of the Americas equally frustrated. When in October 1929 the State Department accepted Panama's invitation to join in a comprehensive review of the treaty they had so laboriously put together, it remained to be seen whether their second shot at an understanding would come any closer than their first.[56]

[56] SD, 811F.244/118, Panama Note of 17.9.29; 711.192/379, Kellogg to South, 14.10.29.

6

The protectorate

Construction decade, 1904–1914

Panama, like Cuba, came to birth as a republic with the United States as its midwife, and like Cuba it became an American protectorate. Both the canal convention and the Panamanian constitution gave Washington the right to intervene in its internal affairs, and throughout the construction period that right was exercised continually – though sometimes ineffectively – to serve American interests.

Yet U.S. intervention had a strictly limited objective: to counteract any instability in Panama which could disrupt the waterway's progress to completion. This was entirely in line with the policy established over the previous half-century whereby the Navy had sent its landing-parties into Panama only to secure the Panama Railroad and whereby the State Department had consistently set its face against involvement in isthmian politics. Pressure for such involvement after 1903 came mainly from Panamanians; very few Americans saw it as other than a tiresome last resort.

Still fewer favoured the even more binding alternative, the annexation of Panama, which some Panamanian Conservatives thought was the only way to make Panama safe from democracy. The cartoonist of the Philadelphia *Record* could show Uncle Sam pondering whether to put Panama in his collection of dependencies, but annexation was a political impossibility with the resurgence of anti-colonialist feeling after the war with Spain. The writer Willis Johnson reflected the mood accurately when he jibbed at adding Panama to 'those alien possessions which were forced upon us by the logic of an unsought war, and which are to us today a "white man's burden" which is heavy and costly to bear'. The colonisation of Panama was unnecessary, however, given the powers already at Washington's disposal. Sovereign rights in the Canal Zone granted the United States everything it needed in the immediate vicinity of the canal, while the protectorate lay in reserve as an additional insurance in case matters got out of hand across the zonal boundary.[1]

The first test of American reflexes came in the autumn of 1904. On 28 October the commander of Panama's army, General Esteban Huertas, demanded the resignation of two members of President Manuel Amador's Conservative cabinet, and a coup seemed on the near horizon. This Washington was determined to prevent, and in military terms the task raised few problems, since the Panamanian army was not exactly a force to be reckoned with. Many of its rifles, Governor George Davis later estimated, 'would not bring more than the price of old iron', and it numbered a mere 250, one-tenth of whom were barefoot boys. But behind the army was the Liberal party, the main political opposition to Amador, and the U.S. chargé d'affaires, Joseph Lee, was at pains to tell one of its leaders that 'no revolutionary methods would be countenanced and . . . all changes in the Government should be made at the ballot box or by voluntary resignations'.[2]

Trouble in Panama had already been anticipated in at least two ways. By the executive order of 9 May 1904 the governor was authorised to call on U.S. naval and military forces to put down disorders in the Zone or the terminals of Panama City and Colón, and a detachment of Marines had been retained at Empire, twelve miles up the railway from Panama City. Their presence, the U.S. minister, John Barrett, believed, killed all chance of a successful rising, but as an extra precaution Davis asked to have the flagship of the Caribbean squadron sent down to Colón. In the event, a Pacific flotilla was despatched under Admiral Caspar Goodrich – the battleship *New York*, the cruiser *Boston*, and the gunboat *Bennington* – arriving off Panama City on 14 November. 'I am glad to know', cabled Davis, 'that the Admiral is in the Bay.' The canal project now seemed safe, and Davis told Goodrich he would not ask for the Navy's support unless the railroad were blocked, canal construction hampered, or order in the Zone disturbed.[3]

Contrast this with the reaction of Hay and Taft in Washington, who viewed the crisis largely in political terms. It was quite intolerable, Hay told Roosevelt, that 'the little blackguard' and his 'falstaff army' should dictate to Amador. The 1903 convention, stated Taft, 'permits us to prevent revolutions. I shall advise

---

[1] Richard, *The Panama Canal in American national consciousness, 1870–1922*, 197. Willis Johnson, *Four centuries of the Panama Canal* (New York, 1907), 360.

[2] The most detailed account of the Huertas affair may be found in McCain, *United States and the Republic of Panama*, 48–60. USD, Lee to Hay, 29.10.04. ICC, 80-G-2, Davis to Taft, 11.1.05. USD, Lee to Hay, 1 and 8.11.04.

[3] BD, 414. USD, Barrett to Hay, 23.8.04. ICC, 80-G-2, Davis to Marriam, undated. USD, Lee to Hay, 14.11.04. ICC, 80-G-2, Davis to Lee, 14.11.04. USD, Lee to Hay, 14.11.04. ICC, 80-G-2, Davis to Goodrich, 14.11.04.

that we'll have no more' in what was 'a kind of Opera Bouffe republic and nation' with an army 'not much larger than the army on an opera stage'. The Marines were accordingly moved up to Ancon, just inside the Zone line and within easy striking distance of the Panamanian capital.[4]

This, in the words of Barrett, produced 'a most excellent moral effect', and the Huertas abscess was quickly lanced. On 18 November the general went into early retirement on a stupendous pension of $500 a month, and the next day the Panamanian army was disbanded. In its place, Lee suggested, the government should set up four or five brass bands 'so that there might be plenty of music every day'. The bands did not materialise, but a police force took the army's place. As we shall see, it was destined to give the ruling powers of both Zone and Republic recurrent headaches for many years to come.[5]

The immediate aftermath of the Huertas episode was uneventful, however. The Marines were returned to their original cantonment on the advice of Barrett. A congressional visitation was imminent which Barrett considered was bound to seize on their bivouac at Ancon as proof of the 'so-called military occupation of Panama by the United States, and consequent imperialistic control'. Taft, in Panama to settle the dispute over the Zone's commercialisation, arranged for the sale of some of the Army's weaponry to Guatemala and the deposit of the remainder in the Zone. As a postscript to his removal, Huertas touched off momentary embarrassment when he told Davis that he had decided to place himself 'under the protection of the glorious starred flag, and, if possible, live on American territory'. But the would-be protégé stayed put on his *estancia*, never again to play a significant role in Panamanian political life.[6]

The departure of Huertas left the Liberal party still very much in business, and for Taft it was an ominous quantity. The Liberals, he told Roosevelt, were much less trustworthy than the Conservatives, and if they came to power it would mean the injection of widespread Negro influence into Panamanian politics. In the spring of 1905 he had Barrett dismissed as an alleged sympathiser with 'the party of the blacks'. Replacing Barrett was Charles Magoon, who, with his recent background as counsel in the U.S. Army's 'colonial office' (the Bureau of Insular Affairs), could be expected to take a sound line.[7]

Given his deep antipathy to the Liberals, it is not difficult to guess Taft's reaction to the petition they handed him on his next visit to the isthmus, in

[4] Hay Papers, Hay to Roosevelt, 14.11.04, and diary entry for 18.11.04. Ralph Minger, *William Howard Taft and United States foreign policy: The apprenticeship years, 1900–1908* (Urbana, Ill., 1975), 106. USD, Loomis to Lee, 15.11.04. ICC, 80-G-2, Walker to Davis, 17.11.04.

[5] USD, Barrett to Hay, 22.11.04 and 21.11.04; Lee to Hay, 1 and 14.11.04.

[6] ICC, 80-G-2, Barrett to Goodrich, undated. USD, Barrett to Hay, 13.12.04. Taft Papers, SWS-OC, Taft to Roosevelt, 19.12.04, and ser. 3, Cromwell to Taft, 28.12.04. ICC, 80-G-2, Davis to Taft, 11.1.05; Huertas to Davis, 21.2.05; Davis to Huertas, 23.2.05.

[7] Taft Papers, SWS-OC, Taft to Roosevelt, 19.12.04 and 13.4.05.

November 1905. In the summer of 1906 the country was to elect the National Assembly, and the Liberals were convinced that Amador would stop at nothing to get a Conservative majority. The petition therefore led off with the question 'Does the American government guarantee public order and constitutional succession in this Republic?' This wording closely followed the phraseology of Article 136 of the Panamanian constitution, which authorised Washington to intervene anywhere in Panama 'to re-establish public peace and constitutional order in the event of their being disturbed'. The Liberals were asking whether Taft was prepared to step in and ensure a meaningful election throughout Panama or stand by and watch as the Conservatives fixed the results. They also claimed to have the impression that the United States was willing to have them 'engage in a revolution if, in their judgement, unfair advantage is taken of them'. Such a righteous upsurge would presumably stir the custodian of the republic to move in to their rescue.[8]

The Liberals' tactics had been anticipated by Senator Joseph Foraker in the 1901 debate on the Platt Amendment allowing Washington to take Cuba in hand in the event of a political breakdown. 'Suppose they have an election,' Foraker conjectured. 'The party that is out is likely to complain, and . . . by making trouble . . . they would lead to an intervention of the United States to put the successful party out.' But relief of the Liberals was the last thing Taft had in mind, and Root agreed. His reply to the petition flatly rejected using Article 136 as a cause for action in Washington's part. The United States would not go beyond its treaty rights, and while guaranteeing Panama's independence under Article 1 of the canal convention, it did not 'purpose to interfere with that independence'.[9]

Root's answer was clearly intended as passive support for the government, yet the nervous Amador was still not reassured, since Root had explicitly limited U.S. concern for peace and order to the Zone and the two terminal cities. The Liberals, he told Magoon, would interpret this as a signal that Root would turn a blind eye to a revolt in the interior. Washington must respond by invoking Article 136 at his request if in its opinion Panama could not cope with the situation – this not just for Panama's sake but because the article was as important to the United States as the Platt Amendment.[10]

In saying this, Amador failed to realise that whereas Washington had manifold interests to protect in Cuba, in Panama its sole preoccupation was the canal, and what went on beyond its environs was a matter of relative indifference. In mid April, however, Taft received reports from Magoon which played on his fears of a race war on the isthmus and in which a senior Conservative was quoted

[8] A detailed account of the 1906 election can be found in Mellander, *United States in Panamanian politics*, 76–125. USD, Magoon to Root, 23.12.05 and 10.11.05.

[9] *CR* (Senate), 27.2.01, 3151. USD, Root to Magoon, 4.12.05.

[10] USD, Magoon to Root, 30.12.05; Amador to Magoon, 9.1.06. On the Platt Amendment, see Chapter 2 at n. 63.

as saying he would be ready to countenance U.S. annexation of Panama 'rather than have it pass into the hands of "niggers"'. Magoon's despatches soon produced the desired effect, and Magoon was told that a Panamanian government request would be enough to prompt the United States 'to lend its aid, by armed force, to suppress an insurrection in any part of the republic of Panama'. Taft's letter was given to the press on 11 May.[11]

The publication of Taft's message devastated the Liberals, as it was intended to do. And a Liberal delegation to Washington was treated to a disingenuous homily from Root in person. 'The day when the Government of the United States appoints citizens of this country as its agents in the territory of the little republic of Panama and pays them from its treasury and gives them instructions to intervene in whatever debates about the electoral or civil rights the Panamanian citizens have, in order that such agents may solve them, on that day you will have lost your sovereignty.'[12]

Worse was to come, from the Liberal point of view. Once again, as in 1904, the big stick was brandished when the Navy pincered the Zone with its war vessels and shipped in a contingent of 400 additional Marines. If the Panamanian police could not handle the situation in the interior, the Marines were to be sent there. Panama City and Colón would be taken over by the Canal Commission police, and the Zone would be secured by sanitary officers and watchmen. In short, Washington was prepared to invert its usual priorities and strip its most vital interest of protection in order to give unconditional backing to the political status quo.[13]

All this in spite of the fact that the Liberals were a paper tiger. When the election was over, Magoon told Taft that the party's 'negro, mestizo and other colored element' was not yet dangerous enough to cause large-scale disorder and that the Liberal leaders were not so very different from their Conservative opposite numbers. They would certainly exploit their non-white following, but they would not let it near the centre of political power.[14]

The Liberals were indeed neither willing nor able to mount an insurgency, and no U.S. troops had to be brought out of the Zone. Magoon was, however, quick to move 300 Marines to the Panama City limits at Amador's request, as well as to make him an express delivery of rifles and ammunition in time for polling day. Given this blatant display of American support, it was not surprising that the Conservatives swept in with a massive majority.[15]

The consequences of the landslide were not everything Washington could have wished. In the judgement of the American chargé, William Sands, the

[11] ICC, 80-G-2, Root to Taft, 21.2.06; Magoon to Taft, 14.4.06; Taft to Magoon, 26.4.06.

[12] Jessup, *Root*, 1: 519–20.

[13] ICC, 80-G-2, Shonts to Magoon, 17.5.06; Magoon to Shonts, 21.5.06.

[14] Ibid., Magoon to Taft, 16.5.06; 80-H-3, Magoon to Taft, 30.7.06. USD, Magoon to Root, 25.7.06.

[15] USD, Magoon to Root, 22.6.06.

Electoral Council set up by the Conservatives in October 1906 was designed to make certain that the party could 'impose its candidate upon the people and continue itself indefinitely in power, making popular elections a mere formality'. This, some Liberals hoped, could duplicate the recent crisis in Cuba, where a Liberal insurrection had brought about a full-dress U.S. intervention to depose the incumbent Cuban administration and to pacify the country under a provisional American government. When he visited Panama in November, however, Roosevelt did not hold out the promise of the USA riding in to save an oppressed opposition. Instead both government and opposition were warned that irresponsible behaviour ultimately meant 'destruction to the republic'. The allusion to Cuba was unmistakable, but Roosevelt had no intention of making the same example of Panama and bringing in an American occupation régime to sort its problems out.[16]

Even so, Washington had come to play an integral part in the politics of its diminutive client. This in turn signified a bruising entanglement with the Panamanian police, which performed a dual function in isthmian life as the supposedly apolitical enforcers of law and order and as the totally politicised muscle-men who served the government at election time. Given American concern for the security of the terminal cities and the emerging role of the United States as Panama's electoral arbiter, the two were destined to come into close and often abrasive contact.

The difficulties of their relationship were already plain to see. When a New York Police Department man was taken on as instructor, his contract was soon cancelled because of 'well-founded suspicions that he protected certain interests'. The Panamanian constabulary meanwhile proved distinctly anarchic. In April 1905 they beat up several West Indian labourers and in February 1906 seriously wounded a Jamaican teamster. In June two U.S. Marine Corps officers and a midshipman from USS *Columbia* were arrested and severely manhandled in Colón. On Christmas Day 1906 Colón was the scene of an ugly riot involving the police and American workers on the canal.[17]

The fault lay on both sides. Central Americans, Magoon considered, were 'liable to these quick and furious exhibitions of uncontrollable rage', but most of the U.S. citizenry the police came up against were from the South 'and [made] no distinction between Panamanians and negroes'. 'The average American', in the view of the Commission's secretary, Joseph Bucklin Bishop, 'has the utmost contempt for a Panaman and never loses an opportunity, especially when drunk, to show it.'[18]

[16] Ibid., Sands to Root, 12.10.06. ICC, 80-H-3, Reed to Taft, 11.10.06. *BD*, 711–12.
[17] *NYT*, 1.4.05, 1/5. USD, Sands to Root, 4.2.06. ICC, 80-G-1, Chiari to Goethals, 29.4.15. USD, Barrett to Hay, 8.5.05; Sands to Root, 15.3.06. ICC, 80-G-2, Taft to Magoon, 4.6.06; 88-A-86, Bishop memo of 27.12.06.
[18] ICC, 80-G-2, Magoon to Taft, 5.6.06. USD, Magoon to Root, 15.6.06. ICC, 88-A-86, Bishop memo of 27.12.06.

If things got worse in Colón, Bishop thought, the ICC would have to take over policing itself. The answer for Magoon's successor as minister, Herbert Squiers, was to deprive the police of their rifles, all-too-lethal weapons 'in the hands of men without either judgment or discretion'. Sands looked much deeper, to 'a thorough modernization of the law courts, police service, jails and penitentiary of this country'.[19]

None of these solutions was acceptable in Washington, however. Maintaining public order in Panama City and Colón under Article 7 of the canal convention was seen as a purely short-term emergency measure. And the kind of drastic house cleaning recommended by Sands would be tantamount to colonisation, an option that had never been on the cards.

The terminals thus confronted the United States with an intractable problem. Too close to the canal to be ignored, inadequately policed by Panama yet unquestionably within its jurisdiction, and well-stocked emporiums of all the vices unavailable in the Zone, they were a standing affront to the regularity the Zone enshrined. The disturbances of 1906 were a small foretaste of the strife they were to produce between the guardian of the isthmus and its ward.

Meanwhile the leading item on Washington's mind was the Panamanian presidential election of 1908. The likeliest successor to Amador was his foreign minister, Ricardo Arias, an ultra-rightist who told Minister Squiers that the advice of the U.S. representative in Panama should be followed on all political matters, 'much the same as the British resident in India'. Squiers was naturally appreciative. Arias, he told Root, was 'not imbued with the deep prejudice against us which is found in so many Latin Americans'; he was 'a conservative and safe man'.[20]

In the light of his recent hostility to the Liberals, it was odd that Secretary Taft did not share this view. Reporting to Roosevelt from Panama in May 1908, he portrayed Arias as a corrupt and unscrupulous figure who would try to rig the election and so spark a Liberal revolt unless Washington stepped in. If the election were 'plainly fraudulent', he would threaten U.S. intervention to 'put the person fairly elected in power'. Looking beyond 1908, he envisaged nothing less than a new treaty giving the United States rights to control the entire electoral process.[21]

Roosevelt backed Taft to the hilt, and Taft conveyed their ultimatum to Amador. The election should have 'no stamp or taint of force or fraud', and if there were malpractice it would bring on U.S. intervention under Article 136. Amador had no choice but to agree to an American-dominated Electoral Inquiry Commission to investigate complaints on the run-up to polling day. On the day itself two U.S. observers would be placed in each election district to watch the

---

[19] SD, 1906–10, 3745, Squiers to Root, 29.12.06. USD, Sands to Root, 15.3.06.

[20] SD, 1906–10, 847/35, Squiers to Root, 9.12.07; 847/44, Squiers to Root, 24.3.08. The 1908 election is covered in Mellander, *United States in Panamanian politics*, 129–86.

[21] Goethals Papers, Taft to Roosevelt, 9.5.08.

voting and to witness the count. By insisting on these measures, Taft was going well beyond the position he had taken in 1906. Nationwide intervention under Article 136 was now to be carried out, not simply proclaimed in principle. He had also reversed his political objective, since intervention of this scope would almost certainly guarantee the success of the candidate endorsed by the Liberal party, José Domingo de Obaldía.[22]

Doubts over the change of direction were widespread. The Liberals, Squiers told Root, would not be happy until the United States occupied the country as it had occupied Cuba, but this would have damaging repercussions on Washington's relations with Latin America, since Cuba 'geographically and commercially belongs to the United States, but Panama is a part of the South American continent'. Commissioner Joseph Blackburn for his part feared that the diffuseness of the commitment to supervision could leave the Zone exposed, and 'unbridled license, loot, and lawlessness' in the terminals would do more harm to the canal work force than yellow fever in one and bubonic plague in the other. In the event, the military focus of the intervention was as narrow as it had been in 1906, with the large Marine Corps reinforcements ordered in by Roosevelt held on standby in the Zone and not stationed at polling places throughout the interior as the Liberals had asked.[23]

Even so, there were several who considered Taft's policy a big mistake. To Alvey Adee of the State Department, U.S. embroilment in the political mêlée could only lead to 'endless trouble and ultimate real intervention as in Cuba'. Congressman Edwin Denby, on mission in the isthmus, conveyed similar forebodings to Root. Hitherto Washington had told the Panamanians that their state was 'a doll house in which they may amuse themselves as long as they do not disturb or annoy us'. Over the election, however, it was 'holding them to an almost higher standard of political purity than we ourselves have ever been able to reach'. And there was no turning back: 'The policy of leading strings having now been established must always be followed.'[24]

Taft was prepared to take the risk for the sake of removing Arias from the scene, and Arias told Squiers he was ready to withdraw from the contest if he were persona non grata, though he was willing to give the Americans anything they wanted to put himself back in their good graces. Unfortunately for Don Ricardo, this was not good enough, and on 3 July he stood down.[25]

[22] TR letters, 6: 1028–9. SD, 1906–10, 847/59, Taft to Amador, 12.5.08. ICC, 80-H-3, Arias to Squiers and Blackburn, 15.5.08; Goethals to Taft, 15.5.08.

[23] SD, 1906–10, 847/70, Squiers to Root, 29.5.08. ICC, 80-H-3, Blackburn to Taft, 27.5.08. TR letters, 6: 1082. Goethals Papers, Russell to Goethals, 12.6.08. ICC, 80-H-3, Goethals et al. to Taft, 20.6.08.

[24] SD, 1906–10, 847/83, Adee to Bacon, 7.7.08. Jessup, Root, 1: 525–6.

[25] Taft Papers, SWS-OC, Taft to Roosevelt, 16.5.08. SD, 1906–10, 847/172, Taft to Roosevelt, 6.7.08; 847/72, Squiers to Root, 20.6.08; 847/92, Squiers to Root, 25.6.08; 847/83, Squiers to Root, 4.7.08.

Squiers was aghast. Now Arias had gone, he predicted that 'the man will win out who is prepared to take advantage of the ignorance of the lower classes of mixed negro and indian blood'. Taft disagreed completely. If the United States had not intervened, he told a correspondent, 'we would have had a man in power . . . who would have thwarted as much as possible our legitimate purposes in the Zone'. Obaldía, the victor by default, he no doubt expected to be considerably more compliant.[26]

But the installation of Obaldía did not usher in a new era of good feelings. In September 1908 a seaman from USS *Buffalo* was killed, and in May 1909 two Americans lost their lives in a murderous affray with West Indian labourers in Colón. Squiers believed the police were implicated in both cases. Their behaviour in the first incident was 'in the highest degree reprehensible', and after the second he reported to Washington that 'the lower classes of this republic hate us, and the police are drawn from that class'.[27]

But the violence was only a symptom of the uproarious climate of the terminal cities, to Senator John Tyler Morgan 'places . . . infested with perhaps every manner of vice, immorality, dissipation, and idleness'. In 1908 no fewer than 351 saloons were open for business in the two townships, as opposed to the much smaller number of bleak stand-up bars in the Zone. Gaming in the Zone was banned by the executive order of May 1904, and prostitution was likewise illegal. But in the terminals gambling joints and brothels were thick on the ground, and the Zone hierarchy was well aware of their explosive potential. The deaths of 1909 had taken place outside a Chinese lottery in Colón, and the Commission chairman, Colonel Goethals, was convinced that the lotteries were ruinous to his men. 'I was stationed at Deadwood, S.D., in 1878,' wrote Squiers, 'but I have never seen prostitution running riot as it is here.' His reference to the Black Hills in the saturnalian days of the gold rush was apt. Panama City and Colón were highly evocative of the wide-open frontier settlements of the late-nineteenth-century West, and all they needed to complete the comparison was an unswerving lawman to make them walk the paths of righteousness.[28]

Theodore Roosevelt would have jumped at the part, but by the spring of 1909 his days in the White House were over. Yet he drew an analogy which was to inspire American policy in this area for the next decade and more. 'If this kind of thing continues,' Roosevelt told Root, 'we shall be obliged to police the cities of Colón and Panama exactly as we take care of their health.' By Article 7 of the canal convention the United States had the right to enforce its own

[26] SD, 1906–10, 847/100, Squiers to Root, 4.7.08. Wilfrid Callcott, *The Caribbean policy of the United States, 1890–1920* (Baltimore, 1942), 257.

[27] SD, 1906–10, 15778, Squiers to Root, 2.10.08; and 847/185, Squiers to Knox, 19.5.09.

[28] *1906 Hearings*, 3: 2766. John Foster Carr, 'The Commission's white workers', *Outlook*, 83 (May–August 1906), 22, and 'Building a state', ibid., 443. ICC, 62-B-164, Goethals to Dickinson, 18.6.09. SD, 1906–10, 847/185, Squiers to Knox, 19.5.09.

sanitary regulations in the two municipalities as well as to restore public order
if the Panamanian authorities failed to cope. What Roosevelt and others after
him asserted was the power to bring moral hygiene to the terminals to crown
the physical disinfection already carried out under American auspices. Yet
laying drains, piping in clean water, and liquidating disease-bearing mosquitoes
was one thing; delivering Panama from evil was quite another.[29]

This was clear throughout the first year of the reform campaign. In December 1908 Panama apparently submitted to American claims over the *Buffalo*
incident. In June 1909, however, when Panamanian promises had not been
made good, Secretary of State Philander Chase Knox threatened that the United
States would begin policing the terminal cities in three months if Panama did
not give satisfaction. Even then the Panamanians merely asked for an American Army officer to instruct the police, not to command them, as Squiers
had wanted. And the only man the Army could suggest was an elderly retired
major. Bringing Panama to order seemed likely to prove an uphill struggle.[30]

The strains underlying the protectorate surfaced yet again in the crisis brought
on by the sudden death of President Obaldía in March 1910. His successor was
Carlos Mendoza, a Liberal and a mulatto. To the chargé at the American
legation, George Weitzel, this made Mendoza a dangerous proposition, since he
naturally suffered from 'a racial inability to refrain long from abuse of power'.
The outgoing minister, Reynolds Hitt, was certain that the white Panamanian
élite would never be reconciled to a president 'partly of African descent' and
thought it wisest to hint privately to Mendoza that he should stand down.[31]

The legation was therefore deeply unhappy about the result of the National
Assembly election in July, when the Liberals romped home after an unsupervised contest with twenty of the twenty-eight Assembly seats. This guaranteed
Mendoza's confirmation as president until the next presidential election in
1912, greatly to the chagrin of a junior officer in the legation, Richard Marsh,
who in spite of his lowly status was to play a key rôle in the development of the
crisis over the coming weeks.[32]

Marsh is perhaps best understood as a tabloid version of Squiers. Mendoza's
power base, he reported to Knox, was black Panamanians, 'mostly ignorant and
irresponsible, unable to meet the serious obligations of citizenship in a Republic'.
In view of their numbers, it would be wrong to encourage them 'in selecting
one of their race to the highest post in the land'. Mendoza, Marsh alleged, was

[29] SD, 1906–10, 15778, Roosevelt to Root, 21.10.08. *BD*, 282.
[30] SD, 1906–10, 15778, Squiers to Root, 15.12.08; Knox to Squiers, 24.6.09, Squiers to Knox,
19.7.09 and 23.7.09; 21344, War Department to State Department, 17.11.09. PC, 80-G-1,
Lefevre to Goethals, 29.4.15.
[31] SD, 1906–10, 847/218, Weitzel to Knox, 1.3.10; 847/230, Weitzel to Knox, 3.3.10; 847/
236, Hitt to Knox, 11.6.10.
[32] SD, 1906–10, 847/240, Marsh to Knox, 28.7.10.

the father of 'numerous illegitimate children'. He would become a dictator like Zelaya in Nicaragua or Estrada Cabrera in Guatemala. Zelaya had recently been deposed with U.S. aid, and Marsh no doubt saw this as a happy precedent. 'Where American influence has dominated in Latin America,' he wrote, 'there prosperity has followed and those countries have been lifted out of the medieval ages into the age of modern civilization.'[33]

On 4 August, in company with Goethals, Marsh discussed with Mendoza's political enemy, de la Guardia, the constitutionality of Mendoza's position. By Articles 82 and 83 of the Panamanian constitution, no president could legitimately succeed himself, and so, de la Guardia contended, the National Assembly could not confirm Mendoza in office when it met in September. On the basis of this transparent piece of casuistry, de la Guardia went on to request U.S. intervention under Article 136 in order to prevent violation of constitutional proprieties. The State Department, anxious to make intervention as discreet as possible, agreed with Marsh that the best course was to put maximum pressure on Mendoza to withdraw and thus relieve Washington of the need to act. On 26 August Marsh reported that Mendoza had submitted his resignation in writing.[34]

The end was not yet, however. Marsh was bent on excluding not only Mendoza but Mendoza's fellow Liberal, Belisario Porras. His particular favourite was Samuel Lewis, like Ricardo Arias an ultra-conservative. On 31 August he wrote to Goethals that if the Assembly failed to choose Lewis, he personally would declare it 'void and null' and ask Washington to appoint a governor-general of Panama, pending a fresh election. Even without State Department backing, he believed it would still be possible to 'ram Lewis down their throats'. On 8 September he was quoted in a local newspaper as saying that if in future Panama refused to bow to the clearly expressed wishes of the U.S. government, the United States could only 'adopt such means to prevent such opposition . . . as occupation and annexation'.[35]

Nothing was farther from Taft's mind, as he assured the Panamanian minister in Washington, Carlos Arosemena. Marsh's 'fussy meddling and loquacity' was a severe embarrassment, and Taft wanted him removed before he did any more damage. He was also convinced by now that it was immaterial who became president of Panama. 'We have such control in Panama', he affirmed, 'that no Government elected by them will feel a desire to antagonise the American Government.' When Arosemena suggested his uncle as a compromise candidate,

---

[33] SD, 1910–49, 819.00/248, Marsh to Knox, 17.8.10; 819.00/253. Marsh to Knox, 15.8.10.
[34] Goethals Papers, Goethals to Dickinson, 13.9.10. SD, 1910–49, 819.00/244, De la Guardia to Knox, 4.8.10; /251, Marsh to Wilson, 20.8.10; Wilson to March, 22.8.10; /255, Marsh to Wilson, 26.8.10. Squiers would have approved of Marsh's caution: A year earlier he had written that 'in the transaction of business with Latin-Americans, I have found that verbal agreements generally prove unsatisfactory': SD, 1906–10, 15778, Squiers to Knox, 2.8.09.
[35] SD, 1910–49, 701.1911/49, Doyle to Dodge, 9.11.10. Goethals Papers, Goethals to Dickinson, 13.9.10. NYT, 9.9.10, 6/7.

Taft posed no objection, and on 14 September Pablo Arosemena was chosen as fourth president of Panama for the remainder of Obaldía's term. Porras replaced Carlos Arosemena as minister on the understanding that he would be the Liberal candidate in the 1912 election. The crisis was finally over.[36]

There were plenty more in store, however, and it was Arosemena who set the pot boiling once again. Having sampled the power of the *presidencia*, he planned to take six months' leave of absence in the first half of 1912 to make himself constitutionally eligible for election. Porras, enraged that Arosemena had gone back on their deal, returned to claim his promised nomination. For Conservatives such as de la Guardia, Porras was a man who might bankrupt Panama as comprehensively as the Khedive Ismail had bankrupted Egypt in the 1870s. To knock him out of the reckoning, they aimed to charge him with treason. They would have done better to put up a strong runner of their own, but Arosemena disqualified himself by taking his leave a month too late, and when Ricardo Arias refused to fight, the relatively unknown Pedro Díaz was left to carry the Conservative banner against Porras as the Liberal nominee.[37]

Through all this confusion both sides besieged Taft with pleas for intervention. Neither Taft nor Secretary of War Henry Stimson saw any reason to supervise the election, but the men on the spot felt a good deal less confident. Goethals asked Stimson to have the Navy postpone the relief of half the Marine Corps garrison; Minister Percival Dodge had always believed that supervision was necessary. Taft gave the order on 13 May, and a supervisory committee was set up on the lines laid down in 1908.[38]

The situation was certainly highly charged. On 10 June the committee discovered a consignment of rifles at Colón, bought by Arias from the U.S. War Department. Under heavy American pressure, Acting President Eduardo Chiari pledged that the weapons would not be issued, that the entire police force would be placed under the committee's authority, and that the police would not be armed on election day. Stripped of his firepower, Díaz pulled out, and the election went to Porras unopposed.[39]

The supervision of 1912 not only decided the result of the election. It also

---

[36] SD, 1910–49, 819.00/285, Taft to Wilson, 9.9.10; /281, Taft to Wilson, 12.9.10; /276, Taft to Wilson, 8.9.10; /278, Marsh to Wilson, 12.9.10; /284 of 14.9.10; 701.1911/49, Doyle to Dodge, 9.11.10.

[37] ICC, 80-H-10, Memo of 20.7.11. SD, 1910–49, 819.00/349, Dodge to Knox, 6.12.11; /361, De la Guardia to Taft, 27.12.11; /372, Dodge to Knox, 8.2.12; /360, Dodge to Knox, 1.2.12; /376, Dodge to Knox, 12.3.12.

[38] SD, 1910–49, 819.00/361, De la Guardia to Taft, 27.12.11; /359, Porras to Taft, 10.1.12; /365, Taft to Porras, 8.2.12; /380, Hilles to Wilson, 22.3.12; /397, Stimson to Arias, 4.4.12, and Arias to Taft, 15.4.12; /387, Dodge to Knox, 25.4.12. ICC, 80-G-12, Goethals to Stimson, 11.5.12. SD, 1910–49, 819.00/362, Dodge to Knox, 25.1.12; /395, Knox to Dodge, 13.5.12.

[39] SD, 1910–49, 819.00/411, Dodge to Knox, 10.6.12. *NYT*, 11.5.12, 2/4, and 13.6.12, 1/2. SD, 1910–49, 819.00/427, Dodge to Knox, 1.7.12; /420, Doyle memo of 1.7.12; /430, Dodge to Knox, 14.7.12.

produced incidents which sucked Washington deeper still into the mire of Panamanian public life. On 4 July, as Americans celebrated their independence in the red-light district of Cocoa Grove, Panama City police stormed in to break up the festivities. An off-duty bartender was bayoneted to death in a cantina, and sixteen servicemen and civilians were wounded. On the same day the police crossed into the Zone to kill a man and abduct a family of three.[40]

There seems little doubt that both episodes were triggered by police resentment at the humiliation of being disarmed, and once again the call went up for American control of the force. In Goethals's view, a recurrence of the trouble should be rendered 'just as remote as it lies within our power to make it'. As a first step, the police commandant was made to resign, and under subsequent pressure Porras was persuaded to contract for two American instructors.[41]

The clean-up did not stop there. When Arosemena had suggested the appointment of an American bishop of Panama, 'as the moral condition of the Panamanian clergy was very low', he was politely ignored. Likewise pigeon-holed was a request from Ricardo Arias that the State Department support the abolition of universal suffrage as an absurdity in a country where over 70 per cent of the population was illiterate. But Conservative plans for fundamental changes in Panama's financial system were given a much more sympathetic reception. These envisaged an American-appointed controller of the Treasury and close surveillance of the National Bank. Dodge had already urged American fiscal supervision as the only way of ending Panama's 'incurable extravagance', and Goethals forwarded the programme to Washington with his personal endorsement.[42]

American concern over Panama's financial misbehaviour had already given the protectorate a third dimension, alongside electoral supervision and control of the police. As early as May 1907 there had been serious disquiet at the National Assembly's reported plans for the so-called Constitutional Fund. Of the $10 million treaty payment for canal rights, $6 million was invested in New York by Article 138 of the constitution, and interest on the investment (close on $300,000) furnished Panama with 12 per cent of its annual revenue. The Assembly aimed to amend the constitution so as to transfer the Fund to a Panamanian mortgage bank, and in the summer of 1909, when the scheme was

[40] SD, 1910–49, 419.11D29/146, De Rappard report of 20.10.16, quoted in *FRUS 1916*, 918–22. SD, 1910–49, 811F.0144/1, Solicitor memo of 30.7.12. *NYT*, 6.7.12, 7/3.

[41] Goethals Papers, Goethals memo of 23.7.12. SD, 1910–49, 819.00/433, Dodge to Knox, 8.7.12. ICC, 62-B-199, Goethals to Stimson, 13.7.12. Goethals Papers, Doyle to Goethals, 24.8.12. SD, 1910–49, 819.1052/10, Andrews to Knox, 27.9.12; /13, Dodge to Knox, 20.1.13.

[42] SD, 1910–49, 819.00/404, Dodge to Knox, 29.11.11, and Knox to Dodge, 3.1.12; /431, Doyle memo of 11.7.12; /435, Arias to Knox, 27.7.12. Goethals Papers, Goethals memo of 23.7.12. SD, 1910–49, 819.00/433, Dodge to Knox, 8.7.12. ICC, 94-A-104, Goethals to Stimson, 8.8.12.

revived, Knox instructed the legation to warn the government off. The transfer was blocked, though nothing could be done to stop the removal of $1.5 million in a current account on Wall Street.[43]

The Fund also featured in a project which took shape in 1911 for a railway from Panama City to David, hundreds of miles to the west in Chiriqui province. Here the Assembly moved to devote the entire Fund to the construction of the line and so avoid a loan which would place the country in pawn to overseas bondholders. Asked to pronounce on the legality of the bill, the State Department solicitor took a firm line. Any attempt to alter the constitution to release the Fund would be an infringement of constitutional order which would bring into play the U.S. right to intervene under Article 136. The next year the solicitor went on to disapprove use of the $250,000 canal annuity as collateral for a railway loan. 'This Government', in the solicitor's view, had 'a direct, and you might say, *personal* interest in seeing that the Government of Panama shall so conduct itself and its finances that it shall not become either a public charge or a charge upon the United States.' In short, Washington should not hesitate to keep Panama on the straight and narrow path of fiscal rectitude. Not even the interest from the Fund could be pledged as security for the railway project, Knox told Dodge. Panama did not sign the contract.[44]

A second contract met with the same American response, and when Porras protested that the revenues were Panama's to spend as it pleased, he was given short shrift. A subsequent attempt to amend the constitution collapsed when Porras was told that the bid would be construed as a threat to the independence Washington had guaranteed under the canal convention: The United States insisted on a veto over any constitutional change affecting its treaty rights.[45]

Early in 1914 Panama was denied a third time. The country, Minister William Jennings Price averred, was 'much more than an independent Republic in this, that her independence was guaranteed by the United States' – saved, that is, from prodigality by her eternally vigilant scrutineer. In November the State Department relented to the extent of letting Panama use the annuity as collateral for a $3 million loan, but the Panamanians were expected to get American

---

[43] SD, 1906–10, 847/21, Squiers to Root, 3.5.07. On the Constitutional Fund, see Chapter 2 at n. 73. SD, 1906–10, 11447, Legation to Knox, 12.10.09, and Knox to Legation, 8.11.09; 1910–49, 819.51/10, Legation to Knox 8.3.10.

[44] SD, 1910–49, 819.77/48, Dodge to Wilson, 4.5.11, and Solicitor memo, undated; /78, Legation to Knox, 9.10.11; /81, Legation to Knox, 11.10.11; /115, Solicitor memo of 4.3.12 (emphasis in original) and Taft to Wilson, 16.4.12; /130, Knox to Dodge, 22.8.12; /133, Dodge to Knox, 3.9.12.

[45] SD, 1910–49, 819.77/145, Knox to Dodge, 7.1.13; /156, Dodge to Knox, 22.2.13, and Knox to Dodge, 28.2.13; /159, Dodge to Knox, 24.2.13; 819.011/1, Solicitor memo of 3.3.13; /2, Dodge to Bryan, 17.4.13.

approval before making any more loan agreements. It was, after all, 'notorious that Latin American officials are apt to be anything but cautious in entering financial obligations'.[46]

Yet if in this area of the protectorate Washington was well able to hold Panama in check, control of the police was another story. The terminal cities went on their rampageous way, and in August 1913 the Commission begged for immediate action to stem the influx of prostitutes and prevent the development of the 'moral conditions which are said to exist at the ports of the Suez Canal'.[47]

After still another riot in September, General Thomas Barry, commander of the Eastern Department responsible for the Zone, looked back for an answer to his time as head of the Army of Cuban Pacification. A detachment of the Army's provost guard should be stationed in both Panama City and Colón to patrol the red-light districts and arrest Americans before the local constabulary could get their hands on them.[48]

Despite the objections of the garrison commander, the patrols were set up, but the long-term solution to the problem of disorder still lay in the appointment of an American police adviser. Major George Helfert arrived to start work on 2 April 1914. He lasted no more than ten weeks. The police hierarchy barely acknowledged his existence, and the government refused to grant him the powers to do his job. On 12 June he was recalled, his mission aborted. Helfert's impotence was underscored in a plaintive report to Secretary of State William Jennings Bryan. He was more than once awakened in the small hours, he told Bryan, by the sound of 'orgies celebrated in the private rooms of the Chief of Police with certain American women [the isthmian name for whores]'.[49]

Soon afterwards Price protested to Lefevre that the trouble in Panama City was almost all fomented in establishments 'permitted, if not protected, by the Government of Your Excellency's Republic'. The complaint was ignored, and though the indefatigable police commandant was replaced, nothing basic had changed. As Helfert had rightly concluded, so long as the police remained the key to government success in elections, no Panamanian administration would ever enact reform. It remained to be seen whether Washington had the will to put through a reform programme of its own and shift its protectorate into a higher gear in this and in other departments.[50]

[46] SD, 1910–49, 819.77/176, Price to Bryan, 5.2.14; /201A, Bryan to Lefevre, 29.6.14; /201, Bingham memo, undated; /212, Bryan to Morales, 7.11.14; /176, Bingham to Long, 14.3.14.
[47] ICC, 80-G-2, ICC memo of 18.8.13.
[48] AG, 1784–1917, 2084148, Barry to Edwards, 8.10.13.
[49] Ibid., Edwards to Barry. SD, 1910–49, 819.1052/32, Price to Bryan, 20.4.14; /34, Price to Bryan, 27.5.14; /37, Bryan to Price, 12.6.14; /45, Helfert to Bryan, 9.7.14.
[50] PC, 62-B-199, Price to Lefevre, 23.6.14; Lefevre to Price, 2.7.14. SD, 1910–49, 819.1052/43, Price to Bryan, 8.8.14; /45, Helfert to Bryan, 9.7.14.

First World War, 1914–1918

During the construction era the Panamanian protectorate had been a relatively minor American preoccupation. Involvement in Panamanian affairs was thought justified only by a threat to the canal generated by anarchy in the terminal cities. As long as the canal was not affected, U.S. tutelage, it was believed, could be limited to those indirect pressures known in the State Department as 'moral influence'.[51]

In practice it was impossible to keep up that degree of restraint, and the construction decade had witnessed U.S. intervention in a number of key areas. By the time the canal went into operation in 1914, the United States seemed ready to step up its control and try to impose higher standards on Panamanian public life. This move towards greater interventionism was fully in tune with the thinking of President Woodrow Wilson and his secretary of state, William Jennings Bryan, who frequently vindicated their approach to Latin America with the argument of the civilising mission. Washington, in their judgement, had a positive duty to rescue the region from a long heritage of misrule and school it in the basics of good government. The main targets of Wilsonian reform in 1914 were the Dominican Republic and Haiti, and in the four years after the canal's opening Panama too was marked down for salvation.[52]

It was the Panamanian police who absorbed the most U.S. attention in 1915. On 14 February they beat up sixteen American soldiers during the carnival in Panama City, and on 2 April shot dead an Army corporal on patrol in Colón. For both Governor Goethals and garrison commander General Edwards, Washington had no alternative but to police the terminal cities under Article 7 of the canal treaty. But Edwards's superior, General Leonard Wood, disagreed – surprisingly, as a former military governor of Cuba. To assume police jurisdiction, he believed, might create a damaging impression in Central America, and it would be better to reach an agreement on the precise status of the U.S. Army provost guard in the terminals. Panama meanwhile came up with a proposal for recruiting American patrolmen to serve in the red-light districts; their senior officer could also act as police instructor.[53]

Goethals balked at both ideas. Hiring American constables would only breed resentment if they put a stop to the collusion between the police and the owners of the down-town dives, and the previous string of American police advisers

[51] SD, 1910–49, 817.00/2081, Weitzel to Knox, 9.10.12, quoted in Whitney Perkins, *Constraint of empire: The United States and Caribbean interventions* (Westport, Conn., 1981), 34–5.

[52] Selig Adler, 'Bryan and Wilsonian Caribbean penetration', *Hispanic American Historical Review*, 20 (1940), 198–226. See also Arthur Link, *Wilson: The struggle for neutrality 1914–1915* (Princeton, N.J., 1960), 495–550.

[53] SD, 1910–49, 319.112c64, traces the aftermath of the 14 February incident; 319.1123L25, the sequel to the 2 April episode. AG, 1784–1917, 2274803, Wood to Adjutant General, 27.4.15; Bliss to Garrison, 7.5.15. SD, 1910–49, 419.11D29/87, Price to Bryan, 17.4.15.

had achieved precisely nothing. To try for a written agreement on U.S. military patrols would amount to an admission that Washington was abandoning its right to intervene under Article 7. The optimum solution was U.S. control of Panama's courts as well as its police, but failing that, the police should lose their high-powered rifles, and – as in the Zone – civilians should not be allowed to carry weapons. But when the State Department took up the idea and pressed Panama to give up the rifles, the response was predictably hostile. With another presidential contest due in 1916, the administration refused to disarm its electoral strike force. In November, Edwards and Goethals were ready to go in and seize the rifles, but they were given no backing for such a drastic move, and stalemate persisted into the new year.[54]

The U.S. bid to tame Panama's excitable gendarmerie was paralleled by the effort to straighten out its erratic finances. Early in 1915 the National Assembly diverted $1 million of the $3 million railway loan to an ambitious programme of public works. The move came partly in response to Panama's heavy loss of customs revenue produced by a sharp fall in imports after the outbreak of the First World War in Europe. But it also reflected a cavalier attitude to the terms of the loan, and President Porras was asked to postpone public works until the end of the war brought a revival in tariff income. Washington was also unhappy about Panama's bid for a further loan of $1.2 million to pay off a number of debts. Yet the loan went through, with interest from the Constitutional Fund as collateral, rather than local assets such as the liquor tax, which the State Department would very much have preferred.[55]

American forbearance was fast evaporating, however. In November 1915 Goethals urged the appointment of a U.S. official to supervise Panama's finances, along the lines of the American financial control set up in the Dominican Republic over the past eighteen months. The managers of the National Bank, he alleged, were lending large sums to political friends without asking for guarantees, and $100,000 had been siphoned off from the railway loan to meet government wage-bills. U.S. banks were being approached for temporary advances to pay a restive police force, and emergency funds were raised through a compulsory levy on administration employees. In January 1916 the legation reported Panamanian plans for devoting the final quarter of the railway loan to a track described by an American surveyor as 'a ridiculous undertaking'. To complete the catalogue of thriftlessness, Panama had run into debt with the

[54] Goethals Papers, Goethals to Boggs, 12.5.15. SD, 1910–49, 819.1052/51, Price to Lansing, 16.10.15; /53, Goethals to Price, 25.10.15; /54, /55, /56, all Price to Lansing, 24.11.15, 17.11.15, 1.12.15.

[55] SD, 1910–49, 819.77/216, Price to Bryan, 27.1.15; 819.51/48, Price to Bryan, 5.10.14; /63, Lansing to Morales, 11.9.15; /69, Morales to Lansing, 13.10.15; /68, Lansing to Price, 15.10.15; /97, Price to Lansing, 8.1.16.

United Fruit Company to the tune of $750,000 and pledged half the revenue from its banana exports in repayment.[56]

Even so, the Porras régime thought it could get along perfectly well without a financial minder. Foreign Minister Ernesto Lefevre, indeed, wanted the entire $6 million Constitutional Fund taken away from the agency of William Nelson Cromwell and used to build up the country's infrastructure. Ample sources of fixed income, he told Minister Price, were 'a continual temptation', and Panama would find it more feasible to live within its means once they had been spent. In April 1916, however, Porras agreed to suspend most public works and to cancel all projected railway development. He had, in Price's diplomatic understatement, shown himself to be 'a dreamer rather than a practical man' in fiscal matters. His successor, due to be elected in July, might prove more responsive to U.S. pressure for retrenchment.[57]

The presidential election was by now well established as a quadrennial pain for Washington, and the 1916 contest was no exception. The battle lines were drawn almost a year in advance, with Ramon Valdés running as Porras's hand-picked successor against the Liberal dissident Rodolfo Chiari. In the late summer of 1915 Chiari sounded out Edwards and Price on the possibility of American intervention under Article 136 of the constitution. There would be mayhem, he warned, if the United States folded its arms and did nothing.[58]

The most obvious American response was to prepare for supervision of the poll, as in 1908 and 1912, but the administration was seriously at odds. The White House and the State Department favoured supervision to avoid the greater evil of full-scale U.S. involvement. Governor Goethals, on the other hand, saw supervision as a mere palliative when what was needed was a fundamental cure for Panama's diseased political system.[59]

Goethals, in fact, had so far lost patience with Panama that he welcomed the chaos an unsupervised election might bring. The way would then be clear for a U.S. Army occupation régime. 'Let them revolute', he told Edwards, 'and the military step in and take over the country.' Edwards, as a former head of the Army's Bureau of Insular Affairs, could not have agreed more, and he looked forward to the same kind of enlightened despotism fostered by the Bureau in the Philippines, Cuba, and Puerto Rico. So too did Goethals's legal adviser,

[56] SD, 1910–49, 819.51/78, Price to Lansing, 6.11.15. On the Dominican Republic, see Dana Munro, *Intervention and dollar diplomacy in the Caribbean 1900–1921* (Princeton, N.J., 1964), 289–90, 296–7, 299, 300, 302–4. SD, 1910–49, 819.51/86, Price to Lansing, 4.12.15; /98, Spencer to Lansing, 19.1.16; /100, Price to Lansing, 10.4.16.

[57] SD, 1910–49, 819.51/87, /82, /100, all Price to Lansing, 29.11.15, 8.11.15, 10.4.16.

[58] SD, 1910–49, 819.00/487, /489, both Price to Lansing, 23.8.15 and 21.9.15. Goethals Papers, Edwards to Goethals, 18.8.15.

[59] SD, 1910–49, 819.00/546, Lansing to Wilson, 11.5.16; /534, Goethals to Baker, 13.4.16; /505, Spencer to Lansing, 22.1.16; /644, Wright memo of 7.2.16.

Frank Feuille. 'If these people cannot hold an election without having us play
the role of "cop" for them,' Feuille wrote Goethals, 'then we should . . . go in
. . . and stay in until the place is completely reorganized.'[60]

Such colonialism had no chance of acceptance in a State Department which
had always sheered away from direct rule. More attractive was the proposition
broached by the young John Foster Dulles, then doing business in Panama on
behalf of Cromwell. This was for a third candidate representing 'the better class
of business and professional men' and 'unofficially approved by local diplomatic,
military and Canal authorities'. The person in mind was Ricardo Arias, whose
hopes of the *presidencia* had been destroyed by Taft in 1908.[61]

But though the Arias solution was given official backing, it was doomed from
the start. It depended on Valdés's agreement to stand down, and that in turn
hinged on a U.S. declaration that the poll would be supervised. When the
decision was taken not to go through with supervision, Valdés knew he was
home and dry. Chiari withdrew, and for the third election in a row the Panamanian presidency was filled by a walkover.[62]

To Price this was 'a very pleasant and peaceful dénouement of the whole
affair'. It was a fatuous conclusion. Panama had avoided bloodshed, but Valdés
was Porras's creature and unlikely to prove more cooperative. The one solid
achievement of U.S. policy in the whole election campaign had been the disarmament of the police in May, leaving only twenty-five rifles for the presidential
guard. But the subsequent Panamanian request for a police instructor was no
more than a gesture, and Panama remained defiantly incorrigible.[63]

The same held true for sanitation in Panama City and Colón, where the
United States had treaty rights to prescribe public health regulations but relied
on Panama to implement them. When the two municipal councils wilfully
ignored their instructions, the Zone's advice was uncompromising: to deprive
the Panamanians of their enforcement powers – as the treaty allowed – and
transfer them to U.S. tribunals sitting in Panama. As with Goethals's call for
an Army take-over, however, this was excessively strong meat for the State
Department to stomach. In the view of the departmental solicitor, the charge
of Panamanian neglect was 'not unlike that which might be brought against the
authorities of some supposedly well-governed American communities, and does
not seem to be of a character beyond prospect of correction by the local

---

[60] GSR, 12621, Edwards to Bliss, 23.5.16. Goethals Papers, Feuille to Goethals, 28.6.16.
[61] SD, 1910–49, 819.00/553, Dulles to Lansing, 18.5.16; /529, Price to Lansing, 3.4.16;
/644, Wright memo of 7.2.16; /576, Lansing to Wilson, 26.6.16.
[62] SD, 1910–49, 819.00/582, Price to Lansing, 1.7.16; Lansing to Wilson, 3.7.16; /587, Price
to Lansing, 6.7.16.
[63] SD, 1910–49, 819.00/573, Price to Lansing, 7.6.16; 819.1052/65 and /98, both Price to
Lansing, 11.4.16 and 18.5.16. PC, 80-G-1, Johannes to Harding, 5.6.16.

authorities, *if a good fire can be built under them*'. The most the department was ready to do was to threaten Panama with action if it refused to respond. A promise of full compliance was enough to defuse the crisis.[64]

Washington, however, was looking for more than promises, as Panama well knew, so in the weeks before Valdés's inauguration it offered a new electoral law to bring in the secret ballot and proportional representation. A team of U.S. police sergeants should take charge of the police. On fiscal matters there was a deafening silence. Price therefore had Valdés annul the appointment of Juan Demóstenes Arosemena as attorney general on the ground of his virulent anti-Americanism, while demanding that the effective commandant of the police should henceforth be a U.S. officer. Goethals made the same point, and he was even more insistent that Washington should also have total control over the Panamanian treasury – the item so conspicuously absent from Panama's agenda.[65]

The drive to place Panama's finances on an even keel produced very little immediate result. By August 1916 the $1.2 million loan had all been spent on debt repayments, but the country was still more than $500,000 in arrears. So another loan was sought – for $600,000, with $80,000 on account; the State Department approved only the $80,000. Soon after Valdés's installation, Price reported that the new régime was accumulating obligations at the rate of close on $100,000 a month. Moreover, it had promised the job of national auditor to the same J. D. Arosemena whom Price had so recently vetoed as attorney general! Price was told to confer with Goethals's successor, Chester Harding, and submit a watertight scheme for reform. As sanctioned by Secretary of State Robert Lansing, this provided for an American financial adviser but saved Panama's face by vesting control in the president. Valdés might thus 'be persuaded perhaps to enforce the plans of the adviser, pressure if necessary being exerted for the purpose'.[66]

That remained to be seen. Meanwhile the battle for solvency rumbled on. The unassigned balance of the annuity was dedicated to whittling down a debt to the Canal which in February 1917 stood at $247,000 and was swelling by up to $15,000 a month. In March, Price stifled yet another bid to repatriate the Constitutional Fund from New York, but he believed that only 'the day

[64] SD, 1910–49, 811F.124/40, Goethals to Garrison, 21.1.16; /41, Feuille to Harding, 9.2.16; /46, Solicitor memo of 17.3.16 (emphasis in original); /43, Lansing to Baker, 24.4.16; /45, Acting Health Officer memo of 12.6.16; Price to Lansing, 19.6.16.

[65] SD, 1910–49, 819.00/633, Stabler memo of 5.9.16; /612, Price to Lansing, 22.9.16; 819.1052/100, Price to Lansing, 26.9.16; 711.19/15, Stabler memo of 7.10.16.

[66] SD, 1910–49, 819.51/103, Price to Lansing, 10.8.16; /104, Lansing to Price, 20.10.16; /112, Price to Lansing, 24.10.16; 711.19/15, Polk to Price, 7.11.16; Lansing to Price, 1.12.16; /16, Price to Lansing, 3.12.16; Lansing to Price, 8.12.16.

of extremity' would make Panama accept alien stewardship. For Harding, 'the evils of grafting upon the public treasury' were so deeply rooted that they would have to be cut out by American surgery.[67]

The operation was postponed, however, by the need to keep Panama closely aligned with the United States as Wilson moved towards war with Germany. Thus Lansing told Dulles that the Constitutional Fund could be made exempt from U.S. federal tax if Panama became a belligerent. In April 1917, after the outbreak of war, the Panamanians were bold enough to ask for an advance of forty annuities – $10 million – as their share of the cost of completing the Chiriqui railway. It could be authorised, they claimed, by the act empowering the secretary of the Treasury to lend to Washington's wartime associates. No mention was made of a financial adviser.[68]

The issue of the police was likewise soft-pedalled, and for the same reason. Feuille, indeed, did not think supervision of the police was essential. The Panamanians understood that the Zone would not hesitate to invoke the powers granted by Article 7, and the presence of the U.S. Army provost guard in the terminals tended to impress this on them. This was an extraordinarily complacent view, but it was shared by Edwards's successor. Wartime relations with Panama were perfectly amicable, he told Washington, and should not be disturbed by raising the vexed question of policing power. When in September 1917 A. R. Lamb of the District of Columbia Police Department was taken on as instructor and inspector of police, the State Department appeared content enough to leave the definition of his authority entirely in the hands of Panama.[69]

The Panamanians immediately tried to exploit the relaxation by setting up a national guard. The idea had been put forward by Edwards's naval adviser, Captain William Pratt, when he suggested raising a Panamanian levy on the model of the Philippine Scouts. The plan was endorsed by Edwards, who maintained that Panama had 'several thousand men of military age, accustomed to riding and the use of fire arms [whose] courage and staying powers have been proved in former revolutions'. This portrayal of a potential nation in arms was glaringly at odds with the fact that soon after U.S. entry into the war the peasants of the interior fled to the mountains to avoid the conscription which had brought them so much suffering in the disastrous rebellion of 1899–1902.

[67] SD, 1910–49, 711.1928/33, Panamana note of 20.11.16; /39, Baker to Lansing, 13.2.17; 819.011/6, Lansing to Price, 29.1.17; /11, Price to Lansing, 15.3.17; 819.51/135, Price to Lansing, 19.3.17; /138, Harding report of 31.3.17.

[68] Thomas Bailey, *The policy of the United States toward the neutrals, 1917–1918* (Baltimore, 1942), 27 n. 43. SD, 1910–49, 819.154/19, Panama Commissioners to Lansing, 27 (?).4.17; 819.77/283, Panama memo of 15.5.17.

[69] PC, 80-G-1, Feuille to Harding, 9.3.17. AG, post-1917, 250.13, Plummer to Adjutant General, 25.7.17. SD, 1910–49, 819.1052/111, /113, /117, all Price to Lansing, 11.8.17, 1.9.17, 6.10.17.

Even so, Valdés proposed a militia 5,000 strong, with Americans as its senior officers. The offer was hailed by the commanding general. 'The habits and virtues inculcated by military training are just the ones that are lacking to these people,' he cabled the War Department. Panama would always be 'difficult to supervise and protect until the qualities referred to are stimulated and developed'.[70]

The reaction in Washington was nowhere near so warm. Equipping the American Expeditionary Force for France had first call on the country's resources, quite apart from 'the disadvantages of creating near the Panama Canal, an alien armed and trained force, with the consequent possible effect of German propaganda'. In the opinion of Jordan Stabler, head of the State Department's Division of Latin American Affairs, the best response would be to bat the issue back and forth until it died of inanition. By the early months of 1918 it had.[71]

So too had a related Panamanian plan to convert 200 of the police into a corps d'élite, to combine the functions of prison guards and presidential janissaries. They would be allowed to carry rifles, but the weapons would 'never be used against American citizens'. Panama also envisaged the detachment as the nucleus of an army which would inhibit the coups predictable in a state 'lying in the heated tropical zone, where men of all climates and races come together'. The State Department took a diametrically opposed view. The disbandment of the army in 1904 had removed a dangerous threat to the civil power in Panama, and Washington was determined that things would stay that way. The only military presence of any significance on the isthmus would be under exclusive American control – namely, the U.S. Army itself. As Price put it, 'Our army was really their army, because they thereby ... possessed an armed force without any of the expenses of maintaining it.'[72]

Yet though the Zone and the Republic had achieved peaceful coexistence, by the end of 1918 relations had hit rock bottom. In part the responsibility lay with the new garrison commander, General Richard Blatchford, who wielded the powers of governor during wartime. Blatchford was determined to root out vice in the terminal cities, bringing on the worst collision with Panama since the protectorate began.

Army concern with the vice problem predated the arrival of Blatchford. In the summer of 1915 Edwards had asked for funds to help suppress the sale of

---

[70] GB, 426–1, Pratt, 'The local defenses of the Canal Zone', 1.6.16. WCD, 6178–56, Edwards report of 31.3.17. SD, 1910–49, 763.72/5324, Price to Lansing, 6.6.17; 819.154/27, Panama memo of 4.5.17. WCD, 7899–6, Memo of 8.5.17. AG, post-1917, 322.8, Memo of 9.5.17.

[71] WCD, 7899–4, Baker to Lansing, 24.4.17; 7899–9, Johnston memo of 18.7.17; 7899–12, Memo of 16.1.18. SD, 1910–49, 819.154/29, Stabler to Brown, 12.9.17.

[72] AG, post-1917, 322.8, Valdés to Plummer, 31.5.17. SD, 1910–49, 819.20, Price to Lansing, 8.9.17; 819.20/1, Garay to Price, 10.10.17; /9, Solicitor memo of 1.2.18; /2, Lansing to Price, 21.11.17; /5, Price to Lansing, 2.11.17.

cocaine to the troops, only to be told that there was no warrant for action.
Washington was similarly deaf to a call for American regulation of Panamanian
brothels and saloons after a circular from the secretary of war ordered 'absolute
repression' of prostitution within a five-mile radius of military training camps.
This was formally on the ground that the National Defense Act did not apply
to the Zone. The real reason was, as Price reported, that the red-light establishments were owned by 'some of the wealthiest and most influential men in
Panama' and the War Department was unwilling to face a confrontation with
them on this issue.[73]

The men on the spot did not see it that way. In May 1918 Blatchford urged
a U.S. take-over of policing and sanitation as the only solution. When approval
from the secretary of state was not forthcoming, he had to try a different tack.
The police did nothing after the stabbing of two U.S. Navy ratings in Cocoa
Grove on 21 May, and Inspector Lamb admitted that whenever he had Panamanians arrested for offences against Americans, judges refused to convict
them. Blatchford therefore issued a general order forbidding officers and enlisted
men of both Army and Navy from entering Panama except on duty. The ban
was to remain in force until vice in Panama was as efficiently controlled as it
was in the Zone. Meanwhile, Panama would be bereft of the spending power of
the armed forces, worth no less than $100,000 a month. On 14 June, Blatchford
tightened the screw still further with a second order prohibiting introduction
into the Zone of alcohol, drugs, and prostitutes.[74]

This fell short of the wholesale action Blatchford wanted, but within a
fortnight events in Panama brought it about. On 4 June the sudden death of
President Valdés triggered a political earthquake. Elections for the National
Assembly were due on 7 July, and the Assembly would choose the man to see
out the remainder of Valdés's term. In panic the government deferred the poll
indefinitely. Porras, as would-be successor to Valdés, telegraphed Lansing that
the postponement was designed to block the victory of the debauchers of the
U.S. Army! Lansing's reply to this impudence was to order the intervention
which he had been so anxious to avoid.[75]

Blatchford seized with both hands the chance to purge Panama of its iniquity.
On 28 June the Panamanian police lost their jurisdiction, saloons and brothels
were closed, and the carrying of fire-arms was banned. At the same time, he

[73] AG, 1784–1917, 2274896, Edwards to Wood, 28.7.15; Judge Advocate General to Adjutant
General, 22.9.15. SD, 1910–49, 819.1151/81, Baker circular of 10.8.17; /11 and /12, Price
to Lansing, 10.10.17 and 27.2.18. WPD, 8082–125, War Plans Division memo of 25.5.18.
[74] SD, 1910–49, 819.1151/31, Wells memo of 25.4.18; Blatchford to Adjutant General, 3.5.18;
Lamb to Blatchford, 28.5.18; Blatchford to Adjutant General, 14.6.18; 811F.124/52, Price
to Lansing, 3.6.18; /54, Greene to Lansing, 19.6.18.
[75] SD, 1910–49, 819.00/651 and 652, Price to Lansing, 4.6.18 and 11.6.18; /657, Greene to
Lansing, 21.6.18; /662, Porras to Lansing, 27.6.18; 819.1151/17, Lansing to Greene, 27.6.18.

planned to deport all foreign prostitutes and seal off the remainder in quarantine camps for medical treatment. Though U.S. forces began to pull out on 9 July, Panama was warned that any recidivism by police or courts would bring back Army control, and the price for withdrawal was a batch of ordinances banning the sale of liquor to servicemen and outlawing the opium traffic. No American forces would be allowed into the terminals until the fumigation was complete.[76]

Yet the central purpose of the intervention had been to restore Panama to constitutionality. Here the outcome was bizarre, to say the least. After an election held under American supervision, preliminary returns gave the opposition twenty seats in the Assembly to the government's thirteen. The way thus seemed clear for an opposition candidate to be selected as president, most likely Ricardo Arias. Moreover, the opposition quickly accepted the demands put to both parties by Lansing, including reform of the police and the judicial system and the end of the national lottery. Porras's reply was evasive by comparison, but Lansing agreed to his request for a special American commission to check the vote for the Assembly. After three weeks' deliberation, the commission reversed the provisional result and made the government the winner. With the State Department's blessing, Porras became president of Panama for the second time.[77]

Blatchford meantime had become a man with the mission of bringing moral hygiene to the Panamanians. 'The United States has rid them of the evils of yellow fever,' he told Washington, 'and why should it not rid them of the greater curse?' This would mean American surveillance 'for . . . as long as this Canal lasts, and it is certain in my mind that the Canal will attain an age equal to that of the pyramids of Egypt, and then some'. It would also mean that the Panamanian oligarchy was not untouchable. 'If there is any real cleanup,' Blatchford wrote, 'it must start with the property owners.' As a first step, an act of Congress should perpetuate the ban of 14 June and keep the Zone bone-dry, dope-free, and clear of whoredom. This would then be followed by the assumption of complete jurisdiction over Panama's police, courts, and gaols.[78]

The State Department's immediate priority, however, was to impose some degree of American control over the police and the budget. In September, Feuille was asked to draft bills for passage by the National Assembly, one for a

---

[76] NYT, 30.6.18, 8/4. WPD, 8082–142, Blatchford to Adjutant General, 28.6.18. SD, 1910–49, 819.00/712, Military order of 9.7.18. NYT, 11.7.18, 10/8.

[77] SD, 1910–49, 819.00/671, Lansing to Greene, 3.7.18; /695, Greene to Lansing, 19.7.18; /661, Greene to Lansing, 23.6.18; /667, Lansing to Greene, 1.7.18; /690, Greene to Lansing, 17.7.18; /708, Greene to Lansing, 23.7.18; /700, Lansing to Greene, 31.7.18; /742, Price to Lansing, 3.9.18; /754, Stabler memo of 10.9.18; /789 Price to Lansing, 12.10.18.

[78] WPD, 8082–149, Blatchford to Adjutant General, 6.8.18. SD, 1910–49, 811F.20/76, Greene to Lansing, 6.8.18; 819.1151/31, Blatchford to Fosdick, 13.8.18; /24, Blatchford to Greene, 24.8.18; /31, Blatchford to Adjutant General, 1.10.18.

police commissioner and one for a fiscal agent. The commissioner would be given 'full power to control, instruct, and guide', and he would be responsible to the president alone. This satisfied the State Department's instinctive preference for obliquity. 'Instead of attempting to force its own will on Panama,' commented Stabler, 'the Government of the United States will induce the President by means of careful suggestions to carry out its policy and save any criticism of an attempt to injure or eliminate the sovereignty of Panama.' In January 1919 Porras signed the bill, and in February Lamb was re-engaged for two years with the title of inspector general.[79]

The bill for the fiscal agent granted him 'control and charge of the national treasury'. He too would deal directly with the president, though Porras had his own very imaginative financial ideas. Liberia, he understood, had been granted a war credit of $5 million. Why not a credit of $2 million for Panama or, better still, a loan of $3 million, put together by discounting twelve annuities? The railway loan could thereby be repaid and the balance used for road construction and an agricultural bank. Panama should also be given $1 million for land requisitioned by the Zone. So far it had had no compensation, and it suffered many other handicaps: the Zone's non-payment of water rates; the Commissary; the tax exemption of U.S. companies operating in the Zone and of the Panama Railroad; and the prospective loss of lottery revenue of up to $200,000 a year. With a man such as this in the *presidencia*, the fiscal agent was likely to have a hard row to hoe, but the bill was signed, and the post went to Addison Ruan, financial adviser to Haiti since July 1916.[80]

There remained the question of what to do about vice in the terminal cities. On Armistice Day, 11 November 1918, the men of the Atlantic bases erupted after nearly six months of enforced abstinence, running wild through Colón in a bacchanalian mob. That evening in the Balboa stadium, Blatchford publicly condemned Panama City and Colón, which he said 'could very readily be renamed – call one Sodom, the other Gomorrah – it will make no difference which is which'. 'If Sodom and Gomorrah were in existence today,' he subsequently affirmed to Washington, 'they would probably sue me for slander.'[81]

Blatchford's Armistice Night speech destroyed any possibility that he would get cooperation from Panama, but he had also made important enemies in the Zone. Governor Harding was wholly out of sympathy with the purification campaign, and he was outraged when the general accused Canal employees of

[79] SD, 1910–49, 819.1052/130, Baker to Lansing, 6.9.18; 819.51/158, Feuille to Harding, 19.10.18; 819.00/782, Stabler memo of 20.9.18; 819.1052/141, Price to Lansing, 14.1.19; /146, Price to Lansing, 20.2.19.
[80] SD, 1910–49, 819.51/158, Feuille to Harding, 19.10.18; 819.00/782, Porras memo of 16.9.18; 819.51/182, Price to Lansing, 31.12.18.
[81] MID, 153–17–2, Memo of 18.1.19 commenting on Winslow letter of 18.11.18. SD, 1910–49, 819.1151/31, Blatchford to Price, 22.11.18; Blatchford to Adjutant General, 12.12.18.

moral laxity. The commanding officer of Coco Solo was likewise furious at the efforts of 'the Army, the Red Cross, the Y.M.C.A. and other Organizations . . . to have the Navy run according to their desires and principles'. In January 1919 Blatchford put out yet another reform decree, but his time was running out. On 23 February the civil administration of the Zone reverted to Harding, who chose not to enforce the ban on bringing liquor in from Panama, while the Navy allowed its libertymen into the terminals. When Blatchford refused to permit his troops to follow suit there was near-mutiny.[82]

Only after Blatchford's departure at the end of April could his successor come to terms. On 19 July the soldiery of the garrison resumed their off-duty pastimes across the Zone line, with one exception. The purchase of hard liquor was forbidden, though in the light of Panama's previous attitudes to law enforcement, that was no more than a gesture. So ended Blatchford's great anti-vice crusade. It had yet to be seen, as the Canal faced up to the post-war years, whether the push to rehabilitate Panama in other areas would also lose its momentum.[83]

The twenties, 1919–1929

At the end of the First World War the protectorate had entered what seemed a much more intensive phase. The Army had stepped in to guarantee the elections and launched an energetic drive against vice, and Americans were brought in as inspectors of police and finance. It was, reported Minister William Jennings Price, 'a gratifying situation and one perhaps unique as compared with that of any other Latin-American country'. Yet the 1920s did not see Washington retain a decisive grip on Panama. Elections went unsupervised, the anti-vice campaign ran out of steam, and the two inspectors were soon no more than ciphers.[84]

The pattern for the decade was set from the start. In January 1920 President Porras resigned to stand for election in July. Convinced that the ballot would be rigged, supporters of his opponent, Ciro Urriola, repeatedly petitioned for U.S. supervision, only to be told the answer was no. Faced with this political death sentence, Urriola pulled out. Porras again entered office by a walkover.[85]

Porras undoubtedly owed a great deal to American willingness to let the corrupt processes of Panamanian democracy take their course. Soon afterwards,

[82] PC, 88-A-86, Blatchford to Harding, 5.12.18. SNGC, 21498:322, Calhoun memo of 30.4.19. PC, 88-A-21, Harding to Flint, 28.2.19; Harding memo of 12.3.19. SD, 1910–49, 819.1151/46, Price to Lansing, 15.3.19.

[83] SD, 1910–49, 819.1151/51, Price to Lansing, undated; /52, Price to Lansing, 16.7.19; /54, Price to Lansing, 23.7.19.

[84] SD, 1910–49, 819.51A/16, Price to Hughes, 9.4.21.

[85] SD, 1910–49, 819.00/878, Price to Lansing, 26.1.20; /950, Price to Colby, 24.5.20; /959, Colby to Price, 21.7.20; /976, Colby to Price, 1.8.20.

however, he survived thanks to a sudden reversal of U.S. inaction, when troops were rushed in to save him from an angry mob besieging the *presidencia*. The occasion was a border dispute with Costa Rica. The frontier had been delimited by two arbitral judgements, the second by Chief Justice Edward White of the U.S. Supreme Court, but Panama had never accepted the White award. In February 1921 Costa Rica took matters into its own hands by seizing the village of Coto. Though it was quickly retaken by a Panamanian expedition, Porras unwisely told the press that he believed war 'over a valueless piece of land' would be an absurdity. Hence the patriotic demonstration and the speedy rescue mission.[86]

Panamanian nationalists planned to draw Washington in even deeper. Acting Governor Jay Morrow was asked to supply weapons for a conscript army, and Secretary of State Charles Evans Hughes was called on to implement the U.S. guarantee of Panama's independence under Article 1 of the canal treaty. Both refused. For Morrow an army would only increase 'the danger of a radical movement of a revolutionary nature'. For Hughes the treaty guarantee would apply only when Panama agreed to the White award. To the argument that the United States could not be neutral where the interests of its protégé were concerned, he responded with the quibble that Article 1 made no reference to Panama's territory. Porras had sixty days to evacuate Coto or face the consequences of an American police action. In August, when Panama had still not budged, a battalion of Marines was despatched to compel withdrawal. Five days later Porras bowed to the ultimatum.[87]

In the immediate aftermath of this capitulation, Porras was anxious to divert popular fury to Washington. Foreign Minister Narciso Garay consequently warned Hughes that feeling was so explosive that the United States might have to invoke Article 7 of the treaty and patrol the terminal cities to prevent an assault on the canal. Morrow was more than ready to oblige and notified Porras that he was poised to order troops in. But he did so without the permission of Secretary of War John Weeks, who made no secret of his displeasure, and the incident opened a lengthy argument over the best way to handle Panama in future.[88]

For Morrow's deputy, Meriwether Walker, Panama was like an American

[86] MID, 2501–19, Cruse reports of 23.2.21 and 28.2.21; Morrow to Baker, 28.2.21. *NYT*, 1.3.21, 1/1. SD, 1910–49, 819.51A/16, Price to Hughes, 9.4.21. The background to the border dispute is covered in McCain, *United States and the Republic of Panama*, 119–41.

[87] MID, 2501–19, Gulick to Nolan, 26.2.21. *NYT*, 27.2.21, 1/1. SD, 1910–49, 718.1915/310, Price to Hughes, 4.3.21. PC, 80-G-7, Morrow to Price, 24.5.21. SD, 1910–49, 718.1915/368A, Hughes to Price, 15.3.21; /438, Garay to Price, 18.3.21; /438, Hughes to Price, 27.4.21. *NYT*, 22.8.21, 1/8, and 24.8.21, 1/4.

[88] SD, 1910–49, 819.00/1053, Lefevre to Hughes, 28.10.21. *NYT*. 4.9.21, 7/5. PC, 80-G-2, Walker to Flint, 23.1.22. SD, 1910–49, 811F.812/914 and 920.

city which had to ask the state or federal government for troops in an emergency. The Zone was cast in the rôle of a state governor empowered to act as law enforcer 'even if the city authorities do not call for aid'. This offered a revealing insight into the Zone's view of its relationship with Panama, and Walker's interpretation of Article 7 was correspondingly sweeping. Intervention would be justified 'if the safety or independence of the Republic . . . were in jeopardy, or if the police force of Panama were unable to properly protect either the citizens of . . . Panama or . . . the United States'.[89]

To Hughes, on the other hand, intervention would be valid only 'if any situation should arise in either of the cities . . . which might imperil the tranquility of the Canal Zone or the orderly operation of the Canal, or expose the life and property of Americans and other foreigners within the two cities themselves to danger'. During the summer of 1922 he denied multiple requests from Morrow and Minister John Glover South for 'some very drastic steps' to curb Porras's arbitrary treatment of his political enemies. And whereas they wanted to install American judges in Panamanian courts, Hughes would countenance intervention 'only in case of very serious rioting wholly beyond the control of the local police and . . . limited to assisting the legally constituted authorities to restore order'.[90]

The same reluctance underlay the department's approach to the 1924 presidential election. Hughes was under no illusions about Porras or his hand-picked successor, Rodolfo Chiari. In the summer of 1923 Porras took leave of absence to validate a contract for a legal textbook, which he had allegedly plagiarised from a work by an American academic. Chiari was said to have debts of over half a million dollars. But Hughes was deaf to South's contention that the U.S. guarantee of Panama's independence 'denies to the people their right to revolt'. This was to take the opposition's hyperbole at face value; and the head of the department's Latin American Division was certain that its programme did not differ from 'the high-sounding bunkum common to opposition parties in the neighborhood'. When in January 1924 Porras told South he would never ask for intervention, that was all right by Hughes.[91]

An additional reason for Washington's inertia was an unwillingness to rock the boat during the treaty negotiations then reaching their climax. The chief U.S. delegate, Francis White, assured his Panamanian counterpart that intervention would take place only if American lives were threatened, as they had recently been in Honduras, where U.S. forces were landed after the outbreak of

[89] PC, 80-G-2, Walker to Flint, 23.1.22.
[90] SD, 1910–49, 819.00/1053, Hughes to Lefevre, 9.3.22; /1063, Hughes to South, 11.8.22; /1065, Morrow to Weeks, 8.6.22; /1078, Hughes to South, 6.9.22.
[91] SD, 1910–49, 819.001.P82/20, South to Hughes, 13.6.23. PC, 80-H-10, Morrow to White, 1.2.23. SD, 1910–49, 819.00/1099, Chargé to Hughes, 26.6.23; /1105, South to Hughes, 22.11.23; /1113, Reed to White, undated; /1110, South to Hughes, 23.1.24; /1111, Hughes to South, 14.3.24.

civil war. White was well aware that Porras was up to all the tricks usual in an election year, but change had to come from within, not be imposed by diktat. As polling day drew near, the department's main preoccupation was to stop Governor Morrow from provoking a crisis by ordering troops in ill-advisedly. Two weeks after Chiari's predictable victory, South's proposal for a new electoral law was dismissed with the comment that it was better to leave things as they were than to exert pressure for reform.[92]

Thus Panama's politics free-wheeled merrily along with only nominal reference to what the United States might think. So too did its finances, in spite of a herculean struggle by the fiscal agent, Addison Ruan, to bring order out of the chaos he found on taking over in 1919. Confronted by an internal debt of some $1.5 million, Ruan proposed to refund it with a loan partly secured by the unpledged $60,000 of the canal annuity. But there were rival claimants to the $60,000. President Porras wanted it for the Chiriqui Railroad, yet since 1916 it had been allotted to the Canal to reduce an accumulated debt for services to Panama which by October 1918 stood at $300,000. After a year of wrangling, the Canal was given priority. The railway extension was again postponed, and Ruan agreed to liquidate the internal debt by dipping into a healthy budget surplus, which at the close of 1920 ran to no less than $2.7 million.[93]

Porras was not short of plans for spending whatever money lay to hand. Without consulting Ruan, he mortgaged the country's main export revenue from bananas to borrow $150,000 from the United Fruit Company for a national archive. His schemes also included warehouses in Panama City, a sanatorium, a penal colony, a secretarial school for women, and a census. Above all, he wanted to put through the ambitious development programme drafted by Clarence Owens, a leading American farm economist. It envisaged an agricultural college with an extension service to educate the peasantry in the field, an agricultural bank offering low-interest credit to farmers, a road network to create a nationwide market, and a Pan-American college of commerce to establish Panama as the centre of hemispheric trade.[94]

Ruan did not share Porras's enthusiasms. For him, wiping out the government's existing liabilities came well before taking on new ones, and Price was

---

[92] SD, 1910–49, 819.00/1120A and 1123, White memo of conversation, 19.5.24 and 18.6.24; /1138, Lamb to South, 24.6.24; /1139, Reed to White, 18.7.24; /1136, South to Hughes, 26.7.24; /1135, Reed memo of 13.8.24. On Honduras, see Dana Munro, *The United States and the Caribbean republics, 1921–1933* (Princeton, N.J., 1974), 126–35.

[93] SD, 1910–49, 819.51/191, Price to Lansing, 20.2.19; 819.51A/24, Ruan to Hughes, 18.12.22; 819.77/291, Lefevre to Lansing, 20.11.18; 819.51/198, Price to Lansing, 20.2.19; /158, Feuille to Harding, 19.10.18; /196, Baker to Lansing, 5.3.19; 711.1928/64, Lefevre to Lansing, 21.3.19; /75, Baker to Lansing, 5.3.19; 819.51/256, Price to Lansing, 14.2.20.

[94] SD, 1910–49, 819.51/197, /223, /221, /238, all Price to Lansing, 12.3.19, 18.6.19, 23.6.19, 3.10.19. *NYT*, 7.5.19, 17/2. MID, Owens report of June 1919. SD, 1910–49, 819.51/230, Owens to Lansing. 4.8.19.

convinced that Porras's cronies would see Owens's grand design as a succulent pork barrel. His suspicions were reinforced by a National Assembly bill requiring the Treasury to cash all drafts submitted by cabinet ministers. This bypassed Ruan, who had so far enjoyed the power to refuse payment of improper claims. When the U.S. legation stamped on the manoeuvre, Porras issued a decree turning over to the Highway Commission the $2.3 million road fund Ruan had built up. He then announced that the law creating Ruan's post (which he himself had signed) was unconstitutional. Under pressure from Washington, Porras gave way, and in March 1921 Ruan's contract was renewed for two years.[95]

His troubles were far from over, however. In May, Porras told Price that he would 'not be treated by our government in everything like a child'. A year later he refused to accept the State Department's condition that the Chiriqui Railroad extension could be built only if the contract were supervised by Ruan and the American engineer on the Highway Commission, R. K. West. Meanwhile, the budget surplus had been reduced to less than $1 million by the commitment to expenditure on roads, and because of the world trade depression, Panama's main source of income, customs revenues, had fallen sharply. But Porras ignored Ruan's warnings that road construction would have to be abandoned unless drastic economies were brought in. The National Assembly for its part believed it could square the circle by releasing the Constitutional Fund from New York and devoting it to the road programme and an agricultural bank. In December, Ruan decided that enough was enough and resigned.[96]

Ruan's departure heightened the feeling in the State Department that the whole policy of fiscal intervention was pointless. Treaty negotiations with Panama were on the horizon, and keeping Panama sweet was more important. While admitting the near-certainty of Panamanian recidivism if U.S. guidance lapsed, the legation opposed a replacement for Ruan with power to override the president. Porras himself made sure of that with a decree which bound the fiscal agent hand and foot. The State Department raised no objection, and in July 1923 the former auditor of the Canal, Judge Walter Warwick, came back to the isthmus to take the job.[97]

By the time of Warwick's arrival, Panama had emptied the road fund and

[95] SD, 1910–49, 819.51/233, /241, /273, all Price to Lansing, 24.8.19, 17.5.19, 29.9.20; 819.154/70, Price to Colby, 11.2.21; 819.51A/1, /4, /9, /14, all Price to Colby, 15.2.21, 21.2.21, 25.2.21, 3.3.21; 819.154/71, Price to Colby, 15.2.21.

[96] SD, 1910–49, 819.51/305, Price to Hughes, 16.5.21; 819.77/316, Hughes to South, 24.5.22; /320, Panamanian legation to Hughes, 10.6.22; /316, South to Hughes, 3.5.22; 819.51/338, /350, /356, /357, all South to Hughes, 18.5.22, 14.9.22, 15.11.22, 15.12.22; 819.51A/24, Ruan to Hughes, 18.12.22.

[97] SD, 1910–49, 819.51A/19, Hughes to South, 7.9.22; /26, Munro memo of 5.1.23; /49, South to Hughes, 25.4.23; /34, South to Hughes, 16.3.23.

borrowed $4.5 million to complete the highway network, a loan guaranteed by income from the Constitutional Fund and the unassigned balance of the canal annuity. Through this commitment, in South's view, Panama had now 'mortgaged her entire patrimony and has no further actual bowering capacity'. She had also acquired a fiscal agent tailor-made to Panamanian specifications. Porras had wanted Warwick rather than Ruan in 1918, and Warwick soon showed why. He had, reported South, 'sat back and allowed the Government to do practically as it has seen fit, even to the extent of purchasing new, expensive automobiles for the use of the President and his Cabinet, including one for the Fiscal Agent himself'. 'I think it is about time we jacked Warwick up,' concluded the State Department's senior Latin Americanist with a sigh in the summer of 1924. It was in fact too late. The pass had been sold, and though the wayward Porras was about to leave office, his successor's disposition for reform was not rated high. The experiment in teaching Panama the rudiments of good husbandry appeared to have run its course.[98]

So too had the effort to remodel the Panamanian police and the associated campaign to clean up the sexual facilities of the terminal cities. The question of vice reared its head once more early in 1921 with the re-establishment of the red-light district in Panama City. This the municipality had set up in June 1918 as a reprisal against the U.S. military occupation of the cities, and the onus of regulating the district was placed on the Canal's health department. The move was made to embarrass the canal administration, in the knowledge that control of prostitution had always been anathema to the Manichaean Anglo-Saxon mind, and it succeeded. Though the State Department believed Washington had the right to combat venereal disease in Panama, the Canal dumped the problem in the lap of the Panamanian authorities, along with drink and drugs. Physical sanitation in the cities was an American responsibility; their moral disinfection was not. All Governor Morrow was prepared to do, as the isthmian whorehouses geared themselves up for a visit by the U.S. fleet, was to bar prostitutes from landing in the Zone.[99]

Cancellation of the visit left the issue hanging fire, but in spite of the rising VD rate among U.S. enlisted men, Washington refused to act. Urged on by the Women's Home Missionary Society to 'do all in your power to close the Brothels and Saloons . . . for the protection of our boys', the Navy Department's only response was that 'any objectionable activities in Panama' were beyond its control. And as long as Panama would neither suppress them nor

[98] SD, 1910–49, 819.51/370, South to Hughes, 16.3.23; /391, Hughes to W. A. Harriman & Co., Inc., 22.5.23; 819.154/103, South to Hughes, 8.12.23; 819.51/172, Price to Lansing, 23.11.18; 819.154/115, South to Hughes, 11.4.24; 819.51/414, Reed to White, 10.6.24.

[99] SD, 1910–49, 819.1151/70, Price to Colby, 22.1.21; /71, Price to Colby, 28.2.21; /57, Lansing to Price, 29.10.19; /59, Feuille to Harding, 18.12.19; /75, Price to Hughes, 17.11.21. SNGC, 28076–49, Morrow memo of 17.11.21.

bring them under more than the laxest supervision, they remained a running
sore in every sense of the word.[100]

Even that, however, was deemed preferable to an expensive, laborious, and
probably futile struggle to scour the moral sink of Panama City and Colón.
Quietism remained the order of the day, even though during the treaty negotiations the State Department was momentarily perturbed by two attempts to
extend U.S. rights at Panama's expense. The first covered sanitation. In response
to a Panamanian bid to get sole power to enforce U.S. sanitary regulations in
the terminals, Morrow submitted a draft article making enforcement an exclusive
American responsibility and allowing Washington the right to control public
health throughout Panama. Secretary of State Hughes, anxious 'not to impose
any conditions which might wound the susceptibilities and amour propre of the
Panamans', kept the substance of Morrow's draft but softened the wording.[101]

The second item concerned jurisdiction over U.S. forces on Panamanian
territory, which had been put in the spotlight by two incidents. In December
1924 a U.S. Army ambulance driver accidentally killed a West Indian while
taking an injured worker to hospital in Colón; six weeks later he was called on
to face a charge of homicide before a Panamanian court. Though the case was
soon dropped, a fracas in Colón involving Navy ratings from the base at Coco
Solo revived the question of the legal status of U.S. servicemen in the republic.
For Minister South and the garrison commander, General William Lassiter,
it was important enough to merit a treaty article. Their draft conferred extraterritoriality on members of the armed forces setting foot in Panama 'in any
official capacity'. Both, however, preferred blanket immunity for all Army and
Navy personnel, off as well as on duty. In that way Lassiter believed he would
spare his troops the humiliation of being arrested on the word of a prostitute or
being forced to share a police cell with coloured detainees. Nothing less would
suffice, in the view of the Army's planners, to uphold 'the dignity of the United
States and the maintenance of American prestige in Central American
countries'.[102]

The State Department did not pursue the idea. Though Panama had readily
waived its jurisdiction over men on duty, it understandably drew the line at
wholesale exemption, and Secretary of State Frank Kellogg agreed. Lassiter

[100] SD, 1910–49, 819.1151/87, Weeks to Hughes, 17.8.23. SNGC, 28076–49, Women's Home
Missionary Society to Denby, 9.3.23, and reply of 14.3.23.
[101] SNGC, 28076–47, State Department to Denby, 4.11.21. SD, 1910–49, 711.192/11A, Hughes
to Weeks, 9.2.24; /18, Morrow memo of 25.2.24; /61A, Hughes to Weeks, 29.5.24; /205,
Meeting of 9.7.24. Text of article is in *BD*, 833–4.
[102] *American Journal of International Law*, 21 (1927), 182–7, gives the Panama Supreme Court's
decision on the December 1924 incident. SD, 1910–49, 819.043, South to Kellogg, 28.3.27.
SNGC, 26283–5739, Irwin to Eberle, 22.4.25. SD, 1910–49, 819.0144/55, South to Knox,
22.5.25. AG, post-1917, 388.1, Lassiter to Adjutant General, 23.5.25; War Plans Division
to Chief of Staff, 12.8.25.

refused to take no for an answer and drew up an elaborate contingency plan for intervention. This authorised the military commander to suppress 'sudden riots or brawls' on Panamanian soil affecting U.S. citizens. The task, Lassiter thought, would not be difficult, since Panama was 'unprovided with arms and [had] no effective anarchistic or revolutionary organization'. Work on the plan, however, did not progress beyond the preliminary discussion stage.[103]

The very idea of martial law was, of course, a sign that the protectorate had failed in the sphere of policing. Lamb's appointment in 1919 had been meant to inaugurate a new model police force, apolitical, incorruptible, and highly disciplined. It was not to be. Part of the problem lay in Lamb himself, who rarely crossed his Panamanian masters, and Lamb's amenability was compounded by the State Department's unwillingness to back him. When the governor urged the sale of rifles bought during the Costa Rica imbroglio, he was told it was 'impractical' to approach Panama at that moment. It was therefore not difficult for Panama to treat Lamb as a nobody. One influential oligarch he brought to trial was acquitted, while the grandson of ex-President Arosemena was released from arrest by his Panamanian deputy. In the 1924 election Lamb was powerless to stop Porras from taking the usual percentage of the police payroll as a campaign contribution for Chiari. The crowning snub came in the law of December 1924 putting the police back under the control of a Panamanian, the former commandant Leonidas Pretelt.[104]

Over the next four years the police became a distinct liability to the Chiari administration. In February 1925 they caused a rising by the Indians of San Blas province after an orgy of rape and torture. In October the president could not rely on them to protect him against the fury of rioting tenants in Panama City's slums. Demoralised, as Chiari put it, through 'overwork and propaganda', they saw their rôle as a security force taken over by the U.S. Army at Chiari's importunate request. In the wake of the riots, a so-called reorganisation brought no serious improvement: As U.S. chargé Munro reported, 'after political influence had been brought to bear, only a few friendless individuals were discharged'. The régime's chief preoccupation seemed to be to hire American drill instructors to train a squad which could 'present a creditable appearance' at the Pan-American Congress of 1926. It was possible, thought Munro, that the instructors 'might be made the entering wedge for the realization of other reforms', but this was too much to hope for. Moreover, Lamb was now an embarrassment whose continued presence on the force, in South's opinion, added nothing to U.S.

---

[103] SD, 1910–49, 819.0144/55, Hughes to Weeks and Denby, 26.5.25. PC, 88-A-20, White Plan draft of 30.6.25.

[104] SD, 1910–49, 819.1052/156, Consul General, Panama City to Price, 27.3.19; /162, South to Hughes, 4.11.21; /165, Weeks to Hughes, 1.2.22; Hughes to Weeks, 15.2.22; /175, Lamb to South, 21.7.22; 819.00/1138, Lamb to South, 24.6.24; 819.1052/184, South to Hughes, 12.1.25.

prestige. The cancellation of his contract in November 1928 thus came as no great disappointment.[105]

The watch on Panama's exchequer fared no better than the police inspectorate. Chiari's Treasury secretary, Eusebio Morales, had described the fiscal agency as 'a system of spying' if the agent considered he was 'not a servant of the Nation, but . . . an Agent of the United States Government sent to intervene in our internal affairs'. The budget for 1925 was prepared without reference to Warwick, and Morales planned to abolish the agency when Warwick's contract expired in June. In the event, the job passed to Ruan's assistant, Floyd Baldwin, though at less than half Ruan's salary, and Morales made it clear that he expected it to be a sinecure. The State Department was not disposed to argue. In Secretary Kellogg's view, the agent no longer served any useful purpose; only bankruptcy might bring Panama to its senses where American paternalism had failed.[106]

On the other hand, Washington was not indifferent to Morales's attack on West, chief engineer of the Highway Commission. In January 1925 a bill was brought in to remove West from the commission, but it was blocked by the threat to review the draft treaty pledge to construct roads for Panama through and beyond the Zone. West stayed on, though Munro was sure that his 'tactless and even offensive utterances' proved he was 'not fitted by temperament to deal with a Latin American government'.[107]

In the context of the State Department's indulgence in the late twenties, the stand taken over West was an aberration, and it reverted to type in its attitude to the revival of the project to extend the Chiriqui Railroad – this despite the knowledge that the scheme was putrescent with graft. The original bidder lost the contract after refusing to pay a $100,000 bribe or to give Panama unfettered control of the work. The Panamanian consulting engineer (and future president), Florencio Harmodio Arosemena, did not have to produce a justification for revising his estimates upwards by no less than $600,000. Yet though the revision almost certainly signified embezzlement on a grand scale, the State Department was in no position to query it, since it had been examined by the acting superintendent of the Panama Railroad and found entirely reasonable. Accordingly there was no objection to a loan of $2.2 million, of which $900,000 was devoted to the railway and $1.3 million to road construction.[108]

[105] SNSCC, 1919–26, 117–46, Commander, Special Service Squadron, to Irwin, 2.3.25. SD, 1910–49, 819.00/1209, Munro to Kellogg, 12.10.25; 819.20/18, Munro to Kellogg, 30.10.25, enclosing Lamb to Munro, 26.10.25; 819.1052/192, South to Kellogg, 19.11.28.
[106] SD, 1910–49, 819.51A/54, Morales speech of 27.9.24; /59, Morales memo of 4.4.25; /56, South to Kellogg, 27.3.25; /58, South to Kellogg, 27.3.25; Kellogg to South, 28.4.25.
[107] SD, 1910–49, 819.154/125, South to Hughes, 1.1.25; /134, Reed to White, 14.2.25; /133, Hughes to South, 31.1.25; /149, Munro to Kellogg, 26.9.25.
[108] SD, 1910–49, 819.77/302, Ruan memo of 12.12.19; /358, Kellogg to South, 24.5.26; /363, Memo of 3.6.26; /366, South to Kellogg, 3.8.26; /371, South to Kellogg, 6.11.26; /513, South to Kellogg, 30.11.26; /515, South to Kellogg, 13.12.26.

An even more compelling reason for the department to hold still was, of course, its anxiety to see Panama ratify the treaty signed the previous July. In January 1927, however, when Panama threw away this advantage by refusing ratification, South took it as the chance to redeem Panama from profligacy. His charge-sheet certainly made remarkable reading: $75,000 transferred out of the road loan by Morales for 'general purposes'; $148,000 diverted to build a wharf for a friend of President Chiari's; misuse of a $1 million bond issue in aid of farmers to fund expensive housing developments in Panama City; Chiari's insistence that he be loaned $350,000 of a second $1 million bond flotation.[109]

The answer, however, or so South believed, was not to arm the fiscal agent with swingeing powers but to press for an austerity budget and a ban on illegal payments. When South did so, Chiari and Morales immediately promised economies, but, as Baldwin pointed out, the only thing that could prompt meaningful reform would be State Department leverage. None was applied, and South was certain that Panama would never learn to be provident as long as it could raise foreign loans.[110]

It was therefore the ultimate expression of the department's unconcern that it did nothing to oppose Panama's biggest loan to date, agreed in 1928. It totalled $12 million, almost half of which was dedicated to the road programme and the remainder to retiring the debt outstanding from the loans of 1914 and 1926. Answering a call from the sponsors for a State Department guarantee, White was at pains to tell them that while Washington had made treaty arrangements to protect the finances of Cuba, Haiti, and the Dominican Republic, and while it enjoyed a special relationship with Nicaragua on financial matters, 'such a relationship does not exist with Panama'. In short, the department was not the watchdog of the Panamanian treasury.[111]

Under the administration of President Arosemena, that rôle seemed to have passed to the contractor of the 1928 loan, the National City Bank of New York. In February 1929 the bank sent a three-man commission down to the isthmus to cast an eye over the Panamanian economy. Its findings told the legation nothing it did not already know: The country was saddled with a grossly overmanned bureaucracy and a president too nerveless to push through reform on the necessary scale. The real power in the land was still Chiari, and he was interested only in finding fresh openings for his henchmen – with some success,

[109] SD, 1910–49, 819.51/519, /527, /534, /539, all South to Kellogg, 7.2.27, 25.3.27, 12.5.27, 13.5.27; 819.00/1336, South to Kellogg, 8.2.27.

[110] SD, 819.51/520, /530, /545, all South to Kellogg, 18.2.27, 8.4.27, 17.6.27; 819.51A/68, South to Kellogg, 19.8.27; 819.51/550, South to Kellogg, 12.7.27; Kellogg to South, 10.8.27.

[111] SD, 1910–49, 819.51/623, South to Kellogg, 14.6.28. McCain, *United States and the Republic of Panama*, 108. SD, 1910–49, 819.51/615, Murray, Aldrich, and Roberts to White, 24.5.28, and reply by White, 29.5.28. Texts of the relevant treaties with Cuba, the Dominican Republic, Nicaragua, and Haiti may be found in Malloy, *Treaties*, 1: 363-4, 418–20; *FRUS 1912*, 1074-5, and *FRUS 1915*, 449–51.

to judge by an annual 'leakage' of $800,000. On their return to the United States, the commissioners looked to the State Department for a remedy, hoping it would not let Panama 'undertake too many extras or float a new loan at this time as they were pretty well over their necks now'. Given the department's complaisance throughout the past decade, this was wildly misplaced optimism. The oligarchy for whom malversation was a way of life need fear no disturbance from that quarter.[112]

Nor need it bother about American interference in the political field. Right through Chiari's term of office the State Department consistently held back from involvement whenever it judged American interests not to be at stake. In February 1925 the San Blas Indians publicly appealed to Washington to save them from the assaults of the police. Supporting the Indian cause was the same Richard Marsh who had threatened Panama with occupation in 1910, and he was not alone in his sympathies. South, who negotiated an interim settlement of the dispute, believed that if Panama went back on it the Army should step in. The Army was not, however, sent to San Blas. Between July 1918 and August 1920 U.S. troops had been put into the even more remote province of Chiriqui, but in that case the action could be justified as a necessary defence of American lives and property. In San Blas there was no comparable American presence at risk and consequently no intervention.[113]

By contrast, the Army was ordered into Panama City in October 1925 to hold the ring in a full-scale political crisis triggered when Panamanian landlords raised rents disproportionately after a minuscule increase in property taxes. The resulting formation of a Tenants' League by the left-wing General Workers' Union soon led to criticism of the Zone as well as the landlords, and the Canal's police chief, Guy Johannes, took it seriously. Quiros, the main spokesman of the League, was 'a radical of the worst type', and if he were not 'hushed up or expelled' there would be trouble. A week later Governor Walker instructed his immigration officers to refuse entry to 'Communist Propagandists', and at the end of August Quiros was deported.[114]

In spite of this, the tenants went on to mount a rent boycott, which escalated into riots and a general strike announced for 12 October. That afternoon, with Chiari's official authorisation, a battalion of U.S. troops took over to quell what a harassed Chiari described as 'a revolt against established order'. Chiari's solution, imploring the landlords to rescind the rent increases and improvising an instant public works programme, produced varied reactions in the Zone

[112] SD, 1910–49, 819.51/78, South to Stimson, 11.4.29; /83, Chargé to Stimson 4.5.29; /84, South to Stimson, 9.5.29; /86, White memo of conversation with Brown, 15.5.29.
[113] NYT, 1.3.25, 7/1. SD, 1910–49, 819.00/1154, South to Hughes, 25.2.25; /1162, Kellogg to Wadsworth, 9.3.25; /1186, South to Kellogg, 30.4.25. McCain, United States and the Republic of Panama, 86–7.
[114] ONI, C-10-M 15772, report of 10.11.25. SD, 1910–49, 819.00/1198, Johannes to legation, 20.7.25; /1199, Johannes memo of 27.7.25.

Figure 2. The face of intervention: U.S. Army troops keep order for
Panama, October 1925. (U.S. National Archives)

establishment. For chargé Munro, who put the outburst down entirely to trade
union agitators, it marked a return to 'the vicious policy of providing the
laboring classes in the city with well paid jobs at the Government's expense
in order to obtain their good will'. For Walker and Lassiter, it came nowhere
near tackling the basic causes of the distress, and Lassiter wanted an extended
occupation to put pressure on Chiari to do so. The battalion commander also
hoped for a long-term stay, but one designed to prod Chiari into carrying out
mass evictions. Both men were to be disappointed. All troops were withdrawn
more than a week before the strike ended; yet again the State Department had
recoiled from an engagement that might take it where it did not want to go.[115]

[115] PC, 80-G-2, Burgess to Flint, 13.10.25. SD, 1910–49, 819.00/1216, /1210, /1213, /1225,
/1220, all Munro to Kellogg, 13.10.25, 14.10.25, 16.10.25, 23.10.25, 23.10.25.

In the wake of the rent strike episode, the department was more than ever determined that it alone should decide intervention policy, above all to keep the governor under control. As things stood, the governor could send the Army into Panama without reference to the minister. His right to call in troops dated from the time the Zone was created, but those days had gone, Munro declared, even though the canal administration did not appear to think so.[116]

The Panamanians too were eager for a change of authority away from the governor and his continual urge to keep them in line and towards the relative laissez-faire of an agency which had always preferred to stay aloof from isthmian politics. But when the idea was put to the Zone, it was dismissed out of hand by Executive Secretary McIlvaine. The State Department was conscious of the Canal 'only as a pawn in the diplomatic chess game', and when it came to intervention the governor was best fitted to set policy.[117]

The Zone was overruled. In March 1928 new instructions empowered the minister to direct the use of American forces 'for police duty or for the maintenance of order in Panama in time of civil disturbances'. They resolved the argument unequivocally in the State Department's favour and delivered a body-blow to the Canal's pretensions from which it never recovered.[118]

The revision came into force as battle lines took final shape for the presidential election in August. The rival candidates were two stalking-horses: Florencio Arosemena, Chiari's straw man, and Jorge Boyd, the stand-in for Porras. The previous year Porras had made his last bid for nomination, only to come up against solid State Department disapproval. Kellogg stood firm on the ground Root had taken to repel Porras's supporters in 1905, and when Porras riposted by quoting Roosevelt's 1908 directive to Taft, it cut no ice. Nor did the invocation of Nicaragua, where Washington had just agreed to supervise elections. In Panama, by contrast, Porras contended, the United States not only denied the opposition the right to rebel; it also allowed the government to rig the poll to stay in power.[119]

This was rich, coming from a man who as president had repeatedly fixed elections, but South agreed. 'By prohibiting subversive movements in Panama,' he told Kellogg, 'the United States has deprived that country of its sole defense against the successive perpetuation of unpopular governments by fraud.' Without American supervision, the vote would be a farce. But the most Kellogg would do was to say that he would not recognise an administration elected dishonestly. Boyd, in Washington to make a personal appeal for intervention,

[116] SD, 1910–49, 819.00/1217, Munro to Kellogg, 13.10.25. *BD*, 414.
[117] AG, post-1917, 336, Panama aide-mémoire of 2.8.27. PC, 80-G-2, White memo of 16.9.27; McIlvaine to Walker, 19.11.27.
[118] WPD, 1652–16, Davis to Walker, 19.3.28; Walker to Flint, 31.3.28.
[119] SD, 1910–49, 819.00/1396, undated; /1408, Kellogg to Porras, 23.12.27; /1401, Porras to Kellogg, 28.12.27.

did not bother to return home for the contest, and Arosemena won hands down.[120]

The protectorate of the 1920s thus ended on the note of restraint that had marked it throughout. It had, of course, been a restraint which very much suited Washington's convenience, and it had considerable propaganda value in answering the mounting Latin charges of U.S. oppression which gathered to a head at the end of the twenties. More important, it foreshadowed the disavowal of interventionism which was soon to come and which was to bring with it a formal abandonment of the suzerainties established during the 'big stick' era, in Panama and elsewhere.

[120] SD, 1910–49, 819.00/1429, South to Kellogg, 14.5.28; /1436, Kellogg to South, 6.6.28; / 1458, Kellogg memo of conversation with Alfaro, 18.7.28; /1470, South to Kellogg, 4.8.28. McCain, *United States and the Republic of Panama*, 75–7.

7

Canal defence

Construction decade, 1904–1914

The canal which the United States cut through Panama had a dual rôle to play: as a thoroughfare for maritime commerce and as a conduit for sea-power. But whereas the trade route was intended for the merchant shipping of the world, the strategic highway was designed with only one battle-fleet in mind: the U.S. Navy. In the judgement of General Tasker Bliss, 'it double[d] the military resources of the United States for operations upon the sea in this hemisphere and considerably increase[d] them for operations in the Orient'. By the time it opened, the canal was seen as an indispensable asset destined to enhance the fleet's mobility substantially by allowing a rapid concentration of strength in either Atlantic or Pacific, according to need. For the American public at large for generations to come, it went without saying that Panama was vital to national security.[1]

Yet opinion was sharply divided on how best to defend the prized new possession. Hay's first canal treaty with Britain in 1900 envisaged a neutralised, unfortified transit open to the ships of all nations in war as well as in peace, exempt from blockade within the three-mile limit, and guaranteed by other canal users besides the United States. The precedents invoked were the Clayton–Bulwer convention of 1850 and the Constantinople convention of 1888 regulating the use of the Suez Canal. Another, not cited but equally relevant, was the 1881 treaty between Chile and Argentina renouncing fortification in the Strait of Magellan and declaring it neutralised in perpetuity.[2]

---

[1] JB, File 325, Bliss memo of 10.6.04. Josiah McKean, *The strategic value of the Panama Canal to the Navy* (Washington, D.C., 1914), 8.

[2] *BD*, 116–17. The text of the 1850 convention is in *BD*, 27–30. The texts of the Constantinople convention and the Chile–Argentina treaty are in Clive Parry (ed.), *The consolidated treaty series*, vol. 171 (Dobbs Ferry, N.Y., 1978), 242–6, and vol. 159 (Dobbs Ferry, N.Y., 1977), 46–7.

The 1900 treaty thus took canal defence out of America's hands, and Hay was convinced that this was right. 'No Government not absolutely imbecile', he later wrote, 'would ever think of fortifying.' An alternative to fortification was, of course, available in the shape of the Navy. As the British Admiralty was to point out, the canal could be shut down by blockade regardless of how well fortified it might be, and Admiral George Dewey's answer was a fleet formidable enough to make certain a blockading force never came within range of the canal's approaches.[3]

One of the military members of the Isthmian Canal Commission set up in 1899 agreed with the Admiralty diagnosis but not with Dewey's prescription. In an article published in 1901, Colonel Peter Hains of the Corps of Engineers claimed that forts were no defence against 'a few men . . . with a few pounds of dynamite', who could disable the waterway indefinitely. And they were irrelevant given the fact that 'the nation that controls the adjoining seas will, in time of war, control passage through the canal, no matter which one has possession. . . . If the canal bristled with guns from one end to the other it would be of no use to the United States, while a powerful hostile fleet dominated the Caribbean Sea.' Given the relative inferiority of the U.S. Navy, Hains's solution was 'a neutral canal with a large area of neutral waters at each terminus'. The Commission drew the same conclusion in its report issued in November 1901.[4]

By this time, however, the United States had a president who would not have dreamed of accepting neutralisation. If a neutralised canal had been open during the war with Spain, Theodore Roosevelt believed, the government would have had to let Spanish warships through, even though they might have been on their way to shell the West Coast. Hay's treaty had to be amended to allow for a defended canal, and defence must be by fortification, not by the Navy. Though Roosevelt was to proclaim that 'our justification . . . for digging the Panama Canal must rest primarily upon our willingness to build and maintain a first-class fighting fleet', the first task of that fleet was to engage the enemy's main force, not to cover the canal. 'One prime reason for fortifying our great seaports', Roosevelt lectured Hay, 'is to unfetter our fleet, to release it for offensive purposes; and the proposed canal would fetter it again, for our fleet would have to watch it, and therefore do the work which a fort should do; and which it would do much better.'[5]

---

[3] Alexander Campbell, *Great Britain and the United States 1895–1903* (London, 1960), 65, quoting Hay to Choate, 27.4.01. Cramond Kennedy, 'The canal fortifications and the treaty', *American Journal of International Law*, 5 (1911), 637–8, quoting Dewey memo of 27.2.00. Charles Campbell, *Anglo-American understanding, 1898–1903* (Baltimore, 1957), 216–17, 357–9, quoting Admiralty memo of 5.1.01.

[4] Peter Hains, 'An isthmian canal from a military point of view', *Annals of the American Academy of Political and Social Science*, 17 (1901), 9, 12. Kennedy, 'Canal fortifications', 621–2, quoting ICC report of 16.11.01.

[5] *TR letters*, 2:1188, 1192; 5:546.

The Senate agreed, and the revised Anglo–American treaty gave the United States the free hand Roosevelt had demanded, while the canal convention of 1903 granted Washington the right to protect the waterway with its armed forces and to build whatever fortifications were necessary.[6]

The first move towards fortification came in 1905 with a board of inquiry into coastal defence. Recommendations for batteries at each terminal were accepted in a report which repeated the Rooseveltian argument that coast artillery was the key to unlock the Navy's offensive power. This was rousing stuff, but the report also gave a more sombre reason for land defences, that is, to offset the consequences of a temporary loss of command of the sea. Fortification, in other words, was insurance against the relative weakness of a fleet which still ranked third in the world after the navies of Britain and Germany. When the General Board concluded that gun emplacements offered the best protection against a hostile raiding squadron, it came close to an admission that the United States did not possess the naval resources to interdict such a force. Roosevelt saw the U.S. base at Guantánamo in Cuba as the first line of the canal's Atlantic defences, but the forts provided an essential inner citadel if that line were breached. By the time Roosevelt made way for his successor, Taft, in March 1909, Washington was poised to transform the Zone into an impregnable redoubt.[7]

The opponents of a militarised canal were still extremely active, however, and they launched a highly charged debate in the new *American Journal of International Law*. There Hains displayed a remarkable faith in covenants without the sword. Article 25 of the Hague convention of 1907 (which the United States was shortly to ratify) forbade naval bombardment of undefended areas, and so, Hains believed, neutralisation of the canal would achieve 'immunity from war and freedom of passage'. He ended by drawing the parallel with Britain and Suez. 'Commanding as she does the Mediterranean and Red Seas [Britain] holds the keys to both entrances to the canal which gives her complete control, and this she could not get from fortifications covering the entrances alone.'[8]

Hains's last comment underscored the lack of a two-ocean fleet comparable to the Royal Navy, and the point was not contested. In an article written specifically to refute Hains, former governor of the Zone General George Davis accepted that for Britain, 'with her great fleet always in the Mediterranean and land forces at Gibraltar, Malta, Aden, and in Egypt, there is no need of defenses at Ports Said and Tewfik'. But fortification, not neutralisation, was the answer,

<hr>

[6] *BD*, 127–9, 287.

[7] AG, 1784–1917, 2266997, Black memo of 22.9.05; Black and Brooke memo of 8.12.05. GB, File 426–1, Report of the National Coast Defense Board, 1.2.06; General Board memo of 29.3.06. *TR letters*, 6:951. *NYT*, 25.5.09, 1/1.

[8] *NYT*, 16.6.06, 1/3. Peter Hains, 'Neutralization of the Panama Canal', *American Journal of International Law*, 3 (1909), 382, 389, 388.

as it was for Admiral Mahan, in whose view the canal should be fortified to such a degree 'as to be indifferent, at a moment of attack, whether the fleet is in its ports or a thousand miles away'. To Mahan, a multilateral pledge of canal security was positively baneful. It would deprive the country of the fundamental right to protect a vital interest single-handed, and it would infringe the Monroe Doctrine by importing alien influences into the Americas.[9]

The Taft administration needed no persuasion. In November 1909 the Panama Fortification Board was set up under General William Wotherspoon, commandant of the Army War College. Even before it sailed for the isthmus, it ordered the installation of two 6-inch guns as 'a formal and technical challenge to those, whether at home or abroad, who may chance to deny the right of the United States to fortify'. In August 1910 the Board proposed a fortification scheme placing four 14-inch and six 6-inch guns at the Atlantic terminal, and six 14-inch and six 6-inch at the Pacific entrance. They would be manned in peacetime by twelve companies of coast artillery, complemented by four infantry regiments, one battalion of field artillery, and one cavalry squadron.[10]

The most influential critic of the plan was the chairman of the Canal Commission, Colonel George Goethals, who believed that the Pacific defences should be more heavily accented to cope with the greater likelihood of an attack by Japan. This would secure the prism of the canal, since, as Goethals argued, 'they will never put ships against the forts'. But it left still another possibility, namely, that a raiding force would land outside the range of the batteries and march through the jungle to envelop the canal from the rear. In Goethals's view, jungle terrain gave no real protection: 'You could get an army through anywhere in that country.' His answer was a close-in defence of the lock areas at Gatún and Pedro Miguel/Miraflores that would turn them into two entrenched camps reducible only by siege. These strong-holds could resist as long as the Russian fortress at Port Arthur had resisted the Japanese in 1904, and reinforcements could be brought in from the United States, because no hostile navy could interrupt sea communications in both oceans simultaneously.[11]

Wotherspoon agreed with Goethals's analysis, as did the chief of staff, General Leonard Wood. But Wood questioned whether Congress would put up the money for the projects Goethals had in mind, and Goethals also had to reckon

---

[9] George Davis, 'Fortification at Panama', *American Journal of International Law*, 3 (1909), 901. Alfred Thayer Mahan, 'The Panama Canal and the distribution of the fleet', *North American Review*, 200 (1914), 417, and 'Fortify the Panama Canal', ibid., 193 (1911), 331.

[10] AG, 1784–1917, 2266997, Rodgers memo of 9.12.09; Haan to Rodgers, 11.12.09; Report of Panama Fortification Board, 12.8.10.

[11] Ibid., Goethals to Wotherspoon, 19.9.10. GB, 426–1, Goethals testimony before House Committee on Naval Affairs, 18.1.13. On the siege of Port Arthur, see Richard Connaughton, *The War of the Rising Sun and Tumbling Bear: A military history of the Russo-Japanese War, 1904–5* (London, 1988), 29–44, 168–207.

with a budget-conscious President Taft, who thought it better to cut out the $5 million earmarked for the 8,000-strong infantry component of the garrison and rely on coast artillery alone to protect the canal. There would be no need for an expensive permanent post, Taft judged, when the infantry could be rushed in as soon as war was declared. As Wood saw it, this ignored the likelihood that 'thirty minutes' possession of the locks by an enemy determined to do harm to them would put them out of use for a year or more', but Taft had his way. In January 1911 the estimates were slashed by more than one-third.[12]

Coastal batteries thus constituted the canal's sole defence, yet Goethals did succeed in prompting a dramatic shift in the pattern of the emplacements. All seven 14-inch weapons were to be at the Pacific terminal, plus a mighty 16-inch piece designed to outrange the new 15-inch gun soon to be introduced into the Royal Navy and doubtless also scheduled for adoption by the Japanese. Construction of the Pacific sites was also to be given priority over completion of the Atlantic forts. This perfected the blueprint for the fortifications, and in January 1912 Goethals's son, Lieutenant George Goethals, arrived on the isthmus to super-intend its realisation.[13]

It remained only to get legislative authority for fortification written into the Act for the permanent government of the Zone, and Goethals went to extraordinary lengths to achieve this. During a visit to Berlin in March 1912 he was given an audience by Kaiser Wilhelm II, who told him that the entire Canal Zone should be fortified. On his return to Washington, Goethals divulged the gist of the conversation to a Senate committee. Though the disclosure kicked up a minor diplomatic storm, he considered it well worth while if it helped squash the remaining opponents of fortification, and the Act went through on the lines Goethals had wished.[14]

It also included a warrant for the president to order the depopulation of the Zone, which Goethals presented as a military necessity. If 'Negroes and foreigners' – 'a very dangerous element' – were allowed to settle on Zone land, they would start cutting down the jungle, 'the greatest safeguard the canal can have'. As we have seen, Goethals did not really believe this. His real purpose was to get total control of land use in the Zone by expelling the undesirable 'mongrel population' currently in the Commission's way. Once the Canal Act

---

[12] AG, 1784–1917, 2266997, Wotherspoon to Wood, 30.9.10; Wotherspoon to Goethals, 1.10.10; Wood to Goethals, 5.10.10; Taft to Dickinson; 23.12.10 and 28.12.10; Dickinson to Taft, 27.12.10 and 10.1.11. Challener, *Admirals*, 326. *NYT*, 14.1.11, 7/1.

[13] AG, 1784–1917, 2314751A, Panama Fortification Board supplementary report of 8.8.11; 2266997, Winslow memo of 12.6.11. Goethals Papers, Goethals to Story, 16.6.11. *NYT*, 5.7.14, sect. II, 5/2.

[14] WCD, 6178–15, Military attaché, Berlin, memo of 26.1.11. SD, 1910–49, 811F.20/31, Leishman to Knox, 1.4.12. Goethals Papers, Goethals to Leishman, 19.4.12.

was passed, he dropped the argument of the jungle as a valuable element in canal defence, though Army planners continued to think of the dense tangle of the rain forest as a virtually impenetrable screen against ground attack.[15]

As the contours of the canal's defence system took shape, the Army sent its first detachment to the isthmus: the 10th Infantry Regiment, which arrived in October 1911. Goethals's reaction revealed the jealousy of a man who had come to see the Zone as his own bailiwick and resented the intrusion of any rival influences. Wood's decision to despatch the regiment was a mistake, thought Goethals, but the chief of staff had 'ambitions of his own', namely, 'the establishment of a Malta or Gibraltar on the Zone'. In May 1912 the chief quartermaster of the Commission resisted Wood's proposal to order in a second batch of troops on the ground that Congress would not stand the expense of housing them. Wood, he told Goethals, seemed to see the Zone as a convenience for units returning from the Philippines which could not be found a posting at home. The move did not take place.[16]

The infantry's first assignment was to familiarise itself with the land approaches to the Zone through manoeuvres and survey work in Panama. Though troop movements in the republic were believed to be justified by the canal convention, Washington went through the formalities of asking Panama's permission, on the understanding that it would not be refused. The War Department also planned to have the men take over police duty in the Zone. The Commission demurred at this, however, while the Marines who had served as the Commission's police auxiliary since 1904 saw themselves being edged out of a job. Their commanding officer had once told Goethals that their presence was 'as essential for the completion of the Canal as the steam shovel', and as the end of construction hove in view the Marines believed they still had a mission to keep the peace not only in the Zone but in 'the numerous scenes of disturbance' throughout nearby Central America. It was not to be, in Panama if not elsewhere. The Marines were withdrawn in January 1914, their rôle in the canal's history over, and the 10th Infantry became the Zone's sole fighting force.[17]

As such, it was decidedly inadequate; and its deficiencies had already been exposed by the Japanese war scare of 1913. The War Department's response was to bring in immediate reinforcements to lift the garrison to its intended

[15] *1911 Hearings*, 7. Goethals Papers, Goethals to Rupprecht, 31.12.12. GB, 426–1, Goethals testimony of 18.1.13 to House Naval Affairs Committee. WCD, 5777–6, Memo for Wood, 25.2.13.

[16] GSR, 7438, Wood to Stimson, 22.8.11. Goethals Papers, Goethals to Fieberger, 22.9.11; Devol to Goethals, 14.5.12.

[17] SD, 1910–49, 811F.20/36, Stimson to Knox, 8.6.12; Knox to Dodge, 29.6.12; /39, Dodge to Knox, 24.7.12. AG, 1784–1917, 1896202, Thatcher to Stimson, 9.7.12; Stimson to Thatcher, 10.7.12. ICC, 88-D-29, Russell to Goethals, 15.1.08. SNGC, 8975:12, Mahoney to Meyer, 15.8.12. GSR, 10853, Daniels to Garrison, 9.1.14.

peacetime strength. Wood meanwhile came up with a desperate expedient: furnishing the Commission with 3,500 rifles to be handed out to volunteers in the canal work force. 'It would be foolish to send any such number of rifles', Goethals was advised, 'unless they should want to arm West Indians.' Yet 2,500 rifles were sent, though there was no support for an idea mailed direct to the White House by a young American newspaperman, Hamilton Foley. A regiment of Panamanians should be raised, Foley told Woodrow Wilson, 'a body of men especially adapted to . . . "jungle" fighting'. The War College Division lost no time in knocking this disturbing proposal on the head, though it was to resurface come the world war.[18]

The most effective way to reduce the Zone's vulnerability was, of course, to build up the Army's manpower, but the 10th Infantry was allowed only to raise its enlisted strength from 985 to 1,500, and the garrison remained severely undermanned. Moreover, it had no autonomy. Goethals saw it as the Commission's servant, best employed in patrolling canal installations. The War College Division could complain that 'guard duty at the Canal is not a good training for war', but during the crisis with Mexico which erupted in April 1914 it was a clear sign of the Army's janitorial status that its chief function was to stand sentry over the new locks. By then the canal was poised to go into operation, but this spectacular addition to American national power was still practically defenceless. When the First World War broke out in Europe two weeks before the opening date, the United States was lucky that Panama was nobody's target.[19]

As the Army laboured to assemble the components of Fortress Panama, the Navy developed its own responses to the onset of the canal. Undoubtedly the greatest impact of the canal on naval policy was over the size and distribution of the fleet. Since 1889 there had been intermittent demands for a 'two-ocean Navy', that is, for a Navy with capital ships in both Atlantic and Pacific. Mahan regularly pressed the argument that the canal's potential to attract conflict justified a fleet second only to the Royal Navy. But though he upheld the expansionist view until his death in 1914, the Navy's General Board took a different line after 1910. Without the canal, coastal defence would require 'a fleet in each ocean sufficiently large to meet a probable enemy on that coast'. With the canal, the total number of warships could be materially reduced, though something markedly bigger than a one-ocean Navy would be needed.

---

[18] WCD, 7820/2, Plan of 15.5.13; War College Division to Goethals, 27.5.13; undated memo for Goethals. Goethals Papers, Goethals to War College Division, 7.6.13. WCD, 7899–1, Foley to Wilson, 8.7.13; War College Division undated memo.

[19] WCD, 8290–1, War College Division to Wood, 22.1.14; Wood to Adjutant General, 24.1.14. AG, 1784–1917, 2140143, War College Division to Wood, 20.2.14; 2152110, Goethals to Garrison, 25.4.14. *NYT*, 25.4.14, 4/5.

Even so, the canal had made it possible to cut back on capital-ship construction, and building programmes were adjusted accordingly.[20]

The canal also exerted great influence on the closely related issue of fleet distribution. With the end of the Russo-Japanese war in 1905, all battleships were stationed in the Atlantic and held there by Roosevelt in spite of calls from the West Coast states for a battleship presence on their shoreline. The Navy, which gave its highest priority to preparation for a war with Japan, supported a westward shift of resources, and in 1910 Mahan came out in favour of putting all battleships in the Pacific. The interim decision was to keep them where they were until the canal opened. Then the two first-class battleship squadrons would operate in the Atlantic from 1 May to 30 September each year. From 1 October to 1 April, one of the two front-line squadrons would serve in the Pacific, and in the event of 'complications' the entire fleet would be concentrated in whichever ocean were threatened. The plan was put up by Navy secretary Josephus Daniels, but it was opposed by Daniels's assistant secretary, Franklin Roosevelt, like his namesake a convinced Atlanticist, and both the ex-president and Mahan were enlisted to block it. In the last article he wrote, Mahan reversed his pro-Pacific stand and argued that, since 'the Caribbean Sea and the Panama Canal form together a great central position', they should be 'the main habitual station of the fleet'. Roosevelt's campaign was a success, and Daniels's scheme was shelved.[21]

Yet while the canal was a key determinant of naval policy, the Navy was only minimally involved in its defence. In the battleship the Navy believed it had a strategic weapon capable of winning a war outright. It was the Army's task to provide safe passage for these monsters as they made their way to Armageddon, and the Navy considered it had larger preoccupations than the minutiae of local defence in Panama. Though in 1903 the department had contemplated naval bases in the vicinity and had made provision for taking them in the canal convention, by 1911 it had lost interest. It was similarly unresponsive to the idea of base development on Costa Rica's Cocos Island or on the Ecuadoran island group of the Galápagos.[22]

U.S. interests could be safeguarded, it was believed, by preventing other

[20] William Braisted, *The United States Navy in the Pacific, 1897–1909* (Austin, Tex., 1958), 6, 151, 173, 200, 212, 236. Robert Seager, *Alfred Thayer Mahan: The man and his letters* (Annapolis, Md., 1977), 497–8. GB, 420–2, VI-359, General Board memo of 28.2.10.

[21] Braisted *USN, 1897–1909*, 117–18, 212, 225–6. Louis Morton, 'War Plan ORANGE: Evolution of a strategy', *World Politics*, 11 (1958–9), 222–3. William Braisted, *The United States Navy in the Pacific, 1909–1922* (Austin, Tex., 1971), 26, 28. Seager, *Mahan*, 501. GB, 420, General Board memo of 21.5.14. Frank Freidel, *Franklin D. Roosevelt: The apprenticeship* (Boston, 1952), 232–5. Alfred Mahan, 'Panama Canal and distribution of the fleet', 411, 413.

[22] SNGC, 14661:14, Moody to Hay, 10.11.03; 21498:13, Naval War College report of 11.11.11. SD, 1906–10, 16698, Navy Department comment of 19.6.09. GB, 414–1, VI, memo of 30.6.09.

powers from acquiring concessions, and over the next two years the policy of denial was twice brought into play. In August 1912, when a Japanese firm sought an agreement with Mexico for rights in Magdalena Bay, Senator Henry Cabot Lodge put through his own corollary to the Monroe Doctrine. Directed against any grant to a non-American corporation which could threaten United States security or communications, it was evidently prompted by fears for the integrity of the canal. Early in 1913 Washington signed a convention with Nicaragua which gave it an option on a canal plus naval stations on both coasts. Though Goethals saw no reason to build a second canal, he agreed that it was wise to preempt a foreign bid and ensure the U.S. monopoly on isthmian traffic which Panama had established.[23]

Inside the Zone the Navy's first concern was over the type of canal Panama was to be. In January 1906 a board of inquiry recommended a sea-level waterway on the ground that it was less vulnerable to sabotage than a lock canal. But the sea-level project was likely to take the best part of two decades to complete and could be prone to all kinds of navigational difficulties once in operation. The Commission's chief engineer, John Stevens, condemned it out of hand as 'nothing less than a national calamity . . . almost equivalent to the inauguration of a foreign war'. Roosevelt too was hostile, and in June 1906 Congress voted for a lock canal.[24]

The dimensions of the locks presented an immediate problem. In 1901 the Canal Commission had envisaged locks 84 feet wide, but the announcement in 1905 of the new British leviathan *Dreadnought*, with an 83-foot beam, made the estimate obsolete overnight. The canal act of 1906 therefore stipulated locks 100 feet in width. Even that, however, seemed inadequate given the scale of the super-dreadnoughts on the drawing-board, and Germany was starting to widen the lock chambers of the Kiel Canal from 81 to 147 feet. Roosevelt himself urged 120 or even 125 feet, which in Goethals's view was the limit for mitring lock gates. In January 1908, however, Congress settled for 110 feet. It was to prove a false economy.[25]

The arrangement of the locks had also been decided by then. Three sets of double chambers were planned. Gatún, at the Atlantic end of the canal, would give a triple lift eighty-five feet up to the level of the neighbouring artificial lake,

[23] Thomas Bailey, 'The Lodge corollary to the Monroe Doctrine', *Political Science Quarterly*, 48 (1933), 223–4. SD, 1910–49, 817.812/6, Weitzel to Knox, undated; Knox to Weitzel, 16.1.13; /8, Goethals to Stimson, 14.1.13.

[24] ICC, 9-A-11, Report of Board of Consulting Engineers, 10.1.06; Taft to Roosevelt, 19.2.06; Shonts to Taft, 5.2.06; 9-A-1, Stevens to Shonts, 19.12.05. *NYT*, 16.6.06, 1/3; 22.6.06, 1/3.

[25] Henry Abbot, 'Present status of the Panama project', *Annals of the American Academy of Political and Social Science*, 31 (1908), 20. *NYT*, 30.6.06, 1/6. GB, 426, V–138, Memo of 29.10.07. *TR letters*, 5:823. Joseph Bucklin Bishop, 'The Panama Canal: Its efficiency and operation', *Scribner's Monthly*, 70 (July–December 1921), 40.

and vessels, after moving through the central cut, would be lowered to the Pacific in two stages, by one step at the La Boca lock and by two more at Sosa. In January 1906 Stevens located the Pacific locks five miles farther inland, the single-lift flights at Pedro Miguel and the double-lift at Miraflores, to shelter them from naval gunfire. The Pacific locks, his successor Goethals believed, were now secure 'against all possibility of distant bombardment' and much better placed to withstand gunboat or torpedo-boat attack.[26]

Navy policy makers also asked for extensive facilities to be put at the fleet's disposal. In August 1910 the General Board called for a first-class base at the Pacific terminus, with full docking and repair services. Comparable installations at the Atlantic entrance would not be needed because of the availability of Guantánamo, but a coal and fuel-oil storage depot was expected, and a drydock. Early in 1912 the ambitious Pacific requirements were scaled down to the more modest level of the Atlantic terminal, but the department insisted on controlling the quality of the coal supplied by the Canal Commission. The Commission, like the Army, so the Navy appeared to think, existed primarily to minister to its needs, even though the Navy's interest in the canal was literally only transitional.[27]

Highest on the list of the Navy's desiderata was a monopoly of radio communications, not only in the Zone but in Panama as well. This was to generate enormous friction with Panama, and already there had been a sharp dispute with the Panamanians over the regulation of cable traffic to and from the isthmus. It grew out of a wrangle between Panama and the U.S.-owned Central and South American Telegraph Company, whose president, James A. Scrymser, claimed that the 1903 canal convention gave the United States absolute jurisdiction over international telegraphy throughout Panama. It would be 'quite useless for the United States Government to fortify its Zone territory', Scrymser later wrote, 'and yet permit foreign telegraph lines, which it cannot control, to operate silently and secretly anywhere within the territory of the Republic of Panama'.[28]

This was barefaced special pleading, but the argument was used to brush aside a Panamanian proposal for joint control of cable services, despite a promise not to offer concessions to other telegraph companies without American approval. Soon afterwards, when Panama contended that Limón Bay, west of Colón, was not in the Zone and that therefore Washington had no power to lay a cable through it, the White House reaction was explosive. 'Panama has no jurisdiction whatever of any kind, sort or description over the waters thru which ships pass in entering the canal,' snapped Roosevelt. The Panamanian claim was inadmissible, and the United States was not prepared even to discuss it.[29]

---

[26] McCullough, *Path between the seas*, 484. ICC, 9-A-1, Goethals to Taft, 9.12.07.

[27] GB, 426–1, VII–48, Reports of 31.8.10, 26.2.12, 19.4.13.

[28] SD, 1906–10, 312, Scrymser memo of 26.10.06. ICC, 43-D-8, Scrymser to Dickinson, 26.5.10.

[29] SD, 1906–10, 312, Bacon to Adee, 10.7.07; Squiers to Root, 12.4.07; Root to Squiers, 8.6.07; Solicitor to Adee, 30.7.07; memo of 29.7.07; Taft to Root, 16.8.07; Roosevelt to Root, 24.12.07.

This was to be precisely the attitude taken by the Navy on the subject of radio communications. The department had been authorised in 1904 to operate government stations in the United States and its possessions, and it demanded nothing less than a monopoly on radio throughout the isthmus. No private wireless company should be allowed in the Zone, and Panama should permit none outside the Zone. But the Navy's bid to rule the roost ran into opposition. In Goethals it faced a man determined to have all the elements of canal operation, including radio, 'under one head who shall be in supreme control', namely himself. One possible compromise, the setting up of two stations, he dismissed as an absurdity. There was no more need for that than there was 'for the construction of two canals, one for commerce and one for the Navy'. For once, however, Goethals was thwarted, and in December 1911 Taft gave the Navy sole responsibility for radio on the isthmus.[30]

To maintain contact with Washington and with fleet units in Atlantic and Pacific, the department called for a high-powered transmitter close to the canal. In Panama it aimed to set up six stations, and naval operators would handle all Panama's radio traffic. No agreement with Panama was necessary, the State Department solicitor advised, since a U.S. monopoly on radio was fully vindicated by Articles 2, 4, and 6 of the 1903 convention. The Joint Army and Navy Board was to find its justification in Article 1 – the American guarantee of Panama's independence! But Taft had been authorised to negotiate with Panama by the Canal Act of 1912, and talks went ahead, though by the summer of 1914 they had failed to produce results.[31]

The radio issue showed how acutely sensitive Washington was to any activity in Panama which could have a bearing on canal defence. The same edginess was well in evidence when it came to railway development in the republic. Three ventures were floated during the construction era, and each one raised American blood pressure whenever it touched the Zone. The first was the ambitious scheme for a line from the capital to David, several hundred miles to the west in Chiriqui province. When originally mooted in 1907, the concession was reportedly on offer to a British syndicate; the State Department's response was an emphatic assertion that no rights could be made over without American consent. The next time the subject cropped up, the Panamanians gave Washington first refusal by suggesting that the track could be laid by the Panama Railroad Company once the canal was finished. This was vastly more acceptable. 'The revolution in Panama and the building of the canal', wrote Minister William Dawson, 'created a certain feeling of apprehension in South American

---

[30] SNGC, 12479:407, Report of 20.4.11. ICC, 43-D-8, Goethals to Adjutant General, 24.5.11. AG, 1784–1917, 1781722, Goethals to Adjutant General, 12.12.11. SD, 1910–49, 819.74/ 2, Knox to Dodge, 15.12.11.

[31] SD, 1910–49, 819.74/7, Navy Department memo of 29.12.11; 819.74/10, Meyer to Knox, 23.1.12; /13, Solicitor memo of 4.4.12. *BD*, 599–600, gives the relevant section of the Canal Act.

countries as to our imperialistic designs in the Caribbean. Such feeling would, however, not be increased by contracting for the David road.' Goethals wholeheartedly agreed. The project would use up surplus equipment, and though he opposed planting American settlers inside the Zone, they would be welcome as 'friendly influences' in the interior as farmers of the rich agricultural land the railway aimed to open up.[32]

Goethals felt quite differently about a second line planned to run inland from a new port on the Atlantic coast only a few hundred feet from the Zone's western boundary. In the hands of an enemy raiding force it would be a priceless short-cut to the locks and the spillway at Gatún, and to allow it to be built would seriously compound the problems of canal defence. Goethals's objection was decisive: The contract was disapproved, and Panama duly cancelled the deal.[33]

It was the third project which stirred the most anxiety. In April 1911 the president of an Anglo–German corporation, August Dziuk, proposed a railway from Chepo, some forty miles east of the canal, to Panama City. To reach the Panamanian capital it would have to cross the Zone, but while Goethals was surprisingly relaxed about the scheme, the new secretary of war, Henry Stimson, was adamant that all foreign businesses should be kept out of Panama.[34]

An agreement with Panama was in prospect whereby Washington would relinquish possession of the Sabanas, a tract of the Zone cutting Panama City off from its eastern hinterland. During a visit to the isthmus in the summer of 1911, Stimson told the Panamanians that there would be no deal over the Sabanas unless the United States was given the right to take over the Chepo railway whenever it considered it necessary. The State Department went even further: If Panama made a contract with Dziuk, it would violate the canal convention. In March 1912 Panama revoked Dziuk's concession in a bid to produce a Sabanas agreement.[35]

The agreement was still a long way off, however. During a second trip to Panama, Stimson demanded the reservation of a half-mile belt of ground for American use, claiming that it was 'of the highest military importance that the Panama Canal Zone should continue to surround and embrace the City of

[32] SD, 1906–10, 3626, Squiers to Root, 4.1.07; Root to Squiers, 4.1.07; 15800, Vice Consul-General, Panama, to Knox, 30.11.09; State Department memo of 1.2.10 quoting Dawson memo of 29.12.09. SD, 1910–49, 819.77/32, Weitzel to Wilson, 9.2.11; /33, Weitzel memo of 17.2.11.

[33] SD, 1910–49, 819.77/147, Dodge to Knox, 27.1.13; /153, Goethals to Boggs, 9.2.13; Knox to Dodge, 13.2.13.

[34] SNGC, 28076:3/1, Galindo to Taft, 4.8.11. SD, 1910–49, 819.77/36, Legation to Knox, 19.4.11; /51, Meyer to Knox, 6.7.11; /42, Legation to Knox, 9.5.11; /57, Stimson to Knox, 21.7.11.

[35] SD, 1910–49, 819.77/58, Stimson to Knox, 19.8.11; Knox to Dodge, 20.9.11; /107, Dodge to Knox, 5.3.12.

Panama'. His successor, Lindley Garrison, dropped the idea of a security cordon but insisted on a U.S. veto on railway construction in the transferred area, together with the right to set up military installations there. In the boundary convention signed on 2 September 1914, therefore, the Sabanas did not pass to Panama free and clear of encumbrances. Along with many other features of U.S.–Panama relations in the past decade, the agreement proved that for Washington canal security immeasurably outweighed the interests of the Panamanians. The First World War did nothing to change that.[36]

First World War, 1914–1918

The opening of the canal came just two weeks after the outbreak of the First World War in Europe. Though the United States was not to go in until April 1917, the war's bearing on the problems of canal defence was inescapable. In the construction era the threat to canal security had seemed remote, but it now took on a much sharper immediacy as the conflict ramified beyond Europe and as the waterway became a potential bone of contention in the struggle for mastery of the oceans it linked.

The first American priority was to get unconditional jurisdiction over radio in Panama. Resistance on Panama's part, Secretary of State William Jennings Bryan instructed Minister South, might 'compel the United States to use force [*sic*] consider the steps necessary to attain that end'. On 29 August, President Porras obeyed via a decree giving Washington 'absolute and permanent control' over every type of wireless communication in the republic.[37]

Enforcement of the canal's neutrality was not so simple. Governor Goethals's request for a guard on every belligerent warship in transit was denied for fear of diplomatic repercussions. Though a belligerent was allowed only six war vessels in Zone waters at any one time, the Army believed Britain would disregard the rule if its ships were in hot pursuit of German raiders. And while restrictions were imposed on belligerents' use of radio in the Zone, the Navy refused to send Goethals a pair of destroyers to monitor the traffic. When Lieutenant Russell Crenshaw dismantled the radio of a British collier in Colón harbour, he was ordered not to shut down a set on board a foreign warship or government-owned vessel in case it led to a violent confrontation. After landing parties from an Australo-Japanese squadron were put ashore to investigate reports of a German wireless operator on Piñas Bay, the formal protest came

[36] SD, 1910–49, 711F.1914/7, Knox to Dodge, 30.1.13; /10, Stimson to Knox, 27.2.13; /11, Dodge to Knox, 1.3.13; /15, Garrison to Bryan, 16.6.13; /17, Garrison to Bryan, 5.8.13; /16, Garrison to Bryan, 11.8.13. *BD*, 733, gives the relevant articles of the boundary convention.

[37] SD, 1910–49, 819.74/55A, Bryan to Price, 13.8.14; /57, Price to Bryan, 23.8.14; Bryan to Price, 25.8.14. See *BD*, 735, for the text of the decree of 29 August.

from Panama, not Washington, in spite of the Navy's unqualified responsibility for the radio issue.[38]

Washington's failure to assert its rights marked a distinct setback for a strict exponent of neutrality like Goethals, but worse was to come. In October 1914 the east bank of the central cut began to slide, and though dredging coped with the obstruction, it could not be suspended for more than a few hours. This placed a serious question over the projected transit of the Atlantic Fleet in July 1915 en route to the San Francisco canal exhibition, and Goethals advised Secretary of the Navy Josephus Daniels against the transfer.[39]

Daniels agreed, and his decision was confirmed by the German sinking of the liner *Lusitania* on 8 May, with the loss of over a hundred American lives. The incident came close to driving the United States into war with Germany, and it was the worst possible time to risk having the country's battleship force unable to steam back into the Atlantic. The wisdom of countermanding the move soon became clear: Early in August the west bank also started to slip, and on 5 October the canal was closed indefinitely, with the cut earthed up for nearly a quarter of a mile.[40]

The closure raised major doubts about the canal's strategic value. It meant that one shoreline would now have to be protected at the other's expense, and in the wake of the *Lusitania's* loss the Atlantic was given priority. This was acceptable as long as the Pacific remained untroubled, but May 1915 also brought on a sudden worsening of U.S. relations with Japan following the Japanese bid to make China its satellite through presentation of the Twenty-One Demands. The 1914 draft of the U.S. plan for war with Japan had concluded that the Pacific was an insurmountable barrier for Tokyo, but the crisis immediately revived calls from the West Coast states for a battleship presence. Daniels told their governors, however, that the nucleus of capital ships was too small to permit its division. Given a war on two fronts, in other words, the Atlantic would have first call on the country's resources.[41]

The most obvious way out of the dilemma was to build the two-ocean navy

[38] SD, 1910–49, 811F.812/586½, Neutrality Board for Lansing, 17.8.14. *BD*, 636–8, has the text of the neutrality proclamation of 13.11.14. SD, 1910–49, 811F.812/590, Judge Advocate General to Garrison, 21.9.14. SNGC, 21498:70, Garrison to Goethals, 12.12.14, and Daniels to Crenshaw, 23.12.14. SD, 1910–49, 819.52G31/9, Flexer to Ridley, 3.6.38. See also *NYT*, 13.12.14, sect. II, 1/5; 15.12.14, 5/1; 16.12.14, 1/3 and 6; 17.12.14, 1/2; 18.12.14, 13/1; 29.12.14, 3/2.

[39] PC, 88-B-7, Goethals to Garrison, 16.12.14. *NYT*, 30.4.15, 4/4.

[40] Goethals Papers, Goethals to Harding, 12.5.15. *NYT*, 11.5.15, 3/6. AG, 1784–1917, 2342929, Boggs memos of 13.10.15 and 18.11.15. *NYT*, 5.12.15, sect. II, 6/1. On the *Lusitania*, see Link, Wilson: *The struggle*, 368–409.

[41] Edward Miller, *War Plan ORANGE: The U.S. Strategy to defeat Japan, 1897–1945* (Annapolis, Md., 1991), 41. GB, 420–1, Daniels to Governor of Washington state, 12.6.15. On the Twenty-One Demands, see Link, *Wilson: The struggle*, 267–308.

which the canal had been designed to avoid. In August 1916 Congress sanctioned a construction programme which aimed to lay down ten battleships and six battle-cruisers by 1919. Six months earlier the Senate had approved a treaty giving the United States rights to an alternative canal through Nicaragua. Both developments were undoubtedly given considerable impetus by the blockage of Panama, and although the waterway reopened to traffic in October 1916, it no longer seemed the axis of American sea-power its creators had intended it to be.[42]

Even so, the Army garrison busied itself energetically with plans for the Zone's land defences. In March 1915 the chief of Coast Artillery, Colonel Adalbert Cronkhite, urged fortification of the Panama Bay islands of Taboga and Taboguilla to add to Pacific emplacements which he believed were vulnerable to naval bombardment and to the heavy artillery of an assailant with a foothold on the coast. The garrison commander, General Clarence Edwards, was also perturbed by the thought of an enemy lodgment and called for an extended infantry defence to meet an assault force on the beach or deny it gun positions within range of the canal line. Edwards envisaged a Japanese attack on the Pacific side of the isthmus as the likeliest contingency, and he wanted defensive cordons set up in Panama more than fifteen miles beyond the Zone border, linked to the Zone by a road reaching out east to Chepo and west to Chame.[43]

Neither proposal found favour with Goethals. If the fleet were knocked out, he told Edwards, the canal could be seized 'without much difficulty' and certainly regardless of the Coast Artillery Corps. During a review of the defences which aimed to draw lessons from the Dardanelles operation, the Army was ready to mount two 16-inch guns on Taboga, whereas he suggested only a mortar battery. And as the arch-protagonist of a close-in defence, he was categorically opposed to Edwards's project for forward lines and their supporting road system.[44]

Edwards was undeterred, and he had many more ideas to press. He believed the Zone should be equipped with aircraft – hydroplanes to be based on Gatún and Miraflores lakes. Before the canal opened, with aerial warfare in its infancy, aircraft had not been taken at all seriously. In 1910 General Wotherspoon had spoken of flying machines as 'minor auxiliaries' of only conjectural value to the defence. Goethals in 1913 told a House committee he lost no sleep over the prospect of an air-raid on the locks. The following August, however, after publication of an aerial photograph of the 16-inch gun emplacement at the

[42] Braisted, *USN, 1909–1922*, 186–90, 197–201. On the Nicaragua treaty, see Arthur Link, *Wilson: The New Freedom 1913–1914* (Princeton, N.J., 1956), 331–46.

[43] AG, 1784–1917, 2265837, Cronkhite to Scott, 8.3.15; 2298940, Cronkhite to Scott, 19.6.15; 2223431, Edwards to Wood, 6.8.15 and 1.12.15.

[44] PC, 88-A-2, Goethals to Edwards, 24.3.15; 47-H-5, Goethals to Assistant Secretary of War, 28.9.15.

Pacific terminal, an executive order required all flights over the Zone to have clearance from the canal administration. In October 1914 the framers of the neutrality rules brought the doctrine of implied powers into play with a vengeance in claiming that since the canal treaty did not mention the Zone's airspace, Washington had the right to regulate it. The neutrality proclamation of 13 November accordingly forbade overflights by belligerent planes. But even if a marauder had tried to bomb the locks, it was the marine superintendent's considered opinion that there was only the remotest chance they could be put out of commission. Such a confident prognosis helped keep the air defence of the canal a low priority, and Edwards's pleas for the immediate despatch of a promised squadron of hydroplanes fell on deaf ears in the War Department.[45]

Edwards was equally unsuccessful with an extraordinary scheme for enlisting the U.S. employees of the Canal as reservists. He wanted a stock of 15,000 rifles ready for the use of a trained volunteer force, but Goethals refused to have his staff enrolled into an organised paramilitary unit. Do that, he told Edwards's superior, General Leonard Wood, and the operation of the canal would be crippled. Wood agreed, though Edwards still insisted on a militia of 15,000, including Panamanians. While aware of the 'probable inadvisability' of issuing them with weapons, he felt it would be wrong to ignore the men from the interior who lived 'away from the debasing influences of the terminal cities and [had been] familiar with arms all their lives'. The answer from Washington, however, was no, and only 5,000 rifles were sent. In Wood's view, these were 'all that could be turned over to people on whom we could depend' – that is, the white Americans of the Gold Roll.[46]

Yet Edwards was not deflated. 'I have not found him to be of a modest or retiring disposition,' Goethals's deputy Harding told him, and in 1916 the general returned determinedly to the charge. He now came up with ambitious plans for the acquisition of land from Panama. Their central feature was the incorporation of Colón into the Zone in exchange for 'a million or two' to pay for road construction in Panama, and transplanting Colón's harbour facilities to a new site at Portobelo. If he had the power to negotiate a canal treaty, he told Goethals, he would demand a Zone thirty to forty miles wide. The canal leadership's response was emphatically adverse. ' "Clarence" ', reported Harding,

[45] AG, 1784–1917, 2318068, Edwards to Wood, 12.8.15 and 21.8.15. WCD, 6178–6, Wotherspoon report of 14.12.10. GB, 426–1, Goethals testimony before House Committee on Naval Affairs, 18.1.13, 691. *NYT*, 11.7.14, 3/1. PC, 88-A-150, Memo for Goethals, 29.4.13. Norman Padelford, 'The Panama Canal in time of peace', *American Journal of International Law*, 34 (1940), 631 n. 116. SNSCC, 1919–26, 197–10, Rodman to Daniels, 14.9.15. AG, 1784–1917, 2318608, Adjutant General to Chief Signal Officer, 9.4.15; Edwards to Wood, 13.12.15.

[46] AG, 1784–1917, 2283996, Wood to Adjutant General, 29.4.15; Adjutant General to Wood, 27.7.15; Edwards to Wood, 12.8.15; Scott to Adjutant General, 24.9.15.

was 'as troublesome as ever, and . . . desirous now of taking over the entire Republic.' Though Edwards went on pushing the idea, it made no further headway.[47]

Nothing daunted, Edwards revived his crusade for a mobile infantry defence of the canal. Late in April he held manoeuvres to prove his claim that an assault force could penetrate the belt of rain-forest between the Pacific coast and the Zone. The significance of the exercise, reported the general's comrade-in-arms, Captain William Pratt, was 'startling when taken in connection with the possibility of a Japanese raid or invasion'. The only answer, Edwards told a press briefing, was a garrison of 20,000 men serviced by a road network passable for field guns and supply caissons. Goethals remained unconvinced, and in Congress too Edwards faced scepticism, coupled with the view that roads were a positive gift to attackers. He thereupon staged an experimental march through the jungle by a unit of over 400 troops and its accompanying pack train, which covered the forty-three miles from the Bayano River to the Pacific locks in under five days at the height of the wet season. It was an impressive feat, but it brought no change in existing defence policy.[48]

By the summer of 1916 Edwards and Goethals were at daggers drawn over practically everything to do with the garrison, not least its accommodation. Neither Goethals nor Harding had any time for the Army's complaints that it was being slighted by comparison with the canal work force. In July 1915 Edwards had reported that the infantrymen guarding the locks were going down with malaria, for the Canal provided them with nothing but tents – and tents without mosquito protection. A year later the position was still as bad, but Harding's reaction was brutally dismissive. The War Department, he guessed, would say, 'We screen houses for Jamaica niggers, why not for the Army?' No mosquito-proof guardhouse was erected, however, and Goethals's solution was to have the infantry relieved by the Canal Zone police on the ground that there were no funds for a proper structure.[49]

Goethals's subsequent replacement by Harding brought no ceasefire between Army and Canal. When Edwards pressed hard for a strategic road network to release the garrison from the clamp of short-range defence, he again ran into solid resistance. The Zone, Harding told Washington, most certainly wanted

---

[47] Goethals Papers, Harding to Goethals, 14.1.15. WCD, 6178–120, Edwards to Adjutant General, 16.2.16. Goethals Papers, Edwards to Goethals, 20.1.16; Harding to Goethals, 20.1.16. WCD, 6178–120, Harding to Adjutant General, 29.3.16; 6178–122, Edwards to Wood, 6.4.16.

[48] *NYT*, 29.4.16, 14/7. GB, 426–1, s.618, Notes by Pratt of 11.5.16. AG, 1784–1917, 2427315, Morton memo of 24.6.16. WCD, 6178–140, Edwards to Wood, 17.8.16; 6178–151, Edwards to Wood, 17.8.16.

[49] Goethals Papers, Edwards to Wood, 10.6.15; Harding to Goethals, 26.7.16. WCD, 9352–26, Memo of 9.11.16.

military roads but not a highway system principally designed to serve Panama's interest in opening the interior to agricultural development. In April 1917 Wood added his considerable weight to the opposition with a stinging critique of the road programme. While accepting that some radial roads should be thrown out from the canal, he saw no reason to question the soundness of Goethals's policy of depopulating the Zone and letting the jungle luxuriate. Edwards's project moved no farther.[50]

Edwards's adversaries were also quick to demolish his renewed bid for a Canal militia. Their task was made easier by unmistakable evidence that Edwards was fast losing touch with reality. 'The time may come', he wrote, 'when the operation of the Canal must be suspended and every available man sent to the front.' Coming from a general whose raison d'être was supposedly the security of the waterway, this was an astounding proposition. Less bizarre but equally objectionable was his idea of using the West Indian labourers as construction gangs for defence works. Harding, like Goethals before him, saw the scheme as a threat to the integrity of the canal organisation and an unwarrantable extension of Army influence. While prepared to allow 1,000 Gold Roll men to serve part-time as a regiment of engineers, he believed that to go beyond that would at the very least interfere with the running of the canal and perhaps even paralyse it. Washington agreed, and at the end of April 1917 the plan dropped into the capacious oubliette of the adjutant general's records.[51]

By this time the canal had moved to a war footing, and the most immediate menace to its security appeared to be sabotage. When America again came to the verge of war with Germany over the torpedoing of the steamer *Sussex* in March 1916, Goethals had advised a number of countermeasures if diplomatic relations were severed. He was especially perturbed at the thought of four German merchantmen refuged in Cristóbal since 1914 trying to ram the Gatún lock gates at night. Edwards for once agreed, convinced of 'the manifest desire of the Germans to do to this Canal what the Lord did in the way of slides'. Goethals's answer was to disable the ships by removing their connecting rods, then have the Zone placed under martial law – and Panama too if it refused to cooperate. In the event, the scare subsided with Germany's acceptance of U.S. demands for restrictions on U-boat warfare. Congress, however, gave the

[50] WCD, 6178–145, War College Division to Scott, 8.1.17. PC, 47-H-17, Harding to Brown, 13.1.17. SD, 1910–49, 819.154/19, Panama Commissioners to Lansing, 27(?).4.17; 819.77/270, Baker to Lansing, 31.1.17. WCD, 6178–156, Wood to Adjutant General, 30.4.17.

[51] AG, 1784–1917, 2425443B, Edwards memo of 5.12.16. WCD, 6178–156, Edwards memo of 31.3.17. PC, 88-A-30, Harding memo of 14.3.17. AG, 1784–1917, 2425443B, Scott to Adjutant General, 27.4.17. See also Edwards's idea of converting the Zone into a vast training camp where volunteers would be drilled daily and then 'turned loose to disport themselves in Panama City and Colon in the evenings': SD, 1910–49, 819.77/259, quoting the *Star and Herald* for 20.10.16.

president powers to exclude anyone from the Zone who might jeopardise canal operations. High on the list of suspects was the erstwhile railway promoter August Dziuk, whom Edwards had recently named as 'a paid German spy'.[52]

Coupled with mistrust of the Germans went a deep phobia of the Japanese. What were ostensibly Japanese fishermen in Panama Bay were believed to be naval officers familiarising themselves with the approaches to the Pacific entrance. But Japan was not yet as willing as Germany to take the United States on, and Washington was right to see Berlin as the clear and present danger. In December, Harding believed the two likeliest moves to watch for were a bid either to dynamite a merchant vessel in a lock chamber or to scuttle one beam-on across the cut. When diplomatic relations were broken off in February 1917, he acted quickly to implement the exclusion order. Germans working in the Zone were sent north to detention on Ellis Island, those on board ships heading through the waterway were taken off before the transit, and all canal installations were placed under heavy guard. Late in March, Secretary of State Robert Lansing's nephew John Foster Dulles was despatched to the isthmus to urge Panama to round up all Germans resident in the terminal cities, who were duly seized and turned over to the Zone for internment. This more than took care of the sabotage problem, and to the end of the war the canal functioned undisturbed by any enemy within.[53]

It was equally untouched by any external challenge. As Harding put it, 'there was at no time the danger of attack . . . by the enemy in force'. This was a considerable mercy, since the defences of the canal were in no condition to stand up to onslaught by a leading military power. In his sardonic commentary on Edwards's grand design for canal security, Wood had marked out three components of the garrison for special treatment: coast artillery; naval patrol and reconnaissance; and air defence. All were seriously deficient when he wrote his report in April 1917, and the war did nothing to improve them.[54]

In February 1917 Edwards was told by his artillery commander that the batteries were now outranged by the latest naval guns and that in consequence both the canal's infrastructure and its through traffic were vulnerable to shelling by modern capital ships. It may have been no more than a coincidence that an identical view had just been stated in a newspaper article by the journalist Rex

[52] PC, 88-H-12, Goethals to Brown, 5.5.16, AG, 1784–1917, 2390305, Edwards to Wood, 21.4.16. Padelford, 'Panama Canal in time of peace', 624–5. On the *Sussex* crisis, see Arthur Link, *Wilson: Confusions and crises 1915–1916* (Princeton, N.J., 1964), 222–79.

[53] GB, 426–1, s.618, Pratt to Operations, 26.6.16; Edwards to Wood, 1.8.16. ONRL, World War, Defensive Plans: Campbell to Daniels, 29.7.16. PC, 88-A-79, Harding to Brown, 5.12.16. MID, 10319–419, War Department press release of 6.1.19. *NYT*, 6.2.17, 2/4; 13.2.17, 5/7; 15.2.17, 10/8. Arthur Link (ed.), *The papers of Woodrow Wilson*, vol. 41 (Princeton, N.J., 1983), 472–3.

[54] WCD, 6278–8, Harding to Baker, 6.12.18; 6178–156, Wood to Adjutant General, 30.4.17.

Beach. Gatún dam, Beach wrote, was within range of a battleship lying beyond the reach of the armament at Fort Sherman. At the Pacific end an enemy fleet could shelter behind Taboga and Taboguilla islands and bombard both the Miraflores locks and the mouth of the canal.[55]

The article triggered a predictable public outcry which Goethals did his best to assuage. Gatún dam, he told the press, was 'nothing more nor less than a miniature mountain', and no barrage of high-explosive shells could destroy it. In private, however, General Wood conceded the weakness of the batteries, especially at the Pacific terminal, where they had been bunched together so closely that a hostile seaborne force could easily converge its fire on them. And the channel in the last half-mile of the Pacific prism was so narrow that U.S. warships would have to stay in column as they debouched and so offer a perfect target to an enemy waiting off Taboga. Heavy guns on Taboga, he believed, would solve both problems. Secretary of War Baker had already approved two 16-inch emplacements for the island, but funding was disallowed. When the item came up again, War Department planners insisted that the requirements of the American Expeditionary Force in Europe must come first. For the rest of the war the faults in the coastal defence of the canal stood unremedied.[56]

So too did the defects in the Navy's contribution, and for many of the same reasons. When the canal opened, the Navy's presence consisted merely of five old C-class submarines. In August 1915, as the earth slides in the cut grew worse, Daniels called for two bases to accommodate the boats, one at each end of the waterway, but the proposal failed to get past the appropriations committees. In January 1917, therefore, Daniels settled for one base only, at Coco Solo, just east of the Atlantic entrance. Its mission would be to deter a close blockade of both termini and to prevent enemy landings near the Zone. The Navy took possession of what its historian called 'this sand-flea pestered point' soon after the declaration of war in April.[57]

Pending completion of the Coco Solo station, the submarines were given a tender, the antique cruiser *Charleston*, which arrived in the Zone in the spring of 1916. Its captain, Commander E.H. Campbell, was aghast at the inadequacy

[55] AG, 1784–1917, 2487411, Cronkhite to Edwards, 20.2.17; 2538347, text of Rex Beach article, 25.2.17. The Navy had already demonstrated the vulnerability of Gatún four years earlier: See GB, 426–1, Report of 28.2.13, 6.

[56] AG, 1784–1917, 2538347, Acting Chief of Coast Artillery to Adjutant General, 23.2.17; 2638801, *Philadelphia Evening Bulletin*, 24.2.17. *NYT*, 4.3.17, sect. I, 7/1. WCD, 6178–156, Wood memo of 30.4.17. AG, 1784–1917, 2407013, Scott to Adjutant General, 24.3.17; 2425443B, Chief of Coast Artillery to Adjutant General, 7.5.17. WCD, 6178–170, War College Division to Bliss, 20.4.18.

[57] SNGC, 21498–160, Campbell to CNO, 17.7.16. WCD, 6178–99, War College Division to Chief of Staff, 3.1.16. AG, 1784–1917, 2314751, Edwards to Wood, 3.12.15. PC, 88-B-1, Memo for Chief of Staff, 27.1.17. OA, NHC, Fifteenth Naval District, *Command Historical Report, 1917 1958*, 1.2.

of the harbour defences: no mines, no nets, no booms in readiness; but in Washington this was not seen as a Navy responsibility. 'Harbors', one commentator pencilled on Campbell's report, 'are supposed to be defended by the army, particularly in a Zone of which they have charge.' On the eve of war in March 1917, only three destroyers had been allocated to the isthmus, and Campbell's request for a detachment capable of maintaining a round-the-clock patrol was denied on the ground that all available craft were earmarked for convoy duty in the Atlantic. Soon afterwards *Charleston* and the destroyers were withdrawn, and though a new unit grandly entitled Naval Forces, Canal Zone, was set up, it comprised only the submarine quintet and an accompanying trio of torpedo boats. Its commander was the Canal's marine superintendent, Commander L. R. Sargent.[58]

In November 1917 Sargent took on a third title. The previous July the Army garrison had been elevated to the status of an autonomous department, and Edwards's successor, General Plummer, wanted to create a naval district for the Zone whose commandant would be the marine superintendent. Plummer visualised a commandant who took orders from him, just as the marine superintendent acted as the governor's subordinate, but the Navy insisted on a district independent of both the Army and the canal organisation. As district commandant, Sargent was to report directly to the chief of naval operations. To clip his wings, however, the Army made sure his writ did not run inside the defensive sea areas set up during the summer. There he exercised responsibility for the protection of shipping, but only as the third-ranking official in the canal hierarchy.[59]

The last of Wood's priorities had been air defence, and this again was given short shrift. In May 1916 Pratt bemoaned the failure to introduce a single aircraft or anti-aircraft gun into the defences. The 'air ship', he felt certain, was more important to the Navy than any weapon bar the submarine, and even the submarine relied on the 'eyes' of aerial reconnaissance. The Navy Department accepted the need for scouting planes and with it Pratt's call for a naval air station in the Zone adjoining the submarine base at Coco Solo. There, however, it drew the line. It was up to the Army to stand guard over the Zone, and provision against air attack, like harbour defence, was entirely an Army function.[60]

Yet the Army Air Service, like the Coast Artillery, was denied first-class resources by the overriding demands of U.S. mobilisation for the war in Europe

---

[58] SNGC, 21498–160, Campbell to CNO, 17.7.16; 21498–212, Daniels to Baker, 5.5.17. ONRL, World War, Defensive Plans: Campbell to Operations, 31.3.17. PC, 88-B-15, Sargent memo of 25.8.19.

[59] AG, 1784–1917, 2256604. GB, 426–1, S.762, General Board to Daniels, 23.8.17; Baker to Daniels, 19.10.17. PC, 88-B-15, Sargent memo of 16.9.18.

[60] GB, 426–1, S.618, Pratt to Operations, 16.5.16; 449, S.569, Bureau of Ordnance to CNO, 10.7.16; General Board memo of 25.8.16.

in 1917. When the 7th Aero Squadron arrived at its base in March, it was equipped only with hydroplanes, and over a year later the Air Service presence in the Zone amounted to no more than six trainers. To meet the fancied threat of attack by planes built in pro-German Colombia, fifteen low-calibre anti-aircraft guns destined for Pearl Harbor were diverted to the Zone. The sortie from Colombia did not materialise, nor did the seaplane raid on the Gatún spill-way feared by the Navy. But the danger of air attack was very much more than the product of a hyperactive military imagination, and in the decade after the end of the war it took over as the leading contingency the canal had to face.[61]

The twenties, 1919–1929

The First World War had exposed disturbing flaws in the canal as a strategic waterway, and in the post-war decade the canal remained less than adequate from the standpoint of national security. The locks were already too small, while the weaknesses of the defence works stood unremedied both in terms of manpower and matériel, particularly against the growing menace of air-power.

The inertia of the 1920s must be seen in the context of a reversion to minimum expenditure on the armed forces with the rapid demobilisation which came after the war. It was justified to some degree by the absence of any immediate threat to the isthmus. Only the British and Japanese navies were capable of attacking the canal, but whatever challenge they posed was believed to have been met by the treaty structure erected at the Washington conference of 1921–2. Adhered to by all three powers, this halted an incipient naval arms race. It also abrogated the Anglo-Japanese alliance, which, if aimed against the United States, would have produced the nightmare of a two-ocean war that not even the canal could have enabled the one-ocean U.S. Navy to win. It was true that American staff officers were busy in the twenties with plans to meet the contingencies of war with Britain (RED), with Japan (ORANGE), and with the two in combination (RED–ORANGE), but there was an air of deep unreality about the exercise as long as the Washington treaty apparatus stayed intact.[62]

There was no doubt that Tokyo, not London, was considered the clearer danger to the canal. As the debate on the League of Nations covenant opened

---

[61] Kathleen Williams, *Air defense of the Panama Canal, 1 January 1939–7 December 1941*, Army Air Forces Historical Studies, no. 42 (Washington, D.C., 1946), 2. WPD, 6178–171, War Plans Division to Bliss, 6.5.18; Baker memo of 9.5.18. SNSCC, 1917–19, C-4-30, memo of 3.5.18.

[62] For the texts of the Washington treaties, see John Grenville (ed.), *The major international treaties 1914–1973* (London, 1974), 87–92. On war planning in the 1920s, see William Braisted, 'On the American Red and Red–Orange war plans, 1919–1939', in Gerald Jordan (ed.), *Naval warfare in the twentieth century, 1900–1945: Essays in honour of Arthur Marder* (London, 1977), 167–85; Morton, 'War Plan ORANGE'; John Major, 'War plan RED: The United States plans for war with Britain', unpublished paper, University of Hull Library.

in the summer of 1919, the former secretary of state, Philander Chase Knox, was insistent on putting in the declaration 'We do not intend that Japan shall obtain a military base in Mexico or anywhere near the Panama Canal.' In December the garrison commander in the Zone urged a U.S. veto on Japanese bids to acquire land in Panama, and the Canal's legal counsel furnished the opinion which formed the basis of the Panamanian refusal.[63]

The most dramatic indication of Washington's attitude, however, was the shift of half the Navy's battleships from the Atlantic to the Pacific in July 1919. The formation of the Pacific Fleet was an unmistakable warning to Tokyo of U.S. determination to have a decisive voice in Asian affairs, and the passage through the canal of the fleet's first detachment – under the command of Goethals's marine superintendent, Hugh Rodman – underscored the cardinal role of Panama in post-war U.S. strategy.[64]

To the Navy Department the fleet constituted the canal's forward line of defence, deterring Japan from a move into the Eastern Pacific by its very presence in the area. Local defence, in and around the Zone, was the Army's business, and apart from aerial patrols the Navy's contribution in the immediate approaches to the canal was limited to the existing handful of small ships. In the unlikely event of an attack, naval planning was confined to the lordly generality that 'such vessels of the Fleet as may be in the vicinity will cooperate in repulsing it'. In other words, the Navy would continue to avoid assigning its battle units to the chore of coastal protection and would count on the military garrison as its insurance if an enemy strike force slipped through the outer screen. The Army would thus serve as the auxiliary of the fleet, to keep the transit open whenever it was needed.[65]

The Army's rôle was, of course, based on the assumption that the canal was a vital adjunct to the Navy. That assumption had been severely shaken in 1916 when the commitment to a huge building programme had pointed to a two-ocean fleet that would make the canal strategically superfluous. In 1919, however, a second programme was scrapped by Congress, and capital-ship construction was suspended by the naval disarmament treaty of 1922. Instead of a projected Navy of thirty-one first-class battleships and twelve battle-cruisers, the United States in 1929 possessed only fourteen battleships and three aircraft carriers. Though the overwhelming bulk of the front-line strength was by then stationed in the Pacific, the canal remained crucial if this relatively limited force had to be redisposed in a national emergency. So it recovered its old pre-eminence, underlined by the fact of its exemption from the defortification clauses of the

[63] CR (Senate), 7.8.19, 3687. ONI, C-10-J 12469, Kennedy to Price, 10.12.19; Price to Lansing, 17.12.19.

[64] Braisted, USN, 1909–1922, 458–60. NYT, 28.7.19, 6/3.

[65] JB, 325, s.84, Navy Planning Committee report of 10.10.19; 325, s.123, Joint Board to March, 10.2.21.

Figure 3. The hinge of strategy: The battleship USS *Nebraska* in Pedro Miguel Lock, July 1919. (U.S. National Archives)

1922 treaty, which halted work on the defences of Guam and the Philippines but allowed fortified bases in Hawaii and the Canal Zone.[66]

Yet while the Washington treaty settlement restored the canal's fortunes, it also prevented its modernisation. In 1919 the beam of the new *South Dakota*-class battleships was limited to 106 feet in order to give them clearance through the 110-foot-wide locks. So long as the ability to transit the canal continued to be a requirement for the Navy's heavyweights, this would inevitably mean the sacrifice of protection by anti-torpedo blisters, and a call for bigger locks went up from the Philadelphia Chamber of Commerce. New locks of up to 150 feet in width were backed by Navy's General Board, but they were opposed by Goethals and by the outgoing Navy secretary, Josephus Daniels. The subsequent 'naval holiday' imposed by the Washington treaty of 1922 shelved the issue, since no more battleships or carriers were to be laid down for a decade. For the time being, therefore, the lockage of the canal stayed as it was when it first went into operation.[67]

This suited the Navy's purposes well enough, but in other respects relations with the Zone were strained. Rodman believed that Harding's successor as governor should be a naval officer, as did the destroyer commander in the Atlantic. Like Oahu, the latter firmly believed, the canal must be under naval control, since whereas it was 'nothing more to the Army than a magnificent monument to the ability and skill of the Army engineers', to the fleet it was 'the Navy's main life artery'. Such views could only envenom the emerging argument between Navy and Canal over the Zone's general support facilities. When traffic fell off in the slump of 1921, Governor Morrow asked the Navy Department to assign repair work to the Canal. The department refused on the ground that thanks to the Gold Roll differential, Zone skilled-labour costs were 25 per cent higher than in its own yards. Nor would it buy coal from the Zone priced at double the stateside rate. Matters came to a head with the approach of the grand manoeuvres set for January 1922, when the fleet aimed to be as self-sufficient as possible but expected the Zone to make up any shortfalls. Morrow's protests fell on deaf ears, and a year later the Navy pigeon-holed a report by Rodman urging the construction of an advance base in the Zone, using the Canal's services as much as possible. This not only smacked of bailing the Canal out but ran completely counter to the long-established policy of devoting minimum resources to local defence and leaving it all to the Army.[68]

[66] Braisted, *USN, 1909–1922*, 419–26. SNSCC, 1919–26, PD 226–103, War Plans Division to General Board, 19.10.21.

[67] GB, 426–1, s.252, Bureau of Ships memo of 25.6.46, WPD, 6278–21, Memo of 13.5.19. JB, 326–1, s.79, General Board memo of 31.7.20. SNSCC, 1919–26, 197–5, Goethals to War Plans Division, 29.10.19. JB, 326–1, s.79, Daniels memo of 25.9.20.

[68] SNSCC, 1917–19, c-42–23, Rodman to Daniels, 29.7.19; 1919–26, PD 198–2, Commander, Destroyer Squadrons, Atlantic Fleet, memo of 26.2.20. PC, 88-B-7, Morrow to Flint, 7.4.21;

The Army's post-war defence planning rested on the worst-case hypothesis of an attack by a Japanese expeditionary force of 75,000 men, but the batteries were now markedly inferior to the latest in big naval guns. In the opinion of Colonel John Gulick of the War Plans Division, 'an enemy fleet could lie in Panama Bay and completely destroy Panama City and the canal fortifications while being completely out of range of the fortifications at the mouth of the canal'.[69]

The solution was to site four 16-inch weapons at the Pacific end of the waterway, either in Fort Amador or on the island of Taboga, ten miles south of the Pacific entrance. Immediately after the Armistice in November 1918, Panama was notified of the intention to turn most of the island into a fortress. The Panamanian reaction was understandably bewilderment: Now peace had come, there was 'not the least fear of an armed attack against the United States and even less in the region of the Isthmus of Panama'. Plans for the emplacements on Taboga went ahead, however, and in May 1920 a huge demonstration in Panama City protested against the scheme during the visit of General of the Army John Pershing.[70]

To the American minister, William Jennings Price, the uproar was not worth taking seriously. Washington would not be 'foolish enough or careless enough to invest in round numbers four hundred millions of dollars . . . in a rather defenseless Canal enterprise in the middle of a foreign country' and then 'place itself in such a position that that foreign country would be able, even in the midst of war or threatened war, so to assert its judgment or its whims' as to block the U.S. right to protect the waterway. But this was to assume that the Taboga design was vital to the canal's security, and it was a questionable assumption. In January 1922 Pershing's staff reported that manpower in the Zone stood at barely more than one-third of its necessary wartime strength. To the commander of the batteries, this undermined the whole basis of his mission: It made no sense 'to build up large fixed armament projects in the tropics with no hope of having anything but limited artillery garrisons engaged principally in caretaking'. To the Navy commandant it was inconceivable that Japan would risk its battleships in an assault on the canal unless it had first taken out Pearl

Denby to Weeks, 7.2.22. SNGC, 21498–421, Lackey for Clark, 30.12.21; Morrow to Weeks, 10.12.21; 21498–440, Morrow to Weeks, 21.2.23; Chief, Bureau of Engineering, to Coontz, 11.6.23; Chief, Bureau of Supplies and Accounts, to Coontz, 22.6.23; 28690–139, Special Board on Shore Establishments to Denby, 12.12.22.
[69] JB, 325, s.84, Report of 10.10.19. SD, 1910–49, 819.52/112, Greene to Rowe, 23.12.19.
[70] AG, Post-1917, 660.2, Office of Chief of Engineers to March, 30.1.20; Panama Canal Department (10–7–21). JB, 326–1, s.191, Joint Planning Committee memo of 1.7.22. WCD, 6178–170, War College Division to Bliss, 20.4.18; 6178–210, War Plans Division to March, 19.5.20. SD, 1910–49, 819.52/81, Price to Lansing, 22.11.18; /131, Price to Colby, 4.5.20. NYT, 4.5.20, 8/3. MID, 153–33, Memo of 20.5.20.

Harbor. The likeliest threat to the debouchment of the U.S. fleet, as he saw it, would come from Japanese submarines, against which heavy guns were useless.[71]

The case against Taboga's fortification was not accepted straightaway, however. In March 1923, after a large-scale exercise laid on to test the canal's Pacific defences, two admirals and the garrison commander all concluded that a 16-inch battery had to be put on the island. But the War Plans Division was now firmly opposed. The scenario of a Japanese Navy offensive was no longer credible, and it was pointless spending $3 million on a bastion that was poorly located to prevent canal installations from being bombarded or to force an enemy expedition to land well away from the Zone. Secretary Weeks agreed and cancelled preparations for the 16-inch batteries.[72]

It was just as well. The conviction that the fate of the canal hung on the outcome of a duel between ships and forts reflected the experience of a generation which had known nothing but land- and sea-power. Since 1914, however, a third dimension of warfare had come into being which was soon to outmode both land-based defence and seaborne attack. In January 1919 Franklin Roosevelt justified U.S. naval expansion on the ground that the nation's shorelines were linked only by 'a strip of canal that one aeroplane could put out of action'. Not long afterwards one Army commentator figured that the canal was less vulnerable to a naval assault than to an air-raid by 'large multi-motored air cruisers'. The following year Captain George Day, USN, predicted a strike 'by fast surface craft or by air plane carriers with the objective of temporarily disabling the canal and thereby dividing our naval force. This could be done – as an extreme case – by one heavy bomb properly placed at one of the spillways.'[73]

The air defence of the Zone was divided between Army and Navy, the Navy taking on long-range reconnaissance and interdiction over the coastal waters on both sides of the isthmus; the Army, close-in defence by aircraft and by anti-aircraft batteries. They operated out of neighbouring bases at the Atlantic terminal, the Army at France Field, the Navy at Coco Solo. Although a joint base would have been more rational, the idea was quickly buried, and in a well-established tradition of mutual animosity the two services went their separate ways.[74]

[71] SD, 1910–49, 819.52/130, Price to Colby, 28.4.20. WPD, 504–1, War Plans Division to Pershing, 27.1.22. SNSCC, 1919–26, PD 197–15, Commanding General, Panama Coast Artillery District, to Sturgis, 3.2.22; Taylor to Sturgis, undated.

[72] WPD, 639–6, Eberle report of 1.3.23. *NYT*, 21.3.23, 4/3. WPD, 1004–3, Sturgis report of 31.3.23; 639–6, War Plans Division to Joint Board, 10.4.23; Weeks directive of 24.7.23.

[73] Michael Simpson (ed.), *Anglo-American naval relations 1917–1919* (Aldershot, 1991), 587. AG, post-1917, 660.2, Panama Canal Department (5–19–19). JB, 326–1, s.117, Day to Craven, 20.9.20.

[74] JB, 326–1, s.180, Report of board on aerial defence, 23.8.21; Chief, Bureau of Aeronautics, to Coontz, 6.1.22; Joint Planning Committee report of 28.4.22.

Disunity persisted in spite of the findings of the two fleet exercises of 1923 and 1924. In the 1923 manoeuvres a lone Navy plane from Coco Solo simulated a surprise attack on Gatún spillway. It flew in unchallenged, and none of the Army's interceptors took off until the raid was over. The incident was proof enough to both Army and Navy planners that money would better be spent on an air defence screen than on the fortification of Taboga. The lesson was again driven home in the 1924 problem, in which the whole fleet made a transit from Pacific to Atlantic. Once more the performance of the Zone's air-defence component left far too much to be desired, but both Army and Navy still balked at collaboration. Instead the Navy pushed ahead with the development of its own air cover, not by reinforcing the Coco Solo station but by making the fleet independent of the Army Air Service by, above all, speeding completion of the carriers *Lexington* and *Saratoga*, with a payload of ninety planes apiece.[75]

The creation of a fleet air arm may just possibly have been influenced by the state of affairs in the Zone. In 1927 the Army's machines at France Field were all of pre-1920 vintage and housed in wooden hangars 'beginning to sag under their own weight'. The ground was a morass for nine months of the year, and aviators were warned that 'habitual cross-wind landings with heavy weights of bombs must be avoided'. And the base was located nearly fifty miles from the Pacific locks which would be one of the first targets of a Japanese raid. Small wonder that Assistant Navy Secretary Edward Warner described the canal's air defences as 'pitifully and extraordinarily inadequate'.[76]

Yet if the Army could not guarantee the air-space of the Zone in the absence of the fleet's carrier umbrella, it asserted the right to control it in principle, and with it the air-space of the republic too. The garrison commander in 1920, General Chase Kennedy, was quoted as having said that 'no ship will ever fly over the whole territory of Panama except American ships', and his successor declared that Washington had overflying rights by virtue of the 1903 convention. When Panama disputed the claim, the response was that unauthorised flights across Panama would be equivalent to an invasion by enemy ground forces. Either U.S. government planes should have a monopoly of air traffic on the isthmus or foreign aircraft should be required to touch down at the outer limits of Panama and embark an American supervisor for the final approach, just as a canal pilot took charge of a vessel in transit.[77]

[75] SNSCC, 1927–39, (SC)A16-3(5-I), Report on Fleet Problem I, 7, 18–23, 72–3, 84, 139. WPD, 639–6, War Plans Division to Joint Board, 10.4.23. SNSCC, 1927–39, (SC)A16-3(5-III), Walsh report of 26.1.24; C-in-C, Battle Fleet, report of 1.2.24; 1919–26, 197–19, Report of 10.6.23.

[76] *NYT*, 23.11.27, 6/5; 7.1.25, 4/2. Williams, *Air defense*, 1–3. AG, post-1917, 660.2 Panama Canal Zone, Revised report on aerial defence, 21.11.22.

[77] SD, 1910–49, 711.1928–436½, Minutes of meeting of 7.8.35. AG, post-1917, 580–81 Panama (7–2–23), War Plans Division to Pershing, 31.8.23. SD, 1910–49, 711.192/14, Joint Board to South, 1.2.24.

In the event, this extraordinary proposal was dropped under State Department pressure, but the power to regulate aviation in Panama was written into the treaty signed in 1926. In peacetime all non-governmental aircraft and airports were to be subject to inspection; American and Panamanian planes and operators were to be licensed; and all private aircraft were to follow prescribed routes and land at designated places. Panama was not to allow flights over territory close to the canal's defences. In time of war or international crisis, Washington alone would decide policy.[78]

Control over radio in Panama was likewise inserted in the treaty after the Panamanians had announced their intention of rescinding the 1914 decree granting Washington carte blanche over wireless transmission. The State Department and the governor both sympathised with the Panamanians' case. But the Navy was adamantly opposed to any infringement on its radio monopoly, and it also insisted on full U.S. sovereignty over all the installations it operated on Panamanian soil. When treaty talks began, it submitted a draft article which effectively validated the status quo. It was softened to some degree by the State Department negotiator, but, like the companion article on aviation, it gave the United States a formidable range of veto powers. Washington was given the right to operate radio stations in Panama, with the sites under Panamanian sovereignty but American jurisdiction. All other stations were to be licensed by Panama, subject to U.S. approval; and they were liable to closure at American behest if deemed to be 'detrimental to the safety or operation of the Canal and its defenses or the operation of the United States Fleets and Forces'. In the event of war or the threat of war, U.S. authority would be unconditional, as with aviation.[79]

Both articles represented large concessions by Panama, but two others sugared the pill by giving substantial aid towards road construction in Panama and by promising either a bridge or a ferry across the Pacific end of the canal. Soon after the war, the Army's chief engineer in the Zone, Colonel Charles Riche, had put up a plan for a network of roads and bridges worth $20 million, and in the summer of 1923 Panama again sought U.S. assistance for a road-building programme. Successive garrison commanders were hostile to both schemes. General William Lassiter saw no military necessity for a trans-isthmian highway, and roads beyond the Zone were condemned on the familiar ground that they gave a raiding force ready-made access to the forward defences. Lassiter was equally opposed to the idea of a bridge near the Pedro Miguel locks, as was

---

[78] Text of Article 10 of the 1926 treaty is in *BD*, 835–6.

[79] SD, 1910–49, 819.74/106, Panama note of 19.12.22; /114, Panama memo of 25.4.23; /106, Hughes to Weeks, 11.1.23; 711.192/106, Morrow to White, 25.3.24, enclosing Morrow to Weeks, 26.2.24; 819.74/108, Taylor to Walker, 20.12.22. AG, post-1917, 311.23, Irwin to Eberle, 31.1.24. SD, 1910–49, 711.192/22, South to Hughes, 27.2.24; /205, Minutes of meetings of 24.4.24, 6.5.24, 8.5.24, and 15.5.24. Text of Article 9 of the 1926 treaty is in *BD*, 834–5.

the canal administration, which saw bridges anywhere as hostages to fortune: an impediment to shipping in normal times and a massive obstruction if blown by saboteurs. So the treaty commitment was to the lesser evil of a ferry, and it opened for business in 1930.[80]

In other respects the treaty did little or nothing for Panama in its defence-related articles. From Panama's viewpoint, one of the most oppressive features of the 1903 convention was the U.S. right under Article 2 to acquire land outside the Zone, and the Taboga furore was proof of its power to whip up a storm of anti-American feeling. Although the clamour over Taboga subsided, there were plenty of other bones of contention to hand, notably the Navy's three radio stations. In October 1920, when a rating at the Puerto Obaldía station shot and wounded 'a drunken and disorderly native', Panama claimed the right to put the assailant on trial. Washington, on the other hand, asserted extraterritorial immunity for its man under the 1903 convention, whereby sovereignty passed to the United States along with title whenever land in Panama was taken for canal purposes.[81]

The only way to break the impasse and to resolve the general issue of land acquisition, so the Panamanians believed, was to make a revision of the 1903 formula part of the new treaty. Panama expected Washington to demonstrate 'the absolute and inevitable necessity' for more land, any transfer must have Panama's advance agreement, and it could be legitimised only by Panamanian warranty.[82]

None of these stipulations found favour in American circles. The necessity for extra land, in Governor Morrow's view, 'will not terminate until canal operation terminates'. Secretary of State Hughes told Minister Alfaro that while he was ready to consider what further tracts might be required for construction, operation, maintenance, and sanitation, the question of land for defence purposes was not open to discussion, because it was impossible to predict coming developments in warfare. When Hughes asked the War Department for an estimate of its future needs, he was told that Article 2 must be preserved to guard against all contingencies. It was a natural precaution, but it left Panama tied to what Alfaro bitterly described as 'an encumbrance in the nature of a floating lien upon the entire territory of the Republic'.[83]

[80] Texts of Articles 2 and 3 of the 1926 treaty are in *BD*, 827–9. PC, 47-H-5, Riche report of 11.1.19. SD, 1910–49, 819.154/283, Alfaro to Hughes, 1.6.23. PC, 47-H-5, Lassiter to Walker, 24.12.25. AG, post-1917, 388.1, Lassiter to Adjutant General, 29.12.25. PC, 94-A-3/1926, Lassiter to Walker, 28.11.25; Walker to Flint, 17.8.26; 47-H-5, Memo of 1.2.19; 9-A-74, Morrow to Harding, 26.1.20. SD, 1910–49, 515.4D5/20, South to Stimson, 15.10.29.

[81] SD, 1910–49, 819.0144/29, Price to Colby, 25.10.20; Colby to Price, 28.10.20.

[82] PC, 80-A-3, Panama memo of 25.11.20. SD, 1910–49, 819.52/150, Price to Colby, 14.12.20; 811F.812/914, Panama note of 24.1.21; 819.0144/49, Panama note of 12.11.21; 811F.812/951, Garay to Morrow, 29.10.23.

[83] PC, 80-A-3, Morrow to Weeks, 7.5.23. SD, 1910–49, 611.1931/157B, Hughes to Alfaro, 15.10.23; 711.192/2/A, Hughes to Weeks, 20.3.24; /197, Weeks to Hughes, 21.3.24; /205, Minutes of meeting of 19.3.24.

Yet though the substance of American rights was not affected, the form of land transfer was changed to suit Panamanian preferences. Up to this point land outside the Zone had been expropriated by fiat: The canal administration served notice on Panama and then took possession. Panama, however, found the notifications peremptory and wanted the legation to handle the transactions instead. This was highly objectionable to a canal directorate who feared the process would bog down in diplomatic negotiation. But Hughes took Panama's side, and Article 1 of the 1926 treaty placed the issue in the State Department's hands. When the treaty was not ratified, Governor Walker reverted exultantly to the old modus operandi, giving Panama a two-week ultimatum to surrender parcels on Taboga and Taboguilla. This provoked just the wave of protest the treaty article had been designed to avoid, and in the spring of 1928 the governor was instructed to turn over responsibility for land acquisition to the minister, in whose bailiwick it henceforth remained.[84]

Given American inflexibility on the fundamentals of the land question, it was extraordinary that Panama should have volunteered to place itself unreservedly at Washington's disposal in defence matters. In May 1924 Alfaro submitted a treaty article which gave permanence to the current ad hoc arrangement for U.S. Army manoeuvres on Panamanian soil in peacetime, but the concession went far beyond that. Panama was also prepared to consider itself in a state of war 'in case of any war in which the United States should be a belligerent'. The republic would then enact whatever measures Washington decreed for internal or external security, and the War Department would have full control of military operations anywhere on the isthmus.[85]

Washington was not slow to accept the offer, but the motivation behind Panama's readiness to make it is hard to fathom. For Governor Walker it merely acknowledged the fact that the United States could occupy Panama whenever it chose, and if Alfaro believed he had something to gain from making the move, he was sadly mistaken. At the final negotiating session in July 1926, the chief U.S. delegate, Francis White, was anxious to assure the Panamanians that the article would not make them bring in military service. Six months later, however, when the treaty came up for ratification, its leading opponent, Harmodio Arias, was able to raise the spectre of conscription. Washington, it was whispered, would recruit the youth of Panama as its foot-soldiers in forthcoming

---

[84] SD, 1910–49, 819.74/92, Price to Colby, 7.10.20; 811F.812/914, Panama note of 24.1.21; /920, Feuille to Harding, 27.4.20; 611.1931/57, White to Hughes, 1.10.23. Text of Article 1 of the 1926 treaty is in *BD*, 823. SD, 1910–49, 711.1914/14, Kellogg to South, 25.7.27. WPD, 1652–16, Davis to Walker, 19.3.28. AG, post-1917, 336, Kellogg to Davis, 30.4.28. Further details on land acquisition may be found in SD, 1910–49, 811F.812/951 and 711F.1914/112 of 13.11.35. See also U.S. Army, Caribbean Defense Command, Historical Section, *Acquisition of land in the Panama Canal Zone* (Quarry Heights, CZ, 1946).

[85] SD, 1910–49, 711.192/205, Minutes of meeting of 8.5.24; 819.0144/49, Panama note of 12.11.21. Text of Article 11 of the 1926 treaty is in *BD*, 836–7.

interventions against Nicaragua and Mexico, and droves of labourers in the
interior made for the hills to escape impressment. When the treaty was lost in
the Assembly vote of 26 January 1927, the defence commitment was an important
nail in its coffin.[86]

But treaty or no treaty, the U.S. military was determined that the Panamanians should stay under strict American control in the realm of defence. Above
all, they should be given no opportunity to call in a foreign patron to undermine
U.S. hegemony. The instincts of the Monroe Doctrine ran as strong as ever.

Some alien infiltrations were taken less seriously than others. In 1924–5 the
Chiari administration granted extensive concessions to British speculators, and
in April 1926 the British-owned Panama Corporation was formed to exploit
their potential. Enter Richard Marsh, the terminator of President Mendoza
in 1910 and champion of the San Blas Indians in 1925. Marsh had recently
explored the isthmus on behalf of Firestone, Ford, and General Motors, pin-
pointing areas suitable for rubber plantations. He was convinced that the British
had promoted the Corporation to block rubber growing in Panama for the U.S.
market. But though Marsh's paranoia was shared by congressional anglophobes
such as Senator William Borah, the flurry soon passed. More alarming was the
Corporation's announcement in 1928 that it had contracted with Panama to
survey the route of a highway from Chepo to Portobelo. The arrangement came
close to eroding the U.S. monopoly on trans-isthmian road construction, and both
State and War were insistent that the monopoly must be upheld. Panama fell
rapidly into line, with its acceptance of Washington's offer to make the survey.[87]

The Army was equally intent on minimising foreign penetration of the burgeoning field of commercial air traffic in and around Panama. In the summer of
1925 General Lassiter tried to amend the treaty text to ensure U.S. control of
civil aviation across an area extending from San José in Costa Rica to Cartagena
in Colombia. Otherwise, he claimed, European airlines with branches in Panama
could reconnoitre the Zone as pathfinders for an attack on canal installations.
Prominent among these was the Colombian–German Air Transport Company
(SCADTA). Lassiter's revision was not adopted, and Panama's non-ratification of
the treaty meant that Washington was left without any formal means of regulating flights across the isthmus. As pressure for admission to Panama mounted
from SCADTA, the Army grew increasingly agitated. U.S. policy, wrote one staff

[86] WPD, 1652–7, Walker to Davis, 13.1.26. SD, 1910–49, 711.192/205, Minutes of meeting
   of 27.7.26; /219 South to Kellogg, 3.8.26; /288, South to Kellogg, 17.1.27; /297, South to
   Kellogg, 24.1.27. NYT, 21.12.26, 1/4; 24.12.26, 4/4 and 14/2.
[87] NYT, 7.4.26, 2/2, 22/3; 5.6.26, 6/1. SD, 1910–49, 819.6341 P19/5, South to Kellogg,
   13.4.26; /8, Interview with Marsh, 4.5.26; /9, Marsh memo of 18.5.26; /6, South to
   Kellogg, 26.4.26; 819.154/242, South to Kellogg, 16.4.28; Kellogg to South 23.4.28; /246,
   Davis to Kellogg, 3.5.28; /223, South to Kellogg, 1.8.28. See also Henry Norton, 'Why
   Britishers in Panama?' World's Work, 59 (November 1930), 29–32.

officer, might appear 'to be dictated by pure commercialism', but American dominance of the air routes to Panama was founded on 'no less a principle than that of our National defense and self-preservation'.[88]

The issue came to a head at the Pan-American conference in Havana in February 1928. There the State Department was faced with a draft convention on air traffic which threatened to give Panama a dangerous degree of latitude, in the provision that every state in the Americas had 'complete and exclusive sovereignty' over its air-space. The U.S. delegation went to Havana in quest of a condition banning any airline from getting landing rights in Panama if run by a non-member of the Pan-American Union. This it proposed to achieve by allowing for bilateral agreements on 'appropriate' regulations. In the teeth of Colombian objections, however, a rider was added stipulating that such an arrangement should 'in no case prevent the establishment of inter-American aerial lines and terminals', and this gave SCADTA the chance to apply for a base at Portobelo, less than twenty miles outside the Zone.[89]

The application was swiftly vetoed by the War Department, which went on to approve the idea of opening a commercial terminal on France Field; its air-mail service to Miami was inaugurated by Charles Lindbergh in February 1929. The Zone was said to be the only possible location, since there were no suitable sites for airport development within a hundred miles of Panama City or Colón. Refusing to accept this self-serving nonsense, Panama made plans to build an airport of its own. The venture was eventually sanctioned, but only if the Canal Zone terminal stayed in business even though its use as a commercial air centre stretched U.S. rights way beyond reasonable limits.[90]

The official Panamanian reaction was understandably bitter, and when the American Legion in the Zone urged a second terminal on the Pacific side, the idea was angrily denounced in the local press. The seal of the Canal should read not 'The earth divided, the world united' but 'The earth divided, the world put at a distance'. Panama's motto should be changed from 'Pro mundi beneficio' to 'Pro U.S.A. beneficio'. To a military establishment whose raison d'être was American security, however, this was no doubt precisely as it should be.[91]

---

[88] AG, post-1917, 580.8, Lassiter to Adjutant General, 5.6.25; 580.81, Lassiter to Adjutant General, 21.8.25. SD, 1910–49, 711.192/151, Acting Secretary of War to Kellogg, 24.8.25. *NYT*, 30.10.27, sect. II, 1/2; 13.11.27, sect. III, 2/5; 19.11.27, 9/1. AG, post-1917, 580.8, Shartle memo of 17.10.27.

[89] Text of the convention of 20.2.28 is in *FRUS 1928*, 1: 585–95. *NYT*, 23.1.28, 3/1; 8.2.28, 4/2 and 3. AG, post-1917, 580.8, Craig to Adjutant General, 20.7.28.

[90] AG, post-1917, 580.8, Davis to Kellogg, 21.7.28 and 7.8.28; Davis to Flint, 10.10.28. Canal Zone Postal Service, *Canal Zone postage stamps* (Mount Hope, CZ, 1961), 233–4. SD, 1910–49, 819.796/29, Report of advisory committee of 31.8.28; 819.7962/1, South to Kellogg, 19.12.28; /19, South to Stimson, 27.9.29; /22, Good to Stimson, 31.10.29.

[91] SD, 1910–49, 819.7962/25, South to Stimson, 17.12.29. AG, post-1917, 580.82, Craig to Adjutant General, 6.8.29.

Yet Panama's subservience was no compensation for the Army's utter failure to persuade Congress to fund the garrison adequately in the twenties. Its storage depot, reported the *New York Times*, was 'housed in tinder boxes which one good fire would wipe out in a few hours'. Its manpower was well below the minimum requirement, and a staple element of this undersized command was the 42nd Infantry Regiment from Puerto Rico – despite the Army's conviction that it was unwise to defend the canal with 'members of an alien race . . . untried in war'. In 1927 the 42nd was disbanded after its quarters were condemned as derelict, and when the commanding general asked the War Department for an appropriation to replace them, the reply could only be that funds would be limited for several years to come. The Zone continued to be protected on a shoestring; symbolic of its appalling state of readiness was the news in 1928 that a 14-inch gun had been shipped in for installation at the Pacific entrance. The weapon was irrelevant now that a fleet bombardment had been discounted, and it had been obsolete even before work on the fortifications began in 1912.[92]

Even though the defences of the canal were at a dangerously low ebb, however, the principle of a defended waterway remained central to U.S. strategy. In the spring of 1927 the Japanese were thought poised to challenge the status quo established by the Washington conference whereby Singapore, Pearl Harbor, and the Canal Zone were all excluded from the freeze on fortification in the Pacific. The response of the service departments was instantly hostile. The United States's willingness to accept the treaty ratio for capital ships was 'premised upon its right to insure the availability of the Panama Canal during war by its adequate protection by fixed and mobile local defense'. Discussion of the Zone at the forthcoming Geneva conference on naval disarmament, Secretary of War Dwight Davis pronounced, would be 'tantamount to permitting the Conference to discuss restrictions upon measures for the defense of the coasts of the continental United States'. The subject did not feature on the conference agenda.[93]

Conformity to the Washington treaty not only prevented the canal's neutralisation, it also countered pressures for its replacement, thanks to the Washington embargo on new capital ships. When enlargement of the locks was ruled out, the notion of a sea-level canal was resurrected, notably by Philippe Bunau-Varilla. In 1924 Bunau-Varilla claimed that no amount of active defence could save the mechanism of the lock canal from bombing or shelling. Only the rugged passive-defence qualities of a seaway could offer the necessary invulnerability.

[92] *NYT*, 7.1.25, 4/2. WPD, 2241, War Plans Division to G-3, 14.5.26; unused War Plans Division memo of July 1925. *NYT*, 28.7.27, 17/1. AG, post-1917, 600.1, Martin to Adjutant General, 11.8.26. *NYT*, 23.3.28, 2/3, 6/2.

[93] JB, s.338, U.S. Mission in Geneva to Kellogg, 23.4.27; Joint Planning Committee memo of 27.4.27. GB, 438, s.1347-8(j), General Board to Wilbur, 25.4.27. WPD, 2938, Davis to Kellogg, 28.4.27.

Both Governor Morrow and his successor, however, were dead against the proposition. The sea-level concept, Morrow told John Stevens, was a hardy perennial which would always have someone to make its case, 'no matter how often the impossibility of realising any such scheme within practicable limits of time and cost may be demonstrated'.[94]

A more attractive possibility seemed to be a second canal, through Nicaragua. This option had been dropped by Harding in 1923 when the Corps of Engineers estimated it might well cost nearly $1 billion, but fresh impetus came with Panama's rejection of the 1926 treaty. It then acquired some important backers, among them Secretary of State Kellogg. Testifying before the Senate's Interoceanic Canals Committee, Kellogg declared that a Nicaragua transit would 'give us two strings to our bow'. This view brushed aside Bunau-Varilla's revival of the argument he had so successfully deployed in 1902 – that the volcanoes of Nicaragua made the very idea of a canal there an absurdity – and in 1929 President Herbert Hoover gave the green light for a feasibility study.[95]

At the same time, however, the investigation was to consider the cheaper alternative of enlarging the traffic capacity of Panama. Already land had been acquired for a storage dam to retain the outflow from Lake Alhajuela, just outside the Zone. The reservoir would guarantee the canal an adequate water supply in the dry season from November to May and provide enough volume to operate a third set of locks, to be built in the 1950s as the existing twin-chamber flights neared the limit of their ship-handling potential. The dam would give the canal an invaluable supplement to its main source in Gatún Lake and together with the new locks was expected to meet all the demands likely to be placed on the waterway for the rest of the century. If the third-locks scheme were adopted in preference to Nicaragua or a sea-level canal, the future of Goethals's masterpiece appeared to be secure.[96]

That is, unless it had first succumbed to an air attack. In its last full-dress exercise of the decade, the U.S. fleet yet again laid bare the defects of the Zone's air defences. At first light on 26 January 1929 the carrier *Saratoga* launched forty-five planes in eleven minutes to 'bomb' the locks at Pedro Miguel and Miraflores. No Army or Navy air patrols were encountered until after the mission had been accomplished, and the canal was deemed to have been put out of action for at least thirty days.[97]

[94] SD, 1910–49, 811F.812/954, Bunau-Varilla to Hughes, 5.2.24. *NYT*, 20.1.24, 20/6. OA, NHC, Papers of Captain Miles DuVal, Memo of 6.6.49, quoting Morrow to Stevens, 31.5.24.

[95] *NYT*, 10.2.23, 15/5. SD, 1910–49, 817.812/433½, Kellogg statement of 3.5.28. *NYT*, 24.2.28, 20/7; 19.6.29, 63/2.

[96] *NYT*, 8.11.27, 54/2. PC, 9-A-11, Burgess to Good, 9.8.29; Burgess memo of 14.10.29, WPD, 3182, Walker to Davis, 17.8.27.

[97] *NYT*, 11.2.29, 14/1. SNSCC, 1927–39, (SC)A16-3(5-IX), Whiting memo of 30.1.29; comment by chief of staff, Scouting Fleet; comment by unit observer, Black Striking Force, of 4.2.29.

The conclusions drawn from Fleet Problem IX were mixed. 'No naval base in the world', wrote the *New York Times*, '. . . is safe from a devastating blow by swift carriers properly supported by a fleet.' To the fleet commander the exercise had shown 'that an air attack upon the Canal once launched cannot be stopped in the air except by a force many times stronger than the attacking force'. The only effective defence was preventive action 'to put enemy carrier decks out of commission before their squadrons take the air'. This view was shared by Admiral William Pratt, an enthusiast for long-range defence since his service on the isthmus in the war. The Navy's offshore reconnaissance, Pratt believed, should be extended well beyond the current 200-mile limit by basing aircraft tenders at the Bahia Honda coaling station in Cuba, in the Pearl Islands archipelago in the Gulf of Panama, and in the Galápagos, a thousand miles out in the Pacific. A less-exalted analyst reached precisely the opposite verdict. Captain M. G. Cook was pessimistic about the chances of early interception, since detection of an attack group heading in at night to mount a dawn strike was virtually impossible in the current state of the art. The only hope, in Cook's opinion, was reliance on intensive close-in defence by torpedo nets and smoke-screens over the locks and the Gatún spillway.[98]

Meanwhile the Army strengthened the inner defence ring by speeding completion of a new air-base at Albrook Field, three miles from the Pacific coast, to improve its reaction time to Japanese warplanes zeroing in across Panama Bay. The building of Albrook marked the most important step forward since the war, but the canal's general preparedness was still rudimentary in the extreme. It would take the cumulative international anarchy of the 1930s to bring it up to scratch.[99]

[98] *NYT*, 11.2.29, 14/1. SNSCC, 1927–39, (SC)A-16-3(5-IX), CINCUS report, 29, 31, 16; remarks by Pratt, *c.* 30.1.29; 1992–4, Cook memo of 8.7.29.

[99] *NYT*, 27.3.28, 2/4; 6.1.29, sect. III, 6/6.

Part III

Changes: 1930–1955

We have two great maritime frontiers, on the Atlantic and the Pacific, connected by a narrow defile which is in our possession – the Panama Canal. . . . So long as we keep the main battle-line strength of our fleet together . . . and so long as we maintain our grip on the Panama Canal . . . we are certain of being able . . . to transfer our fleet quickly from ocean to ocean, while denying a like privilege to an enemy. . . . The keystone of our arch of security is . . . the Panama Canal.

(George Fielding Eliot, *The ramparts we watch* [1938])

The strategic importance of the Panama Canal . . . is largely based on its economic value to our commercial shipping. So far as actual naval operations are concerned, [it] is of a secondary nature. . . . The ability to move naval forces from the Atlantic to the Pacific or vice versa via the canal is not as important as it was prior to World War II [and] crippling the canal would not be a decisive blow to our defense. . . . I do not believe that permanent closure of the canal would jeopardize the national security.

(Admiral Daniel Gallery, September 1947)

8

The Zone régime

In its second quarter-century the canal establishment went through the trauma it had escaped after the Connor inquiry of 1921 – a wholesale reorganisation which turned it inside out. Though in the end it came out of the experience surprisingly resilient, it was a painful operation which left a multitude of scars.

Early on in the period there was little sign that the sacrosanctities of the Goethals régime were in any serious danger. Exposure of the lack of any meaningful anti-sabotage precautions in the spring of 1934 convinced Army planners that the old order was not fit to be entrusted with the security of the waterway. Their conclusion, like that of General Wood in 1917, was to vest the governorship permanently in the garrison commander, in peace as well as in time of war. But the idea was soon dropped when the drawbacks were weighed up. The Corps of Engineers would not give up control without an almighty struggle, and it had many powerful allies in Congress. Above all, the military's take-over bid might backfire disastrously if President Franklin Roosevelt took his predilection for the Navy so far as to put a naval governor in charge. Better things as they were than that nightmare scenario. Sleeping dogs were consequently allowed to lie.[1]

Later in the year a heavyweight study of the canal administration was published which levelled at it many of the same criticisms as Connor. The canal's accounting system, wrote its author, Marshall Dimock, 'violates some of the most important of the accepted canons of financial management', that is, in having its auditor act simultaneously as its budget director. But the Zone was in no mind to fall in line with bureaucratic orthodoxy. Testifying before a Senate subcommittee, the head of the Canal's Washington office was adamant that federal agents had no right to check on the purchases of the Zone's

---

[1] WPD, 3741, War Plans Division to MacArthur, 30.4.34. For the 1934 scare, see Chapter 12 at nn. 6–8.

business arm, the Panama Railroad. At the end of 1934 the auditor's title was changed to comptroller, but he continued to work both sides of the street, and the Canal went on its own idiosyncratic fiscal way.[2]

It was no more receptive to Dimock's thought that Canal and Railroad would best be merged into a single corporation. This, Dimock claimed, would liberate the Zone from the strait-jacket of congressional appropriations, since the revenues of the new partnership would derive entirely from its earnings. But the Zone leadership judged that Congress would keep hold of the purse-strings and that if Railroad proceeds were reckoned part of Canal income, its funding would be pruned. As it was, the Railroad's profits were an invaluable bonus which made it possible to sustain high living standards for the Zonians and avoid an increase in tolls which would make the Panama route less attractive to merchant shipping. Here too, therefore, Dimock was ignored, although in 1938 tolls were raised for the first time since the canal opened.[3]

Yet while the Zone stayed intact in its basic structure, it was marginalised as an influence on Washington's Panama policy. In the unratified treaty of 1926 it succeeded in minimising the commercial concessions made to Panama, and it acquired the New Cristóbal section of Colón. But it was cut out of the negotiations for the treaty signed in 1936, which left New Cristóbal with Panama and acknowledged in principle the Panamanian stake in a canal enterprise hitherto the governor's exclusive sphere.[4]

Worse was to come. On 5 September 1939, just four days after the outbreak of the Second World War, a presidential executive order assigned control of the Zone to the Army garrison commander. The move touched off deep resentment in the Zone directorate. The Panama Canal Act of 1912 prescribed an Army take-over only when the United States itself was at war or when war was imminent, and in the First World War the Army had not assumed control until after U.S. entry, that is, two years and eight months after the war began. Governor Clarence Ridley therefore questioned the legality of the order, but the Army found sufficient justification in an obscure clause of the Canal Zone Code of 1934 whereby the president could delegate authority to the governor 'and such other persons as he may deem competent' to run the Canal and the Zone. The staff at Balboa Heights were appalled at the chicanery and at the prospect of military rule. 'Should the Canal ever be placed under the War Department,' a senior official had stated in 1930, 'this would be well nigh

[2] Norman Padelford, *The Panama Canal in peace and war* (New York, 1942), 226–7. Dimock, *Government-operated enterprises*, 131, 134, 37.

[3] Dimock, *Government-operated enterprises*, 217. Padelford, *Panama Canal*, 303, 256–7. Emory Johnson, 'Panama Canal revenues and finances', *Proceedings of the American Philosophical Society*, 87 (January–June 1943), 177. André Siegfried, *Suez and Panama* (New York, 1940), 339.

[4] See Chapter 5 at n. 51 and Chapter 18 at n. 21.

disastrous.' But Army Chief of Staff George Marshall was advised that objections to the code were inadmissible, and he tersely informed Ridley that 'those in the Zone must conform to the necessities of the Zone'.[5]

The conformity was prolonged way beyond the end of the war. After the Armistice of November 1918 the governor recovered his powers in less than four months; not so after the Japanese surrender of August 1945. Commanding General Willis Crittenberger believed that putting the governor back at the helm would be 'temporizing with the fundamental question of responsibility for the overall security of this area'. A new executive order should be issued giving the Army charge of all aspects of canal defence in peacetime, so far the governor's prerogative.[6]

In the event, the order was not put through, but the 1939 directive remained in force, and on formation of the Caribbean Defense Command in November 1947 the governor was instructed to place himself at its disposal. For two years more the jurisdictional dogfight raged, until in February 1950 the dispute was resolved in the governor's favour. The 1939 order was rescinded, and Goethals's system came into its own again.[7]

Yet not for long. The Zone's reversion to civil government was only one of a batch of recommendations made to President Truman by his Bureau of the Budget, which took the ancien régime straight out of the frying pan of Army hegemony and into the fire of a managerial revolution.

Its origins lay in a visitation to the isthmus early in 1947 by a pair of Bureau investigators, Messrs Moore and Seidman, who returned to Washington to pen a scathing report on the Canal–Railroad organism. The Zone, they believed, still displayed 'many of the characteristics of an Army Camp run by an absolute Governor', and its insularity had stiffened a tendency 'to crystalize tradition and develop a general resistance to change'. Contributing heavily to the pervasive inertia was 'the predominance of "old-timers" in key jobs', and the machinery of government could only be described as 'a museum of administrative antiquities'.[8]

Twice the governor was urged to put his own house in order, but nothing

[5] Padelford, *Panama Canal*, 635. WPD, 4193-2, Judge Advocate General to Chief of Staff, 13.11.39. The clause in question was Section 5, Title 2, of the Canal Zone Code of 19 June 1934: See Executive Order 8232 of 5.9.39 in *3CFRC (1938–43)*, 569, and POD, 381, Case 57, Crittenberger to Plans and Operations, 26.3.48. PC, 2-C-124, Flint to McIlvaine, 24.5.30. WPD, 4193-2, Marshall to Ridley, 11.12.39.

[6] OpD, 384 CDC, Crittenberger to War Department, 19.11.45. POD, 381, Case 57, Crittenberger to Eisenhower, 15.8.46.

[7] POD, 381, Case 57, Royall to Mehaffey, 14.11.47; Crittenberger to Plans and Operations, 26.3.48. SD, 1950-4, 911F.5301/3-250, citing Executive Order 10107 of 8.2.50 in *3CFRC (1949–53)*, 300.

[8] PC, 65-J-3/M, Mehaffey to Rossbottom, 11.2.47. BB, Memo by Seidman and Moore, 30.4.47. *1950 Hearings*, 50.

Figure 4. The high command: Governor Joseph Mehaffey and his
department heads, April 1948. (Panama Canal Commission)

was done, in spite of a serious financial crisis. On the governor's own admission,
operating expenses had doubled since 1932 while revenues remained static. His
answer, however, was not structural reform but a rise in tolls, from the ninety
cents a ton prescribed in 1938 to one dollar a ton. When American shippers
balked at the increase, Truman postponed it and directed the Bureau to mount
a searching inquiry into the Canal apparatus.[9]

The Bureau's recommendations were based on a blueprint already drawn up
by the Commission on the Organization of the Executive Branch of Government,
headed by former president Herbert Hoover. In February 1950 Truman approved
them all, except for a proposal to transfer the Canal to the secretary of commerce. Henceforth the business activities of the Canal and the Railroad would
be brought together under the corporate aegis of a new Panama Canal Company. The Canal's municipal functions would be taken over by a body entitled
the Canal Zone Government.[10]

The crux of the reorganisation was the revolution it envisaged in finance.
The Company was to bear the net expense of civil administration, health, and

[9] BB, Seidman memo of 27.7.48 and Donnelly memo of 24.2.49. *NYT*, 14.12.49, 63/5; 15.3.49,
     55/8; 24.8.49, 25/1; 26.8.49, 8/5. *BB Report*, 2.
[10] *NYT*, 2.2.50, 51/5.

sanitation, and these costs would be met out of the revenues of the enterprise as a whole. Hitherto they had been covered exclusively by tolls, leaving income from Canal and Railroad businesses untouched. In other words, tolls were subsidising the Zonians and making it possible for them to enjoy an artificially high standard of living. These happy days were now drawing to an end. Seidman made it clear that in future toll income would be expected to pay for no more than 50 per cent of municipal expenditure, the remainder coming from the Zone's ancillary operations. In order to maximise receipts from both sectors, U.S. government vessels would lose the privilege of free transit, while fees would be imposed for such services as schooling, and charges would be levied on the armed forces as well as on Company personnel. In short, the Company was expected to become self-sufficient and to place itself on a strictly commercial footing.[11]

To Governor Francis Newcomer the changes marked 'a violent departure' from the previous principles of canal management, and an Army Department report drew the conclusion that the Zone was 'of necessity . . . a paternalistic dictatorship'. All to no avail. The Canal Zone Government Act went on the statute book in September 1950, though the provision on the apportionment of costs did not embody the fifty–fifty formula set out by Seidman. Tolls were to carry only 'an appropriate share' of the net costs of the Canal Zone Government, and in calculating that share no more than 'substantial weight' would be given to the ratio of toll income to the Company's total revenue. Imprecision such as this left ample room for manoeuvre over future cost allocations. To that extent, at least, the Zone's congressional allies had given it the means to fight another day.[12]

The Zone was also able to fend off an Army bid to put the canal back under the sway of the garrison commander. This was partly justified by accusations that the governor had given inadequate backing to the government's anti-communist loyalty programme and failed to enforce the Internal Security Act by keeping undesirable aliens under surveillance. All the Army got after months of infighting was an order decreeing that in the event of a conflict of view on canal defence, the judgement of the military should prevail.[13]

The brush with Caribbean Command was nothing, however, in comparison with the bruising contest which opened up over the implementation of the 1950

---

[11] *BB Report*, 13–16. *NYT*, 31.1.50, 45/8. *1950 Hearings*, 45–8.

[12] *1950 Hearings*, 42. WNRC, RG 335, OSA 320 Panama Canal (9–20–50), Report by W. T. Comer of 4.4.50. Text of Public Law 841 of 26 September 1950 may be found in *United States statutes at large*, 64/1 (1951), 1032–7.

[13] WNRC, RG 335, OSA 381 Panama Canal (12–20–50); CD 092 Panama, General Counsel, Department of Defense, to Director, Bureau of the Budget, 8.1.51. POD, 350.09 Panama, Staff study of 29.1.51. WNRC, RG 335, OSA 381 Panama Canal (3–2–51). POD, 350.09 Panama, Morris to Collins, 21.9.51. Richard Baxter, *The law of international waterways*, 86, citing Executive Order 10398 of 26.9.52 in *3CFRC (1949–53)*, 899.

Act. Stepping into the ring on Washington's behalf was Karl Bendetsen, assistant secretary of the Army and from September 1951 chairman of the Company. Seidman, the instigator of the purge, strongly approved of Bendetsen as 'a fighter who does not hesitate to overrule the Governor on occasion when a good case is proved'. Bendetsen certainly seemed a man after the Bureau's own heart. His first move was to recommend the dismissal of the heir-apparent to the governorship, the chief of the Canal's Washington office, and the vice-president of the Railroad and their replacement by businessmen attuned to the new management style. Soon thereafter he was deep in two wrangles with the Zone establishment, both products of the drive to make the Canal pay its own way.[14]

The first stemmed from the February 1951 proposal for a steep increase in the tuition fees charged by Canal Zone schools to parents living outside the Zone. There was, of course, the alternative of raising the price of goods and services to shipping, and in June Governor Newcomer announced a toll increase. But he was overruled by Washington, and the Canal faced protests from both American and Panamanian sources over the new school fees. Anxious to smooth Panama down, the State Department asked the Company board for some concession, but in the wake of the veto on a tolls rise, the board did not disguise its anger. To the department's representative at the conference, Tapley Bennett, the board members 'sounded like Grade-7 crane operators when they got going. . . . Social evolution stopped in 1908, if not earlier, for most of these gentlemen.' When Bennett stressed the importance of an American education for Panamanians, he was asked to comment on 'the influence on recent events in China [the communist revolution] of United States use of the Boxer indemnity for the education of Chinese students'. In December, however, Bendetsen relented, and the previous tuition rates for non-resident Panamanian and American pupils were restored.[15]

The second imbroglio centred on the Bureau's determination to raise rents on Canal Zone housing. Newcomer jibbed at putting any extra burden on Company employees; the money would be found by doubling the rents charged to other U.S. government personnel. In October he compounded this defiance by asking Bendetsen who was running the Canal, the board of the Company or the Bureau of the Budget? Bendetsen's reply was a magisterial reprimand. 'Neither you nor any member of the Board', he told Newcomer, 'has any vested or proprietary interest in the Canal Company. We are all working for the same employer – the Government of the United States. We should never

[14] SD, 1950–4, 811F.43/9–1751. WNRC, RG 335, OSA 320 Panama Canal (1–15–51), Bendetsen to Pace, 15.1.51.
[15] SD, 1950–4, 811F.43/2–2351. WNRC, RG 335, OSA 350 Panama Canal (7–11–51) and (12–20–51). NYT, 8.6.51, 55/4. SD, 1950–4, 811F.43/4–2451, /9–1751, and /8–2552.

presume to place ourselves beyond the administrative influence of our employer, nor waste time in resistance to that overlying authority.' Goethals, the creator of gubernatorial autonomy, was no doubt revolving in his grave.[16]

Two months later, in January 1952, Bendetsen went on to produce a survey of the Zone which revealed extensive duplication of facilities between the Canal and the armed forces and suggested gross incompetence in some areas. The Commissary, according to an admirer of Bendetsen's, was being administered by 'a former school teacher who gives every evidence of being overwhelmed by his task'. Again Bendetsen urged the introduction of businessmen on the Company board to bring a measure of professionalism to this snug little isthmian fraternity.[17]

Yet Bendetsen took the Company's side on the vexed question of Canal Zone Government finance. Rented accommodation was relieved of any liability for contributing towards the cost of Zone administration, and Bendetsen proposed to exempt commissaries and clubhouses too. He did so on the thesis that all dealings with employees were 'transactions within the company', which had the same kind of obligation towards its work force as a lumber camp in the backwoods providing its loggers with bed and board.[18]

The Bureau saw this move as a stratagem in conflict with the 1950 Act, and when Bendetsen's scheme was adopted by the board, it again called for the organisation to be taken out of the Army's hands and placed under the Department of Commerce. The Army retained control, but the Bureau's co-inquisitor, the General Accounting Office, launched an immediate offensive in a report demanding widespread economies. Governor Newcomer was incensed at what he described as a 'mass of misstatements of fact, unjustified innuendos, and irresponsible opinions', but his term of office was expiring, and Washington saw to it that his designated successor, Lieutenant-Governor Herbert Vogel, did not take up where he left off. The astounded Vogel was passed over in favour of General John Seybold; it was the first time since 1914 that the engineer of maintenance had not become governor.[19]

In September, Seybold began to prove his worth with the announcement of a rent increase averaging 34 per cent. In October the Army Department urged him to consider stepping up tolls, and pending that review Seybold introduced

[16] PC, 65-J-3/M, Bendetsen to file, 16.5.51; Newcomer to Bendetsen, 1.6.51; 65-H-1, Memo of 29.6.51. WNRC, RG 335, OSA 620 Panama Canal, Newcomer to Board, 31.8.51; Bendetsen to Pace, 10.10.51; Newcomer to Pace, 22.10.51. PCC, 65-J-3, Bendetsen to Newcomer, 2.11.51.

[17] WNRC, RG 335, OSA 091 Panama Canal, Bendetsen to Pace, 16.1.52, with Inclosure 'B', 10, and Inclosure "E"; OSA 320 Panama Canal, Robinson to Pace, 16.1.52.

[18] WNRC, RG 335, OSA 091 Panama Canal, Bendetsen to Pace, 16.1.52, with Inclosure 'B', 4, 8–9; OSA 320 Panama Canal, Memo of 26.6.52.

[19] BB, Undated analysis of Bendetsen report of 16.1.52; Seidman to Donnelly, 27.2.52, Seidman for Truman, 8.4.52. WNRC, RG 335, OSA 320 Panama Canal, Bureau of the Budget to Secretary of the Army, 29.7.52; Newcomer to Ives, 6.3.52.

stiffer rates for marine bunkering, the railway, the docks and piers at the terminals, and the steamship line under the Company flag.[20]

To the Zonians this was nothing short of a cataclysm. Ambassador Wiley caught the mood in his graphic résumé of the response to Vogel's erasure: 'When the Ming Dynasty was overthrown in China, or when Louis XVI took abrupt exit from official life, the impression could not have been deeper.' The *New York Times* wrote of a community bewildered at the sudden demotion of the father-figure of the governor and the usurpation of the Zone by 'cold businessmen' operating by remote control from stateside. After the bombshell of the rent hike, the Zonians hit back with demands for an investigation. Perhaps the truest gauge of their thirst for revenge, however, was the support they threw behind Panama's renewed demand for a larger annuity and their equally unprecedented backing for the claims of the non-white majority of the Company's work force. This fellow feeling was short-lived, but it was a tell-tale sign of the chagrin the *aggiornamento* had produced.[21]

Over the next three years the GAO kept up its pressure through annual audits of the Company–Government. The report published in September 1953 – written in collaboration with Bendetsen's former aide in the Zone, Colonel Peter Beasley – revealed that duplex services still functioned undisturbed and that no less than 79 per cent of the costs of administration were met by canal users – a far cry from the 50 per cent the Budget Bureau had expected. 'The Company's policy of establishing relatively low prices for employee services', the GAO concluded in 1954, 'has resulted in fringe benefits to Canal organization employees and a corresponding burden to ship operators and other customers.' In 1955 the GAO alleged that the Company was contravening the 1950 Act by charging the losses from its business operations to toll income.[22]

To Ambassador Wiley the entire approach of the GAO was misguided, 'accounting hocus pocus based on the concept of competitive business practices'. The 1953 report aimed 'to convert the Canal Zone hierarchy into a political plum orchard' and to make it 'an integral and succulent part of the spoils system'. Turning the Canal into a corporation could also have dangerous consequences if Panamanian nationalists imitated their counterparts in Iran and Egypt. 'The vicissitudes of the Anglo–Iranian Oil Company and the Suez

[20] WNRC, RG 335, OSA 548.2 Panama Canal, Assistant Secretary of the Army to Seybold, 24.10.52. SD, 1950–4, 811F.06/11–752. PCC, 65-J-3/M, Paxton memo of 18.9.52; Seybold to Chairman, House Committee on Appropriations, November 1952.

[21] SD, 1950–4, 711F.11/5–852, Wiley to Siracusa, 8.5.52. *NYT*, 11.9.52, 63/1 WNRC, RG 335, OSA 620 Panama Canal, Shackleford to Pace, 20.10.52. SD, 1950–4, 811F.06/11–752.

[22] SD, 1950–4, 911F.5301/7–3053, Wiley to Sowash, 30.7.53. U.S. General Accounting Office, *Report on audit of the Panama Canal Company and the Canal Zone Government for the fiscal year ended June 30, 1952, by the Comptroller-General of the United States* (1953), 10–11, 13. Ibid. for the year ended June 30, 1953 (1954), 51. *NYT*, 12.7.55, 52/2.

Canal Company should have been enough to dissuade us from increasing the vulnerabilities of the Canal by emulation of their corporate structure.'[23]

The Company, however, was safe from nationalisation by a Panamanian élite which aimed to maximise their takings from it, not to run it themselves. And as American shipowners proved in the late 1950s, it was also beyond the reach of the General Accounting Office. In 1955 the shippers brought suit against the Company for $27 million, contending that it was overcharging them for its transit services because of the subsidies tolls were giving to the Zonians. Nine months later the case was dismissed when the federal government claimed 'sovereign immunity' from prosecution, and though the Court of Appeals reversed the decision, in 1958 the Supreme Court came down conclusively against the shipping interests.[24]

The Eisenhower régime too had thrown its weight behind the Company. The issue, according to the solicitor general, was whether it had the right to set toll levels or whether it must make policy in keeping with the 'theories' of the comptroller general of the GAO. The Company also had solid backing in Congress. 'The present practice of allocating the major part of overhead supporting services to the account of tolls', stated the House Merchant Marine and Fisheries Committee in 1960, 'is proper and is in full compliance with the law as it now stands.' In 1976 a legal analyst of the Zone noted that, thanks to the funds siphoned off from tolls income, it could sustain 'a profusion of government services . . . of tenuous relationship to the actual operation of the Canal'.[25]

Twenty-five years earlier, when the Company was formed, that demiparadise had seemed at serious risk, but the Zone weathered the storm of the mid-century purge. It also succeeded in blunting a challenge to the status quo which developed in the final year of the Eisenhower presidency. Prompted by Eisenhower himself, it looked to a State Department observer on the Company board, primacy for the ambassador on everything touching Panama, and a civilian governor instead of the usual general of the Corps of Engineers. While Army Secretary Brucker yielded to the first two propositions, he balked at the third. Faced with Eisenhower's call for a civilian incumbent of Balboa Heights endowed with 'qualities of tact and diplomacy' and giving off a less palpable 'aura of colonialism', Brucker refused to create an opening for 'a run-of-the-mill politician'. To the State Department's argument that it was important 'to avoid

[23] SD, 1950–4, 911F.5301/7–3053, Wiley to Sowash, 30.7.53; 611.19/3–953, Wiley to Sowash, 9.3.53.
[24] See Marjorie Whiteman (ed.), *Digest of international law*, vol. 3 (Washington, D.C., 1964), 1204–8. *NYT*, 26.4.57, 4/1; 14.9.55, 70/6; 18.9.55, sect. v, 10/6; 30.6.56, 36/8; 9.4.57, 66/1; 29.4.58, 58/1. 'America's troubled canal', *Fortune*, 55 (January–June 1957), 160, 162.
[25] *NYT*, 15.10.57, 65/1. Lyman Tondel (ed.), *The Panama Canal: Background papers and proceedings of the sixth Hammarskjöld Forum* (Dobbs Ferry, N.Y., 1965), 25. Martha Shay, 'The Panama Canal Zone: In search of a juridical identity', *New York University Journal of International Law and Politics*, 9 (1976), 59.

the image of military occupation', his answer was that Latin Americans 'had a tremendous respect for U.S. Army officers'. He closed by reminding all present that the nominee for the governorship would have to be confirmed by Congress, 'where of course the Corps of Engineers was very powerful'. The idea was stopped in its tracks.[26]

The episode said a great deal about the Zone's tenacity under fire from Washington. Early in the 1950s an enthusiast for the new order brought in by Truman urged it to prove that 'tradition can be broken in the interest of what is right'. But the staying power of Zonian conservatism outmatched that radical zeal. Since its inception the Canal Zone had been irreducibly sui generis, and it was to stay that way for the rest of its remarkable lifetime.[27]

[26] *FRUS 1958–1960*, 5 (1991), Microfiche Supplement, ARA/OAP files, Lot 63D127, 'Panama 1960', Minutes of meeting of 29.3.60; TAB C, Memo of 16.2.60; TAB B, Minutes of meeting of 21.3.60; TAB E, Undated Policy Planning Staff Study. SD, post-1954, 719.00/4–660; 611.19/9–160. Eisenhower's brother returned from his visits to the isthmus in 1958 and 1959 convinced that the ambassador, and not the governor, should handle relations with Panama: See Milton Eisenhower, *The wine is bitter: The United States and Latin America* (New York, 1963), 225–6.

[27] WNRC, RG 335, OSA 320 Panama Canal, Robinson to Pace, 16.1.52.

9

The labour force

From depression to war, 1930–1939

The economic catastrophe which disabled the United States throughout the 1930s inevitably left its mark on the Canal, above all when it came to employment. At midsummer 1929 the full-time work force stood at 15,712; five years later it had fallen to 12,020, a drop of nearly 23 per cent. In this fearful slump, the most vulnerable of the Zone's employees were the West Indians on the Silver Roll. They were under heavy pressure from the Americans on the Gold roster, who coveted their semi-skilled positions when force reductions loomed, and by Panamanian Silvers, who had been given a formal promise that they would not be the first to go when cutbacks began. This convergence of the job-hungry was to be the cardinal feature of the Canal's labour relations during the entire depression decade.[1]

The Americans were the first to move in for the kill in the spring of 1931, with a bid by the Metal Trades Council for 3,800 semi-skilled West Indian posts. Not for themselves – Americans in work were slightly up on 1929 – but to provide a living for their unemployed offspring. Governor Burgess's reply was predictably negative. 'A great colony of white people' would be 'sociologically . . . the greatest thing that could happen to Panama', but the MTC claim could only be met by the repatriation of the West Indians and their dependents, and that meant a bill for over $2 million. New Gold-standard facilities would cost $26 million and running expenses nearly $7 million a year. These figures, moreover, were based on the assumption that the newcomers would be paid at Silver rates. Burgess's deputy, Julian Schley, foresaw either a clamour for higher wages or 'great dissatisfaction with the status of permanent inferiority'.

---

[1] Figures are taken from *Force – Company/Government, 1904–1968*, a statistical sheet issued by the Personnel Bureau of the Panama Canal Company – Canal Zone Government.

Though the chief of the Bureau of Statistics, Seymour Paul, argued that the current handful of white American Silvers 'wherever practicable . . . are pushed into positions of superiority', the potential for trouble with almost 4,000 touchy U.S. citizens on that roll was clear.[2]

Burgess's answer was to temporise by ordering the gradual replacement of all West Indian office clerks by young Americans. Schley, after he became governor, took an unequivocal stand against an MTC- sponsored bill to require the government to transfer every single Silver post to the Gold Roll. The Canal's labour policy did not mean 'that aliens already in employ should be discharged in order to give their positions to Americans'. The canal administration had steered a middle course between the extravagance of an all-American work force and the parsimony of silverisation by adopting the dual employment system, and to do what the MTC were asking would be prohibitive. The union leadership could not see that its members' agreeable life-style was only made possible by the cheapness of Silver labour, and the bill posed a stark choice. On an all-Gold work force, Americans would either keep their 25 per cent differential and price the canal out of the shipping market, or they would have to give up the differential and accept a cut in living standards. The bill did not go through.[3]

The onslaught on the West Indians from the Panamanian lobby fared no better. In Burgess's view, the Canal employed 'very few Panamanians of the lower classes who measure up to the average West Indian'. To one senior canal official, the 1914 order protecting Panamanians vis-à-vis West Indians in a force reduction was a dead letter because of their unimpressive work record. The Panamanians themselves had admitted their inferiority as labourers by amending the 1926 exclusion act to admit West Indians to harvest bananas if local men were 'not available'. As the Act had demonstrated, their solution to the West Indian problem was to stem immigration to the terminal cities and to discourage the existing communities there from staying on. So in 1931 West Indians were forbidden to seek naturalisation, and a hefty financial guarantee was required of all applicants for an entry visa. At the same time, Panama pressed Washington to repatriate all West Indians who were either retired or unemployed.[4]

Repatriation had already been tried between 1914 and 1917, without much success. Now in response to the Panamanian request Executive Secretary McIlvaine proposed setting up a repatriation fund to pay for assisted one-way

[2] PC, 2-E-11/P, MTC to Assistant Secretary of War, 18.4.31; 2-E-11/L, Burgess memo of 11.9.31; 2-E-11/A, Hurley to Rayburn, 18.1.32; 2-E-11/L, Schley to Flint, 8.1.32; 2-E-11, Paul to Smith, 3.12.31.

[3] PC, 2-E-11/A, Minutes of Silver Rates Board, 27.3.32; McIlvaine to heads of department, 29.10.32; Schley to Dern, 30.10.33 (draft). SD, 1910–49, 811F.504/112, Schley to Dern, 22.11.33.

[4] PC, 2-E-12, Burgess to Davis, 16.7.32; Mehaffey memo of 18.5.33. SD, 1910–49, 819.504/ 5 and 6, South to Kellogg, 13.12.26 and 7.2.27; 819.55/130, Davis to Stimson, 25.8.31; 819.55/135, Vice-Consul, Panama City to Stimson, 12.12.31. Conniff, Black labor, 77.

passages to the islands. Burgess took the idea up a year later only after the eruption of a second rent strike in Panama City and Colón. While Panamanian landlords were the target of the protest, the West Indian minority was more than likely to be next in line, and the last thing the canal authorities wanted was race riots in the terminals. Burgess therefore called on Secretary of War Patrick Hurley to ask Congress for a repatriation fund of $150,000.[5]

Waiting for the incoming régime of Franklin Roosevelt to take action, the Panamanian envoy in Washington, Ricardo Alfaro, claimed that repatriation was vital to save Panama from 'serious disturbances of a communistic nature'. This was calculated hyperbole, but the terminal cities were certainly simmering with unrest, and the first hundred days of Roosevelt's New Deal only served to bring them closer to the boil when the Canal's budget was slashed and more men were fired. Soon a Panamanian Fascist movement had emerged which targeted the West Indians as enemies of the republic and which had undoubted popular support. Among the few discernible opponents of repatriation were the landlords of the city tenements where most West Indians lived. Their stand was far from principled. As the U.S. minister, Roy Tasco Davis, put it, they were largely motivated by fear that 'such a reduction of the colored population would materially reduce the large incomes they derive from renting filthy rooms in ramshackle buildings at high prices'.[6]

Though he too was a man of property, President Harmodio Arias pushed on. The United States, he told Davis, had made a convenience of Panama 'as a labor camp for the Canal Zone', and the burden of the West Indians was now insupportable. Failing American agreement to fund repatriation, he would deport them into the Zone. The threat elicited a promise from Roosevelt to request the fund if Panama gave assurances that it would prevent future immigration and re-entry. The deal was clinched during Arias's visit to Washington, and Congress approved an expenditure of $150,000 in May 1934.[7]

Repatriation turned out to be an emphatic flop. The slow take-up rate was evident as early as August 1934, and Panama was quick to switch to another tack. As Arias started negotiations for a new treaty, he presented a draft stipulating full equality between U.S. and Panamanian citizens in the employment field. This covered both Gold and Silver rolls and extended to eligibility, pay, promotion, holidays, retirement benefits, and accident insurance. In addition

[5] PC, 46-D-8, Morrow memo of 25.11.21. SD, 1910–49, 811F.504/103, Schley to Dern, 7.8.33. PC, 46-D-8, McIlvaine to Burgess, 4.9.31; 80-A-3, Burgess to Hurley, 7.9.32; 2-E-12, Paul memo of 8.7.33. On the 1932 rent strike, see Demetrio Porras, 'El movimiento inquilinario', Revista Lotería, nos. 212–13 (October–November 1973), 169–98; also SD, 1910–49, 819.00/1658 to 1678, 4.8.32 to 27.10.32, and Conniff, Black labor, 82–3.
[6] SD, 1910–49, 811F.504/87, Alfaro memo of 24.2.33; /91, Wilson memo of 10.6.33; /93, Davis to Hull, 10.6.33; 819.00/1698, Military attaché, Costa Rica, memo of 27.10.33; 819.00B/30, Finlay memo of 10.7.33; 811F.504/100, Davis to Hull, 3.7.33.
[7] SD, 1910–49, 850.4/855, Davis to Hull, 11.6.33; 811F.504/106, U.S. note of 26.9.33. The Roosevelt–Arias joint statement of 17.10.33 is in BD, 870. PC, 46-D-8, 7.5.34.

Panamanians were to be given preference over West Indians both when appointments were being made and when the work force was being reduced.[8]

Panama's initiative ran into objections on several counts. Governor Schley foresaw the State Department being drawn 'too intimately into the management of the Canal' by dealing with treaty claims made by Panama through diplomatic channels. The chief of the department's Division of Latin American Affairs meanwhile deployed precisely the same argument against Panama. A treaty commitment would offer Panama 'an excuse to pry into the administration of the Canal on every occasion'. The governor, the department, and the president all asserted – with more than a touch of sophistry – that to give treaty status to equality for Panamanians while denying it to British subjects (the West Indians) would be a violation of the most-favoured-nation principle which would bring down irrefutable protests on Washington's head.[9]

As the treaty talks reached their conclusion, therefore, the U.S. negotiator, Under Secretary Sumner Welles, suggested putting the agreement in the form of a note, that is, an affirmation without the contractual force of a treaty. Alfaro gave way on condition that it did not include 'any hint of an equality of a Panamanian with a Jamaican or a Negro'. It did not, but written into it was a proviso which Alfaro could not persuade Welles to strike out. The United States, read the note, 'maintains and will maintain as its public policy the principle of equality of opportunity and treatment . . . consistent with the efficient operation and maintenance of the Canal and its auxiliary works and their effective protection and sanitation'. That, as Alfaro well knew, was to give the Canal the latitude to do precisely as it chose, and it marked a decisive setback to Panamanian aspirations.[10]

The Americans on the Gold Roll meanwhile battled on with their congressional campaign to commandeer Silver jobs, now fixing on the 3,200 semi-skilled assignments held mostly by West Indians. The Golds were a frustrated body of men. Between 1931 and 1935 they had made a net gain of only forty posts at the expense of aliens, and legislation was their only hope of quick aggrandisement, given the government's denial of their right to strike. Yet strong as their links with Congress were, not one of their bills was destined to go through.[11]

In the summer of 1936 the blue-collar MTC tried to find another way round the impasse by changing the structure of labour policy in the Zone, but to no

[8] PC, 46-D-8, 21.4.37 and 14.10.46; 2-E-12, Wilson to Schley, 6.12.34. SD, 1910–49, 711.1928/297½, Alfaro memo of 1.12.34.
[9] PC, 94-A-3/1936, Schley to Gruber, 6.10.34. SD, 1910–49, 819.74/303A, Wilson memo of 26.9.34. PC, 2-E-12, Schley to Wilson, 11.12.34. SD, 1910–49, 711.1928/237½, Legal Adviser memo of 4.10.34; /436½, Minutes of meeting of 25.7.35.
[10] SD, 1910–49, 711.1928/436½, Minutes of meetings, 17.12.35, 19.12.35, 21.12.35. BD, 899, has the text of the note on employment of 2.3.36.
[11] PC, 2-E-11/P, McConaughey and Paul memo, 20.11.35.

avail. Part of the explanation for their failure, in the view of the governor's public relations officer, H. H. Railey, was the low calibre of their leadership. 'The Metal Trades Council,' wrote Railey, 'put brutally, is a tiny outpost of organized labor with ballooned pretensions, activated by a lust for power but bereft of the wisdom to wield it if won.' The main reason was the fact that they were up against an autocrat. As Railey put it, their demands were 'in reality but appeals to the Governor, whose decisions in reference to them are quite final'. Governor Clarence Ridley immediately proved Railey's point by rejecting the MTC proposal for a labour relations board and telling the MTC he would not be bound even by its unanimous findings. In December 1936 Ridley ordered the MTC's Washington representative, Charles Wahl, not to lobby for semi-skilled positions, and when Wahl did so revoked permission for him to remain in Washington on unpaid leave.[12]

Ridley's defence of the status quo was many-sided. The Canal's employment system was unequivocally based on colour, and putting Americans to work alongside blacks would almost certainly result in 'friction and possible humili-ation'. Combatting the argument that the West Indians were a security risk, he pointed to a contingency plan to tighten white supervision of black subordinates and replace aliens in sensitive positions with teenage Zonians. But there were also principles at stake. 'To turn [the West Indians] out en masse on the world with no place to go and no opportunity to earn a living', he wrote the MTC, 'would be a dictatorial act of shameful cruelty which would become a national scandal.'[13]

Ridley's avowed solicitude was notably at odds with the Canal's actual treatment of its Caribbean dependents during the 1930s. In 1930 the all-white Classification Committee decided against transferring West Indians on the Gold Roll to Silver but made them forfeit a recently agreed wage rise. The Silvers were also refused paid leave, and in 1934 their rent subsidies were phased out. And West Indians still had no retirement benefit unless they worked for the Panama Railroad. Their spokesman Samuel Whyte had called for a gratuity of $20 a year for each year of service, but when Congress finally enacted a super-annuation bill in 1937 it conceded much less: $1 a month for every working year up to a maximum of $25 a month, and despite inflation the ceiling was not raised until a new treaty was implemented in 1958.[14]

---

[12] PC, 28-B-48/Enclosure 7, H. H. Railey, 'Relations of the Panama Canal with its employ-ees', 8.6.36, 20, 12; 2-P-46, Ridley to MTC, 2.7.36.

[13] PC, 2-E-11/P, Ridley to Clark, 21.4.38; 2-E-11/L, Ridley to Verhou, 8.12.38; 2-P-46, Ridley to MTC, 27.1.39.

[14] PC, 2-F-14, Gold Rates Board, 24.5.30; and Classification Committee, 11.7.30. Conniff, *Black labor*, 77, 85, 79–80. PC, 2-E-11, Paul memo of 23.6.34; 2-P-70, Schley to White, 30.1.35; 2-E-11/L, White to Ridley, 28.12.34. *BD*, 999, 1039, gives texts of the changes to the 1937 legislation put through in 1955 and 1958.

In their education too the West Indians were severely disadvantaged. Although Whyte made repeated pleas for vocational training at secondary level, no high school was provided. Primary schooling was deemed quite enough for children who could never expect a skilled position. In the view of the superintendent of schools, Ben Williams, the role of the coloured primary schools was to teach 'proper attitudes . . . that will not make each graduate feel that he or she should occupy only a white-collar job'. The black principal of the primary teacher training college, Alfred Osborne, was also painfully aware of the deference demanded from the West Indian work force. 'Young people', Osborne wrote in his curriculum guide, 'must be told that keeping one's head, keeping one's mouth shut, and being courteous to superiors and subordinates will pay large dividends in the end.'[15]

Black Americans found themselves in the same boat. They too could not hope for high-school education, since the Zone high schools were for white Americans only. J. E. Moore, manager of the Gatún Silver Clubhouse, ran into a brick wall when he tried more than once to send his children to secondary school. 'It has not been our policy', wrote Williams, 'to accept in the white schools children who have unmistakable negroid characteristics and certainly not when one of the parents is found to be black and of the negro race.' Their admission would create 'widespread and bitter resentment' and step up pressure for general desegregation of public facilities. Four years later when Moore tried again, Williams needed only to cite the example set by Washington, D.C.: 'In the shadow of the Capitol dome they find it necessary to maintain a strict separation in the schools on the basis of color.'[16]

Petitioning Ridley late in 1939, Whyte protested that it was 'uncharitable and inhumane to so ruthlessly narrow our field of opportunities' by the systematic discrimination practised in the Zone. Whyte was writing soon after the outbreak of the Second World War, which the United States was eventually to enter as the champion of a New Deal on a universal scale. By the time it ended, the labour policies preserved intact since the construction era would have faced their most searching challenge yet.[17]

Second World War, 1939–1945

The war which broke out in September 1939 gave a decisive impetus to the decolonisation of the European overseas empires, and the outpost of American empire in the Canal Zone was not exempt from the process. The most salient emblem of U.S. colonialism, the Gold and Silver employment system, was to

[15] PC, 46-D-8, White to Ridley, 14.8.37; 2-P-70, Williams memo of 5.12.39. Conniff, *Black labor*, 94–5.
[16] PC, 28-B-233, Williams memo of 2.10.33; Williams to McIlvaine, 6.3.33; Williams memo of 29.3.37.
[17] PC 2-P-70, White to Ridley, 26.10.39.

come under increasing fire, and as the self-styled champion of freedom in the struggle against the Axis, the United States was awkwardly placed to meet the onslaught.

As war approached, these political repercussions were still some way in the future, but labour relations on the isthmus were immediately affected by the huge lock-building scheme to which the Roosevelt administration had just committed itself. A six-year project, it was bound to absorb a vast number of men, and the American unions moved straight into action to persuade Congress that only U.S. citizens be hired to carry it through.

The Canal authorities put up their usual stiff resistance. To import American common labour would be like relieving unemployment by sending construction gangs to 'Africa or . . . the North Pole'. It would add enormously to the cost, since unskilled Americans would have to be paid much more than the local rate, and they would 'occupy an anomalous position in the general social organiza-tion of the tropics where lower-grade work is done by natives'. An all-American force would also violate the successive pledges of equality Washington had given Panama, and when in August 1939 congressional authorisation for the locks stipulated a U.S. monopoly of jobs, Roosevelt was quick to reassure Panama by warning that he would fight an appropriation bill containing the proviso.[18]

Keeping white Americans off the Silver Roll did not, however, mean taking on Panamanians. Nor black Americans, who would bring in 'subversive and troublesome elements', and the National Association for the Advancement of Colored People was sharply discouraged when it pressed the Canal to hire them. Puerto Ricans raised the difficulty that they could not easily be categor-ised as white or black. Best of all for Governor Ridley were the 'generally quiet and docile' West Indians, despite virulent Panamanian prejudice against them. To soothe Panamanian feelings, Ridley made a survey of the republic's manpower resources, proving that it simply could not meet the imminent demand for labour. He also planned to conciliate Panama by confining the new intake entirely to the Zone, off duty as well as on, and by making certain the recruits were repatriated as soon as the work was completed.[19]

The canal hierarchy's determination to keep the West Indians under tight control was no doubt heightened by the bid of the Congress of Industrial Organizations to unionise the Silver force. Ridley certainly did everything in his power to cripple the activities of the CIO delegate, Harvey Stoudt. In July 1939

[18] SD, 1910–49, 811F.812/1096, Ridley to Smith, 12.7.39. PC, 2-E-11/A, Ridley to Smith, 10.6.39. SWCF, Smith to Ridley, 24.4.39. SD, 1910–49, 811F.812/1099, Dawson to Hull, 14.8.39.
[19] SD, 1910–49, 811F.504/155, Woodring to Hull, 24.10.39;/203, Duggan memo of 23.1.40; 819.4016/5, Finlay to NAACP, 19.10.30. PC, 46-D-8, Vietheer memo of 27.9.39; 2-E-11, Vietheer memo of 24.7.39. SD, 1910–49, 711.1928/819½, Dawson to Chapin, 26.7.39; 811F.504/163, Woodring to Hull, 3.1.40. PC, 2-E-11, Ridley to Woodring, 12.8.39.

Stoudt was told he could not hold meetings in the Zone without giving an absolute no-strike guarantee. When he eventually did so, Ridley threw the secretary of the organising committee off the Canal payroll and denied the jurisdiction of the National Labor Relations Board when a charge of unfair labour practice was filed. In October the governor placed close restrictions on the committee's meetings yet, though Stoudt accepted them, invented new reasons for objecting to the CIO campaign.[20]

Stoudt, he told the secretary of war, had been described by the House Un-American Activities Committee as a communist and should be required to show he was not. Even when the head of the Canal's Civil Intelligence Section, Captain Leo McIntire, discounted the threat of communist-induced sabotage or strike action, Ridley was still not satisfied. An extra condition should be imposed on Stoudt, namely, that 'no member of your organization shall be a Communist, nor shall be one who believes, advises, or teaches, or has membership in or affiliates with any organization that believes, advises, advocates or teaches the overthrow by force or violence of the Government of the United States or of all forms of law'.[21]

Though the War Department had by then already sanctioned union meetings, this was a body-blow to Stoudt, and the anti-union measures were capped in May 1940 by an executive order outlawing strikes against either the government or its private contractors. Strikers, or the inciters of strikes interfering with the canal, were to be deported forthwith, and when Jamaicans at Gatún downed tools the following September the order was immediately invoked. The week-long Gatún stoppage was to be the only strike of the war in the Zone.[22]

This still left the Canal facing the claim for an exclusively American work force on the third locks. When the money bill for the locks began to be framed in February 1940, the author of the anti-alien clause, Senator Pat McCarran, toned it down to reserve only skilled positions for U.S. citizens. In April the State Department persuaded McCarran that he would risk nothing by adding in Panamanians. As Roosevelt had told a recent press conference, Panamanian skilled labour was 'a drop in the bucket compared to the total'. In June the appropriation act incorporated the so-called McCarran Amendment restricting employment on the project after 1 May 1941 to Americans and Panamanians and to West Indians with at least fifteen years' service.[23]

[20] PC, 2-P-71, Police report of 30.3.39; Ridley to Smith, 1.6.39; Ridley to Smith, 12.7.39; McIlvaine to Stoudt, 17.7.39; Stoudt to McIlvaine, 29.8.39; Standard to Ridley, 20.9.39; Stoudt to Ridley, 3.10.39; Stoudt to Ridley; 19.10.30; Bentz memo of 28.11.39; Ridley to Stoudt, 25.10.39; Stoudt to Ridley, 6.11.39.

[21] Ibid., Ridley to Woodring, 1.12.39; Ridley to Adjutant General, 5.2.40. MID 1766-R-22, McIntire memo of 13.12.39.

[22] PC, 2-P-71, Ridley to Burdick, 20.5.40. Executive Order 8417 of 22.5.40 in 3 CFRC (1938–43), 660–1. MID, 2736-M-14, Memo of 8.4.41.

[23] SD, 1910–49 811F.504/207, Duggan memo of 8.2.40; /208, Roosevelt to Woodring, 8.2.40; /234 and /238, Memo of 16.3.40; /255, McCarran to Hull, 5.4.40. PC, 2-E-11/A, Panama

The compromise satisfied Panama but not the Canal or the Navy Department. The McCarran Amendment, in the Navy's eyes, would make construction work 'exceedingly difficult and costly, if not impossible', and Roosevelt was urged to disregard it 'in time of war or national emergency if he should deem such course to be in the public interest'. Governor Glen Edgerton got the agreement of labour leader Sidney Hillman, and in March 1941 the McCarran section of the Canal appropriation act for the coming fiscal year was suspended in its entirety. Thereafter suspension was annually brought into play to ensure that government agencies could hire as many aliens as they chose.[24]

Legalising the recruitment of foreign labour was paralleled by the even more delicate task of convincing Panama that West Indians had to be part of the force. When the Panamanians were told this in January 1940, their reaction was schizoid: anger at the prospect of a black influx and chagrin that keeping the newcomers in 'concentration camps' in the Zone would rob Panama of their spending power. But racism was stronger than cupidity, and Panama cast about for a more ethnically acceptable alternative.[25]

The garrison commander, General Daniel Van Voorhis, believed he had found it in a revival of the Civilian Conservation Corps, whose youthful labour battalions had done so much construction work under Army supervision during the New Deal. Van Voorhis's troops in the Canal Zone were doing precisely that kind of work. In the words of the official Army history, soldiers 'carried concrete sacks, sand, and crushed rock up steep hills to emplacements where even mules could not be used . . . and . . . put in long hours under the tropical sun in pick and shovel gangs'. But the Canal would never take that option, and Roosevelt backed the Canal strongly en route to the isthmus in February. Americans, he confided to newsmen, were 'all right for supervisory labor but they cannot do back breaking shovel work in the sun'. Van Voorhis's solution was consequently ruled out of court.[26]

Roosevelt's own preference was for Hispanic labour, and in a shipboard conference with President Boyd he suggested importing 500 Spaniards and Puerto Ricans. Governor Ridley wanted neither, especially not the Spaniards. If they were introduced, he insisted they be 'of a peasant type from a district in Spain where there is less likelihood of getting persons of objectionable character', that is, potential saboteurs. What he wanted urgently was 600 Jamaicans, but

Canal Appropriation Act of 24.6.40. *Complete press conferences of Franklin D. Roosevelt*, vol. 15 (New York, 1972), 170. The full text of the McCarran Amendment may be found in *FRUS 1947*, 8: 953–4.

[24] PC, 2-E-11/A, Chief, Bureau of Yards and Docks, to Knox, 23.7.40; Edgerton to Burdick, 28.7.40; Burdick to Edgerton, 5.12.40. Stimson Diary, entry for 5.2.41. PC, 2-E-11/A, Hushing to Edgerton, 28.3.41. Executive Order 8719 of 22.3.41 in *3 CFRC (1938–43)*, 916–17. Executive Order 8797 of 18.6.41 in ibid., 955–6.

[25] SD, 1910–49, 811F.504/168, Panama note of 6.1.40; /201, Welles to Roosevelt, 11.1.40.

[26] SD, 1910–49, 811F.504/202, Dawson to Hull, 19.1.40. *HPCD*, 2: 62. *Press conferences*, 15: 170.

Roosevelt was reluctant to authorise the shipment. 'While I realize that Jamaican labor is highly efficient,' he told Secretary of State Cordell Hull, 'I believe that we should respect the insistent desire of the Republic of Panama that the bulk of the labor brought in should be of white or near white blood.' Though he gave his consent, he remained deeply resistant to West Indian recruitment. In September, however, when Secretary of War Henry Stimson passed on the governor's request for 1,000 more Jamaicans, Roosevelt again agreed, and in November Stimson secured White House permission for a further 2,000. Given the president's previous attitude, Stimson noted, this was 'quite an achievement'.[27]

Panama likewise acquiesced, under protest. In October newly inaugurated President Arnulfo Arias 'winced at the figure of two or three thousand' but none the less gave way. Yet the hostility of his régime to the West Indian community was evident. The new constitution of January 1941 took away the citizenship of all English-speaking black children born since 1928, and in the twelve demands presented to Washington the same month, Arias called for a halt to the importation of West Indian workers. In the eventual agreement reached in May 1942, Washington promised to try to meet its labour requirements from territories whose people Panama had not listed as prohibited immigrants. The pledge was made good: Of the 22,265 contract employees brought in to work for the Canal after 1940, only 5,000 were Jamaican; 12,773 came from El Salvador, 2,248 from Costa Rica, and 2,244 from Colombia. Moreover, as the 1942 accord also stipulated, the Jamaicans were confined to the Zone and repatriated once their job was done.[28]

By this time the social configuration of the Zone was very different from what it had been in 1939. As early as June 1940 the head of the Bureau of Personnel had complained that the myriad demarcation lines of the Gold and Silver system were threatening to dissolve under the rising tide of newcomers, who upset the rules of the game so meticulously worked out since the construction decade. Two years later, with over 70,000 alien staff to be pigeon-holed, the situation seemed to be running out of control.[29]

In the face of incipient chaos, the Canal strove mightily to preserve the standards of the 1900s. White-collar alien employees of wartime agencies which did not function via Gold and Silver categories were segregated on racial lines by the Central Labor Office in order to decide which facilities they were entitled to use. In the screening process some were told to take their clothes off

[27] WPD, 1652–32, Van Voorhis to Adjutant General, 29.2.40. SD, 1910–49, 811F.504/266, Woodring to Hull, 16.4.40, and Roosevelt to Hull, 19.4.40; /274, U.S. note of 25.4.40. Stimson Diary, entries for 8.10.40, 8.11.40, 12.11.40.

[28] SD, 1910–49, 711F.504/356, Dawson to Hull, 18.10.40. Conniff, *Black labor*, 98–9. SD, 1910–49, 711F.1914/237½, Panama memo of 29.1.41; 811F.504/387, De Roux to Wang, 13.3.41. See *BD*, 939, for the agreement of 18.5.42. PC, 46-D-8, gives the figures for contract labour.

[29] PC, 28-D-233, Paul to Lombard, 18.6.40. *HPCD*, 74.

to have their skin examined. Nothing could more graphically have revealed the insularity of a régime oblivious of the world beyond its tiny confines.[30]

Related to the effort to keep up the old stratifications was a fight to hold the Panamanians in check. In June 1942 Edgerton rejected an Army proposal for a propaganda offensive highlighting the material benefits of the war for the isthmus. Warned by McIntire that the campaign would have to be handled with extreme care 'to prevent providing a basis upon which Panamanian labor would demand raises of pay or other special privileges', the governor could not have agreed more. 'Stressing the opportunities for Panamanians in employment on the Canal Zone', he wrote, 'would bring out pointedly the relatively small numbers employed in the higher positions.' A year later a senior canal official pounced on a move to alter the phraseology of the McCarran Amendment in order to create up to nearly 1,200 more Gold positions. However many new Gold jobs there would be, some were bound to go to Panamanians, and for the Canal this was highly unwelcome. So far it had restricted Panamanian membership of the Gold fraternity to a mere 20 (out of 8,357), and if more were to be let in, the dikes would seem to be crumbling.[31]

The struggle to damp down Panamanian expectations was accompanied by dour resistance to interference by Washington in the realm of labour policy. In the spring of 1941 the Civil Service Commission was persuaded to rescind its ruling that Panamanians could take examinations for U.S. government jobs. The commission had based its action on the McCarran Amendment, but it was told that the suspension of the amendment voided the guarantee. What was more, the Civil Service itself had a regulation that 'no person shall be admitted to examination unless he is a citizen of or owes allegiance to the United States'. The outcome was eminently satisfactory to Charles Wahl of the AFL, whose long experience had taught him, the State Department reported, that 'the more [the Panamanians] received the more they wanted; and that civil service status was, if he could help it, one of the things which they would not get'.[32]

Nor was more than minimal co-operation given to the Committee on Fair Employment Practice set up in June 1941. Unlike the National Labor Relations Board, the FEPC had responsibility for government employees, and the Canal authorities could not deny its competence. They could, however, stonewall it into futility. In the autumn of 1941, when the committee passed on allegations of segregationism from the National Association for the Advancement of Colored People, the Canal's Washington office was told to reply that 'amalgamation of all races and nationalities is an abstract ideal that cannot be realized for many

---

[30] SD, 1910–49, 819.504/55, Muccio to Hull, 17.2.44 (copy in OF, 25-i).
[31] PC, 2-P-12, Edgerton to Burdick, 6.5.42; 80-A-3, Burskin memo of 21.5.42; McIntire to Edgerton, 12.6.42; Edgerton memo of 16.6.42; 2-E-11/A, Rankin memo of 4.10.43. ONI, C-10-L 14602, Report of 5.7.43.
[32] PC, 2-E-11/A, Edgerton to Burdick, 7.5.41. SD, 1910–49, 811F.504/395 and 407.

years, at best'. In May 1942, in answer to a request for information on black employment in the Zone, Edgerton maintained that it was 'impracticable' to go into detail. Without a positive response from the Zone, the FEPC could make no impact whatever on its affairs.[33]

During the closing stages of the war, the challenge to the status quo took on more formidable proportions. In September 1943 the president of the Confederation of Workers of Latin America, Vicente Lombardo Toledano, stopped over in Panama to rally the forces on the isthmian labour front. His audience was the Association of Workers in the Service of the United States Government, led by Victor Urrutia. Admission to this grouping was restricted, as Captain McIntire had put it, to 'the lighter-colored members of the better families of Panama' with their eyes on the prize of Gold Roll jobs. Urged on by Lombardo, Urrutia drafted a petition addressed to Roosevelt which attacked the Zone's employment policies at length. The high principles of the FEPC had been turned into 'a cruel mockery' by the American craft unions in concert with the antiquated canal bureaucracy 'established during the "big stick" era'. The chief culprits, the governor and his executive secretary, should be replaced by '"new dealers" above suspicion' who enjoyed Roosevelt's confidence.[34]

The Zone's reaction to the document was furious. Urrutia's dossier described him as 'a turncoat, treacherous and sly' who acted 'like a Leftist'. As for Lombardo, he had reportedly been 'hired' by the Soviet minister in Mexico to plant the seeds of future trouble. The Canal's pay structure was perfectly justifiable, and Silver rates were a decided improvement on the minimal wages paid by Panamanian employers. In view of its maltreatment of the West Indians under its own jurisdiction, Panama was in no position to censure racialism in the Zone.[35]

The State Department saw things quite differently. The appeal to Roosevelt, thought Robert McGregor, encapsulated everything Latin Americans resented about the USA: 'race discrimination; "Yankee Imperialism"; color barriers; wage differentials; exclusive privileges'. The Canal's arrogance in its dealings with Panama, so the U.S. Embassy believed, could do considerable damage to American interests not only in Panama but throughout the hemisphere.[36]

How then to field this hot potato? Roosevelt chose not to pass it across to FEPC but instead to drop it in the lap of his assistant Jonathan Daniels, whose

[33] Executive Order 8802 of 25.6.41 in 3 CFRC (1938–43), 957. PC, 28-B-233, Ethridge to Edgerton, 20.9.41; Edgerton to Burdick, 3.10.41; Edgerton to Ethridge, 1.5.42; Mehaffey to Ethridge, 27.10.42 (not sent).

[34] SD, 1910–49 810.504/290. PC, 2-P-68, McIntire to Edgerton, 5.3.42. SD, 1910–49, 811F.504/448B, Urrutia to Roosevelt, 3.10.43.

[35] SD, 1910–49, 810.504/328. PC, 2-P-68, Memo of 12.11.41. MID-R, 1933–44, 2300, Memo of 26.4.44. SD, 1910–49, 811F.504/456, Edgerton memo of 15.4.44.

[36] SD, 1910–49, 811F.504/454, McGregor to Daniels, 16.3.44; 819.504/55, Muccio to Hull, 17.2.44 (also OF, 25-i).

task became even trickier when Panama took the issue to the conference of the International Labour Organisation in Philadelphia at the end of April. There the Panamanian union delegate, Diógenes de la Rosa, made a direct approach to the U.S. secretary of labor, Frances Perkins, for an investigatory commission on the Zone, and the conference ended by adopting a resolution in which labour relations featured prominently. Recommendation 70 covered 'minimun standards of social policy in dependent territories', including pay and conditions of work. Members of the ILO were called on to give all their workers 'equitable treatment' and to ban discrimination on grounds of race or colour.[37]

Failure to live up to these injunctions could well put Washington in the dock, though not for the moment. Calling in at the State Department after the conference, Lombardo agreed that it would be 'unwise to publicize current labor practices in the Zone because of the strategic importance of that area during a time of war'. Even so, Daniels felt something had to be done to limit the damage the Canal's 'military colonial officials' could inflict. The answer was a letter from Roosevelt to the new governor, Joseph Mehaffey, ghosted by Daniels in collaboration with McGregor. The president did not want the matter stirred up in an election year, Daniels explained, and McGregor saw the letter as 'a very adroit way of getting out from under'. Few would have guessed that from Roosevelt's sermonising tone. The Canal Zone, he informed Mehaffey, was 'a continuing and dramatic demonstration of the American attitude in Latin America to the peoples of all races and nationalities in those countries'. There must be no cause for saying that in the Zone Washington dealt 'with its neighbors of any race or nation in anything less than the fairest and most neighborly spirit'. Ambassador Avra Warren was delighted. With a man such as Roosevelt in the White House, Panama's charges would be taken seriously. The response of the president would be ' "humanitarianism" together with the "good neighbor policy" . . . combined with the spirit of the Atlantic Charter'.[38]

This was more true of Roosevelt as a maestro of inspirational rhetoric than as a genuine reformer, though he did back a number of improvements in the employment sector. These all related to the West Indians, who had actually criticised the Urrutia petition for ignoring their own claims on the canal administration. Their requests for jobs at U.S. rates, better housing, vocational training, and paid leave had been repeatedly cold-shouldered by Edgerton, and in 1943 when they petitioned both Vice-President Wallace and Roosevelt himself,

[37] OF, 25-i, Roosevelt to Daniels, 1.3.44. SD, 1910–49, 811F.504/455, Muccio to Hull, 22.4.44. PC, 2-P-68, De la Rosa to Perkins, 6.5.44. International Labour Organisation, *International Labour Conference: Conventions and recommendations, 1919–1949* (Geneva, 1949), 561–77. SD, 1910–49, 500C115 28th Conf./362.

[38] OF, 25-i, Daniels to Roosevelt, 13.5.44. SD, 1910–49, 811F.504/458, McGregor memo of 10.5.44. OF, 25-i, Roosevelt to Mehaffey, 16.5.44. SD, 1910–49, 811F.504/461, Memo of conversation with Warren, 14.6.44.

Edgerton refused to support their case. In a briefing paper for Mrs. Roosevelt in March 1944 the governor spoke of renovating the Silver elementary schools but not about building the high school Whyte had hoped to discuss with her. And while he planned to double Silver housing in the Zone, this was not out of benevolence but to remove the West Indians from 'the subversive influence of self-serving or misguided agitators of the demagogue type, who find fertile and profitable fields for the cultivation of discontent in the crowded terminal cities'.[39]

One such rabble-rouser, from the Zone's standpoint, was Diógenes de la Rosa, who was believed to be preparing a general strike for September 1944. In countering the threat, the canal authorities had a persuasive deterrent in their hands, as one observer pointed out. There would be no real difficulty 'so long as the Canal Zone government has the power to fire a man from his job, which in addition loses him commissary privileges, his home and his right to enter any Canal Zone facility'. But Washington also held out a number of carrots. In June, Mehaffey told Stimson that Roosevelt had given him funds for building repairs to 'help tone down the trouble'. In July, Daniels asked Jacob Crane of the National Housing Agency to look into the housing problem, and in August Roosevelt signed an executive order authorising the governor to employ up to 200 West Indians at the minimum Gold rate.[40]

These were no more than palliatives, however, and they did not challenge the Zone's segregationism, which was forcefully upheld by the garrison commander and wartime governor, General George Brett. In May, Brett had justified the Army's withdrawal of the 25 per cent pay differential from its Panamanian employees by saying that the 1936 note on equality applied to the armed forces only by inference. He went on to instruct all government agencies in the Zone to take a hard line on employment – especially the Navy, which had so far ignored the suspension of the McCarran Amendment and implemented its guarantee of non-discrimination for Panamanian workers.[41]

The Panamanian foreign minister, Samuel Lewis, therefore faced a solid wall of resistance when he came to Washington in December to plead for basic reforms in working practices. Brett and Mehaffey stood shoulder to shoulder in asserting that 'strict adherence to the treaty provisions of "equal opportunity and equal treatment" would result in chaos'. In Mehaffey's view it was not feasible to tamper with the Gold and Silver dispensation, and to put new labels

[39] SD, 1910–49, 811F.504/457, Muccio to Hull, 28.4.44. PC, 2-E-11, Edgerton to Whyte, 14.12.40. Conniff, *Black labor*, 96–7; 101–2. FDR Library, President's Secretary's File, Box 64, Edgerton to Brett, 24.3.44.

[40] OSS, 80432C, Military attaché report of 27.5.44; 91541R, Report of 25.8.44. Stimson Diary, entry for 20.6.44. PC, 28-B-44, Crane to Mehaffey, 3.10.44. Executive Order 9467 of 19.8.44, in *3 CFRC (1943–48)*; 329–30. PC, 2-P-70, Mehaffey to Whyte, 21.10.44.

[41] SD, 1910–49, 811F.504/459, Brett to Muccio, 18.5.44. PC, 2-E-11/P, Mehaffey to Perkins, 26.2.45. OpD, 384 CDC, Brett to Marshall, 10.1.45. SD, 1910–49, 811F.504/12–1644.

on the two categories would provoke uproar when the underprivileged realised that the change was merely cosmetic. Crowning the opposition came a statement from Daniels that his master was 'cool on the question of abolishing the gold and silver roll system'. So much for Roosevelt's resounding exhortation to make the Canal a showcase of American values.[42]

Yet the Canal's modus operandi was still under scrutiny. When Mehaffey returned to the isthmus he faced an ILO questionnaire on social policy in the Zone that wanted to know how far it measured up to the standards set by Recommendation 70. He sent it back unanswered. Since the Zone contained no ' "native population" or "dependent peoples" ', it was not a dependent territory and consequently not within the scope of the recommendation.[43]

A second scatter of fall-out from the ILO conference came in a request from Secretary of Labor Perkins for a report on the Canal's employment policy. Hardly had Mehaffey mailed his lengthy vindication than a vituperative critique of the Zone landed on his desk. Its author was a U.S. employee of the Anglo-American Caribbean Commission in Washington, Paul Blanshard. Comparing the Gold and Silver apparatus to the institutionalised racism of South Africa, Blanshard described Mehaffey's reply to Perkins as 'a polite and fundamentally evasive letter which should be cross-indexed under the heading of *Official Baloney*'. His attack was the product of just five days on the isthmus, but it was only the latest in a series of assaults on the Zone's handling of labour relations, some from inside the government itself. They had begun to put the canal administration under siege, and it was to stay embattled throughout the post-war decade.[44]

Cold war, 1945–1955

The wind of change which had begun to blow across the Canal Zone in the Second World War went on shaking its deeply rooted working practices in the post-war years. Pressure for change came from a number of quarters. In January 1946 President Harry Truman ordered an inquiry into Zone discrimination against the West Indians when told that the blacks of the Caribbean were receptive to communist influence. It was carried out by Ambassador Frank Hines, who was in fact more concerned with the need to find skilled jobs for Panamanians. That perspective was fully shared by his first secretary, Lansing

[42] SD, 1910–49, 811f.504/12–1244, /12–744, /12–944. PC, 80-A-3, Mehaffey to Burdick, 5.12.44.
[43] PC, 2-P-68, Mehaffey to Burdick, 6.1.45.
[44] Ibid., Perkins to Mehaffey, 27.1.45; 2-E-11/P, Mehaffey to Perkins, 26.2.45. SD, 1910–49, 819.4016/3–645, Paul Blanshard, 'Notes on the West Indian negro and racial policy in Panama', 6.3.45. Conniff, *Black labor*, 107. OpD, 291.21.

Collins, who keenly appreciated 'the political desirability of giving your opponent a responsible position in your organization to silence him'.[45]

Governor Mehaffey could not have agreed less. The objective of the anti-discrimination drive, he told Hines, seemed to be 'an amalgamation of all races and nationalities into one harmonious group. . . . This is a Utopian dream that runs counter to nature and the facts and realities of life.' The Canal had 'no mandate to raise the standard of living in Panama or elsewhere, nor any money to indulge in socialistic experiments'. If segregation were eliminated, half his U.S. staff would quit within a month and the remainder would be badly disaffected.[46]

Mehaffey's reaction was a classic instance of the tactics deployed by successive governors since 1914. Whenever one of the three components of the work force pushed for an advantage, the interests of the others were invoked to block the move. Earlier in the year Mehaffey had countered a renewed bid by the Americans of the Gold Roll to snatch extra posts via the McCarran Amendment with the argument that it would stir up a hornets' nest among the Panamanians and the West Indians. And when a new Silver union was founded embracing West Indians and Panamanians, Mehaffey was convinced that their incompatibility would soon split it apart.[47]

The union in question was the Canal Zone Workers' Union (CZWU), formed in July 1946 as Local 713 of the United Public Workers of America, an affiliate of the CIO. This was a watershed in the history of unskilled labour in the Zone, and it marked the end of the Panama Canal West Indian Employees' Association and its deferential leader, Samuel Whyte. Ironically, the CZWU came to birth at a time when West Indians had gained several concessions. They were now entitled to up to 10 per cent of jobs paying the basic Gold rate, and the secondary education they had so long begged for arrived with the building of two vocational high schools. But the West Indian community was no longer prepared to accept whatever the Canal was pleased to give, and the prospect of militancy loomed.[48]

For the U.S. establishment it was a disturbing outlook. If the CZWU succeeded in mobilising even one-third of the 30,000-strong Silver force, Hines told Washington, the Canal would be 'beset with labor difficulties of the first order'. Mehaffey was even more agitated, though he took comfort from the

[45] SD, 1910–49, 811F.504/2–2146, Braden to Hines; /5–1646, Hines to Byrnes; /6–1146, Collins to Wise.
[46] SD, 1910–49, 811F.504/5–1646, Mehaffey to Hines, 1.5.46. PC, 80-A-3, Meeting of 23.7.46.
[47] PC, 2-E-11/A, Mehaffey to Coles, 29.6.46; 28-B-233, Mehaffey to Hines, 31.8.46; 2-P-70, Mehaffey to Wood, 25.10.46.
[48] PC, 2-P-71, Goldsmith to Mehaffey, 21.7.46. SD, 1910–49, 811F.504/4–2446. PC, 2-P-12, Memo of 6.12.48. Conniff, *Black labor*, 119–20.

thought that the intelligence services would keep the union under constant scrutiny. And – a remarkable comment in view of the fact that the 1936 treaty had renounced the right of intervention in Panama – the U.S. Army was on hand 'to preserve order under any conditions'.[49]

The assault on the status quo from inside the Zone might thus be thrown back by an adroit mixture of repression and exploitation of the deep-set rivalries within the labour force. The onslaught from beyond the isthmus was more difficult to repel. At the Mexico City conference of the International Labour Organisation in April 1946, the call for an ILO investigation into the Zone's labour code was deflected only when the Department of Labor promised to take up the issue. This came on top of a demand by the United Nations for members to submit reports on economic, social, and educational conditions in their dependencies under Article 73(e) of the UN Charter. The Canal Zone was on the list, and returns were due by 30 June 1946.[50]

Only after a reminder from Truman himself did the War Department reply by offering to submit the governor's annual report, a decision which kicked up a furious storm in the State Department. The ultra-nationalist assistant secretary for American republic affairs, Spruille Braden, saw no more reason for submitting a report on the Zone than for presenting one on the District of Columbia. The head of the department's United Nations office, Alger Hiss, on the other hand, believed that a refusal to respond would encourage the European colonial powers to do likewise. When Hiss was given the firm backing of Under Secretary Dean Acheson, the report went in. The submission was not repeated, however. Panama was no happier than Braden at seeing the Zone discussed by the UN, and after 1946 it was kept out of the organisation's purview.[51]

At the same time, the Zone remained in the spotlight of the ILO, and Hines beseeched Mehaffey to come up with some gesture to save the U.S. delegation embarrassment at the ILO's Montreal conference in September. Mehaffey, implacably hostile to the ILO as a would-be 'inquisitorial super-state', made his concession minimal. Gold and Silver signs were to be discreetly removed when circumstances showed 'that their continued use is unnecessary to accomplish the purpose for which they were originally posted'. But in the wake of the conference the governor was persuaded to accept a labour relations adviser,

[49] SD, 1910–49, 811F.504/7–246. PC, 2-P-70, Mehaffey to Wood, 25.10.46.

[50] SD 500C115 Mexico City/4–1646. *YBUN 1946–47*, 570–3.

[51] Hiss Papers, Patterson to Byrnes, 28.6.46. PC, 2-P-68, Patterson to Mehaffey, 1.8.46. SD, 1910–49, 811.014/10–746, Braden to Acheson; /9–446, Hiss memo of 4.9.46. Spruille Braden, *Diplomats and demagogues: The memoirs of Spruille Braden* (New Rochelle, N.Y., 1971), 354–5. Hiss Papers, Meeting of 18.10.46. SD, 1910–49, 811.014/12–1346. PC, 79-A-6/U, Memo of 28.8.47.

General Frank McSherry, whose assignment was to produce a report on Zone employment in time for the next ILO meeting in Geneva in June 1947.[52]

McSherry's findings were submitted on 1 June. The Gold and Silver denominations should be scrapped, he advised, and a single payroll structure set up. The pre-war system of cash relief for retired unskilled workers should be replaced by a proper pension scheme. There should be a conclusive interpretation of the intent of the 1936 note on equality, and personnel policy in the Zone should be decided by an interdepartmental committee sitting in Washington.[53]

McSherry's reform package was warmly welcomed in the State Department. The United States's leadership of the Western democracies, wrote Tapley Bennett, demanded 'that we make the Canal Zone a show place as regards our labor practices and our treatment of non-U.S. citizens'. The canal authorities did not see it that way, and Mehaffey told Hines that no governor could do his job properly 'if there were a board in Washington issuing directives'. He was upheld by Secretary of Defense James Forrestal. In March 1948 the Zone's Personnel Board pigeon-holed McSherry, and when the State Department asked for a progress report six months later, nothing had been done. In November the terms 'Gold' and 'Silver' were officially dropped and replaced by 'U.S. rate' and 'local rate', but the move meant nothing substantive. 'The road to reform on the Isthmus', wrote Bennett, 'has many blind turns and disheartening detours.'[54]

Yet though McSherry had been side-tracked, Mehaffey faced another irritant in the shape of a 1947 order giving Panamanians the right to take examinations for Civil Service positions in the Zone. This instantly raised hackles in the Gold Roll, where, as in 1941 when the question had last come up, it was condemned as a threat to canal security. Mehaffey reassured a Senate hearing that sensitive posts could be earmarked for American citizens alone, and all Panamanians would be passed through the elaborate screening process of the recently introduced loyalty programme. Panamanians therefore took the examination, and nearly 200 qualified as clerks and typists.[55]

[52] SD, 1910–49, 811F.504/9–2446, Wise to Hines, 24.9.46; Mehaffey to Hines, 18.9.46. PC, 28-B-233, Wang circular of 30.9.46. SD, 1910–49, 500C115 Montreal/10–1546, Morse memo of 1.10.46; /10–446, Byrnes to Schwellenbach, 20.11.46.

[53] WNRC, RG 335, OSW 230 Panama (6–12–47), McSherry report, 167–70.

[54] SD, 1910–49, 819.504/7–2547; 811F.504/10–3147 and 12–1847. WNRC, RG 335, OSA 004.06 Panama Canal (12–17–47), Report of 9.3.48 and Ohly to Royall, 21.10.48. SD, 1910–49, 811F.504/3–1748, Marshall to Gray, 7.9.49. PC, 28-B-233, Newcomer circular of 19.11.48. SD, 1910–49, 811F.504/12–848.

[55] SD. 1910–49, 811F.504/3–547, Executive Order 9830 of 24.2.47 in 3 *CFRC (1943–48)*, 606–24. POD, 230, Crittenberger to Eisenhower, 10.5.47. SD, 1910–49, 811F.812 Protection/5–2647. PC, 2-E-12, Paul memo of 12.1.48. On the Truman loyalty programme, see Leonard White, 'The loyalty program of the United States government', *Bulletin of the Atomic Scientists*, 7 (1951), 365–6, 382.

The underlying objection to the order was, as the personnel director, Seymour Paul, put it, that it could be 'an opening wedge for equalization of pay scales all the way down the line'. This was a dire prospect for Darwinian die-hards such as Paul, to whom holding down Panamanians 'on the tropical alien basis' had 'the justification of nature'. But, as the head of the Canal's Washington office remarked, passing the examination did not necessarily mean that a Panamanian would get a job 'even though he may be number one on the list'. With that caveat in mind, Panamanians were allowed to keep their eligibility, but by December 1949 only 14 of the 333 who jumped the examination hurdle had been taken on the Canal payroll.[56]

Even so, it was unsettling for the Zone establishment to have the Civil Service issue resurface, since it revealed how meaningless the 1936 note on equality was in practice. By the governor's own admission, not more than 1 per cent of the Gold Roll in the spring of 1947 was Panamanian. In 1936 such minimalism had been acceptable to the State Department, but times had changed, and Acheson maintained that the note implied 'an intent to establish a pattern for the future'. This meant prompting the Canal to give it a more liberal interpretation and, in Hines's view, extending its application to all other U.S. agencies in the Zone, above all the armed services.[57]

But the Pentagon flatly refused to be governed by the note. Garrison commander Matthew Ridgway took satisfaction in a Civil Service Commission opinion that the 1936 statement did not touch the Army, and Secretary of Defense Louis Johnson declared that the Department of Defense operated a dual wage scale in all its overseas commands and that any departure from that norm in the Zone would set off damaging repercussions worldwide.[58]

The response from the Canal was equally negative. In Governor Francis Newcomer's exegesis of the note, 'equality of opportunity' signified no more than eligibility, not a right to employment or to preferential treatment in the selection process. 'Equality of treatment' merely denoted 'absence of discrimination during employment'. And whatever equality the note conferred was modified by the reservation the American treaty negotiators had been careful to write into it.[59]

A tabloid version of Newcomer's comment came from Seymour Paul. In May 1948 Paul was to explore the possibility of using an electronic 'colour eye'

[56] PC, 2-E-11, Paul memo of 18.6.47. *HPCD*, 81. PC, 2-E-11/A, Burdick to Mehaffey, 6.5.48. SD, 1910–49, 811F.504/4–2348. PC, 28-B-233, Executive Order 9980 of 26.7.48 in 3 *CFRC (1943–48)*, 720–1. WNRC, RG 335, OSA 004.06 Panama Canal (12–19–49), Report of Civilian Personnel Policy Committee of Department of Defense by George Vietheer, 31.10.49, 152.

[57] SD, 1910–49, 811F.504/4–947, Memo by Mehaffey; /5–847, Acheson to Clark, 9.5.47. PC, 80-A-3, Hines to Marshall, 21.3.47.

[58] SD, 1910–49, 811F.504/12–848, Memo by Bennett; /4–1449, Johnson to Acheson.

[59] SD, 1910–49, 711.19/7–1249, Memo of Newcomer.

to separate the Gold sheep from the Silver goats, as it would help to 'remove the personal factor and develop consistency in records'. To a mind such as his, equality ran counter to 'ordinary national principles'. Panamanians were admitted to Gold status 'on a personal basis', that is, by the grace and favour of American supervisors, and that was how it should stay 'unless we are absolutely beaten down by the treaty obligations'.[60]

Rufus Lovelady, spokesman of the American Federation of Government Employees, took much the same view and had his own intriguing answers to the problem. Why not, he suggested to the embassy, classify two-thirds of U.S.-rate jobs as security-related and therefore closed off to aliens? Alternatively, introduce an apportionment system based on population ratios, which would grant Panamanians 7 or 8 of the 1,500 Civil Service appointments. A 'compromise' on these lines would 'not violate the Treaty and . . . at the same time [would] ease the local situation'.[61]

Ambassador Monnett Davis was not persuaded. As part of his 'constructive program' to improve relations between Washington and Panama, he had called for progress on the employment issue, and the chargé at the embassy was quick to point out what a propaganda gift it was handing the Soviet bloc. Thanks to the Canal, the United States could plausibly be depicted as 'a hypocritical nation which advocates fair play but, in her own back yard, indulges in the most venal and vicious of employment practices'. At a meeting in September the State Department took the view that the 1936 treaty note was as binding as the treaty itself. Soon afterwards the Defense Department's own investigator of Zone labour conditions felt that to discriminate against Panamanians through a literal reading of the note would be 'an extremely weak and tenuous excuse upon which to base an exclusion policy'. In January 1950 Under Secretary of State James Webb asserted that the note committed Washington to the position that 'its administrative acts in the Zone carry and will carry out the policy of equality'.[62]

Yet the Canal remained proof against reform, and action was postponed *sine die*. At the same time, it secured exemption from a statute which would have given the 25 per cent wage differential only to heads of families – even though this would have saved over $1.5 million a year. The Zone continued to look after its own, and Panamanians stayed on the outside looking in.[63]

[60] PC, 28-B-233, Paul to Pittsburgh Glass Co., 26.5.48; 2-E-11, Paul memos of 18.6.47 and 12.8.48; 2-E-12, Paul memo of 12.1.48.

[61] SD, 1910–49, 811F.017/2–749.

[62] SD, 1910–49, 711.19/2–349, Davis to Acheson. OpD, 091 Panama, Case 18, 10.6.49 to 6.9.49. SD, 1910–49, 711.1928/7–2049, Chargé to Acheson. PC, 2-E-12, Whitman memo of 14.9.49. Vietheer Report (see n. 56), 165. SD, 1910–49, 811F.06/1–1750, Webb to Johnson.

[63] USNA, RG 330, CD 10-1–1, Johnson to Acheson, 6.6.50. WNRC, RG 335, OSA 230 Panama Canal (1–30–50), Bendetsen memo of 30.12.49; OSA 248.3 Panama Canal (12–16–49). Public Law 491 of 22.7.49 and Executive Order 10,000 of 16.9.48 in *3 CFRC (1943–48)*, 792–7.

This was most true of the West Indians, since 1945 full citizens of the republic under the new constitution. Fewer than 300 of the more than 900 who qualified for the basic Gold rate had been given it by 1948. And when McSherry revived his proposal for full retirement benefits for the unskilled, Newcomer struck back with venom. Washington should 'not try to appease the Communists by doing something that, except for their criticisms, we would not otherwise do'.[64]

Newcomer's outburst was directed at all those who, like McSherry, believed the best way to limit communist influence was to remove the economic and social malignancies which gave communism a breeding ground. Curiously enough, this belief appeared to be shared by none other than J. Parnell Thomas, chairman of the House Un-American Activities Committee. Returning from a visit to the isthmus in February 1948, Thomas wrote that 'our government should indeed bow its head in shame at the conditions under which it forces some of the Canal workers to live. . . . We couldn't do more to encourage Communism if we offered Communist party cards to all Canal Zone employees. . . . One thing we can do without delay to counteract Red propaganda is to improve . . . wage and housing conditions'.[65]

In the view of the canal hierarchy, on the other hand, the answer was to prevent the development of any serious challenge to the established order from the work-force rank and file. The likeliest source of such a challenge was the newly formed Canal Zone Workers' Union. The Canal Zone police had it under close surveillance, and the right-wing journalist Ralph DeToledano denounced it as a threat to 'the jugular vein of our system of defense'. To Ambassador Davis its leadership was open to the now familiar charge of 'Communist associations'. Under the loyalty programme introduced by Truman in March 1947, such associations were grounds for dismissal from federal employment, and several leading U.S. figures on the isthmus were glad to use the programme to destroy opposition on the labour front.[66]

One such was the Zone's district attorney, Daniel McGrath, who successfully prosecuted one CZWU official for criminal libel. In March 1949 the regional director of the United Public Workers of America, Max Brodsky, was expelled from Panama at the instance of Ambassador Davis, and four possible successors were denied passports by the State Department. At the same time, Davis had the Panamanian Partito del Pueblo placed on the attorney general's list of subversive organisations. This, Davis admitted, was a questionable move

[64] Conniff, *Black labor*, 119–20. PC, 2-E-11, Paul memo of 12.8.48. WNRC, RG 335, OSA 230.64 Panama Canal (10–9–50), Newcomer memo of 3.1.51.

[65] J. Parnell Thomas, 'Reds in the Panama Canal Zone', *Liberty*, 25 (1948), 54.

[66] SD, 1910–49, 819.5043/9–2546, Mulliken to Newbegin, 25.10.46; /11–546, Newbegin to Mulliken. Ralph DeToledano, 'Stalin's hand in the Panama Canal', *Plain Talk*, November 1946, 31. SD, 1910–49, 819.00B/10–1847 and 12–847, Davis to Marshall.

in view of the fact that the party functioned entirely within the jurisdiction of another sovereign state, but it was justified by the 'unique relationship' with Panama.[67]

To Governor Newcomer much of this was overkill. He was happy enough about the way Brodsky had dealt with him and saw no good reason for his deportation. The leaders of the union, he felt, were harmless, as were the forty-odd employees who belonged to the Partito del Pueblo. They were all being kept under observation and could be rounded up quickly if need be; meanwhile they were being fired piecemeal so as to avoid a protest over mass dismissal. This was the language of an autocrat confident enough to keep his dissidents on a long leash, and Newcomer was just as illiberal as his predecessors. In January 1949 the Zone was visited by delegates from the AFL-sponsored Inter-American Workers' Confederation in a vain bid to persuade the AFL's all-white American affiliates to accept black and Hispanic members. The reply of the president of the Metal Trades Council, Davis reported, was 'punctuated by imprecations and insults leveled at Panamanians in general'. Newcomer did nothing to break down the MTC's resistance to solidarity. 'Segregation is going to stay in the Canal Zone', he told the IWC mission, 'and will have to continue as long as white American workers refuse to live together in the same locality or housing project with colored people.'[68]

A year later the governor's position vis-à-vis the alien section of the work force was strengthened even further by the collapse of the CZWU. In February 1950 the United Public Workers of America was expelled from the CIO as an allegedly communist-dominated body, and after a virtual ultimatum from Newcomer the Zone branch withdrew from the UPWA. By July it had split between a left-wing rump and a moderate majority which formed up as Local 900 of the Union of Government and Civic Employees under the West Indians Ed Gaskin and George Westerman.[69]

In September, Gaskin presented an extensive list of demands which echoed the McSherry report of 1947. Prominent among them were a single wage scale to replace the existing dual payroll; equal pay for equal work by eliminating nationality as the main criterion for making appointments; greatly improved retirement benefits; and the end of racial segregation as the Zone's public policy.[70]

Newcomer's response was uncompromising. Segregation on the isthmus was

[67] PC, 2-P-71, McGrath to Clark, 4.8.48; Clark to Royall, 12.8.48. SD, 1910–49, 811F.5043/ 7–2949, 2–1549, 3–1049, 4–2649, and 8–3049; 819.111/11–2349; 819.00B/5–1149 and 6–1649.

[68] SD, 1910–49, 819.77/10–1749; 711F.1914/10–2649; 811F.504/1–2149 and 1–2849. PC, 2–P-12, CIT committee report of 24.1.49.

[69] SD, 1950–4, 819.062/3–150, 3–350, 3–2750, 4–650, 4–1950, 6–1450, and 7–1950.

[70] PC, 2 P-72, Gaskin to Newcomer, 8.9.50.

'more or less natural and, in general, preferred by the majority of those directly concerned'. And wage increases were out of the question, given the impending change in the canal's administrative structure. On 1 July 1951 the Panama Canal Company was to come into being, and it was expected to be financially self-sufficient. Pay rises could only be met by putting up tolls, and increases in the running costs of the canal would not be tolerated by the powers that be.[71]

The Canal had indeed been put on a new footing in order to save money, but part of the savings were supposed to come from replacing at least some Americans with cheaper local workers. This was the burden of a White House meeting attended by Karl Bendetsen, assistant secretary of the Army, and his aide, Colonel Peter Beasley. Bendetsen had been placed in charge of the reorganiza- tion, and he believed the Company should adopt the practice of U.S. firms in Panama, which engaged Panamanians at all levels, and so create openings cur- rently denied to local-rate personnel. In a report which made pointed reference to the Connor board's identical recommendations in 1921, Truman's fiscal watchdog, the General Accounting Office, called for maximum use of local labour to bring in economies of $2 million a year. The president himself, speaking through an aide, urged 'phasing out of the picture . . . U.S. rate em- ployees as attrition occurs, to be replaced by Panamanians'.[72]

True to tradition, Newcomer was appalled that Washington presumed to teach the Zone its business. The planned replacements 'on a basis of job equality' would, 'conceivably, result in a breakdown of operations in units affected because of social and racial antagonisms'. The classification scheme introduced in 1948 had made it possible for more Panamanians to climb to the upper strata, and 150 were now paid at the U.S. rate. This for Newcomer denoted progress, though those Panamanians represented under 4 per cent of the total on the U.S. roll.[73]

At the end of the year his successor as governor, John Seybold, reported difficulties: Slotting Panamanians into higher positions posed 'many problems relating to extension of training and the absence of [relevant] skills and techni- cal qualifications'. This was in sharp conflict with Bendetsen's recent statement that no ceiling would be placed on job opportunities, and in July 1953 a General Accounting Office audit written with the advice of Beasley noted that the coloured high-school curriculum had not yet been revised to include training for skilled posts. In the realm of employment the Canal was evidently a tough nut to crack.[74]

[71] Ibid., Newcomer to Gaskin, 27.11.50; minutes of meeting of 24.1.51.
[72] SD, 1950–4, 811F.061/12–2051, WNRC, RG 335, OSA 091 Panama Canal, Bendetsen report of 16.1.52, Inclosure C; OSA 320 Panama Canal (3–6–52); OSA 320 Panama Canal (2–15–52).
[73] PCC, 80-A-3, Newcomer to Bendetsen, 21.3.52.
[74] PCC, 65-J-3/M, Seybold report of November 1952. SD, 1950–4, 811F.06/11–752, Labor developments in the Canal Zone, January 1951 to October 1952.

Over housing and education, by contrast, the Company was ready to bow to the pressure for retrenchment – this because it could do so with negligible damage to the interests of the powerful American unions and almost entirely at the expense of the West Indians, who had no lobbyists on Capitol Hill. In 1950 Newcomer had approved a ten-year housing plan which aimed to gather the bulk of West Indian workers into the Zone. In 1952, however, when drastic trimming of the programme was demanded as part of the general economy drive, Governor Seybold willingly complied. There was no longer any need for West Indians to be housed in the Zone to keep them away from the turbulent ambience of the terminal cities, Seybold explained. Their place was henceforth in Panama: 'These employees are citizens of the Republic and should be assimilated into its environment and culture, to grow and expand with their country and join its economic welfare.'[75]

Seybold's words marked a turning point in the Canal's attitude to its West Indian workers. For nearly half a century it had seen them in quite a different light from the Panamanians on the force, as wards to be kept under a paternalistic wing. Now they were to lose that protected status, and the decision to scrap their housing development was a clear sign that the Zone was abandoning its old responsibilities.

The point was confirmed by Seybold's comment on West Indian schooling. 'We educate [the West Indian] as an American', Seybold declared, 'and then place him uninitiated into a greatly dissimilar community.' No action on the educational front was taken until the beginning of 1954, however, when policy was changed as a device to avoid the racial integration of Canal Zone schools. When a Pentagon directive banned segregation in schools attached to its installations, the National Association for the Advancement of Colored People pressed the Army to desegregate the schools in the Zone. The Company's initial reaction was to argue that the Zone fell outside the scope of the decree, but Seybold had an ingenious alternative to hand. It was unfair to put West Indian children through an American syllabus, he told the U.S. ambassador, when they should be taught to become fully Panamanian. Instead, local-rate schools would teach the Spanish-language Panamanian curriculum and be renamed 'Latin American' schools; 'U.S. citizen' schools would continue much as before.[76]

So the integration ordered in May was adroitly side-stepped and effective segregation perpetuated. At the same time, the West Indian community was given a decisive push in the direction of Panama with the announcement that

---

[75] SD, 1950–4, 611.1913/4–2450; 811F.02/1–2552. WNRC, RG 335, OSA 320 Panama Canal (3–6–52), GAO report of 28.2.52; OSA 620 Panama Canal, Seybold to Board, 25.11.52. Conniff, *Black labor*, 124–5.

[76] WNRC, RG 335, OSA 620 Panama Canal, Seybold to Board, 25.11.52. PCC, 28-B-233, NAACP to Stevens, 17.2.54, and draft of reply; Army to NAACP, 7.5.54. SD, 1950–4, 611.1913/2–1854; 811F.43/3–1954 and 6–1854.

the Company aimed to shift all but its most essential West Indian workers out of Zone housing. Coming in tandem as they did, the measures signalled a marked readjustment in relations between the Zone and the republic.[77]

So too did the negotiations then in train for a new treaty between Panama and the Eisenhower administration. High on Panama's wants list was 'effective application' of the principles of the 1936 note, that is, 'opening up the entire scale of Zone jobs to Panamanians, without the dual rates now prevailing, . . . to see that Panamanians obtain higher jobs'. But that would signify the end of labour policy as the Zone had known it, and Governor Seybold soon lodged his objections. 'Equality of opportunity' as Panama construed it was unacceptable, since it meant that the upper echelons would no longer be reserved for American citizens, and 'equality of treatment' must continue to be subject to the caveat in the note. Finally, in Seybold's view, the note gave no justification for a single wage scale based on U.S. rates, as Gaskin had recently proposed. Gaskin had been easily rebuffed, but Seybold clearly feared it would be much more difficult to prevent the State Department from making a deal with Panama at the Company's expense.[78]

The diplomats by no means intended to concede complete equality over pay, promotion, leave, and pensions, but they were ready to move a good deal farther than the Company. At a White House meeting with President José Antonio Remón in the autumn of 1953, Eisenhower promised to give 'full effect' to the 1936 note. In the State Department's view, this should involve a merger of the two wage scales: paying the same rate for a given job regardless of nationality. There should also be uniform labour standards for all U.S. government agencies in the Zone and the introduction of retirement benefits for all non-American personnel. At the same time, American union leaders were told that their people would have to give up the old practice 'of reserving the training schools largely for their own children and of having Americans replaced by their children or other Americans as they die or retire'. To soften the impact of these hammer blows, they would be allowed to keep the 25 per cent differential as well as tax, leave, and travel privileges. The single wage scale, Secretary of State John Foster Dulles assured Secretary of Defense Charles Wilson, 'would simply involve a combining and dovetailing of the existing two wage schedules and would not in itself increase Panamanian wages'. In other words, there was no question of a single scale where everyone was paid a U.S. rate.[79]

[77] NYT 12.4.54, 18/1.
[78] SD, 1950–4, 611.19/4–753 and 7–2053; 611.1913/6–253. PCC, REP.7(1955)-9, Bentz memo of 19.4.54. SD, 1950–4, 811F.062/3–653. PCC, 2-P-12, Seybold to Gaskin, 12.2.53.
[79] SD. 1950–4, 611.19/10–753. The Eisenhower–Remón statement of 1.10.53 is in BD, 984. PCC, REP.7(1955)-9, State Department memo of 14.10.53. SD, 1950–4, 611.19/2–1554, Smith to Eisenhower; 811F.061/12–153, Minutes of meeting of 1.12.53; 611.19/2–2654, Dulles to Wilson, 25.3.54. PCC, REP.7(1955)-9, Whitman to Seybold, 2.6.54.

Even so, the State Department proposals were a bitter pill to swallow. The new single scale, according to the Defense Department, would cost nearly $7 million more a year to implement. Better by far than caving in to the Panamanian clamour for 'equal pay for equal work' would be maximum job opportunity. Measured by the Company's yardstick, however, this would not amount to much, since Panamanians would be excluded from 'key positions, as determined by the U.S.': security-related posts and 'positions requiring skills which are not available locally among non-U.S. citizens'. But these sweeping exceptions were not allowable, and the State Department package was eventually accepted.[80]

The reasons for the apparent climb-down became clear during hearings on the treaty a year later. The single wage scale was not in fact the end of the world. Its purpose, as Assistant Secretary of State Henry Holland candidly described it, was 'to eliminate the appearance of discrimination'. The reality would remain largely untouched, and the Army was satisfied that the single scale would preserve the Pentagon's long-established policy of 'fixing the pay for particular occupational categories on the basis of the prevailing rates of pay in the basic area of recruitment'. Jobs for which employees 'must' be found in the United States would be U.S.-rate, and those filled by applicants from the isthmus would be local-rate. In other words, the two original scales stayed in being but tacked end to end to give the semblance of a single wage ladder. The U.S. commitment, in the Army's view, 'merely require[d] that the basic wage ... apply alike to United States citizens and citizens of Panama occupying identical positions'.[81]

This, of course, was far short of the equality Panama had wanted, and the Panamanians had to be offered several inducements to accept it. One of them was aid to resettle West Indians leaving the Zone, a gesture made to offset Seybold's provocative decision to move 125 West Indian families next door to an expensive apartment block in Colón. Another was to raise the canal annuity by $1.5 million. Yet, as in 1936, Washington refused to put the agreement on labour policy into the treaty. Instead it featured as the leading item in a so-called Memorandum of Understandings Reached. Treaty and memorandum were signed in January 1955.[82]

In July they were rapidly approved by the U.S. Senate against very little opposition. The principal losers were those Americans doing semi-skilled work,

---

[80] SD, 1950–4, 611.19/2–2654 and 6–554. PCC, REP.7(1955)–9, Minutes of meeting of 29.3.54. SD, 1950–4, 611.19/4–1054, Undated Company paper. PCC, REP.7(1955)–9, Roderick memo of 24.7.54. SD, 1950–4, 611.1913/7–3054.

[81] U.S. Congress, Senate, Committee on Foreign Relations, *Hearings on Executive F, the treaty of mutual understanding and cooperation with the Republic of Panama*, 84th Cong., 1st sess. (1955), 44, 70–2, 181–7.

[82] SD, 1950–4, 611.1913/8–1254; 611.1931/8–1254; 611.19/6–1154, 8–1654, 3–3054, and 4–2154; 811F.06/5–854 to 5–3154; 611.1913/9–254 and 12–2054. Text of memorandum is in *BD*, 999–1000.

who would henceforth be classified as local-rate and have their pay cut almost by half. But they were expendable: Although the State Department received a quantity of protest mail from the angry victims, the American unions put up only a token fight on their behalf. They were doubtless well aware that they had little to complain about. The commanding heights of the Zone's employment structure remained overwhelmingly in U.S. hands, and the new settlement made no fundamental changes in the system inaugurated half a century earlier. Americans still officered the canal, and Panamanians were still their subordinates. It would be some time yet before that dispensation was altered decisively in Panama's favour.[83]

[83] *BD*, 1022–3. SD, 1950–4, 611.1913/1–1955 and 5–2555.

10

The Commissary

From depression to war, 1930–1939

In the realm of commercial relations the entire decade of the 1930s was taken up with the negotiation and ratification of a substitute for the aborted treaty of 1926. The starting point was an American draft put together early in 1930. As with the 1926 agreement, it bowed to the Zone authorities in retaining sales to ships and bonded warehouses, and above all in demanding jurisdiction over New Cristóbal – in Governor Burgess's view 'the heart of the new treaty'. But the compensation for New Cristóbal was now to go as high as the full cost of the trans-isthmian highway, and the draft made the significant concession of recognising what was described as Panama's 'reversional sovereignty' over the Zone.[1]

This formulation, of course, represented yet another effort by the State Department to balance the conflicting interests of the Zone and Panama, but for Panama the stumbling block was still New Cristóbal. 'No territory in the City of Colón was needed for Canal purposes,' the American chargé was told, 'and . . . Panama would never cede any territory in that city to the United States.' In the face of the Panamanian refusal to give up New Cristóbal, Secretary of War Patrick Hurley was not disposed to discuss a trans-isthmian road. And the revival of Panamanian complaints over the Commissary showed how little give there was in the canal administration. Though Burgess was willing to stop the sale of luxuries to vessels in transit, he claimed that the 1903 treaty gave Washington 'a complete right to operate for the general public, as well as for its own employees and for passing ships'. In the absence of any movement over New Cristóbal he was perfectly happy to forgo a new accord and stand pat on the 1903 position.[2]

[1] SD, 1910–49, 711.192/382½, U.S. treaty draft of 1.1.30; /384½, Draft of 26.5.30.
[2] SD, 1910–49, 711.1914/30, Muse to Stimson, 28.2.30; 819.154/312, White memo of 24.6.31; /335, Hurley to Stimson, 2.1.32; 811r.244/156, Burgess memo of 30.9.31.

It was not until the advent of the Franklin Roosevelt presidency in March 1933 that the Panamanians themselves began to address the issues of their commercial future seriously. They were prompted by two pieces of legislation, the 'Buy American' Act of 3 March, which enjoined government purchasers to give preference to U.S. goods, and the Act of 22 March which ended prohibition on beer. Both were bound to damage the Panamanian economy by cutting out local suppliers, and in July President Harmodio Arias asked for an excise tax to be kept on American beer shipped down to the Zone and for a surcharge of 25 per cent on sales to ships. In September he cabled his minister in Washington, Ricardo Alfaro, to request an invitation from Roosevelt to discuss the whole question of Panama's share in the business created by the canal.[3]

As Arias later depicted it, the appeal to Roosevelt was a desperate last resort to extricate the country from a severe economic crisis. To the U.S. chargé the overture was only the latest admission of Panama's refusal 'to evolve any considerable source of budgetary income other than the taxes and duties on merchandise consumed by the Canal and its personnel and visitors'. Even so, he accepted that if Arias did not return home with something solid to show for his visit, 'we must face the likelihood of his succession here by a strongly nationalistic President placed in power on an anti-American platform'. Secretary of State Cordell Hull was similarly anxious to respond to Panama in the spirit of the good neighbourliness which Roosevelt had proclaimed as the essence of his approach to Latin America. Arias, he advised the president, should be met more than halfway, and at the very least their conversations 'would serve the useful purpose of allowing "steam to be blown off"'.[4]

In preliminary talks on 9 October, Arias asked for closure of the Commissaries to the 9,000-odd men on the Silver payroll and for an excise tax on cigarettes. Sales in the Zone were proportionately five and a half times higher than in the USA, and clearly smuggling into Panama was taking place on an outrageous scale. Two days later he demanded restrictions on Commissary sales of luxuries, the suspension of sales to ships and of the bonded warehouse business, the 'delivery' to Panama of Railroad land in Colón not needed for the canal, permission for Panama to complete the trans-isthmian highway, and greater Panamanian access to the Zone market for such items as beef and building materials (Arias himself had interests in cement and cattle ranching).[5]

---

[3] SD, 1910–49, 811F.244/193, Memo of 26.4.33; /194, Davis to Hull, 22.4.33, enclosing Panama note of 19.4.33; 611.1931/109, Davis to Caffery, 27.7.33; 819,001 Arias, H./51, Memo of conversation of 11.9.33. Texts of the two Acts are in *United States statutes at large*, 47/1 (Washington, D.C., 1933), 1520–1, and 48/1 (Washington D.C., 1934), 16–20.

[4] SD, 1910–49, 711.1928/331, Chargé to Hull, 11.2.35; 819.001 Arias, H./60, Chargé to Hull, 30.9.33; /72, Chargé to Hull, 4.10.33, and Hull to Roosevelt, 25.9.33.

[5] SD, 1910–49, 819.74/257, Memo of conference, 9.10.33; 711.19/175, Arias memo of 11.10.33.

Once again, as in the 1920s, a sharp cleavage opened up within the administration in its answer to the Panamanian case. Roosevelt passed down the word 'that we grant as many of these points as could properly be done', and the Army was convinced that the State Department 'apparently had no interest in our position and only wished to make as many concessions as possible'. Whereas Hull was ready to see the curtailment of sales to ships and looked forward to the termination of the bonded warehouse trade, Secretary of War Dern insisted that both should carry on much as before. Moreover, Dern unblushingly told Hull, 'there is nothing sold in the commissaries that does not come under the term "necessary and convenient"' as prescribed by Article 13 of the 1903 treaty.[6]

The joint statement put out by Roosevelt and Arias at the end of the discussions gave little away to Panama. Though it promised to limit the Zone's commercial activities to some degree, the changes proposed left the main problems untouched. At the same time, three declarations of principle advanced by Arias were carefully modified to make it impossible for Panama to box Washington into general commitments in the treaty talks to which the White House summit now seemed the prelude.[7]

Throughout the negotiations which began in April 1934, the antagonism between the State Department and the Zone was, if anything, even more pronounced than it had been during the making of the 1926 treaty. The only thing of importance the Zone wanted from Panama was New Cristóbal. On the eve of the first negotiating round, Governor Julian Schley proposed its acquisition in exchange for granting Panama authority to build the trans-isthmian road and for conveying to Panama title to two million dollars' worth of Railroad land in Colón. In May 1934 the chief U.S. spokesman, Sumner Welles, made the offer of the land transfer, only to be told by Alfaro that the cession of New Cristóbal was out of the question.[8]

Roosevelt therefore instructed Hull to drop the request for the area, and the canal leadership found itself isolated. Dern could not understand why the governor and his entourage attached so much importance to the take-over, and the inadequate Panamanian police protection given to American residents produced a resolution by the blue-collar Metal Trades Council for them all to be evacuated into the sanctuary of the Zone – this after American women were said to have been 'subjected to the grossest indecencies and physical handlings by hoodlums, in most cases . . . in broad daylight'. For Schley the absorption of the quarter into the Zone was the only long-term solution, as it was for that veteran of the Goethals era Judge Frank Feuille. In June 1934 Feuille proposed

[6] SWCF, Gruber memo of 11.10.33. SD, 1910–49, 711.19/175, Hull to Roosevelt, 13.10.33; /178, Dern to Hull, 12.10.33.

[7] SD, 1910–49, 711.19/175A and 183, Legal Adviser memo of 11.10.33. BD, 869–70.

[8] PC, 94-A-3/1926, Schley to Gruber, 30.10.33. SD, 1910–49, 819.77/403, Schley to Dern 17.1.34. PC, 94-A-3/1936, Schley to Welles, 26.3.34. SD, 1910–49, 711.1928/436½, Minutes of meeting of 3.5.34.

seizure by exercising the hitherto unused right of eminent domain conferred by Bunau-Varilla in 1903. When eminent domain in the terminal cities was surrendered in the negotiations, Feuille bounced back with the notion of extraterritoriality: New Cristóbal would become 'a special residential district' akin to the foreign settlements in China's treaty ports. This too came to nothing, though the Zone's ambition to incorporate the section was still unquenched.[9]

Roosevelt's abandonment of the claim to New Cristóbal did not mean the withdrawal of its quid pro quo, now an offer to sell Panama all Railroad land in Panama City and Colón not required for government purposes. On the other hand, Washington dismissed Arias's contention that the Railroad's leasehold property in Colón should revert to Panama. Arias then maintained that when the canal convention came into force the Railroad owned only four blocks in Colón, the remainder of the municipality being swampland not in its possession. Though the Railroad had since reclaimed the tract and built on it, its title none the less remained with Panama. This ingenious proposition too was denied, along with Arias's simultaneous assertion that all Railroad property in the terminals not used for the company's own needs was subject to Panamanian taxation. Colombia's 1867 contract with the Railroad had granted it tax exemption in return for free transportation for local residents. Because the United States had assumed the Railroad's privileges through the canal treaty, the Panamanians were told, there was no chance of liability short of a revision to the treaty which the U.S. Senate would almost certainly strike down.[10]

That said, Roosevelt was willing to shed the Railroad lots and to renounce the Railroad's monopoly over a trans-isthmian road – this in spite of the Railroad's deep reluctance to see a highway come into being which would compete with the rail service. In the company's view Panama should be permitted to have the road only if it were forbidden to introduce tolls and if the Zone were given exclusive rights to operate bus and haulage lines. Dern's price was cancellation of the Panamanians' right to free railway travel, worth over $45,000 a year. But the waiver of the monopoly was made without strings, and Panama agreed to complete the road, apart from two short links which the Zone would build; virtually all the expense was to be borne by Panama.[11]

[9] SD, 1910–49, 711.1928/271A, Hull to Dern, 4.10.34. PC, 94-A-3/1936, Rossbottom to Schley, 22.9.34; 2-P-46, MTC resolution of 28.10.34. SD, 1910–49, 819.0144/74, Summerlin to Hull, 12.1.35. PC, 94-A-3/1936, Feuille to Schley, 5.6.34; Panama note of 12.3.35. BD, 876. SD, 1910–49, 819.0144/84, Schley memo of 10.4.35.

[10] SD, 1910–49, 711.1928/271A, Hull to Dern, 4.10.34. PC, 33-E-8, Gonzalez memo of conversation, 5.1.34. SD, 1910–49, 711.1928/208, Arias memo of 12.2.34; 819.77/403, Schley to Flint, 17.1.34; 711.19/182, Gonzalez memo of 7.2.34. BD, 37. SD, 1910–49, 711.1928/436½, Minutes of meeting of 26.4.34.

[11] BD, 35. PC, 94-A-3/1936, Walker to Schley, 2.10.34; Rossbottom to Schley, 22.9.34. SD, 1910–49, 819.154/406½, Flint to Wilson, 13.3.35. PC, 94-A-3/1936, Schley to Dern, 20.12.35. Text of Trans-Isthmian Highway convention is in Bevans, *Treaties and other international agreements*, 10: 778–80.

A further concession to Panama came after the full repeal of prohibition in 1934. In January, as the end of the 'experiment noble in purpose' hove in sight, Panama called for its monopoly on supplying alcohol to be made permanent. No less than a fifth of government revenue was raised from customs and excise taxes on drink, and Alfaro predicted financial disaster for the republic if the Zone became completely 'wet'. This, however, appeared to be precisely what Governor Schley had in mind. In March he told Washington that he envisaged selling duty-free alcohol not only in the Zone but to ships in transit. The sale of drink to ships in fact contravened the agreement reached by Roosevelt and Arias, and Welles was quick to knock the idea on the head. Shortly after repeal went through in June, he advised the president that the Zone should buy all its stocks from Panama, as before. During his state visit to Panama the next month, Roosevelt intimated to Arias that an arrangement could be worked out along these lines.[12]

When rumours of the suggested deal began to circulate, there was uproar. In 1933 the Metal Trades Council had written to the White House asking that the U.S. community on the isthmus not be called on 'to contribute to the welfare of a foreign nation to whom they are not in any sense obligated'. The Council now lobbied Dern, demanding the right to buy duty-free alcohol in the Zone. The Army commander had also warned that the imposition of a U.S. excise tax on American beer 'might result in unfortunate incidents', and feeling ran even higher on the subject of hard liquor. Pressured by both constituencies, Dern found it impossible to accept the compromise put forward by Schley. This proposed that the Zone go on selling beer and light wines duty-free, but that all stronger drink be bought in Panama, where it would be subject to the Panamanian tariff.[13]

To Roosevelt, however, this was an eminently reasonable solution, and he imposed it on Dern in a pontifical directive. 'Liquor is a luxury,' the president decreed, 'and I see no reason for the Government to supply it in the Zone as though it were a food necessity.' In March 1935 Schley's proposal was adopted as official policy and given the force of a presidential executive order.[14]

Panama was singularly ungrateful for the concession, because the Zone's sale of duty-free beer was expected to hit the terminals' entertainment business hard. As the treaty took final shape in February 1936, Alfaro called for restoration of the full Panamanian monopoly on beer as well as on wines and spirits.

[12] SD, 1910–49, 811F.114 Liquor/1, Panama memo of 12.1.34; 711.1928/436½, Minutes of meeting of 26.4.34. PC, 59-G-1, Schley to Flint, 3.3.34. SD, 1910–49, 811F.114 Liquor/4, Wilson to Merrell, 6.4.34; Dern to Hull, 13.4.34. OF, 110, Welles to Roosevelt, 25.6.34. SD, 1910–49, 711.19/200, Gonzalez to Hull, 18.7.34.

[13] OF, 110A, Horle to Roosevelt, 23.10.33. PC, 59-G-1, MTC to Dern, 27.7.34. SD, 1910–49, 811F.244/224, Dern to Roosevelt, 2.1.34. PC, 59-G-1, Schley to Dern, 29.9.34.

[14] OF, 25-I, Roosevelt to Dern, 29.12.34. Executive Order 6997 of 25.3.35 in *Executive Orders*, Supplement no. 28 (Mount Hope, CZ, 1935), 477–8.

The move was opposed by the garrison commander, General Lytle Brown, 'in the interest of our manufacturers at home and . . . more than twelve thousand American soldiers far from home', and the order stood unchanged. Even then, it rankled for a long time to come. 'President Roosevelt gave away our rights in 1935,' one Army officer bitterly observed nearly three years after Roosevelt's death, and the military establishment was to fight the concession throughout the post-war decade.[15]

The Army's sense of betrayal was shared by the Canal when it came to the commercial clauses of the treaty. In June 1934 Welles counselled Roosevelt to let Panama sell foodstuffs to ships, and during his talks with Arias the following month Roosevelt suggested that the Zone restrict itself to the sale of ship's stores, that is, coal, fuel oil, paint, hardware, rope, and cable. Panama went still further, demanding a ban on all ship sales bar coal and oil, plus the end of sales from the bonded warehouses. In the governor's view the administration was coming dangerously close to accepting Panama's criticisms of the Canal's commercial activities.[16]

By the close of 1934, indeed, the canal hierarchy had become morbidly suspicious of Roosevelt and Welles. General Counsel Frank Wang was fearful that they had both been persuaded that U.S. rights in the Zone were finite, not absolute. Schley for his part complained to Dern that neither of the first two U.S. drafts secured the Canal's entitlement to conduct business operations. Whatever franchises were conceded to the merchants of Panama, he told Welles, should not be cast in the iron mould of a detailed treaty article but set out in general terms and 'subject to change when considered advisable by the United States'.[17]

The whole trouble, Schley confided to Feuille, was that Roosevelt had evolved 'a big brotherly sympathetic feeling toward Panama'. He had a tendency to 'turn his good ear toward the State Department', and he seemed to feel that appeasement would make Panama 'a happy booster for the United States . . . and thus greatly affect Latin America's sentiment toward us and thereby improve trade relations'. Schley particularly disliked the final sentence of Article 1 of the U.S. draft of 11 December 1934, which echoed the phraseology of Panama's own first article and which Roosevelt himself had written. It pledged both governments to ensure 'the full and perpetual enjoyment of the benefits of all kinds which the Canal should afford the two nations that made its construction

[15] SD, 1910–49, 711.1928/436½, Minutes of meetings of 30.3.35 and 1.2.36; 811F.114 Liquor/25, Summerlin to Hull, 24.4.35; /31, Brown memo of 13.3.36; /1–248.
[16] OF, 110, Welles to Roosevelt, 25.6.34. SD, 1910–49, 811F.244/242, Roosevelt to Hull, 23.7.34; 711.1928/273½, Legal Adviser comment on Panamanian draft, 4.10.34. WPD, 1652–20, Schley memo of 26.12.34.
[17] PC, 94-A-3/1936, Wang memo of 8.6.34. JB, 326–1, s.558, Joint Planning Committee memo of 6.11.35. PC, 94-A-3/1936, Schley to Welles, 20.11.34 and 7.12.34.

possible'. This, Schley believed, implied 'a partnership between the United States and Panama in the pecuniary profits from the Canal', whereas it ought to be 'a partnership in service rather than a partnership in selfish profit'.[18]

Roosevelt's willingness to take on Panama as a co-participant had its limits, however. In April 1935 Alfaro asked for a share in the canal's gross proceeds from tolls – a due renounced in the treaty of 1903. The payment was to acknowledge Panama as an associate in what Roosevelt had described as 'joint trusteeship' of the waterway. The initiative put Roosevelt's rhetoric to the test and found it wanting. Nothing was done to examine an alternative option put up by the U.S. legation, namely, that the Canal turn over to Panama a fixed percentage of the Commissary's annual profits; and the Canal's dismissal of the Panamanian bid was accepted without argument. Panama, growled Schley, was 'not from any point of view' entitled to revenue sharing, and the treaty should contain no wording which could be interpreted as a recognition that Panama might have 'inherent unliquidated interests in the Panama Canal and certain rights other than those expressly reserved and granted to her by treaty'. In November, Welles refused to link acceptance of the subsidiary radio convention with the tolls issue, and two weeks before the treaty was signed the Panamanian appeal was rejected on the ground that Washington alone was responsible for spending the funds invested in the canal.[19]

Yet the united front over the tolls dividend did not extend to other items on the treaty agenda, and in the closing months of the negotiations the rift between the Canal and the State Department widened still further. In August 1935 Schley complained to Dern about a speech by Welles which had defined the purpose of the new agreement as ending 'the inequities and injustices which may exist in our relations with Panama'. Worse still, the head of the Washington office reported that Welles 'has the President's ear, and . . . it will be difficult to make any change in the provisions of the treaty as they have now apparently been agreed to'. Hull was to tell Dern that 'no step whatsoever has been taken which has not had the full knowledge and approval of the President', adding for good measure a sharp rebuke to the Canal for its unaccommodating attitude.[20]

In truth, the Canal had been cut out of the treaty-making process. When

---

[18] PC, 94-A-3/1936, Schley to Feuille, 7.12.34. See *BD*, 872, for text of Article 1. PC, 94-A-3/1936, Schley memo of 26.12.34.

[19] SD, 1910–49, 711.1928/359, Panama memo of 23.4.35. See *BD*, 43, for Article 15 of Wyse Concession; pp. 210 and 286 for the renunciations under the 1903 treaties. SD, 1910–49, 711.1928/436½, Minutes of meeting of 24.4.35; /387, GRM to Welles; 811F.244/254, Summerlin to Hull, 31.5.35, enclosing memo by Burdett; 711.1928/412½, Heimer memo of 2.8.35. PC, 94-A-3/1936, Dern to Hull, 15.8.35, quoting Schley memo of 22.5.35. SD, 1910–49, 711.1928/436½, Minutes of meetings of 20.11.35 and 17.2.36.

[20] SD, 1910–49, 711.19/210, Dern to Hull, 30.8.35. PC, 94-A-3/1936, Heimer to Schley, 3.9.35; Hull to Dern, 15.10.35.

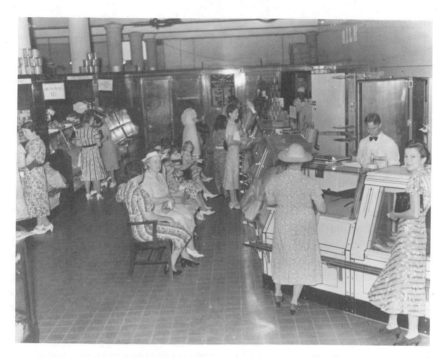

Figure 5. The company store: Zonian housewives stock up on the duty-free wares of the Balboa Commissary, late 1930s. (Panama Canal Commission)

Roosevelt visited the Zone in October, Schley was disturbed to find that he had been kept ignorant of important amendments to the treaty text. When he asked for a copy of the latest draft, he was told that the U.S. legation had instructions not to show it to anyone, and though it was eventually handed over, the project made unpalatable reading. During his audience with Roosevelt, Schley had detected the same tendency to 'play the "Lady Bountiful" role' that he had castigated a year earlier, and he was shaken to discover that none of the criticisms he had entered since then had made any impact.[21]

In the final agreement signed on 2 March 1936, Commissary sales were to be restricted to Canal and Railroad staff, the Army and Navy, and employees of contractors and auxiliaries resident in the Zone. Sales to ships were to be sharply curtailed by having the Commissary place a surcharge on sea stores, that is, consumer goods for passengers and crew. Bonded warehouses were to

[21] PC, 94-A-3/1936, Schley to Summerlin, 17.10.35; Ridley to Schley, 1.11.35; Schley to Dern, 19.10.35; Schley memo of 17.12.35.

remain in business until Panamanian facilities became available at 'reasonable' rates, but Welles told Alfaro it was Roosevelt's decision that 'private business is to cease to exist in the Canal Zone except insofar as it relates to the operation and protection of the Canal'. To Schley's protest that Washington had materially undermined the attractiveness of the canal to international shipping, the State Department's reply was that Panama's interests came first. Panama was to have the guarantee that the Zone would not be set up as a commercial centre. In other words, the promise made by Roosevelt's namesake in 1904 was at last to be made good.[22]

The Zone accepted its defeat with extreme bad grace. In April 1936 Dern told Schley that there was no more need to inflate the Commissary's prices to protect Panamanian retailers against unfair competition. A year later the War Department began to step up its purchases from the Commissary rather than buy from Panama. Schley's successor, Clarence Ridley, stated flatly that Panama's suppliers enjoyed 'no preemptive right to business profits obtainable at the expense of Governmental Agencies and Personnel resident in the Zone'.[23]

The War Department was equally difficult over the matter of the Railroad's holdings in Colón, which Roosevelt was still determined it should offload. As part of his campaign to promote divestment, he ordered an investigation into a long-standing charge that brothels were being run on Railroad leaseholds. Assistant Secretary Harry Woodring's report, while admitting prostitution on two blocks of Railroad property, advised that 'we should not stir up the question by any action whatever'. In July 1937 the congressional resolution authorising disposal of the Railroad's Colón estate included a clause providing for the Zone's annexation of New Cristóbal in exchange for transfer to Panama of title to whatever Railroad land was not required for U.S. government purposes. Thus the Canal resurrected a scheme which Welles believed the treaty had killed off. In the summer of 1938 Woodring told Hull he planned to open negotiations for an exchange agreement in the teeth of Welles's conviction that there was no issue more likely to inflame Panamanian opinion.[24]

When Roosevelt's treaty came into force in July 1939, therefore, it confronted a grudging canal establishment whose pretensions to commercial hegemony were dented but still basically intact. Though the settlement was hailed as a triumph for good-neighbour diplomacy, much of its success in practice would depend on the Zone's willingness to make it work. In the light of the Zone's stance over the past thirty-five years, the outlook was not promising.

[22] Text is in *BD*, 873–4, 891–3, 887. SD, 1910–49, 711.1928/436$\frac{1}{2}$, Minutes of meeting of 17.12.35. PC, 94-A-3/1936, Schley memo of 17.12.35. SD, 1910–49, 711.1928/456$\frac{1}{2}$, 16.

[23] SWCF, Dern to Schley, 17.4.36; Ridley to Smith, 3.5.37.

[24] SWCF, Dern to Woodring, 21.3.36; Woodring to Dern, 14.4.36. Public Resolution No. 54 of 10.7.37 is in *United States statutes at large*, 50/1 (Washington, D.C., 1938), 511. SD, 1910–49, 819.77/464, Welles memo of 14.6.37. SWCF, Woodring to Hull, 17.6.38.

Second World War, 1939–1945

The argument over the scope of commercial activity in the Zone fell silent for most of the Second World War. The heat was taken out of the situation largely by the surge of prosperity which washed over the isthmus as the United States expanded the garrison to man an extensive new anti-aircraft network and brought in tens of thousands more labourers to build defence installations and excavate a third set of locks for the Navy. The result was a bonanza even greater than Panama had known in the construction decade, and as long as it lasted grievances over the Zone's business operations receded into the background.

Even so, a residual tension lay not far below the surface, and it broke through continually as a reminder that for both sides the conflict still smouldered. In December 1939 Panama revived the perennial complaint that Commissary goods were being smuggled across the Zone line and demanded they be marked to show their provenance. To the U.S. Embassy this dodged the real issue, namely, the uncompetitive pricing of commodities in Panama thanks to the inordinate tariffs clapped on such imported staples as rice, potatoes, sugar, and canned vegetables. The remedy was obvious enough – tariff reduction – but this was easier said than done. In 1934 Harmodio Arias had eliminated the duties on luxuries, but he had not gone farther because the government could not break its heavy dependence on tariffs as a source of revenue. True, Arias had already turned to the alternative of an income tax, but the rates were kept minuscule to placate the rich, and the tax applied chiefly to foreigners and the employees of foreign contractors. If tariffs were now to be lowered on basic foodstuffs, it would inevitably mean a steeper income tax, and the political reaction was bound to be explosive. Until the Panamanian oligarchy grasped this nettle, all it could do was to rely on the Zone to bail it out.[25]

The Zone, however, was not disposed to be generous. When Panama asked for restrictions on the Commissary and on Army post exchanges, the Army tersely rejected 'the amazing proposition that the cost of living of all military and Canal Zone personnel be increased for the benefit of the Republic of Panama'. From December 1939 all meat, eggs, butter, cheese, and potatoes imported from the United States were bought only from the Commissary, cutting out Panamanian wholesalers. Secretary of State Cordell Hull consoled Panama with the thought that the flow of money from projected U.S. government spending would more than compensate.[26]

---

[25] SD, 1910–49, 811F.504/166, Dawson to Hull, 6.1.40. John Biesanz, 'The economy of Panama', *Inter-American Economic Affairs*, 6 (1952–3), 8. SD, 1910–49, 811F.244/296, Muccio to Duggan, 15.12.39; 819.00/1904, Legation to Hull, 10.8.36; 819.5123/45, Wilson to Hull, 14.10.41.

[26] WPD, 1652–32, War Plans Division to Adjutant General, 20.2.40. SD, 1910–49, 811F.24/43, Dawson to Hull, 7.11.39; Dawson to Hull, 2.3.40; /50, Woodring to Hull, 16.3.40; /58, Hull to Garay, 3.6.40.

Hull's confidence was amply justified. In September 1939 the garrison numbered 14,000 officers and men; by December 1942 it had swollen to 67,000. Aliens employed by all U.S. government departments totalled over 71,000 in July 1942, as compared with the 38,000 serving with the ICC and the Railroad in 1913. The financial impact on Panama was phenomenal. By 1943 the country's gross receipts from the Zone were four times the pre-war average, and since 1940 income per head of population had tripled. The cheap emporiums of the terminal cities raked in unprecedented takings, along with the gambling joints, the bars, and the whore-houses. Panama had never had it so good.[27]

In these flush circumstances, renewed Panamanian protests against the 'terrible scourge' of Zone competition smacked of synthetic indignation and met with a sceptical response in the State Department. When Panama in January 1941 again took up the question of contraband, the department thought it 'not unreasonable to believe that even the merchants can report gains in the resale of smuggled merchandise'. And the defence establishment refused either to eliminate luxuries from the PXS or to introduce surcharges, on the ground that 35 per cent of the Zone payroll went into Panamanian tradesmen's pockets.[28]

Faced with this blank wall, the Arias administration put through a law reducing import duties on mass consumer goods and bringing in an income tax much more far-reaching than the taxation introduced in 1933. Prosperity made the Act a dead letter, however. The new tax rates were not enforced, nor were tariffs lowered. Instead the government turned a blind eye to the influx of contraband which kept body and soul together for people too poor to buy the exorbitantly priced provender in local stores. No use was made of the existing provision for a joint anti-smuggling inspectorate. At the same time, Panamanian traders felt little need to sell to ships, and meetings with Canal officials to co-ordinate policy on ship sales lapsed after June 1940.[29]

Yet the State Department still believed that Panama deserved some consideration. A call from American blue-collar workers for the sale of duty-free hard liquor in the Zone was rejected as an insult to a loyal ally. When the Army dispensed with the services of the Panamanian wholesalers, Welles fought to have their business restored, but without success. The department had once noted 'a tendency from top to bottom in the military and naval hierarchy to scoff at any regulations aimed to improve the Panamanian economy', and

[27] HPCD, 4: 1 and 2: 80. Panama Canal Company – CZ Government, Personnel Bureau, *Force – Company/Government 1904–1968* (Balboa Heights, CZ, 1969). Biesanz, 'Economy of Panama', 5–6.

[28] SD, 1910–49, 711.1914/325, Panama memo of 2.6.41; 711F.1914/189, Panama note of 29.1.41; /234, Undated study of the Twelve Points; 811F.244/319, Army–Navy memo of 18.4.41; 711F.1914/189, Panama note of 7.5.41. WPD, 4452–4, Stimson to Hull, 14.6.41. SD, 1910–49, 711F.1914/314. Minutes of meeting of 14.6.41.

[29] SD, 1910–49, 711.1928/973, Wilson to Hull, 6.9.41; 819.5123/45, Wilson to Hull, 14.10.41; 819.51/9–944; 619.003/3–345; 811F.244/6–845; 711.19/1–2346. *BD*, 889–90, 937. PC, 58-A-6, Mehaffey to Hines, 24.12.45.

nothing since had changed that view. 'I know by long and bitter experience', Welles lamented, 'that at every opportunity the War Department will undertake to disregard the spirit animating the agreements . . . between this Government and that of Panama, and every time the War Department has conceded one inch they go on to ask for the proverbial mile.'[30]

For the duration of the wartime boom Panama could afford to be indifferent to this antipathy. When it tapered off in the closing months of 1943, Panamanian economic nationalism resurfaced, but it had to vent its frustrations on foreign concerns in the republic itself. In January 1944 a decree-law placed manifold restraints on the business activities of non-Panamanians. As before, the prime targets were the Chinese who controlled the grocery trade, and exemption for American businesses was soon forthcoming. But the passage of the law was ominous, and it was followed early in 1945 by a new draft constitution envisaging the nationalisation of commerce, which could place U.S.-owned companies in jeopardy.[31]

Panama's price for amending these clauses was a commercial treaty, but when Washington refused to haggle, the requisite immunity was granted unconditionally. Now that American interests were safeguarded, the embassy advised, the idea of a commercial treaty could be shelved. Panama did not demur, and what had seemed likely to become a troublesome issue in U.S.-Panama relations was to lie dormant for the greater part of the post-war decade.[32]

Cold war, 1945–1955

The Panamanian quest for a larger slice of the commercial business generated by the canal had subsided during the boom years of the Second World War, and it continued to be a side-issue well into the post-war era. Government pressure for commercial concessions was quite remarkably sporadic, and the only systematic attack on the Zone's mercantilism came from an opposition figure, former Foreign Minister Ricardo Alfaro, in a series of lectures given at the National University in the summer of 1948. There he redeveloped the thesis that American rights in the Zone were qualified, not plenary. But Alfaro was given no official support, and he was decidedly persona non grata in American circles, thanks to the ultra-nationalist stand he had taken over the

[30] SD, 1910–49, 811F.114 Liquor/44, Hushing to Stimson, 5.12.41; Hull to Stimson, 3.2.42; 811F.24/66, Wilson to Hull, 22.4.42; /68, Welles to Stimson, 28.5.42; 711F.1914/234; 811F.24/74, Welles to Bonsal, 28.8.42.

[31] MID-R, 2320, quoting FBI report of 10.8.43. ONI, C-10-M, 15772C, Report of 22.3.44. OSS, 77340S, Military attaché report of 23.5.44. SD, 1910–49, 819.5034/91 and 94. ONI, C-10-M, 24220. SD, 1910–49, 819.011/2–2845, Embassy to Stettinius, 28.2.45; on the laws of 1934 and 1941, see 819.111/178, 179, 181, and 187 and 819.5034/15, 20, 26, and 29.

[32] SD, 1910–49, 819.5034/6–545; 819.011/10–145, Hines to Byrnes, 1.10.45; 819.5034/2–2346 and 2–2646; 711.192/1–1546, Hines to Byrnes, 15.1.46.

bases agreement. As far back as 1922 he had been described as 'untrustworthy and intensely anti-American', and thirty years on he retained his reputation as 'one of the most influential enemies of the United States in the Republic'.[33]

One senior U.S. official anxious to counter the 'Alfaro Doctrine' was Ambassador Monnett Davis, with his 'constructive program' of February 1949. Davis's masters, however, were not as willing to conciliate Panama as they had been in the days of Sumner Welles. When negotiations for a post-war defence agreement began, the idea of throwing in a package of economic inducements, as in 1942, was emphatically ruled out. And whereas settlement of the unresolved El Encanto claim was not made a condition of the bases agreement of 1942, in 1945 it was held up as the prerequisite to a commercial treaty. When Panama rejected the new bases agreement in December 1947, the spirit of charity in the State Department dwindled to an all-time low.[34]

It shrank close to vanishing point in the Pentagon, still smarting over Roosevelt's order banning Zone sales of duty-free hard liquor from home. President Truman's military aide, General Harry Vaughan, had recently passed on the word that several of his friends in the Zone 'have written to me very tearfully about the difficulty they have in getting a supply of whiskey'. The Army therefore tried to get the order revoked to deprive Panamanian liquor stores of their 'Jesse James profits' and 'put things back on the track'. Though the bid failed, it was revived periodically over the next five years, and while the fuss seems trivial, the financial consequences of revocation would have been very serious for Panama. Ambassador John Wiley was not joking when he reported that if the Panamanians ever knew he supported the order's cancellation 'it would be necessary for the Department at once to buy me a one-way ticket out. My position would become completely untenable.'[35]

The Army was similarly ill disposed to Panama in another respect. The so-called 'Buy American' Act of 1933 fixed a price differential of 25 per cent in favour of U.S. goods, but when the Army was pressed by the State Department to waive it, the response was minimal. When Davis called for government agencies not to apply the Act to purchases in the Zone, the Army refused to make a blanket exemption for Panamanian products. Panama need expect no consideration from that quarter.[36]

[33] SD, 1910–49, 711F.1914/12–2346; 819.00/2–1551; 711.1928/9–1448; 711.19/10–148; 701.1911/172, South to Hughes, 22.6.22; 611.1913/11–1252, Wiley to Acheson, enclosing Alfaro article in *La Estrella* of 9.11.52. For the bases agreement, see below, 316–20.
[34] SD, 1910–49, 711.19/2–349, Davis to Acheson, 3.2.49; 711F.1914/12–2346, Byrnes to Hines, 27.12.46; /547 of 22.9.42; /562 of 9.10.42; 711.192/10–3145 and 12–445.
[35] POD, 012, Norstad memo of 18.7.47. SD, 1910–49, 811F.114 Liquor/1–248; 819.50/2–2448, Hines to Wise, 24.2.48. SD, 1950–45, 811F.531/7–2651, Pace to Acheson, 26.7.51; /9–2751, Acheson to Pace, 20.11.51; 411F.196/2–1853; 411F.19/12–1152, Wiley to Miller, 11.12.52.
[36] SD, 1910–49, 811F.244/3–1449, Webb to Royall, 29.4.49; /9–1249. SD, 1950–4, 411F.1931/5–850; 611.19/10–650.

Nor from the canal administration. The 'necessary and convenient' phraseology of Article 13 of 1903 was still interpreted as a licence to import and sell any items 'not luxuries by American standards'. The reference in Article 3 of 1936 to goods 'produced or manufactured' in the Zone was taken as an effective admission by Panama that the Zone was entitled to run its own farms, workshops, and processing plants. In the view of the Canal Company's general counsel, Paul Bentz, the 1936 treaty had not intended 'to concede the legitimate Canal Zone market to the commerce and industry of Panama'. Nor had it prescribed curbs, 'express or implied', on the degree of Commissary and post-exchange operations. If Washington should choose to make concessions to Panama, it must take care to insert in them 'proper qualifications or escape clauses'.[37]

Panama, however, had inescapable changes in mind. In November 1952 President José Antonio Remón spoke of going to Washington to launch negotiations for basic treaty revision with the incoming Eisenhower régime. Such summit diplomacy recalled Harmodio Arias's visit to Roosevelt in 1933, but Remón recruited public opinion behind the cause much more boldly than Arias had done. In March 1953 he opened an elaborate propaganda campaign with a speech culminating in the slogan 'We want justice, not millions, not charity'. First and foremost, this entailed 'a fair share of the profits from the canal' and a larger annuity, though Foreign Minister José Ramón Guizado had recently suggested to Ambassador Wiley that instead of increasing the annuity Washington might consider a grant for building a new presidential palace and ministerial offices on Paitilla Point.[38]

Wiley turned down the feeler as a blatant piece of pork-barrelling, yet he agreed that something had to be done to relieve the United States of 'the onus of merely having and holding in an antiquated, colonial fashion'. It should not be treaty revision: 'To open the door on that would be to lift the lid on Pandora's box.' 'The status of Great Britain in certain British crown colonies', Wiley advised Secretary of State John Foster Dulles, 'demonstrates vividly the disastrous cumulative effect of small concessions granted seriatim over long periods of years.' Far better, he believed, to augment the Point Four programme of aid for Panamanian agriculture by $5 million a year for ten years, and Dulles took up the idea, urging it on the Pentagon as the agency responsible for canal affairs.[39]

The canal directorate, however, was more interested in contesting Panama's

[37] SD, 1910–49, 811F.812/9–2849, Snow to Bennett, 28.9.49. SD, 1950–4, 611.19/8–652, Bentz to Seybold, 26.6.52.
[38] SD, 1950–4, 611.19/11–2052; 719.00/3–2353. SD, 1955–60, 611.1913/2–1055, Report of the Panamanian negotiating mission, 26.1.55, 4. SD, 1950–4, 611.19/4–753; 819.10/11–2552, Wiley report of conversation with Guizado on 21.11.52.
[39] SD,1950–4, 611.19/11–3052, Wiley to Bennett, 30.11.52; 911F.5301/11–652, Wiley to Sowash, 6.11.52; 611.19/3–2053, Wiley to Dulles, 20.3.53; 819.00TA/2–2853, Dulles to Wilson, 28.2.53.

claims. The 1936 treaty, Governor Seybold told Wiley, did not bear out the argument that the Canal had a permanent responsibility to guarantee Panamanian welfare through continual treaty revision. It would be especially dangerous if the annuity were subject to periodic increases, as this could 'jeopardize the perpetual grants of the 1903 Convention by tending toward the substitution of something more nearly resembling leases'.[40]

Equally alarming was the notion that Panama should be given a percentage share in canal revenues as Narciso Garay had proposed the preceding November. Washington had been quick to stamp on the proposal in 1935 and again in 1941 when it was briefly floated during the base negotiations. For the canal leadership a share dividend was the first step along the road to nationalisation. It would involve Panamanians in all too many aspects of management, and it was particularly ominous against the background of Guizado's comments on the U.S.-owned Power and Light Company. 'The day of the foreign concession operating independently in the field of public utilities in a foreign country has ended,' Guizado proclaimed, and it was time for Panama to be awarded a 50 per cent interest. The parallels with recent events in Iran and Egypt were far too close for American comfort. In Iran, Western oil companies had been sequestrated in 1951, while in Egypt, which already received 23 per cent of the net profits of the Suez Canal Company, the new revolutionary régime had set its sights even higher. 'We are not Egyptians,' Guizado assured Wiley, yet Wiley believed Washington might well find itself with 'still another burr under the saddle blanket'.[41]

In the treaty proposals presented in September, however, Panama proved considerably more than an irritant. The Panamanian opening position constituted nothing less than a frontal attack on American prerogatives in the Zone, which, if accepted, would have made the canal organization a Panamanian dependency.

The centre-piece was the stipulation that the United States recognise the principle of Panamanian sovereignty over the Zone and accept a restrictive definition of its sovereign rights there. In consequence, mixed tribunals were to be set up to judge disputes involving Panamanians; the Panamanian flag was to be flown on Zone territory and on vessels in transit; and Spanish was to become an official language. Panama was to be given the power to tax all of its residents working in the Zone, plus all its citizens and non-U.S. government employees

[40] PCC, REP.7(1955)-1, Seybold to Wiley, 27.5.53; REP.7(1955)-4, Position paper of 19.6.53.
[41] SD, 1950–4, 611.1913/11–2152. See above, n.19. SD, 1910–49, 711.1914/325, Panama memo of 2.6.41; /336, Legal Adviser memo of 14.6.41; /337, Edgerton to Van Voorhis, 28.6.41. PC, 80-A-3, memo. of 16.6.41. PCC, REP.7(1955)-4, Position paper of 24.8.53. SD, 1950–4, 819.2612/9–153. Douglas Farnie, *East and west of Suez: The Suez Canal in history, 1854–1956* (Oxford, 1969), 671–2. SD, 1950–4, 611.19/8–353, Wiley memo of conversation with Guizado; /8–1853, Wiley memo of conversation with Harmodio Arias.

resident there. The perpetuity of American tenure was to go, and the duration of all existing U.S.–Panama treaties set at ninety-nine years. To drive home the point that relations had changed decisively, a new treaty was to be concluded whereby the United States would become no more than Panama's concessionaire for the Canal.[42]

These jurisdictional demands were accompanied by equally wide-ranging economic conditions, headed by the call for a $5 million annuity derived from up to 20 per cent of the canal's gross income from tolls. The Zone's commercial activities were to be severely hamstrung: Only 'indispensable' articles might be sold in U.S. government stores, and sales to individuals were to be limited to 1 per cent of an employee's salary. U.S. federal agencies alone were to import goods into the Zone, and the only non-Panamanian products shipped in must be produced in the United States. Only drink bought in Panama was to enter the Zone, and none was to be sold there. Panama was to take over the provisioning of ships, and manufacturing in the Zone was to cease. To boost the Panamanian economy still further, the 'Buy American' Act was not to apply to Panama, and Panamanian exports were to have preferential quotas in the USA. Finally, all U.S. government property in Panama except Madden Dam was to be conveyed to Panama gratis; and Washington was to build docks at Colón and to construct and maintain a bridge or a tunnel at both terminals.[43]

As Assistant Secretary John Moors Cabot pointed out, this ambitious package 'cut straight across our treaty position in the Zone'. But in Dulles the Panamanians faced a man who considered the 1903 convention a model of its kind, who refused to think of treaty revision or renegotiation, and who would contemplate neither an increase in the annuity nor the smallest inroads on U.S. jurisdiction. Indeed, when Remón met Eisenhower, Dulles even went so far as to say that new treaties with Spain did not touch on Florida, nor those with the USSR on Alaska. In other words, he saw the Zone as United States territory (which it was not) and therefore none of Panama's business.[44]

Eisenhower, however, displayed a much more open mind. He had been stationed in the Zone in the early 1920s, he told Remón, and in an unwitting comment on the Canal's perennial conservatism, admitted that 'the same old problems that he remembered from his service there still seemed to exist'. All proven abuses, he promised, would be corrected. Though the State Department believed the president had taken Remón's assertions at face value when they 'should be quoted a lot below par', Eisenhower was undeflected. When Remón

[42] SD, 1955–60, 611.1913/2–1055, 3–6. SD, 1950–4, 911F.7301/9–1553; 611.19/10–753. The Panamanian demand for equality in the field of employment is treated in the chapter on labour relations; see Chapter 9 at nn. 78–83.

[43] SD, 1950–4, 911F.7301/9–1553.

[44] SD, 1950–4, 611.1913/10–1953, Cabot to Smith, 19.10.53; 611.19/9–853; /9–2853.

protested at the wording of the final joint communiqué, Dulles rewrote it at Eisenhower's dictation to restate the general principles of 1933 and 1936 on which Panama based its entire case.[45]

The concessions Eisenhower's chieftains had in mind were relatively few. Dulles was ready to accept Panama's bid to widen its taxation powers, and the Army to relinquish Paitilla Point in exchange for manoeuvre rights at the old Rio Hato base. The governor was willing to evacuate New Cristóbal (after moving in hundreds of West Indians), to give up sanitary regulation of the terminal cities, and to see a bridge at the Pacific entrance. But both he and the Army rejected Cabot's idea of putting a sales tax on PX and Commissary goods, and the Army declined absolutely to stop selling luxuries at its stores. It persisted in its refusal even after the revelation that the Nicaraguan dictator Anastasio Somoza had been allowed to go on an unbridled shopping spree in the Albrook Field PX – though the credibility of the Panamanians' protest was destroyed by the fact that he had been escorted onto the premises by their own motor-cycle police![46]

Dulles was equally resolved not to budge on the annuity, sharing Seybold's neurosis that to increase it could vitiate the U.S. title to the Zone. In the wake of Remón's departure, therefore, the search for an innocuous alternative became the treaty makers' central preoccupation. A suggestion by Wiley that the annuity be commuted into a single lump-sum payment of some $25 million was turned down with the reflection that if it were squandered Panama would be back 'with an outstretched palm and a new demand for "justice"'. Instead Cabot revived Wiley's plan for a ten-year aid programme, reduced to $2 million a year. The response of the Navy commandant was glacial: Panama had grown used to living off 'parasitic pickings and gleanings on the transit trade', and aid on this scale would only prolong the welfare mentality. Even so, the offer was made, though cut back still further to $1 million a year. To the Panamanians this nowhere near matched their bid for a $5 million annuity, and when two-thirds of their proposals were rejected as a misguided attempt to infiltrate the 'inviolable line' of Article 3, negotiations came to the verge of breakdown.[47]

Yet the deadlock forced a reappraisal of U.S. policy. Both Ambassador Selden Chapin and the leader of the U.S. negotiating team, John Muccio, believed the time had come for a revaluation of the annuity, to as much as $2 million if need

---

[45] SD, 1950–4, 611.19/9–2853; /9–2953; /9–2953, State Department comment; /10–853, Remón speech of 7.10.53. *BD*, 984, gives text of Eisenhower–Remón statement of 1.10.53.

[46] SD, 1950–4, 611,1913/9–2453; 611.19/10–2053, Minutes of meeting of 14.10.53; 611.1913/ 12–1553; 611.19/10–2053; 611.1913/11–1253, Johnson to Cabot, 3.11.53; /12–753. *NYT*, 20.11.53, 6/5.

[47] SD, 1950–4, 819.10/9–1853; 611.19/10–2353; 611.1913/11–1253. PCC, REP.7(1955)–4, Seybold memo of 4.12.53 and position paper of 22.12.53. SD, 1950–4, 819.00TA/2–2654, Chapin to Muccio and Muccio to Chapin. SD, 1955–60, 611.1913/2–1055, 11–13. SD, 1950–4, 611.1913/2–2754 and 3–1254.

be, and Dulles agreed. Yet strings were attached: Cabot's successor, Henry Holland, was instructed to tie the increase to an explicit statement that it did not signify recognition of Panama's claim to share sovereignty and did nothing to change existing treaty rights and obligations. A week later Holland added the further condition that Panama should agree not to reopen the annuity issue and an even more far-reaching proposal emanating from Dulles. This was for a new treaty providing for a larger annuity 'and in all other respects carrying forward the treaty of 1903'. It would supersede the 1936 accord and its 'vague declarations', that is, its references to partnership and the opportunities due to Panama by virtue of geography. In other words, it would destroy the theoretical basis of Panama's demand for more equitable treatment.[48]

The State Department's legal adviser had previously considered that Panama would probably think of such a deal as 'trading her rights for a mess of pottage', and Muccio warned Holland that it would spell political suicide for any Panamanian leader to put his name to it. Yet the Panamanian negotiators in Washington were ready to accept the provisos, while Foreign Minister Guizado told Chapin that he would agree to the cancellation of the 1936 treaty: Harmodio Arias and Alfaro regarded it as their sacred cow, but Remón had overruled them. The way to a final settlement now seemed clear, though the Panamanian price was once again an annuity of $5 million.[49]

Dulles would not go anywhere so high; he offered instead an extra $1 million on the annuity plus $10 million in aid spread over ten years. When Remón talked of a second descent on the White House to ask for more, the secretary rapidly headed him off, cutting out the aid programme but stepping up the annuity to $1.93 million. He also dropped the idea of scrapping the 1936 treaty, but he was adamant that Panama must accept wording which nullified Panama's contention that it had the right unilaterally to reopen any of its canal treaties with Washington. Without such a safeguard Americans might someday face 'the situation which has confronted the British in Suez', where the Anglo-Egyptian treaty of 1936 had recently been revised to promise a British military evacuation. Dulles had encouraged the withdrawal from Egypt, but he had no intention of allowing Egypt to set any kind of precedent for Panama.[50]

---

[48] PCC, REP.7(1955)-4, Whitman to Seybold, 4.6.54. SD, 1950–4, 611.1913/3–1054. *FRUS 1952–4*, 4: 1433–7, Muccio to Cabot, 5.3.54. PCC, REP.7(1955)-4, Runnestrand to Whitman, 11.6.54; Runnestrand to Whitman, 21.6.54. SD, 1955–60, 611. 1913/2–1055, 19–20. Marjorie Whiteman (ed.), *Digest of international law*, vol. 3 (Washington, D.C., 1964), 1160. SD, 1950–4, 611.19/6–1154, Holland to Chapin, 23.6.54.

[49] SD, 1950–4, 911F.5301/4–1554, Legal Adviser memo of 15.4.54; 611.19/6–1154, Muccio to Holland, 11.6.54 PCC, REP.(1955)-4, Runnestrand to Whitman, 21.6.54. SD, 1950–4, 611.1913/6–2554. Whiteman, *Digest*, 3: 1160.

[50] SD, 1950–4, 611.1931/8–1254, Dulles to Chapin, 12.8.54; 611.19/8–1654; 611.1931/8–2654, Chapin to Dulles and Dulles to Chapin; 611.1913/8–2754, 8–2854, and 9–1354; / 2–1755, Sowash to Cabot, 17.2.55; /10–2254. Farnie, *Suez*, 705–11.

During the final negotiating round in Panama City, the Panamanians put up a strenuous fight against Dulles's behest. In Alfaro's view the United States had never imposed such terms, even on a defeated enemy. Remón, thought Ambassador Roberto Huertematte, would rather have no treaty at all, since acceptance of the American stipulation would be tantamount to keeping 'perpetual silence'. In the end the offending article was deleted and replaced by a clause in the preamble recognising that treaties between the two countries could be modified only by mutual consent. Both sides also acknowledged 'the absence of any obligation' on the part of either to change the amount of the annuity. On this basis the agreement was initialled on 20 December. Remón did not live to witness its signature five weeks later; he was assassinated on 2 January 1955.[51]

The treaty he had prompted gave Panama a good deal less than it had hoped for. The annuity was fixed at $1.93 million, Panama was granted the right to tax Panamanians in the Company's employ, and Americans alone were to be allowed to buy from the Commissary. An accompanying 'memorandum of understandings' included the transfer to Panama of sales to ships and the exemption of Panamanian products from the 'Buy American' Act. New Cristóbal was to be conveyed to Panama along with Paitilla Point, and the two outstanding obligations from the 1942 agreement were to be fulfilled: the railway station in Panama City would be consigned to the republic, and a bridge would be built at the Pacific terminal. In return Panama made two significant concessions to the Pentagon: allowing visiting military personnel from 'friendly' third countries to use the PXS and undertaking to give a 75 per cent reduction in import duty on liquor sold to the Zone as long as Roosevelt's 1935 executive order remained in effect.[52]

In coming to this arrangement, Washington had given way only on inessentials; the core of its position was still intact. To most Americans on the isthmus, however, the treaty was a capitulation, and they pinned the blame for it squarely on the president and his foreign-service advisers. 'Already', wrote one angry Zonian to Eisenhower, 'many Panamanians are saying "Queremos la zanja" [We want the ditch] . . . and if the fallacious thinking of the . . . Department of State prevails the Panama Canal will eventually be given to Panama scott free.' Eisenhower's government, another told him, was 'placing the U.S. citizens in the Zone in a state of bondage to please the greed of Panama'.[53]

The Senate did not share that hostility. Once Panama had cleared its debt to the Canal Company, the Foreign Relations Committee recommended approval of the treaty after a mere three days of hearings, and it entered into force in August. Like the pact which Franklin Roosevelt had fostered in the 1930s, it

[51] SD, 1950–4, 611.1913/9–2954 and 10–2254; 611.19/11–954; 611.1913/11–1454 and 11–1754. BD, 988. NYT, 3.1.55, 1/8, 14/3, 15/1.
[52] Details are in BD, 987–1006.
[53] SD, 1950–4, 611.1913/5–2555.

was seen by U.S. diplomats as a masterly piece of adaptation whereby tactical concessions to Panama had done nothing to flaw the imperative of complete American control. 'We felt we could not agree to do anything', Holland had testified, '. . . which could be construed a hundred years hence as receding one millimeter' from the insistence on full sovereign rights. Only Eisenhower's fuming correspondent, perhaps, would have suspected that within twenty-five years of its passage the Canal Zone would have ceased to exist and the canal itself been scheduled for transfer to Panama.[54]

[54] On the ratification process, see Larry LaRae Pippin, *The Remón era: An analysis of a decade of events in Panama, 1947–1957* (Stanford, Calif., 1964), 145–50. Text of Foreign Relations Committee report is in *BD*, 1008–30. See also U.S. Congress, Senate, Committee on Foreign Relations, *Hearings on Executive F*, 84th Cong., 1st sess. (1955), 164, and id., *Executive sessions of the Senate Foreign Relations Committee*, Historical Series, vol. 7, 1955, 95th Cong., 2d sess. (1978), 707–15.

11

Partnership politics

From depression to war, 1930–1939

In the 1930s the United States put a different face on its approach to Latin America by repudiating Theodore Roosevelt's corollary to the Monroe Doctrine and embracing Franklin Roosevelt's Good Neighbor policy. Both moves were meant to indicate abandonment of the interventionism which had provoked so much hostility south of the Rio Grande. For Panama they meant the formal end of the protectorate set up in 1903 and the start of a new era of partnership with Washington.

The first and most dramatic signal of change on the isthmus was the coup d'état which ousted President Florencio Arosemena. It came after some stupendous malpractice on Arosemena's part. Early in 1930 he had floated the idea of suspending the constitution, with American backing, in order to 'cure the sickness of this country' but it was Arosemena himself who was the seat of the infection. His sponsor Chiari had been given $250,000, the now elderly Porras a retainer of $40,000-plus. Of a proposed $1 million loan, $350,000 was earmarked for a grandiose palace of justice. In short, as U.S. military intelligence put it, Panama was being run 'very much as gang leaders have been running Chicago'.[1]

Standing outside the vicious ruling circle was the radical movement Acción Comunal, led by Harmodio Arias Madrid and Francisco Arias Paredes. In the light of repeated U.S. refusals to guarantee a straight presidential election, they drew the obvious conclusion that the only way to achieve power was to mount a coup. It ran like clockwork. During the night of 1–2 January 1931 Arosemena

---

[1] SD, 1910–49, 819.00/1512, Muse to Stimson, 18.2.30; /1543, White memo of 3.1.31; /1513, Muse to Stimson, 24.2.30; 819.51/662, Davis to Stimson, 23.8.30. MID, 2657-M-239, Memo of 12.1.31.

was seized in an assault on the *presidencia*, taken unawares very largely because greed had outstripped fear as the motive force of the régime. The pay of more than 130 police officers was being drawn by Arosemena's friends and relatives, and he had thereby crippled his first line of defence in a crisis.[2]

And though Arosemena hoped for deliverance from the United States, he was disappointed. In the small hours of 2 January he pleaded with Minister Roy Tasco Davis to bring U.S. troops to patrol the city, but after conferring with the garrison commander and the governor's deputy, Davis declined to act. U.S. neutrality meant Arosemena's survival, but the price was his resignation. In his place the Supreme Court nominated Panama's envoy in Washington, Ricardo Alfaro.[3]

American reactions to the coup were mixed. The news was greeted by President Herbert Hoover's cabinet with general merriment. 'There is, of course,' noted Secretary of State Henry Stimson, 'no real danger to American interests because of our treaty with Panama and the presence of our troops in the Canal Zone.' Davis, however, was well aware that the removal of Arosemena was a good deal more than a non-event. While reassuring Stimson that Acción Comunal was 'not in any way connected with the International Communist movement', he and the Army were both clear that 'irresponsible elements' had demonstrated 'what a comparatively few determined men can do in a few hours' – and presumably could do again. Moreover, the Zone as well as Arosemena had been caught on the hop through inadequate intelligence. Looking back on the decision not to intervene, Davis did his best to make a virtue of necessity. Up until the coup the United States had been open to the charge of condoning an undemocratic status quo. On 2 January, Washington had proved its statesmanship and shown to the world that the days of the big stick in Panama were over.[4]

The intervention issue was far from dead, however. By the summer of 1931 violent factionalism had developed within Acción Comunal. In August, Harmodio Arias's younger brother Arnulfo was wounded by a gunman in Colón, and when Francisco Arias lost the presidential nomination to Harmodio, he rushed to buy quantities of arms in the United States. For commanding general Preston Brown this immediately raised the possibility of a U.S. police action, though this would mean putting his troops into the narrow streets around the presidential palace, where their rifle fire 'would penetrate building after building'. But Brown was ordered to make no such commitment without clearance

[2] MID, 2657-M-239, Memo of 3.1.31. PC, 80-H-10, Burgess memo of 5.1.31. SD, 1910–49, 819.00 Revolutions/29, Davis to Stimson, 6.1.31; 819.105/6. Military attaché, Costa Rica, memo of 21.1.31.

[3] SD, 1910–49, 819.00 Revolutions/29, Davis to Stimson, 6.1.31; 819.001 Arias, H./1, Davis to Stimson, 2.1.31.

[4] Stimson Diary, entry for 2.1.31. SD, 1910–49, 819.00 Revolutions/29, Davis to Stimson, 6.1.31; 819.00/1546, Davis to Stimson, 31.1.31. MID-R, 3020, Report of 7.1.31. SD, 1910–49, 819.00/1552, Davis to Stimson, 23.3.31.

from the White House, and his subsequent bid for authority to send in small detachments to guard American lives and property was filed and forgotten.[5]

At the same time, Washington gave no encouragement to Alfaro's plan to organise an army of 250 men independent of the police. Davis appreciated the logic of the argument that if Washington had now forsworn intervention the Panamanian government would need some means of defending itself, yet he feared the political consequences of a military force. The State Department agreed, and it would only sanction 'a presidential guard or a corps d'élite of police for purposes of protection against subversive activities'. Alfaro thereupon dropped the idea, though with a presidential election scheduled for June 1932 the prospect of trouble was very real.[6]

In the event, election day passed off quietly, in spite of the fact that the all-powerful Electoral Board was still controlled by Chiari. But the Chiaristas did not tamper with the results, no doubt because embezzlement charges against Chiari and Arosemena were dropped, even though Alfaro admitted that they had probably defrauded the country of huge sums. Nor did Francisco Arias bring his recently acquired weaponry into play to reverse his defeat by Harmodio. Stimson sent congratulations on a good, clean fight, while his officials were quick to point out that for the first time in the history of presidential contests in Panama neither party had requested American intervention.[7]

The tranquillity was short-lived. By the summer of 1932 the Panamanian economy was suffering deeply from the depression. The slump inevitably heightened social tensions among the tenants of the city slums, and a rent strike started on 1 August. In tackling the situation, Alfaro had serious doubts not only about the reliability of the police but about the allegiance of the fire brigade, which had kept order during the strike of 1925. When the fire chief told the president that '95 per cent would turn out for a fire but . . . not 5 per cent for any other purpose', Alfaro turned to Davis. Told by Davis that American support was out of the question, he tried to buy arms from the Zone. Washington's refusal left him on his own: Non-intervention remained the order of the day.[8]

The Zone even continued to stand aside when riots broke out in the capital

[5] SD, 1910–49, 819.00/1579, Davis to Stimson, 26.8.31; /1580, Davis to Stimson, 24.8.31; 819.24/10, Davis to Stimson, 25.9.31. AG., post-1917, 000.24 Panama, Brown to Adjutant General, 26.9.31. WPD, 3556, War Plans Division memo on White Plan, Panama Canal Department, 24.11.31. MID, 2657-M-246, Memo by G-2, Panama Canal Department, 27.2.32.

[6] SD, 1910–49, 819.20/21, Davis to Stimson, 20.1.32; Stimson to Davis, 27.2.32; /23, Davis to Stimson, 7.3.32.

[7] SD, 1910–49, 819.00/1552, Davis to Stimson, 23.3.31; /1597, Wilson memo of conversation, 4.11.31; 819.77/396 and 397, Davis to Stimson, 2.6.31 and 6.5.32; 819.00/1647, cutting from Panama American, 11.6.32.

[8] NYT, 16.6.32, 19/1. SD, 1910–49, 819.00/1658, Davis to Stimson, 4.8.32. AG, post-1917, 000.51, Brown to Adjutant General, 5.8.32.

after the Assembly went back on a bill to implement rent reductions. Davis was studiously non-committal when asked if tear-gas could be supplied, and General Brown was appalled when feelers were thrown out for the Army to instruct the police in using it for crowd control. 'Any action which might connect the United States Army with the use of gas against a Latin American populace', he advised the War Department, 'could bring forth throughout Latin America a storm of protest.' The War Plans Division whole-heartedly agreed: There might well be 'unpleasant eventualities should the population of Panama be given the idea that the military stores of the Panama Canal Department are subject to call by the civil police in order to enforce discipline'. Once again Panama was left to work out its own salvation.[9]

With the advent of the Franklin Roosevelt administration in 1933, the practice of non-intervention was elevated into a high principle by the proclamation of the Good Neighbor policy. Already in 1930 the State Department had publicly revoked the Roosevelt Corollary whereby the United States had asserted a right to police the hemisphere on behalf of the international community. Under the Good Neighbor régime the process of retraction was taken a stage further. At the inter-American conference at Montevideo in December 1933 Secretary of State Cordell Hull signed a convention on the rights and duties of states which, among other things, avowed that 'no state has the right to intervene in the internal or external affairs of another'. This was soon followed by negotiations with Cuba for the abrogation of the Platt Amendment, which had given Washington a warrant to intervene in Cuba's domestic politics. When the U.S. Senate instantly approved cancellation of the amendment in May 1934, there was a widespread assumption that Roosevelt would go on to renounce the protectorate over Panama.[10]

The initiative in fact came from Panama. Its draft treaty planned to end the protectorate by annulling Article 1 of the 1903 convention – the guarantee of Panama's independence – and the last paragraph of Article 7, granting the United States emergency police powers in the terminal cities. Objections were raised mostly by the secretary of war, George Dern. The licence to intervene,

[9] MID, 2657-M-250, Report by military attaché, Costa Rica, 4.11.32. SD, 1910–49, 819.00/1681, Davis to Stimson, 28.10.32. AG, post-1917, 471.6, Brown to Adjutant General, 22.11.32; War Plans Division to MacArthur, 14.12.32.

[10] The text of Roosevelt's Good Neighbor speech of 12 April 1933 is in Samuel Rosenman (ed.), *Public papers and addresses of Franklin D. Roosevelt; 1933* (New York, 1938), 129–33. On the discarding of the Roosevelt Corollary, see L. Ethan Ellis, *Frank B. Kellogg and American foreign policy, 1925–1929* (New Brunswick, N.J., 1961), 101–4, and Robert Ferrell, *American diplomacy in the great depression: Hoover–Stimson foreign policy, 1929–1933* (New Haven, Conn., 1957), 220–3. The text of the Montevideo convention is in *FRUS 1933*, 4:215. On the rescission of the Platt Amendment, see Irwin Gellman, *Roosevelt and Batista: Good neighbor diplomacy in Cuba, 1933–1945* (Albuquerque, N.M., 1973), 103–9. *NYT*, 2.6.34, 1/7.

he told Hull, discouraged 'riots and disorders in opposition to the established Panamanian authorities' and acted as 'a positive insurance against the danger of introducing within the Canal Zone conditions such as those which existed along the Mexican border during the Carranza and Huerta Governments'.[11]

Dern's judge advocate general, however, was happy enough at the prospect that 'we shall be only bystanders', and in the Zone, Canal, Army, and legation were all agreed. 'With our present policy of friendliness toward Latin America,' chargé William Burdett told Hull, 'certain concessions are unavoidable,' and the intervention which had taken place 'was never vitally necessary'. The entitlement might as well be renounced 'inasmuch as any Panamanian disturbances would provoke armed repression if they injured the Canal Zone or its inhabitants'.[12]

During the treaty negotiations Under Secretary of State Sumner Welles was therefore ready to agree to Panama's demands, though at a price. This was a modified version of the 1926 treaty article giving Washington the right to put its troops into any part of Panama to protect the canal. The proposal was unacceptable to Panama as carte blanche for a U.S. military occupation, which might well be directed against a troublesome Panamanian government, not an external threat to the waterway. The offending formula was consequently dropped, but it was replaced by another which the Panamanians found almost equally hard to stomach, and at the same time Welles made sure to stifle two further bids to encroach on American prerogatives. As in 1924, Panama was denied exclusive authority to enforce public health regulations, and when its spokesman, Ricardo Alfaro, called for the deletion of Article 24 of the 1903 convention (which immunised U.S. treaty rights against changes in Panama's law and constitution), Welles cautioned him to leave well alone.[13]

Just as in the case of Cuba, then, the essentials of American hegemony remained intact, and, passing through the canal in October 1935, Roosevelt assured Governor Julian Schley that the new article on defence 'would clearly make it possible for this Government to take such action as it might consider necessary in the event of any imminent danger to the neutrality or security of the Canal'. This naturally included intervention in Panama City and Colón. When the War Department refused to accept Roosevelt's confident assumption and insisted on retaining the intervention clause, it was overridden. The clause was an anachronism, in the State Department's view, and its abrogation was 'calculated to remove a sore spot' which was 'apt to have unfavourable results'

---

[11] SD, 1910–49, 819.74/303A, Wilson comment on Panamanian draft of 22.9.34; 711.1928/313, Dern to Hull, 11.1.35.

[12] PC, 94-A-3/1936, Fiske memo of 16.1.35; Ridley to Flint, 29.12.34. SD, 1910–49, 711.19/205, Burdett to Hull, 8.12.34.

[13] SD, 1910–49, 711.1928/436½, Meeting of 21.11.34; 819.74/303A, Wilson memo of 26.9.34; 711.1928/4361/2, Meetings of 4.3.35, 9.3.35, and 27.5.35; 711.1928/273½, Memo of 4.10.34.

not only in Panama but throughout the Americas. Clothing the reality of American power in the language of good neighbourliness would reap handsome diplomatic rewards.[14]

An additional bonus from the formal abandonment of intervention was the lift it offered a Panamanian régime beset by horrendous economic difficulties. A telling gauge of Panama's desperation was the introduction of an income tax in February 1933. Originally exempting unearned income from land, rent, and investments, the tax bill was hastily redrafted under the threat of a general strike. The revenue was to go into a public works fund, but Arias needed more to stave off further trouble. In May 1933 he procured it by reducing interest payments on the 1928 loan by two-thirds. Without the default, he told Davis, 'he would not have a cent on hand to meet Government expenses', the most pressing of which was the cost of bringing the police back up to sufficient strength to prevent a repetition of the 1931 coup.[15]

Arias may well have been piling on the agony, but Washington did not want to make matters worse. Only token pressure was applied to dissuade Panama from channelling the loan interest into day-to-day expenditure and no support was given to the luckless American creditors, who had been left high and dry. And in the autumn of 1933 Roosevelt went out of his way to prop up Arias by making a number of concessions to boost Panama's commercial income from the Zone.[16]

American generosity had its limitations, however, and this was made clear over the issue of the canal annuity. The 1903 convention stipulated that the yearly payment be made 'in gold coin of the United States', but in January 1934 Roosevelt reduced the gold content of the U.S. dollar by 40 per cent, and this placed an immediate query over the annuity's true value. The position was further complicated by the fact that the entire sum was pledged to the two loans of 1923 and 1928, but in June 1933 an Act of Congress had declared that an obligation to require the repayment of loans in gold was 'against public policy'.[17]

Panama took the view that the U.S. government's treaty commitment to pay

[14] SD, 1910–49, 711.1928/444, Hull to Summerlin, 29.10.35. PC, 94-A-3/1936, Schley to Summerlin, 17.10.35. WPD, 1652–20, Miles memo of 25.11.35. SD, 1910–49, 711.1928/466½, Dern to Hull, 13.12.35; /456½, pp. 22, 23. On the defence article, see p. 286.
[15] SD, 1910–49, 819.5123/1, Davis to Stimson, 4.1.33; /3, Davis to Stimson, 14.2.33; 819.00 General Conditions/92, Davis to Hull, 23.3.33. MID, 2657-M-246, Brown to Adjutant General, 11.2.33. NYT, 5.2.33, sect. IV, 8/4. SD, 1910–49, 819.51/732, Davis to Hull, 12.5.33; /735, Davis to Hull, 12.5.33.
[16] SD, 1910–49, 819.51/729A, Hull to Davis, 6.5.33. On the origins of the treaty negotiations, see Chapter 10 at nn. 3–7.
[17] BD, 284. On the devaluation of gold, see Rosenman, Public papers of Roosevelt, 1934 (New York, 1938), 67–76. Text of the Act of 5 June 1933 is in United States statutes at large, 48/1 (Washington, D.C., 1934), 112–13.

the annuity in gold was not affected by the 'gold clause' statute. The annuity
was still due on the basis of the dollar's gold content at the time the canal
convention was ratified in 1904 and should be increased to take account of the
1934 devaluation. Panama's loan instalments, on the other hand, were governed
by the 1933 legislation and would be delivered not in gold but in legal tender.
In other words, Panama was aiming to benefit by 40 per cent each way, as
creditor and as debtor.[18]

While Washington accepted the need for a compensatory revaluation of the
annuity, it rejected the argument that Panama's debts to the holders of the loan
bonds were now abated. The U.S. Supreme Court, however, came to a decision
on the 1933 law which favoured Panama both ways. Debts owed by governments
to private institutions could be serviced in cash, but obligations by one government to another had to be met in gold. Soon after the judgment, Welles and
Alfaro were able to agree on an annuity of $430,000. This figure, it is worth
noting, was more than a million dollars less than the annual payment which the
Suez Canal Company was to make to Egypt in 1937 – some $1,448,000 at the
current exchange rate.[19]

The outcome was unsatisfactory for Panama in this and a number of other
ways. Foreign Minister Juan Demóstenes Arosemena had complained to the
legation in 1933 that the annuity was 'ridiculously small', but when Welles
offered $430,000, Alfaro did not ask for more. The Panamanians also suffered
from insisting on payment in gold: Washington would render it only by cheque,
and from February 1934 on, the cheques were returned uncashed. They were
further hamstrung by the fact that the annuity was a treaty issue and therefore
subject to whatever delay there might be over ratification. When the deal with
Welles was clinched, Alfaro tried in vain to have it divorced from the negotiations and handled quickly by administrative action. As a result, it was impossible to make progress towards a resolution of the 1928 loan problem. The best
Arias could offer the bondholders was to reduce their interest by 1 per cent.[20]

In other words, charity began at home, and Arias's priorities were sharply
reinforced by the onset of the 1936 presidential election. By the summer of
1935 the Treasury had built up a surplus of nearly $1.5 million, most of it from
the defalcation on the 1928 loan, and Arias began to spend it generously on
behalf of his chosen successor, Arosemena, and to take the public's mind off
his political troubles. In July he had overcome high-level disaffection within

[18] SD, 1910–49, 711.1928/206⅚, Wilson memo of 28.2.34; 206⅘ Hull memo of 21.2.34.

[19] SD, 1910–49, 711.1928/214½, Wilson to Welles, 25.1.34; /207, Legal Adviser opinion of
8.2.34. Lawyers' Cooperative Publishing Company, *Cases argued and decided in the United
States Supreme Court*, 79 (Rochester, N.Y., 1935), 885–907, 912–33, 1763, 1835, 1862–3.
SD, 1910–49, 711.1928/436½, Meetings of 29.4.35 and 2.3.36. Farnie, *Suez*, 607–8.

[20] SD, 1910–49, 711.1928/195, Chargé to Hull, 15.8.33. *NYT*, 2.3.34, 3/3. SD, 1910–49,
711.1928/436½, Meetings of 17.4.35 and 3.5.35; /365, Hull to Summerlin, 29.4.35; /367,
Summerlin to Hull, 1.5.35; 819.51/788, Alfaro to Foreign Bondholders' Protective Committee, 14.6.35.

the police, but he soon faced another challenge. Late in August a quantity of weapons was stolen from the U.S. Army barracks at Corozal. The instigator was said to be Francisco Arias; the objective, to secure the wherewithal for a rising on 1 September, the centre-piece of which was to be the assassination of Arosemena.[21]

The conspiracy was quickly nipped in the bud, and after the event Arias could feign nonchalance. 'Any government set up by the use of machine guns stolen from the American Army', he told a member of the legation over drinks at the Union Club, 'would never be recognized by the United States and without such recognition could not stand for twenty-four hours.' To make assurance double sure, however, he asked for the immediate transfer from the Zone of three machine guns, six automatic rifles, and 50,000 rounds of ammunition. Washington's response was in notable contrast to the flat refusal given to Alfaro's call for arms in 1932. The guns were handed over at once, though only 2,400 rounds went with them.[22]

The Army was reluctant to fortify Arias because of the feud then raging between it and Arias's close political adviser, the editor of the *Panama American*, Nelson Rounsevell. Rounsevell was one of the more bizarre notabilities on the isthmus. 'Married' five times, he had among other things fled New York State after a knifing incident in 1898, been expelled from Chile and Peru, and finally settled in Panama in 1925. In his editorial column on 12 July 1935 he penned an outrageous attack on the commanding officer of the Army base at Fort Clayton, 'the "Simon Legree" of the Panama Canal Department, whose cruel and relentless driving of his men by day and indifference to their Marijuana smoking by night has earned for his command the title "SUICIDE POST"'. The Army's reaction was to sue Rounsevell for criminal libel, and Governor Schley and Minister Summerlin were equally adamant that the case against him must be prosecuted 'with utmost force'. Rounsevell had fomented immense bad feeling against the Zone, and the legation saw his possible acquittal 'as a grave danger to our national defense and to our standing in Latin America'. This vastly overrated Rounsevell's importance, but it reflected the chagrin within the American community at a fellow citizen who had betrayed U.S. interests and defected to the other side. Come the trial, however, Rounsevell was denied the martyrdom he may have sought and given a suspended sentence.[23]

[21] SD, 1910–49, 819.00/1749, Legation to Hull, 31.8.35; 819.105/12, Legation to Hull, 15.7.35; 819.00/1740, Legation to Hull, 17.7.35; 811F.24/2, Summerlin to Hull, 31.8.35. ONI, C-10-M 15772, Reports of 7.9.35 and 14.9.35.
[22] SD, 1910–49, 811F. 24/21, Summerlin to Hull, 18.9.35; /25, Hull to Woodring, 20.9.35; /20, Summerlin to Hull, 23.9.35.
[23] SD, 1910–49, 811F.24/25, Memo of 18.9.35; 819.911/23. MID-R, 2810, Rounsevell biography. Nelson Rounsevell, *The life story of 'N.R.'; or 40 years of rambling, gambling and publishing* (Panamá, 1933). SD, 1910–49, 811F.22/4, Legation to Hull, 15.7.35. SWCF, Schley to Dern, 6.8.35. SD, 1910–49, 811F.22/16, Schley to Dern, 9.8.35; 811F.22/18, Summerlin to Hull, 20.8.35; /43, Summerlin to Hull, 5.10.35.

With the Rounsevell imbroglio behind him, Arias pulled out every available stop to get Arosemena elected. After Arosemena's win, Arnulfo Arias went on to form a National Civil Guard of hand-picked storm-troopers to discourage any thoughts of a putsch, but, once inaugurated, Arosemena dissolved it. Incensed at losing his political strike force, Arnulfo sailed for Europe as envoy to London and Paris, and Arosemena made his own security arrangements. In 1937 a presidential guard was raised to defend the chief executive's palace and other government buildings. Largely comprising mestizos from Chiriqui, this household brigade was considered by U.S. military intelligence more dependable than 'their cousins of negroid blood in the Capital City', but the mainstay of the régime remained the police. They were now housed in a headquarters made of reinforced concrete, proof against a replay of the seizure accomplished by the revolutionaries of 1931. Impregnable in its new redoubt, this strong right arm kept Panama in order for Arosemena throughout his administration.[24]

With all quiet on the political front, the chief focus of attention in the late 1930s was the economy, and above all settlement of the two American loans. A prominent feature of yet another refunding plan was the liquidation of the Constitutional Fund, whose keepership had just passed from William Nelson Cromwell to the Chase National Bank. The income from the Manhattan mortgages in which the fund was invested had sagged by nearly 30 per cent in the depression, and Panama aimed to sell them off to retire the 1923 loan. The maturation of the 1928 loan would be postponed, and its subscribers would see their interest drop by a quarter. To the State Department's economic adviser, Herbert Feis, however, the scheme seemed 'unskillful and ill-considered, impudent in effect if not in intent, and indefensibly disregardful of the contractual rights of Panama bond-holders'.[25]

State Department solicitude for the bondholders was something new, but it failed to make an impression on the U.S. Senate. In May 1938 Arosemena declared a moratorium on the 1923 loan and vowed there would be no more debt service until the arrears of the annuity were handed over. The move was an expression of Panama's understandable anger at the lack of progress towards treaty ratification in the Senate, and the bondholders too were losing patience. When the Senate Foreign Relations Committee reported favourably on the treaty in June, Welles implored Roosevelt to put his name to a resolution authorising payment of the arrears. Though Roosevelt immediately did so,

---

[24] SD, 1910–49, 819.00/1847, Summerlin to Hull, 6.7.36; 711.1928/573, Summerlin to Hull, 15.5.36; 819.00/1921, Chargé to Hull, 10.10.36. *NYT*, 1.12.36, 12/5. MID-R, 3917, 21.6.37; 2710, October 1937.

[25] SD, 1910–49, 819.51/885, Chargé to Hull, 23.10.37; /892, Panamanian note of 30.11.37, Feis comment of 15.12.37, and U.S. reply of 30.12.37. MID-R, 5000, G-2 memo of 22.5.41.

opposition in the Senate was still too strong, and the bid to break the impasse came to nothing.[26]

Frustrated over the treaty, Panama began to lash out at American economic influence in general, in a burst of the most assertive nationalism the country had yet experienced. Its driving force was Arnulfo Arias, recently returned from Europe. On his departure in 1936 Arias had affirmed his faith in right-wing statism, and his European sojourn had only reinforced his admiration for Hitler, Mussolini, and Franco. 'His', reported U.S. military intelligence, 'is definitely a totalitarian complex.' Arias quickly went ahead with a project for a new constitution which lengthened the president's term from four years to six and enhanced his powers at the expense of the Assembly. The draft also reflected a strong xenophobia in its provision that aliens living in Panama might be placed on a different legal footing from Panamanians themselves.[27]

Arias went on to develop the attack on foreign interests in a variety of ways. Cromwell, whose stewardship of the Constitutional Fund had been found un-impeachable in 1937, was now accused of irregularities to the tune of nearly $2 million. A provision in the income tax law of December 1938 was targeted at overseas businesses operating on the isthmus and was seen in Washington as a device to raise revenue from a source more open to a squeeze than the repub-lic's own tax-evading citizenry. The pièce de résistance, however, was a bill to require foreign banks, utilities, and oil companies to buy $6 million worth of 'guarantee bonds'. To the manager of the Panama City branch of Chase Na-tional, the proposition was nothing more nor less than 'a rationalised hold-up', and it was accompanied by a strident government letter to the banks ordering instant compliance. This the banks refused to give, and when they also declined to make a short-term loan of $2 million, the scheme was dropped.[28]

The failure of the forced loan was proof that Panama was bound to lose in any such confrontation with Washington, and in January 1939 Arosemena made the concessions on defence policy which led to Senate approval of the treaty the following July. This at once released the $2.58 million arrears of the annuity, and the State Department rightly predicted 'a merry legal scramble' for the money between the bondholders and Panama. Under a new refunding plan, the arrears were to be placed in escrow for the benefit of the bondholders. They

---

[26] SD, 1910–49, 819.51/930, Chargé to Hull, 24.5.38; /932, 24.5.38; 711.1928/725½, Welles to Roosevelt, 14.6.38; /688, Corrigan to Hull, 15.1.38.

[27] *NYT*, 1.12.36, 12/5. MID-R, 3610. SD, 1910–49, 819.011/55, Corrigan to Hull, 23.9.38; /56, Corrigan to Hull, 23.9.38.

[28] SD, 1910–49, 819.51/948, Chargé to Hull, 30.9.38; /989, Chargé to Hull, 15.12.38; 819.5123/ 19, Luthringer memo of 30.9.38; /23, Department of Commerce memo of 23.11.38; 819.51/ 950, Chargé to Hull, 10.10.38; 711.1928/883, Memo of 5.10.39; 819.51/955, Chargé to Hull, 24.10.38; /980, Chargé to Hull, 21.11.38; /983, Chargé to Hull, 2.12.38.

were not happy about this arrangement, especially the stipulation that an agency fee of $530,000 was to be deducted, plus a remittance of $860,000 to Panama. At the final treaty negotiating session the entire amount of the arrears had been committed to them, and they expected to receive the full $2.58 million.[29]

In the event, they were given a good deal less than their due. In September, Panama asked for $1.5 million to be paid to the Chase National Bank for transmittal to the bondholders, plus a further $220,000 for the bank to distribute among them, and for $860,000 to be paid direct to the Panamanian government. A week later Washington put the cheques in the mail, and when Chase National returned the $220,000 on the ground that it could not be made responsible for deciding on a share-out, it was handed over to Panama at Arosemena's request. In reply to a protest from the bondholders, the Panamanian chargé was flatly dismissive: They had been paid $1.5 million, 'and that was all his Government was committed to pay'. This, of course, was quite untrue, but Assistant Secretary of State Adolf Berle backed him up when he told the bondholders that the $180,000 augmenting the old annuity was 'an additional grant to Panama made in consideration for grants made to the United States in the Treaty of 1936'. The head of the Division of American Republics, Laurence Duggan, had wondered earlier whether the department was to follow the interests of the bondholders or the wishes of Panama. The answer was now clear.[30]

Why did Washington act as Panama's accomplice in cheating the bondholders out of their entitlement? The explanation lies in the use the Panamanians said they wanted to make of the $860,000. They intended to pledge it as collateral for a $2.5 million loan from the Export–Import Bank to finance their share of the cost of a sixty-mile road from Chorrera to Rio Hato, a prospective air-base south-west of the canal. Though the Army attached little importance to the road, Roosevelt encouraged its development to offset Panamanian irritation at the Senate's blocking of the treaty. Despite a warning in June 1939 from commanding general David Stone that Panama was 'more than usually desperate for ready cash' and would have to be watched carefully in its handling of the funds, the transaction went ahead, and the annuity arrears were disbursed the same day the Ex–Im credit was approved.[31]

President Arosemena did not live to enjoy the fruits of this gratifying outcome. He died on 16 December 1939 – though it was perhaps remarkable that he had

[29] SD, 1910–49, 819.51/1035½, Memo of 28.7.39; /1007, Memo of 16.3.39; /1027½, Memo of 2.6.39; /1036, Dawson to Hull, 8.8.39; /1048, Memo of conversation of 22.8.39.

[30] SD, 1910–49, 711.1928/860, Hull to Panamanian chargé, 19.9.39; /878, Chase National Bank to Hull, 22.9.39; /880, Welles to Morgenthau, 20.11.39; /882, White to Hull, 26.9.39; /878¼, Finley memo; /893, Berle to White, 27.10.39; /863½, Duggan memo of 7.9.39.

[31] SD, 1910–49, 819.51/932, Chargé to Hull, 24.5.38; 711.1928/709, Evans to State Department, 6.4.38; /866½, Barber memo of 14.9.39; 819.154/452, Chapin memo of 1.11.38; /453, Duggan to Welles, 7.11.38; /454, Chapin to Welles, 17.11.38; /462, Chapin memo of 14.6.39; 819.51/1050A, Hull to Dawson, 19.9.39.

survived so long. In March 1938 U.S. military intelligence had predicted the imminent demise of a man whose 'normal daily consumption of liquor is said to be at least a quart of Scotch. The President rides around in a new Buick car and he forces his driver to run at a reckless rate of speed on all his trips through the country – that he has not met with an accident so far is nothing short of a miracle.'[32]

Arosemena's death came as a thunderbolt to the Panamanian oligarchy, especially to Ambassador Augusto Boyd in Washington, who now became his successor, and to Arnulfo Arias, the favourite to win the 1940 election, en route to Panama to begin his campaign. The Arias entourage was highly disconcerted when Boyd was flown in by U.S. Army bomber, and demanded that Arnulfo be airlifted from his liner to reach the isthmus at the same time. Welles turned down the idea, and Boyd was in position before Arias landed at Cristóbal. The incident was an ironic finale to a decade marked throughout by American determination to stay out of Panamanian politics, and it showed how much the Panamanian élite still saw the United States as the arbiter of their power struggles. The protectorate established in 1903 was officially a thing of the past, but Washington's rôle in Panama's affairs remained as central as ever.[33]

Second World War, 1939–1945

The renunciation of the protectorate via the 1936 treaty by no means signalled the end of U.S. involvement in Panamanian affairs. For one thing, as Arnulfo Arias was to put it, the Canal Zone and Panama were 'Siamese twins', and the symbiosis made each of them hypersensitive to the other's reactions. For another, the outbreak of a second world war only heightened Washington's determination to inhibit hostile foreign influences throughout the hemisphere, particularly in an area of such vital strategic importance as the isthmus.[34]

Given its understandable concern for canal security, the Army was hotly interventionist. 'Action by the United States in Panama', wrote the commandant of the Army War College, 'must be based on hard practical facts, rather than any fatuous illusions of fraternalism. . . . While Panama, to date, appears to cooperate . . . for the protection of the Canal Zone, a small country with the temperamental instability characteristic of mixed races is not too dependable.'[35]

It was a view shared by the garrison commander in the Zone, General Daniel Van Voorhis, who in March 1940 drew up a blueprint for an emergency

[32] SD, 1910–49, 819.00/1974, Muccio to Hull, 18.12.39. ONI, C-10-M, 15772A, G-2 report of 16.3.38.
[33] SD, 1910–49, 819.001 Boyd, Augusto/3, Muccio to Hull, 17.12.39; /10, Welles to Harmodio Arias, 18.12.39.
[34] SD, 1910–49, 811F.504/356, Dawson to Hull, 18.10.40.
[35] MID-R, 'A strategic study of Panama', 2.8.40.

take-over of Panama, using as his justification Article 10 of the 1936 treaty. Under this top-secret 'Panama Plan' the Army was to assume all the draconian powers of a military occupation. It would police the streets, regulate traffic, supervise local businesses, 'seize and silence' communications, disarm all possible insurgents, and, if the government refused to collaborate, control personal movement and ban strikes and public meetings.[36]

A month before the election it looked as though the Army might get its chance. The leading contender, Arnulfo Arias, was conducting a brutal campaign against his opponent, Ricardo Alfaro, and the Canal's intelligence officer predicted that ships in transit might soon be trapped in factional crossfire. But the State Department was highly sceptical of the argument that the 1936 treaty justified intervention, and it had already rejected a plea from Alfaro to step in under Article 136 of the Panama constitution. Van Voorhis was instructed to make no move without reference to Washington, and Ambassador Dawson was told that troops would not be sent in even if Panama asked for them. Shortly before polling day Alfaro fled into the Zone for sanctuary, and Arias became president by the familiar walkover.[37]

One of Arias's most lasting achievements was the final settlement of the loans from the 1920s. In March 1940 Panama had accepted a plan to retire the 1923 bonds with a loan issue of nearly $4 million and the 1928 loan with another worth over $11 million. The take-up rate by the bondholders was disappointing, however, and in December Arias approached Washington as an alternative source of aid and comfort. Some weeks earlier, negotiations had started for the acquisition of sites in Panama for the long-range air defence of the canal, and Arias hoped that in return for the lease of the sites the United States would wipe Panama's slate clean. This would entail either a $20 million loan to cover the entire foreign debt or the advance of fifty canal annuities. When the State Department refused both options, the feelers were withdrawn. In March 1941 the refunding plan was adopted, though the underwriters were said to have 'a nervous fear that any particular issue may come out on the same day that the morning newspapers report the Germans have landed at Dover or the Japanese at Singapore'.[38]

---

[36] HPCD, 2: 241–5. AG, post-1917, Registered Documents 309-F, The Panama Plan. This version is dated 7 July 1947; the original was drafted on 30 March 1940.

[37] SD, 1910–49, 819.00/2015, Dawson to Hull, 2.5.40, enclosing report by McIntire; /1991, Dawson to Hull, 12.2.40, and Hull to Dawson, 20.2.40; /2021, Duggan memo of 9.5.40; /2020, Hull to Dawson, 13.5.40. WPD, 3509–3, War Plans Division to Adjutant General, 9.5.40. SD, 1910–49, 819.00/2031, Dawson to Hull, 25.5.40.

[38] SD, 1910–49, 819.51/1069, Memo of conversation, 28.10.39; /1099, Panamanian note of 14.3.40; /1155, Hull to Dawson, 30.11.40; /1165, Dawson to Hull, 9.12.40; /1161, Memo of conversation, 19.12.40; /1172, Dawson to Hull, 23.12.40; 711F.1914/179½, Finley memo of 13.1.41; 819.51/1227, Panamanian note of 13.3.41 and U.S. note of 15.3.41; /1225, Memo of 28.2.41.

Failing the $20 million credit, Arias had a good many other ideas for extracting compensation for the sites, quite apart from their rental. In January 1941 he presented a twelve-point shopping list with an estimated price tag of $25 million. Among other things, the water and sewerage systems of Panama City and Colón were to be made over to Panama, together with the site of the Panama Railroad terminus in Panama City. The full cost of the road to Rio Hato would be borne by the United States, and a bridge or tunnel would be constructed at the Pacific entrance to the canal. Finally, Panama would be given all the land owned by the Railroad in the terminal cities not needed for canal purposes.[39]

Under Secretary Sumner Welles's reaction to the demands was confused. After first saying that Panama had no right to ask for inducements, he accepted every item in question bar the bridge/tunnel, which Roosevelt disapproved. And after describing Arias's negotiating tactics to Roosevelt as 'blackmail of the cheapest variety', he put together an extra package of largesse for road construction costing over $9 million. Together with the commitment Roosevelt had taken on in 1940 to pay for Panama's share of a trans-isthmian highway, the whole deal was worth nearly $28 million.[40]

Its centre-piece was the transfer of the Panama Railroad land, whose book value was some $11.5 million and which was generating rent income of $300,000 a year. Here Welles ran into strenuous opposition from Governor Edgerton and Secretary of War Stimson. The lots included the New Cristóbal quarter of Colón, which the Canal had been trying to incorporate into the Zone for over twenty years, and Edgerton saw no good reason to surrender them. But Roosevelt ordered Stimson into line with a homily on the need to move with the times. The Railroad property represented 'one of the "unusual and outmoded relationships" inherited from the past'. Washington had no place as the landlord of Colón and should now 'get out of the real estate business in that city'. When Stimson agreed to the conveyance only if Panama granted jurisdiction over New Cristóbal, Welles would not hear of it.[41]

The financial appeasement of Arias did not make him any less of a pest for Washington, however. From the moment of his election the U.S. establishment had known he would prove an exceedingly awkward customer as president. He had the reputation, reported Dawson, of being 'strong-willed, courageous,

---

[39] SD, 1910–49, 711F.1914/237½, Panamanian note of 28.2.41.

[40] Ibid., /170, Dawson to Hull, 3.1.41. WPD, 2674–31, Van Voorhis to Marshall, 3.1.41. SD, 1910–49, 711F.1914/178, Welles memo of conversation, 31.1.41; /189, U.S. note of 7.5.41; /301½, Welles to Roosevelt, 19.6.41; /347, Minutes of meeting of 23.6.41; 819.154/581, Roosevelt memo of 15.8.40.

[41] SD, 1910–49, 711F.1914/234, Undated study of the Twelve Points; /211, Edgerton Memo of 26.2.41. WPD, 4452–41, Roosevelt to Stimson, 8.5.41. SD, 1910–49, 711F.1914/305, Stimson to Hull, 24.6.41, and Hull to Stimson, 30.6.41; /329, U.S. note of 8.7.41; /336, Memo of 17.7.41.

impulsive, unscrupulous, selfish, and vindictive'. In the view of the broker of
the loan settlement, George Train, he was 'a prima donna with an inverted
inferiority complex'; to the U.S. military attaché in neighbouring Costa Rica,
a 'problem child'. The creed underpinning his political programme was
Panameñismo, a drive against all manifestations of non-Hispanic influence, which
the new president promoted with fanatical zeal.[42]

Arias's most prominent target was, of course, the USA, and his anti-
Americanism came over loud and clear from the day he took office. The orig-
inal text of his inaugural address was so provocative that Ambassador Jorge
Boyd threatened resignation if it were delivered as it stood. The speech was toned
down after a telephone call from Welles, but Arias retaliated by seating General
Van Voorhis in the back row at the swearing in, and the Navy commandant,
Admiral Frank Sadler, was required to speak Spanish when he paid a courtesy
call on Foreign Minister Raúl de Roux. In January 1941 Boyd told Welles that
Arias had decided to go for broke. As Arias saw himself, he was 'not a statesman
nor diplomat, but a mere surgeon, and . . . as such he was going to perform the
operation of cutting the leg off the patient if he as a medical man thought it
best, without consulting the patient nor anyone else'. In June he spoke to
Ambassador Edwin Wilson of his resentment at South American jibes 'that
whenever the United States called the turn Panama jumped into line'. His
policy was consequently out to prove Panama's independence at all costs, and
he was sure he was beyond the *norteamericanos*' power: 'They chew me, but
they cannot swallow me.'[43]

Measures introduced in the first months of President Arias's term did stick
momentarily in Washington's throat. The new constitution of January 1941
placed American treaty rights in doubt. A bill allowing non-Panamanian businesses to operate only under licence was seen as 'a serious potential menace to
numerous and substantial American interests'. And Arias revived a personal
vendetta against the U.S.-owned Power and Light Company, which supplied
the terminal cities with gas and electricity and ran their telephone and streetcar
services. But the multiple assault gained little ground. Both the constitution
and the commerce bill were amended to meet American objections, though
Panama still asserted the right to tax residents who worked for private firms in

[42] SD, 1910–49, 819.00/2069, Dawson to Hull, 19.8.40. MID, 2657-M-342(59), Train
remarks of 1.11.40; (58), Military attaché, Costa Rica, report of 27.10.40. Felipe Escobar,
Arnulfo Arias, o el credo panameñista, 1930–1940: Ensayo psico-patológico de la política panameña
(Panamá, 1946).
[43] SLC, Meeting of 6.10.40. SD, 1910–49, 819.00/1–1845, Chargé to Stettinius. PC, 80-H-10,
Police memo of 7.11.40. FDR Library, President's Secretary's File, Box 64: Panama, Boyd
to Welles, 31.1.41. SD, 1910–49, 711.19./270, Wilson to Hull, 30.6.41. ONI, C-9-C, 21743A,
Report of 20.5.41.

the Canal Zone, and the Power and Light Company's tariffs were reduced by presidential decree.[44]

Much more disturbing from Washington's standpoint was the cumulative evidence of Arias's pro-Axis sympathies. Dawson believed Arias was an opportunist, and it did not necessarily follow that he 'would favour any extension of German influences in Panama or elsewhere in the Americas'. But in a script prepared for a radio broadcast to the United States the day after his inauguration he was scheduled to say that though Panama might be small and weak, it could, 'as a reprisal, affect the high interests of the Unites States by granting concessions upon its territory to other powerful nations which would have the material force for defending it'. The sentence was deleted, but it was published in the Spanish edition of his brother Harmodio's paper, the *Panama American*.[45]

The incident showed how close Arnulfo Arias would go to the edge, and it convinced Sumner Welles that a serious problem was in the making. That same week Welles told a high-level committee in Washington that Arias had appointed 'two Nazis' to his cabinet and that his private secretary – who reportedly kept an autographed photo of Hitler by his bed – was 'completely pro-Nazi'. In November the *Panama American*'s New Zealand–born editor, Ted Scott, was served a formal warning after taking the microphone in a beer garden where the Italian minister was dining to fanfare the latest British victory over the Italian fleet, and two months later he was deported. In May 1941 the governor was told that intercepted cables and letters showed that Panama was in regular touch with 'high officials of our prospective enemy nations'. 'What has developed in Panama', reported Ambassador Wilson, 'is about as near an approach to Hitlerism as the characteristics of Latin Americans and the peculiar circumstances affecting Panama could be expected to permit.'[46]

Arnulfo's new order made him some important enemies in Panama. His brother Harmodio and others in the oligarchy were alarmed that the new constitution would damage their business interests. Harmodio himself was presented with a demand early in 1941 either to sell the *Panama American* or to appoint an Arnulfista as editor. If the president went on like this, Welles considered, he might be faced with a revolution, and in April Ambassador Boyd

[44] SD, 1910–49, 819.011/72½, Legal Adviser memo of 28.10.40; 819.5123/26, Dawson to Hull, 4.12.40; 819.5034/15, Dawson to Hull, 14.2.41; 819.00/2106, quoting G-2 report on Arias of 7.10.40; /2096, Dawson to Hull, 18.12.40; 819.011/80A, Hull to Dawson, 20.11.40; 819.5034/26, Dawson to Hull, 22.3.41; 819.5123/35, Wilson to Hull, 11.9.41. ONI, C-10-L, 14602, Report of 29.10.41.

[45] SD, 1910–49, 819.00./2069, Dawson to Hull, 19.8.40. PC, 80-A-3, Memo of 5.10.40. SD, 1910–49, 819.911/49, Corrigan to Hull, 16.9.38.

[46] SLC, Meeting of 6.10.40. ONI, C-10-M, 15772A, Report of 6.1.41. SD, 1910–49, 819.911/62, Dawson to Hull, 5.12.40. ONI, C-10-M, 15772A, Report of 31.1.41. SD, 1910–49, 711F.1914/351, quoting McIntire report of 14.5.41; 711.19/270, Wilson to Hull, 30.6.41.

suggested to him that this would solve everyone's problems. Indeed, Harmodio's son, Roberto, had earlier told Dawson that he and his father were thinking of a coup, which 'could be accomplished for fifty or sixty thousand dollars'.[47]

Everything, of course, hinged on the U.S. reaction. Dawson was convinced that the opposition was 'only too disposed to look to us to pull their chestnuts out of the fire', but others were quite willing to lend a helping hand. The chief of the Canal's intelligence service, Captain McIntire, believed the Panamanian police would be ready 'to throw out the crooked pro-Axis officialdom' if promised American backing. The American editor of the *Star and Herald*, Albert McGeachy, went still further. 'The use of the big stick, even in disguised form, might produce salutary effects', that is, bring in 'a 100% Pro-American Government'.[48]

The feelings of the Zone were tested yet again in the summer via two long interviews given by Harmodio to the ambassador and the chief of military intelligence. By this time Arnulfo was in serious trouble. He had made the critical mistake of alienating the police, first by dismissing the commandant, Colonel Manuel Pino, and appointing an unpopular Guatemalan, Fernando Gomez Ayau. He had then antagonised the police even more by setting up an independent secret police. In September, when he refused to replace Gomez Ayau with his deputy Colonel Rogelio Fábrega, Pino and Fábrega concerted plans with the disaffected oligarchs for a weekend coup on the night of 11 October.[49]

The overthrow was rapidly brought forward after the president's unexpected departure for Cuba in the early hours of 7 October. The previous day he had refused Washington's call to arm merchant ships under Panamanian registry. Whether he did so as a final gesture of defiance before jumping overboard is impossible to tell. Ambassador Wilson was to note that Arnulfo suffered from 'periods of "blackouts" when he apparently does not know . . . or does not care what he is doing'. But if Arias thought he was unassailable, he could not have been more wrong. The minute he flew to join his mistress in Havana, the Zone police passed the word to the revolutionary junta, and within twenty-four hours they had nominated as Arias's successor the minister of government and justice, Ricardo Adolfo de la Guardia. At a conference with de la Guardia, McIntire

[47] SD, 1910–49, 819.011/76, Dawson to Hull, 29.10.40; 819.00/2134½, Wilson to Welles, 2.7.41. SLC, Meeting of 3.1.41. SD, 1910–49, 819.00/2123, Boyd to Welles, 15.4.41; /2–841.

[48] SD, 1910–49, 819.00/2093, Dawson to Hull, 14.12.40; 711F.1914/351. MID, 2657-M-242(66), Report of 4.6.41.

[49] SD, 1910–49, 819.00/2134½, Wilson to Welles, 2.7.41. MID-R, 3000, quoting Office of Naval Intelligence report of 8.9.41. MID, 2030–16, Report of 17.10.40. SD, 1910–49, 819.00/2143, quoting Military Intelligence Division report of 25.8.41; 819.105/35, Dawson to Hull, 11.3.41; 819.00/2201, Wilson to Hull, 14.11.41. Jules DuBois, *Danger over Panama* (Indianapolis, Ind., 1964), 138–9.

gave him the necessary assurance of U.S. support. 'While the United States authorities here would never, under any circumstances, use any influence . . . , I was sure that . . . the accession to authority . . . of a man of known pro-U.S. sentiments . . . such as himself, would be acceptable if not welcomed.'[50]

In the wake of the putsch, de la Guardia sped to merit the tribute. Gambling concessions worth a small fortune to the ex-president's entourage were cancelled and the Arnulfista youth movement disbanded. Ships under the Panamanian flag were armed and preparations made for the round-up of Axis citizens as enemy aliens on the outbreak of war. When Arnulfo tried to bargain his way back to office, he was unceremoniously sent into exile, and an attempted counter-coup by his erstwhile henchmen fizzled when the police withstood a bid to suborn them.[51]

Even then there were doubts in some quarters as to the loyalty of the new régime. McGeachy yearned for a leader 'who has pro-Americanism grafted in his soul', preferably Francisco Arias, 'a real Latin Gringo if ever there was one'. Military intelligence for its part urged 'a thorough fumigation' whereby U.S. values would be 'indoctrinated in the school children from the kindergarten to the university . . . so that never again will we ever face the danger of having to tolerate an anti-American Administration in Panama'. When de la Guardia failed to put through an instant purge of Arnulfo's men, McIntire seized the opportunity to try to expand his own modest department to guard against spies, saboteurs, and fifth columnists. But the $10,000 for counter-espionage was allocated to the Army, and McIntire went without, though his existing network of contacts helped keep Arnulfo's following quiet for the duration of the war.[52]

De la Guardia was, of course, just as interested as Washington in muzzling Arnulfo's partisans, and he was manifestly more cooperative than his intransi-gent predecessor. The immediate reward was a rental for the air-defence sites in the republic of some $288,000 a year and the simultaneous clinching of a deal on the Twelve Demands. In order to bypass the Senate, it took the form of an executive agreement, against the strident opposition of Senators Hiram Johnson and Gerald Nye. Some items, notably the commitment to the bridge/tunnel and the conveyance of the Panama City railway station, were deferred until after the war. In the State Department's view it was 'desirable to keep some-

[50] *NYT*, 19.10.41, 4/2. SD, 1910–49, 819.001 Arias, A./114, Wilson to Hull, 10.10.41; 819.00/2202, McIntire report of 11.10.41.

[51] MID-R, 3020, Galloway memo of 10.10.41. SD, 1910–49, 819.00/2182, Wilson to Hull, 23.10.41. ONI, C-10-M, 15772B, Report of 22.10.41. MID-R, 3020, Report of 21.10.41. WPD, 4319–5, Marshall to Welles, 27.10.41. ONI, C-10-M, 15772B, McIntire report of 21.10.41. SD, 1910–49, 819.00/2209, Wilson to Hull, 24.11.41.

[52] MID-R, 3000, Report of 28.10.41. SD, 1910–49, 819.00/2220, Military Intelligence Division report of 15.10.41. MID-D, 350.09, McIntire to Edgerton, 2.1.42; Wilson to Welles, 21.2.42; Lee memo of 27.2.42.

thing dangling before the noses of our Panamanian friends. There is no profit
to us in giving the present administration all of the gravy.'[53]

Washington thus did not plan to take its liberality too far, and there was stiff
War Department resistance to the idea that Panama be furnished Lend–Lease
aid on top of the bounty already served out. In November 1941 de la Guardia
asked for 200 Thompson submachine-guns, but though every other Latin
American state bar Argentina was receiving Lend–Lease supplies, the Army
drew the line at Panama. The police were already sufficiently well equipped,
and 'in the last analysis, United States troops will maintain order should conditions become critical'. Once give way to this demand, Colonel Matthew
Ridgway believed, and there would be no stanching the flood of importunity. 'If
we consider it necessary,' Ridgway told Welles, 'we send them modest amounts
of rifles or something like that.'[54]

In March 1942 de la Guardia tried once more. The legal objection to allocating
Panama Lend–Lease was that it had no army. The president therefore hinted
at conscription and sent in a request for enough arms to fit out a police force
which had now grown to 1,600 officers and men. The War Department recoiled
at the prospect of all this weaponry in the hands of an unfriendly Panama,
though the force of its argument was weakened by its low estimate of the martial prowess of the police, namely, that 'if a battle were to turn against them, the
majority would run'. Even so, the answer was still no.[55]

Washington was equally deaf to de la Guardia's call for a $1.5 million Lend–
Lease credit to fund public works. Irrepressible, Panama renewed its plea for
the machine-guns, and chargé John Muccio believed something could be done
to comply: a few machine-guns, perhaps, plus a brace of patrol boats and a
handful of jeeps. While realising that his superiors might consider the Panamanian
wants list 'very very childlike to say the least,' wrote Muccio, 'you must have
known school children who preferred a red lollipop to a crisp dollar bill'. Hull
therefore offered fifty machine-guns and fifteen jeeps, but strictly for cash.
Since Panama had expected to get its matériel 'on British terms' – that is, free
– nothing more was heard.[56]

Muccio's proposal was no doubt partly designed to mollify de la Guardia
after the slights he had recently suffered at the hands of the U.S. Army. His car

[53] For documentation on the defence-sites agreements of 18 May 1942, see *BD*, 926–43. OpD,
381 Panama, Eisenhower to Stimson, 16.5.42. SD, 1910–49, 711F.1914/616, Johnson–Nye
views of 30.11.42; /6–2344, Bonsal to Duggan.
[54] SD, 1910–49, 819.24/73, Wilson to Hull, 14.11.41. WPD, 4298–1, Memo of 25.11.41. SD,
1910–49, 819.24/73, O. Wilson memo of 5.12.41 SLC, Meeting of 13.12.41.
[55] MID-R, 5900, Memo of 6.4.42. SD, 1910–49, 819.24/123, Panamanian note of 17.4.42;
819.20/55, Combat estimate of 10.6.42.
[56] SD, 1910–49, 819.51/1303, Jaén Guardia to Hull, 11.6.42; /1316, Bunn memo of 1.7.42;
819.24/741, Muccio to Hull, 18.10.43 and 18.11.43; /770, Muccio to McGregor, 10.12.43;
/772, Hull to Panamanian chargé, 14.3.44; /245, Hawkins memo of 21.12.42.

had twice been stopped by Army sentries, who showed scant respect for the very important occupant. Each time, the incident drew a vehement protest note from Foreign Minister Octavio Fábrega, and the garrison commander, General George Brett, saw the second note as a personal attack on himself. Like Blatchford in 1918, he had launched a big crackdown on venereal disease, and prostitution, he alleged, was a business from which 'several of the highest ranking officials in the Panamanian Government derive the major part of their income'. Whatever the truth of the accusation, it did not save him from a mild reprimand from Chief of Staff George Marshall, and Roosevelt himself had to make de la Guardia a fulsome apology.[57]

Against their common enemy, however, the Zone and the de la Guardia régime worked in close harmony. In January 1943 McIntire helped foil an Arnulfista plot to kidnap police commandant Rogelio Fábrega and, more important, his deputy José Antonio Remón, the real mainstay of de la Guardia's power. A cowed National Assembly thereupon voted the president two more years in office. For their part in the cause, both Fábrega and Remón were decorated with the Legion of Merit, Remón by Eleanor Roosevelt during her visit to the isthmus in March 1944. 'Through his broad vision, resourcefulness, tact, spirit of cooperation, and unswerving devotion to the ideals of democracy,' ran Remón's citation, 'he rendered services of inestimable value.'[58]

Shortly after the First Lady pinned the medal on Remón's tunic, Colonel Jules DuBois of Zone military intelligence reported that Fábrega and Remón were likely to stand by de la Guardia in a forthcoming political crisis, since they were both doing so well from graft. In January 1945 the National Assembly was due to decide who should complete the final stretch of Arnulfo's six-year term. DuBois forecast that the president would dissolve the meeting in advance to pre-empt Harmodio Arias, allegedly poised to buy a majority of deputies, electing a complaisant proxy before taking over the presidency himself in 1946.[59]

De la Guardia behaved exactly as predicted, suspending the constitution on 29 December. But he could not count on the unconditional support which DuBois hoped Washington would extend, and Harmodio's mobilisation of the student movement plus a general strike helped push him into retreat. He agreed to stay on until a constituent assembly met in June, and after elections to the

[57] MID-G, Report on incidents of 3.7.43 and 22.11.43. ONI, C-9-C, 21743A, Report of 29.12.43. MID-R, 5940, Brett memo of 31.12.43. OpD, 336 Panama, Marshall to Brett, 4.1.44. FDR Library, President's Secretary's File, Box 64: Panama, Roosevelt to de la Guardia, 31.12.43.

[58] SD, 1910-49, 819.00/2309A, quoting Office of Naval Intelligence report of 14.11.42; /2311, Wilson to Hull, 6.1.43; /2322, quoting Office of Naval Intelligence report of 5.1.43; 819.105/50, Wilson to Hull, 21.6.43. ONI, C-9-C, 21743A, Report of 25.3.44.

[59] MID-R, 3020, DuBois memos of 25.3.44 and 7.3.44.

Assembly went against him, stepped down in favour of Enrique Jiménez, named as provisional president until September 1948.[60]

This was strictly an interim settlement of the struggle to shape Panama's destiny as it emerged from the Second World War. It served only to postpone the collision between the two main rivals for power: Arnulfo Arias, who returned from four years of exile in October 1945, and José Remón, who had by then become the decisive force in Panamanian affairs. Between them, these two were to dominate the politics of the post-war decade.

Cold war, 1945–1955

The years after the Second World War saw Panama's politics stoke up the vehemence that had begun to mark them since the coup of 1931. A crudely fraudulent election was followed by a crisis in which the police made and unmade governments at will, a would-be revolution from above ending in a welter of violence, and the assassination of the president – all this against the background of the Cold War with Soviet Russia in which the United States was transfixed by the spectre of communist penetration of the hemisphere.

Washington's main concern in the immediate aftermath of the war was the return from Argentinian exile of its bête noire, Arnulfo Arias, whose excited supporters were reported to be salivating at the prospect of a come-back, with 'a taste for "blood" and the desire to replenish their pocketbooks'. To combat the Arnulfista challenge, one FBI man was in place as 'technical adviser' to the Panamanian secret police and another as 'legal attaché' in the U.S. Embassy with the mission of countering the activities of 'foreign agents and subversive elements'. In late 1945 Arias unquestionably headed that list, and in December he was thrown in gaol on a charge of inciting armed revolt. Eight months later, however, he was out on bail and by early 1947 had re-established himself as the dominant figure on the political scene, to the point of becoming the favourite to win the presidential election of 1948.[61]

The run-up to the election brought the first post-war test of U.S. reflexes when President Jiménez asked the Army for six armoured cars. They were not provided. In 1945 the State Department had balked at General Brett's call to organise and equip the Panamanian police as a paramilitary force. As the election loomed, it was not disposed to change that view, especially with warnings

---

[60] SD, 1910–49, 819.00/12–2944, Warren to Stettinius, 29.12.44; /12–3044; 819.01/12–3044. ONI, C-10-M, 15772C, Report of 9.2.45. *NYT*, 30.12.44, 4/8, and 31.12.44, 17/1. SD, 1910–49, 819.00/5–1045, Chargé to Stettinius; /6–1545.

[61] ONI, C-10-G, 19629, Report of 25.10.45. OSS, XL 32910, Military attaché report of 13.12.45. MID-G, Report of 3.8.45 and Shipp memo of 8.8.45. SAPF, Patterson to Byrnes, 2.2.46. SD, 1910–49, 819.00/10–2945. *NYT*, 23.12.45, 6/2; 3.5.46, 5/1; 11.8.46, 14/1. SD, 1910–49, 819.00/2 2047, Hines to Marshall.

from the embassy that Remón – now police commandant – was 'drinking heavily and appears anxious to provoke incidents with the Arnulfistas'. So it looked the other way while Jiménez threw the election to Arias's opponent, Domingo Díaz. Washington was well aware that Díaz had, as Ambassador Hines put it, been 'successfully railroaded . . . into office', but it gave no backing to the National Assembly when it voted to annul the election and unseat Jiménez. And to prove its neutrality it declined to respond when Jiménez and Anastasio Somoza of Nicaragua asked its blessing on a joint invasion of Costa Rica, where Arnulfo had fled for sanctuary. Díaz was duly inaugurated on 1 October and survived an Arnulfista bomb to embark on his presidential term.[62]

Díaz did not live long to enjoy the fruits of office. He died in August 1949, to be succeeded by the first vice-president, Daniel Chanis. Chanis, however, was soon in extremis after he was unwise enough to offend one of the most powerful combines within the ruling class. The Díaz and Jiménez families through their control of the National Cooperative dominated the market in beef cattle, which they imported from Somoza. The beasts were given priority for slaughter at the Panama City abattoir, which formed part of Remón's business empire, and this cosy arrangement badly damaged the interests of domestic cattle breeders such as Harmodio Arias. When on 19 November Chanis dismissed Remón for refusing to apply a Supreme Court decision holding the slaughterhouse contract unconstitutional, Remón forced him out and installed his cousin Roberto Chiari in the *presidencia*.[63]

Forty-eight hours later the game took an unpredictable turn when Chanis withdrew his resignation and Harmodio mobilised the students against Remón. To bring the merry-go-round to a stop with the most surreal gyration of all, Remón replaced Chiari with Arnulfo Arias, the man he had helped disqualify in 1948. This black joke was played with the police in a disturbingly irrational mood. If Arnulfo dared fire their commanders, Hines reported, they were poised to move on his house, 'arrest all its inmates and, if the chiefs were really resigning, throw them in the carcel [gaol] too, shoot up the town and declare a military dictatorship'. The threat was unnecessary, and Arnulfo had the satisfaction of seeing the Electoral Jury reverse its 1948 verdict and pronounce him president by right.[64]

[62] OpD, 336 Panama, Brett to Adjutant General, 26.9.45. SD, 1910–49, 810.20 Defense/10–3145, Furniss to Dreier and Wise, 17.10.45; Wise to Cochran, 31.10.45; 819.24/4–2048, Hall to Marshall; 819.00/4–2748, Marshall to Hall, 29.4.48; /4–648; /5–748; /6–148; /6–2648; /7–448; /7–1348; /8–748; /8–1448; /8–1948; /10–2548; 12–3048. NYT, 26.10.48, 13/1. SD, 1910–49, 719.00/2–1551.
[63] NYT, 24.8.49, 25/1; 20.11.49, 1/6; 21.11.49, 1/6. SD, 1910–49, 819.00/10–2949; /11–2249; /11–2349; /11–2849, Wise memo.
[64] NYT, 23.11.49, 1/4; 24.11.49, 1/7; 25.11.49, 1/5. SD, 1910–49, 819.00/11–249; /11–2849, Sowash memo; /11–2649.

The dénouement came as unwelcome news to Washington. To the State Department, Chanis was still the legal president, and the last person it wanted to see in power was Arnulfo. But there was no realistic chance that Remón would allow Chanis to return, and Hines strove to convince himself that Arias was a changed man who had put behind him 'the intense nationalism and totalitarian concepts which he flaunted so boldly in his earlier term'. On 14 December Arnulfo's régime was given diplomatic recognition, and he set out on his second presidency a little over eight years after he had so bizarrely terminated his first.[65]

High on Arias's agenda was the state of the nation's finances. The war had left Panama solvent as never before, and in June 1945 Jiménez inherited a budget surplus of over $5 million. He then put in for a loan from the Export–Import Bank of no less than $30 million, and his optimism was undimmed even when it was explained that the bank had resources of only $30 million in toto. The Díaz administration was equally sanguine when it revived the loan project late in 1948, though a World Bank mission found the presentation of its case more than a little hazy, with no 'clear cut, well thought out, amply documented programs' to back up its claims.[66]

In July 1949 Panama came up with the required precision. Instead of the bridge or tunnel promised in 1942, it asked Washington to fund a concrete road from Rio Hato to the Costa Rica border, as part of the Inter-American Highway. This was far beyond what Sumner Welles had agreed to, and the State Department soon discovered that Panama had something even more creative in mind. The department, Ambassador Octavio Vallarino suggested, could get the Ex–Im Bank to arrange a $30 million loan and then after a decent interval ask Congress to cancel repayment 'as a friendly act to Panama'. 'Even . . . old hands at Panamanian "gimme" tactics', wrote Tapley Bennett, 'found themselves blanching at this proposal', and the idea was hastily dropped.[67]

There was an alternative up Panama's sleeve, however. Successive governments had tried to get their hands on the $6 million Constitutional Fund, and the liquidation of the fund was part of a new plan to refund the foreign debt put forward by Alfonso Manero of Glore, Forgan, promoters of the last debt consolidation in 1941. When Arias dispensed with Manero's services, he alleged that the fund was likely to be repatriated into the pockets of the president and his cronies via 'shady side-line transactions'. Whatever the truth of that, the fund stayed put in New York for the time being, though Washington sanctioned

[65] *NYT*, 23.11.49. 1/4; 26.11.49, 4/6; 27.11.49, 1/4; 15.12.49, 1/2. SD, 1910–49, 819.01/ 12–849 and 12–1349.

[66] SD, 1910–49, 819.51/9–944; /7–2045; /1–2846; /7–946; /8–3046; /9–2546; /12–748; /4–1449.

[67] SD, 1910–49, 711.19/7–2549, Hall to Acheson; 819.154/7–149, Wise memo; /7–2849, Bennett memo.

the use of the canal annuity as collateral for a $10.5 million loan to redeem the bonds outstanding from the 1941 credit.[68]

U.S. approval chimed well with Ambassador Monnett Davis's repeated call for a 'constructive program' to combat both Panamanian nationalism and infiltration by 'Communist-influenced subversive elements'. It included American aid for road development and increased technical assistance for agriculture in line with President Truman's Point Four plan, launched in 1949. At the same time, Davis wanted to see Washington make good its commitments to build a bridge or tunnel at the Pacific end of the canal and to hand over the railway terminus in Panama City.[69]

Panama was mainly interested in getting the United States to pay for the expansion of its highway network, avowedly to link town and country, in reality to generate jobs and therefore government patronage. Assistant Secretary of State Thomas Mann gave Davis small encouragement, however, while the Army saw Panama's prize objective, the Inter-American Highway, as no more than a marginal convenience. Davis feared the consequences of U.S. indifference, 'bearing in mind that it is Arnulfo Arias with whom we have to deal', and Bennett too was apprehensive. Since 1945, he told Mann, Washington had been involved in 'the difficult and thankless task of bringing Panama down stage by stage from the policy of unlimited generosity which they enjoyed during the Roosevelt administration. The present stage of the cure cannot go much farther without a real deterioration of the patient.'[70]

The response came in the form of a $600,000 grant towards the cost of the Inter-American Highway, provided Panama appropriated matching funds of $375,000. Though less than the Panamanians had hoped for, it was supplemented by an agreement to include Panama in Point Four. The accord built on the precedent of the U.S. aid mission operated by the Institute of Inter-American Affairs since 1942, and the scheme begun in 1950 was also run partly by the IIAA, with the Agricultural Institute at Divisa under an American director, specifically at Panama's request.[71]

The first Point Four report echoed what Owens had said back in 1919 – that the farms needed an efficient road system branching out from the axis of the Inter-American Highway. As it was, Panama suffered from excessive dependence on the canal. Direct receipts from the Zone had accounted for no less than

[68] SD, 1910–49, 819.51/Bondholders/5–2449. SD, 1950–4, 819.10/8–2250, Memo of conversation with Manero; /9–1550, Sowash to Siracusa; /9–2050.

[69] SD, 1910–49, 711.19/2–349, Davis to Acheson.

[70] SD, 1950–4, 611.19/5–550; 819.2612/1–3050 and 11–1750; 611.19/7–1150; 611.1913/10–1450.

[71] SD, 1950–4, 819.2612/3–2151 and 3–2251; 819.00TA/12–3050. Almon Wright, *The United States and Panama, 1933–1949* (U.S. Department of State, Bureau of Public Affairs, Research Project no. 499, August 1952), 172–4, 283–7. SD, 1950–4, 819.20A/8–1150 and 12–1250.

40 per cent of the national income in 1944, and although agriculture employed half the republic's work force, it contributed only 6 per cent of national income. Panama should therefore diversify by stepping up food production. Belief in the canal as the fount of all welfare had so far prevented diversification, but now there were signs of change. Panama's application for Point Four assistance stemmed from a decree issued in May 1950 which looked to the development of the interior as a government priority. Whether this was anything more than words and how much effort Washington was ready to put into making it a reality remained to be seen.[72]

As Davis had emphasised, an American aid programme would have a political as well as an economic objective, namely, the demolition of communism in Panama. Here he could count on the enthusiastic cooperation of the Arias regime. In April 1950 Arias's cabinet signed a resolution outlawing the Communist People's party and used it as the basis of a decree-law denying government jobs to 'persons dedicated to propaganda, activities, or agitations of a Communist character'. The edict was aimed principally at schoolteachers and academics at the National University, including Republican refugees from the Spanish Civil War, and it was hailed by Davis as 'a brilliant political stroke'. Shortly afterwards it led to the resignation of the education minister, Maximiliano Arosemena, who refused to dismiss a number of leading suspects, including Vicente Bayard, director of the teacher training college at Santiago. But in September the Supreme Court ruled that the cabinet resolution had no legal force, and the following April the Court declared part of the decree unconstitutional. For the moment the witch-hunt came to a halt.[73]

The chief threat to Panamanian democracy in 1951 was not communism, however, but President Arias. Arias had several times been reported to be planning a coup, and on 7 May he struck. The 1946 constitution was abrogated to make way for the return of the 1941 constitution Arnulfo himself had introduced. The National Assembly was dissolved and a 'de facto' presidential government set up, with all appointments in Arias's own hands. At the same time, over 120 political enemies were arrested, including Arnulfo's nephew, Roberto Arias, and ex-president de la Guardia, who had recently been gaoled for *lèse majesté* and beaten up by the secret police.[74]

But Arias had miscalculated disastrously, and within three days his bid was in ruins. In Ambassador John Wiley's view the administration was nothing more than 'a group of opportunists shot through with nepotism, ruthless

[72] SD, 1950–4, 819.20A/2–751. Biesanz, 'Economy of Panama', 5, 8, 17, 6. SD, 1950–4, 819.00/5–1250, decree of 10.5.50.

[73] SD, 1950–4, 719.00/4–3050; 710.001/5–1050, 5–2550, and 1–952; 719.13/7–2750 and 8–1850; 719.00/9–750 and 4–1351.

[74] SD, 1950–4, 719.13/8–150; 719.00/8–2250, 11–1550, 4–351, and 5–751. *NYT*, 11.3.51, 13/3.

self-interest and machiavellian slyness who are determined to milk the country as thoroughly and as long as possible', and all Arias's pleas for U.S. backing were summarily denied. Bereft of American support, Arnulfo found himself besieged inside the *presidencia*, faced with a general strike, and then impeached by the National Assembly, which administered the presidential oath to Alcibíades Arosemena.[75]

His last hope was the police, and Remón stood by Arnulfo until almost the last moment. But the commandant was finally persuaded to move against him, and when the police stormed the presidential palace in the afternoon of 10 May, Arias surrendered. As he left the building he shot dead the commander of the palace guard. Two weeks later the Assembly dismissed him as president and banned him from public office for life.[76]

In the wake of Arnulfo's collapse, Wiley was highly nervous about Panama's future. A radical such as the Colombian Jorge Eliécer Gaitán might emerge, and then 'perhaps the vested interests will not retain their vested interests'. And though the State Department had rightly discounted Arias's claim that his putsch was mounted to save the republic from communism, Wiley fancied there was a communist fringe around the Arosemena government which made it alarmingly similar to the reformist administration of Jacobo Arbenz in Guatemala, by then increasingly suspected of taking a pro-communist line. In December 1951 Wiley concluded that Washington had only one choice – to work for the election of Remón, who had recently declared himself a candidate for president and who in Wiley's opinion was 'the sole anti-Communist leader in the entire political panorama'.[77]

To put the election result beyond doubt, Wiley proposed a credit of $500,000 for public works. And – even though he had recently said the Panamanians must learn that 'the Canal Zone is not operating primarily . . . as a first aid station for the political and economic ills of their nation' – he urged the Canal Company to dip into its coffers to help bring in a 'firm' government. On this he ran into solid resistance from Assistant Secretary of the Army Karl Bendetsen, who was currently imposing a series of drastic economies on the Zone and who told Wiley there was no chance of paying out the subsidies he had in mind.[78]

The State Department, on the other hand, was remarkably receptive to Wiley's thinking. It had already authorised a $1.5 million Export–Import loan for the new Hotel El Panamá, as well as an extra $560,000 for the Inter-American Highway, and it was now ready to disburse even more. When Wiley suggested a $2 million grant for various development projects, to be

[75] SD, 1950–4, 719.00/5–851, Siracusa to Mann and Wiley to Acheson; /5–851; /5–951; /5–1051, Wiley to Acheson.
[76] SD, 1950–4, 719.00/10–2351, 5–1551, and 5–2651.
[77] SD, 1950–4, 819.00/8–2451; 719.00/7–2051; 719.001/12–2651.
[78] SD, 1950–4, 719.001/12–2651; 819.00/8–2451; 719.00/1–1152.

administered via Point Four, the idea was enthusiastically pursued, though Point Four's director, Jonathan Bingham, objected to his programme being used as a political convenience. While the payment could not be processed before the election, it was to be held in reserve 'as leverage for obtaining in return certain tangible concessions'.[79]

In May 1952 Remón was safely elected, but Wiley doubted whether he would survive 'the Politburo's efforts to achieve a global extension of its political system'. 'Colonel Remón', he told Washington, 'is to the Communists what General Razmara was to them in Iran. The General was eliminated.' Razmara had in fact been assassinated by an Islamic fundamentalist, but to Wiley the world was threatened exclusively by 'the great Communist conspiracy'. Its isthmian stronghold was higher education, where 'the Communists have worked like Cascarets – while we have slept'. A senior member of the embassy staff, Murray Wise, told Wiley that the rector of the National University, Octavio Méndez Pereira, might be 'a big and important cog in the Communist mechanism', and Wiley believed that seeds were being sown in the university 'that will flourish and fester for long years to come'.[80]

Meantime Wiley impatiently anticipated the moment of Remón's inauguration in October. In an expansive mood after dinner one evening Remón informed Wiley that he proposed tackling the university head-on. Pending that day, Wiley did what he could, making sure that the former education minister, Max Arosemena, was dropped as consultant to the Point Four mission. When its director, Ernest Jeppsen, supported Arosemena, Wiley attacked him as 'completely unsuited for any employment in a responsible position in a Latin American country'. Wiley was also furious with Jeppsen when he questioned a Panamanian government order to remove the 200 male students at the co-educational teacher training college at Santiago from its supposed communist ambiance. It was only after the exodus that Wiley discovered the real reason behind it. The secretary to the archbishop of Panama had wanted the sexes at Santiago put asunder to end a flush of pregnancies. Given the inadmissibility of birth control, separation was the only answer and the tale of rescuing the trainees from communist brainwashing merely a cover story.[81]

Besides his anti-Marxist onslaught on the educational front, Remón planned an offensive against the communist movement in general. Though he had a decade of experience behind him as the republic's chief warder, he ingratiated himself with Wiley by requesting 'technical guidance' on control measures and shortly after his installation notified the embassy that he aimed to outlaw the People's party. To Wiley this was objectionable because it would not deal with

[79] SD, 1950–4, 819.10/7–2751; 819.2612/9–351 and 10–2451; 719.001/12–2651, Acheson to Wiley, 11.1.52; /1–2452; 719.5MSP/3–1052; 819.00TA/3–1352 and 3–2852.
[80] SD, 1950–4, 719.001/8–2852; 719.00/5–1952; 819.00TA/6–1352; 719.00/1–1452.
[81] SD, 1950–4, 719.11/7–2852, 611.19/7–1452; 819.43/7–852, 6–3052, and 9–1552.

the 'crypto Commies and conspiratorial elements'; better to follow the American model whereby the party remained legal but conspiracy against the state was made a criminal offence. Asked by Mann for advice on what kind of statute would most effectively drive the communists out of political life, Wiley replied that in Panama the law was frequently what those in power chose it to be. 'Such an attitude, while not commendable, would make a complex law perhaps simple in function.'[82]

Satisfactory though Remón was as a political ally, however, he was less than adequate as an economic reformer. Under Arias, as we saw, Panama had begun to recognise the need for diversification. With things as they were, over 60 per cent of the nation's foodstuffs had to be imported at a cost of $11 million a year out of an annual budget of $40 million, and Remón's election seemed to offer Panama the chance to reorder its economic priorities.[83]

The turnaround could be achieved, in Wiley's view, only if the United States took charge of the operation through 'a policy of paternalism', which should not be 'eleemosynary, but hard-headed, practical and dynamic'. Just how paternalistic Wiley was prepared to be became clear when he opposed a gambling concession at the El Panamá hotel as a likely opening for the Mafia. To the State Department this was interventionism gone mad, as absurd as rebuking Portugal for running the casino at Estoril. Bossing Panama's development was similarly ruled out of court. 'Panama . . . belongs to the Panamanians and not to us,' Wiley was reminded. 'It is impossible for us to pick other countries up by their boot straps. . . . The realm of the possible . . . cannot be greater than the potentiality of Panama.' In exchange for dropping the demand for the bridge/tunnel project and in return for 'specific action to show a determination to curb communist expansion', Panama should get $15 million spread over five years: $6 million for the Inter-American Highway and $9 million for agriculture. The Panamanians themselves would implement the schemes.[84]

Shortly before taking over in October, Remón accepted a recent World Bank report as the basis of his economic planning. Heading the bank's demands were debt reduction, precedence for agriculture, and higher taxes on income and property to make up for the expected shortfall in tariff revenue. As matters stood, very few Panamanians paid income tax, and the 5 per cent levied on incomes of more than $12,000 a year brought in very little, thanks to widespread tax evasion.[85]

---

[82] SD, 1950–4, 719.001/7–1452; 719.00/11–352; 719.3/1–853, Mann to Wiley, 24.12.52, and Wiley to Mann, 8.1.53.

[83] SD, 1950–4, 611.19/2–1353.

[84] SD, 1950–4, 819.00TA/5–1452; 819.45/7–2852 and 8–252; 819.00TA/5–1452, Miller to Wiley, 26.5.52 /5–1252, Siracusa to Miller.

[85] SD, 1950–4, 819.10/9–2352; 819.00/10–2952; 819.10/10–1651 and 6–2052. Biesanz, 'Economy of Panama', 24–5.

Yet the impetus for reform slackened from the moment of Remón's first cabinet meeting, when a new National Assembly building was approved at a cost of $750,000 – a commitment wholly at variance with the World Bank's insistence on expenditure cutbacks, as was the Assembly's endorsement of a $1.5 million bond issue to fund the completion of the national racecourse. As for the promotion of agriculture, the Agrarian Bank had just come badly out of an inquiry into maladministration, and Remón sought full control of the Agricultural Institute on the ground that 'we have to take care of our friends'. Moreover, as Wiley noted, Point Four's rural development projects were 'frequently regarded as a thing apart by the poorer city inhabitants and something which does not benefit them as individuals'. And the auditing firm which was reorganising the tax system rapidly withdrew when the government failed to shield it from political pressures.[86]

The road programme likewise showed that Panama was still indulging in bad financial habits. In July 1952 Wiley told Washington that progress on the Inter-American Highway was 'woefully slow'. Only 80 of its 335 miles had been completed – all by U.S. civil engineers – and work was going ahead on a mere 20 miles more. Some of the reasons why were made plain in the World Bank's response to a road-loan application. The Panamanian case was found to be 'completely unrealistic and unacceptable in that with one exception, the proposed routes had not been inspected, let alone surveyed; the cost estimates were arbitrary and unrelated to the specific requirements of each road location; and there was neither an adequate highway, or road organization nor satisfactory maintenance and other equipment'.[87]

Wiley's reaction is difficult to fathom. Early in November 1952 he had said that aid would neither encourage Panama to put through the necessary reforms nor buy its goodwill. Yet within weeks he was urging funds for the Inter-American Highway 'irrespective of the Panamanian attitude toward the United States and American interests'. Though this raised eyebrows in the department, Wiley's next proposal was adopted by the new Secretary of State, John Foster Dulles, who took office under the Eisenhower administration in January 1953. It was for an agricultural development grant of $5 million a year for ten years, to be channelled through Point Four. This, Wiley believed, would be 'bread upon the water' and the indication of a readjustment between Washington and Panama comparable to 1936 or 1942, the years of Roosevelt's treaty and the settlement of the Twelve Demands.[88]

Remón too was convinced that the advent of the Eisenhower régime presented

[86] SD, 1950–4, 819.10/10–1652 and 12–753; 819.20/7–152; 819.00TA/11–1252; 719.00/ 9–1652; 611.19/11–2552.
[87] SD, 1950–4, 819.2612/7–1752; 819.10/9–1554.
[88] SD, 1950–4, 911F.5301/11–652; 819.2612/11–2452; 611.19/11–3052 and 2–1353; 819.20/ 2–1353; 819.00TA/2–2853.

a golden opportunity to put things on a new footing. But his objectives were very different from Wiley's. In January 1953, it is true, an Economic Development Institute was founded to remodel Panamanian farming. Yet Remón continued to look to the canal for economic salvation, as a painless alternative to fundamental reform.[89]

In doing so, he displayed the parasitism which had been such a marked characteristic of the ruling oligarchy in its dealings with Washington. But he was also careful to pay homage to the urge for independence which constituted the other face of the Panamanian response to American dominance – this by liquidating the Constitutional Fund through sale of the New York City properties acquired by Cromwell in the republic's name. The fund's repatriation was more than a short-term capital gain for Remón and his lieutenants. It symbolised Panama's claim to alter the arrangements made over its head by Hay and Bunau-Varilla, and it foreshadowed the demand for full-scale revision of the old canal convention in the treaty negotiations which opened in September 1953. Even after that treaty went into force at the end of the post-war decade, relations between Washington and Panama were still essentially those of master and servant. It was to take another generation to put them on a radically different footing, with the American abandonment of the Zone and the promised assignment to Panama of the canal Americans had thought was theirs forever.[90]

[89] SD, 1950–4, 819.00/2–353; 611.19/11–2552.
[90] SD, 1950–4, 819.10/1–1353; 611.19/11–2052.

12

Canal defence

From depression to war, 1930-1939

As the world moved towards war in the 1930s, the United States withdrew even more decidedly into isolation. At the same time, it was compelled to look to its national security and the protection of vital interests, such as Panama. Defence issues thus took up the foreground of U.S. canal policy, in the treaty signed in 1936 and in a series of measures to make the waterway fitter to survive in a menacing world environment.

Improvements were slow to take shape, notably in air defence. The Army Air Corps unit in the Zone, the 19th Wing, had a capability which, in the understated view of an Air Corps historian, was 'at best questionable'. In 1931 the garrison commander informed Washington that the new base at Albrook Field was unusable by bombers in the six-month rainy season because loaded machines would bog down on its unconcreted runways. The Navy's air station was equally below par. 'It is a matter for concern', wrote the chief of naval operations to the district commandant in 1934, 'that although there are thirty-six patrol planes based at Coco Solo whose major weapon is the bomb, there are no bombs for those planes in the Canal Zone.'[1]

Anti-aircraft guns and their crews were likewise hard to come by. In 1930 the chief of coast artillery noted that at the rate Congress was doling out appropriations it would take at least twenty years to complete the current programme. In 1934 Army war planners reported that the four batteries approved in 1929 were only now being manufactured under a grant from the New Deal's Public Works Administration. During a 1930 exercise a simulated bombing raid on Fort

---

[1] Williams, *Air defense of the Panama Canal*, 5. HPCD, 1: 69–70. WPD, 3531, Sampson to Simonds, 16.5.31. SNSCC, 1927–39, NB/NDI5, Standley to Crosley, 10.8.34.

Amador by only twelve planes was unopposed by anti-aircraft fire because there were not enough troops to man the existing emplacements, even though the entire garrison was concentrated on the Pacific side. 'Had both entrances to the Canal been involved,' judged the chief umpire, 'the defending forces would have constituted merely a forlorn hope.'[2]

At the same time, it was clear that the Zone was much too narrow as a defensive cordon against air attack. As early as 1925 one coast artillery officer had demanded the widening of the Zone for military purposes to embrace the whole of Panama, and in the early thirties successive Army spokesmen called for installations in the republic as the forward line of the canal's inner screen. In 1933 Panama agreed to lease private land for emergency airstrips, and in 1935 the Army began renting a large tract at Rio Hato, some sixty miles south-west of the Zone. Consideration was also given to the idea of advanced air-bases on the Costa Rican Cocos Island and the Ecuadoran Galápagos.[3]

As yet, however, no action was taken. In answer to a query from the White House as to why no modern planes were based on the isthmus, the reply came that it was standard practice to send down obsolescent types because aircraft fabric soon rotted in tropical conditions. This made the Zone's air component, as one senior officer put it, 'antiquated and of practically no value . . . against modern up-to-date weapons, either ground or air'. The latest models were reserved for the General Headquarters Air Force, held in the continental United States ready to be flown out to the Zone in a crisis. To Colonel Sherman Miles, the policy of rapid reinforcement was dangerously mistaken. The Zone's air squadrons should be modernised, even at the expense of the GHQ spearhead, and the anti-aircraft command brought up to strength, since it was currently impossible 'to maintain the equipment in serviceable shape, to say nothing of manning it in action'. But again nothing was done.[4]

Washington snapped out of its torpor when it came to a more immediate security problem: sabotage. The threat had been highlighted in 1925 with the publication of a disquieting piece of futurology – the tale of a Pacific war between the United States and Japan, prefaced by a Japanese merchantman blocking the canal by blowing itself up in the Gaillard Cut. Eight years later, after the Japanese conquest of Manchuria, fiction seemed poised to become

[2] AG, post-1917, 354.21 (7–10–30), Chief of Coast Artillery to Adjutant General, 16.7.30. WPD, 1992, War Plans Division to MacArthur, 17.1.34. AG, post-1917, 354.21 (7–10–30), Urwin report of 8.3.30.

[3] WPD, 2501–34, Dyer memo of 25.6.25; 2674–30, Van Voorhis to Marshall, 12.11.40. SD, 1910–49, 819.7962/40, Panama note of 27.4.33. U.S. Army, CDC, Historical Section, *Acquisition of Land*, 106–9. WPD, 3782, Memo of 4.10.34; 3782–1, MacArthur to Sheppard, 27.6.35. SNSCC, 1919–26, 218–2, Gleaves to Daniels, 20.9.19; Daniels to Lansing, 30.12.19; Lansing to Daniels, 17.1.20.

[4] SWCF, Woodring to Dern, 17.6.36. Williams, *Air defense*, 5. WPD, 3803, Miles report of 25.2.35.

reality. The editor of the *Panama American*, Nelson Rounsevell, denounced the small Japanese colony on the isthmus as a nest of subversion, a phobia shared by Army Intelligence. In the words of one G-2 officer, 'the spectacle of 8,000 men gazing out to sea for an enemy who is operating behind their backs, destroying the very thing they are sent to protect, would not be too pleasant'.[5]

Fears of a Japanese coup de main climbed to a new pitch early in 1934 as the fleet prepared to transit from Pacific to Atlantic. In February a former yeoman of signals told Navy Intelligence he had been approached to help disable the canal after the last warship had cleared the Atlantic terminal. His story was taken seriously, with a White House directive ordering an instant review of anti-sabotage precautions. The survey revealed that there was no provision for ship inspection or for transit guards. The Army had posted no sentries on the locks since 1918, and at night each pair of chambers was left in the care of 'a couple of indifferent, sleepy watchmen'. As for intelligence gathering, the existing security organisation was 'perhaps less than that, say, for a tobacco warehouse in North Carolina'.[6]

By any standard, this was an alarming situation, yet no agreed response emerged. The Army and Navy identified Panamanian hostility as a major obstacle to American counter-espionage measures, but when the State Department asked them to cultivate friendlier relations with Panama, the idea met with a cool reception. When the services proposed a liaison man in the legation with special responsibility for the surveillance of aliens, the reply was that 'such activity . . . would be highly improper'. Searches of ships, as Governor Schley saw it, could be carried out 'only in cases of evident suspicion', since they were bound to trigger explosive diplomatic repercussions. The only certain way to avoid a disaster, in the opinion of all concerned, was to cancel the transit and hold the exercise in the Pacific.[7]

In the event, the movement went ahead, with the fleet given a monopoly of the canal for forty-eight hours; all mercantile traffic was held up until it had completed the transfer. Schley took this decision with extreme reluctance, and he was deeply embarrassed when British shippers objected at the delay to their cargoes. Both he and the State Department were sensitive to the charge of discrimination, but when the department suggested parity of treatment for

[5] Hector Bywater, *The Great Pacific War: A history of the American–Japanese campaign of 1931–33* (London, 1925), 21–5. SD, 1910–49, 894.20219/21, Davis to Hull, 26.4.33. MID, 1766-T-22(6), Memo of 30.8.33.

[6] MID, 1766-R-2(17), Smith to MacArthur, 14.2.34. OA, NHC, SPD, ser. III, Measures for protection of Panama Canal 1934, Memo of 26.3.34. SD, 1910–49, 811F.812 Protection/5. MID, 1766-R-22(21), Military attaché, Costa Rica, memo of 23.2.34. SD, 1910–49, 811F.812 Protection/11, Gonzalez to Hull, 15.4.34.

[7] SD, 1910–49, 811F.812 Protection/8, Green memo of 31.3.34; /9, Schley to Flint, 22.3.34. MID, 1766-R-22(55), War Plans Division memo of 31.3.34.

foreign battle-fleets, the Navy was adamant that it must continue to have privileged access.[8]

The scare over the 1934 transit made the defence establishment even more nervous about Japan, and during the next twelve months it fought to prevent Panama from granting fishing rights to Japanese concessionaires in the Pacific approaches to the canal. Here again it ran into opposition from the diplomats, but when in March 1935 a new Panamanian law allowed unrestricted Japanese immigration, they suddenly became more sympathetic. It now seemed possible that a substantial Japanese community could settle in Panama, as it had in Hawaii, all too close to a second major defence base. So Panama was warned off, while Roosevelt had a bill introduced in Congress to control Japanese fishing in the territorial waters of Hawaii, the three West Coast states, and the Canal Zone, and to stymie the operations of trawlers whose real business was to 'follow the Fleet and not the fish'.[9]

Significant as these local developments were in forcing on a higher state of readiness, however, they were dwarfed by Japan's denunciation of the naval disarmament treaties in December 1934. This meant that from the close of 1936 Tokyo would not consider itself bound by limitations on warship tonnage or by the freeze on base fortification in the Western Pacific. To the War Department the move diminished at a stroke the security of the 'strategic triangle' of the Canal Zone, Hawaii, and Alaska. The garrisons at all three points, Secretary of War George Dern told Roosevelt, must be brought up to strength at once.[10]

The build-up did not take place, but other concrete advances began to register. In March 1935 the Canal was urged to take on 'a high grade, experienced, enthusiastic – almost fanatical – sleuth', and he was duly appointed in the person of Captain Leo McIntire. In June 1936 Sumner Welles endorsed a scheme for collecting information on Japanese citizens throughout Central America. By this time too an interdepartmental board had begun to devise detailed plans for counteracting sabotage by ships in the locks. Gradually the canal authorities were gearing themselves to cope with an emergency.[11]

[8] SWCF, Schley to Dern, 26.10.34; Flint to Dern, 24.4.34, enclosing Schley to steamship agent, n.d. JB, 326–1, s.562, Acting Secretary of State to Joint Board, 20.7.35; Joint Planning Committee memo of 30.7.35.

[9] SD, 1910–49, 819.628/15, Swanson and Dern to Hull, 24.12.34; Wilson to Welles, 26.12.34; Hull to Swanson, 31.12.34. JB, 326–1, s.545, Joint Board to Dern, 13.2.35; Welles to Dern, 26.3.35. SD, 1910–49, 819.628/23, Dern and Swanson to Hull, 13.4.35. SWCF, Woodring to Flint, 14.5.35.

[10] WPD, 3804, Dern to Roosevelt, 27.12.34.

[11] MID, 1766-R-22(124), Military attaché, Costa Rica, memo of 28.3.35. SD, 1910–49, 811F.812 Protection/23, Summerlin to Hull, 1.8.35; 894.20219/89, Military Intelligence Division to Wilson, 17.3.36, and Welles circular of 4.6.36. OA, NHC, SPD, ser. III, Measures for protection of Panama Canal 1936, Minutes of meeting of 29.4.36.

For the Navy this did not mean the development of elaborate local facilities. Though in 1931 Secretary Charles Adams revived the Rodman board's plea for a destroyer and submarine base at Balboa, nothing came of it. When Roosevelt in July 1934 put up a proposal for a huge fleet berth at the Pacific terminal, the admirals showed only polite interest, and after some three years the project was forgotten. The canal hierarchy, meanwhile, continued to display scant concern for the Navy's existing requirements. In 1936 the commander of the Special Service Squadron complained that the squadron was looked on merely as 'a nuisance to be tolerated' and left to make shift. In 1937 the district commandant accused the Zone administration of being so preoccupied with the canal's commercial performance as to let the Navy go by the board. Housing, in particular, was so inadequate that no more men should be drafted to the Zone until things were made good.[12]

In one critical respect, however, the Canal did promote the Navy's interests: It demanded the waterway's modernisation. In December 1931 both the findings of the Army's Nicaragua survey and the governor's review of the various options for Panama were published. The Nicaragua alternative was effectively ruled out in advance after an earthquake destroyed Managua, and the project for a sea-level canal at Panama was also a non-starter. There was no economic way of excavating rock down to the necessary depth, and an air strike was thought well capable of blocking a seaway by sinking ships in transit. An improved lock canal, on the other hand, equipped with an extra water supply and a third set of wider locks, would deal with all foreseeable traffic demands, and the locks would be an important strategic bonus. Sited well away from the existing flights, they would reduce the chance of a knock-out blow by aerial bombing, and they could put through the Navy's biggest vessels in comfort. As it was, the carriers *Lexington* and *Saratoga* each had less than four feet of clearance, and their passage through the chambers was a slow and nerve-racking process with constant danger of serious damage to the ships and to the locks themselves.[13]

Even so, the need for the third locks was not seen as urgent, though the damming of Lake Alhajuela was approved and construction of the dam begun in 1932. The pressure for new lockage became irresistible, however, after the breakdown of naval arms limitation, which raised the prospect of capital ships

[12] OA, NHC, SPD, ser. III, Naval Districts, Panama, Naval aide to president to Standley, 13.7.34; Bryant memo of 9.8.34; Swanson to Dern, 27.6.35. SWCF, Dern for Flint, 17.12.34; Dern to Swanson, 3.5.35. SNSCC, 1927–39, NB/ND15, Adams to Hurley, 12.8.31; AO-1/FF8, Supplementary annual report of Special Service Squadron, 8.7.36; NB/ND15, Marshall to Leahy, 28.1.37 and 4.2.37.

[13] *NYT*, 12.12.31, 39/1; 2.4.31, 2/7. PC, 9-A-11, Burgess to Hurley, 19.8.30; Schley to Burgess; 9.1.31, Burgess to Hurley, 4.8.31; Moore memo of 21.5.31; Mehaffey to Gross, 18.7.31. WPD, 3182, Burgess to Hurley, 4.8.31.

much too big for the old locks to handle. Early in 1936 Congress agreed to fund a detailed study of improvements to the canal, with the third locks foremost among them. Together with the evolving anti-sabotage programme, it represented the genesis of a response to an international crisis which, if it deepened still further, was likely to pull the canal into its vortex.[14]

It was ironic, therefore, that just as the tempo of preparedness quickened, Washington signed a treaty which in the judgement of the armed forces materially reduced their power to defend the canal. One of the most controversial features was the article on land acquisition. In September 1934 Panama proposed an immediate end to land transfers. The Panamanians now contended that Article 2 of the 1903 convention referred only to land needed for the actual building of the canal, and President Harmodio Arias claimed that the joint statement he and Roosevelt had issued in October 1933 supported the Panamanian case in saying the canal had been constructed. Abrogation of the 1903 entitlement was vital to get the treaty through the National Assembly, Arias later maintained: 'With the menace of Article II hanging over Panama, the people would feel that they were being sold out.'[15]

Roosevelt's advisers could not have disagreed more. The chief American negotiator, Sumner Welles, told his counterpart, Ricardo Alfaro, that the United States could not possibly surrender the right to take land over, and a rejoinder to Arias put out in Roosevelt's name asserted that land was bound to be required from time to time as the canal's facilities expanded to meet future demand. In conference with Welles, Governor Schley stressed the point forcefully, besides noting that 'the increase in importance of aviation made it evident that distant tracts might be needed for defense'.[16]

The offers made through Welles consequently included the proviso that Panama must continue to transfer whatever land the U.S. government considered essential. When Alfaro rejected them, Roosevelt changed tack. Land for enlargement of the canal's capacity could be obtained by negotiation 'in the event of some now unforeseen contingency' such as 'a geological disturbance which might cause Lake Gatun to dry up'. Negotiation would be justified by Article 1 of the new treaty, which established Washington and Panama as partners in a 'joint trusteeship' of the waterway.[17]

This was a concession a good deal more apparent than real. As both Roosevelt

[14] PC, 9-A-11, Memo of 25.8.34. SD, 1910–49, 811F.812/1062, Dern to Hull, 6.2.36.
[15] SD, 1910–49 711.1928/436½, Minutes of meeting of 23.4.34; 819.74/303A, Wilson memo of 26.9.34; 711.1928/436½, Minutes of meeting of 14.3.35; /285B, Statement of 19.10.34; / 331, Chargé to Hull, 11.2.35.
[16] SD, 1910–49, 711.1928/436½, Minutes of meeting of 23.4.34; /285B, Statement of 19.10.34. PC, 94-A-3/1936, Schley memo of conversation with Welles, 14.11.34.
[17] SD, 1910–49, 711.1928/436½, Minutes of meetings of 9.4.35 and 24.4.35 ONI, C-9-C, 21743A, Memo of 10.12.36. DuBois, *Danger over Panama*, 182–3.

and Alfaro knew, the damming of Lake Alhajuela would give the canal an adequate water supply for the next seventy or eighty years, and no more land would be required for that purpose. Moreover, the concept of joint trusteeship did not extend to protection: It was, Welles told the Panamanians, only 'vis-à-vis the commerce of the world', and acquisition of land for defence must remain an absolute American prerogative. Yet when Alfaro declared that a Panamanian régime which was unwilling to allow its territory to be used for canal defence would be guilty of treaty violation, Welles gave way, with Roosevelt's full support. The power of requisition was renounced completely, and henceforth all additional land taken from the republic was to be acquired by agreement.[18]

As part of the settlement of the land issue, Panama dropped its objections to another controversial defence article. In November 1934 Welles had insisted, as the price for ending the U.S. protectorate, on Panamanian acceptance of an amended version of Article 11 of the 1926 accord. This now stipulated that Panama would consider itself 'in a state of war in case any power at war with the United States attacks or threatens the Panama Canal'. It also gave the U.S. Army the right to manoeuvre its troops in Panama in peacetime, and it incorporated the American view that Article 23 of the 1903 convention allowed Washington to deploy its forces at any time throughout Panama and not just in the Zone, as Panama contended.[19]

This was unacceptable to Panama. President Arias had opposed the 1926 treaty partly because it placed Panama so completely at the disposal of the U.S. military, and he was certain that the revival of the 1926 commitment would again destroy any chance of ratification. Instead there should be U.S.–Panamanian agreement on the defence measures to be taken if the isthmus were threatened by 'international conflagration' or outright aggression.[20]

Welles, however, would not recognise Panama as an associate in canal defence: An arrangement such as the Panamanians had in mind 'might by the delay involved prove fatal to the safety of the Canal'. The most he was prepared to concede was that Panama would be consulted if a crisis blew up, but Alfaro was instructed to insist on Panamanian agreement to whatever action were taken. Alfaro himself bent over backwards to be accommodating, accepting that 'consultation' might not be possible during a night attack and that 'agreement' could come after the event rather than before. The deadlock was broken only by the deal over the land issue, and Panama was granted mere consultancy status on defence matters.[21]

---

[18] SD, 1910–49, 711.1928/436½, Minutes of meetings of 6.3.35, 26.4.35, 3.5.35, 10.5.35, 17.5.35, and 22.5.35. Text of the relevant article is in *BD*, 872–3.

[19] SD, 1910–49, 711.192/382½, U.S. draft of new treaty, 1.1.30; 711.1928/436½, Minutes of meetings of 21.11.34 and 4.3.35. PC, 94-A-3/1936, Schley memo of 26.12.34.

[20] SD, 1910–49, 711.1928/331, Chargé to Hull, 11.2.35; /436½, Minutes of meetings of 4.3.35 and 9.3.35.

[21] SD, 1910–49, 711.1928/436½, Minutes of meetings of 9.3.35, 25.3.35, 27.3.35, 16.3.35, 15.4.35, 11.1.35. Text of Article 10 on defence measures is in *BD*, 880.

The two articles on land acquisition and canal defence were negotiated without reference to the armed forces. It was not until November 1935 – six months after they were clinched – that the new agreements were revealed to the service departments. Their reaction was predictably seismic. 'If the United States intends sometime in the future to turn the Canal in its entirety over [to Panama],' Navy commandant Albert Marshall advised the chief of naval operations, the draft formed 'a prefect preliminary phase for such eventuality.' 'American blood', General Lytle Brown believed, 'will be unnecessarily shed in recouping what we relinquish with the scratch of a pen.' Land transfers, Brown insisted, 'should not be at the whim of a political group in Panama nor should such acquirement be subject to protracted and dilatory negotiation'. The provision on land, in Marshall's view, would work only *provided the Panamanian government will invariably agree to U.S. desires*. Likewise, the obligation to consult Panama in a crisis could stand only 'with the knowledge that when an emergency arises it will be willfully violated by the U.S. authorities'. In December, Dern and Navy Secretary Claude Swanson gathered all these arguments and more together in a lengthy critique of the treaty presented to Roosevelt at a stormy White House conference.[22]

Their salvo was accompanied by an onslaught on Roosevelt's draft of a supplementary convention outlining the future of radio on the isthmus. This brought to a head a conflict which had been rumbling on for the past five years between a U.S. Navy determined to retain the monopoly on wireless conferred on it by Panama in 1914 and a Panamanian government equally fixed on having its own independent broadcasting network. The sympathies of the State Department were almost entirely with Panama. When in December 1930 Panama abrogated the 1914 decree, the department saw no good reason why the Navy should not give up absolute control. Countering the Navy's claim that commercial stations in Panama would set up intolerable interference, it cited the situation in New York City, where communications at the Brooklyn Navy Yard functioned despite the surrounding presence of 245 stations operating on 326 frequencies. And though the Army ultimately sided with the Navy, it too was on record as a supporter of liberalisation, if only to hit back at the admirals 'so bitterly engaged in endeavoring to destroy Army overseas radio facilities'.[23]

None of this was more than a preliminary skirmish, however, compared with the full-scale battle which soon opened up for control of wireless transmissions to and from ships in transit through the canal. In June 1933 an application to handle ship–shore traffic was submitted by the Tropical Radio Telegraph

[22] PC, 94-A-3/1936, Marshall to Standley, 17.12.35 (emphasis in original); Brown to Schley, 16.12.35. WPD, 1652–23, Brown to Adjutant General, 10.12.35. SD, 1910–49, 711.1928/466½, Dern and Swanson to Roosevelt, 13.12.35.

[23] SD, 1910–49, 819.74/183, Davis to Stimson, 1.1.31; /189, Dawson to Thurston, 14.2.31. AG, post-1917, 311.23, Stimson to Adams, 26.3.32; MacArthur to War Plans Division, 25.11.31.

Company, a subsidiary of United Fruit licensed to operate in Chiriqui province. When the Navy put up its usual objections, the Harmodio Arias régime lost patience. If Navy Department policy were applied to aviation, Arias told the U.S. minister, all planes in Panama's air-space would have to be flown by Navy pilots. The radio issue consequently featured high on Arias's agenda during his visit to Washington in October for talks with Roosevelt.[24]

Immediately after the summit, Roosevelt urged the Navy to agree that radio, like civil aviation, would be controlled by a joint U.S.–Panama board and to allow private companies a share of the traffic with ships. The Navy's spokesman on radio, Captain Stanford Hooper, who had been ordered by the chief of naval operations, Admiral Standley, 'not to yield an inch in our stand', was appalled. The State Department, which did not 'care a rap about our own defense', was the source of all the trouble. The General Board, however, advised compliance, and Secretary Swanson accepted the White House directive with the understanding that Washington would reserve the right to close commercial stations down if they interfered with Navy transmissions.[25]

When Panama insisted on being given full control of radio in peacetime, Welles had a struggle to persuade the defence establishment to make more than the most token concessions. The Navy, he was told, was eaten up by a cancerous feud between itself and United Fruit, a supposition borne out by the district commandant's charge that Panama was merely the company's mouthpiece. To accept the Panamanian proposals would be 'an acknowledgement that the United Fruit Company [had] defeated three Departments of the United States Government'. General Charles Kilbourne, for his part, wondered out loud 'how much Japan was interested in Panama's chiseling', in other words, whether the Panamanians were in Tokyo's pay. Hooper, meantime, was adamant that Navy jurisdiction over radio was part and parcel of the U.S. guarantee of Panama's independence and that if Panama did not come into line Washington should withhold the canal annuity! In the end, however, a compromise was reached which offered Panama the semblance of control but left Washington the final arbiter. In July 1934 Roosevelt also conceded that private stations must be barred from ship–shore traffic, and on that basis the Navy approved his scheme.[26]

[24] AG, post-1917, 311.23, Hull to Dern, 20.7.33. SD, 1910–49, 819.74/253, Gonzalez to Hull, 10.9.33; 711.19/177, Alfaro to Hull, 21.9.33.
[25] GB, 426-1, s.1633, Roosevelt to Swanson, 18.10.33; Memo of Hooper–Caffery conversation, 7.10.33; Hooper to Standley, 12.10.33; General Board to Swanson, 3.11.33. SD, 1910–49, 819.74/263, Swanson to Roosevelt, 11.12.33.
[26] SD, 1910–49, 819.74/279½, Panama memo of 18.4.34; /287⅔, Wilson to Welles, 9.6.34; /287⅓, Crosley to Gonzalez, 11.5.34; /287⅞, Minutes of conference with War Department, 25.5.34; /287⅓, Hooper to Fawell, 15.5.34; /287⅝, Minutes of conference of 28.6.34. WPD, 1652-19, Draft of 3.7.34. SD, 1910–49, 711.1928/436½, Minutes of meeting of 21.8.34; 819.74/297, Swanson to Hull, 28.8.34.

It was still unacceptable to Panama, which demanded a completely free hand, and the deadlock persisted into the summer of 1935, with Alfaro resisting the radio board as 'a sort of super-government'. There was a strong element of disingenuousness in this stance if the Aviation Board served as a precedent: The board dealt only with minutiae, its meetings were few and far between, and the Panamanian members had been decidedly uncooperative. But whether or not Alfaro was posturing, he was immovable. He was also well able to expose Hooper's brief as the 'unsupported assertion' the State Department had once said it was, but Hooper had now convinced Welles that any breach of the Navy's monopoly would, as Welles put it, be a 'monkey wrench thrown into the efficient operation of the canal'.[27]

In August, Alfaro pointed a way through the impasse by suggesting that private stations might be admitted to ship–shore business provided they were based at least 125 miles from Panama City and Colón. Roosevelt adopted the idea, setting aside an alternative draft by Hooper which allowed merely for possible future discussions on the feasibility of licensing commercial stations for mobile traffic. In order to evade Senate disapproval of the radio convention, the restricted area was defined in a note, which Welles assured Alfaro could not be abrogated unilaterally. To emphasise that the arrangement was not fixed for all time, the convention held out the prospect of changes in Panama's favour. A month later the last outstanding issue in the sphere of defence was also settled with a verbal agreement to continue the practice of asking and granting permission for manoeuvres by means of ad hoc notes, and treaty and conventions were signed on 2 March 1936.[28]

As the negotiating process reached its climax, the State Department issued a lengthy vindication of its policy in response to a final broadside from Schley. The treaty, it claimed, pledged Panama to 'a cooperative attitude in everything relating to the defense of the Canal'. In the past Washington had acted arbitrarily, without reference to Panamanian interests; in future Panama would freely take on a wide range of obligations now that it had served its time as a U.S. protégé. The new dispensation ensured that on defence issues no Panamanian government would choose to be obstructive, and it held considerable significance for Latin Americans in general: 'If their fears regarding our alleged

---

[27] SD, 1910–49, 819.74/303A, Wilson comment on Panama draft, 26.9.34; 711.1928/436½, Minutes of meeting of 7.6.35. PC, 43-D-8, Schley to Crosley, 12.4.34. SD, 1910–49, 711.1928/436½, Meetings of 6.7.35 and 8.7.35. OF, 110, Memo of 13.3.34. SD, 1910–49, 711.1928.436½, Meeting of 12.7.35.

[28] SD, 1910–49, 711.1928/436½, Meetings of 2.8.35 and 6.8.35. WPD, 1652–19, Hooper memo of 17.10.35. SD, 1910–49, 819.74/330, Hooper to Standley, 17.10.35. WPD, 1652–20, Hooper to Welles, 27.11.35. SD, 1910–49, 711.1928/436½, Meetings of 31.12.35, 2.1.36, 1.2.36. Text of radio convention and notes are in USNA, RG 11, Unperfected treaties, File 012 (Executive C, 74th Cong., 2nd sess.) SD, 1910–49, 711.1928/436½, Meeting of 2.3.36.

Figure 6. Good Neighbours: Franklin D. Roosevelt and Harmodio Arias in
Panama, July 1934. (U.S. National Archives)

imperialistic policies of aggression are allayed or replaced by a feeling of confidence, then our problems of defense in the Western Hemisphere become
materially simplified.'[29]

Yet behind this optimism was a realistic awareness of how overgenerous the
treaty might seem to public opinion. The full text was not published, and the
official press release glossed over the true meaning of the article on land acquisition and made no mention whatever of the commitment to consult Panama
over emergency defence measures. As Schley rightly observed, 'What the public knows today is what the State Department has given to it, and in the form

[29] PC, 94-A-3/1936, Dern to Hull, 8.1.36, transmitting Schley memos of 17.12.35 and 20.12.35.
    SD, 1910–49, 711.1928/456½, Undated State Department memo, 27, 11, 12, 37, 38, 40, 42.

in which the Department wished to present it.' Only at the end of April was a so-called uncorrected text printed in the *New York Times*, revealing the details hitherto kept back.[30]

By that time the Army and Navy appeared to have been reconciled to the settlement. From a fishing holiday in the Caribbean, Roosevelt had cabled Hull to impress on them both that it would 'maintain military necessity of exercising troops in Panamanian territory', give Washington 'full freedom of action in event of war or threat of war', and guarantee 'prevention of ship to shore radio except through United States or Panamanian government control'. The chairman of the Senate Foreign Relations Committee, Senator Key Pittman, for his part asserted that any Panamanian violation would nullify the treaty and revive the plenary powers of the 1903 convention, which remained 'in full force and effect' except as modified by the terms of 1936. On 8 April, Hull was told that as a result of a careful 'restudy', the new defence provisions were found acceptable.[31]

Enemies of the treaty in the Senate, such as William Borah and Hiram Johnson, however, were still in no hurry to bring it to a vote. Better, they told Pittman, to wait for Panamanian ratification before taking up the treaty in committee. But when Panama duly ratified the treaty in December, there was no move to give it consideration, and 1937 saw further delay as Roosevelt was locked in conflict with the Senate over his plan to reform the Supreme Court. Despite a warning from Welles that opinion in Panama was starting to become restive, the president refused to add to his problems and chance a rebuff. In May 1938 a personal appeal from President Arosemena roused him to get the accord reported out of the subcommittee which had it under scrutiny, but there the momentum was lost. Opposition on the Senate floor was strong enough to ensure recommitment even if the full committee produced a majority in favour, and so the stalemate persisted into yet another congressional session.[32]

Doubts on the wisdom of the treaty revolved mainly around questions of security, in particular the fact that the procedure for manoeuvres and the meaning of 'consultation' rested on verbal undertakings. To bring in the required two-thirds majority in the Senate, therefore, explanatory notes were drafted for Panama to accept. At a heated cabinet meeting in January 1939, Arosemena denounced Roosevelt for 'attacking the Nazi persecution of Jews [after

[30] ONI, C-9-C 21743, State Department press release of 2.3.36. PC, 65-J-3, Schley to Gruber, 9.3.36. *NYT*, 26.4.36, 1/4, 35/1.

[31] SD, 1910–49, 711.1928/544, Roosevelt to Hull, 29.3.36. WPD, 1652–27, Pittman to Dern, 25.3.36. SD, 1910–49, 711.1928/563½, Dern and Andrews to Hull, 8.4.36.

[32] USNA, RG 46, Records of the United States Senate, SEN 76-B-B20, Pittman to Hull, 22.4.36. SD, 1910–49, 711.1928/617, Summerlin to Hull, 25.12.36. USNA, RG 46, SEN 76-B-B20, Welles to Roosevelt, 10.6.37. SD, 1910–49, 711.1928/655, Hull memo of 21.9.37; 713½, Welles memo of 16.5.38. WPD, 1652–28, Roosevelt to Woodring, n.d. USNA, RG-46, SEN 76-B-B20, Borah to George, 21.5.38. SD, 1910–49, 711.1928/688, Corrigan to Hull, 15.1.38.

Kristallnacht], yet . . . exercising the same kind of domination against the Panamanian nation'. Soon afterwards, however, the notes were agreed, and the Foreign Relations Committee recommended the treaty for passage. In a brief two-day Senate debate, it ran into the inevitable flak of die-hards like Johnson. 'Why is it necessary right now,' he asked, 'when fires are burning all over the earth, to say that the United States Government shall yield any part of its power over the Panama Canal?' Few shared Johnson's view: The treaty went through by the handsome margin of sixty-five votes to sixteen on 25 July, less than six weeks before the outbreak of a second world war.[33]

The war marked the final collapse of an international order under increasing strain for the past decade, and the closing stages of the disintegration concentrated the minds of U.S. defence planners wonderfully. In July 1937 Japan began the conquest of China, and the canal's security was a steady preoccupation throughout the Far Eastern crisis.

The most immediate concern was the continued presence of Japanese trawlers in Panama Bay, ostensibly fishing but in fact making charts of the Pacific approaches to the canal. As in 1934, Hull was urged to impress on Panama the need to refuse fishing concessions to foreign companies, and despite a belief that some of the Panamanian élite were all too closely involved with Japanese businesses, the appropriate decree was issued in January 1938. It was designed to prove, in the words of the president's brother, Leopoldo, that Panama was with Washington 'lock, stock and barrel'. But the disappointed concessionaires were ready to fight the decree's constitutionality, and meanwhile they put their boats under Panamanian registry while having themselves taken on as 'employees'. And the Japanese community in the terminal cities was still seen as a breeding ground for spies and saboteurs.[34]

Equally suspect were Japan's Axis partners, the Germans, who were reportedly aiming to buy land for a settlement in Piñas Bay on the Caribbean coast east of the canal. The bay had been identified by the commander of the Special Service Squadron as one of a number of places 'where submarines or aircraft might be provisioned with little chance of it becoming known to American forces in the Canal Zone, until it was too late', and the Army high command was absolute that the sale must not go through. Panama once more loyally obliged, buying the property to keep it out of alien hands. The quid pro quo was $1.5

[33] SD, 1910–49, 711.1928/763½, Chapin to Welles, 3.1.39; /765½, Arosemena to Boyd, 10.1.39. MID, 2657-P-497, G-2, Panama, Memo of 13.1.39. WPD, 1652–30, Stone to Adjutant General, 16.1.39. Documentation on the notes of 1.2.39 is in *BD*, 902–4. *NYT*, 15.6.39, 7/1 and 8/6. See also Whiteman, *Digest of international law*, 3: 1215–18. CR (Senate), 24–5 July 1939, 9833–45, 9903–4.

[34] ONI, C-10-L, 14951, Commander, Special Service Squadron, to Leahy, 23.11.37. WPD, 3730–12, Leahy and Woodring to Hull, 18.8.37. SD, 1910–49, 819.628/42, Corrigan to Hull, 25.1.38. MID, 2655-M-131(118), Stone to Craig, 10.1.38; (121), G-2, Panama Canal Department, Memo of 20.1.38.

million of U.S. aid towards the cost of the first stretch of the Inter-American Highway running west from the Zone border to Costa Rica.[35]

The third precaution against an enemy within was Governor Clarence Ridley's plan for countering sabotage by ship. It too was given dramatic stimulus by the Japanese onslaught on China. During Anglo-American naval conversations in January 1938, the British assumed that in the event of a joint blockade of Japan the canal would be closed to Japanese shipping to prevent the catastrophe of a merchantman blowing itself sky-high in transit, 'For any nation of a certain type of psychology,' Ridley judged, 'such a suicide venture is possible in view of the invaluable results that might be gained.' In the light of Japan's known capacity for fanatical self-sacrifice in war, it was no far-fetched prediction.[36]

Ridley's response was a scheme for ship inspection and transit guards; for a ban on cargoes containing more than a prescribed amount of high explosive; and for the use by foreign vessels of one side only of the twin-chambered lock flights. He went on to introduce a cluster of additional safeguards, including nets and fenders in the locks, the bombproofing of lock operating machinery, and the installation of emergency dams and power plants. In May 1939 U.S. diplomats were instructed to report on ships bound for Panama, taking note of all suspicious details: bows strengthened for ramming lock gates, seacocks added to speed up the rate of scuttling, outlets fitted below the waterline to discharge mines in passage. Security consciousness had sharpened unmistakably since the alarm over the fleet transit in 1934.[37]

The Army too had identified sabotage as a serious threat to the waterway, and it also moved to tighten the canal's air defences. In April 1937 the planners at last scrapped the mission worked out in 1919, which had postulated defence by a large mobile ground force of infantry and field artillery. Instead they envisaged a garrison whose first duties would be anti-sabotage and defence against air attack. Their prognosis was not shared by the commanding general, David Stone, who was nowhere near sufficiently air-minded for the commander of the 19th Wing, General Brett, who was convinced that unless the wing were brought up to strength 'the Air Force would be neutralised and we would play golf the balance of the war'. Brett was firmly backed by the chief of the Air Corps, who after an inspection trip to the Zone in May 1938 urged immediate reinforcements and the construction of an extra air-base at the

[35] SD, 1910–49, 811F.812/1069, U.S. Consul General to Hull, 20.3.37. ONI, C-10-L, 14951-A, Commander, Special Service Squadron, to Leahy, 26.1.38. SD, 1910–49, 819.52G31/9, Corrigan to Hull, 4.6.38, and /19, /21, /23, /25. See also Almon Wright, 'German interest in Panama's Piñas Bay, 1910–38', *Journal of Modern History*, 27 (1955), 61–6.
[36] John Haight, 'Franklin D. Roosevelt and a naval quarantine of Japan', *Pacific Historical Review*, 40 (1971), 217. WPD, 3730–12, Ridley memo of 18.4.38.
[37] WPD, 3730–12, Ridley memo of 18.4.38; Craig to Ridley, 15.7.38. SWCF, Ridley to Woodring, 23.12.38. SD, 1910–49, 811F.812 Protection/55, Woodring to Hull, 3.5.39; Hull memo of 8.5.39.

Pacific terminal to supplement Albrook, which was already reaching the limit of its capacity.[38]

Air Corps interest in the canal's security was not motivated by the need to keep it operational in a Pacific war with Japan, the Navy's chief concern. From early 1938 Washington focussed increasingly on the defence of the hemisphere, the traditional priority for Army strategists. In this context the canal had the highest significance, and its fate seemed to depend on the ability to enforce the Monroe Doctrine so completely as to nullify Axis penetration of the Americas. It followed that no Axis power should be allowed to establish a presence in any Latin American state which would place it within striking distance of Panama.[39]

The Army Air Corps gave itself an ambitious rôle in that policy. In the B-17 bomber it believed it held the shield against Axis intervention, patrolling hundreds of miles out at sea to interdict violators of hemispheric integrity. Though these pretensions were at first squashed by the combined enmity of a jealous Navy and a conservative Army staff, they were given an enormous impetus by the second great watershed of the pre-war biennium, the Anglo-French capitulation to Germany over Czechoslovakia at Munich in September 1938. Within weeks Roosevelt had sanctioned a galvanic expansion of U.S. air power by no fewer than 5,500 planes, and the new chief of the Air Corps, General Henry Arnold, saw this as authorisation for his men to take over long-range coastal reconnaissance of the Americas from the Navy. At the same time, military and naval planners were ordered to examine the contingency of a two-front war, fought in the Hemisphere as well as in the Pacific.[40]

For some, the prospect of a shift towards the hemisphere was decidedly unsettling. On the day of the Munich conference, the Army's Pacific Sector commander in the Zone wrote that 'so long as our Navy is definitely preponderant in the Pacific *and is present in the Pacific*, any effort against the Canal is a remote probability'. He was clearly aware that the resurgence of Germany had undermined that assumption, and it was also challenged by the strategy review when it reported in April 1939. It envisaged the canal as the prime target for such bombers as the German Heinkel 111, if based in Brazil at Natal or Manaos. Such a lodgment would demand prompt U.S. intervention, since any lengthy blockage of the canal could open the way to Axis triumph in Latin America at large. And if Washington were to face a two-front war, then first call should go

[38] JB, 325, S.598, Joint Planning Committee to Joint Board, 26.4.37. WPD, 3558–7, Stone to Adjutant General, 27.6.38; 4129, Brett memo of 7.4.38. Williams, *Air defense*, 6.

[39] AG, post-1917, 336 (Classified), G-2 to Craig, 18.4.38. See also Stetson Conn and Byron Fairchild, *The framework of hemisphere defense* (volume of *The U.S. Army in World War II: The Western Hemisphere*) (Washington, D.C., 1960), 3–5.

[40] John Major, 'The Navy plans for war', in Kenneth Hagan (ed.), *In peace and war: Interpretations of American naval history, 1775–1978* (Westport, Conn., 1978), 242–3. Library of Congress, Papers of Frank Andrews, Memo of 21.11.38 with comment by Arnold.

to the Caribbean and Panama. Much of this was in close accord with Air Corps thinking, but in a pointed dismissal of the Corps' claims, the survey concluded that in the defence of the hemisphere's Atlantic shoreline 'fundamental reliance' was to be placed on the Navy.[41]

The aviators refused to let it go at that and mounted a study of their own. 'Establishment of airdromes in the north-western part of Brazil', it stated, ' . . . would place Nazi–Fascist bombers less than 1000 miles from the Panama Canal, well within their operating radius of action with heavy loads of bombs.' Air-bases should therefore be acquired at Natal and in the British West Indies colony of Trinidad, and to give maximum cover the Air Corps should be equipped with a four-engined bomber bigger than the B-17.[42]

The main object of this exercise was undoubtedly to get procurement of a new long-range bomber force which would supersede the battleship fleet as the nation's strategic deterrent, and it ran into predictable resistance from the Navy on this score. At the same time, the Navy's high command was not persuaded of the need to devote significant resources to the Atlantic. The chief of naval operations, Admiral William Leahy, saw the canal's best defence in the continued presence of the fleet's first-rate capital ships in the Eastern Pacific. Germany and Italy, he reasoned, would not make a move against South America as long as the British and French navies remained in being. Yet as Leahy took retirement in July 1939, priority in war planning was given to a project for the defence of the hemisphere north of 10° S. – in other words, the Atlantic approaches to the canal – while in and around the Canal Zone itself preparations were already in train for strengthening the waterway's air-defence cordon.[43]

Following Roosevelt's request to Congress in January 1939, $27 million had been authorised to house an expanded anti-aircraft command. Another $22 million went to boost the Army's air force in the Zone from 107 combat planes to 356 and so 'relieve the Navy of any concern in this respect'. To accommodate the extra squadrons, more bases were needed – and bases in Panama beyond the confines of the Zone, where the recently opened Howard Field could offer only a temporary easement of the pressure on Albrook. The most desirable locale was the vast tract at Rio Hato, and in February General Stone reported that Panama was willing to approve a 999-year lease on the property. Outright purchase was no longer possible because of the abandonment of land expropriation under the 1936 treaty. On this basis Stone asked Ambassador William Dawson

---

[41] WPD, 4100–2, Smith memo of 29.9.38 (emphasis in original). JB, 634, Report by Clark and Crenshaw of 21.4.39, IV: 12, I; V: 2, I; IV: 14.

[42] WPD, 3748–17, 'Air defense of the Western Hemisphere', 21, paraphrase of TAB X². AAF: CDF, Ser. 2, Air Adjutant General, 686, Air bases, West Indies, Arnold to Craig, 8.2.39. WPD, 3748–17, TAB C, 5.

[43] John Major, 'William Daniel Leahy', in Robert Love (ed.),*The Chiefs of Naval Operations* (Annapolis, Md., 1980), 108–9, 113–14, 115.

to begin negotiations for Rio Hato and nine ancillary areas picked out as sites for aircraft warning stations.[44]

Given the danger of carrier attack, Stone also believed the detection system must be pushed out far into the Pacific via U.S. possession of bases on Cocos Island and the Galápagos. But Roosevelt's say-so was not forthcoming. In December 1938 he had put forward a devious solution to the question of the Galápagos: 'a trusteeship of certain American States, guaranteeing the security (and military inviolability) of the Islands as a wild life sanctuary under international control and the Ecuadorean flag'. Now, in response to Stone's petition, the word came down through Welles that the president did not favour the acquisition of territory from sister republics, and the White House veto halted any further discussion of the issue for the time being.[45]

Even so, the canal's air-defence network had made distinct progress by the summer of 1939, as had the third-locks scheme – and not a moment too soon for the Navy. The 1938 refit of *Lexington* and *Saratoga* had been critically affected by lock widths of 110 feet. Given their beam of 106 feet, it had been possible to add an anti-torpedo blister on only one side. Likewise, the 35,000-ton *North Carolina*–class battleships laid down in 1937 had had to be limited to a beam of 108 feet (unblistered on either side), as had the forthcoming 45,000-ton *Iowa* class. New locks 135 feet across, on the other hand, would give clearance even to the 128-foot-beam *Montana*-class leviathans on the drawing board. Moreover, since they would be reserved for American warships in emergencies, they would eliminate the risk of sabotage by a vessel in transit. They would also come at less than one-third the cost of a Nicaragua canal, whose partisans staged a last-minute lobby as the locks project came before the legislature. But the president was as hostile to the case for Nicaragua as his namesake had been in 1902, and the bill went through rapidly. Signed by Roosevelt on 11 August 1939, it heralded a new era for the canal as the world stood three weeks away from the outbreak of a second global war.[46]

Second World War, 1939–1945

The Second World War faced the canal with its severest test. In response, the isthmus was turned into an unassailable strongpoint, and the waterway's operational capacity was stretched to the limit. Yet while Panama came through with flying colours, the building of a two-ocean fleet threatened to make it irrelevant,

[44] WPD, 4132, Woodring to Roosevelt, 10.1.39; press release of 6.7.39; 3807–31, Brief for hearings of 16.5.39; 2674–19, 22, 30; 1992–77, Stone memo of 24.2.39. SD, 1910–49, 711.1928/841, Dawson to Hull, 11.8.39. WPD, 2674–30, Stone to Dawson, 8.8.39.
[45] WPD, 3782–3, Stone to Adjutant General, 5.1.39. SLC, Meeting of 16.12.38. WPD, 3782–6, Welles to Woodring, 12.5.39.
[46] PC, 9-A-11, Ridley to Smith, 27.12.38. SNSCC, 1927–39, QH(15)Panama/A1-1 (380822), Bureau of Construction and Repair to Leahy, 2.3.39. SD, 1910–49, 817.812/780, State–War–Navy conference of 16.2.39; /781, Bureau of the Budget to Hull, 6.3.39.

and it had long been technologically outmoded. It was also extremely vulnerable to aerial bombing – above all to the nuclear weapons that brought the conflict to an end. Though its wartime performance was invaluable, its post-war future was highly uncertain. The war thus marked both the apogee of the canal as a key element in American national security and its rapid eclipse by the very forces Washington had brought into being to ensure victory.

There was already a general awareness that the canal was obsolescent when war broke out. Some, like Congressman Melvin Maas, believed the only long-term solution was to opt for a two-ocean Navy of monster capital ships: As Maas put it in December 1939, 'Go to 60,000 or 80,000 tons and forget the Panama Canal.' But the Navy stood by new locks 140 feet wide, which it claimed would suffice 'for many years to come'. The House Appropriations Committee was not convinced. The third locks could not be ready before 1946, and the committee voted less than $1 million to start work on a project with 'questionable standing as an urgent defense measure'. On 1 July 1940, however, the scheme got under way with the first preliminary dredging.[47]

It went ahead in spite of the simultaneous decision to opt for a two-ocean Navy. This was the fevered reaction to the desperate crisis of May and June 1940, when France collapsed beneath the German blitzkrieg and when Britain seemed doomed to go under as well, leaving the United States to confront Germany alone. The battleships in the programme would not be completed much sooner than the new locks, and the two-ocean fleet was no more of an answer to the nation's clear and very present danger, but both projects moved forward in tandem in the headlong rush to get the country on a war footing.[48]

Yet the opening year of the war generated precious little team spirit among the various agencies of the Zone. Governor Ridley's head of counter-espionage, Captain McIntire, and Captain Jules DuBois of Army Intelligence were both soon at loggerheads with the FBI agent assigned to the Zone and succeeded in having him recalled in less than six months. More seriously, at the height of the crisis surrounding the fall of France in June 1940, the Navy refused point-blank to accept orders from commanding general Daniel Van Voorhis. Told by Chief of Staff George Marshall to take every possible anti-sabotage precaution in case the fleet had to be brought to the Atlantic, Van Voorhis directed the district commandant and the commander of the Special Service Squadron to place themselves at his disposal. They both declined, in replies heavily laced with venom, and Marshall was left fuming. The canal, he reminded the chief of naval operations, Admiral Harold Stark, could not be defended 'with a debating society'.[49]

[47] *NYT*, 23.12.39, 1/4, 4/2. OA, NHC, CNO/SN 1940–7, (SC)HG/A16-1, Edison to Woodring, 24.2.40. *NYT*, 28.2.40, 1/4, 8/4. Padelford, 214.

[48] John Major, 'Navy plans for war', 250–1.

[49] SD, 1910–49, 811F.812 Protection/114, FBI report of 17.11.39; /245, Muccio memo of 10.4.41. PC, 62-A-7. *NYT*, 13.12.45, 1/2. OA, NHC, CNO/SN 1940–7, (SC)HG, Marshall to

The Navy's contribution to the local defence of the Zone remained marginal, however. The Army was compelled to supply transit guards, as there were not enough Navy personnel on hand to do the job. Nor could the commandant provide ships to guide merchant vessels through the mine-fields outside the terminals. In August, when the Special Service Squadron left the Zone, the sole craft available for harbour protection were one minesweeper and two patrol boats, and Van Voorhis's calls for a destroyer flotilla were as unavailing as Goethals's appeal for destroyers in 1914.[50]

In only one area was Van Voorhis given satisfaction, and then to no real purpose. He was highly alarmed about the 1,000-strong foreign community on the isthmus, the bulk of them in Panama City. As France was brought to its knees, he told Washington that the aliens in Panama must be put under lock and key. But the 134 suspects despatched to Ellis Island in September were refugees from Europe, many of them Jews. Citizens of the Third Reich, Fascist Italy, and the Japanese empire all stayed in situ.[51]

The Zone was thus by no means proof against internal threats, and it was also uncomfortably exposed to a strike from the air. When war broke out in 1939, one possible source of danger was removed when Bogotá agreed to put a Colombian co-pilot on board each SCADTA plane flown by a German – on the assumption that every German pilot on the company's payroll was an officer in the Luftwaffe reserve. This still left the basic structure of the Zone's air defence network undetermined, however. In September 1939 the chief of the Army Air Corps decided to hold to the set policy of sending out reinforcements in an emergency. His directive was strongly contested by General Stone and by the commander of the 19th Wing, General Herbert Dargue. Both wanted to expand the current early warning line, whose 200-mile radius could give only forty minutes' notice of an incoming bomber force flying at 300 miles an hour – this through bases on Cocos Island and the Galápagos whence interceptors could reach out and 'destroy the wasps in their nests before they ever begin to fly'.[52]

For Dargue the mission of long-range reconnaissance had to be taken from the Navy and handed to the Air Corps, but to minimise the Army's chances of usurping the Navy's rôle, Stark ordered the Atlantic Scouting Force not to remove its Patrol Wing from the Zone. To Van Voorhis, who took over from Stone in January 1940, Stark's pledge was unreliable. He also feared that if

Van Voorhis, 17.6.40; Van Voorhis to Sadler, 20.6.40; Sadler to Van Voorhis, 21.6.40; Marshall to Stark, 8.7.40. WPD, 4326, Marshall to Van Voorhis, 20.6.40; Van Voorhis to Marshall, 24.6.40; Marshall to Strong, 3.7.40.

[50] WPD, 4326, Memo of 28.6.40; Van Voorhis to Marshall, 23.7.40 and 22.8.40.

[51] WPD, 4319, Van Voorhis to Marshall, 11.6.40; Van Voorhis to Adjutant General, 18.6.40. SD, 1910–49, 811F.504/298, Dawson to Hull, 13.6.40; /299, Dawson to Hull, 19.6.40.

[52] WPD, 3326–30, Memo of 2.9.39. AAF: CDF, Ser. 2, Air Adjutant General, 400 Panama–Caribbean, Arnold memo of 9.9.39; Dargue to Arnold, 19.9.39; 452.1 Panama–Caribbean Airplanes, Stone to Arnold, 9.10.39. WPD, 4186, Stone to Adjutant General, 16.6.39; 3782–6, Stone to Adjutant General, 17.6.39.

Washington eventually entered the war, demands to protect the continental USA would drown out the claims of outposts such as Panama. Arnold disagreed, and no new planes were sent to Panama. Instead, twenty-five 3-inch anti-aircraft guns were shipped out to improve the hitting power of batteries designed in the mid twenties to tackle marauders closing in at what by 1940 was a plodding 150 miles an hour.[53]

By the autumn of 1940 this makeshift gave way to the co-ordinated response to air attack which successive commanders in Panama had been urging for years. The Nazi defeat of France had weakened the British control of the Atlantic on which so many of Washington's strategic dispositions had rested. A stop-gap defence of the canal was no longer an acceptable risk, and far-reaching changes in the anti-aircraft system at last began to materialise. In the Caribbean, Puerto Rico was designated as a heavy bomber station, and the destroyers deal with Britain in September opened the way for a base on Trinidad. In the Pacific, negotiations began for Navy airstrips on Cocos Island and the Galápagos, though Stark sanctioned only 120 planes for long-range scouting. Air Corps strength in the Zone was augmented by the arrival of the 9th Bombardment Group, though it consisted of no more than outdated B-18 medium bombers. In the sombre view of the air commander in the Zone, General Frank Andrews, not only were his fighters second-rate, but 'you know the price we would pay operating B-18s in daylight against anything modern'.[54]

The growth of the garrison's air power also exposed the inadequacy of the Zone's existing base facilities. The surface of France Field had already been condemned as unfit, while both Albrook and Howard Field would soon be oversubscribed. 'If we are not able to deploy the projected five hundred planes from the congested area of the Canal Zone,' Van Voorhis told Marshall, 'we will be caught like so many flat-footed policemen.' Auxiliary landing fields would have to be acquired in Panama, plus emergency runways, stations for the Aircraft Warning Service, searchlight positions, and in particular the immense area of Rio Hato.[55]

All these defence sites, however, now had, under the terms of the 1936 treaty, to be obtained through agreement with Panama, and from October 1940 Washington faced a hard bargainer in President Arnulfo Arias, who quickly made it clear that negotiations would be no mere formality. Arias's conditions for the sites reflected a bold assertiveness: Panamanian jurisdiction over all but the U.S. military serving on them; a lease solely for the six-year term of his

[53] WPD, 4270, Van Voorhis to Adjutant General, 12.2.40; 1992–114, Van Voorhis to Strong, 13.4.40; 3689–14, Arnold memo of 3.3.40; 1992–94, Marshall memo of 15.2.40; 4270, War Plans Division to Marshall, 17.4.40.

[54] Conn and Fairchild, *Framework of hemisphere defense*, 18, 249, 61. *NYT*, 5.9.40, 12/2, 13/1. OA, NHC, CNO/SN 1940–7, (SC)HG/A16–1, Sadler to Stark, 29.8.40; Stark to Sadler, 21.10.40. AAF: CDF, Ser. 2, Air Adjutant General, 676.3, Andrews to Brett, 15.1.41.

[55] AG, post-1917, 381 National Defense (1–6–38), Stone to Craig, 6.1.38. WPD, 2674–30, Van Voorhis to Marshall, 12.11.40.

presidency; and generous compensation from Washington. To Ambassador Dawson this was not unreasonable. The Panamanian flag, he thought, could fly on the sites as a reminder of Panama's sovereignty, and if some tracts were needed after Arias left office, 'there would be no difficulty in negotiating renewals'. To an incandescent General Van Voorhis, on the other hand, it was straight appeasement. In March 1940 he had demanded plenary American jurisdiction over the sites, and both he and Marshall insisted on a ninety-nine-year lease – the tenure of the bases acquired from Britain in the destroyers deal. The State Department agreed: Short-term leases were a device to shake Washington down whenever they came up for renewal, and the tracts should be held for as long as necessary. At the end of the year Hull reminded Arias that Panama had taken on defence obligations under the 1936 treaty and should now fulfil them. If Arias refused, Roosevelt instructed Hull 'to try some strong arm methods on him'.[56]

By this time the War Department was seething with impatience, all the more so since it had now persuaded itself that the treaty entitled it to do whatever it chose to defend the canal. In an emergency, the judge advocate general advised Marshall, the Army could 'occupy and utilize' such land as the president might deem necessary for canal protection, and without reference to Panama. Arias for his part threatened resignation if the Army took the bases unilaterally. Panama's treaty commitments, he argued, were contingent on a 'threat of aggression', and Washington had not yet told Panama it existed. To answer this quibble, the relevant treaty articles were formally invoked, and when that failed to produce results, Van Voorhis drafted orders to set Panama out of bounds to all servicemen and civilians quartered in the Zone. 'The prohibition', commented a State Department observer, 'has never had to be maintained for more than two or three days to bring about a happier situation.' On 5 March, Arias authorised the Army to move on to the sites, and a month later the land for nine airfields and two Aircraft Warning Service stations was occupied.[57]

Arias was not prepared to hand over the sites unconditionally, however, and the effort to reach agreement over the terms of the lease was to last for more than a year. So much for the State Department's confident prediction that Panama as a co-partner in the canal enterprise would be more than willing to collaborate in its defence.[58]

[56] SD, 1910–49, 711F.1914/156, Dawson to Hull, 9.11.40; /159, Dawson to Welles, 12.11.40. WPD, 2674–30, Van Voorhis to Marshall, 12.11.40; 2674–28, Woodring to Burdick, March 1940. SD, 1910–49, 711F.1914/135, Dawson to Hull, 20.3.40. SLC, Meeting of 23.11.40. SD, 1910–49, 711F.1914/160, Bonsal memo of 17.12.40; /162, Hull to Dawson, 27.12.40. Stimson Diary, entry for 9.1.41.
[57] SASF, Judge Advocate General to Marshall, 4.2.41. SD, 1910–49, 711F.1914/195, Dawson to Hull, 24.2.41; /182, Panama note of 13.2.41; /183, Hull to Dawson, 17.2.41; /214, Finley memo. of 28.2.41. WPD, 4451, Memo of 27.2.41. SD, 1910–49, 711F.1914/202, Dawson to Hull, 5.3.41.
[58] WPD, 2674–34, War Plans Division to Marshall, 10.3.41.

In the jurisdictional field, Panama demanded the right to bring Panamanian citizens before its own judiciary, whatever the allegation against them. The Army, on the other hand, had recently been granted sweeping judicial powers over the Caribbean bases leased from Britain, and it expected Panama to be similarly obliging. By September 1941, however, six months of talks between Under Secretary Sumner Welles and Foreign Minister Raúl DeRoux had failed to settle the issue.[59]

They had also deadlocked over the subject of compensation. DeRoux was asking a rental of $4,000 a year per hectare for private lands. This was a figure based on what Panama claimed Washington was paying for land on its British West Indies bases. It did not apply to Rio Hato, perhaps because the president's brother Harmodio had a considerable financial interest in the tract, and since there was no love lost between them, Arnulfo was determined to minimise Harmodio's proceeds from the lease. Even so, the rent from the rest of the privately owned terrain needed for defence purposes would come to more than $22 million a year, whereas the payment the State Department originally contemplated for all the lands required was no more than $24,000 a year. Here again, then, the negotiations faced impasse.[60]

Crowning the disagreement came an unbridgeable difference of view over the extent of the lease. For Panama, it would be for the length of the current 'international conflagration', that is, until the end of the European war. For the United States, it had to be for the open-ended period of the 'unforeseen contingency' cited as the justification for taking extra land. There can be little doubt that what Welles had in mind was permanence. While not so categorical as the leading authority on the waterway, Professor Norman Padelford, who proclaimed that the sites must be held 'for the duration of American tenure of the Panama Canal' – that is, in perpetuity – he made it clear that Washington would not subscribe to a deadline. At best, the land would revert to Panama only when the provisions of the 1936 treaty no longer held good; in other words, at some point in the indefinite future. Progress on this front too, therefore, ground to a halt.[61]

Yet the sites were in American hands, and their development was spurred on by an international situation increasingly dangerous from Washington's point of view. The previous guarantor of the eastern approaches to the canal, the Royal

[59] WPD, 2674–38, Stimson to Hull, 15.4.41. SD, 1910–49, 711F.1914/358, Panama draft of 20.8.41; /361, U.S. draft of 30.9.41. Text of the Anglo-American lease agreement of 27.3.41 is in *United States statutes at large*, 55/2 (1941), 156off.

[60] For the Twelve Points, see Chapter 11 at n. 39. SD, 1910–49, 711F.1914/297. Memo of conversation with DeRoux of 2.6.41; /373, Bonsal to Welles, 27.8.41; /361, Wilson to Hull, 21.8.41; /432, Wilson to Hull, 9.3.42; /237, Finley memo of 8.3.41; /463, Memo of 27.4.42.

[61] SD, 1910–49, 711F.1914/202, U.S. draft of 26.3.41; /381, Wilson to Bonsal, 11.9.41; /291, Finley memo of conversation with Briceño of 11.6.41. MID-R, 3850, Padelford memo of 18.4.41. SD, 1910–49, 711F.1914/286 and 298, Welles meetings with DeRoux, 4.6.41 and 9.6.41; /361, U.S. draft of 30.9.41.

Navy, was suffering grievous losses in the battle of the Atlantic. To counter any possible pro-Axis coup, the commanding general in the Zone was therefore empowered to rush paratroops to Colombia, Ecuador, Venezuela, and the republics of Central America. In 1905 Elihu Root had declared that the acquisition of the canal would 'require us to police the surrounding premises'. Old-style intervention – uninvited if need be – remained basic to Roosevelt's Latin American policy whenever the canal was thought to be at risk.[62]

Nervousness over German capabilities heightened dramatically with the news that the Luftwaffe had succeeded in closing the Suez Canal by dropping parachute mines. And morale was further undermined when the Atlantic fleet laid claim to the Navy's aircraft in the Zone, which could no longer be committed to search operations around the isthmus. The loss of naval air reconnaissance was especially disturbing in the light of reports that France had granted Germany facilities at its West African port of Dakar, all too close to Brazil. The chance of a German descent on Brazil, however, was reduced to nil by Hitler's invasion of the Soviet Union. From mid 1941 the spectre of a German air strike against Panama, which had absorbed so much attention over the past three years, vanished never to return.[63]

The threat from Japan endured, in terms of both sabotage by ship and air attack. The ultimate defence against ship sabotage was, of course, to deny transit to Japanese vessels, and in February 1941 consideration was given to abrogating the promise in the Hay–Pauncefote treaty to grant all canal users unhindered passage. Early in July, however, when the Navy told Roosevelt that a Japanese bid to block the canal might be imminent, the decision was to discriminate against Japanese traffic de facto, not de jure, and so avoid giving Tokyo a possible casus belli. Japanese merchantmen arriving at Cristóbal were told they could not be handled because the waterway was undergoing 'urgent repairs'. By 22 July no Japanese shipping remained in Zone waters, and the trauma of closure via a mercantile coup de main had been lifted from Washington's mind.[64]

Not so the fear of a Japanese air-strike. Part of the problem lay with the commanding general. Like many ground commanders, Van Voorhis was deeply hostile to the Air Corps and in April 1940 infuriated General Dargue by ending the Corps' exclusive use of the Rio Hato air-base. He also clashed repeatedly

---

[62] Conn and Fairchild, *Framework of hemisphere defense*, 186–90. Jessup, *Root*, 1: 471.

[63] WPD, 4507, Military attaché, Cairo, report of 19.3.41; 4452–3, Lynd report of 1.5.41. Conn and Fairchild, *Framework of hemisphere defense*, 110–27.

[64] SD, 1910–49, 811F.812 Protection/257, Memo of 20.2.41; 811.812/1086, Legal Adviser memo of 16.3.39. Whiteman, *Digest of international law*, 3: 1178–80. WPD, 3730–22, War Plans Division to Adjutant General, 9.7.41. Stetson Conn and Byron Fairchild, *Guarding the United States and its outposts* (volume in *The U.S. Army in World War II: The Western Hemisphere*) (Washington, D.C, 1964), 335–7.

with Dargue's successor, General Andrews, who had submitted a scathing report soon after his appointment in December 1940. 'I can't get people down here', Andrews told Van Voorhis, 'to realize that we are in a war and that we must prepare our mental attitude to just that. Everything here seems to be planned on what may happen two or three years from now instead of next week or next month.' There then developed a running battle between the two, and when both appealed to Marshall, the sympathies of the chief of staff were undisguised. 'You lack the flood of daily irritations and disturbances that we have every hour,' Marshall wrote Van Voorhis in June 1941, 'which eventually produces either prostration or a case-hardened front to the world.' In September, Van Voorhis was removed and his replacement by Andrews signalled the inauguration of a defence structure for the canal in which air power would at last be paramount.[65]

The air defences, moreover, were to be provided almost entirely by the Army. When commandant Sadler called for 360 patrol planes to scout the Pacific, Stark told him the request was completely disproportionate. The canal was secured by its distance from Japanese bases and by the presence of the U.S. Pacific Fleet at Pearl Harbor. Marshall agreed, placing his confidence in the Army's fighters in the Zone and its anti-aircraft batteries clustered around the locks and storage dams.[66]

Andrews objected strenuously to this last-ditch approach, especially in view of the still glaring deficiencies of the inner ring. There were no troops to man the 90-mm anti-aircraft guns currently being sent down to the isthmus, and there was sufficient ammunition for only one minute of fire by each of the 37-mm guns in position. Some of these gaps began to be plugged with an immediate 40 per cent increase in the garrison, but that continued to leave the canal without the distant early warning line which Andrews knew was its best safeguard. The lack of a forward line became even more critical after the outbreak of the Pacific war blew Stark's assumptions sky-high. Two-thirds of the Pacific Fleet's battleships were put out of action in the Japanese strike on Pearl Harbor, and if Japan chose to launch a carrier assault against the canal, there was frighteningly little standing in its way.[67]

Faced with the prospect of a second disaster, the administration scrambled to make the air-defence screen impenetrable. On 13 December, Roosevelt formally vested long-range surveillance of the Pacific approaches in the Army.

[65] Conn and Fairchild, *Guarding the U.S.*, 316, 331–5. AAF: CDF, Ser. 2, Air Adjutant General, 381 War Plans, Andrews to Van Voorhis, 11.1.41. WPD, 4270–8, Marshall to Van Voorhis, 12.6.41.

[66] WPD, 3730–42, Stark to Marshall, 25.10.41; Marshall to Stark, 14.10.41.

[67] WPD, 3558–25, War Plans Division to Marshall, 31.10.41; 4544–13, Andrews to Adjutant General, 29.11.41; 3558–26, Memo of 26.12.41; 3730–42, Andrews to Adjutant General, 17.9.41.

Army air stations were to be set up at three points along a 1,000-mile arc centred on the Zone: Guatemala City, the Galápagos, and Salinas in Ecuador. Pending completion of these outposts, the War Department rushed to strengthen the cordon in and around the Zone. Secretary of War Stimson knew all too well that the Army's radar equipment was incapable of giving enough warning of incoming aircraft. During talks with the British radar pioneer Robert Watson Watt, he admitted that in a recent exercise planes had got within fifteen miles of the canal before being spotted and that low-flying attackers could not be detected at all. In Watson Watt's view, the first priority was to fit airborne radar in the squadrons of the long-range patrol, and Stimson had already asked for urgent delivery of new ground-based installations to Panama. The first consignment was on its way when Stimson made an inspection tour of the Zone in March and became convinced that they would arrive not a moment too soon. Piloted by Andrews over the Gatún Dam, he touched down shaken by his realisation of the canal's vulnerability to heavy bombing – 'more possible than I had believed'.[68]

Yet the crisis did remarkably little to speed an agreement on terms for the bases in Panama. General Andrews was even more uncompromising than Van Voorhis, while the ousting of President Arias in October 1941 did not produce a Panamanian administration with a softer negotiating stance. The régime of Ricardo Adolfo de la Guardia was perfectly willing to countermand Arias's refusal to arm Panamanian-flagged ships and to round up Axis nationals after Pearl Harbor, but it too placed stiff conditions on the lease of the bases, and talks dragged on for a further seven months before a settlement was reached.[69]

In the realm of jurisdiction, Ambassador Wilson agreed, with heavy sarcasm, that it would be more convenient for Washington if Panama 'ceased to exist as a sovereign republic and complete jurisdiction by the United States could be extended over [its] entire territory'. Panamanian legal powers had to be given some recognition, however, if only as a reward for the abandonment of Arias's neutralism. This the War Department moved heaven and earth to stop, and though Panamanian civil authority was guaranteed in the agreement signed in May 1942, Stimson introduced an enabling bill into Congress a year later conferring judicial competence over the bases on the Canal Zone District Court. Denounced by Panama as a bid to set up 'little Canal Zones' throughout the republic, it was eventually withdrawn by a military establishment reluctantly

---

[68] Stimson Diary, entry for 12.12.41. WPD, 2917–34 and 35, Memos of 12.12.41 and 16.12.41. Conn and Fairchild, *Guarding the U.S.*, 339–43, 424–8. Sumner Welles, *Seven major decisions* (London, 1951), 103. WPD, 1992–121, Minutes of conference of 23.2.42. Stimson Diary, entries for 13.2.42, 21.2.42, 23.2.42, 11.3.42. Stimson Papers, Meeting of 23.2.42. SASF, Stimson to Roosevelt, 14.3.42.

[69] SD, 1910–49, 711f.1914/413, Wilson to Hull, 24.1.42.

persuaded that its political damage potential outweighed any possible jurisdictional advantage.[70]

Striking a bargain over the annual rental for the sites was comparatively smooth going. Foreign Minister Octavio Fábrega was ready to come down to $100 a hectare for both public and private lands, exclusive of Rio Hato. Since this would reduce the annuity from over $22 million to under $800,000, it seemed 'eminently reasonable' to Wilson, but when Fábrega called 'with considerable vehemence' for $100 a hectare on Rio Hato too, Washington faced a severe hike in its rental from $2,400 a year to $767,000. The only alternative, in the Panamanian view, was to backdate the rent to 1935, when the area was first leased as an airfield. At first sight these were exorbitant requirements, but they fell into perspective against a report that the Navy leased an hotel on Waikiki Beach for $210,000 a year. In the final agreement Fábrega settled for $10,000 a year for Rio Hato, $50 a hectare on other private holdings, and a peppercorn rent of $1 a hectare on public lands.[71]

The most intractable point at issue was the duration of the lease. 'I feel that the time will never come', General Andrews told Wilson, 'when the majority of the sites under consideration can be evacuated.' But Wilson felt it would be wrong to demand permanence, and Welles agreed: 'bad faith, sharp practice, and politically inexpedient'. Better, in Wilson's view, to accept de la Guardia's suggestion for withdrawal from the bases one year after the signature of the peace treaty ending the war. Though he told de la Guardia that certain sites must be kept 'for all time hereafter', their status could be renegotiated once the war was over. In the May 1942 bases agreement, therefore, termination of the lease was set at 'one year after the date on which the definitive treaty of peace which brings about the end of the present war shall have entered into effect'. If during that year the two governments considered that there was still 'a state of international insecurity', they were to make a new agreement.[72]

The War Department was deeply unhappy with this arrangement. If the Axis surrendered unconditionally, Stimson told Hull, 'our prestige and military power will be so great that Panama is almost certain to do our bidding without haggling and without consideration of price'. But if the war ended by negotiation,

[70] Ibid., /407, Wilson to Hull, 17.1.42; /418, Wilson to Hull, 17.2.42. WPD, 2674–44, Judge Advocate General memo of 25.2.42. OpD, 381 Panama, Memo of 15.6.43; 381 Panama Canal Department, Memo for the record of 17.11.43; Brett to Adjutant General, 17.12.43. See *BD*, 927, for final text.

[71] SD, 1910–49, 711F.1914/407, Wilson to Hull, 17.1.42; /413, Wilson to Hull, 24.1.42; /407, Hull to Wilson, 13.2.42; /432, Wilson to Hull, 9.3.42; /461, Wilson to Hull, 28.4.42; /390. See *BD*, 931, for final text.

[72] SD, 1910–49, 711f.1914/397, Andrews to Wilson, 14.11.41; /396, Wilson to Hull, 29.10.41; Welles memo of 12.11.41; /432, Wilson to Hull, 9.3.42; /434, Wilson to Hull, 10.3.42. See *BD*, 926–7, for final text.

Panama could 'prejudice, perhaps even . . . nullify, our entire military position'. In the event of a Panamanian refusal to come to a post-war agreement on the bases, 'the American right to use Panamanian soil for military purposes lapses, and our forces are legally obliged to retire into the Canal Zone'.[73]

Stimson's dissatisfaction was natural for a man convinced that Panama was 'the one spot external to our shores which nature has decreed to be most vital to our national safety, not to mention our prosperity'. But the Second World War was to undermine many of the strategic axioms of Stimson's generation, among them the certainty that the canal was essential for American security. Already in 1940 the move to a two-ocean fleet had pointed to a future in which it would no longer be indispensable to the Navy, and within days of the signing of the bases agreement, another blow fell with Roosevelt's suspension of work on the third locks.[74]

The possibility of discontinuing the locks had been raised shortly after Pearl Harbor, but the project went on even though it imposed a huge drain on shipping resources. In April 1942, however, the decision was taken to stop building the 60,000-ton *Montana*-class battleships for which the locks had been intended, and postponing the locks' completion was the logical sequel, author-ised by the White House on 23 May.[75]

This left a canal whose existing lockage was inadequate to transit a growing number of the Navy's largest vessels. The carrier *Saratoga* and three front-line battleships were all too broad after refits placing anti-torpedo blisters on both beams. The three new *Midway*-class carriers on the stocks would likewise be unmanageable, given the width of their flight decks. If the canal were to retain its strategic significance, it would have to be given a new lease of life by some form of modernisation.[76]

The consummation of the third-locks scheme was one answer, but there were alternatives. For General Andrews the best was a sea-level canal. A seaway too had weak points vulnerable to aerial bombing – its flood-control barrages and tidal gates – but Andrews believed it was immeasurably more viable than the lift-lock canal. Above all, it would eliminate dependence on Lake Gatún. If the Gatún dam were breached, the water in the lake would be drained and the canal

[73] SD, 1910–49, 711F.1914/514, Stimson to Hull, 21.7.42, and /536 for an unsent reply by Hull attacking Stimson's depiction of a victorious USA as 'the sort of false portrayal of our policy which the Nazi propagandists have been making use of, and which we should seek to combat rather than stimulate'.

[74] Henry Stimson and McGeorge Bundy, *On active service in peace and war* (New York, 1948), 183. SWCF, Stimson to Edgerton, 23 May 1942.

[75] WPD, 3182–7, Edgerton to Stimson, 23.12.41; Stimson to Edgerton, 22.1.42. OA, NHC, CNO/SN 1940–7, (SC)HG, Moreel to Horne, 4.5.42; Knox to Stimson, 7.5.42; memo of 9.5.42. SWCF, Marshall and King to Roosevelt, 21.5.42.

[76] GB, 426–1, S.252, War Plans Division for Kalbfus, 17.3.44; Kalbfus memo of 15.3.44.

put out of commission for at least two years. The mechanism of a sea-level canal could be repaired comparatively quickly.[77]

Rivalling the sea-level plan was a quite different project, elaborated in 1943 by the Navy's port captain at Balboa, Commander Miles DuVal. This envisaged a lock canal with symmetrical arrangements on either side of the central cut. DuVal contended that the two-lock system on the Pacific side was a fundamental design error which had made the Pedro Miguel chamber a dangerous bottleneck. He proposed instead a single Pacific set of locks, as at Gatún. Also mirroring Gatún would be a Pacific-terminal lake for use as a traffic reservoir and anchorage. The result, DuVal claimed, would be a canal easier to navigate than either a seaway or the third-locks development, which would simply reproduce all the drawbacks of the present configuration.[78]

DuVal drafted his blueprint at a time when the canal seemed out of danger for the remainder of the war. At the battle of Midway in June 1942 the tide of Japanese expansion had been decisively turned, and Panama was secure from carrier attack. After the close of 1942 the Zone was no longer rated as a first-rank theatre of war. In November, Andrews moved on, and from January 1943 a progressive reduction of the garrison began. Many American troops were replaced by Puerto Ricans and a number of defence sites abandoned.[79]

With the rundown came a predictable slackening of discipline. In December 1943 *Newsweek* reported that the Zone resembled Oahu on the eve of Pearl Harbor, high on 'a spirit of carefreeness and gayety that one doesn't associate with an all-out war effort'. The social life of the armed forces had clearly improved since the day when Andrews had endorsed an unsuccessful proposal to bring in large numbers of young women in uniform to make up for 'the almost complete lack of white American girls'. Andrews's successor, General George Brett, was consequently warned by Marshall to keep his men up to the mark, but, as Stimson noted in December 1944, Brett had a hard row to hoe. His was 'a rather discouraging command because the menace of a Japanese surprise attack which livened up the situation two and a half years ago now is dim in the distance as the Japanese fleet has been pounded to pieces across the Pacific'. Once a vital citadel, Panama had become a military backwater.[80]

In these circumstances the only immediate defence issue of any note was

---

[77] OpD, 600.12 Panama, Andrews to Marshall, 17 and 18.5.42. WPD, 4452–19, Andrews to McNair, 15.1.42.

[78] PC, 9-A-11, DuVal memos of 25.2.43 and 25.3.43. Miles DuVal, 'Isthmian canal policy–an evaluation', *U.S. Naval Institute Proceedings*, 81 (1955) 268–70.

[79] *HPCD*, 4: 1.

[80] OpD, 000.7/109, Hull to Brett, 7.12.43. AG, post-1917, 333.1, Draper to Marshall, 25.11.41. WPD, 4452–13, War Plans Division memo of 10.12.41. Stimson Diary, entries for 17.10.42 and 14.12.44.

control of Panama's air-space. As early as October 1939 Panama had objected strongly to a new executive order regulating flights across the Zone, complaining that its planes were barred from entry just like those of the European belligerents. U.S. pilots, in contrast, ranged freely over Panama in spite of Sumner Welles's confirmation of national sovereignty over air-space at the recent inter-American conference in Panama City. The order also seemed to ignore the Panamanian Aviation Board set up in 1929 to co-ordinate policy with the Zone authorities.[81]

Panamanian tolerance finally snapped in the summer of 1941. Following the U.S. decision to permit a commercial air terminal at Albrook Field, Arnulfo Arias first abrogated the 1929 agreement and then denied Washington's right to allow aviation companies to do business in the Zone. Implicit in the denial was the familiar assertion that Panama retained sovereignty over the Zone in regard to everything not specifically relinquished by treaty, and the argument was elaborated in a Panamanian court opinion in September 1943.[82]

Like all previous challenges to American sovereign powers, this too was given short shrift. Learning that Pan American Airways planned to leave Albrook for Panama, Stimson had the State Department bring pressure on it to hold still. Wartime supervision of air traffic must be kept up, he told Hull, 'either through the continued use of U.S. Army air bases, or through the establishment of an ironclad military control of all airplanes and operations at any base to be constructed in Panama territory'.[83]

Others went still further. Ambassador Wilson was convinced that 'even in any "normal" period in the future the United States will have to exercise at all times . . . control regarding all aviation coming to the Isthmus'. General Brett demanded exclusive authority over the air-space of Panama in peace as well as war, and insisted that U.S. officials must be stationed at any eventual Panamanian national airport to process all travellers to and from the Zone. For Governor Joseph Mehaffey this was much too heavy-handed: A new Aviation Board would suffice, where the Panamanians would be expected to follow the lead of the American co-members. Given the inflammability of Panamanian nationalism, this was highly optimistic, but the problem was not urgent, and the quest for a solution could be left until the war was over.[84]

The closing years of the war were thus something of an extended anticlimax

[81] SD, 1910–49, 811F.7961/84, Legation to Hull, 2.3.39; Division of International Communications memo of 18.3.39; /107, Dern to Hull, 21.11.39; /106. USNA, RG 43, 1939 Conference, U.S. draft resolution on aviation. SD, 1910–49, 810.154/1381½, Memo of 16.8.39; 819.76/56, Embassy to Hull, 7.8.39.

[82] SD, 1910–49, 819.7962/51, Panama note of 3.6.41; 811F.7962/11, Wise memo of 11.6.41; 819.7962/60, Panama note of 17.9.41; 811F.7961/178A, Hull to Embassy, 16.12.43; /180, Chargé to Hull, 5.1.44.

[83] SD, 1910–49, 819.7962/81, Stimson to Hull, 24.12.43; /2–2244, Young to Berle.

[84] SD, 1910–49, 819.7962/68, Wilson to Hull, 21.4.42. OpD, 580.82 CDC, Joint Committee report to Brett of 19.10.44. SD, 1910–49, 819.796/11–1144.

for the canal. If the Japanese Navy had had its way, the finale could have turned out very different. The discovery of the wrecks of two midget submarines in the Pearl Islands in 1973 suggests an abortive bid to destroy Miraflores Lock, while an attack by torpedo planes launched from monster U-boats was planned to block the transfer of U.S. troops to the Pacific after the German surrender in May 1945. It was abandoned, however, and the waterway came through the war untouched.[85]

Its contribution to the war effort is impossible to calculate, but if the much longer subcontinental route around Cape Horn had had to be used, Washington might well have been forced to choose between limiting the protection of Atlantic convoys and reducing shipments to the Pacific theatre. The canal removed the necessity for that choice, and combat vessels and supply ships could be shuttled through at will from one ocean to the other. The resulting gain in flexibility was priceless, and the canal took the strain with remarkable ease. Between July 1941 and June 1945 more than 23,000 transits were recorded, an average of nearly sixteen per day. Panama had more than justified itself as one of the nation's most crucial assets.[86]

The way the war came to an end, however, placed a huge question mark over the canal's long-term value to the country. In June 1945 Stimson confided to his diary the fear that the new 'high explosives' under development were likely to make it 'dangerous and easily destroyed'. He was writing about the atomic bomb, and the annihilation of Hiroshima and Nagasaki in August was a sombre warning of what lay in store for the equally friable structures of Panama in the event of a nuclear strike. Unless a remedy could be found, the canal which had just served American interests so well would have no strategic future.[87]

Cold war, 1945–1955

In terms of its military value to the United States, the Panama Canal came out of the Second World War fatally flawed. The creation of a two-ocean Navy made it redundant, and its locks were in any case too small to accommodate the new generation of fleet carriers. Above all, the arrival of the atomic bomb in August 1945 made its obliteration a certainty if ever a nuclear strike found its target. The post-war decade did nothing to change this situation, and while the canal retained a powerful symbolic importance, it had irretrievably lost the standing of a critical national interest.

[85] Letter to the author from Colonel Robert Sprague, 12.2.82. Zenji Orita and Joseph Harrington *I-Boat captain* (Canoga Park, Calif., 1976), 318–19. E. John Long, 'Japan's "underseas carriers"', *U.S. Naval Institute Proceedings*, 76 (1950), 609. *The Imperial Japanese Navy*, vol. 12; *Submarines* (Tokyo, 1990), 137–96, 242–53.
[86] PC, 9-A-14, ICS memo of 28.5.48, 18, 20. *NYT*, 18.11.45, sect. VI, 6.
[87] Stimson Diary, entry for 7.6.45.

No thought of such a demotion had crossed the mind of General Brett when in the spring of 1945 he drafted a long-term plan for the post-war defence of the canal. This contemplated maintaining most of the wartime anti-aircraft network in the Pacific approaches, with first-class bases at Rio Hato, Aguadulce, Chorrera, David, and the Galápagos. When Japan capitulated in August, the last vestige of a threat from the Pacific disappeared, but the plan found justification in the advent of the atomic bomb, high-speed jets, and supersonic missiles. All three compounded the problems of interception enormously, but the commander of the 6th Air Force believed they made an elaborate early warning system even more essential. The Joint Chiefs of Staff were in full agreement. Their October 1945 survey of future requirements for U.S. air-bases gave high priority to the Canal Zone, with outstations in Panama and the Galápagos. Negotiations for base facilities, they urged, should start immediately.[88]

It soon became clear, however, that Panama's consent would be hard to come by. On 6 November, Foreign Minister Ricardo Alfaro declared that American tenure of defence sites in Panama must end on 1 September 1946, that is, one year after the Japanese signature of unconditional surrender terms aboard the USS *Missouri*. The 1942 agreement on the bases had stipulated that the lease would expire one year after a peace treaty came into force, but for Alfaro 'treaty' signified 'whatever pact, agreement, act or instrument . . . definitely terminated the hostilities inherent in the state of war'. His statement reflected a mounting restiveness, in Panama and elsewhere, at the victor powers' continued occupation of allied territory after the rationale for their presence had apparently ceased to exist. Pressure was also growing in Ecuador for an American withdrawal from Salinas and the Galápagos, and the issue was clearly capable of being exploited by the USSR, particularly since Washington itself was currently pushing for an early departure of Soviet troops from China and Iran.[89]

The prospect of relinquishing the Panamanian bases was decidedly unwelcome to Brett's successor, General Willis Crittenberger. He too saw Rio Hato as the centre-piece of his defence network with its acreage doubled to give space for a manoeuvre ground as well as a bomber field. He also wanted it in perpetuity, but, persuaded by a nervous U.S. Embassy that the demand would bring any Panamanian government down, trimmed it to ninety years. As it had been during the war, the canal would be secured by 'continuous Aircraft Warning

[88] *HPCD*, 4: 49–50, 54. AG, post-1917, Administrative Services Division, Operations Branch, Special Projects, War Plans 'COLOR', 'A long-term strategic plan for the defense of the Panama Canal', 22.6.45. *HPCD*, 4: 45. JCS, 570/40 of 25.10.45: 'Overall examination of United States requirements for military bases and base rights'. Michael Sherry, *Preparing for the next war: American plans for postwar defense, 1941–45* (New Haven, Conn., 1977), 44–7. James Schnabel, *The history of the Joint Chiefs of Staff*, vol. 1 of *The Joint Chiefs of Staff and national policy* (Wilmington Del., 1979), 299–321.

[89] SD, 1910–49, 711F.1914/11–745, Hines to Byrnes, 7.11.45. DuBois, *Danger over Panama*, 154–6, gives an English translation of the Alfaro statement. *NYT*, 19.9.45, 14/4.

System coupled with a "round-the-clock" fighter aviation and ground antiaircraft defense' plus 'an air bombardment striking force to destroy hostile surface forces'.[90]

Crittenberger's plan, however, was a classic instance of 'localitis', a bid to breathe new life into a justifiably inactive command, and its bearing on reality was tenuous. By his own definition, Panama was faced with only the remote possibility of 'suicidal attacks by submarine-based aircraft, or attacks by naval craft operating by stealth, or by aircraft operating from hidden bases in near-by jungles'. These were precisely the measures Japan had been contemplating during the last year of the war, and the entire project seemed dedicated to securing the canal against a vanished threat.[91]

It was also in conflict with the military and diplomatic needs of the immediate post-war situation. In January 1946 the new Army chief of staff, Dwight D. Eisenhower, confirmed that garrisons at places such as the Canal Zone were being 'cut to the bone' to provide manpower for occupation duty in Germany, Austria, Japan, and Korea. At the same time, the ambitious requirements of the Joint Chiefs came under severe criticism from the State Department as a wants list postulated on an early showdown with both Russia and Britain, not continued co-operation. The Joint Chiefs therefore termed only six locations essential, although they included Panama and the Galápagos.[92]

In June 1946 Crittenberger appeared to bow to the revision. But he was insistent that Panama must be nailed down by a hard-and-fast new agreement on base facilities so that the Army would not have to rely on 'the unpredictable attitude of a vacillating government to provide [them] when needed'. In Crittenberger's judgement, backed by Ambassador Frank Hines, it was pointless to dispute Alfaro's contention that the 1942 agreement would lapse on 1 September, and negotiations for a renewal of the lease should start at once.[93]

The State Department, however, was perfectly happy to sit tight. 'We are not too concerned ... over any September 1 deadline,' wrote one seasoned Panama hand, Murray Wise. The reference to a peace treaty as the terminal point of the 1942 agreement had been chosen deliberately, Wise recalled, 'to obtain after the war a period of delay which it was thought conceivably might mean a period of five or six years'. The Azores bases agreement with Portugal

[90] SD, 1910–49, 711F.1914/11–945, Hines to Byrnes; /11–1445; 711.19/1–2346. AG, post-1917, 381 Panama, Panama Canal Department Basic War Plan, 10.2.46.
[91] AG, Post-1917; 381 Panama, Panama Canal Department Basic War Plan, 10.2.46.
[92] Louis Galambos (ed.), *The papers of Dwight David Eisenhower* vol. 7 (Baltimore, 1979), 799, Eisenhower to MacArthur, 28.1.46. *FRUS 1946*, 1: 1125–8. JCS, 570/62 of 15.5.46, 451, 454.
[93] POD, 686 TS, Memo of 13.5.46; 381, Case 17, Memo of 19.6.46; 381 Panama Section 1-A (ABC File), JPS 684/24 and JPS 684/24, Appendix B of 22.6.46. JCS, 570/71, Appendixes A and B of 2.7.46. POD, 381 Panama Section 1-A (ABC File), Crittenberger to Eisenhower, 13.3.46. SD, 1910–49, 711F.1914/4–2546, Hines to Byrnes.

had stipulated U.S. withdrawal nine months after the end of hostilities, and in January 1946 Secretary of State James Byrnes accepted the Portuguese argument that hostilities ceased with the Japanese surrender; the bases were consequently handed back on 2 June. Panama got very different treatment.[94]

Midway through the war one foreign service officer had predicted a closely fought round of bargaining over the defence sites once the war was over. 'The Panamanians are of course hard traders,' observed Orme Wilson, ' . . . naturally aware . . . that their most profitable extractive industry is that of extracting concessions from Tio Sam.' By standing on the letter of the 1942 agreement, Panamanian voracity could be held at bay, and yet another roadblock was erected to postpone negotiations still further. In August 1945 Assistant Secretary Nelson Rockefeller told Alfaro that no issue of any importance could be broached until Panama had first paid out on the so-called El Encanto claim. The claim had not been allowed to stand in the way of the wartime agreement, but its resurrection now was a transparent spoiling tactic, and Hines was directed to make a claim settlement the precondition of any discussion of a new bases agreement.[95]

Hines ignored the instruction. On 29 August he took it upon himself to tell Panama that Washington was ready to deal, and his initiative was not repudiated. In answer to a note from Alfaro leaving open the possibility of a new accord, Byrnes promised to give reasons why the bases were still needed and called for negotiations to take place soon.[96]

The conclusion that the Zone could not be defended without forward positions in Panama was one token of the enduring belief in what the Joint Chiefs of Staff planners described as the 'strategic essentiality' of the canal. Another was the debate on canal modernisation which ran in parallel with the bases issue. After the suspension of work on the third locks in May 1942, the sea-level project had come back into vogue, and Commander Miles DuVal had introduced his plan for a restructured lock canal. A choice between these mutually exclusive approaches could not be made until the war was over, but in December 1945 Governor Joseph Mehaffey was authorised to conduct a full-dress inquiry as to which could best serve the interests of American national security and international maritime trade. Shortly afterwards the Navy mounted an independent investigation, looking, like Mehaffey, to report its findings by the end of 1947.[97]

[94] SD, 1910–49, 711F.1914/8–2846 and 11–1645; 811.34553B/1–3046, Byrnes to Crocker, in *FRUS 1946*, 5: 962.

[95] SD, 1910–49, 711F.1914/8–1743, Wilson to Bonsal; /8–745. POD, 680.4, Case 14, Memo of 30.8.46.

[96] SD, 1910–49, 711F.1914/8–3146, Hines note of 29.8.46; /9–146, Panama note of 31.8.46; /9–346, Byrnes note of 3.9.46.

[97] POD, 381 Panama, JPS 684/24 of 22.6.46. *NYT*, 27.11.45, 4/3.

In the opening phase of the study it was the sea-level concept which made the running. As early as June 1945 Stimson told Mehaffey that completing the third locks was 'only a palliative'; a seaway alone, he felt, could stand up to the explosive power of an atomic bomb. The ruins of Hiroshima and Nagasaki seemed to bear out that prediction to the full in August, and top-ranking officials in the Zone all drew the conclusion that the bomb had made Goethals's pride and joy militarily obsolete overnight. As the Canal's consulting engineer, General Hans Kramer, was to put it, the sea-level design was 'no longer a second choice'.[98]

The two rival versions of a modified lock canal, meanwhile, battled it out in the framework of the Navy's review body. When DuVal was appointed to head it in April 1946, his ideas seemed destined to be given Navy Department blessing. DuVal believed it was not feasible to build locks wider than the 140 feet fixed on in 1940, and he had the apparent support of the General Board. When asked to report whether the capacity to transit should continue to be a requirement for the Navy's biggest vessels, the board leaned towards a fleet where numbers counted for more than size. It would provide not only global coverage but dispersion to guard against a second Pearl Harbor, and if giant lock chambers were to be prohibitively expensive, the Navy could make a virtue of necessity by scrapping its plans for mammoth ship construction and building within the limitations imposed by a more modest scale of lockage.[99]

Yet this verdict flatly contradicted the board's view six months earlier that the widest possible locks were imperative. In September 1945 the planned width of the third locks was increased from 140 feet to 154 feet, but in June 1946 the Bureau of Aeronautics told the chief of naval operations, Fleet Admiral Chester Nimitz, that it had a new carrier in mind with a flight deck 154 feet across. Nimitz therefore came out in favour of a lock width of 200 feet to take care of 'the largest ships now extant or contemplated'.[100]

Nimitz's recommendations thus marked a victory for the third-locks scheme over the DuVal project, and DuVal could only take comfort in Nimitz's comment that if Congress balked at funding locks as big as he wanted, then he would settle for something closer to the 140 feet DuVal still called for. But that did not signify acceptance of correspondingly smaller ships. As the doyen of the carrier admirals of the Pacific war, Nimitz was not about to let carrier evolution be hampered by lock dimensions. Bigger vessels would be built even if it meant

[98] Stimson Diary, entry for 7.6.45. OA, NHC, CNO/SN 1940–7, HG 1946, DuVal memo of 1.5.46.
[99] OA, NHC, CNO/SN 1940–7, HG 1946, DuVal draft letter of 13.8.46. GB, 426–1, S.252, DuVal to Nimitz, 1.8.46; 426–1, S.305, General Board to Forrestal, 4.12.46.
[100] GB, 426–1, S.252, Bureau of Ships to King, 24.8.45; Bureau of Aeronautics to Nimitz, 6.6.46; General Board to Nimitz, 4.6.46; CINCPAC to General Board, 13.12.46; Forrestal to Patterson, 24.12.46. OA, NHC, CNO/SN 1940–7, HG 1946, McRea to Nimitz, 20.12.46.

they could not transit, because this would be preferable to 'indefinite dependency upon the existing canal'.[101]

It followed that Nimitz was no less indifferent to a sea-level waterway. Recent studies indicated that a nuclear strike on the existing canal would cause what were blandly described as 'serious casualties and disruption of operation', as well as lingering contamination from radioactive fall-out. But they also showed that any type of canal would be vulnerable to atomic attack. Consequently, he did not deem the construction of a seaway mandatory.[102]

The sea-level project lived on, however. In October 1946 General Crittenberger had set up a board to look into the problems of defending sea-level and lock canals. In December, just three weeks after Nimitz's hostile finding, it brought in its 'inescapable' conclusion that a sea-level canal was 'inherently more secure than a lock canal and requires fewer troops and less equipment for its defense'. The cost of protecting a lock canal would be mountainous, and it could never have the intrinsic passive defence qualities of a seaway.[103]

It was thus against a favourable backdrop that Governor Mehaffey issued his draft report in July 1947. As expected, he recommended a sea-level canal, even though the price-tag would be $2.5 billion. The choice was made on strategic grounds: Denial of Panama to the Navy 'would be to halve its strength at a stroke', and only the sea-level canal offered viability in a nuclear war. Even if hit by two 20-kiloton A-bombs, it would be closed for only four weeks after repairs began; such an attack on a lock canal would block it for four years.[104]

During the next three months the draft was examined by the Navy, the Joint Chiefs of Staff, and the Atomic Energy Commission, whose imprimatur Mehaffey felt was essential. In the event, the AEC's comments were curiously muted, but its statement that 'a nearby or contact explosion . . . would almost certainly wreck any of the townsites and related service features essential to a lock canal' was undoubtedly grist to the governor's mill. So too was the pronouncement of the Joint Chiefs' planners that a sea-level cut would offer 'the maximum security attainable against sabotage and weapons of the foreseeable future'.[105]

The Navy's verdict was equally pro–sea-level. Two witnesses at the General

[101] GB, 426–1, S.252, Forrestal to Patterson, 24.12.46.
[102] OA, NHC, DuVal Papers, Nimitz to Shafroth, 7.12.46.
[103] POD, 381, Case 89, Crittenberger to Eisenhower, 19.1.47, enclosing report of 28.12.46. OA, NHC, War Plans Division memo of 10.4.47, 'Cost estimates of the defense of a Panama Sea-Level Canal'.
[104] GB, 426–1, S.310, Mehaffey to Shafroth, 24.7.47. SD, 1910–49, 811F.812/12–2747, Mehaffey report of 21.11.47.
[105] POD, 381, Case 89, Mehaffey to Burdick, 6.9.47. U.S. Atomic Energy Commission, Lilienthal to Royall, 15.10.47. The first draft of this letter, dated 10.10.47, predicted that 'a nearby or contact explosion would wreck any of the essential features of a lock canal' and was quoted by Mehaffey in his final report of 21.11.47. POD, 381 Panama (17 July 1945), Section 1-B (ABC File). JCS, 1778/1 of 1.10.47, Appendix to Inclosures A and B.

Board's hearings in September came out against it. Admiral Daniel Gallery, indeed, saw no need for a canal at all as long as the Soviet navy remained as negligible as it was in 1947. Not even the permanent closure of the waterway would threaten American security, since rounding the Horn was now a routine operation. As head of the Navy's rocket programme, Gallery believed that the funds asked for the sea-level project would be far better spent on missile research and development.[106]

Admiral William Parsons appeared, without much doubt, as the spokesman for DuVal, and he testified as the navy's leading authority on nuclear weapons. Parsons believed that Crittenberger's committee had understated the vulnerability of a sea-level canal to a nuclear strike and that the seaway's flood-control dams were its Achilles' heel. The security it offered was therefore highly debatable, and at best it would be no more than a 'Maginot-line type of defense'.[107]

All the other admirals coming before the Board supported the sea-level project, however. They did so in spite of uncertainties over Moscow's will and capacity to destroy the canal. Admiral Forrest Sherman estimated that an effective assault would come only if 'one power' should seize control of Europe. Meanwhile the immediate threats to Panama were gauged to be 'sporadic air attack by stealth from places in South America or attack by missiles brought to the vicinity . . . by submarines'. Even when the USSR obtained nuclear weapons and a delivery system for them, major American seaports such as New York were thought more profitable targets than the canal. 'Once the potential enemy acquires the use of the atomic bomb,' remarked Admiral William Callaghan, 'any type of canal will be of relatively minor strategic importance.' Yet the sea-level was still seen as an absolute requirement.[108]

This was partly because of its supposed ability to survive a nuclear attack and partly because Washington had to have the means of transiting the largest ships the Navy had in prospect. As things were, no carrier above 15,000 tons could pass through the locks without damage. And even if – given the two-ocean fleet – the canal were not needed to shuttle front-line vessels back and forth, it remained a vital link in the Navy's supply lines. Sherman predicted that in a future war fought in the Atlantic and Mediterranean, Panama would handle as great a volume of shipments as it had put through in the Second World War. Closure of the lock canal would rob Washington of this freedom, but an ever open seaway would guarantee it.[109]

At the end of September the General Board submitted a pro–sea-level report. DuVal was highly chagrined. Acceptance of the sea-level scheme represented 'a

[106] GB, 426–1, s.310, Statement of Admiral Daniel Gallery.
[107] OA, NHC, CNO/SN 1940–7, HG 1946, Parsons memo of 14.7.47. GB, Hearings, 1947, 3: 592–4.
[108] GB, Hearings, 1947, 3: 576, 572, 575, 602, 582.
[109] Ibid., 582, 573–4, 572.

gigantic national expenditure of human energy, resources and money' without an assurance that the seaway would function as well as the canal it was going to replace. All this and more he hoped Navy Secretary John Sullivan would convey to Mehaffey, but Sullivan accepted the board's findings, and on 1 December President Truman sent Mehaffey's report to Congress.[110]

Despite fears that the legislature would hesitate to spend billions on canal improvements resulting only in 'certain advantages to shipping interests and . . . a desirable plaything for the Military', there was good reason to believe that a sea-level construction programme would be financed. On 22 December, however, the Panamanian National Assembly voted unanimously to reject the defence agreement on U.S. bases in the republic, and the reaction on Capitol Hill was furious. The chairman of the House Defense Appropriations Subcommittee vowed he would have funds withheld from canal development until Washington was given rights to defend the isthmus. Senator William Knowland spoke up on behalf of a Nicaragua waterway, with the enthusiastic support of President Anastasio Somoza. The possibility of a new canal in Panama seemed to have disappeared from sight.[111]

The miscarriage of the bases agreement came after more than a year of hard and often bitter negotiations beginning in the autumn of 1946. From the outset there was intense conflict between a Panama more than ever determined to assert its national rights and a United States as convinced as it always had been that the interests of canal defence overrode whatever claims Panama might enter.

The standard-bearer of Panamanian nationalism was Foreign Minister Alfaro. As preliminary discussions got under way, Alfaro warned that if Washington spent a great deal of money on the bases, it would be 'just the same as building a battleship which might be sunk at any moment'. Tenure of the sites would be for only one year at a time, and they must be placed under joint U.S.–Panamanian control.[112]

This was bad enough, but it also seemed possible that Alfaro would raise the bases issue at the United Nations General Assembly in New York. The Soviet Union had recently made mischief by questioning the presence of British and American forces on friendly terrain, and Ambassador Hines felt that a token concession might persuade Alfaro not to air the subject in public. Panama should be given a symbolic share in the operation of the bases, pending a new

[110] GB, 426–1, S.310, General Board report of 26.9.47. OA, NHC, CNO/SN 1940–7, CNO–HG, DuVal memo of 3.10.47. GB, 426–1, S.310, Sullivan to Royall, 16.10.47. NYT, 2.12.47, 24/6.

[111] PC, 9-A-14, Manning to Stratton, 9.4.47. NYT, 28.12.47, 10/1; sect. IV, 4/3; 24.12.47, 1/8; 25.12.47, 14/2, 20/3.

[112] SD, 1910–49, 711F.1914/9–1146, Chargé to Byrnes; /10–1246, enclosing Panama note of 8.10.46.

agreement, by bringing in one or two Panamanian officials and by hoisting Panama's flag over the sites. When Alfaro left for New York at the end of October, Hines tried but failed to work out an arrangement on these lines with his deputy, Carlos Sucre.[113]

Hines's efforts ran into immediate opposition. To Murray Wise it was highly inadvisable for the State Department 'to sacrifice principle in order to save Panamanian "face"', yet merely to sit tight and prove that 'Uncle Sam is not afraid of being bullied by small boys with a pea shooter' was unlikely to bring a solution closer. One answer might be an 'invitation' from Panama for U.S. detachments to stay in place while fresh terms were worked out, but that was too much for General Crittenberger to stomach. He objected to anything which detracted one iota from existing U.S. rights, and his own draft envisaged expanding the already huge base at Rio Hato, allowing U.S. troops to man-oeuvre throughout the republic, and giving Washington full control of Pan-ama's airways, roads, and telecommunications. The whole package, in Wise's view, went beyond even the voracious provisions of the 1903 canal treaty, and it stood no chance of acceptance.[114]

The deadlock was momentarily broken by a wholly unexpected intervention. Speaking at the United Nations on 21 November, Alfaro announced that Panama would protest if the United States failed to evacuate the bases promptly, and soon after privately threatened to tell the General Assembly that they were being held against Panama's wishes. His declaration, he believed, would gratify the Russians. When a report of the conversation reached the White House, Truman was said to have asked his foreign policy aide, Fleet Admiral Leahy, 'Why don't we get out of Panama gracefully before we are kicked out?' On 9 December, Truman instructed Byrnes to tell Alfaro that U.S. forces would withdraw from the bases forthwith. After a rushed Army briefing, Byrnes made no such promise but prevailed on Alfaro not to give Moscow ammunition in the General Assembly debate. Back in Washington he was quoted as saying that there was 'a lot more to Alfaro's complaints than the State Department had led him to believe'. In future the bases could perhaps be occupied under the doctrine of 'joint trusteeship', devised by Roosevelt to conciliate Alfaro during the negotiations for the 1936 treaty.[115]

Byrnes's foreign service advisers did not share his view. To Assistant Secretary

---

[113] YBUN 1946–47, 409. SD, 1910–49, 711F.1914/9–1746 and 10–2146.

[114] SD, 1910–49, 711F.1914/9–1746; 711.1928/10–2546. POD, 091 Panama, Crittenberger to Eisenhower, 26.9.46 and 25.10.46; 680.4, Case 4, Crittenberger to Eisenhower, 8.12.46. SD, 1910–49, 711F.1914/1–948, Wise memo of 13.1.48.

[115] NYT. 22.11.46, 18/4 SD, 1910–49, 711F.1914/12–846, Hines to Byrnes; /12–1146, Wise memo. POD, 381 Panama, Section 1-B (ABC file), Lincoln memo of 11.12.46. SD, 1910–49, 740.00119 Council/12–1246, Byrnes memo; 811.002/12–2446, Minutes of State–War–Navy meetings of 11.12.46 and 18.12.46; 711F.1914/12–1846.

Braden the resort to trusteeship was nothing short of appeasement, and he reckoned Alfaro had put one over on Byrnes. To offset the damage, he had Byrnes make it clear that Washington would not look at a lengthy set of Panamanian requests – including a call for a $25 million loan – until an agreement on the bases had been worked out. That said, the Army was persuaded to suspend the demand for more land at Rio Hato and to offer improvements in the Balboa ferry service so as to release Washington from the expensive commitment to build a bridge or a tunnel at the Pacific terminal. With these concessions up his sleeve, Wise was despatched to Panama to see if there were room for a compromise which would not only 'get around Dr Alfaro' but also circumvent the equally recalcitrant General Crittenberger.[116]

The Wise mission did not pull off the intended deal. For one thing, Sucre ignored the refusal to consider Panama's shopping list and continued to ask a rent which would raise the cost of Rio Hato from $10,000 to $350,000 a year. At the same time, President Enrique Jiménez wanted a form of trusteeship for the bases which Crittenberger found unacceptable. A Panamanian decree would sanction joint administration of the sites, which would thus be founded on 'consultation and mutual agreement rather than on a basis of the United States "requesting" and Panama "giving"'. The hard fact of ultimate American authority was to be discreetly buried in secret ancillary notes, and in Crittenberger's eyes this tortuous arrangement gave Panama a golden opportunity to trespass on U.S. jurisdiction. In December he had told Eisenhower that 'the only possible way for Panama to share in this responsibility to any sizable extent is to contribute willingly and patriotically the use of its sovereign soil as defense sites for the troops designated to do the fighting if such becomes necessary'. When Assistant Army Secretary Howard Petersen observed that 'the number one lesson about joint military command was demonstrated at Pearl Harbor', he was speaking for Crittenberger. Although the State Department went on to meet Panama halfway on the trusteeship issue, the general was still unreconciled.[117]

The other main obstacle to a settlement likewise remained in place. At the first negotiating session on 9 May, the other Panamanians present were visibly agitated when Alfaro insisted that trusteeship should give Panama a substantive role in the operation of the bases. While he relented soon afterwards, he refused to contemplate an extendable lease. He also made plain his determination not to be side-lined by an invitation to join a United Nations mission to hear a petition

[116] SD, 1910–49, 711F.1914/12–1746, Braden to Byrnes. POD, 091 Panama, Lincoln memo of 19.12.46. SD, 1910–49, 711F.1914/12–2346, Hines to Byrnes, 23.12.46; Byrnes to Hines, 27.12.46. POD, 686 TS, Crittenberger to Plans and Operations, 31.12.46. AG, post-1917, 091 Panama, Byrnes to Patterson, 14.1.47. POD, 091 Panama, Memo of 21.1.47. SD, 1910–49, 711F.1914/1–2147, Marshall to Wise, 24.1.47; /1–3047; /6–2348, Wise memo of 23.6.48.

[117] SD, 1910–49, 711F.1914/2–2047, Hines to Marshall; /2–1347; /2–447. POD, 091 Panama, Crittenberger to Eisenhower, 11.2.47. SAPF, Crittenberger to Eisenhower, 8.12.46. SD, 1910–49, 711F.1914/4–2547, Wise memo; /5–547, Crittenberger to Hines, 1.5.47.

for self-government from American Samoa – an assignment which would have put him out of circulation for months to come.[118]

Alfaro's assertiveness was an irritating thorn in Washington's side, but foreign ministers elsewhere were just as sensitive to the political repercussions of having U.S. bases on their soil. In October 1946 the American right to use the transatlantic staging post in Iceland was renewed for no more than five years. Portugal likewise granted only three to five years' tenure of the transit stop in the Azores, by the agreement eventually signed in February 1948. Denmark by that time was still reluctant to authorise air-base facilities in Greenland. All these negotiations were immensely frustrating to a country which had recently acquired the Pacific island clusters of the Marshalls, the Carolines, and the Marianas as a strategic trust territory in perpetuity, and which in March 1947 entered into a ninety-nine-year lease on bases in its erstwhile colony the Philippines. As another one-time protégé, Panama was expected to display similar generosity, and Alfaro's disobliging failure to meet American requirements was consequently hard to brook.[119]

Yet the Army's reaction was not to urge pressure on Panama, as General Van Voorhis had done in 1941. Instead Alfaro's intransigence fed growing doubts about the value of the bases. For one thing, it was unlikely that manpower and funds would be available for the elaborate anti-aircraft screen Crittenberger wanted. For another, the increasing possibility that a sea-level canal would replace the existing transit pointed to a defence structure which could afford to discard outlying bases because of the supposed impregnability of a seaway.[120]

Both points were made by General Robert Berry, Crittenberger's chief of staff, during a visit to Washington on the eve of the talks with Panama, and Alfaro's obstinacy in the opening sessions confirmed the feeling that a crossroads had been reached. On 20 May, Crittenberger was told to revise the current defence plan on the supposition that within the next ten years the main dangers to the canal from Russia would be sabotage, submarine-launched rocket attack, and a small air-strike. Since the planned air-defence net would be virtually useless against any of these contingencies, the risk of giving up the Panama bases could be taken. Not even the key site of Rio Hato was essential, and if it could not be kept on a thirty-year lease, it should be returned to Panama.[121]

Crittenberger felt bound to agree. The main reason for getting base rights

[118] SD, 1910–49, 711F.1914/5–1247, Collins memo of 10.5.47. POD, 091 Panama, Hines memo of 14.5.47. SD, 1910–49, 711F.1914/5–1747, Hines to Marshall.

[119] On Iceland, see *NYT*, 21.9.46, 1/4; on Portugal, 4.6.46, 11/3, and 4.2.48, 17/6. On Denmark, see *FRUS 1947*, 3: 657–87. On the Strategic Trust Territory in the Pacific, see *YBUN 1946–47*, 394–400. On the Philippines, see *NYT*, 15.3.47, 1/2.

[120] On Van Voorhis, see Chapter 12 at n. 57. POD, 381 Panama, Section 1-B (ABC file), Berry memo. of 7.5.47.

[121] POD, 686 TS, P & O to Crittenberger, 8.5.47; P & O memo of 9.5.47. POD, 091 Panama, Crittenberger to Eisenhower, 13, 17, and 22.5.47. POD, 686 TS, P & O to Crittenberger, 20.5.47.

was to develop the canal's defences in the period beyond the next decade, that is, when Russia had acquired the capability to mount a strategic onslaught on the isthmus via bombers or missiles. If Panama were unwilling to concede long-term tenure, negotiations might as well be broken off. American forces could then either be pulled back to the Zone or stand fast under the 1942 agreement.[122]

The advice was not taken. Ambassador Hines believed that withdrawal would provoke Panamanian charges of bad faith, and staying put was an equally unviable option. In July, Egypt had gone before the United Nations to claim that its 1936 alliance treaty with Britain did not entitle the British to keep bases on Egyptian soil, and the head of the State Department's UN office, Dean Rusk, predicted extensive political damage if Panama followed Cairo and arraigned Washington before the Security Council. So the negotiators pressed on, fortified by a helpful assurance from the Joint Chiefs that Panama remained a base area 'vital to the security of the United States'.[123]

The decision to keep talking eventually bore fruit. The main sticking point was the term for the lease of Rio Hato, which Alfaro insisted could not be more than ten years, and when Alfaro invoked student opposition to a new agreement, Marshall tried out a misguided piece of gunboat diplomacy. Why not send the battleship *Missouri* on a flag-showing visit to Panama and win over the students by inviting them on board? No doubt mindful that *Missouri* was where the Japanese had signed themselves into unconditional surrender, Alfaro declined the offer, and Marshall immediately changed tack. He had already chided his State Department advisers for letting the Army sell them 'a bill of goods' on the tenure issue when it could 'do with much less without serious harm'. In conference at the Pentagon he pronounced that fifteen years was as long as was necessary. If the defence establishment went on pursuing a thirty-year agreement, Alfaro might go public in the United Nations, and other negotiations could be prejudiced – almost certainly the discussions with Denmark over the much more important question of base facilities for the Air Force in Greenland. From this point on, Marshall was in sole charge, and the figure eventually settled on for Rio Hato was ten years, with the option of ten years more. On 10 December, Panama signed the agreement on these terms after Alfaro's resignation the previous day.[124]

Yet this was not the end of the story. Large-scale student demonstrations

[122] POD, 686 TS, Crittenberger to Eisenhower, 8.6.47, enclosing revision of JCS, 570/71.
[123] SD, 1910–49, 711F.1914/8–1247, Hines to Marshall. On Egypt, see *YBUN 1947–48*, 356, and *NYT*, 12.7.47, 1/4. SD, 1910–49, 711F.1914/8–3047, Rusk to Wright. JCS, 570/83 of 12.8.47.
[124] POD, 381 Panama, Section 1-B (ABC file), Memo of 20.8.47. Full text of Crittenberger draft is in *FRUS 1947*, 8: 906–12. SD, 1910–49, 711F.1914/9–1947, Crittenberger to Hines, 18.9.47; /9–1747; /9–2347, Memo of Marshall–Alfaro conversation; 819.2612/8–2250, Bennett memo; 711F 1914/9–2947, 10–1247, and 12 547.

erupted against the agreement, marshalled by Harmodio Arias. On 22 December, when the National Assembly gathered for its ratification vote, the galleries were crammed with hostile onlookers and the building surrounded by a vast intimidating mob. 'Nobody will vote for the bases', the Assembly's president had said, 'when he can look out the window and see ten thousand boys sharpening their knives.' He was right. The agreement was rejected unanimously, and Washington appeared to have suffered a stinging humiliation.[125]

Who was to blame? General Crittenberger was not alone in judging that the upsurge had been 'inspired and exploited by Communists'. The *New York Times* correspondent, Crede Calhoun, ascribed it, in part at least, to 'leftist labor leaders and professional anti-American agitators' who had closely followed 'the line laid down by . . . Soviet Foreign Secretary Molotov'. But Calhoun also saw a deeper reason for the rejection in the strains imposed by the presence of a rich foreign enclave in the heart of a state with a wretchedly low standard of living. So too did Murray Wise. The whole trend of U.S. policy since 1903 bore some of the responsibility: 'insufficient respect for Panamanian sovereignty' and more recently 'some lack of foresight in the psychological approach to a small country, the people of which have become extremely sensitive concerning matters of national pride'. Most culpable of all were the Zonians, who had nurtured 'an ingrown provincial Americanism which has been severely critical and even disdainful of Panamanians'. Seen in this light, the Assembly vote manifested an explosion of resentment against everything the Zone stood for, and at a time when anti-colonialism was on the march it was an uncomfortable augury for future relations between Washington and Panama.[126]

Meanwhile recriminations flew back and forth at high speed. Wise condemned the Army for allowing an intransigent Crittenberger to call the tune for so long. Senator Arthur Vandenberg, for his part, zeroed in on the State Department. Why, he asked one hapless official, had the department put its name to such an obviously unacceptable deal? It was a body-blow to pan-American solidarity when one of the smallest members of 'the family' refused to grant the use of its territory for hemisphere protection and the supposedly binding Rio defence treaty now appeared to be 'meaningless'.[127]

Panama certainly seemed to have inflicted a sharp defeat on Washington when, the day after the Assembly vote, the decision was taken to evacuate the bases forthwith. The move was naturally presented to the American public as

[125] SD, 1910–49, 711F.1914/12–1347; 819.4212/12–1547. On the students in 1945, see Chapter 11 at n. 60. SD, 1910–49, 819.00/11–2348, Bennett memo of 8.12.48; 711F.1914/12–1547 and 2–2648. *NYT*, 28.12.47, 10/1; sect. IV, 4/3. SD, 1910–49, 711F.1914/12–2347.
[126] POD, 091 Panama, Crittenberger to Eisenhower, 23.12.47. *NYT*, 28.12.47, 10/1. SD, 1910–49, 711F.1914/1–948, Wise memo.
[127] SD, 1910–49, 711F.1914/1–948, Wise memo; /12–2447, Newbigin memo of conversation with Vandenberg.

a statesmanlike act of policy, via James Reston of the *New York Times*. If the Pentagon had refused to budge from Panama, explained Reston, 'the whole moral argument against Soviet tactics in the Dardanelles, Iran and Eastern Europe would have been challenged, and nobody here was prepared to pay that price for the bases'.[128]

This gloss concealed the fact that the military establishment was far from disconcerted by the way things had turned out. Behind the scenes the Army confided to the State Department that it felt 'no dissatisfaction about the evacuation'. When the withdrawal was completed, Marshall noted that the Zone commanders felt the failure of the agreement 'probably was a blessing in disguise'. The Air Force was interested only in acquiring a few sites as radar stations and in using Rio Hato for transit and technical stops. In January the long-range air defence of the canal moved to the outer perimeter of the Caribbean, with the transfer of B-29 reconnaissance bombers to Waller Field, Trinidad, where, of course, the United States enjoyed a ninety-nine-year lease dating from the destroyers-for-bases deal of September 1940.[129]

Panama's repudiation of the bases agreement was nothing less than a watershed in the history of canal defence. Not even the confrontation with Russia over the Soviet blockade of West Berlin which began in the spring of 1948 was enough to revive American interest. Army Chief of Staff Omar Bradley brushed aside the idea of new negotiations, and though the possibility of denying passage to Soviet and East European vessels was discussed, the only precaution believed necessary was a thorough search to forestall sabotage. Since Moscow had no other means of reaching the waterway, this was enough.[130]

Come the autumn, when commanding general Matthew Ridgway submitted a list of sites required in an emergency, there was again no inclination to approach Panama, though the new régime of Domingo Díaz was reported to see a bases agreement as critical to the republic's economy. After the Assembly's vote, the veteran newspaperman Nelson Rounsevell wrote that the Panamanians had 'killed the goose that has laid the only golden eggs dropped on the Isthmus in half a century [and] bitten their economic nose off to vent their spite against the Gringos'. That was characteristic Rounsevellian hyperbole, but it was certainly true that the financial importance of the bases to Panama now far outstripped their military value to Washington. In February 1949 Secretary of State Dean Acheson told Ambassador Monnett Davis that negotiations had been shelved indefinitely. The following October, Ridgway indicated that the Defense Department would actually be embarrassed if Panama broached the

[128] POD, 091 Panama, P & O memo of 23.12.47. *NYT*, 24.12.47, 1/8.
[129] SD, 1910–49, 711F.1914/1–1248, Bennett memo; /2–1948, Marshall to Lovett. POD, 091 Panama, P & O memo of 28.1.48. *NYT*, 30.12.47, 7/2.
[130] JCS, 570/95, Bradley memo of 17.5.48. SD, 1910–49, 811F.812 Protection/5–648, 5–748, 5–1048, and 5–2548. POD, 560 TS, P & O memo of 2.8.48.

issue again, since it would be forced into a public denial of its need for any installations outside the Zone.[131]

As it happened, there was no call for such a statement, since the defence establishment had already publicised its downgrading of Panama. Writing in the *Saturday Evening Post* in October 1948, the journalist Sidney Shalett stated that 'we are taking the calculated risk of leaving the canal virtually without airplanes, radar, anti-aircraft batteries and ground soldiers, on the theory that we can rush them down there in a hurry if anything happens first in Berlin or Korea'. All this – as Admiral Daniel Barbey told Shalett – because the Navy no longer saw the canal as one of its foremost assets.[132]

The same message was passed to the defence correspondent of the *New York Times*, Hanson Baldwin, who reported that to the Navy the canal's significance was logistical, not strategic. It remained necessary, but not so much for the passage of its warships as for shuttling its transports in order to relieve the burden on the transcontinental railways. For the Army the isthmus was now important mainly as 'a good listening post and intelligence center for much of Latin America', and it did not greatly miss the Panama bases. They would probably be required in wartime, 'but today the United States does not have the men to man them, even if their use were granted'.[133]

It followed that plans for canal modernisation were now so much waste paper. In August 1948 the Joint Chiefs' planners affirmed that funds for bigger locks could not be justified. And although a bill for a sea-level waterway was introduced into the Senate in May 1949, it made no progress.[134]

Assessing the status of the canal in midsummer 1949, Captain DuVal concluded that the isthmus was 'no longer the strategic center of the Americas for war' and that the importance of Panama had dwindled with 'the consolidation of potential land powers, the increasing destructiveness of modern weapons, and the relocation of the industrialization of the United States'. The security of the United States did not depend on an impregnable trans-isthmian canal; on the contrary, the security of the canal hinged on American military and industrial might. In saying this, DuVal was primarily interested in driving another nail into the coffin of the sea-level project, but his analysis was sound none the less. A waterway built for the Navy of a previous era had lost its strategic rationale, and in a world where Washington had taken on manifold responsibilities its relevance was secondary at best.[135]

---

[131] POD, 091 Panama, P & O memo of 22.10.48. SD, 1910–49, 711F.1914/10-948; /1–2148, quoting Rounsevell in the *Nation* for 20.1.48; /2–349, Acheson to Davis, 28.2.49; /10–1049, Bennett memo.

[132] Sidney Shalett, 'Can we defend the Panama Canal?' *Saturday Evening Post*, 9 October 1948, 16, 162–3.

[133] *NYT*, 5.3.49, 6/4; 6.3.49, 12/3–4.

[134] JCS, 1778/6 of 14.9.48 and 30.3.49. PC, 9-A-11, S.1917 of 23.5.49.

[135] OA, NHC, DuVal Papers, DuVal memo of 6.6.49.

In this recessional climate, the only defence-related accord of any substance was the civil aviation agreement concluded in March 1949, and even this was less concerned with canal protection than with keeping Panama on its traditional leash. The Army's draft agreement framed in 1946 gave the Zone authorities effective supervision of the national airport the Panamanians had said they would start building at Tocúmen soon after the war was over. Air traffic control, customs and immigration to the Zone, sanitation and quarantine, and handling of passengers, baggage, cargo, and mail were all to be under the direction of a joint board whose American members would have the decisive say. When the draft was presented in 1948, the Panamanians immediately demanded changes, and Governor Mehaffey, who had consistently opposed the Army's heavy-handed approach, was in broad sympathy. Commanding General Ridgway most emphatically was not, urging a revocable arrangement which would allow the Zone to re-establish a civil air terminal at Albrook whenever it chose. But he was overruled: The agreement was modified, and at the end of August 1949 all U.S. airlines using Albrook transferred to Tocúmen.[136]

A companion agreement on radio communications did not materialise. The radio convention of 1936 had not been approved by the Senate, but the Navy did not press for ratification. Its indifference contrasted markedly with the impassioned interest it had taken in the subject during the thirties, and it was yet another indication of the way in which the canal had slipped down the defence hierarchy's scale of priorities over the past decade.[137]

The outbreak of the Korean war in June 1950 did nothing to change this attitude. Over the next three years, no less than 54 million tons of cargo and 22 million tons of petroleum products went through the canal to the United Nations forces under American command. But this logistical triumph did not bring with it the revival of the isthmus as an armed camp. In August, President Arnulfo Arias made a number of offers in the hope of setting Panama back in the forefront of U.S. strategic thinking, but only one of them was taken up. Use of the 950 merchant ships sailing under the Panamanian flag was accepted, and in the summer of 1951 Panama – if only after considerable American pressure – agreed to ban ships under its registry from trading directly or indirectly with Communist China and North Korea.[138]

The other tenders were politely declined, among them volunteers for the UN army in the field. The Joint Chiefs of Staff refused to mobilise a Latin

[136] POD, 091 Panama, Draft of 17.1.46. SD, 1910–49, 711.1927/7–3146. POD, 091 Panama, Memo of 29.3.48, Mehaffey comments of 30.4.48, revised draft of 7.6.48, and Ridgway to Bradley, 18.1.49. SD, 1910–49, 711.1927/3–3149; 711.19/7–149.

[137] POD, 676.3, Crittenberger to Eisenhower, 7.8.46; 091 Panama, Case 20, Hanson to C-in-C, Caribbean Command, 12.7.49; Ridgway to Bradley, 30.9.49.

[138] 1960 Hearings, 92–3. SD, 1950–4, 795B.5/8–250; 795.00/8–750. NYT, 4.8.50, 7/2. SD, 1950–4, 795B.5/10–1050; 919.537/6–2551, 8–1451, and 8–651. NYT, 20.8.51, 37/1.

American brigade of unorganised irregulars, and Haiti, Honduras, Costa Rica, and Panama were all deemed incapable of raising effective ground forces. Nor did the Pentagon welcome Arias's proposal that Rio Hato and its vicinity become a training area for UN troops. The cost of reactivating the Rio Hato complex would be prohibitive, and no foreseeable use now existed for bases in Panama.[139]

In the treaty signed in January 1955, the Army leased Rio Hato as a manoeuvre ground, but the negotiating time the deal took up was fractional in comparison with the man-hours put into defence issues in past agreements. This was a telling index of the strategic importance attached to the canal in the mid 1950s. Already in serious doubt at the beginning of the post-war decade, by its end it had shrunk irreversibly. Marginalised by the two-ocean Navy, dwarfed by the super-carrier, and defenceless against a nuclear strike, the waterway had become no more than a monument to the era when Washington first stepped decisively on to the international stage. Then it had linked the United States' divergent commitments in the Pacific and the hemisphere. Now, with the defeat of the Axis, the onset of the cold war, and the break-up of Europe's overseas empires, American preoccupations were nothing short of global and immensely more demanding than the effort to reconcile the competing claims of Atlantic and Pacific through the medium of Panama. The canal remained an impressive emblem of American power, but it would never again be its mainstay.[140]

---

[139] SD, 1950–4, 795B.5/7–2750, 9–1250, 9–2350, and 10–1050 (Acheson to Marshall, 1.11.50).
[140] SD, 1950–4, 611.1913/9–1354, 9–1554, and 10–1854. Text of the relevant article of the 1955 treaty is in *BD*, 995–6.

Part IV

Recessional: 1956–1979

The basic problem . . . is the exercise of American control over a part of the territory of Panama in this age of intense nationalist and anticolonialist feeling. . . . It seems to me entirely proper and necessary for the United States to take the initiative in proposing new arrangements that would redress some of Panama's grievances. . . . Surely, in a confrontation so unequal, it is not unreasonable to expect the United States to go a little further than half-way in the search for a fair settlement.

(William Fulbright, *Old myths and new realities,*
1964)

The future security and well-being of the United States are threatened by the administration's proposed abandonment of sovereignty over the Panama Canal and the Canal Zone. . . . A U.S. retreat from Panama would prob-ably put the last nail in the coffin of the Monroe Doctrine. . . . If we will not stand fast in our own backyard, if we compromise and equivocate and retreat about an issue as vital as the Panama Canal and an area as strategic as the Caribbean, where will we stand?

(Hanson Baldwin, *AEI Defense Review*, 1977)

13

The reluctant handover

In the 1955 treaty with Panama the fundamentals of Washington's position in the Canal Zone remained unshaken. The treaty it signed in 1977, on the other hand, liquidated the Zone and promised the transfer of the canal itself to Panama in 1999. This was nothing short of a revolution. How did it happen?

The starting point came when the Egyptian nationalist leader, Colonel Nasser, expropriated the Suez Canal Company in July 1956. The seizure immediately sharpened American fears that the Panamanians would revive the extreme claims they had entered in the recent treaty negotiations. On the eve of the Egyptian nationalisation, indeed, President Eisenhower himself had warned his secretary of defense, Charles Wilson, that Washington 'must be exceedingly careful that the future years do not bring about for us, in Panama, the situation that Britain has to face in the Suez'.[1]

Eisenhower was writing after months of strained relations with Panama caused by the U.S. Army's demand for radar sites on Panamanian territory at a time when Congress was in no apparent hurry to enact implementing legislation for the new treaty. To some the blame for the unpleasantness rested entirely with Panama, which Ambassador Julian Harrington was convinced wanted posts in the canal's managerial structure as a first step towards outright take-over. The remedy, in his view, was 'a good scare such as the threat of a completely in-dependent operation in the Zone with a fence around it and non-Panamanian people working inside it. . . . The Panamanians should not rely too heavily on our traditional generosity and tendency to be soft.' Eisenhower, for his part, preached conciliation. The United States, he told Wilson, should be '*more than*

---

[1] On Suez, see William Roger Louis and Roger Owen (eds.), *Suez 1956: The crisis and its consequences* (Oxford, 1989), and Keith Kyle, *Suez* (London, 1991). See also Herman Finer, *Dulles over Suez: The theory and practice of his diplomacy* (London, 1964). Eisenhower to Wilson, 25.7.56, is quoted in *FRUS 1955–1957*, 7: 281.

ready to meet them halfway', though '*without* incurring the risk of divided control beclouding our clear title to ownership'. Two weeks later Nasser's bombshell had torn a large hole in this moderation. Told by Secretary of State John Foster Dulles that Panama was in close diplomatic contact with Egypt, Eisenhower exploded with the promise that 'if we left the Panama Zone, we would take the locks with us'. Negotiations on a Nicaragua canal, moreover, now began to seem an attractive bargaining counter 'so that we would not be subject to blackmail'.[2]

The administration's displeasure was also conveyed in Panama's exclusion from Dulles's briefing for Latin American ambassadors in Washington on 7 August. Nor was Panama invited to the conference of Suez Canal users which opened in London shortly afterwards, in spite of the fact that a high percentage of the world's merchant shipping sailed under its registry. Panama's omission from the guest list was designed to prevent it from making a nuisance of itself in the international forum which the London conference provided, and on 29 August Dulles agreed with Eisenhower that its 'conniving with Nasser' should be punished by starting up talks on a Nicaragua canal.[3]

It followed that President Ricardo Arias's bid for a seat on the board of the Panama Canal Company was instantly rebuffed. Nor was any notice taken of the Panamanian statement that the republic sought 'royalties' from the Company's proceeds equal to the increased annuity granted in 1955. In brushing Panama aside, of course, Washington knew it ran no risk. As the London *Times* commented, 'Panama's only military force is its lightly armed National Guard, . . . and a physical grab, in emulation of Colonel Nasser, can thus be written off.' Panama could do no more than put its case on the record at every available opportunity. At a conference of jurists in March 1957, ex-foreign minister Octavio Fábrega urged that agreements in perpetuity, such as the canal convention of 1903, should be declared invalid, since they were inconsistent with national sovereignty. In May the ambassador to Britain, Roberto Arias, pointed out that whereas Egypt after 1949 had received 7 per cent of the Suez Company's gross income from tolls, Panama got no such revenue. In December the Panamanian representative at the United Nations contrasted Panama's fee from the waterway with the 50 per cent share of profits passed on by Western oil companies to Venezuela and the states of the Middle East.[4]

Panama's awareness of its comparatively poor return was coupled with rising

---

[2] SD, 1955–60, 611.1913/10–1955. *NYT*, 11.8.56, 2/3–5. *FRUS 1955–1957*, 7: 268, 281, 291 (emphasis in original).

[3] Finer, *Dulles*, 131–2. *NYT*, 5.8.56, 1/8; 16.8.56, 2/3–5. U.S. Department of State, *The Suez Canal problem: July 26 – September 22, 1956* (Washington, D.C., 1956), 301. *FRUS 1955–1957*, 7: 302.

[4] PCC, 65-J-3/M, Boyd to Harrington, 12.9.56. *NYT*, 21.8.56, 4/5. *Times*, 17.4.57, 9/5. *NYT*, 31.3.57, 15/1. *Times*, 1.5.57, 11/5. *NYT*, 28.12.57, 24/1.

anger at the continuing tardiness of Congress in reforming the Zone's inequitable employment system, as pledged by the 1955 treaty. On 2 May 1958 Panamanian students protested by marching into the Zone to plant fifty national flags, and though the irruption was dismissed by the canal authorities as theatrical nonsense, within three months an employment Act was on the statute book.[5]

The new arrangement fell well short of Panama's expectations, however, and Panamanian leaders made their disappointment plain to the president's brother, Milton Eisenhower, during his visit to the isthmus. He returned to Washington convinced that more was needed to take the edge off their resentment and to counter an Egyptian legation in Panama City 'trying subversively to promote a "Suez situation"'. His answer was a package of goodwill offerings: subsidies for low-cost housing in Panama; modest wage increases for the Company's unskilled Panamanian workers; consideration of loans for economic diversification; and an agreement to fly the Panamanian flag at selected sites in the Zone on ceremonial occasions.[6]

Though the concessions were accepted by the White House, they were too much for Congress, the Army, and the canal directorate and were immediately blocked. Early in October 1959, however, after reports that trouble was brewing in Panama, the president called for an urgent review of the Zone's pay structure. It revealed that Panamanians held only 15 per cent of white-collar jobs and that there was a significant gap between the lowest point on the U.S.-rate scale and the highest rung on the local-rate ladder. It reminded him, Eisenhower said later, of the Army at the time he was commissioned in 1915, when an inexperienced second lieutenant was better paid than a top master sergeant. But there was no time to act, and on Panama's independence day, 3 November, the terminal cities erupted in a massive anti-American protest.[7]

What began as an attempt by former Foreign Minister Aquilino Boyd and the historian Ernesto Castillero Pimentel to plant the Panamanian flag in the Zone soon escalated into widespread rioting. Seen in conjunction with the Cuban revolution inaugurated by Fidel Castro the preceding January, the episode marked a serious challenge to American power, and though on Cuba Eisenhower took a hard line, on Panama he worked for an accommodation. At a meeting on 27 November he recalled that after the Suez crisis of 1956 he and Dulles had discussed Panama repeatedly and sought to head off anything 'comparable to what had occurred in Egypt'. This now meant treaty adjustments 'to insure that our provisions stand for right and not for mere letter of the law'. Among other

[5] *NYT*, 3.5.58, 4/3. The text of the statute of 25 July 1958 is in *BD*, 1034–40.
[6] Milton Eisenhower, *The wine is bitter: The United States and Latin America* (New York, 1963), 213, 215–16, 221–3.
[7] Eisenhower, *Wine is bitter*, 223. *DDRS, 1981*, 449A, briefing on 12.10.59. *DDRS, 1982*, 1377 and 1379, conferences with Eisenhower of 12.10.59 and 27.11.59. *FRUS 1958–1960*, 5: MS, 611.19/10–1259 and 10–2859. *NYT*, 3.11.59, 13/3; 4.11.59, 1/3.

things, the Panamanian flag should be flown 'in some ceremonial spot along with the American flag' in token of the U.S. recognition that Panama had titular sovereignty in the Canal Zone. A few days later he made his view public at his regular press conference.[8]

Yet again, however, Eisenhower ran into stubborn resistance. In 1906 the first governor of the Zone, General George Davis, had doubted whether his administration had the right to fly the Stars and Stripes. Half a century later such scruples were long since a thing of the past, and Eisenhower's opponents were adamant that the Panamanian *bandera* must not be allowed on Zone territory. 'If that flag goes up,' predicted Congressman Daniel Flood, 'you are a dead pigeon sooner or later. . . . The day it is formally hoisted marks the beginning of the end of exclusive U.S. control over the Panama Canal.' Governor William Potter was sure that flying the flag was 'not an ultimate step; it [was] merely the next step [in] a constant 50-year erosion of our position'. The Zone authorities were said to be ready to bow to the display of both national colours only if Panama agreed that this would be 'a virtual quit claim for further Panamanian sovereignty ambitions in the Zone' – a stipulation they knew full well no Panamanian government could possibly accept. Nothing less would have satisfied the House of Representatives, which had overwhelmingly endorsed a resolution that no Panamanian flag should fly in the Zone unless a new treaty were first approved by the Senate.[9]

Given the strength of feeling on Capitol Hill, Eisenhower bypassed Congress in making his response to Panama. In April 1960 a presidential directive promised more skilled and supervisory posts to Panamanians, gave unskilled and semi-skilled workers a 10 per cent wage rise, and funded 1,000 new houses for Panamanians on U.S. payrolls. At the same time, a State Department planning paper had much more fundamental changes in mind, as Secretary of State Christian Herter put it, 'to avoid particularly the increase of sentiment favorable to Castro in Panama where there was much social pressure on the part of unhappy elements'. The new deal would also serve to build the 'politico-psychological atmosphere' needed to clinch a treaty for a sea-level canal across the isthmus. The project had just been recommended by the Company after a year's study initiated by Eisenhower, and its revival came after more than a decade in the wilderness. Three times in the 1950s the Joint Chiefs of Staff had reaffirmed that it was not a vital strategic requirement, but for Herter its justification was political, since it would be a key part of the effort to prevent a Castroist revolution in Panama. Once completed, it would render the old lock

[8] *FRUS 1958–1960*, 5: MS, 719.00/11–2759. *DDRS, 1982,* 1379. *BD*, 1046, 1047. Milton Eisenhower had recommended display of the Panamanian flag in the Zone on his return from his visit to Panama in the summer of 1958: See Eisenhower, *Wine is bitter*, 221–3.

[9] *1906 Hearings*, 3: 2260. *1960 Hearings*, 12, 4, 74, 43, 45. *NYT*, 22.2.60, 3/6; 3.2.60, 18/5.

canal superfluous, and so the State Department was prepared to contemplate its transfer to Panama as soon as the new seaway was in operation.[10]

The plan raised a host of imponderables. For one thing, would Panama be content to take over a canal which would effectively be a white elephant? For another, would Congress be willing to fund a scheme with an estimated price-tag of more than $2.5 billion when improvement of existing facilities would cost much less? Most important, would Congress stomach the abandonment of a possession for generations the emblem of American glory? In June the House Committee on Merchant Marine and Fisheries gave its answer: The waterway should be modernised, not replaced, and it must be kept under complete American control.[11]

Battle between executive and legislature over future canal policy was thus squarely joined, but the most immediate bone of contention between them was the flag issue. Eisenhower was acutely sensitive to what he called the 'jingoistic criticism' coming from the Hill, and in August he told Herter he aimed to make a move 'the day after Congress which would keep Flood from going crazy'. This he did by prescribing that American and Panamanian flags be flown daily side by side in Shaler's Triangle, a small plot of Zone land jutting into Panama City close to the Tivoli Hotel. He signed the order knowing it had all the appearance of action under duress, and with the gloomy prediction that 'some other type of blackmail will follow'.[12]

Assistant Secretary Ray Rubottom had put it rather differently. Flying the Panamanian flag 'would not curtail for long the demands [nor] ease the pressures over the long run in Panama'. He was entirely correct. In the autumn of 1961 President Roberto Chiari asked Eisenhower's successor, John Kennedy, for treaty revision and a bigger annuity, and the National Assembly then set out a long series of claims on Washington. Most of them repeated the maximalist petition of right presented back in 1953. A new treaty should scrap the perpetuity clause of the 1903 convention and make U.S. tenure finite. Meanwhile Panamanian sovereignty over the Zone should be recognised and Panama be granted complete jurisdiction over the terminal ports. Mixed courts should be

[10] BD, 1050–1. FRUS 1958–1960, 5: MS, 711.19/4–660; ARA/OAP Files, Lot 63D127, 'Panama 1960', meeting of 29.3.60; Eisenhower Library, Whitman File, Cabinet Series, Minutes of Cabinet meeting of 22.5.59. DDRS, 1980, 365B, memo for Radford of 23.10.56. DDRS, 1981, 166B, Joint Strategic Plans Committee to Joint Chiefs of Staff, 21.10.57. FRUS 1955–1957, 7: 348–9, Cutler to Adams, 19.11.57. NYT, 10.7.60, 1/6; 12.8.60, 5/2. FRUS 1958–1960, 5: MS, ARA/OAP Files, Lot 63D127, 'Panama 1960', meeting of 29.3.60, TAB E, undated study by Policy Planning Staff.

[11] Georgetown University, Center for Strategic Studies, Panama Canal: Issues and treaty talks (Washington, D.C., 1967), 81. NYT, 15.6.60, 3/1. BD, 1374.

[12] FRUS 1958–1960, 5: MS, 611.19/9–160; Eisenhower Library, Herter Papers, Telephone Conversations, 9.8.60. BD, 1058. DDRS, 1983, 1941, memo of 13.9.60. DDRS, 1984, 1164, Eisenhower conversation with Farland, 9.8.60. DDRS, 1977, 255B, conference of 1.9.60.

established in the Zone and Panama given a 'fair share' of canal revenues and 'effective equality' for its citizens in Zone employment. The Panamanian flag should fly on all public buildings in the Zone and on all ships in transit through the canal. Disputes between the United States and Panama should go to arbitration.[13]

Acceptance of these far-reaching proposals would, of course, have destroyed the entire U.S. position in the Zone, and Kennedy told Chiari that while he was prepared to discuss liberalisation of existing treaties, he would not consider their basic revision. Or not, at least, until Washington had investigated the feasibility of excavating a sea-level canal with nuclear explosives, an inquiry that was expected to take five years.[14]

Kennedy's willingness to explore the sea-level project was entirely in line with Eisenhower's thinking, but there were sizeable doubts as to its viability. In October 1959 Eisenhower had remarked that 'one good missile with an atomic warhead could knock out one whole end of the Canal structure', and soon afterwards Admiral James Russell testified that there was no appreciable difference between a lock canal and a sea-level waterway when it came to their vulnerability to a nuclear strike. And though in December 1960 the National Security Council recommended nuclear excavation of a seaway, to be completed by 1980, its report admitted that in the current state of the art nuclear devices 'could not be used within 50 miles of any densely populated area'.[15]

Both Kennedy's Latin America Task Force and an interdepartmental review group concluded, however, that the sea-level probe had value as a means of keeping dialogue with Panama off the high ground of fundamentals. Meanwhile, as Kennedy himself put it, Washington could come forth with a number of sweeteners: 'an appropriate flow of concrete results in order to contain Panamanian pressure for immediate and radical treaty revision'.[16]

In the event, such concrete results as emerged from the discussions were negligible: a few concessions on employment and an agreement to raise the two national flags wherever the civilian authorities in the Zone flew the Stars and Stripes. The talks were wound up at Panama's request on 23 July 1963, and Panamanian disappointment turned to anger when the United States signed the test-ban treaty on 5 August. Although the treaty permitted underground tests,

[13] *1960 Hearings*, 74. *NYT*, 12.9.61, 15/5; 18.11.61, 9/2. Eisenhower, *Wine is bitter*, 225.

[14] *DDRS*, *1981*, 505A, NSAM no. 152 of 30.4.62. *DDRS*, *1983*, 1445, Kennedy to Chiari, 30.4.62. *DDRS*, *1985*, 1165, memo of 8.5.62. William Jorden, *Panama odyssey* (Austin, Tex., 1984), 32–4.

[15] *DDRS*, *1982*, 1377, Eisenhower memo of 12.10.59. *1960 Hearings*, 97, 100. *DDRS*, *1984*, 1280, NSC 6026 of 29.12.60.

[16] Margaret Scranton, 'Changing United States foreign policy: Negotiating new Panama Canal treaties, 1958–1978' (doctoral diss., University of Pittsburgh, 1980), 146, 148–9, 150–1, 154. *DDRS*, *1981*, 505B, NSAM no. 164 of 15.6.62.

it prevented the Atomic Energy Commission from developing cratering technology to the point where it could be proven safe and cost-effective. The Panamanians had not been warned of this, and they had based their consent to postpone full treaty negotiations on the premise of nuclear excavation. Now they felt betrayed, in company with the U.S. ambassador, Joseph Farland, who resigned on 2 August, and Kennedy added insult to injury by ignoring Chiari's appeal for 'interim compensation' of $50 million over the five years he had supposed would be the prelude to negotiations proper. The slight was coupled with a sharp American U-turn over the key issue of perpetuity. In June 1962 a joint U.S.–Panama memorandum had stated that the decision on whether or not to go ahead with a sea-level canal 'will make the question of perpetuity obsolete because a new treaty will have to be negotiated in either case'. After the collapse of the talks, however, the review group concluded that 'no changes should (though they could) be made regarding perpetuity'. In other words, the central Panamanian demand for wholesale revision of the 1903 convention was still an impossibility as far as Washington was concerned.[17]

Relations between Washington and Panama were thus at a low ebb when the worst crisis of their sixty-year history exploded in January 1964. It was touched off by the highly charged issue of flags. The agreement to display both flags at civilian locations in the Zone had been interpreted by Governor Robert Fleming as applying to seventeen designated sites. These did not include schools, and the American pupils at Balboa High School defied government policy by hoisting their flag outside the school building. A counter-demonstration by Panamanian students on 9 January swiftly led to large-scale riots in Panama City and Colón which left at least twenty-two dead, three of them Americans.[18]

In the view of Governor Fleming, blame for the calamity lay on the American side. Fleming saw the flag protest as 'the perfect situation for the guy who's 150 percent American – and 50 percent whiskey'. In his judgement it was 'the extremists among the Zonian population whose actions set the stage for the January blowup', but he also targeted Washington for failing to take 'more positive action on obvious and frequently reported problems before these ballooned up to become unmanageable'.[19]

President Lyndon Johnson was acutely sensitive to this charge. Fearing he

---

[17] BD, 1066–8. Scranton diss., 164. Georgetown University, Panama Canal, 18, 55. NYT, 26.4.63, 8/4; 3.8.63, 5/1. DDRS, 1988, 258–61, Review Group memos of 23.4.63, 7.6.63, 12.7.63, 24.10.63. DDRS, 1984, 400, status report of 11.6.63. Jorden, Panama odyssey, 33 quoting joint memo of 15.6.62.

[18] Jorden, Panama odyssey, 34–53. See also the report on the riots by the International Commission of Jurists in BD, 1099–142.

[19] Trevor Armbrister, 'Panama: Why they hate us – More than one torn flag', Saturday Evening Post, 7 March 1964, 77. DDRS, 1983, 2666, Fleming to Adair, 12.4.66.

might be accused of 'knowing exactly what was going to happen and not doing anything', he did not want 'to have a Pearl Harbor type situation on his hands'. But as in 1941, recriminations were engulfed in the rush to cope with the immediate fall-out of the débâcle. The violent Panamanian response to the flag incident almost certainly had the tacit blessing of President Chiari, whose party faced an election in May and who quickly proclaimed that the January martyrs must be requited by complete revision of the existing treaties. Johnson, who was also up for election, rejected the idea of revision point-blank. Chiari, he wrote in his memoirs, was exploiting the disturbances 'to try to exact a new treaty from me by force', and he was not about to give Panama that satisfaction.[20]

As reported by the ambassador to the United Nations, Adlai Stevenson, Panama wanted nothing short of a treaty which abandoned perpetuity, recognised its sovereignty over the Zone, and gave it an equal share of benefits from the waterway. There was no mention of Panama taking on any operating responsibility, since nobody in Panama was thought to be suggesting that Panamanians were capable of handling the complex canal mechanism. Even so, acceptance of the Panamanian demands would signify the end of a long chapter in U.S. history, and for the great majority of Americans that was unthinkable. Very few indeed would have gone along with Senator William Fulbright's call to rewrite the 1903 convention 'and disabuse ourselves of the myth that there is something morally sacred about it'. The most Johnson was prepared to say was that the convention 'perhaps would require adjustment', and the policy response sketched out behind the scenes gave little away. A civilian governor would be appointed, together with a Panamanian advisory committee for a Company board which, in the diplomatic words of Under Secretary of State George Ball, was 'now not attuned to the situation in Panama'. The Zonian élite of the work force would be put on short-term contracts to break down their deep-rooted attachment to the status quo. Panama would be offered better job opportunities, plus the right to open shops and warehouses in the Zone, and the annuity would be substantially increased, but that was all. Agree to thorough-going revision, predicted Assistant Secretary Thomas Mann, 'and the Panamanians will demand new changes before the ink is even dry on the new treaty'.[21]

Mann saw the answer to revisionism in the project the test-ban treaty seemed to have killed off: the sea-level canal. It also held considerable attraction for the Pentagon, and, once resurrected, it remained at the centre of U.S. negotiating strategy throughout Johnson's tenure. In 1960 Governor Potter had seen the

[20] DDRS, 1987, 003558, Smith memo of meeting of 13.1.64. NYT, 11.1.64, 1/3, 1/4, 1/8. Lyndon Johnson, The vantage-point: Perspectives of the presidency, 1963–1969, (London, 1972), 180.

[21] DDRS, 1978, 426D, Stevenson memo of conversation, 21.1.64. DDRS, 1979, 44A, memo of 12.2.64. NYT, 26.3.64, 1/2; 1.3.64, 31/1. DDRS, 1987, 001501, memo of 17.1.64; 003558, Smith memo of meeting of 13.1.64.

merits of a transit which would require only a hundred American personnel to run it. It would thus eliminate that affluent community which Army counsel Joseph Califano was to identify as a root-cause of the 1964 riots, juxtaposed as it was next to the underprivileged masses of the terminal cities. The sea-level cut would be sited well away from the main population centres. Like Suez, it would have no 'buffer area', and, once in operation, the defunct lock canal, together with the Canal Zone, could safely be transferred to Panama. Until then both must stay under effective U.S. authority.[22]

The administration's negotiating position was developed further as soon as relations with Panama had been restored to normal on 3 April, through a Panama Review Group chaired by Mann, with Secretary of the Army Stephen Ailes; Johnson's special representative, Robert Anderson; and his White House aide, Walt W. Rostow, as members. Its junior counterpart on the isthmus comprised Governor Fleming, Ambassador Jack Hood Vaughn, and the garrison commander in the Zone, General Andrew O'Meara.[23]

The Pentagon's outline of a treaty was submitted to Johnson in midsummer. It envisaged an increased annuity, appointment of some Panamanian directors to the Company board, the conveyance to Panama of whatever tracts of Zone land were not used for Company purposes. In return, Panama would subscribe to a Status of Forces Agreement (SOFA) which would set no limits on the U.S. right to protect the canal. The sea-level waterway built to replace it would remain under American control for at least fifty years, and the SOFA would be extended to maintain U.S. defence rights over the seaway for as long as need be.[24]

None of this touched the cardinal issues of sovereignty or perpetuity. Nor did the blueprint drafted by Mann. The present canal, in Mann's opinion, was 'a wasting asset which will become obsolete in a relatively short period of time'. But that was no reason to hand it over to Panama lock, stock, and barrel. Only tactical concessions were in order – the Panamanian flag on merchant ships in transit, Spanish as an official language in the Zone, the use in the Zone of Panamanian postage stamps. A Panamanian citizen and an American resident in Panama could sit on the board of directors, a labour advisory committee for the governor could be set up, Panamanian businesses could be permitted to operate in the Zone, Panama could be given a free water supply. In all other respects American prerogatives would stay inviolate.[25]

In Anderson's judgement this was no longer a realistic basis for negotiation. The Panamanians had made it clear they were not interested in anything less

[22] *DDRS, 1987*, 003558, Smith memo of meeting of 13.1.64. Jorden, *Panama odyssey*, 88. Scranton diss., 117. *DDRS, 1979*, 220, Kenny to Bundy, 17.11.65. Tondel, *Panama Canal*, 50.

[23] *DDRS, 1983*, 1446, NSAM no. 296 of 25.4.64.

[24] Scranton diss., 206–7, 215.

[25] *DDRS, 1987*, 001381, Mann for McNamara, 19.11.64. A similar list of minor concessions can be found in *DDRS, 1989*, 2181, undated (probably September 1966).

than the dismantling of the unequal treaty of 1903, and in December Anderson told Johnson they would not be satisfied with 'patchwork'. The treaty would have to go, and with it perpetuity and American sovereign rights in the Zone. A new treaty would take its stead, incorporating three sections. The first would govern the lock canal, giving the United States powers to operate and defend it pending the construction of a sea-level waterway. It would lapse as soon as the seaway opened, whereupon the old canal and the Zone would pass to Panama. The second would regulate the sea-level canal, and the third would be a SOFA ensuring the retention of a U.S. Military presence on the isthmus both before and after the building of the seaway.[26]

Johnson endorsed Anderson's approach and made the gist of it public on 18 December, with one significant addition. In March the Joint Chiefs of Staff had urged that in any new arrangements Washington 'should seek to maintain the military base complex in Panama considered essential for hemispheric security'. This was the Defense Department's huge offshoot, Southern Command, which had no standing under existing treaties. 'There is no pretending', Jan Morris later wrote, 'that this base is there for the defense of the canal itself, as the original treaty allowed. Its purpose is strategic, a command post for the whole of Latin America, a staging point, a training camp, a military laboratory.' In the Pentagon's view it was vital to keep these installations to combat 'the growing threat of Castro-communist subversion', and in his statement Johnson declared that the new treaty 'should provide for effective discharge of our [US and Panamanian] common responsibilities for hemispheric defense'. So the stage was set for talks to begin, with Anderson as leader of the American delegation.[27]

In the course of the next nine months the discussions produced two important changes. For one thing, the single treaty was split into three, with the safeguard of 'three or none' – in other words, Panama would be expected to accept or reject them as a whole. In the second place, the Panamanians now demanded a share in the running of the canal, something they had not asked for a year earlier. The issue had consequently been given no thought and threw up serious problems. The canal executive had never dreamed of admitting Panama to management posts, and the Zone had numerous allies in the Senate, where the final verdict on the treaties would be reached.[28]

[26] Jorden, *Panama odyssey*, 94–5, 100. *DDRS*, *1983*, 1447, Anderson memo of 2.12.64. *DDRS*, 1986, 1034, minutes of White House conference of 2.12.64.

[27] Jorden, *Panama odyssey*, 100–2. *DDRS*, *1981*, 470A, JCSM-1052–64 of 16.12.64, quoting JCSM-157–64 of 2.3.64. Jan Morris, 'Panama, an imperial specimen', in *Destinations: Essays from 'Rolling Stone'* (Oxford, 1980), 71. *BD*, 1143–5. LaFeber, *Panama Canal*, 146–7. *DDRS*, *1978*, 191C, NSAM no. 323 of 8.1.65. See also *DDRS*, *1989*, 2180 of 16.9.66, where the importance of the Southern Command bases is again given high emphasis.

[28] Jorden, *Panama odyssey*, 107–9. *DDRS*, *1983*, 1993, Johnson to Anderson, undated. *DDRS*, *1984*, 860, Department of Defense memo of 8.1.65. On the question of joint authority in the 1940s, see Chapter 12, at nn. 115, 117.

By early September, Anderson believed he had found a compromise. Panamanians would not go on the board of directors but would be given a rôle in the administration of the canal, subject to the exercise of a veto by both presidents. Each president could also act unilaterally to guarantee the waterway's security. The new treaty would thus allow Washington to use military force 'to ensure the operation or defense of the Canal against hostile Panamanians'. Shortly afterwards, on 24 September, Johnson announced that the basis of an agreement had been laid and that it would now be worked out in detail.[29]

The texts of the three treaties were eventually initialled in June 1967. The settlement for the lock canal did away with the 1903 convention and the treaties of 1936 and 1955. The Zone thereby ceased to exist, and taking its place was a Canal Area, to be governed by a so-called Joint Administration of five Americans and four Panamanians. Within the Area, Panama was sovereign, and its laws were to be introduced there. Judicial power would be in the hands of an Administration court, presided over by four American and four Panamanian judges. The Administration was to allow Panamanians to do business in the Area, and after five years it would close down the Commissary. The annuity to Panama would be paid out of toll revenues, and the remaining proceeds from the canal would be shared equally. Disputes between the two associates would be resolved by arbitration. The treaty would lapse on 31 December 1999, or up to ten years later if work on a sea-level canal were started before 1999. On its expiry the operation of the canal and all the property of the Administration would be transferred to Panama.[30]

The treaty for the sea-level canal granted the United States the right to construct the waterway, which was to be operated by a Panama Interoceanic Canal Commission, headed by five Americans and four Panamanians. Its termination date was 31 December 2067.[31]

The defence treaty made canal protection nominally a joint responsibility, but Washington alone could deploy troops. The rôle of Panama was confined to furnishing 'Defense Areas', not only for the canal, but for 'related security purposes', that is, for Southern Command. The treaty applied not only to the lock canal but to the projected seaway, and its duration was infinite.[32]

Yet though the triad guaranteed Washington's operational control of the existing canal for the rest of the century and its strategic interests into the indefinite future, public reaction was mixed. Speaking to the *New York Times*, former President Eisenhower noted that Theodore Roosevelt (of all people!) had handed down the following dictum to posterity in his book *The Winning of*

---

[29] Jorden, *Panama odyssey*, 109–11. DDRS, *1979*, 444B, Anderson to Johnson, 2.9.65. BD, 1146–7.

[30] Text of the canal treaty is in *BD*, 1149–254.

[31] Text of the sea-level treaty is in *BD*, 1319–70.

[32] Text of the defence treaty is in *BD*, 1255–318.

the West: 'No treaties, whether between civilized nations or not, can ever be regarded as binding in perpetuity; with changing conditions, circumstances may arise which render it not only expedient, but imperative and honorable, to abrogate them.' But Roosevelt's statesmanlike sentiments (published nearly a decade before he gladly embraced the perpetuity of the 1903 convention) were not universally shared. Two ultra-conservative opponents of change, Professor Donald Dozer and Admiral Thomas Settle, had averred that the status quo in Panama was 'more vital to this nation than victory in Vietnam'. To slacken control might well 'trigger communist takeovers of governments in Latin America'. Panama should surrender many of the grants it had been made in 1936 and 1955, and the United States should be given permanent title to the entire watershed of the Chagres – as recommended by General Edwards fifty years before. 'There is a difference between 1903 and 1967,' Secretary of State Dean Rusk remarked. Super-patriots such as Dozer and Settle did not appear to see it.[33]

Nor were they alone. Congressional opposition to Johnson welled up passionately when the treaty texts were leaked to the press in July, and he decided to postpone the effort to get Senate approval until after the 1968 presidential elections in both Panama and the United States. In Panama too the treaties came under fire as an unacceptable compromise, and President Marco Robles agreed that ratification would have to wait until the new National Assembly met.[34]

Deferment did not improve the treaties' chances. The winner of the U.S. election was Richard Nixon, who in 1964 had said that Washington should negotiate with Panama on 'the little irritating things' but not on essentials. 'If the United States retreats one inch in this respect, we will have raised serious doubts about our bases throughout the world.' The treaties were unacceptable to him, and they were equally friendless under the new régime in Panama. This was not the presidency of Arnulfo Arias, inaugurated for the third time on 1 October 1968. Ten days later, Arias had been removed in a National Guard coup led by Colonel Omar Torrijos. Torrijos's military junta saw themselves as the redeemers of the nation and the treaties as only the latest betrayal of Panamanian interests by the compliant oligarchy they had displaced.[35]

In September 1970 Torrijos rejected the treaties outright. The defence treaty reintroduced perpetuity in its failure to set a precise deadline for U.S. withdrawal. It also nullified gains made by Panama in 1936 by giving Washington carte

[33] *NYT*, 27.7.67, 13/3. Theodore Roosevelt, *The works of Theodore Roosevelt*, vol. 9, *The winning of the West*, II (New York, 1926 edn), 56. Georgetown University, *Panama Canal*, 71, 75–83.

[34] *NYT*, 4.9.67, 15/1; 7.11.67, 35/4.

[35] Stephen Rosenfeld, 'The Panama Canal negotiations: A close-run thing', *Foreign Affairs*, 54 (1975–6), 2. Jorden, *Panama odyssey*, 148.

blanche to use land in Panama for military purposes and to carry out manoeuvres there. American commercial activities in the Zone banned by the 1936
treaty would now be 'whitewashed and revalidated'. The direct benefits from
the 1967 package were not good enough, while Panama's indirect proceeds from
U.S. employment of its labour and from the purchase of its farm products
would nose-dive if the lock canal closed and a sea-level waterway took its place.
Finally, if past experience were any guide, arbitration of disputes would be
confined to secondary issues and exclude those 'related to the defense of the
sovereignty and dignity of the Republic'.[36]

If Torrijos expected Washington to improve on the 1967 agreements, he was
mistaken. During the next two years Nixon took a significantly harder line than
Johnson. In June 1970, before the Panamanian refusal, he had been ready to
share canal administration on the 1967 model, but when Anderson's report on
the sea-level project was published in December he went into reverse. Most of
the report was taken up with the recommendation to build a sea-level waterway
ten miles west of the Zone, but it touched incidentally on the shape of a
prospective canal treaty. Washington, so Anderson believed, should be the real
director of canal operation and keep absolute control of canal defence for the
foreseeable future. After negotiations reopened in June 1971, Nixon himself
insisted on a lock-canal treaty with at least a fifty-year life-span and up to fifty
years extra if a seaway were put through. In addition Panama was to promise to
ask for no more than 'reasonable' tolls, as well as to do nothing to hamper the
efficient working of the transit.[37]

Torrijos did not take kindly to this approach. 'The moment Panama feels let
down at the negotiating table,' he proclaimed on the third anniversary of his
coup, 'the moment has come for one generation to offer its lives so that another
generation can live in a free country.' But when Panama broke off negotiations
in December 1972 there was no repetition of the government-sponsored mayhem
of 1964. Instead, as a first step, senior foreign adviser Jorge Illueca made an
inflammatory exposé of the U.S. treaty proposals to reveal how far they fell
short of Panama's bid to recover its patrimony.[38]

Panama had asked for an agreement with a 1994 deadline; Washington had
proposed fifty to ninety years. Panama had called for jurisdiction over the Zone
within five years; Washington had stipulated fifteen to fifty. Washington had
made no more economic concessions than in 1967 and was prepared to transfer
only one-third of Zone territory. Panama claimed a decisive voice in framing
labour policy, plus 85 per cent of the pay roll for its workers; Washington had
said no. In the realm of defence, the United States had pressed for a 'Canal air

[36] Panamanian statement of 2 September 1970 is in *BD*, 1386–95.
[37] *DDRS, 1982*, 742, Nixon memo of 5.6.70. *BD*, 1407–8, 1405. *DDRS, 1982*, 744, Nixon memo
    of 13.9.71.
[38] *NYT*, 12.10.71, 6/1. Jorden, *Panama odyssey*, 173–4. *NYT*, 24.12.72, sect. IV, 3/1.

zone' 200 miles wide and, if need be, control of all Panama's air-space. Its forces were also to have the power to take emergency action in the canal's vicinity. Panama, on the other hand, wanted non-intervention written into the treaty, plus the removal of Southern Command. As far as the sea-level project was concerned, Panama would neither allow the United States to exercise jurisdiction over it nor military bases to protect it. And whereas Washington had expected rights to a seaway without making a hard-and-fast commitment to build it, Panama refused to deal on these terms. As one of its officials had once said, 'You want us for a mistress, and we want marriage with no possibility of a divorce.'[39]

Illueca's bravura performance drew little public attention, but it was followed by a remarkable dramatisation of the Panamanian case played out before an international audience. In March 1973 the United Nations Security Council met in Panama City. It had recently come together in Addis Ababa, where Panama's delegate, Aquilino Boyd, compared the Zone to European colonialism in Africa. The Panama City meeting served to put Washington's canal policy still more conspicuously under a world spotlight, and for Torrijos it turned out to be a huge propaganda success. On 21 March the United States placed itself in a minority of one, vetoing a resolution which called for a 'just and fair' treaty to 'fulfil Panama's legitimate aspirations and guarantee Panama's effective sovereignty over all of its territory'.[40]

The Security Council vote was a turning point in the tedious saga of the treaty negotiations. Soon afterwards Nixon publicly called for a 'fresh look' at the problem of the canal and in July named the veteran diplomat Ellsworth Bunker as his envoy in lieu of Anderson, who stepped down after nine grinding years of non-achievement. At the same time, having scored their public relations victory, the Panamanians mellowed notably. On 24 May, Foreign Minister Juan Antonio Tack put his name to eight principles designed to give future negotiations a comprehensive frame of reference. The sixth allocated canal operation, maintenance, and defence during a canal treaty's lifetime to the United States alone, a distinct retrocession from the 1967 scheme of joint responsibility. Bunker in turn proved equally accommodating. The final version of the principles not only restored Panama's share in canal management but also promised it an active role in the protection of the waterway, something the 1967 defence treaty had not envisaged. When Secretary of State Henry Kissinger signed the resulting agreement in February 1974, the road towards the long-sought treaty settlement suddenly appeared open.[41]

---

[39] Text of Illueca speech of 12.12.72 is in U.S. Department of Commerce, *Foreign Broadcast Information Service, Central America*, 6 (13.12.72), M1–M12, and 6 (14.12.72), M1–M4. Georgetown University, *Panama Canal*, 34.

[40] *NYT*, 12.11.72, 18/1; 1.2.72, 3/5; 17.1.73, 3/4. Text of the resolution is in *YBUN 1973*, 168. Jorden, *Panama odyssey*, 189–96.

[41] Jorden, *Panama odyssey*, 199, 206, 204–5, 695–6, 211–23. Text of the final version of the principles is in *BD*, 1478–9.

The Kissinger–Tack principles marked an effective return to the position reached in 1965, and the subsequent trio of so-called threshold agreements initialled in November 1974 largely echoed the terms of the 1967 treaties, with one very significant exception. Conspicuous by its absence from the negotiators' breakthrough was the sea-level canal. Doubts over a seaway had been growing progressively over the past decade. As early as 1966 a seminar on the canal had judged that if nuclear excavation were out of the question, a sea-level project at any site might be ruled out for economic reasons, and Anderson had pronounced nuclear blasting unfeasible in a preliminary report issued in 1969. In 1971 a National Security Council committee noted concern over its ecological impact and could see no compelling defence or foreign policy reasons for building it. So the seaway proposal lapsed. Torrijos accepted that it was moribund, while Bunker felt that insistence on exclusive U.S. rights should be dropped, as the cost was now prohibitive. In instructions to Bunker in August 1975 President Gerald Ford made it clear that Washington no longer planned to construct a sea-level canal.[42]

Ford's directive was an attempt to bridge the wide differences between the State Department and the Department of Defense, and the sea-level's demise marked a big set-back for the Pentagon. Hitherto, in the view of Ambassador Vaughn, it had used the seaway as a spoiling device to postpone an agreement indefinitely. But giving up the sea-level scheme did not slacken the military's drive to get a treaty that safeguarded its interests to the hilt. Indeed, the loss of South Vietnam to the communist North in April 1975 only reinforced its determination. 'When Saigon fell,' the *New York Times* later reported, 'the attitude tightened considerably.' The administration was called on to 'stand up if tested and be firm', and for some intransigents perpetuity was 'not long enough' to safeguard U.S. interests. In the August brief Bunker was authorised to concede a canal treaty terminating in 1999. But he was also told to demand a defence treaty lasting at least forty years and an American 'right in principle' to a rôle in canal defence after the treaty expired. When, following Panamanian objections, Bunker asked only for a pledge to discuss a longer-term arrangement, the Army was furious, and at the end of the year, with another presidential election on the horizon, negotiations were put into cold storage.[43]

The decision to suspend the treaty talks was prompted by vociferous opposition in Congress. As his party's nominee for the presidency in 1976, Ford knew

[42] Text of the Johnson–Robles statement is in *BD*, 1146–7. Text of the three conceptual agreements is in *CR* (House), 121 (6 October 1975), 31874–6. *DDRS, 1983*, 385, NSC Under Secretaries' Committee memo of 10.6.71. Georgetown University, *Panama Canal*, 57. *BD*, 1375. *NYT*, 4.2.75, 7/1. Jorden, *Panama odyssey*, 277, 289, quoting National Security Decision Memorandum of 18.8.75.
[43] Jack Hood Vaughn, 'A Latin-American Vietnam', *Washington Monthly*, October 1973, 34. *NYT*, 16.9.75, 11/1. Jorden, *Panama odyssey*, 288–91, 304–5, 308–9; detail of the 1974–5 round of negotiations is given on pp. 249–309 passim.

there were no votes in a canal treaty, and Bunker's diplomacy had already been punctuated by the boom of diehard salvoes from Capitol Hill. In March 1974 a resolution calling for 'retention of undiluted United States sovereignty over the Canal Zone', sponsored by Senators Strom Thurmond and John McClellan, garnered thirty-four names, enough to kill a treaty. In June 1975 a House motion to stop the use of federal funds 'to negotiate the surrender or the relinquishment of any United States rights in the Panama Canal Zone' was carried by a handsome margin. During his campaign for the Republican nomination, Ronald Reagan drew rapturous applause for his florid claim 'We bought it, we paid for it, it's ours, and we should tell Torrijos and company that we are going to keep it.'[44]

The administration did what it could to counter Reagan's charlatanism with the truth. 'We bought Louisiana; we bought Alaska,' Bunker declared. 'In Panama we bought not territory, but rights.' After giving Reagan a tutorial on American prerogatives, Kissinger told the columnist James Reston that he had seldom had to deal with 'a more gullible pupil with less knowledge of the subject'. Yet the ignorance of Reagan and his public was proof even against the fact that the canal was long since past its prime. On its sixtieth birthday in 1974 it was described as showing signs of 'technological arteriosclerosis', and Governor David Parker had recently admitted that less than 1 per cent of the U.S. gross national product passed through it. A study published in 1976 concluded that its economic value was significantly overstated, and the Panamanian diplomat Carlos López-Guevara made a shrewd point when he observed that if the canal really had been vital to Washington, Panama would have stood no chance of a new treaty. But Ford was compelled to adjourn the treaty-making effort until after election day.[45]

When the contest went to Ford's Democratic opponent, Jimmy Carter, he too faced deep hostility over the canal. A conservative such as Captain Paul Ryan, USN, echoed what Admiral Mahan had said in 1912 when he wrote that 'pragmatists of the *realpolitik* school will reason that Panama's lot can be roughly equated with that of Finland, Sweden, Vietnam, Cambodia, and other small nations. It is linked inexorably to that of a major nation.' The former defence correspondent of the *New York Times*, Hanson Baldwin, who in 1957 had correctly stated that 'the Canal Zone today is in low strategic priority', saw it in a very different light after the advent of a Soviet-backed Castro. Cession of the

[44] *NYT*, 30.3.74, 3/1. Rosenfeld, 'Panama Canal negotiations', 9. LaFeber, *Panama Canal*, 185–9. Jorden, *Panama odyssey*, 316.

[45] *BD*, 1496. *NYT*, 5.5.76, 41/5; 11.8.74, 52/8. Thomas Franck and Edward Weisband, 'Panama paralysis', *Foreign Policy*, no. 21 (Winter 1975–6), 180. *NYT*, 17.5 76, 20/5 and 43/2. LaFeber, *Panama Canal*, 223.

Zone, he told Ryan, would reactivate the domino theory and 'encourage penny-dictators and minor aggressions everywhere'. Few on the right shared the view of William Buckley when he urged that Washington should get out of Panama 'while the initiative is still clearly our own. That is the way great nations act.' This was a conclusion reached mainly by liberals, such as Sol Linowitz. In December 1976 Linowitz put his name to a report which counselled 'adjusting to nationalist aspirations rather than confronting them' and which saw American policy on the canal as the touchstone of the United States's approach not only to the hemisphere but to the Third World as a whole.[46]

Carter agreed with Linowitz's analysis, so much so that he named him as Bunker's co-negotiator. In Linowitz's judgement, Carter approached the task of treaty making 'with no great enthusiasm'. But he; his secretary of state, Cyrus Vance; and his national security adviser, Zbigniew Brzezinski, were all convinced that it had to be cleared out of the way before the mid-term elections of 1978.[47]

They were no less certain that if they did not bring off a settlement quickly the Zone would become untenable. As Johnson's secretary of the Army, Vance had witnessed the backwash of the 1964 flag incident, and this had led him to believe that 'sooner or later Panama would resort to major violence, even to the point of destroying the canal'. Asked his likely reaction if a mass demonstration were mounted against the Zone, Torrijos had replied: 'Two courses are open to me. To smash it or to lead it, and I am not going to smash it.' This could have been a bluff. It was clearly not in the republic's interest to damage a key source of its national income. But Egypt had not hesitated to block Suez in 1956, and Torrijos's threat was taken seriously enough for the Pentagon to make contingency plans for canal defence against Panama, including one scheme entailing the use of 100,000 troops.[48]

For one figure outside government circles the challenge had to be met head-on. Hanson Baldwin acknowledged 'the distinct possibility of a physical

[46] Paul Ryan, 'Canal diplomacy and U.S. interests', *U.S, Naval Institute Proceedings*, 103 (1977), 52, 47. For Mahan, see Chapter 2, at n. 79. *NYT*, 28.4.57, 44/1. William Buckley, 'On the right', *National Review*, 12 November 1976, 1253, quoted in LaFeber, *Panama Canal*, 214. Commission on United States–Latin American Relations, *The United States and Latin America: Next steps* (Washington, D.C., 1976), 1–6, quoted in Lafeber, *Panama Canal*, 194–5, and in George Moffett, *The limits of victory: The ratification of the Panama Canal treaties, 1977–1978* (Ithaca, N.Y., 1985), 4.

[47] Sol Linowitz, *The making of a public man: A memoir* (Boston, 1985), 150. Jimmy Carter, *Keeping faith: Memoirs of a president* (London, 1982), 156. Zbigniew Brzezinski, *Power and principle: Memoirs of the national security adviser 1977–1981* (New York, 1983), 54. Cyrus Vance, *Hard choices: Four critical years in managing America's foreign policy* (New York, 1983), 33.

[48] Carter, *Keeping Faith*, 155. Brzezinski, *Power and principle*, 136. Vance, *Hard choices*, 141. *NYT*, 28.7.75, 3/5, 8. SCFR, *Hearings*, 1: 180–3, McCloskey to Clark, 30.6.76. See also Jorden, *Panama odyssey*, 322–3.

confrontation – perhaps an armed one. . . . but for some things we must be prepared to fight. . . . Somewhere the line must be drawn. . . . Panama is the place and now the time.' Government officials saw things very differently, however. Remembering the U.S. Army's massacre at My Lai in Vietnam, one senior Army Department spokesman remarked that 'the last thing in the world we want now is to be ordered to start shooting into a crowd of Panamanians'. Far better, as the State Department had argued in 1936, to guarantee the canal's security by having it operate in a sympathetic environment where Panamanians and Americans were partners in the waterway, not forever on the verge of collision.[49]

Negotiations began on 15 February 1977, and to speed the process Carter appointed Linowitz for only six months. For the U.S. delegation the top priority was a defence agreement giving Washington a permanent right to guarantee the canal's security after the canal treaty expired at the end of 1999. The Pentagon had already devised a formula which granted the United States the power to defend the canal unilaterally if need be. It allowed for an elaborate consultation procedure on defence matters; if that broke down, either party was to take 'such other diplomatic, economic or military measures as it deems necessary, in accordance with its constitutional processes'. But Carter's secretary of defense, Harold Brown, was as unhappy about the idea of consultation as the Army had been when it featured so prominently in the 1936 treaty. Instead the two signatories would jointly underwrite the canal's neutrality for the indefinite future.[50]

Brown's simplification was completely unacceptable to the Panamanians. Quite apart from the fact that the guarantee of neutrality held good only for the canal and not for Panama as a whole, it gave Washington freedom to send in troops in any circumstances. This to Panama was a licence for intervention and the basis for a second protectorate. Panama was equally disturbed by the U.S. demand for permanent defence arrangements, which, as Linowitz admitted, 'put us back into the world of perpetuities'. The Panamanians wanted sole control of canal defence after 1999, subject only to a short-term mutual security treaty directed exclusively at threats from third countries – that is, with no application to an attack coming from Panama itself.[51]

[49] Hanson Baldwin, 'Con: The Panama Canal – Sovereignty and security', *AEI Defense Review*, no. 4 (August 1977), 12–34, repr. in *SCFR*, *Hearings*, 1: 107–27 (quotation from p. 123). Franck and Weisband, 'Panama paralysis', 187. For the State Department comment of 1936, see Chapter 12 at n. 29.

[50] Linowitz, *Public man*, 153–5. US Congress, Senate, Committee on Armed Services, *Hearings on defense, maintenance and operation of the Panama Canal, including administration and government of the Canal Zone*, 95th Cong., 1st sess. (1978), 201–2, gives the text of the 1976 formula. See also Jorden, *Panama odyssey*, 368–9n, 368–9, 351.

[51] SCFR, *Hearings*, 3: 477–9, for Escobar speech of 19.8.77 revealing details of the negotiations. Jorden, *Panama odyssey*, 351–5. Linowitz, *Public man*, 155.

Faced with this impasse, the American team made two highly important concessions. Hitherto the Joint Chiefs of Staff had planned to hold on to some bases in Panama after 1999; it was now clearly impossible to get Panamanian approval for them. Accordingly, the Joint Chiefs made a virtue of necessity, accepting that the Army could make a rapid deployment of combat troops from the continental United States if a crisis blew up. On 9 May, Bunker offered to pull out American forces at the end of 1999 and consequently gave up the quest both for a security pact and for a nucleus of military installations.[52]

This was a remarkable readjustment, and it was followed by another two days later. Up to this point the Pentagon had fought to retain a Canal Area for the new administration not much smaller than the existing Zone and to have American civilian employees of the Canal granted the same extraterritorial rights as U.S. servicemen. These provisions showed an extraordinary insensitivity to Panamanian irredentism. For generations the Panamanians had been outsiders in their own heartland, as Jan Morris had recently observed, gazing into the Zone like the poor 'looking through the lodge gates at some unapproachable estate'. Ambassador William Jorden was to put the Panamanian case graphically when he asked how Americans would feel if the Mississippi and a belt of land on each bank were under foreign jurisdiction, and he worked hard to persuade the Defense Department to be less unyielding. On 11 May the generals gave way: U.S. civilians would be subject to Panamanian law after a brief transition period, and large tracts of the Zone would be conveyed to Panama. The terminal ports of Balboa and Cristóbal were to be transferred, together with the whole of Ancon Hill, which housed the headquarters of Southern Command and towered over Panama City as an inescapable reminder of American power.[53]

There was, of course, a price to pay in the shape of Panamanian agreement to swallow the neutrality guarantee as stipulated by Secretary Brown and the Joint Chiefs, to be incorporated in a treaty separate from the accord on the canal. Though the chief Panamanian negotiator, Rómulo Escobar Bethancourt, insisted that it must not allow the United States to take military action as a result of political developments inside Panama, this was not spelled out in the treaty text. Panama was left to rely entirely on American discretion, and Torrijos could only say he was certain Washington would not make 'an incorrect or unwise use of this authority'.[54]

With the neutrality treaty apparently settled, the focus switched to the treaty for the canal. Washington's objective hitherto had been, in the words of Ambler

---

[52] Diane Bendahmane and John McDonald (eds.), *Perspectives on negotiation: Four case studies and interpretations* (Washington, D.C., 1986), 47, 27. Jorden, *Panama odyssey*, 368.

[53] Linowitz, *Public man*, 159–60. Jorden, *Panama odyssey*, 351, 370, 372–3, 380, 473–4. Morris, 'Panama', 77.

[54] Linowitz, *Public man*, 162–3. Jorden, *Panama odyssey*, 369, 382–5. SCFR, *Hearings*, 3: 479.

Moss, a leading member of Carter's team, 'to make sure that it would, in fact, be able to operate the Canal unilaterally (without saying so in so many words)'. Carter's blueprint for canal administration during the treaty's lifetime indicated the same preference: a U.S. government agency with a joint advisory board attached. In the event, the precise form of the organisation that would run the waterway through the remainder of the century was left to be defined by statute, and the treaty simply established a body entitled the Panama Canal Commission, headed by five Americans and four Panamanians. Until the close of 1989 the administrator was to be a U.S. citizen, at which point a Panamanian national would take over. During the 1980s and the 1990s Panamanians would progressively assume more managerial responsibility against the day when the canal would pass fully into Panama's hands.[55]

The administrative structure was agreed by 23 June, and the final weeks of the negotiations were largely taken up with the much hotter topic of monetary compensation. On 30 May, Escobar had asked Linowitz for a breathtaking amount: no less than $1.02 billion in a lump sum and an annuity of $300 million. Although Linowitz made it clear that the Senate would not stomach such astronomical figures, they were proposed again on 24 June. In addition Panama demanded military assistance to the tune of $50 million over the next few years. The deal eventually struck gave the Panamanians bounty on nothing like this scale, but vastly more than the annuity of $2.3 million they currently enjoyed. The annuity was stepped up to $10 million, with the promise of $10 million more if canal revenues could sustain it. A further $10 million a year would be paid for municipal services, and this would be inflation-proofed. So too would the annual payment of thirty cents per net ton for all vessels in transit charged with tolls; this was calculated to give Panama an income of some $53 million a year. On top of these proceeds from the treaty, Panama was to receive nearly $350 million in loans and guarantees during the first five years after the treaty went into force.[56]

By the end of July only one item remained on the agenda. Early in the month Senator Mike Gravel of Alaska sold Carter the idea of a sea-level canal whereby Alaskan crude oil could be shipped in supertankers to refineries on the Gulf of Mexico and the Atlantic coast. So the project which had apparently been buried in 1974 was resurrected, and Carter pressed for an exclusive option on it. When Panama refused, he had to be content with a U.S. veto until 1999 on development of a seaway by any other country (most probably Japan). The agreement removed the last main obstacle to an overall settlement – though on 8 August Panama tried to slip through a number of changes in the hope they would be unnoticed

---

[55] Bendahmane and McDonald, *Perspectives*, 23, for the Moss comment. Jorden, *Panama odyssey*, 388–90, 397, 409. Treaty terms are in *BD*, 1525–8, 1533–5.

[56] Linowitz, *Public man*, 164–70. Jorden, *Panama odyssey*, 13–14, 17–18, 393–4, 409, 413–22, 425–6, 429, 432. Details of treaty payments are in *BD*, 1527, 1538.

in the rush to close the bargain. On 10 August the two treaties were completed in Panama and signed in Washington a month later, on 7 September, in the presence of political leaders from states throughout the hemisphere. Almost thirteen years of laborious diplomatic endeavour had finally borne fruit.[57]

The texts still had to be ratified in both countries, however, and the campaign for ratification added yet another agonising chapter to the story. It began with legislative hearings focussing mainly on the neutrality treaty and asking one key question again and again. Did the treaty give the United States the right to act against a threat to the canal from Panama itself, either by dissident extremists or a hostile Panamanian government? Administration witnesses were quick to assert that Washington could do anything to safeguard the waterway, even from its co-guarantor, though they were more inhibited than Brzezinski. Asked by a congressional delegation what would happen if after 1999 the Panamanian government said it was closing the canal 'for repairs', the national security adviser replied that Washington would 'move in and close down the Panamanian government for repairs'. Fears that the neutrality treaty was unsatisfactory were confirmed, however, by publication of remarks made by Escobar the previous month. According to Escobar, it did not give United States 'the right of intervention'. Nor did it say that the United States could determine whether neutrality was violated or not. Moreover, the clause entitling U.S. warships to transit 'expeditiously' conceded only 'the right to as rapid a passage as possible'.[58]

In saying this Escobar was trying to persuade Panama that the treaty was not a device to institutionalise American domination. The clause on expeditious passage was phrased to conform with a pledge not to discriminate among canal users, and the treaty did not validate intervention for the simple reason that it would have been superfluous to do so. Johnson, Escobar pointed out, had sent U.S. troops into the Dominican Republic in 1965 without asking the Dominican government, and Panama was similarly exposed. 'A country like the United States can land in Panama whenever if feels like it after the year 2000 with or without a neutrality pact.'[59]

The Carter administration, however, needed more than the justification of power politics to face down any critics of an expedition to the isthmus. In the words of Secretary Brown, the treaty provided 'the diplomatic, international and moral underpinning' for whatever military action had to be taken. Escobar's commentary threatened to knock away those valuable props, and in the view of

[57] Jorden, *Panama odyssey*, 6–7, 16–19. Bendahmane and McDonald, *Perspectives*, 28–9, for comment by Wyrough. Jorden, *Panama odyssey*, 429–31. Linowitz, *Public man*, 171. Jorden, *Panama odyssey*, 433–7, 453–6.
[58] U.S. Congress, House of Representatives, Committee on International Relations, *Hearings on proposed Panama Canal treaties*, 95th Cong., 1st sess. (1978), 244, 245, 250, 263. SCFR, *Hearings*, 1: 12, 39, 131, 183. Brzezinski, *Power and principle*, 136. SCFR, *Hearings*, 1: 77.
[59] SCFR, *Hearings*, 1: 77, 133.

Senator Howard Baker, if it represented the official Panamanian position, the chances of a positive Senate vote were gravely reduced. The only way to save the situation appeared to be a Senate reservation to the treaty, which Panama would be required to accept.[60]

Linowitz balked at this idea, preferring to have an interpretive declaration put out by Carter and Torrijos. Accordingly Torrijos was invited to Washington to approve a 'statement of understanding' drafted by Linowitz and Escobar. Issued on 14 October, it proclaimed that both countries were entitled 'in accordance with their respective constitutional processes' to defend the waterway against 'any threat to the regime of neutrality', that is, 'any aggression or threat directed against the Canal or against the peaceful transit of vessels through the Canal'. This did not signify 'a right of intervention of the United States in the internal affairs of Panama', and no U.S. action would ever be aimed at Panama's territorial integrity or political independence. As for the expeditious–passage clause, this meant that U.S. and Panamanian warships were to be handled 'as quickly as possible, without any impediment, with expedited treatment, and in case of need or emergency, to go to the head of the line of vessels in order to transit the Canal rapidly'.[61]

The statement gave concessions to both sides. It confirmed, as Torrijos himself had said at the signing ceremony, that Panama was to be placed 'under the protective umbrella of the Pentagon'. But Torrijos had also warned that the treaty could, 'if . . . not administered judiciously by future generations, become an instrument of permanent intervention', and, as Ambassador Jorden observed, to most Panamanians intervention meant 'foreign troops coming in, killing their people, removing their government . . . , taking over and running the show'. With Panama poised to vote on the treaties in a national referendum, the pledge of respect for Panama's sovereignty was a necessary boost for ratification, and in his presentation of the statement to the Foreign Relations Committee, Linowitz told its members that it was designed to assure the Panamanians that 'we would not be assigning troops to the isthmus to invade the country or annex any territory'.[62]

On 24 October the plebiscite came out two to one in support of the treaties, but Baker believed the Carter–Torrijos manifesto would have to be entered verbatim as an amendment to the neutrality treaty, that is, as an integral part of the document with full legal validity. Only then could ratification be clinched. Carter agreed, and the amendment was submitted by the majority leader, Senator Robert Byrd, on 7 February 1978, the eve of the Senate's debate.[63]

[60] Ibid., 134, 57.

[61] Ibid., 84, 484. Jorden, *Panama odyssey*, 477–80. Linowitz, *Public man*, 190–1, 192–4. Text of Carter–Torrijos statement is in *BD*, 1620.

[62] *BD*, 1512. SCFR, *Hearings*, 1: 306. Jorden, *Panama odyssey*, 479.

[63] *NYT*, 25.10.77, 3/1. *Sen. Deb.*, 2: 1291–2. *NYT*, 28.1.78, 2/3. *Sen. Deb.*, 1: 1029.

Yet although the Byrd–Baker resolution attracted as many as seventy-eight supporters, it by no means settled the outcome. The opposition found it impossible to live with even the façade of partnership which the resolution denoted and vastly preferred the formula the Pentagon had wanted Ford to endorse. This had given the United States the ultimate right to intervene in Panama 'as it deems necessary', and it was leaked by Ford's deputy defense secretary, William Clements, just before the neutrality treaty went to the Senate. This hostile move was followed up with several wrecking amendments introduced by Senators James Allen and Robert Dole. They called for the maintenance of U.S. bases in Panama after 1999, the removal of any conditions on the passage of U.S. warships through the canal, and an absolute American right to intervene.[64]

The treaty's promoters were painfully aware that insistence on an unfettered power of intervention might well sink the treaty and provoke a wild reaction from Panama. Soon after negotiations ended, the columnists James Reston and Tom Wicker undoubtedly reflected the administration's view when they argued that if the Senate failed to endorse the treaty it could lead 'not merely to some kind of violence with the Panamanians but with volunteers from all over Latin America', that is, 'a lingering and unwinnable guerrilla war'. 'The Canal Zone, if this issue is not handled properly,' Senator Frank Church declared in his opening speech, 'has the potential of becoming a military nightmare, another Vietnam.' The garrison commander, General Dennis McAuliffe, had spoken of the risk to shipping from mortars and sniper fire, and in Church's opinion 'those ships are not going to transit the canal if their captains doubt that they can safely step out onto their decks during passage'. 'How easy it would be', Linowitz later wrote, 'for a single Panamanian National Guardsman with a bazooka to put the great locks out of commission for months.'[65]

These warnings cut no ice with the irreconcilables, however, and they were numerous enough to put the treaty on a knife-edge. The amendments entered by Allen and Dole secured an average vote of thirty-six, two more than the thirty-four required to block approval. Since the administration's average score on the same twelve votes was fifty-three, it had to work assiduously to swing the uncommitted over to its side. It did so partly, as Vance described it, by encouraging waverers 'to "improve" the treaties by adding conditions so that they could justify a yes vote to their constituents'. This was done with the proviso that the revisions would take the form of innocuous reservations and understandings which would leave the core of the treaty untouched. By such means nine men were brought into the fold: Bellmon, Brooke, Cannon, DeConcini, Heinz,

---

[64] *Sen. Deb.*, 1: v; 2: v–vi; 3: v–vi. See n. 50 above for the Clements formula, on which see also Jorden, *Panama odyssey*, 509–11. Texts of Allen's amendments are in *Sen. Deb.*, 2: 2058, 2260–1, 2449, 2591, 3151, 3293, 3404, 3454. Texts of Dole's amendments, 2: 2572, 3355.

[65] *NYT*, 17.8.77, 1/3, 21/1; 30.8.77, 29/1. *Sen. Deb.*, 1: 1467, 1151; 2: 3075. Linowitz, *Public man*, 195.

Long, Nunn, Randolph, and Talmadge. As the decisive vote on 16 March hove in sight, a government victory began to seem possible.[66]

To put a majority beyond doubt, Carter had to make two final deals. The first was a motion submitted in the name of Senator Nunn which allowed for negotiations on U.S. military bases in Panama after 1999. Drafted in conjunction with Warren Christopher of the State Department, it was given the status of a condition, that is, a qualification (like reservations and understandings) without the force of an amendment. 'Everybody knows what a condition is,' explained Byrd. 'If the other party does not accede to that condition, then all bets are off.' The anti-treaty forces knew full well that since the Nunn addendum made base negotiations hinge on Panamanian agreement, it was a nullity. It was carried none the less by a huge margin.[67]

Far more serious was the government's capitulation to Senator Dennis DeConcini, who on 9 February had submitted an amendment stating that 'if the Canal is closed, or its operations are interfered with, the United States . . . shall have the right to take such steps as it deems necessary to reopen the Canal or restore the operations of the Canal, as the case may be'. In his gloss on the text DeConcini defined the reasons why Washington might take action as 'labor unrest and strikes; the actions of an unfriendly government; political riots or upheavals'. This was a direct contradiction of the Carter–Torrijos statement, and it revived the spirit of an imperialism which Carter and his supporters had said was now exclusive to the USSR. 'Let us make it clear to the world', proclaimed Senator Church, 'that we are not seeking for ourselves the kind of rights the Soviets claimed in Czechoslovakia in 1968.' DeConcini appeared to be doing precisely that.[68]

Yet so desperate was Carter to get DeConcini into the pro-treaty camp that he accepted an even more harshly worded version of the proposal which went so far as to give explicit authorisation to the use of American military force in Panama. It was softened by Christopher through Panama's inclusion as associate in the guarantee and, more important, by being presented, like the Nunn resolution, as a condition rather than an amendment, thus being gutted of anything more than nominal significance. Even so, it was considered an outrage by the Panamanians, who protested vehemently that 'no government could

[66] Details of the votes on the twelve amendments by Allen and Dole are in *Sen. Deb.*, 2: 2092, 2312, 2463, 2866, 3154, 3256, 3338, 3365, 3367, 3426, 3435, 3559. Vance, *Hard choices*, 151. See also Jorden, *Panama odyssey*, 511–30. On the distinctions among amendments, reservations, and understandings, see *Sen. Deb.*, 1: 935–7; 2: 3207–10, 3876. See also Louis Henkin, *Foreign affairs and the Constitution* (New York, 1975), 133–6, and George Haynes, *The Senate of the United States: Its history and practice*, vol. 2 (New York, 1938), 604–25.

[67] *Sen. Deb.*, 2: 3606, 3675, 3622, 3614–15, 3684–7, 3693–7, 3707–8, 3708–9. Jorden, *Panama odyssey*, 530–6.

[68] *Sen. Deb.*, 1: 1390–1; 3: 4834.

grant such a right to another nation and maintain its national pride'. But
DeConcini made the rider the price of his vote, and Carter had no choice but
to go along.[69]

Likewise Torrijos, whose immediate response to Carter's surrender had been
to demand a second leadership amendment offsetting the DeConcini condition.
Given the delicate balance of forces in the Senate, this would almost certainly
have lost the treaty, and Torrijos was persuaded to give up the idea. On 16
March, DeConcini's proposition was easily carried, and soon afterwards the
treaty itself squeaked through by sixty-eight to thirty-two, only one vote more
than the requisite two-thirds majority.[70]

By this time the Senate debate had taken up twenty-two working days –
twice as many as were devoted to the North Atlantic treaty in 1949 – but the
canal treaty still had to be considered, and here too the struggle was hard
fought. Although the neutrality treaty had successfully run the gauntlet, the
two agreements stood or fell together, and if the canal treaty were struck down,
the neutrality pact was doomed to become a dead letter. The opposition therefore
had everything to play for, and once more the administration was compelled to
pull out all the stops to procure the necessary votes.[71]

Its task was complicated by the need to meet the renewed Panamanian call
for some means of neutralising the DeConcini condition. The answer was a
leadership reservation, tortuously constructed in six days of intensive talks with
the Panamanians and put before the Senate on 18 April, the day of the final vote
on the treaty. It affirmed that, 'pursuant to its adherence to the principle of
non-intervention', any action taken by Washington to guarantee the canal's
neutrality 'shall not have as its purpose nor be interpreted as a right of intervention in the internal affairs of Panama or interference with its political independence or sovereign integrity'. As a crowning touch, DeConcini himself
was wheeled forward to give the wording his seal of approval.[72]

With DeConcini's imprimatur on it, the leadership reservation was home
and dry, and with it the canal treaty, which passed by the same margin as the
neutrality treaty, sixty-eight to thirty-two. The vote brought to an end a debate
which in many ways had been what Senator Claiborne Pell described as 'a
public relations minuet'. Both sides had postured energetically for the benefit of
their respective electorates, and the forgone conclusion of a settlement on the

[69] Jorden, *Panama odyssey*, 517–18, 520, 532–5, 537, 539–51. Moffett, *Limits of victory*, 97.
Sen. Deb., 2: 3476–8, 3782–5.
[70] Jorden, *Panama odyssey*, 545–8. *Sen. Deb.*, 2: 3804, 3892–4.
[71] Full list of amendments, reservations, and understandings is in *Sen. Deb.*, 3: v–vi. On the
course of the debate, see Jorden, *Panama odyssey*, 560–620.
[72] Jorden, *Panama odyssey*, 562–3, 565–7, 571–3, 579–82, 586–7, 590–3, 595–604. *Sen. Deb.*,
3: 5443, 5398–5401, 5482–4.

terms agreed in 1977 was privately never in doubt, whatever may have been said for general consumption.[73]

Given the news that the canal treaty had won through, Torrijos's first comment to the media was that 'today, the canal was placed within two votes of being destroyed'. The transit, he had told his British admirer Graham Greene, was easy to sabotage. 'Blow a hole in the Gatún Dam and the Canal will drain into the Atlantic. It would take only a few days to mend the dam, but it would take three years of rain to fill the Canal.' Panama could make life very unpleasant for the Zone, and 'for the first time since the Civil War American civilians would be in the firing line'. In his memoirs published four years later, Carter disclosed that this was no mere bravado. Torrijos's subsequent claim that he had ordered special units of the National Guard to disable the waterway in the event of an unfavourable Senate vote was borne out by intelligence reports. And the threat of violence, Torrijos believed, must be held continuously in reserve to deter U.S. intervention: 'That capacity to destroy should never be renounced by the National Guard or by future generations.'[74]

Whether Panama would indeed have put its national pride before its economic interest is unknowable. What is certain is that the Senate's consent to the treaties marked the close of an era for the United States. Some Americans welcomed the passing of the old order. Others were in shock. When Carter flew down to the isthmus to exchange ratifications with Torrijos, he was given a cool reception by several of his fellow citizens in the Zone. Their mood was understandable, in the view of one treaty supporter. 'I think it's traumatic for the Zonians,' explained Senator Donald Riegle, 'who have always had a cocoon situation, to have that taken away.' As in Algeria in 1962, as in Rhodesia in 1979, the sense that the metropolis had betrayed its kith and kin ran deep throughout the Zonian community.[75]

Carter's enemies in Washington struck back to some effect in the enabling act for the canal treaty hammered out in 1979. Resentment at the terms of the treaty was strongest in the House of Representatives, which had been highly piqued at its exclusion from the ratification process. Although the Constitution undoubtedly gave the Senate a monopoly of jurisdiction over treaties, the House claimed a constitutional voice in the transfer of government property. Sixty Congressmen consequently brought suit against Carter to prevent him from disposing of federal assets in the Zone without the assent of the House.

[73] Sen. Deb., 3: 5584–6. SCFR, Hearings, 1: 133.

[74] Jorden, Panama odyssey, 623. Graham Greene, Getting to know the general: The story of an involvement (London, 1984), 61–2. Carter, Keeping Faith, 177. NYT, 19.4.78, 1/5–6, 16/1.

[75] Jorden, Panama odyssey, 654–5. NYT, 18.6.78, 1/6.

The action failed on appeal, and the Supreme Court refused to consider it further. Thwarted on this front, the opposition switched its attack to the implementing legislation, due to be agreed before the treaties went into operation on 1 October 1979.[76]

Bills did not go before Congress until the start of the new session in January 1979. It was already clear by then that the House had very different views from the White House on the organisational structure for the canal in the 1980s and 1990s. Carter wanted a Canal Commission which would take the same form as the existing Company, that is, as a semi-autonomous government corporation raising its own funds and responsible only to the president. Representative John Murphy – a sworn foe of the treaties – planned to make the Commission an adjunct of the Pentagon and dependent for all its expenses on congressional appropriations.[77]

When the rival projects came to a vote, the administration's bill was rejected and Murphy's adopted in preference. This placed the nine-member Commission under the Secretary of Defense, required the five American commissioners to vote in accordance with Defense Department wishes, and stipulated that in a quorum of five only two could be Panamanian. In time of war or threat of war the U.S. military would run the canal. Congress would hold the Commission's purse-strings and would also control property transfers. The $10 million discretionary payment on top of the canal annuity was not to be made unless unexpended funds were first used to defray the costs of treaty implementation.[78]

This last item reflected the influence of the shipping lobby. Tolls had been raised twice in the last five years, by 19 per cent in 1974 and by another 19 per cent in 1976. Although the increases were a necessary response to an operating deficit, the shipowners foresaw crippling losses if tolls became 'a revenue machine for Panama' and were upped continually to cover the huge new treaty payments. Hence the caveat on the annuity bonus. Hence too Murphy's additional provision that tolls must not go on subsidising the Canal's manifold

[76] William Furlong and Margaret Scranton, *The dynamics of foreign policymaking: The president, the Congress, and the Panama Canal treaties* (Boulder, Colo., 1984), 157, 135, 136–7. Jorden, *Panama odyssey*, 665–6. *NYT*, 7.4.78, 5/5; 16.5.78, 20/2. 'Transfer of the Panama Canal by treaty without House approval: *Edwards* v. *Carter*', *Harvard Law Review*, 92 (1978–9), 524–35. Wilbur Hamlin, 'Panama Canal: Legal issues involved in the transfer of the Canal to Panama', *Harvard International Law Journal*, 19 (1978–9), 279–328. The delay in the treaties' entry into force stemmed from a reservation entered by Senator Edward Brooke; text is in *Sen. Deb.*, 3: 5585.

[77] Jorden, *Panama odyssey*, 660. *NYT*, 10.5.78, sect. II, 4/3; 14.5.78, 37/3. Jorden, *Panama odyssey*, 664–5. *NYT*, 26.12.78, 3/4.

[78] Furlong and Scranton, *Dynamics*, 158–9. U.S. Code, *Congressional and administrative news. 96th Congress, 1st Session, 1979*, vol. 2, *Legislative history of the Panama Canal Act of 27 September 1979* (1980), 1044–5, 1050–1, 1063, 1073–4, 1065–6, 1075.

fringe benefits for its work force. And to make certain they were not ignored, the shippers were to have their own man on the Commission, alongside a specialist on port facilities and a labour relations expert.[79]

This was anathema to the canal directorate. Murphy's bill was a frontal assault on its cherished independence, and the claim that his proposals were modelled on the Goethals régime was absurd. Governor Goethals and his successors had been practically a law unto themselves, and they had functioned with only incidental reference to Congress. Now, it seemed, the legislators would have a finger in every pie, and the officiousness of Washington, which had briefly sunk its talons into the Zone after the reform of the Goethals system in 1951, would have to be endured for the next twenty years. Small wonder that Governor Harold Parfitt opposed the Murphy bill root and branch – but to no purpose, and when the House voted it through, Carter suffered an important defeat.[80]

He no doubt took some consolation from the fact that Panamaphobes more rabid than Murphy failed to carry the House with them. Congressman Philip Crane's amendment to postpone the conveyance of all U.S. property to Panama until after 1999 was thrown out by a big majority. But Representative George Hansen's motion requiring Panama to pay most of the cost of treaty implementation was lost by only six votes, and an even more provocative condition was passed with Murphy's support. During a secret session on 20 June, Hansen's comrade-in-arms Robert Bauman alleged that Torrijos had been sending aid to the Sandinista rebels then on the verge of bringing down Murphy's good friend the Nicaraguan dictator Anastasio Somoza. In a forlorn gesture of solidarity with Somoza, Murphy tacked on a clause denying any payments to Panama if it were found that Panama was 'interfering with the internal affairs of any other state'.[81]

When House and Senate conferees came together to reach an agreed text in August and September, the House delegates did not insist on keeping this inflammatory item, but 'Murphy's Law' went on the statute book substantially intact. It marked a damaging blow to the treaty makers of both states, and in signing it Carter went out of his way to assure Panama that the Act would be interpreted and applied by the executive branch 'in strict conformity with the terms and the intent of the treaties'.[82]

[79] *NYT*, 12.7.74, 2/5; 12.5.76, 67/1. Moffett, *Limits of victory*, 183–7, 188–9, 195, 198, 200. U.S. Code, *Legislative history*, 1065–6, 1075, 1045.

[80] U.S. Code, *Legislative history*, 1042 and 1090–105 (Parfitt to Murphy, 28.3.79). *NYT*, 22.6.79, 1/4.

[81] Jorden, *Panama odyssey*, 666, 674–5, 670–1. Furlong and Scranton, *Dynamics*, 160.

[82] Jorden, *Panama odyssey*, 676–7, 679–81. Furlong and Scranton, *Dynamics*, 161–2. *Public papers of the presidents of the United States: Jimmy Carter, 1979* (Washington, D.C., 1980), 1777. For Panamanian protests against the Act, see Furlong and Scranton, *Dynamics*, 160–1, 162, and for complaints by both Panama and the Commission, see *NYT*, 17.12.80, 3/1.

On 1 October 1979 the settlement took effect and the Canal Zone created three-quarters of a century earlier ceased to exist. As Panama redeemed the territory most Americans had thought of as their own inalienable domain, the U.S. community was heavy with the sense of bereavement. 'The past is dead,' lamented one inconsolable Zonian. 'Teddy Roosevelt is in the ground.'[83]

[83] *NYT*, 1.10.79, 1/4.

Part V

Epilogue

The rights of the United States [are] held in trust for the commerce of the world. . . . We took the responsibility upon ourselves alone, to do for civilization what otherwise all the maritime powers would have united in requiring. . . . We will dig the canal, not for selfish reasons, not for greed of gain, but for the world's commerce [and] we shall render inestimable service to mankind.

(Elihu Root, 'The ethics of the Panama question',
22 February 1904)

14

'Mandate from civilization'?

In January 1904 that same Teddy Roosevelt proclaimed to Congress that 'if ever a Government could be said to have received a mandate from civilization to effect an object the accomplishment of which was demanded in the interest of mankind, the United States holds that position with regard to the interoceanic canal'. Washington and Panama he was later to describe as the waterway's 'joint trustees for all the world'.[1]

In saying this Roosevelt was repeating what successive American administrations had maintained throughout the nineteenth century, beginning with Henry Clay's admonition in 1826 that the benefits of an isthmian transit 'ought not to be exclusively appropriated to any one nation'. In 1850 the French government was told that the United States 'would not, if they could, obtain any exclusive right of privilege in a great highway which naturally belonged to all mankind'. In 1885 President Grover Cleveland spoke of the project for a Nicaragua canal as 'a trust for mankind, to be removed from the chance of domination by any single power'.[2]

Yet this altruism simply made a virtue of necessity – the fact that the country was still too weak to monopolise canal development. Most Americans looked forward to the day when it would be strong enough to brook no rivals. The nationalism at the heart of U.S. policy was visible as early as 1846 in the treaty with Bogotá granting Washington the right-of-way over Panama. It was even more evident in the draft of 1849 giving the United States alone the concession to operate and defend a Nicaraguan crossing. But for the next half-century control of any future route had to be shared with Britain under the Clayton–Bulwer treaty of 1850, and the vision of an all-American enterprise was not fulfilled

---

[1] *BD*, 316, 711.

[2] *BD*, 3. Luke Lee, 'Legal aspects of internationalization of interoceanic canals', *Law and Contemporary Problems*, 33 (1968), 160. James Richardson (ed.), *A compilation of the messages and papers of the presidents, 1789–1897*, vol. 8 (Washington, D.C., 1898), 539.

until Roosevelt's day. In 1901 Britain acknowledged that a Central American seaway would come entirely within U.S. jurisdiction, and the 1903 canal convention signed with Panama gave the United States the complete mastery it had previously insisted no one state should ever be allowed to hold.[3]

Roosevelt's claim to act as agent of the world community thus rang hollow, and it was as bogus as the notion that the Suez Canal had been internationalised by the Constantinople convention of 1888. Britain took good care not to let the convention detract from its absolute authority over Suez, and Washington was determined to clamp no less tight a grip on Panama.[4]

The canal was consequently glorified as the emblem of American national might. In 1912 Franklin Roosevelt took infinite pride in 'this wonder of the world, greater than the Tower of Babel or the Pyramids'. To the doyen of U.S. navalists, Admiral Alfred Thayer Mahan, American dominion in Panama was as sacrosanct as the Monroe Doctrine. Senator Claude Swanson was to affirm that 'our national prestige and safety demand that the canal should be under our control and ownership. That is a national policy as fixed as the eternal stars. For its maintenance there is no sacrifice we would refuse.'[5]

Control was enforced via three concentric circles of U.S. power. The innermost ring was the Canal Zone, where Washington stood sovereign. Beyond that lay the protectorate over Panama, and then a far-flung perimeter encompassing the Caribbean and Pacific approaches. During the year following the seizure of Panama, Roosevelt formulated his corollary to the Monroe Doctrine, asserting a unilateral American claim to police the republics of the hemisphere on behalf of their foreign creditors. But fiscal order was intimately bound up with canal security: The canal's defence would be promoted by keeping shaky Latin American finances out of unfriendly alien hands. As Roosevelt's secretary of state, Elihu Root, observed, 'The inevitable effect of our building the canal must be to require us to police the surrounding premises.' It was essential, Root later noted, 'that there should be no hostile control of the route between our great Atlantic and Pacific ports and the Isthmus. . . . For that reason it is of special importance that the people inhabiting the islands and shores of the Caribbean shall maintain independent, peaceful and prosperous governments. . . . In that region . . . the United States must exercise a dominant influence. It is there that the true justification and necessity for the Monroe Doctrine is to be found.'[6]

[3] BD, 7–10, 16–21, 51, 127–9, 279–88.

[4] Text of the Constantinople convention is in Clive Parry (ed.), The consolidated treaty series, 171 (Dobbs Ferry, N.Y., 1978), 242–6. Farnie, Suez, 341.

[5] Elliott Roosevelt (ed.), The Roosevelt letters, vol. 2 (London, 1950), 161, 162. NYT, 2.4.12, 1/4. CR (Senate), 14.7.19, 2537.

[6] BD, 280. TR letters, 4: 801, Roosevelt to Root, 20.5.04. Theodore Roosevelt, Works, 15: 177. Jessup, Root, 1: 471. William Adams, 'Strategy, diplomacy and isthmian canal security, 1890–1917' (doctoral diss., Florida State University, 1974), 175.

This so-called Panama Policy was seldom compared with the colonialism which then held sway in Africa and Asia. Roosevelt could say that Japan had 'a paramount interest in what surrounds the Yellow Sea just as the United States has a paramount interest in what surrounds the Caribbean'. Root once remarked à propos the Japanese sphere in southern Manchuria that 'such a state of affairs is only natural to occur where one nation has special interest and influence. The condition of affairs in the Panama Canal Zone is another example.' But the Russo-Japanese partition of Manchuria also made nonsense of Washington's Open Door policy of standing up for China's rights. So Root was constrained to point out that if there were to be 'a broad belt of sovereignty drawn through the center of Manchuria, Russian at the one end, Japanese at the other, like our Canal Zone across the Isthmus of Panama, it may be very serious'. Root's successor, Philander Chase Knox, went very much farther. In November 1909 he was to call for the transfer of the Russian- and Japanese-owned Manchurian railway system to an international consortium. The same year a campaign was mounted by the American peace movement to have the canal declared neutral on the ground that it had been 'conveyed *in trust* to us for the benefit of the world's commerce'. But for Knox the two cases were entirely distinct: Depriving other powers of their strategic assets was a worthy cause; neutralisation of a vital American interest was strictly taboo.[7]

The U.S. establishment agreed. In 1912 Mahan was to write that 'the Isthmus of Panama, because of its interoceanic possibilities, was and is a world concern, in so far that if there be maladministration the world will interfere. If the United States do not give good administration and security she will hear from the world, though she be a strong state.' But when the idea of a multilateral guarantee of the canal's security was raised, Mahan protested that this would be 'to constitute over ourselves a kind of protectorate'. Neutralisation of the canal under international auspices, wrote the president of the Army War College, was 'fraught with all those dangers growing out of foreign entanglements and alliances so studiously avoided by our statesmen in the past'.[8]

Many Americans were ready to accept this double standard through their belief in the nation's moral superiority, among them Elbert Farman, the former U.S. consul-general in Cairo. In a book pointedly entitled *Egypt and Its betrayal*, Farman asserted that 'the conditions under which we are completing the Panama Canal furnish a marked and characteristic instance of the difference

---

[7] *TR letters*, 4: 830, Roosevelt letter of 13.6.04. Michael Hunt, *Frontier defense and the Open Door: Manchuria in Chinese–American relations, 1895–1911* (New Haven, Conn., 1973), 151. Raymond Esthus, 'The changing concept of the Open Door, 1899–1910', *Mississippi Valley Historical Review*, 46 (1959–60), 446, quoting Root remarks of 26.3.08. *FRUS 1910*, 234–5. Hains, 'Neutralization of the Panama Canal', 365 (emphasis in original).

[8] Mahan, 'Was Panama "a chapter of national dishonor"?' 568, and 'Fortify the Panama Canal', 331. WCD, 6178–6, Wotherspoon to Wood, 14.12.10.

between our manner of treating the small powers of America and the treatment of Oriental non-Christian countries by the European governments'. 'There is more than one "guaranteed" state in Europe,' wrote Willis Johnson after his visit to the isthmus in 1904. 'Moreover, such guarantees in Europe are largely for selfish purposes and for the maintenance of a "balance of power", while ours over Panama is made with the disinterested design of maintaining peace and order and of facilitating the commerce of the world.'[9]

Fortified by this strong self-righteousness, American politicians saw no trace of hegemony in the intense proprietary feeling the canal aroused. In March 1909 the Senate approved a further treaty with Panama with the proviso that no issue be submitted to arbitration touching the interests of the United States in 'the construction, operation, maintenance, sanitation and protection of the Panama Canal'. In 1912 Congress passed the Panama Canal Act, which exempted American coastal shipping from the payment of tolls. By Article 3 of the 1901 treaty with Britain, Secretary of State John Hay had accepted a version of the rules of the Constantinople convention as the basis of the canal's neutralisation. Under Rule 1 the canal was to be 'free and open to the vessels of commerce and war of all nations observing these rules, on terms of entire equality'. Now in the 1912 Act the promise of equal treatment had gone by the board. Washington, claimed President William Howard Taft, 'enjoys absolute rights of ownership and control, including the right to allow its own commerce the use of the canal upon such terms as it sees fit'. Confronted by a sustained British protest and by considerable disquiet from such figures as Root, Taft's successor, Woodrow Wilson, gave way, and the exemption of coastwise trade was repealed. In the regulations adopted for the canal's operation in 1914, however, transit was stated to be a privilege, presumably conferred by American grace and favour.[10]

Having won the battle over tolls, the British were ready to live and let live. When the subject of international waterways came before the Paris peace conference in January 1919, British spokesman Lord Robert Cecil steered well clear of the Panama Canal. It was 'property of the United States, and it must be for that country to say how it shall be controlled'. The matter did not end there, however. The American 'inquiry' team of experts on the manifold issues due to be thrashed out in Paris had just recommended internationalisation of the Kiel Canal, and Secretary of State Robert Lansing was apprehensive that the proposal might start an embarrassing discussion of Panama's status. He

[9] Elbert Farman, *Egypt and its betrayal: An account of the country during the periods of Ismail and Tewfik pashas, and of how England acquired a new empire* (New York, 1908), 211. Willis Johnson, *Four centuries of the Panama Canal*, 255.

[10] SD, 1910–49, 711.1928/1. BD, 128, 598, 608, 635. SD, 1910–49, 811F.812/300, 304, 320, 355, 400. Jessup, *Root*, 2: 262–9, covers Root's opposition to the exemption. Padelford, 'Neutrality, belligerency, and the Panama Canal', 64, and 'The Panama Canal in time of peace', 611–16.

consequently made certain that it was dropped, and when the question reached the Council of Four in April, only Clemenceau pressed for internationalisation and with it defortification. Kiel, professed the U.S. chief of naval operations, was of no concern to the outside world, and neutralisation would be excessive: 'To go into a country and make special provision for a Canal was very similar to going in and taking its railways.' Both the United States and Britain, of course, had done precisely that in Panama and Egypt, respectively, but as long as they stood shoulder to shoulder there was no chance their control would be shaken.[11]

It followed that a Panamanian appeal to Wilson on the eve of the conference got nowhere. In 1904 the diplomat Eusebio Morales had urged that the wrangle with Washington over the scope of U.S. sovereignty in the Zone be referred to the Permanent Court of Arbitration at The Hague. He now argued that the projected League of Nations should take over both the administration of the canal and the guarantee of Panama's independence.[12]

Nothing could have been less attractive to American opinion. Wilson's opponents in the Senate during the debate on the Versailles treaty and the League covenant refused to go to war to uphold the new world order, but they were certain that Washington would be bound to fight to protect the integrity of Panama and with it the free operation of the canal. And since the Monroe Doctrine was outside the scope of the covenant, not even Wilson's most dedicated supporters suggested that the guarantee should become a League responsibility.[13]

With the Senate's rejection of Versailles and United States membership of the League, the determination to keep the world body out of inter-American affairs hardened still further. In March 1921, when Panama tried to refer its border dispute with Costa Rica to League headquarters in Geneva, the State Department blocked the overture. By the autumn the Panamanians had been brought sternly to heel, their plea to go before the League's Permanent Court of International Justice turned down, and a detachment of Marines sent south

---

[11] *NYT*, 25.1.19, 3/6; 22.2.19, 1/4. Lawrence Gelfand, *The inquiry: American preparations for peace, 1917–1919* (New Haven, Conn., 1963), 197–8. SD, 1910–49, 184.00101/35, Meeting of 20.3.19 of Lansing, White, and Bliss; 180.03401/120, Minutes of meeting of Council of Four, 25.4.19. See also Link, *Papers of Woodrow Wilson*, 59: 123, and Etienne Mantoux, *Les délibérations du Conseil des Quatre, 24 mars – 28 juin 1919*, vol. 1 (Paris, 1955), 372–6. Kiel was ultimately governed by Articles 380–6 of the Versailles treaty, for which see Clive Parry (ed.), *The consolidated treaty series*, 225 (Dobbs Ferry, N.Y., 1981), 371–2.

[12] SD, 1910–49, 763.72119/3602, Price to Lansing, 6.1.19. Eusebio Morales, 'El canal de Panamá y la Liga de las Naciones', *Revista Nueva*, 6 (1919), 65–78. *Revista Loteriá*, 276 (February 1979), 36, Amador to Morales, 26.7.04.

[13] *CR* (Senate), 11.6.19, 956, statement by Senator Thomas Walsh; 12.8.19, 388, statement by Senator Henry Cabot Lodge. *NYT*, 15.7.19, 2/2; 10.8.19, 9/1. Text of Article 21 of the covenant excluding the Monroe Doctrine from the League's purview is in Parry, *Consolidated treaty series*, 225: 202.

to compel Panamanian acceptance of the frontier. Washington, a U.S. Army officer in the Zone proudly claimed, had acted as 'a League of Nations of its own' and done what League peacekeepers might themselves do some day, 'using a display of force to prevent a useless war'.[14]

The League was again ignored in a brief scuffle over the U.S.–Panama treaty of 1926. Article 11 committed Panama to war whenever the United States itself was a belligerent, and League officials took this as a slight, since it overrode Panama's obligations under the covenant. In a speech to the League Assembly the following year, Morales rejected the charge but claimed that if differences over the prickly issue of sovereignty could not be settled bilaterally, 'the two nations would still have the resource of submitting this and any other dispute to an impartial Court of Justice for its decision'. Construing the proposal as a bid to involve the Permanent Court in the Zone's affairs, the State Department immediately denied the League's competence to act, and the Senate weighed in with the flat statement from Swanson that Congress 'will not permit this sovereignty to be questioned'. At a banquet in honour of the visiting U.S. battle fleet commander, President Chiari was quick to offer the assurance that all disagreements could be ironed out without recourse to 'foreign intervention'.[15]

Yet though the idea of the League as a counterpoise to Washington was so decisively smothered, Panama kept up the search for some form of international arbitration – and with a certain amount of support from the State Department. When Panama's Washington envoy, Ricardo Alfaro, asked Secretary of State Charles Evans Hughes in 1923 for arbitration of the meaning of an article in the canal convention, the request was peremptorily dismissed. At the Pan-American conference in Havana five years later, however, Hughes's successor, Frank Kellogg, approved Alfaro's plan for a system of tribunals to adjudicate interstate disputes in the hemisphere. The abrogation of the Roosevelt Corollary was already in the making, and State Department blessing for Alfaro's scheme was thus in line with a general readiness to conciliate Latin opinion. In January 1929 the initiative blossomed into a general treaty of inter-American arbitration, but in the view of the department's treaty division, it served mainly 'as a *beau geste*' with little more substance than a public relations exercise.[16]

The point escaped the Senate, which in 1932 disembowelled the treaty with

[14] SD, 1910–49, 718.1915/356, Price to Hughes, 11.3.21. *NYT*, 26.7.21, 2/4; 2.8.21, 8/7; 26.9.21, 6/2.

[15] See *BD*, 836, for Article 11 of the 1926 treaty; text of Articles 12 and 13 of the covenant is in Parry, *Consolidated treaty series*, 255: 199. *NYT*, 23.12.26, 2/6. League of Nations, *Records of the eighth ordinary session of the Assembly* . . ., special supp. no. 54 (Geneva, 1927), 10.9.27, 8–9. *NYT*, 13.9.27, 1/1; 17.9.27, 3/5.

[16] *FRUS 1923*, 2: 710, Hughes to Alfaro, 13.10.23. *NYT*, 11.2.28, 6/3; 12.2.28, 10/1. Connell-Smith, *United States and Latin America*, 149–58. Text of the 1929 convention is in Manley Hudson (ed.), *International legislation: A collection of the texts of multipartite international instruments of general interest*, vol. 4 (Washington, D.C., 1931), 2625–33. SD, 1910–49, 710.1012 Washington/548, Treaty Division to White, 29.8.32.

a reservation excluding from arbitration any question touching Washington's sovereign rights over the canal. This, in the words of Senator William Borah, would squash the Panamanian contention that the United States 'never secured title in fee simple to the Canal Zone, that we simply secured a right of way, an easement'. The reservation was distinctly unwelcome to the State Department, but the Senate was not to be moved, and the treaty went unratified in consequence.[17]

So when the Franklin Roosevelt administration began talks with Panama on a treaty to supplement the 1903 convention, it was in the certain knowledge that it would not be endorsed by the Senate if it contained a commitment to arbitration. The proposal by President Harmodio Arias that economic disagreements should be settled by a third party was therefore watered down to the joint statement that Washington would 'sympathetically consider' requests from Panama for the arbitration of any 'purely economic' issue. Although the subject came up several times during the negotiations, it was never taken far. Panama's talk of referring the question of U.S. control of wireless traffic on the isthmus to the tribunals set up by two international radio conventions remained no more than talk. When the Panamanians complained that there was no provision for adjudication of key articles of the treaty, the chief American negotiator, Under Secretary Summer Welles, told them that such vital U.S. interests as the canal were not open to the process. If, as they seemed to wish, relations were to be based on international law, then Washington would be entitled as the wielder of sovereignty to do exactly as it chose with the Canal Zone. In 1937, when Panama called for arbiters to pronounce on its claim to reversionary rights to Panama Railroad land in Colón, Welles demurred for fear of damaging the treaty's chances in an already antagonistic Senate.[18]

In 1934 Roosevelt had described the United States as 'a trustee for all the world' in respect of the canal. This was, of course, sheer rhetoric, echoing his namesake's declamation on the mandate thirty years before. Though Roosevelt later spoke of Washington and Panama as associates in a 'joint trusteeship', he avoided putting the term into the treaty's wording. Unlike the mandatories of the League of Nations, the United States was not to be held responsible to any external body, and by the same token Panama was not to be given the chance of appealing to that body. The two were to continue locked in an exclusively

[17] SD, 1910–49, 710.1012 Washington/544, 545, 546, 547, 548, 549, and 550. See CR (Senate), 19.1.32, 2311, for Borah statement.

[18] See BD, 865, 869, for Panama memo of 21.9.33 and Roosevelt–Arias statement of 17.10.33. SD, 1910–49, 711.19/183; 819.74/183, 192, 253, 287⅓, 310, and 311; 711.1928/436½, Minutes of meeting of 22.10.35; 819.77/454 and 464. See also 711.1928/436½, Minutes of meeting of 29.10.35, and PC, 94-A-3/A, Wang to Schley, 24.10.34; 33-E-5, Rossbottom to Schley, 3.4.36; Wang to Ridley, 28.10.36; Smith to Ridley, 12.8.37; Woodring to Hull, 23.8.37. Texts of the conventions of 1927 and 1932 are in Hudson, International legislation, vol. 3 (1931), 2197–2210, and vol. 6 (1937), 109–33.

bilateral relationship, and Welles bluntly reminded the Panamanians that they had no choice but to rely on American goodwill.[19]

Panama could be treated in this high-handed way for a number of very basic reasons. In the first place, it was impossible for a country with the population of North Dakota and the territorial area of South Carolina to challenge a nation as gigantic as the United States. Moreover, Panama had no alternative patron, in the shape of a great power or an international organisation, to turn to for support outside the hemisphere. There was, finally, the undeniable fact that the local oligarchy was in most ways content enough to accept American tutelage, since there were rich pickings to be got from the canal, and their nationalism expressed itself in a drive to sluice off a bigger percentage from this bounteous source, not to waste time in a vain bid to take it over.

The plight of Panama comes into fuller perspective when a comparison is drawn with Egypt. In the treaty it signed with Britain in 1936, Egypt too was confirmed as a satellite, yet it gained the right to appeal to the League of Nations in the event of a dispute with its suzerain. This was a concession denied to Panama, given Washington's determination to keep the isthmus completely beyond the reach of any influence but its own. Egypt, however, with twelve times the area and thirty times the population of Panama, was altogether harder to handle, and the backing it received from Fascist Italy in the 1930s was a factor which had to be taken into account in planning for the defence of Suez. More important, in Egypt Britain confronted a state which had once been a considerable regional power, which had gone down fighting against military occupation in 1882, and many of whose leaders aimed at full independence from British rule. By 1919 Egyptian extremists were prepared to take their resistance movement to the point of terrorism, and five years later they assassinated the British commander-in-chief of their army. Nothing about Panama made it such a poisonous thorn in Washington's side.[20]

At worst, it seemed, the Panamanians were capable of nothing more than a spiteful ingratitude towards Americans, who saw themselves as their benefactors. 'The Panamanian has little love for the United States or its people,' wrote a former Zone police officer, 'which is the customary thanks any man or nation gets for lifting a dirty half-breed gamin from the gutter.' The apparent Panamanian friendship for the United States, remarked the naval district commandant in 1937, was 'only a surface veneer' concealing 'their true hatred of our government and our people'.[21]

---

[19] *NYT*, 12.7.34. sect. VI, 4. On 'joint trusteeship', see Chapter, 12 at nn. 17 and 18. SD, 1910–49, 711.1928/436½, Minutes of meeting of 22.10.35.

[20] Text of 1936 Anglo-Egyptian treaty is in *American Journal of International law*, 31 (1937), Official Documents, 77–94. On Egypt, see Tom Little, *Modern Egypt*, (London, 1967), 30–47, 70–85.

[21] Franck, *Zone policeman*, 230. ONI, C-9-C, 21743A, Marshall to Leahy, 21.1.37.

The Zone could live with this animosity, however, and Panama could be kept on a relatively loose rein. In 1925 U.S. Army Intelligence observed that 'the United States exercises what might be classed as a very liberal protectorate over Panama. Independence of action is permitted only so long as the acts do not threaten the safety of the canal.' Panamanians, in short, were treated as minors, and the experience inevitably promoted an institutional mentality. As chargé John Muccio put it in 1944, Panamanians tended to look instinctively to American authority for a solution to their political problems. Washington's influence was pervasive and inescapable, 'even though we should be able to keep our mouths tightly shut and take no overt action. . . . The question is not so much what we actually do, as what they think we do'.[22]

It was, in other words, a profoundly unequal relationship. 'If they really tried,' wrote a State Department desk officer in 1954, 'the Panamanians could make life difficult for us . . . [but] we could make life even more difficult for the Panamanians.' An anonymous Panamanian diplomat, speaking to the press in 1927, drew a bleak conclusion. 'When you hit a rock with an egg, the egg breaks. Or when you hit an egg with a rock, the egg breaks. The United States is the rock. Panama is the egg. In either case, the egg breaks.'[23]

The treaty promoted by Roosevelt and Welles was designed to make this fragility more tolerable to Panama through a judicious measure of appeasement. In this it called to mind Jan Christiaan Smuts's description of the mandate policy he fostered for the League in 1919: 'reform of the colonial system which, short of abolishing sovereignty, would take the sting out of it'. But just as Panamanians found it hard to break the habit of obedience, so Americans persisted in seeing Panama as a fiefdom where Panamanian interests would always come second to the requirements of U.S. national security. This attitude was heavily reinforced by another world war, when the defence of the canal became an even more critical element in Washington's dealings with Panama. Welles, for example, in 1942 looked forward to a post-war world in which the British base at Singapore would come under international control, but not the Canal Zone. In 1944 the Panamanian delegation to the Chicago conference on civil aviation was swiftly discouraged from proposing a multinational board with power to regulate flights over the isthmus.[24]

Perhaps the most outstanding wartime revelation of basic American assumptions about the canal came in a paper by an authority on Suez, Professor

[22] MID, 3750, Memo of 10.2.25. SD, 1910–49, 819.00/6–644, Muccio to Bonsal, 6.6.44.
[23] SD, 1950–4, 611.1913/5–1854, Memminger memo of 18.5.54. *NYT*, 2.10.27, sect. IX, 5/1.
[24] W. Keith Hancock, *Smuts: The sanguine years, 1870–1919* (London, 1962), 499. Christopher Thorne, *Allies of a kind: The United States, Britain, and the war against Japan, 1941–1945* (London, 1978), 215. OPD, 580.82 CDC, Operations Division memo of 17.11.44. Lawrence Ealy, *The Republic of Panama in world affairs, 1903–1950* (Philadelphia, 1951), 147.

Halford Hoskins. 'It is nothing less than ironical', stated Hoskins, 'that the
Canal which was constructed through Egyptian soil so largely at Egyptian
expense not only remained from the outset commercially and politically in
European hands but also held Egypt in a state of dependence from which it has
not entirely escaped.' Looking to the future, it was difficult to suppose that as
long as the canal remained a vital strategic asset to Britain there would not be
'an expectation of retaining a share in the direction of Canal affairs'. If Egypt
were to be given full operational control of the canal, there would be a danger
of intervention by other states, and this had been 'at the bottom of British
determination to maintain a protective position relative to the Canal and even
with reference to Egypt itself'. Mutatis mutandis, most of what Hoskins said
about Suez applied equally to Panama, but no parallel was drawn. Instead, there
was an apparent blindness to the fact that Washington too had a vassal and
a sublime confidence that, unlike Britain, it would face no problems from its
underling's burgeoning nationalism in the post-war era.[25]

The war gave a sharp stimulus to Panamanian aspirations, however, and it
also brought outside influences into play from which the canal had largely been
screened by the United States' self-imposed isolation. The war had committed
Washington to a central rôle in world events, and its continuing involvement in
the post-war arena made such American interests as the canal the focus of an
international attention only rarely experienced before the 1940s.

The chief object of international concern was the Zone's segregationist employment policy, which came under fire at the International Labour Organisation's
conference in the spring of 1944. When the ILO called for a ban on discriminatory
employment practices by member states, the Zone bristled at interference from
a body whose authority it denied outright. In January 1945 Governor Joseph
Mehaffey refused to answer an ILO questionnaire, and Secretary of War Henry
Stimson did not overrule him.[26]

International interest did not fade, however. In January 1946 the United
Nations too called for information from members on conditions in their dependencies, including the Canal Zone. In October the Zone was reported to the
UN, but not until a heated dispute had been fought out between those who
saw the canal entirely as an American national interest and those who took
the concept of a mandate seriously. To the State Department's senior Latin
Americanist, Spruille Braden, the Zone was no business of the UN's. To the
head of its United Nations office, Alger Hiss, Washington had a firm obligation
to co-operate with the world community. But though the report was submitted,

[25] SD, Records of Harley A. Notter, 1939–1945, Box 63, T, Document 302, Halford Hoskins,
'The Suez Canal and Egyptian interests', 1.4.43.
[26] See Chapter 9 at n. 37. The issue is covered in detail in John Major, ' "Pro mundi beneficio"?
The Panama Canal as an international issue, 1943–8', *Review of International Studies*, 9 (1983),
17–34.

it was not sent in again, since Panama also jibbed at UN involvement; and the initiative was not repeated. When the ILO simultaneously relaxed its pressure for reform of Zone employment practices, the threat from what Mehaffey had seen as a nascent 'inquisitorial super-state' appeared to have been fended off.[27]

Yet the canal could not be divorced from the world at large. Like the Paris conference of 1919, the Potsdam summit of 1945 did not discuss the waterway, but in 1946 and 1947 the spotlight continually fell on Panama. When Washington opposed the Soviet bid to control the Dardanelles, there were some who condemned the Truman administration for refusing the USSR what the USA itself possessed on the isthmus. 'The Russians', declared Senator Claude Pepper, 'have as much right in there as we have to be in Panama.' The difference, for Secretary of the Navy James Forrestal, however, lay between the benevolent American stewardship of Panama and imperialistic Soviet designs on Turkey.[28]

Russia's riposte to Forrestal was to call – as it had done as early as 1917 – for the internationalisation of Panama and Suez, 'instruments in the struggle of the Anglo-Saxon bloc for a dominant role in the world'. The rejoinder also pointed to the nationalist unrest in both Panama and Egypt, where demands for the withdrawal of American and British troops had been made repeatedly since the end of the war. The Egyptians took their case to the United Nations, and in 1951 their claims on Suez were enormously heightened after Iran's nationalisation of Western oil concerns. By the end of the year Cairo had abrogated the 1936 treaty and launched a campaign of guerrilla warfare against the British garrison.[29]

The repercussions of both Middle East crises put Washington in a highly uncomfortable fix. In November 1951 Ambassador John Wiley reported that events in Iran and Egypt had not gone unnoticed in Panama. The United States could not therefore follow its anti-colonialist instincts and encourage Egypt without risking a Panamanian onslaught on its own position. And its aversion to supporting Egyptian insistence on a decisive voice in the operation of Suez was compounded by Cairo's refusal to allow Israeli vessels through the canal after the Arab–Israeli war of 1948–9. In August 1951 the U.S. delegate to the United Nations protested against the ban and stressed the international character of Suez as a transit no single government had the right to control.[30]

In doing so, however, he laid himself open to the charge that Washington would react in exactly the same way to stop enemy ships using Panama. Moreover,

[27] Ibid.

[28] SD, 1910–49, 811F.812/7–345, Donnelly to Stettinius, 3.7.45. In August 1956 former president Truman claimed he had urged the internationalisation of the Suez, Panama, and Kiel canals at Potsdam, but the documentation of the conference shows no evidence of this; see NYT, 10.8.56, 7/1; 6.10.46, sect. IV, 5/7; 18.4.47, 1/2.

[29] NYT, 22.10.17, 2/4. SD, 1910–49, 811F.812/1–1147. NYT, 11.1.47, 4/7. Farnie, Suez, 636–9, 662, 691–4, 697–702.

[30] SD, 1950–4, 719.00/11–751; 911F.5301/4–152; 911F.7301/2–752. YBUN 1951, 293–9.

in emphasising the status of Suez as an international waterway, the State Department was painfully aware that it would immediately be asked why Panama too should not be internationalised. This would have put Washington unequivocally on the spot, but it was spared the embarrassment. During the treaty negotiations of 1953–4 Panama made no attempt to raise the issue beyond a proposal that both parties should submit all disputes to the International Court of Justice and accept its verdict. The idea was summarily rejected, and Panama did not pursue it, apart from a momentary rumble from President Remón which soon passed over.[31]

Yet two years later Suez came back to haunt Washington with a vengeance. In July 1956 the revolutionary régime of Colonel Nasser nationalised the Suez Canal Company, in which Britain was the leading shareholder. The British expected the American backing they had got in Iran three years earlier when the Central Intelligence Agency fostered the removal of the radical leadership which had confiscated their oil interests. After a pointed reading from the *Annual Register* for 1903 on the subject of Theodore Roosevelt's master stroke, Viscount Hinchingbrooke told the House of Commons he believed 'that when the United States looks upon the isthmus of Suez in the same way as her history must look upon the isthmus of Panama . . . she should feel herself compelled . . . to come to our aid with the least possible delay'.[32]

Not so. Hinchingbrooke had evidently forgotten the cool reception given by Congress to Prime Minister Winston Churchill's plea in January 1952 for a token American detachment to help guard the canal against the insurgency Egypt had recently launched, and no rescue mission was forthcoming. When Secretary of State John Foster Dulles flew to London on 31 July, it was not to concert measures to restore the status quo ante. Instead Dulles proposed a multinational authority for Suez, a dénouement which would make Nasser 'disgorge' but which would not allow the Company to repossess. It would, pronounced Dulles, be 'intolerable that an international waterway should be under the domination of one country without international control and supervision', and clearly his finding applied to Britain just as much as it did to Egypt.[33]

Internationlisation had no bearing on Panama, however, where, as far as Dulles was concerned, 'international interest [was] really limited to the tolls

---

[31] SD, 1950–4, 911F.5301/2–2152; 911F.54/3–452; 611.19/7–1053, Sowash to Woodward; 611.19/7–1053, Memo to Egypt Desk; 811F.06/6-554.

[32] U.K. Parliament, *Parliamentary debates* (Commons), 5th ser., 1955–6, vol. 557., col. 1638.

[33] *NYT*, 18.1.52, 1/8, 4/5. Martin Gilbert, '*Never Despair': Winston S. Churchill 1945–1965* (London, 1988), 676, 679–80, 684–5, 689. *FRUS 1955–1957*, 16:95. Professor Hoskins suggested an international Suez Canal commission as early as 1944: See Halford Hoskins, 'The Suez Canal and the outlook for Egypt', *American Political Science Review*, 38 (1944), 117.

agreement with the U.K.', that is, Wilson's abandonment in 1914 of toll-free passage for American coastal shipping. 'Our own position in Panama', Dulles told the British premier, Anthony Eden, 'was dependent upon a treaty and if we accepted the view that merely because a waterway had international use the world generally was able to deal with it and control it, we would be cut away from our moorings in Panama.' Moreover, as he later put it to President Eisenhower, unlike Egypt in its treatment of Suez, Washington was not exploiting Panama 'to further some grandiose plan of aggrandizement'. Both observations were in piquant contrast with what the young Dulles had said at the height of the tolls controversy. Addressing the American Society of International Law in 1913, he had declared that because Panama was 'affected with an international use', the United States was not entitled 'to use the canal as a club, to impose American policies on the world'. To have come out with such liberalism in 1956 would have given Panama ammunition for a damaging assault on U.S. treaty rights, and a devotee of the 1903 treaty like the intensely illiberal old Dulles was the last man to do that.[34]

Eden bowed to internationalisation, but there can be little doubt where his true preferences lay. In 1933 he had been present in Geneva on the day the League condemned Japan's seizure of Manchuria and voted for international supervision of the area under League auspices. Washington and London had both approved, and the Japanese delegate did not hide his bitterness. 'Would the American people agree to such control over the Panama Canal?' he asked. 'Would the British people permit it over Egypt?' In 1946 Eden had voiced a similar concern when he told the Commons that the Canal Zone was 'United States territory, but nobody doubts that the continuation of this state of affairs is not only an American interest, but a world interest' like the Soviet neutralisation of Finland or British paramountcy in Egypt. Dulles's projected multilateral agency for Suez thus directly undercut Eden's assumption that great powers were members of a select brotherhood who should respect each other's strategic prerogatives.[35]

In 1919 Dulles's uncle Robert Lansing had closed ranks with Britain to snuff out talk of internationalising Panama and Suez, but Dulles broke that Anglo-American solidarity, as did Eisenhower at his news conference on 1 August 1956. Invited to comment on whether calls to internationalise Suez might not put like pressure on Panama, the reply was that 'the conditions aren't the same'. The line that the two were on quite different legal footings had been maintained for more than half a century, but there were immediate reasons for restating the

[34] FRUS 1955–1957, 16: 95, 99, 199. John Foster Dulles, 'The Panama tolls question', Proceedings of the American Society of International Law, 7 (1913), 193, 196.
[35] Christopher Thorne, The limits of foreign policy: The West, the League and the Far Eastern crisis of 1931–1933 (London, 1972), 336. U.K. Parliament, Parliamentary debates (Commons), 5th ser., 1945–6, vol. 423, col. 705.

American case. Soviet Russia was once more making mischief by querying why
Washington should pick out Suez for internationalisation while saying nothing
about 'other not less important sea straits and canals'. Nasser himself was
floating the idea that Panama, the Dardanelles, the Strait of Gibraltar, and the
Gulf of Aden should all be put under United Nations jurisdiction. At the same
time, Panama was redeveloping the thesis first advanced by Harmodio Arias in
1911, namely, that Suez and Panama were fundamentally analogous in that both
were operated by the rules of the Constantinople convention. And, as Harmodio's
son Roberto later contended, the Egyptian canal grant of 1854 and the Panama
treaty of 1903 were each 'a contract of concession for an international public
service'.[36]

The administration found all such arguments profoundly disturbing. When
Nasser touched on Panama in conversation with the U.S. ambassador in Cairo,
he was instantly warned that he was 'treading on dangerous ground indeed in
any reference to the Panama Canal. If as he predicted Egypt and Russia might
end up side by side in an effort to place international control over all restricted
waterways, including the Panama Canal, he would have the wrath of all America
against him.' 'Thinking of our situation in Panama,' Eisenhower had told Dulles
at the outset of the crisis, 'we must not let Nasser get away with this action.'
Dulles for his part was said to have threatened to discipline any of his officials
who even verbally drew a parallel between the one and the other.[37]

Perhaps the most revealing evidence of high-level disquiet was a State Department circular to all U.S. diplomatic posts in Latin America instructing
them to avoid 'any precedent or step which might result in demands, from
Panama or any other source, for internationalization of the Panama Canal being
considered in the UN or OAS [Organization of American States] forums'.
Although Panama owed its very existence to Washington, 'and its transformation
from a miserably misgoverned and backward province of Colombia', it was still
not satisfied. It continually sought 'to encroach upon our exclusive jurisdiction
. . . with a view . . . to terminating [it] by the establishment of joint control and
administration of the Canal or by its internationalisation'. At the root of this
drive was the Panamanian determination to curtail American sovereign powers,
and to acquiesce in that would bring 'administrative chaos within the Zone and
imperil the efficient operation and security of the Canal'.[38]

Dulles's response was to push for a Suez settlement entirely within the

---

[36] *Public papers of the presidents of the United States: Dwight D. Eisenhower: 1956* (Washington,
D.C., 1957), 627. *NYT*, 10.8.56, 1/8, 2/4. Sarvepalli Gopal, 'India, the crisis and the non-
aligned nations', in William Roger Louis and Roger Owen (eds.), *Suez 1956: The crisis and
its consequences* (Oxford, 1989), 176–7. Harmodio Arias, *The Panama Canal: A study in
international law and diplomacy* (London, 1911), 147. *Times*, 1.5.57, 11/5.
[37] *FRUS 1955–1957*, 16: 133, 65. *NYT*, 9.9.75, sect. IV, 15/6.
[38] SD, 1955–60, 611.1913/8–956, Circular to all ARA missions, 9.8.56, 7, 4, 5, 7.

framework of the Constantinople convention, whose nine signatories were charged with monitoring its implementation, and which bound Egypt to carry out its provisions. This was internationalisation up to a point, but Dulles refused to go beyond that point for fear of the repercussions on Panama. If any bid were made to supersede the convention and have the United Nations require Egypt's acceptance of a new agreement, there might then be a move 'to impose a treaty on the United States with respect to the Panama Canal'. A supervisory régime based on the convention would steer clear of that unwelcome contingency and of the subsequent need for an American veto in the UN Security Council. At the end of August, Dulles set out the government view at a State Department briefing, asserting that Suez was already internationalised by Constantinople, whereas the status of Panama derived wholly from the bilateral treaties of 1901 and 1903, which gave Washington an unchallengeable monopoly of control. The citadel built by Hay and Bunau-Varilla stood unshaken, and the notion of the canal as a trusteeship held on behalf of the world at large had been stamped on in no uncertain terms.[39]

In the crisis which exploded in January 1964 over the flag issue, Washington was also quick to stifle Panama's attempt to give its call for treaty revision international significance. 'The question might be raised', wrote one American commentator, 'whether the treaty [of 1903] has long since lost in part its bilateral character and become, in respect to the United States, an obligation to all the world.' But 'larger interests' were at stake than 'the appeasement of the nationalistic feelings of the people of Panama'. They were not spelled out, but prominent among them without any doubt was the appeasement of the nationalistic feelings of the people of the United States, for whom the canal continued to be a totemic symbol of American power.[40]

To head off a Panamanian resort to the United Nations, the conflict was put in the hands of the Inter-American Peace Committee of the Organization of American States. When it failed to produced a settlement and Panama planned to charge Washington with aggression under the Rio treaty of 1947, the OAS Council was persuaded instead to set up an investigating committee. This also was intended as a mere analgesic, but its peace formula was too much for Republican leaders in Congress to stomach, since it implied a commitment to rewrite the 1903 treaty ab initio. President Lyndon Johnson thereupon destroyed the initiative, but Panama did not turn to the UN, as it had threatened to do if

[39] Full text of the Constantinople convention of 29 October 1888 is in *Hertslet's commercial treaties*, 18 (London, 1893), 369–73, *FRUS 1955–1957*, 16: 65, 412, 49. Text of Dulles statement of 28 August 1956 is in U.S. Department of State, *The Suez Canal problem: July 26 – September 22, 1956*, Pub. 6392 (1956), 301. See also Baxter, *Law of international waterways*, 176.

[40] Charles Fenwick, 'Legal aspects of the Panama case', *American Journal of International law*, 58 (1964), 440.

recourse to the OAS led nowhere. Relations with Washington were resumed in a remarkably short time.[41]

The episode revealed a good deal about the attitudes of both states towards the bearing of the international community on the canal. For Assistant Secretary Thomas Mann, the OAS Council committee was simply a nuisance which had to be prevented from carrying out 'an investigation of the facts . . . or other important action'. Told at the outset of treaty negotiations in 1953 that Panama was enlisting diplomatic support in the hemisphere, Mann had curtly informed Ambassador Roberto Huertematte that 'the United States does not respond to pressure of this kind'. U.S. missions in Latin America were subsequently told that the department regarded U.S.–Panama relations as 'strictly bilateral: public endorsements of Panama's claims by other American republics are considered improper and inadmissible'.[42]

Yet Panama's campaign for Latin American involvement had its limits. In the aftermath of the Suez war, the Panamanian commentator Domingo Turner had argued that 'if Latin America were for the Republic of Panama what the Arab world was for Egypt, Panama would undoubtedly take a clear stand, more forceful, decisive and in agreement with its international interests'. But when in 1959 the Costa Rican president, José Figueres, suggested that Washington transfer the canal to an OAS administration, Panama immediately turned down the idea. If it had ever become a serious negotiating proposal, the same reception would certainly have been given to the scheme thought up by Kennedy's Latin America Task Force in 1961. This was for a sea-level canal operated by a multinational agency effectively under American control and protected by an inter-American defence force mostly comprising U.S. troops and under the command of a U.S. Army general – in short, the ancien régime beneath a thin hemispheric veneer.[43]

[41] *NYT*, 11.1.64, 1/3, 1/4, 1/8; 21.1.64, 1/2, 10/4, 11/1; 29.1.64, 1/7, 14/4; 7.2.64, 1/7, 12/1. *BD*, 1069–95. Texts of relevant Rio treaty articles are in James Gantenbein (ed.), *The evolution of our Latin American policy: A documentary record* (New York, 1950), 823–6. Eric Goldman, *The tragedy of Lyndon Johnson* (New York, 1969), 74–5. Jorden, *Panama odyssey*, 82–3.

[42] Walter LaFeber, 'Latin American policy', in Robert Divine (ed.), *Exploring the Johnson years* (Austin, Tex., 1981), 69. SD, 1950–4, 819.11/3–3153; 611.199/4–753; 611.1913/6–2653.

[43] Domingo Turner, 'Foster Dulles y el Canal de Panamá', *Humanismo*, 5 (1957), 33–4 (author's translation). Mercer Tate, 'The Panama Canal and political partnership', *Journal of Politics*, 25 (1963), 135. Furlong and Scranton, *Dynamics of foreign policymaking*, 46. In 1964 Senator Fulbright put up a proposal, similar to the Kennedy Task Force blueprint, for an international consortium with some representation for the OAS *and* including the Soviet Union if need be. This, he claimed, would spare Washington 'the extremely sensitive political problems connected with being the sole proprietor of an international thoroughfare across the territory of another country'. See J. William Fulbright, *Old myths and new realities* (New York, 1964), 21–4.

In January 1964, when Ambassador Aquilino Boyd went before the UN Security Council to demand either the return of the Canal Zone or internationalisation with special rights for Panama, it seemed clear to one State Department man that for Panama the second option was not viable. 'I doubt GOP [Government of Panama] would be willing to take risk of possible ultimate "internationalization",' wrote the anonymous annotator of Adlai Stevenson's memorandum of his conversation with Boyd. 'GOP knows it can better deal with USG [U.S. Government] and would not want to diffuse its leverage among 18 others in OAS or 110 others in UN!'[44]

It was not an unbiassed judgement. Washington unquestionably preferred to have Panama facing it alone across the negotiating table. But it hit the mark. For Panama, as for the United States itself in the early nineteenth century, support for internationalism was the only policy open to a powerless state. Both embraced the cause not for its instrinsic merits but because they lacked the strength to secure their interests independently. When Torrijos staged the Security Council meeting in his capital nine years later, it was to dramatise Panama's claims, not to place the canal under UN or OAS control.

Caught in a minority of one when the Council took its vote, the United States ultimately came to terms on treaties handing the canal over to Panama at the end of the century and ensuring its neutrality indefinitely thereafter. But the urge to keep the outside world at bay did not subside. In the closing months of the negotiations, Torrijos was told that a United Nations guarantee of neutrality was unacceptable, and the arbitration formula worked out as the treaty came up for signature was carefully non-committal. And though a treaty opponent such as Professor Hans Smit was to argue that Washington alone could not send in troops to uphold neutrality because of its overriding obligations under the UN charter and the charter of the OAS, this was no more than disingenuous legalism. As Senator Ernest Hollings was to put it on the final day of the ratification debate, 'No language will force us in or force us out. It depends on . . . the intent, the steel, the determination, and the will of a national Congress.'[45]

So while the United States relinquished its mandate to operate the canal, the mandate to defend it stood, through an everlasting watch on the isthmus, beyond the moment of American withdrawal. The price of Panamanian liberty,

[44] *DDRS, 1978*, 426D, Stevenson memo of conversation with Boyd, 21.1.64.

[45] Jorden, *Panama odyssey*, 345, 442–3. The more binding arbitration clause in the 1967 draft treaty may be found in *BD*, 1219–20, 1347–8. The difference between it and the 1978 arrangement was pointed out by Senator Robert Griffin: See SCFR, *Hearings*, 1: 266–7. Hans Smit, 'The proposed Panama Canal treaties: A triple failure', *Columbia Journal of Transnational Law*, 17 (1978), 2, 7–10. For the text of Article 2(4) of the UN charter, see *YBUN 1946–47*, 831; for that of Article 15 of the OAS charter, see Inter-American Institute of International Legal Studies, *The inter-American system: Its development and strengthening* (Dobbs Ferry, N.Y., 1966), 344. *Sen. Deb.*, 3: 5460.

as after 1903, was to be eternal American vigilance. Though General Manuel Noriega momentarily called into question Washington's power to chart the destiny of the republic, the U.S. invasion which removed him in 1989 proved that the American urge to dominate was as strong as ever. The 1977 treaties had shown, wrote one of their most enthusiastic partisans, 'that we are sincere in our desire to relegate hemispheric paternalism and hegemony to the history books'. That claim has already been impaired, and the century to come will continue to put it to the test, in Panama and in the Americas at large.[46]

[46] Gale McGee, 'After Panama: Some lessons and opportunities in the aftermath of the canal treaties debate', *South Atlantic Quarterly*, 78 (1979), 7.

Appendix A: Full-time civilian work force, 1904–1979

Year	Gold/U.S. Rate	Silver/Local rate	Total
1904	46	700	746
1905	2,705	14,250	16,955
1906	3,700	13,300	17,000
1907	5,544	23,902	29,446
1908	5,403	25,328	30,731
1909	5,009	28,484	33,493
1910	5,275	30,303	35,578
1911	5,078	27,612	32,690
1912	4,940	30,017	34,957
1913	5,671	37,679	43,350
1914	4,257	25,416	29,673
1915	3,593	23,304	26,897
1916	3,492	19,970	23,462
1917	3,549	20,597	24,146
1918	3,108	16,157	19,265
1919	3,290	17,071	20,361
1920	4,608	17,023	21,631
1921	3,506	10,035	13,541
1922	2,553	7,623	10,176
1923	2,583	8,418	11,001
1924	2,810	8,701	11,511
1925	2,885	9,385	12,270
1926	2,879	9,940	12,819
1927	2,936	10,467	13,403
1928	3,038	10,884	13,922
1929	3,225	12,487	15,712

Year	Gold/U.S. Rate	Silver/Local rate	Total
1930	3,344	11,780	15,124
1931	3,276	10,624	13,900
1932	3,148	9,120	12,268
1933	3,028	9,575	12,603
1934	2,934	9,086	12,020
1935	3,087	9,365	12,452
1936	3,233	9,675	12,908
1937	3,418	10,159	13,577
1938	3,386	10,413	13,799
1939	3,511	11,246	14,757
1940	5,258	18,891	24,149
1941	7,260	25,994	33,254
1942	8,550	28,686	37,236
1943	8,357	26,293	34,650
1944	6,974	23,040	30,014
1945	6,685	24,347	31,032
1946	5,918	21,944	27,862
1947	5,418	19,276	24,694
1948	5,020	17,716	22,736
1949	4,779	16,559	21,338
1950	4,322	14,470	18,792
1951	4,214	14,519	18,735
1952	4,358	13,881	18,239
1953	3,987	12,405	16,392
1954	3,860	10,951	14,811
1955	3,726	10,147	13,873
1956	3,596	9,719	13,315
1957	3,536	9,313	12,849
1958	3,621	9,584	13,205
1959	3,531	8,946	12,477
1960	3,606	9,161	12,767
1961	3,686	9,660	13,346
1962	3,688	9,975	13,663
1963	3,766	10,370	14,136
1964	3,794	10,277	14,071
1965	3,821	10,444	14,265
1966	3,873	10,519	14,392
1967	3,970	10,870	14,840
1968	4,010	11,314	15,324
1969	3,986	11,146	15,132
1970	3,965	11,089	15,054
1971	3,892	10,635	14,527
1972	3,845	10,551	14,396
1973	3,795	10,495	14,290
1974	3,805	10,628	14,433
1975	3,949	10,442	14,391
1976	3,531	9,635	13,166

Year	Gold/U.S. Rate	Silver/Local rate	Total
1977	3,467	9,929	13,396
1978	3,465	10,095	13,560
1979	3,327	9,090	12,417

Note: All figures are for June, except for 1904, 1905, and 1906, which are for May, November, and November respectively. The figures for these years exclude employees of the Panama Railroad, who are included for the years 1907–79.

Appendix B: Chief Canal administrators, 1904–1979

John Walker	9.5.04 to 31.3.05
Theodore Shonts	1.4.05 to 3.3.07
John Stevens	4.3.07 to 31.3.07
George Washington Goethals	1.4.07 to 10.1.17
Chester Harding	11.1.17 to 27.3.21
Jay Morrow	28.3.21 to 15.10.24
Meriwether Walker	16.10.24 to 15.10.28
Harry Burgess	16.10.28 to 20.10.32
Julian Schley	21.10.32 to 26.6.36
Clarence Ridley	27.6.36 to 10.7.40
Glen Edgerton	11.7.40 to 15.5.44
Joseph Mehaffey	16.5.44 to 19.5.48
Francis Newcomer	20.5.48 to 26.5.52
John Seybold	27.5.52 to 26.5.56
William Potter	27.5.56 to 30.6.60
William Carter	1.7.60 to 31.1.62
Robert Fleming	1.2.62 to 31.1.67
Walter Leber	21.2.67 to 2.3.71
David Parker	3.3.71 to 23.3.75
Harold Parfitt	24.3.75 to 1.10.79

Appendix C: Garrison commanders, 1914–1979

Clarence Edwards	16.11.14 to 11.4.17
Edward Plummer	12.4.17 to 13.8.17
Adalbert Cronkhite	14.8.17 to 30.8.17
George Landers	31.8.17 to 27.2.18
Richard Blatchford	28.2.18 to 27.4.19
Chase Kennedy	28.4.19 to 23.5.21
Edwin Babbitt	24.5.21 to 21.10.21
Samuel Sturgis	22.10.21 to 18.9.24
William Lassiter	19.9.24 to 12.1.26
William Martin	13.1.26 to 1.10.27
William Graves	2.10.27 to 31.3.28
Malin Craig	1.4.28 to 9.8.30
George Irwin	10.8.30 to 23.11.30
Preston Brown	24.11.30 to 13.11.33
Harold Fiske	14.11.33 to 9.11.35
Lytle Brown	10.11.35 to 29.7.36
Henry Butner	30.7.36 to 9.2.37
Frank Rowell	10.2.37 to 11.4.37
David Stone	12.4.37 to 7.1.40
Daniel Van Voorhis	8.1.40 to 18.9.41
Frank Andrews	19.9.41 to 8.11.42
George Brett	9.11.42 to 14.10.45
Willis Crittenberger	15.10.45 to 28.6.48
Matthew Ridgway	29.6.48 to 30.9.49

William Morris	1.10.49 to 31.3.52
Horace McBride	1.4.52 to 14.6.54
William Harrison	15.6.54 to 31.12.56
Robert Monrague	1.1.57 to 1.3.58
Truman Landon	2.3.58 to 31.3.58
Ridgely Gaither	1.4.58 to 31.7.60
Robert Sink	1.8.60 to 31.1.61
Andrew O'Meara	1.2.61 to 28.2.65
Robert Porter	1.3.65 to 28.2.69
George Mather	1.3.69 to 30.9.71
George Underwood	1.10.71 to 31.1.73
William Rosson	1.2.73 to 30.9.75
Dennis McAuliffe	1.10.75 to 1.10.79

Appendix D: Heads of diplomatic mission, 1903–1982

William Buchanan	17.12.03 to 2.2.04[1]
John Barrett	17.3.04 to 13.5.05
Charles Magoon	3.7.05 to 25.9.06
Herbert Squiers	20.10.06 to 3.8.09
R. S. Reynolds Hitt	21.12.09 to 19.7.10
Thomas Dawson	24.6.10 to 1.12.10
H. Percival Dodge	6.7.11 to 10.6.13
William Jennings Price	20.8.13 to 28.12.21
John Glover South	8.10.21 to 5.1.30
Roy Tasco Davis	16.12.29 to 10.9.33
Antonio Gonzalez	28.8.33 to 9.1.35
George Summerlin	10.12.34 to 7.7.37
Frank Corrigan	9.8.37 to 14.6.39
William Dawson	23.3.39 to 21.4.41
Edwin Wilson	11.2.41 to 23.9.43
Avra Warren	21.3.44 to 5.1.45
Frank Hines	17.8.45 to 20.2.48
Monnett Davis	26.2.48 to 24.1.51
John Wiley	20.6.51 to 27.11.53
Selden Chapin	22.1.54 to 29.5.55
Julian Harrington	27.7.55 to 14.7.60
Joseph Farland	24.6.60 to 31.8.63
Jack Hood Vaughn	8.4.64 to 27.2.65
Charles Adair	6.5.65 to 6.9.69

Robert Sayre   15.9.69 to 14.3.74
William Jorden   8.4.74 to 25.8.78
Ambler Moss   23.9.78 to 1.8.82

[1] Dates are dates of appointment and of departure from Panama.

Bibliography

UNPUBLISHED SOURCES

Private papers

Franklin D. Roosevelt Library, Hyde Park, N.Y.

Papers of Franklin Roosevelt: Official File, 25-i, 110, 110A; President's Secretary's File,
Box 64
Diary of Henry Morgenthau, Jr.: vols. 128, 214

Library of Congress, Washington, D.C.

Papers of Frank Andrews
Papers of Philippe Bunau-Varilla
Papers of George Washington Goethals
Diary and Papers of John Hay
Diary of William Leahy
Papers of Theodore Roosevelt
Papers of Elihu Root
Papers of William Howard Taft

Nimitz Library, U.S. Naval Academy, Annapolis, Md.

Papers of William Moffett

*Operational Archives, Naval Historical Center, Washington Navy Yard,
Washington, D.C.*

Papers of Miles DuVal

Stanford University Libraries, Stanford, Calif.

Papers of Francis Loomis

Sterling Memorial Library, Yale University, New Haven, Conn.

Diary and Papers of Henry Stimson

Government documents

U.S. National Archives, Washington, D.C.

Record Group 11, Unperfected Treaties: File 012
Record Group 18, Army Air Forces: Central Decimal Files, 1939–42, Series 2, Air
    Adjutant General, 360.01, 381, 400, 452.1, 676.3, 686; Air Adjutant General, Bulky
    Files 1942–4, Foreign, Panama
Record Group 38, Office of Naval Intelligence: C-9-C 21743, 21743A; C-10-G 19629;
    C-10-J 12469; C-10-L 14602, 14951, 14951A, 14951B, 14951C, 14951D; C-10-M
    15772, 15772A, 15772B, 24220; L-4-B 7338
Record Group 43, International Conferences, Commissions, and Expositions: 1939
    Conference
Record Group 45, Office of Naval Records and Library: World War–Defensive Plans
Record Group 46, United States Senate: 76-B-B-20
Record Group 51, Bureau of the Budget: Series 39–37
Record Group 59, Department of State
    1863–1903
Despatches from Ministers, Colombia, vols. 24, 29, 33, 35
Instructions to Ministers, Colombia, vol. 16
Notes from Foreign Legations, Colombia, vol. 6
Notes to Foreign Legations, Colombia, vols. 6, 7
    1903–1906
Drafts of Treaties, vol. 4: Isthmus countries, Italy
Despatches from U.S. Ministers in Panama
Diplomatic Instructions of the Department of State: Panama
Notes From the Legation of Panama
    1906–1910: Numerical File
        234, 243, 312, 637, 847, 862, 1502, 3626, 3739, 3745, 5067, 5430, 5747, 8438, 9271,
        9684, 11447, 14975, 15354, 15778, 15800, 16133, 16698, 17095, 17704, 21344,
        21419, 23103, 23185
    1910–1949: Decimal File
        033.1100, 1110, 1119, 111.16 Welles, 121.5419, 124.196, 180.03401, 183.9 Panama,
        184.00101, 319.112C64 319.112R15, 319.1123L25, 419.11D29, 419.11 El Encanto,
        500C115 28th Conference, 500C115 Mexico City, 500C115 Montreal, 501BB, 501RA,
        515.4D5, 600.11F232, 611.1924, 611.1931, 619.0012, 619.002, 619.0024, 619.003,
        619.11, 619.1171, 619.11F, 701.1900, 701.1911, 701.1962, 701.511, 701.5119,
        701.6219, 702.5111F, 710.1012 Washington, 710G, 710H Agenda, 711.17, 711.19,

711.1911, 711.1914, 711.192, 711.1927, 711.1928, 711.21, 711F.1914, 718.19, 718.1915, 719.21, 719.94, 740.0011 AR, 740.0011 EW 1939, 740.00119 Council, 763.72, 763.72119, 800.20210, 810.20 Defense, 810.154, 810.54, 811.001 Roosevelt Visits, 811.002, 811.014, 811.114, 811.1927, 811.2319, 811.24517, 811F.00, 811F.0144, 811F.017, 811F.06, 811F.114 Liquor, 811F.114 Narcotics, 811F.124, 811F.1541, 811F.20, 811F.22, 811F.24, 811F.244, 811F.502, 811F.504, 811F.5041, 811F.52, 811F.796, 811F.7961, 811F.7962, 811F.812, 811F.812 Protection, 811F.8123, 811F.815, 817.812, 819.00, 819.00 Bolshevik, 819.00 General Conditions, Revolutions, 819.001 Arias, Arnulfo, 819.001 Arias, Harmodio, 819.001 Boyd, Augusto, 819.001P82, 819.002, 819.01, 819.011, 819.012, 819.0144, 819.02, 819.0443, 819.105, 819.1052, 819.111, 819.113, 819.1151, 819.154, 819.20, 819.24, 819.4016, 819.404, 819.4202, 819.50, 819.502, 819.5032, 819.5034, 819.504, 819.5043, 819.51, Advisers, 819.51 Bondholders, 819.5123, 819.52, 819.52G31, 819.53, 819.55, 819.602, 819.628, 819.6341P19, 819.74, 819.76, 819.77, 819.796, 819.7961, 819.7962, 819.8503, 819.851, 819.911, 850.4, 862.20219, 894.20219, 894.628

1950–1954: Decimal File

CD 091.6, 411.19, 411.199, 411F.006, 411F.19, 411F.1931, 411F.196, 611.19, 611.1913, 611.193, 611.1931, 611.199, 611F.19, 611F.1913, 701.1911, 711F.00, 711F.11, 711F.43, 711F.55320, 711F.57, 719.00, 719.001, 719.11, 719.13, 719.14, 719.21, 719.3, 719.5, 719.5MSP, 795.00, 795B.5, 811F.02, 811F.06, 811F.061, 811F.062, 811F.112, 811F.411, 811F.43, 811F.5301, 811F.531, 819.00, 819.00TA, 819.01, 819.06, 819.062, 819.10, 819.11, 819.112, 819.14, 819.19, 819.20, 819.20A, 819.261, 819.2612, 819.2614, 819.2615, 819.411, 819.413, 819.43, 819.431, 819.45, 819.50, 819.501, 819.51, 819.53, 819.556, 911F.530, 911F.5301, 911F.54, 911F.7301, 919.512, 919.537

Papers of Alger Hiss
Records of Harley A. Notter, 1939–45
Record Group 80, Secretary of the Navy
  General Correspondence, 1897–1915 and 1916–26: 8975, 12479, 14344, 14661, 21393, 21498, 26283, 28076, 28690
  Secret and Confidential Correspondence, 1917-19: C-3–880, C-4-30, C-42–23
  Secret and Confidential Correspondence, 1919–26: 117–45, 117–46, 162–78, 197–2, 197–5, 197–10, 197–11, 197–14, 197–15, 197–19, 197–23, 198–1, 198–2, 198–35, 218–2, PD 226–103
  Secret and Confidential Correspondence, 1927–39: 1992, A9-1/FF8, A16-1/ND15, A16-1/QH(15)Panama, A16-3(5–I), A16-3(5–III), A16-3(5–IX), A0-1/FF8, EF53/A14-7, NB/ND15, QH(15)Panama/A1–1
Record Group 94, Adjutant General of the Army 1784–1917: 1776695, 1781722, 1896202, 2049731, 2068560, 2084148, 2140143, 2152110, 2187310, 2188679, 2197449, 2198726, 2223431, 2256604, 2263553, 2265837, 2266997, 2274803, 2274896, 2283996, 2289124, 2298712, 2298940, 2303473, 2314751A, 2318068, 2327880, 2339118, 2340998, 2342929, 2349493, 2356510, 2390305, 2407013, 2411702, 2412935, 2425443, 2427315, 2430381, 2458356, 2462264, 2642429, 2487411, 2538347, 2574834, 2588144, 2597285
Record Group 107, Secretary of War: Classified File; Secretary of the Army Subject File 1940–2; Secretary of the Army Project File 1946–7
Record Group 127, Marine Corps: General Correspondence 1904–12: Cases 872, 8724, 11309, 11517, 14723

Record Group 165, General and Special Staffs of the Army
  General Staff Reports 1903–17: 818, 4102, 7438, 8835, 8941, 8952, 9097, 9540, 10853,
    11592, 11782, 11900, 12376, 12403, 12621, 13309, 13336, 13700, 14628
  General Staff, Secretary, Series 30, Minutes of the Standing Liaison Committee
    1938–41
  Military Intelligence Division (pre–August 1941); 153–28, 153–33, 1766-R-22, 2030–
    16, 2501–19, 2501–45, 2257-M-67, 2271-M-79, 2280-B-95, 2655-M-131, 2656-M-103,
    2656-M-250, 2657-M-5, 2657-M-10, 2657-M-20, 2657-M-25, 2657-M-39, 2657-M-40,
    2657-M-46 2657-M-96, 2657-M-195, 2657-M-238, 2657-M-239, 2657-M-242, 2657-M-
    246, 2657-M-259, 2657-M-287, 2657-M-313, 2657-M-342, 2657-P-497, 2736-M-14,
    2736-M-15, 2736-M-16, 10058-D-3, 10218–48, 10634–672
  Military Intelligence Division (post–August 1941)
    Decimal File 1941–5
    G-2 Geographic Subject File 1940–46, Latin American Branch
    See also entry under Washington National Records Center
  War College Division, 1903–17: 1766, 5777, 5791, 6178, 6278, 7113, 7113B, 7820,
    7899, 8082, 8290, 9339, 9352, 9748, 9756, 9934, 10802
  War Plans Division, 1917–42: 242–39, 446, 470–16, 504–1, 580–11, 639–6, 816, 1004,
    1162, 1470, 1652, 1992, 2241, 2501, 2674, 2875, 2917, 2939, 3182, 3326, 3531, 3550,
    3556, 3558, 3674, 3680, 3689, 3730, 3741, 3748, 3782, 3786, 3793, 3803, 3804, 3807,
    3827, 4068, 4100, 4124, 4129, 4132, 4186, 4193, 4225, 4247, 4250, 4270, 4319, 4326,
    4402, 4410, 4451, 4452, 4507, 4544, 4622, 6178, 6278, 8082
  Operations Division, 1942–6: 000.7, 291.21, 336 Latin America, 336 Panama, 336.2
    Panama, 381 Panama, 381 Panama Canal Department, 384 Caribbean Defense
    Command, 452.1 Caribbean Defense Command, 580.82 Caribbean Defense Com-
    mand, 600.12 Panama, 611 Panama
Record Group 218, Joint Chiefs of Staff: 570/40, 570/62, 570/71, 570/83, 570/95,
    570/98, 1778/1, 1778/6
Record Group 225, Joint Board of the Army and Navy, 1903–38: 325, s.84, s.228, s.546,
    s.598; 326–1, s.47, s.79, s.117, s.180, s.191, s.202, s.203, s.231, s.235, s.292b, s.545,
    s.558, s.562, s.634; 338
Record Group 226, Office of Strategic Services: 12326, 17066, 23202, 77340S, 80432C,
    91541R, 108608, XL32910, XL41034, XL41655, XL41657
Record Group 313, Naval Operating Forces: Instructions for Army–Navy exercise off
    the Panama Canal, March 1939
Record Group 319, Army Staff: Plans and Operations Division 1946–50: 012, 091
    Panama, 230, 291.2, 313.5, 320.2 Top Secret, 346, 350.09 Panama, 370.02, 381, 381
    Caribbean Defense Command (ABC File), 381 Panama Section 1-A (ABC File), 381
    Panama Section 1-B (ABC File), 381 RD, 381 Top Secret, 384, 560, 560 Top Secret,
    611, 676.3, 680.4, 686 Top Secret
Record Group 330, Office of the Secretary of Defense: CD 10–1–1
Record Group 350, Bureau of Insular Affairs: 13815-55A
Record Group 407, Adjutant General of the Army post-1917: 000.1, 000.1 Panama, 000.2
    Panama, 000.24 Panama, 000.24 Panama Canal Department, 000.4, 000.51, 040TPC,
    041.211 Panama, 041.391 Panama, 091 Panama, 092, 230 Panama, 230.6, 245, 250.1
    Panama, 250.13, 286 Panama, 311.23, 319.12 PD, 320.2, 322.8, 333.1, 336, 336

Panama, 350.09, 353.2, 353.5, 354, 354.2, 354.21, 370.26, 380.1, 381, 381 Classified, 381 Panama, 381.5 Plans, 383.4, 388.1, 388.1 Panama, 471.6 Panama, 580.8, 580.81 Aviation, 580.81 Panama, 580.82, 584 Panama, 600.1, 600.12 Panama, 601 Panama, 601 Panama Canal Department, 601.1, 601.1 Panama Canal Department, 601.4, 602.1 602.5, 611 Panama, 620 Panama Canal Department, 660.2, 660.2 Panama, 660.2 Panama Canal Department, 660.2 Panama Canal Zone, 676.3, 686, 686 Panama, 821 Panama, 821.1, 821.1 Panama Canal, 823, Registered Documents 309F (The Panama Plan); Administrative Services Division, Operations Branch, 'A long-term strategic plan for the defense of the Panama Canal' (22.6.45)

Washington National Records Center, Suitland, Md.

Record Group 165, Office of the Director of Military Intelligence, Regional File 1933–44: 2030, 2300, 2320, 2710, 2800, 2810, 3020, 3110A, 3610, 3700, 3750, 3830A, 3850, 3917, 5000, 5900, 5940, 5990, 6000, 6400, 6550, 8000, 9185, 'A strategic study of Panama' (2.8.40)
Record Group 185, Isthmian Canal Commissions, 1904–14, The Panama Canal 1914–51, and The Panama Canal Company 1951–60: 2-C-55, 2-C-124, 2-C-129, 2-D-4, 2-D-6, 2-D-40, 2-E-1, 2-E-2, 2-E-2/Jamaica, 2-E-2/Martinique, 2-E-11, 2-E-11/A, 2-E-11/L, 2-E-11/P, 2-E-12, 2-F-14, 2-P-12, 2-P-46, 2-P-49/P, 2-P-59, 2-P-68, 2-P-70, 2-P-71, 2-P-72, 5-D-25, 9-A-1, 9-A-11, 9-A-14, 9-A-74, 13-Q-1, 23-C-2, 28-B-5, 28-B-44, 28-B-48, 28-B-233, 33-E-5, 33-E-8, 43-D-8, 46-D-8, 47-H-5, 47-H-16, 47-H-17, 58-A-1, 58-A-3, 58-A-4, 58-A-6, 58-A-13, 58-A-20, 58-A-50, 58-A-501, 59-G-1, 59-G-3, 62-A-7, 62-B-14, 62-B-164, 62-B-199, 62-B-209, 62-B-248, 62-D-8, 64-Y-4, 65-J-3/M, 79-A-6/U, 79-A-11, 79-F-5, 79-F-5/U, 79-F-8, 80-A-3, 80-A-4, 80-C-5, 80-G-1, 80-G-2, 80-G-7, 80-H-3, 80-H-10, 88-A-2, 88-A-2/A, 88-A-2/B, 88-A-11, 88-A-20, 88-A-21, 88-A-30, 88-A-79, 88-A-83, 88-A-86, 88-A-150, 88-A-165, 88-A-207, 880-A-220, 88-B-1, 88-B-7, 88-B-15, 88-D-1/L, 88-D-2, 88-H-3, 88-H-12, 88-H-13, 91-A-39, 94-A-3, 94-A-3/A, 94-A-3/T, 94-A-3/1926, 94-A-3/1936, 94-A-78, 94-A-104, REP.7(1955)-1, REP.7(1955)-2, REP.7(1955)-4, REP.7(1955)-9, BLD6 of 19.6.79 ('Latin American Communities Study' by Robert Jeffrey)
Record Group 319, Army Staff: 000.2, 000.24, 336, 350.09
Record Group 335, Secretary of the Army:
OSW 230 Panama, OSA 004.06 Panama Canal, 091 Panama Canal, CD 092 Panama, OSA 230 Panama Canal, OSA 230.64 Panama Canal, OSA 248.3 Panama Canal, 320 Panama, 320 Panama Canal, 350 Panama Canal, 381 Panama Canal, 400.1913, OSA 548.2 Panama Canal, 620 Panama Canal, 813.4 Panama Canal

Operational Archives, Naval Historical Center, Washington Navy Yard, Washington, D.C.

General Board of the Navy: 404, S.472, S.1939; 414, S.1318; 414–1, VI-113, VII-92; 414–3; 419, S.1534; 420; 420–1; 420–2, VI-359; 422–1, VI-488; 425, S.315, S.1963; 426, S.1204, III-236, V-138; 426–1, S.252, S.305, S.310, S.618, S.762, S.1382, S.1633; 432; 438, S.1280, S.1347–8(j); 449, S.569; Letterbooks I and II; Hearings, 1947, vol. III

Chief of Naval Operations/Secretary of the Navy, 1940–7: CNO-HG, HG 1946, (SC)HG, (SC)HG/A16-1
War Plans Division/Strategic Plans Division: SPD, Series II, B31; SPD, Series III, Naval Districts, Panama; SPD, Series III, Measures for protection of Panama Canal, 1934; SPD, Series III, Measures for protection of Panama Canal, 1936; 'Cost estimates of the defense of a Panama Sea-Level Canal' (10.4.47)

U.S. Atomic Energy Commission, Washington, D.C.

Lilienthal to Royall, 10 and 15 October 1947

PUBLISHED SOURCES

General works of reference

Bevans, Charles (ed.), *Treaties and other international agreements of the United States of America, 1776–1949*, vol. 10, *Nepal–Peru* (Washington, D.C., 1973)
Bray, Wayne, *The controversy over a new canal treaty between the United States and Panama: A selective annotated bibliography of United States, Panamanian, Colombian, French, and international organization sources* (Washington, D.C., 1976)
Cardoze, Nydia, and Tempone, Consuelo, *Guia para investigadores de Panamá* (Panamá, 1978)
Conte-Porras, Jorge, *Diccionario biográfico de Panamá* (Panamá, 1975)
Hackworth, Green (ed.), *Digest of international law*, vol. 2 (Washington, D.C., 1942)
Hedrick, Anne, and Hedrick, Basil, *Historical dictionary of Panama* (Metuchen, N.J., 1970)
Langstaff, Eleanor, *Panama: A bibliography* (Oxford, 1982)
Library of Congress, Congressional Research Service, *Background documents relating to the Panama Canal* (Washington, D.C., 1977)
Malloy, William, *Treaties, conventions, international acts, protocols and agreements between the United States and other powers, 1776–1909*, vols. 1–2 (Washington, D.C., 1910)
Subject catalog of the Panama Canal Collection of the Canal Zone Library–Museum (Boston, 1964)
Whiteman, Marjorie (ed.), *Digest of international law*, vol. 3 (Washington, D.C., 1964)

Press

New York Times, 1903–79 (all entries under the headings 'Canal Zone', 'Panama', 'Panama Canal')

General secondary works

Alfaro, Ricardo, *Los canales internacionales: Panamá* (Panamá, 1957)
  Medio siglo de relaciones entre Panamá y los Estados Unidos, new edn (Panamá, 1959)
Arosemena, Diógenes, *Documentary diplomatic history of the Panama Canal* (Panamá, 1961)

Baxter, Richard, *The law of international waterways: With particular regard to interoceanic canals* (Cambridge, Mass., 1964)

Bemis, Samuel, *The Latin American policy of the United States: An historical interpretation* (New York, 1943)

Biesanz, John, 'Cultural and economic factors in Panamanian race relations', *American Sociological Review*, 14 (1949), 772–9

'The economy of Panama', *Inter-American Economic Affairs*, 6 (1952–3), 3–28

'Race relations in the Canal Zone', *Phylon*, 11 (1950), 23–30

'Social forces retarding development of Panama's agricultural resources', *Rural Sociology*, 15 (1950), 148–55

'Uncle Sam on the Isthmus of Panama: A diplomatic case history', in Alva Wilgus (ed.), *The Caribbean: Contemporary trends* (Gainesville, Fla., 1953), 185–202

Biesanz, John, and Biesanz, Mavis, *The people of Panama* (New York, 1955)

Biesanz, John, and Smith, Luke, 'Panamanian politics', *Journal of Politics*, 14 (1952), 386–402

'Race relations in Panama and the Canal Zone: A comparative analysis', *American Journal of Sociology*, 57 (1951), 7–14

Blanco, Boris (ed.), *Relaciones entre Panamá y los Estados Unidos* (Panamá, 1974)

Bray, Wayne, *The common law zone in Panama: A case study in reception with some observations on the relevancy thereof to the Panal Canal Treaty controversy* (San Juan, P. R., 1977)

Burdick, Bernard, 'The Panama Canal and the Canal Zone: Their character, functions, government and laws', *Federal Bar Association Journal*, 3 (1937), 89–92

Canal Postal Service, *Canal Zone postage stamps* (Mount Hope, CZ, 1961)

Canal Zone postage stamps 1961–1979 (Mount Hope, CZ, 1979)

Canal Zone Information Office, *The Panama Canal, fiftieth anniversary: The story of a great conquest* (Mount Hope, CZ, 1964)

Carillo, Ramón, and Boyd, Richard, 'Some aspects of social relations between Latin and Anglo Americans on the isthmus of Panama', *Boletín de la Universidad Interamericana de Panamá*, 2 (1945), 703–84

Castillero Pimentel, Ernesto, *Panamá y los Estados Unidos* (Panamá, 1953)

Política exterior de Panamá (Panamá, 1961)

Connell-Smith, Gordon, *The United States and Latin America: An historical analysis of inter-American relations* (London, 1974)

Conniff, Michael, *Black labor on a white canal: Panama, 1904–1981* (Pittsburgh, Pa., 1985)

Panama and the United States: The forced alliance (Athens, Ga., 1992)

'Panama since 1903', in Leslie Bethell (ed.), *The Cambridge history of Latin America*, vol. 7 (New York, 1990), 603–42

Davis, Raymond, 'West Indian workers on the Panama Canal: A split labor market interpretation' (doctoral diss., Stanford Univesity, 1981)

DeCambell, Carolina, and Hooper, Ofelia, 'The middle class of Panama', in Theo Crevenna (ed.), *Materiales para el estudio de la clase media en la América Latina* (Washington, D.C., 1950)

de la Rosa, Diógenes, 'Alfaro, sujeto historico', *Revista Lotería*, 184 (March 1971), 7–16

El mito de la intervención (Panamá, 1927)

DeSalamín, J., and DeSalamín, M., *La concepción oligarquía de las negociaciones entre Panamá y los Estados Unidos* (Panamá, 1976)

Dimock, Marshall, *Government-operated enterprises in the Panama Canal Zone* (Chicago, 1934)

DuVal, Miles, 'Isthmian canal policy – an evaluation', *U.S. Naval Institute Proceedings*, 81 (1955), 263–75

Ealy, Lawrence, 'The development of an Anglo-American system of law in the Panama Canal Zone', *American Journal of Legal History*, 2 (1958), 283–303

The Republic of Panama in world affairs, 1903–1950 (Philadelphia, 1951)

Yanqui politics and the isthmian canal (University Park, Pa., 1971)

Farnsworth, David, and McKenny, James, *U.S.–Panama relations, 1903–1978: A study in linkage politics* (Boulder, Colo., 1983)

Garay, Narciso, 'Les relations extérieures et le statut de Panama', *Séances et travaux de l'Union Juridique Internationale*, 6 (1929)

Goldrich, Daniel, 'Panama', in Martin Needler (ed.), *The political systems of Latin America* (New York, 1970), 151–66

Haizlip, John, 'Panama Canal defense: Influence of international law' (manuscript, U.S. Naval War College, Newport, R.I., 1968)

Hanrahan, David, 'Legal aspects of the Panama Canal Zone – in perspective', *Boston University Law Review*, 45 (1965), 64–87

Harper, Alda, *Tracing the course of growth and development in educational policy for the Canal Zone colored schools, 1905–1955* (Ann Arbor, Mich., 1979)

Harris, Louis, 'Panama', in Ben Burnett and Kenneth Johnson (eds.), *Political forces in Latin America* (Belmont, Calif., 1970), 159–91

Howard, Harry, *Military government in the Panama Canal Zone* (Norman, Okla., 1931)

Hoyt, Edwin, 'Law and politics in the revision of treaties affecting Panama', *Virginia Journal of International Law*, 8 (1966), 289–309

National policy and international law: Case studies from American canal policy (Denver, Colo., 1967)

Johnson, Emory, 'Panama Canal revenues and finances', *Proceedings of the American Philosophical Society*, 87 (January–June 1943), 175–88

Kane, William, *Civil strife in Latin America: A legal history of U.S. involvement* (Baltimore, 1972)

King, Thelma, *El problema de la soberanía en las relaciones entre Panamá y los Estados Unidos* (Panamá, 1961)

Knapp, Herbert, and Knapp, Mary, *Red, white and blue paradise: The American Canal Zone in Panama* (San Diego, Calif., 1985)

Kron, Norman, 'Applicability of Federal statutes to non-contiguous areas', *University of Pennsylvania Law Review*, 97 (1949), 866–77

LaFeber, Walter, *The Panama Canal: The crisis in historical perspective* (New York, 1990 edn)

Landa, Ronald, 'U.S. policy toward Panama, 1903–present. Questions of recognition and diplomatic relations and instances of U.S. intervention: A tabular summary', *Department of State Bulletin*, 70 (22 April 1974), 433–44

Langley, Lester, 'The United States and Panama: the burden of power', *Current History*, 56 (1969), 13–18, 51

Lee, Luke, 'Legal aspects of internationalization of interoceanic canals', *Law and Contemporary Problems*, 33 (1968), 158–68

Leonard, Thomas, 'The Commissary in United States–Panamanian relations' (doctoral diss., American University, Washington, D.C., 1969)

'The Commissary issue in United States–Panamanian relations, 1900–1936', *The Americas*, 30 (1973), 83–109

'The 1977 Panama Canal treaties in historical perspective', *Journal of Caribbean Studies*, 2 (1981), 190–209

Liss, Sheldon, *The Canal: Aspects of United States–Panamanian relations* (Notre Dame, Ind., 1967)

McCain, William, *The United States and the Republic of Panama* (Durham, N.C., 1937)

Major, John, 'The Panama Canal Zone, 1904–1979', in Leslie Bethell (ed.), *The Cambridge history of Latin America*, vol. 7 (New York, 1990), 643–70, 722–7

Prize Possession: The United States and the Panama Canal, 1903–1979 (New York, 1993)

'The United States, Japan, and the Panama Canal', in Robert Love (ed.), *Pearl Harbor: A fifty-year perspective* (New York, 1993)

Méndez Pereira, Octavio (ed.), *Antología del Canal, 1914–1939* (Panamá, 1939)

Morales Padrón, Francisco, 'El caso de Panamá', *Revista Loteriá*, 336–7 (March–April 1984), 5–25

Mount, Graeme, 'American imperialism in Panama' (doctoral diss., University of Toronto, 1969)

Padelford, Norman, 'American rights in the Panama Canal', *American Journal of International Law*, 34 (1940), 416–42

'Neutrality, belligerency, and the Panama Canal', ibid., 35 (1941), 55–89

The Panama Canal in peace and war (New York, 1942)

'The Panama Canal in time of peace', *American Journal of International Law*, 34 (1940), 601–37

Panama Canal Company – Canal Zone Government, Personnel Bureau, *Force – Company/Government 1904–1968* (mimeograph, Balboa Heights, CZ, 1969)

Paz, Sadith, 'The status of West Indian immigrants in Panama from 1850–1941' (master's thesis, University of Massachusetts at Amherst, 1977)

Revista Lotería, 317 (August 1982) [issue on Ricardo Alfaro]

Richard, Alfred, *The Panama Canal in American national consciousness, 1870–1922* (New York, 1990; repr. of 1969 Boston University diss.)

Ridley, Clarence, 'Commitments of the Republic of Panama with respect to the Canal Zone' (mimeograph, Army War College, 1931)

Ropp, Steve, *Panamanian politics: From guarded nation to National Guard* (New York, 1982)

Ruben, Carlos, *La evolución de la política de empleo y salarios en la Zona del Canal y el desarollo económico de Panamá* (San Pedro Sula, Honduras, 1970)

Sepulveda, Melida, 'El tema del Canal en la novelística panameña', *Montalbán*, 4 (1975), 217–80

Shay, Martha, 'The Panama Canal Zone: In search of a juridical identity', *New York University Journal of International Law and Politics*, 9 (1976), 15–60

Siegfried, André, 'Les canaux internationaux et les grandes routes maritimes mondiales',
    Recueil des cours de l'Académie de Droit International de La Haye, 74 (1949), 1–72
    Suez and Panama (New York, 1940)
Smith, Darrell, *The Panama Canal: Its history, activities, and organization* (Baltimore, Md.,
    1927)
Turner Morales, David, *Estructura económica de Panamá: El problema del Canal* (México,
    1958)
United States, Army, Caribbean Defense Command, Historical Section, *Acquisition of
    land in the Panama Canal Zone* (Quarry Heights, CZ, 1946)
    Control of venereal disease and prostitution (Quarry Heights, CZ, 1947)
    History of the Panama Canal Department, 4 vols. (Quarry Heights, CZ, 1947)
United States, Navy, Fifteenth Naval District, *Command Historical Report, 1917–1958*
    (Balboa, CZ, 1959)
Universidad de Panamá, *Panamá y los Estados Unidos ante el problema del Canal* (Panamá,
    1966)
Valdés, Manuel, *Las intervenciones electorales en Panamá* (Panamá, 1932)
Vega Méndez, D., *El panameñismo y su doctrina* (Panamá, 1963)
Weiner, Richard, 'Sovereignty of the Panama Isthmus', *New York University Intramural
    Law Review*, 16 (1960), 65–76
Westerman, George, *Fifty years of treaty negotiations between the United States and the
    Republic of Panama* (Panamá, 1953)
    'Historical notes on West Indians on the Isthmus of Panama', *Phylon*, 20 (1961),
    340–50
    Los inmigrantes antillanos en Panamá (Panamá, 1980)
    'La otra versión de las relaciones entre Panamá y los Estados Unidos', *Revista Lotería*,
    51–2 (May–June 1960), 90–106
    'School segregation on the Panama Canal Zone', *Phylon*, 15 (1954), 276–87
    A study of socio-economic conflicts on the Panama Canal Zone (Panamá, 1948)
Wilson, Arnold, 'The Suez and Panama canals: A comparison', *Journal of the Royal Society
    of Arts*, 81 (1933), 679–94
Wilson, Lowell, et al., *Schooling in the Panama Canal Zone, 1904–1979* (Panama Canal
    Area, 1980)
Wright, Almon, *Panama: Tension's child, 1502–1989* (New York, 1990)

Visual

Charlson, Carl, *A man, a plan, a canal, Panama* (television documentary for WGBH,
    Boston, 1987)
Foster, Roman, *Canal diggers* (television documentary for PBS, Washington, D.C., 1984)
Keller, Ulrich, *The building of the Panama Canal in historic photographs* (New York, 1983)
Laval, Jerome, *Panama and the building of the canal: Photographs from the Keystone–Mast
    stereograph collection* (Fresno, Calif., 1978)
Panama Canal Photograph Collection 1904–1939 (U.S. National Archives, Washington,
    D.C.)
Pennell, Joseph, *Joseph Pennell's pictures of the Panama Canal* (Philadelphia, 1913)
Wiseman, Frederick, *Canal Zone* (television documentary for WNET, New York, 1977)

1826–1903

Alessandria Camacho, Thaís, *La política de los Estados Unidos de América frente a la construcción de un canal por Panamá 1826–1873* (Panamá, 1983)

Ameringer, Charles, 'The Panama Canal lobby of Philippe Bunau-Varilla and William Nelson Cromwell', *American Historical Review*, 68 (1962–3) 346–63

Anguizola, Gustave, *Philippe Bunau-Varilla: The man behind the Panama Canal* (Chicago, 1980)

Barrows, Chester, *William M. Evarts: Lawyer, diplomat, statesman* (Chapel Hill, N.C., 1941)

Bourne, Kenneth, 'The Clayton–Bulwer treaty and the decline of British opposition to the territorial expansion of the United States, 1857–60', *Journal of Modern History*, 33 (1961), 287–91

Bourne, Kenneth, and Watt, Donald (eds.), *British documents on foreign affairs: Reports and papers from the Foreign Office confidential print*, pt I, ser. C, *North America*, vols. 4, 9, 10, 11 (Bethesda, Md., 1986–7)

Campbell, Alexander, *Great Britain and the United States, 1895–1903* (London, 1960)

Campbell, Charles, *Anglo-American understanding, 1898–1903* (Baltimore, 1957)

Chester, Colby, 'Diplomacy of the quarterdeck', *American Journal of International Law*, 8 (1914), 443–76

Clayton, Lawrence, 'The Nicaragua Canal in the nineteenth century: Prelude to American empire in the Caribbean', *Journal of Latin American Studies*, 19 (1987), 323–52

Collin, Richard, *Theodore Roosevelt, culture, diplomacy and expansion: A new view of American imperialism* (Baton Rouge, La., 1985)
  Theodore Roosevelt's Caribbean: The Panama Canal, the Monroe Doctrine, and the Latin American context (Baton Rouge, La., 1990)

Colombia, Ministerio de relaciones exteriores, *Libro azul: Documentos diplomáticos sobre el canal y la rebelión del Istmo de Panamá* (Bogotá, 1904)

Congressional Record (Senate), 9 March 1903, 14–16, 22; 17 March 1903, 107–10.

Crowell, Jackson, 'The United States and a Central American canal, 1869–1877', *Hispanic American Historical Review*, 49 (1969), 27–52

Daley, M. C., 'The watermelon riot: Cultural encounters in Panama City, April 15, 1856', *Hispanic American Historical Review*, 70 (1990), 85–108

DuVal, Miles, *Cadiz to Cathay: The story of the long diplomatic struggle for the Panama Canal* (Stanford, Calif., 1947 edn)

Farman, Elbert, *Egypt and its betrayal: An account of the country during the periods of Ismail and Tewfik pashas, and of how England acquired a new empire* (New York, 1908)

Farnie, D. A., *East and west of Suez: The Suez Canal in history, 1854–1956* (Oxford, 1969)

Grenville, John, 'Great Britain and the isthmian canal, 1898–1901', *American Historical Review*, 51 (1955–6), 48–69

Hagan, Kenneth, *American gunboat diplomacy and the old Navy, 1877–1889* (Westport, Conn., 1973)

Howe, George, 'The Clayton–Bulwer treaty: An unofficial explanation of Article VIII in 1869', *American Historical Review*, 42 (1936–7), 484–90

Huberich, Charles, 'The trans-isthmian canal: A study in American diplomatic history (1825–1904)', *Bulletin of the University of Texas*, 1 (March 1904), 3–31

Johnson, Willis, *Four centuries of the Panama Canal* (New York, 1907)

Kemble, John, *The Panama route, 1848–1869* (Berkeley, Calif., 1943)

Kemble, John, 'The Panama route to the Pacific coast, 1848–1869', *Pacific Historical Review*, 7 (1938), 1–13

Lawyers' Co-operative Publishing Company, *Cases argued and decided in the Supreme Court of the United States*, 45 (Rochester, N. Y., 1920), 1106–28

Lockey, Joseph, 'A neglected aspect of isthmian diplomacy', *American Historical Review*, 41 (1936–7), 295–305

Lowrie, Walter, 'France, the United States, and the Lesseps Canal: Renewed rivalry in the Western Hemisphere, 1879–1889' (doctoral diss., Syracuse (N.Y.) University, 1975)

McCullough, David, *The path between the seas: The creation of the Panama Canal, 1870–1914* (New York, 1977)

Mack, Gerstle, *The land divided: A history of the Panama Canal and other isthmian canal projects* (New York, 1944)

Mahan, Alfred Thayer, 'The isthmus and sea power', *Atlantic Monthly*, 72 (July–December 1893), 459–75

'The United States looking outward', ibid., 66 (July–December 1890), 816–24

Manning, William (ed.), *Diplomatic correspondence of the United States: Inter-American affairs 1831–1860*:

Vol. 3. *Central America: 1831–1850* (Washington, D.C., 1933)

Vol. 4. *Central America: 1851–1860* (Washington, D.C., 1934)

Vol. 5. *Chile, Colombia* (Washington, D.C., 1935)

Vol. 7. *Great Britain* (Washington, D.C., 1936)

Vol. 8. *Mexico: 1831 – June 1848* (Washington, D.C., 1937)

Vol. 9. *Mexico: June 1848–1860* (Washington, D.C., 1937)

Marks, Frederick, 'Morality as a drive wheel in the diplomacy of Theodore Roosevelt', *Diplomatic History*, 2 (1978), 43–62

Miner, Dwight, *The fight for the Panama route: The story of the Spooner Act and the Hay–Herrán treaty* (New York, 1940)

Morgan, John Tyler, 'The choice of isthmian canal routes', *North American Review*, 174 (January–June 1902), 672–86

Morison, Elting (ed.), *The letters of Theodore Roosevelt*, vols, 1–2 (Cambridge, Mass., 1951)

Naylor, Robert, 'The British role in Central America prior to the Clayton–Bulwer treaty of 1850', *Hispanic American Historical Review*, 40 (1960), 361–82

Offutt, Milton, *The protection of citizens abroad by the forces of the United States* (Baltimore, 1928)

Parks, E. Taylor, *Colombia and the United States, 1765–1934* (Durham, N.C., 1935)

Parry, Clive (ed.), *A British digest of international law, compiled principally from the archives of the Foreign Office: Phase I, 1860–1914*, vol. 2B (London, 1967)

Penfield, Frederic, 'Why not own the Panama isthmus?' *North American Review*, 174 (January–June 1902), 269–74

Pérez Venero, Alec, *Before the five frontiers: Panama from 1821–1903* (New York, 1978)

Pierson, William, Jr, 'The political influences of an interoceanic canal, 1826–1926', *Hispanic American Historical Review*, 6 (1926), 205–31

Revista Lotería, 292 (July 1980): Issue on the French canal project

Richardson, James (ed.), *A compilation of the messages and papers of the presidents, 1789–1897*, vols. 7–10 (Washington, D.C., 1898–9)

Rippy, J. Fred, 'Diplomacy of the United States and Mexico regarding the isthmus of Tehuantepec, 1848–1860', *Mississippi Valley Historical Review*, 6 (1919–20), 503–31

'Justo Rufino Barrios and the Nicaraguan canal', *Hispanic American Historical Review*, 20 (1940), 190–7

Russel, Robert, *Improvement of communications with the Pacific coast as an issue in American politics, 1783–1864* (Cedar Rapids, Iowa, 1948)

Schott, Joseph, *Rails across Panama: The story of the building of the Panama Railroad, 1849–1855* (Indianapolis, Ind., 1967)

Senior, Olive, 'The Colón people', *Jamaica Journal*, 14 (1980), 62–71, 87–103

'The Panama railway', ibid., 14 (1980), 66–77

Sewell, Mike, 'Political rhetoric and policy-making: James G. Blaine and Britain,' *Journal of American Studies*, 24 (1990), 61–84

Skinner, James, *France and Panama: The unknown years, 1894–1908* (New York, 1989)

Smith, Joseph, *Illusions of conflict: Anglo-American diplomacy toward Latin America, 1865–1896* (Pittsburgh, Pa., 1979)

United States, Congress, Senate, *Correspondence in relation to an interoceanic canal between the Atlantic and Pacific oceans, the Clayton–Bulwer treaty and the Monroe Doctrine, and the treaty between the United States and New Granada of December 12, 1846*, 56th Cong., 1st sess., S. Doc. 237 (1900)

Senate, *Use by the United States of a military force in the internal affairs of Colombia*, 58th Cong., 2d sess., S. Doc. 143 (1904)

Senate, Committee on Foreign Relations, *Report* [on the Hay–Pauncefote convention of 5 February 1900], 56th Cong., 2d. sess., S. Doc. 268 (1900)

Senate, Committee on Interoceanic Canals, *Hearings . . . on H.R. 3110* [the Spooner Bill], 57th Cong., 1st sess., S. Doc. 253 (1902)

United States, Department of State, *Diplomatic history of the Panama Canal: Correspondence relating to the negotiation and application of certain treaties on the subject of the construction of an inter-oceanic canal, and accompanying papers* 63/2 S. Doc. 474 (1914)

Papers relating to the foreign relations of the United States:
1866 (1866)
1874 (1874)
1881 (1882)
1882 (1883)
1900 (1901)
1901 (1902)
1902 (1903)
1903 (1904)

Use by the United States of military force in the internal affairs of Colombia. . . . Message from the President of the United States, transmitting, in response to Senate Resolution No. 73 of January 22, 1904, reports from the Acting Secretary of State and the Secretary of the Navy, with accompanying papers (1904)

United States, Isthmian Canal Commission, *Reports of the Isthmian Canal Commission, 1899–1902* (1904)

Van Aken, Mark, 'British policy considerations in Central America before 1850', *Hispanic American Historical Review*, 42 (1962), 54–9

Van Alstyne, Richard, 'Anglo-American relations, 1853–1857: British statesmen on the Clayton–Bulwer treaty and American expansion', *American Historical Review*, 42 (1936–7), 491–500

  'British diplomacy and the Clayton–Bulwer treaty, 1850–1860', *Journal of Modern History*, 11 (1939), 149–83

  'The Central American policy of Lord Palmerston 1846–1848', *Hispanic American Historical Review*, 16 (1936), 339–59

Weld, Stuart, 'The isthmian canal and American control', *Atlantic Monthly*, 64 (July–December 1889), 289–303

  'The isthmian canal and our government', ibid., 63 (January–June 1889), 341–53

Wicks, Daniel, 'Dress rehearsal: United States intervention on the isthmus of Panama, 1885', *Pacific Historical Review*, 49 (1980), 581–605

Williams, Mary, *Anglo-American isthmian diplomacy, 1815–1915* (Washington, D.C., 1916)

Williams, Thomas (ed.), *Hayes: The diary of a president, 1875–1881* (New York, 1964)

Woolsey, Theodore, 'An interoceanic canal from the standpoint of self-interest', *Yale Review*, 4 (1896), 357–64

  'An interoceanic canal in the light of precedent', ibid., 4 (1896), 246–55

  'Suez and Panama – A parallel', *American Historical Association Report for 1902*, 1 (1902), 305–11

                              October 1903–May 1904

Abbott, Lyman, *Reminiscences* (Boston, 1915)

Ameringer, Charles, 'Philippe Bunau-Varilla: New light on the Panama Canal treaty', *Hispanic American Historical Review*, 46 (1966), 28–52

Arbena, Joseph, 'Colombian reactions to the independence of Panama, 1903–1904', *The Americas*, 33 (1976), 130–48

Aufricht, Hans, 'On relative sovereignty', *Cornell Law Quarterly*, 30 (1944), 137–59

Bunau-Varilla, Philippe, *Panama: The creation, destruction, and resurrection* (London, 1913)

Castillero Reyes, Ernesto, *El profeta de Panamá y su gran traición* (Panamá, 1936)

Chamberlain, Leander, 'A chapter of national dishonor', *North American Review*, 195 (January–June 1912), 145–74

Clapp, Margaret, *Forgotten first citizen: John Bigelow* (Boston, 1947)

Clymer, Kenton, *John Hay: The gentleman as diplomat* (Ann Arbor, Mich., 1975)

Collin, Richard, *Theodore Roosevelt's Caribbean: The Panama Canal, the Monroe Doctrine, and the Latin American context* (Baton Rouge, La., 1990)

Colombia, Ministerio de relaciones exteriores, *Libro azul: Documentos diplomáticos sobre el canal y la rebelión del Istmo de Panamá* (Bogotá, 1904)

Congressional Record (Senate), 20 February 1904, 2131–41; 23 February 1904, 2261

Cortissoz, Royal, *The life of Whitelaw Reid* vol. 2 (London, 1921)

Cullom, Shelby, 'The Panama situation', *Independent*, 55 (July–December 1903), 2787–90

Dennett, Tyler, *John Hay: From poetry to politics* (New York, 1933)

Dennis, William, 'The Panama situation in the light of international law', *American Law Register and Review*, 52 (1904), 265–306

Escobar, Francisco, 'President Roosevelt's message and the isthmian canal', *North American Review*, 178 (January–June 1904), 122–32

Fox, George, *President Roosevelt's coup d'état: The Panama affair in a nutshell* (New Haven, Conn., 1904)

Freehoff, Joseph, *America and the canal title: or, An examination, sifting and interpretation of the data bearing on the wresting of the Province of Panama from the Republic of Colombia by the Roosevelt administration in 1903 in order to secure title to the Canal Zone* (New York, 1916)

Friedlander, Robert, 'A reassessment of Roosevelt's role in the Panamanian revolution of 1903', *Western Political Quarterly*, 14 (1961), 535–43

Gatell, Frank, 'The Canal in retrospect – Some Panamanian and Colombian views', *The Americas*, 15 (1958), 23–36

Gordy, J. P., 'The ethics of the Panama case', *Forum*, 36 (July–December 1904), 115–24

Graham, Terence, *The 'interests of civilization'? Reaction in the United States against the 'seizure' of the Panama Canal Zone, 1903–1904* (Lund, 1983)

Granger, Henry, 'The stain on our flag', *Independent*, 71 (July–December 1911), 347–55

Herwig, Holger, *Germany's vision of empire in Venezuela, 1871–1914* (Princeton, N.J., 1986)
The politics of frustration: The United States in German war planning, 1889–1914 (Boston, 1976)

Hill, Howard, *Roosevelt and the Caribbean* (Chicago, 1927)

'Historicus', 'The fifty miles order', *North American Review*, 178 (January–June 1904), 233–45

Jessup, Philip, *Elihu Root*, vol. 1 (New York, 1938)

Johnson, Emory, 'The Panama Canal: The title and concession', *Political Science Quarterly*, 18 (1903), 197–215
'The Panama Canal question', *Independent*, 55 (July–December 1903), 3098–101

Johnson, Willis, 'Justice and equity in Panama', *Forum*, 36 (July–December 1904), 125–37

Lael, Richard, *Arrogant diplomacy: U.S. policy toward Colombia, 1903–1922* (Wilmington, Del., 1987)

Lemaitre, Eduardo, *Panamá y su separación de Colombia* (Bogotá, 1971)

Lodge, Henry Cabot (ed.), *Selections from the correspondence of Theodore Roosevelt and Henry Cabot Lodge 1884–1918*, vol. 2 (New York, 1925)

Mahan, Alfred Thayer, 'Was Panama "a chapter of national dishonor"?' *North American Review*, 196 (July–December 1912), 549–68

Major, John, 'Who wrote the Hay–Bunau-Varilla convention?' *Diplomatic History*, 8 (1984), 115–23

Morey, William, 'International right of way', *American Lawyer*, 12 (1904), 54–9

Morison, Elting (ed.), *The letters of Theodore Roosevelt*, vol. 3 (Cambridge, Mass., 1951)

Muhleman, Maurice, 'The Panama Canal payment', *Journal of Political Economy*, 12 (1903–4), 473–94

Nikol, John, and Holbrook, Francis Xavier, 'Naval operations in the Panamanian revolution of 1903', *American Neptune*, 37 (1977), 253–61

Patterson, John, 'Latin American reactions to the Panamanian revolution of 1903',
    Hispanic American Historical Review, 24 (1944) 342–51
Peirce, Clyde, 'The Panama libel cases', *Indiana Magazine of History*, 33 (1937), 171–86
    *The Roosevelt Panama libel cases: A factual study of a controversial episode in the career
    of Teddy Roosevelt, Father of the Panama Canal* (New York, 1959)
Peterson, Harold, *Diplomat of the Americas: A biography of William I. Buchanan (1852–
    1909)* (Albany, N.Y., 1977)
Pringle, Henry, *Theodore Roosevelt: A biography*, new edn (New York, 1956)
Richards, Henry, *The Panama Canal controversy* (Oxford, 1913)
Roosevelt, Theodore, 'How the United States acquired the right to dig the Panama
    Canal', *Outlook*, 99 (September–December 1911), 314–18
    The works of Theodore Roosevelt, vol. 15, *State papers as governor and president 1899–
    1909* (New York, 1926)
        Vol. 20, *An autobiography* (New York, 1926)
Root, Elihu, 'The ethics of the Panama question', in *Addresses on international subjects*
    (Cambridge, Mass., 1916), 175–206
Schoonover, Thomas, 'Max Farrand's memorandum on the U.S. role in the Panama-
    nian revolution of 1903', *Diplomatic History*, 12 (1988), 501–6
Thayer, William Roscoe, 'John Hay and the Panama Republic, from unpublished papers
    of John Hay', *Harper's Magazine*, 131 (July–December 1915), 165–75
    The life and letters of John Hay, vol. 2 (Boston, 1915)
    Theodore Roosevelt: An intimate biography (London, 1919)
Tompkins, E. Bradley, *Anti-imperialism in the United States: The great debate, 1890–1920*
    (Philadelphia, 1970)
Turk, Richard, 'The United States Navy and the "taking" of Panama, 1901–1903',
    Military Affairs, 38 (1974), 92–8
United States, Congress, House of Representatives, Committee on Foreign Affairs, *The
    story of Panama: Hearings on the Rainey resolution*, 62d Cong., 2d sess. (1913)
United States, Department of State, *Papers relating to the foreign relations of the United
    States*:
        1903 (1904)
        1904 (1905)
Vivian, James, 'The "taking" of the Panama Canal Zone: Myth and reality', *Diplomatic
    History*, 4 (1980), 95–100
Weisberger, Bernard, 'The strange affair of the taking of the Panama Canal Zone',
    American Heritage, 27 (October 1976), 6–11, 68–77
Woolsey, Theodore, 'The recognition of Panama and its results', *Green Bag*, 16 (1904),
    6–12

                                1904–1914

Abbot, Henry, 'Present status of the Panama project', *Annals of the American Academy
    of Political and Social Science*, 31 (1908), 12–35
    Problems of the Panama Canal (New York, 1907)

Adams, William, 'Strategy, diplomacy and isthmian canal security, 1890–1917' (doctoral diss., Florida State University, 1974)

Adamson, William, 'Needed Panama Canal legislation', *Independent*, 72 (January–June 1912), 610–14

Arias, Harmodio, *The Panama Canal: A study in international law and diplomacy* (London, 1911)

Austin, H. A., 'The fortification of the Panama Canal', *Forum*, 49 (January–June 1911), 129–41

Bailey, Thomas, 'The Lodge corollary to the Monroe Doctrine', *Political Science Quarterly*, 48 (1933), 220–39

Bakenhus, Reuben, Knapp, Harry, and Johnson, Emory, *The Panama Canal, comprising its history and construction, and its relation to the Navy, international law and commerce* (New York, 1915)

Baker, Ray Stannard, 'The glory of Panama: How the Big Ditch, dug on honor, is a great example of the new idealism in public service', *American Magazine*, 76 (November 1913), 33–7

'Goethals: The man and how he works', ibid., 76 (October 1913), 22–7

Barrow, Robert, 'The first Panama Canal crisis, 1904', *Caribbean Studies*, 5 (1965–6), 12–27

Bennett, Ira (ed.), *History of the Panama Canal: Its construction and builders* (Washington, D.C., 1915)

Bigelow, Poultney, 'Our mismanagement at Panama', *Independent*, 60 (January–June 1906), 9ff

Bishop, Joseph Bucklin, 'A benevolent despotism', *Scribner's Monthly*, 53 (January–June 1913), 303–19

Notes and anecdotes (New York, 1925)

'Personality of General Goethals', *Scribner's Monthly*, 57 (January–June 1915), 129–52

Bishop, Joseph Bucklin, and Bishop, Farnham, *Goethals, genius of the Panama Canal: A biography* (New York, 1930)

Bourne, Kenneth, and Watt, Donald (eds.), *British documents on foreign affairs: Reports and papers from the Foreign Office confidential print*, pt I, ser. C, *North America*, vol. 15 (Bethesda, Md., 1987)

Braisted, William, *The United States Navy in the Pacific, 1897–1909* (Austin, Tex., 1958)

The United States Navy in the Pacific, 1909–1922 (Austin, Tex., 1971)

Browning, Robert, *Two if by sea: The development of American coastal defense policy* (Westport, Conn., 1983)

Callcott, Wilfrid, *The Caribbean policy of the United States, 1890–1920* (Baltimore, Md., 1942)

Campbell, John, 'Taft, Roosevelt and the arbitration treaties of 1911', *Journal of American History*, 53 (1966–7), 279–98

Carr, John Foster, 'Building a state', *Outlook*, 83 (May–August 1906), 433–45

'The Chief Engineer and his work', ibid., 83 (May–August 1906), 265–70

'The Commission's white workers', ibid., 83 (May–August 1906), 21–4

'The silver men', ibid., 83 (May–August 1906), 117–20

Challener, Richard, *Admirals, generals and American foreign policy, 1898-1914* (Princeton, N.J., 1973)

Chamberlin, Eugene, 'The Japanese scare at Magdalena Bay', *Pacific Historical Review*, 24 (1955), 345–59

Chandler, Alfred, 'Theodore Roosevelt and the Panama Canal: A study in administration', in Elting Morison (ed.), *The letters of Theodore Roosevelt*, vol. 6 (Cambridge, Mass., 1952), 1547–57

Coker, William, 'The Panama Canal tolls controversy: A different perspective', *Journal of American History*, 55 (1968–9), 555–64

Conte-Porras, Jorge, 'Porras y el Tratado' [memorial of 9.11.04], *Revista Lotería*, 240–1 (February–March 1976), 75–133

Costello, Daniel, 'Planning for war: A history of the General Board of the Navy, 1900–1914' (doctoral diss., Tufts University, 1968)

Coudert, Frederic, 'The evolution of the doctrine of territorial incorporation', *Columbia Law Review*, 26 (1926), 823–50

Cox-Sinclair, E., 'The international status of the Panama Canal', *Law Magazine and Review*, 38 (1912), 1–15

Davis, George, 'Fortification at Panama', *American Journal of International Law*, 3 (1909), 885–908

Dennis, Alfred, *Adventures in American diplomacy, 1896–1906* (New York, 1928)

Dulles, John Foster, *The Panama Canal controversy between Great Britain and the United States* (New York, [?], 1913)

'The Panama tolls question', *Proceedings of the American Society of International Law*, 6 (1913), 189–96

DuVal, Miles, *And the mountains will move: The story of the building of the Panama Canal* (Stanford, Calif., 1947)

Franck, Harry, *Zone Policeman 88: A close range study of the Panama Canal and its workers* (New York, 1913)

Fraser, John Foster, *Panama and what it means* (London, 1913)

Freidel, Frank, *Franklin D. Roosevelt: The apprenticeship* (Boston, 1952)

Ghent, William, 'Labor and the Commissary at Panama', *Independent*, 66 (January–June 1909), 1129–36

'Work and welfare on the canal', ibid., 66 (January–June 1909) 907–14

Gibson, John, *Physician to the world: The life of General William G. Gorgas* (Durham, N. C., 1950)

Goethals, George Washington, *Government of the Canal Zone* (Princeton, N. J., 1915)

Goethals, George Washington (ed.), *The Panama Canal: An engineering treatise* (New York, 1916)

Gorgas, Marie, and Hendrick, Burton, *William Crawford Gorgas: His life and work* (New York, 1924)

Gorgas, William, *Sanitation in Panama* (New York, 1915)

Grenville, John, and Young, George, *Politics, strategy and American diplomacy: Studies in foreign policy, 1873–1917* (New Haven, Conn., 1966)

Hains, Peter, 'An isthmian canal from a military point of view', *Annals of the American Academy of Political and Social Science*, 17 (1901), 1–12

'The labor problem on the Panama Canal', *North American Review*, 178 (January–June 1904), 42–54

'Neutralization of the Panama Canal', *American Journal of International Law*, 3 (1909), 354–94

Haskin, Frederic, *The Panama Canal* (New York, 1913)

Healy, David, *Drive to hegemony: The United States in the Caribbean, 1898–1917* (Madison, Wisc., 1988)

Hill, Roscoe, 'The Nicaraguan canal idea to 1913', *Hispanic American Historical Review*, 28 (1948), 197–211

Hogan, J. Michael, 'Theodore Roosevelt and the heroes of Panama', *Presidential Studies Quarterly*, 19 (1989), 79–94

Jessup, Philip, *Elihu Root*, vols. 1–2 (New York, 1938)

Johnson, Emory, 'Necessary Panama Canal legislation', *North American Review*, 194 (July–December 1911), 714–22

Johnson, Willis, *Four centuries of the Panama Canal* (New York, 1907)

Kaplan, Edward, 'Wiliam Jennings Bryan and the Panama Canal tolls controversy', *Mid-America*, 56 (1974), 100–8

Kennedy, Cramond, 'The canal fortifications and the treaty', *American Journal of International Law*, 5 (1911), 620–38

'Neutralization and equal terms', ibid., 7 (1913), 27–50

Kim, Jin 'An anatomy of the Hearst press campaign to fortify an American isthmian canal' (doctoral diss., University of Maryland, 1982)

Knapp, Harry, 'The Navy and the Panama Canal', *U.S. Naval Institute Proceedings*, 39 (1913), 931–48

'The Panama Canal in international law', ibid., 39 (1913), 96–126

'The real status of the Panama Canal as regards neutralization', *American Journal of International Law*, 4 (1910) 314–58

Lael, Richard, 'Dilemma over Panama: Negotiation of the Thomson–Urrutia treaty', *Mid-America*, 61 (1979), 33–45

Latané, John, 'The effects of the Panama Canal on our relations with Latin America', *Annals of the American Academy of Political and Social Science*, 54 (1914), 84–91

'The Panama Canal Act and the British protest', *American Journal of International Law*, 7 (1913), 17–26

Le Prince, Joseph, *Mosquito control in Panama* (New York, 1916)

Lewis, Lancelot, *The West Indian in Panama: Black labor in Panama, 1850–1914* (Washington, D.C., 1980)

McCullough, David, *The path between the seas: The creation of the Panama Canal, 1870–1914* (New York, 1977)

Mack, Gerstle, *The land divided: A history of the Panama Canal and other isthmian canal projects* (New York, 1944)

McKean, Josiah, *The strategic value of the Panama Canal to the Navy* (Washington, D.C., 1914)

Mahan, Alfred Thayer, 'Fortify the Panama Canal', *North American Review*, 193 (January–June 1911), 331–9

'The Panama Canal and sea power in the Pacific', *Century Magazine*, 82 (January–June 1911), 240–8

'The Panama Canal and the distribution of the fleet', *North American Review*, 200 (July–December 1914), 406–17

Mellander, Gustavo, *The United States in Panamanian politics: The intriguing formative years* (Danville, Ill., 1971)

Minger, Ralph, 'Panama, the Canal Zone and titular sovereignty', *Western Political Quarterly*, 14 (1961), 544–54

  William Howard Taft and United States foreign policy: The apprenticeship years, 1900–1908 (Urbana, Ill., 1975)

Morales, Eusebio, 'El tratado del canal: Su historia y interpretación', *Revista Lotería*, 276 (February 1979), 59–64 [written for publication in *North American Review*, issue of November 1904]

Morison, Elting (ed.), *The letters of Theodore Roosevelt*, vols. 4–8 (Cambridge, Mass., 1951–4)

Munro, Dana, 'Dollar diplomacy in Nicaragua, 1909–1913', *Hispanic American Historical Review*, 38 (1958), 209–34

  Intervention and dollar diplomacy in the Caribbean, 1900–1921 (Princeton, N.J., 1964)

Neary, Peter, 'The Panama Canal tolls dispute', *Journal of Transport History*, 7 (1965–6), 173–9

Newton, Velma, *The Silver Men: West Indian labour migration to Panama, 1850–1914* (Kingston, Jamaica, 1984)

Olney, Richard, 'Fortification of the Panama Canal', *American Journal of International Law*, 5 (1911), 298–301

Oppenheim, Lassa, *The Panama Canal conflict between Great Britain and the United States: A study* (Cambridge, 1913)

Parry, Clive (ed.), *A British digest of international law, compiled principally from the archives of the Foreign Office: Phase I, 1860–1914*, vol. 2B (London, 1967)

Patterson, David, *Toward a warless world: The travail of the American peace movement, 1887–1914* (Bloomington Ind., 1976)

Payson, Howard, *The Boy Scouts at the Panama Canal* (New York, 1913)

Pepperman, Walter, *Who built the Panama Canal?* (New York, 1915)

Pomeroy, Earl, 'The Navy and colonial government', *U.S. Naval Institute Proceedings*, 71 (1945), 291–7

Pratt, Julius, *America's colonial experiment: How the United States gained, governed, and in part gave away a colonial empire* (Gloucester, Mass., 1964)

Price, A. Grenfell, 'White settlement in the Canal Zone', *Geographical Review*, 25 (1935), 1–11

Richardson, Bonham, *Panama money in Barbados 1900–1920* (Knoxville, Tenn., 1986)

Roberts, G. W., 'Emigration from the island of Barbados', *Social and Economic Studies*, 4 (1955), 245–88

Roosevelt, Elliott (ed.), *The Roosevelt letters*, vol. 2 (London, 1950)

Roosevelt, Theodore, 'Arbitration and Panama', *Outlook*, 103 (January–April 1913), 111–13

  'The Monroe Doctrine and the Panama Canal', ibid., 105 (September–December 1913), 745–54

The works of Theodore Roosevelt, vol. 15, *State papers as governor and president, 1899–1909* (New York, 1926)

Sands, William, and Lalley, Joseph, *Our jungle diplomacy* (Chapel Hill, N.C., 1944)

Seager, Robert, *Alfred Thayer Mahan: The man and his letters* (Annapolis, Md., 1977)

Semonche, John, *Ray Stannard Baker: A quest for democracy in modern America* (Chapel Hill, N.C., 1969)

Sibert, William, and Stevens, John, *The construction of the Panama Canal* (New York, 1915)

Slosson, Edwin, and Richardson, Gardner, 'The Republic and the Zone', *Independent*, 60 (January–June 1906), 778–85

Stevens, John, *An engineer's recollections* (New York, 1936)

A sketch of the Panama Canal: Its past, present and possible future (New Haven, Conn. [?], 1908)

Stimson, Henry, 'The defense of the Panama Canal', *Scribner's Monthly*, 54 (July–December 1913), 1–6

Some problems of the Panama Canal (Washington, D.C., 1911)

Taft, William Howard, 'The Panama Canal: Why the lock-system was chosen', *Century Magazine*, 73 (July–December 1906), 300–13

The physical, political and international value of the Panama Canal (Albuquerque, N.M., 1979)

Tower, Charlemagne, 'The treaty obligations of the United States relating to the Panama Canal', *Proceedings of the American Philosophical Society*, 52 (1913), 234–42

Turk, Richard, 'United States naval policy in the Caribbean, 1865–1915' (doctoral diss., Tufts University, 1968)

United States, Board of Consulting Engineers on the Panama Canal, *Report of the Board of Consulting Engineers for the Panama Canal* (Washington, D.C., 1906)

United States, Congress, Senate, *Coast defense of the United States and the insular possessions*, 59th Cong., 2d sess., S. Doc, 248 (1906)

Senate, Committee on Interoceanic Canals, *Investigation of Panama Canal matters: Hearings . . . in the matter of the Senate resolution adopted January 9, 1906, providing for an investigation of matters relating to the Panama Canal*, 4 vols., 59th Cong., 2d sess., S. Doc. 401 (1907)

Senate, Committee on Interoceanic Canals, *Hearings . . . on . . . a bill to provide for the opening, maintenance, protection and operation of the Panama Canal, and the sanitation and government of the Canal Zone*, 62d Cong., 2d, sess. (1912)

Senate and House of Representatives, Committees on Appropriations, *Extracts from hearings . . . relative to pay, allowances, health and other conditions of employment of skilled labor on the Panama Canal: Fiscal years 1907–1915 inclusive*, 63d Cong., 2d. sess. (1914)

United States, Department of State, *Papers relating to the foreign relations of the United States*:

1904 (1905)
1906, vol. 2 (1909)
1907, vol. 2 (1910)
1908 (1912)
1909 (1914)

1910 (1915)
1911 (1918)
1912 (1919)
1913 (1920)
1914 (1922)

United States, Isthmian Canal Commission, *Annual report* [for the years ending 1 December 1904, 1905, and 1906, and for the fiscal years 1907 to 1914 inclusive] (Washington, D.C., 1904–14)

United States, President, *Executive orders relating to the Panama Canal (March 8, 1904, to December 31, 1921)* (Mount Hope, CZ, 1922)

Waldo, Fullerton, 'Organization and personnel in the building of the Panama Canal', *Engineering Magazine*, 26 (1903–4), 488–93

'The Panama Canal work, and the workers: A personal study of actual conditions', ibid., 32 (1906–7), 703–16

Wallace, John, 'Plain facts about the Panama Canal', ibid., 30 (1905–6), 801–15

Wambaugh, Eugene, 'Exemption from Panama tolls', *American Journal of International Law*, 7 (1913), 233–44

'The right to fortify the Panama Canal', ibid., 5 (1911), 615–19

Williams, Mary, *Anglo-American isthmian diplomacy, 1815–1915* (Washington, D.C., 1916)

Wood, Robert, 'The working force of the Panama Canal' in George Goethals (ed.), *The Panama Canal: An engineering treatise*, vol. 2 (New York, 1916), 189–204

Zadow, F., 'A German view of the strategic importance of the Panama Canal', *U.S. Naval Institute Proceedings*, 40 (1914), 803–7

1914–1929

Adler, Selig, 'Bryan and Wilsonian Caribbean penetration', *Hispanic American Historical Review*, 20 (1940), 198–226

Alfaro, Olmedo, *El peligro antillano en la América Central: La defensa de la raza* (Panamá, 1926)

Alfaro, Ricardo, *Costa Rica y Panamá: En defensa de los que quieren paz y amistad* (Panamá, 1927)

'Historia documentada de las negociaciones para la celebración del tratado de 1926', *Revista Lotería*, 248–9 (October–November 1976), 51–64

Anderson, Chandler, 'The Costa Rica–Panama boundary dispute', *American Journal of International Law*, 15 (1921), 236–40

Bailey, Thomas, 'Interest in a Nicaragua canal, 1903–1931', *Hispanic American Historical Review*, 16 (1936), 2–28

The policy of the United States toward the neutrals, 1917–1918 (Baltimore, 1942)

Baker, George, 'The Wilson administration and Nicaragua, 1913–1921', *The Americas*, 22 (1966), 339–76

'The Wilson administration and Panama, 1913–1921', *Journal of Inter-American Studies*, 8 (1966) 279–93

Bishop, Joseph Bucklin, 'The Panama Canal: Its efficiency and operation', *Scribner's Monthly*, 70 (July–December 1921), 33–52

Bonnet, Georges-Edgar, *Le canal de Panama: Rapport de mission* (Paris, 1929)

Braisted, William, 'On the American Red and Red–Orange war plans, 1919–1939', in Gerald Jordan (ed.), *Naval warfare in the twentieth century, 1900–1945: Essays in honour of Arthur Marder* (London, 1977), 167–85

The United States Navy in the Pacific, 1909–1922 (Austin, Tex., 1971)

Bywater, Hector, *The Great Pacific War: A history of the American–Japanese campaign of 1931–33* (London, 1925)

Charles, L. D., 'An account of the Panama–Costa Rica boundary dispute', *Fortnightly Review*, 110 (1921), 615–22

Colby, Everett, 'The United States and the Coto dispute between Panama and Costa Rica', *Journal of International Relations*, 12 (1921–2), 372–8

Coletta, Paolo, 'William Jennings Bryan and the United States–Colombia impasse, 1903– 1921', *Hispanic American Historical Review*, 47 (1967), 486–501

Congressional Record (Senate), 11 June 1919, 956; 14 July 1919, 2537; 12 August 1919, 388; 14 May 1921, 1456–7

Crenshaw, Russell, 'Naval radio stations of the Panama Canal Zone', *U.S. Naval Institute Proceedings*, 42 (1916), 1209–18

Cuevas, Alexander, 'El movimiento inquilinario de 1925', *Revista Lotería*, 213 (October– November 1973), 133–61

Edge, Walter, 'The Nicaragua trade route', *Saturday Evening Post*, 11 May 1929, 155–7

Fisher, J. B., 'Diplomatic aspects of the Nicaragua canal', *U.S. Naval Institute Proceedings*, 56 (1930), 381–6

Franck, Harry, 'Eight Years later', *Century Magazine*, 101 (July–December 1920), 222–8

Gasteazoro, Carlos Manuel, 'Presentación de Narciso Garay', *Revista Lotería*, 281 (July 1979), 1–45

Goldingham, C. S., 'The Panama Canal: The problem of its defence in a future war', *United Service Magazine*, 55 (1917), 189–97

Goldsberry, Kenneth, 'The strike of 1920: A study of the black labor movement in the Canal Zone' (unpublished paper in Panama Canal Collection, Panama Canal Commission Library)

Gompers, Samuel, 'Conditions of life and labor on the Panama Canal Zone', *American Federationist*, 31 (1924), 209–21

Grieb, Kenneth, *The Latin American policy of Warren G. Harding* (Fort Worth, Tex., 1977)

Hardmann, R. C., 'The highway program of Panama', *Pan-American Magazine*, 37 (1924), 273–8

Howe, James, 'Native rebellion and U.S. intervention in Central America', *CS Quarterly*, 10 (1986), 59–65

Johnson, Emory, *The Panama Canal and commerce* (New York, 1916)

Lansing, Robert, *War memoirs of Robert Lansing, secretary of state* (New York, 1935)

League of Nations, *Records of the eighth ordinary session of the Assembly. Plenary meetings. Text of the debates. Official journal*, Special Supp. no. 54 (Geneva, 1927)

Le Cesne, J., *Situation juridique et rôle économique du Canal de Panama* (Paris, 1919)

Leonard, Thomas, 'The United States and Panama: Negotiating the aborted 1926 treaty',
    Mid-America, 61 (1979), 189–203
Link, Arthur, *Wilson: The struggle for neutrality 1914–1915* (Princeton, N.J., 1960)
Lodge, Henry Cabot, *The Senate and the League of Nations* (New York, 1925)
MacDonald, Donald, *Some engineering problems of the Panama Canal in their relation to
    geology and topography* (Washington, D.C., 1915)
Miller, Hugh Gordon, *The isthmian highway: A review of the problems of the Caribbean*
    (New York, 1929)
Millett, Richard, 'The State Department's navy: A history of the Special Service
    Squadron, 1920–1940', *American Neptune*, 35 (1975), 118–38
Moffett, Cleveland, *The conquest of America: A romance of disaster and victory* (New York,
    1916)
Morales, Eusebio, 'El canal de Panamá y la Liga de las Naciones', *Revista Nueva*, 6 (1919),
    65–78
Morrow, Jay, *A great people's great canal* (Mount Hope, CZ, 1923)
    The maintenance and operation of the Panama Canal (Mount Hope, CZ, 1923)
    'Needs of the canal', *Outlook*, 138 (September–December 1924), 443–5
    'Our business dominions – Panama', *American Industries*, 23 (November 1922), 5–8
Morton, Louis, 'War Plan ORANGE: Evolution of a strategy', *World Politics*, 11 (1958–9),
    221–50
Muñoz, Hernando Franco, *El movimiento obrero panameño, 1914–1921* (Panamá, 1979)
Munro, Dana, *Intervention and dollar diplomacy in the Caribbean, 1900–1921* (Princeton,
    N.J., 1964)
    The United States and the Caribbean republics, 1921–1933 (Princeton, N.J., 1974)
'A Naval Expert', 'Can we defend the Panama Canal in a crisis?' *Century Magazine*, 94
    (January–June 1917), 919–28
Norton, Henry, 'Why Britishers in Panama?' *World's Work*, 59 (November 1930), 29–32
O'Hern, Edward, 'Guns, ammunition and accessories', *Journal of the United States
    Artillery* (March–April 1915), 161–4, 167, 178–9
Panama, Supreme Court of Justice, 'The Republic of Panama against Wilbert L.
    Schwartzfiger: Involuntary manslaughter', *American Journal of International Law*, 31
    (1927), 182–7
Pereira Jiménez, Bonifacio, 'Historia de la controversia de limites entre Panamá y Costa
    Rica', *Revista Lotería*, 92 (September 1962), 7–126
Perkins, Whitney, *Constraint of empire: The United States and Caribbean interventions*
    (Westport, Conn., 1981)
Poindexter, Miles, 'Our rights in Panama', *Forum*, 68 (1921), 129–44
Porras, Belisario, and Filós, Francisco, *Estudio sobre el tratado del canal* (Panamá, 1920)
Reeves, Jesse, 'Clearing the way for the Nicaragua canal', *American Journal of Inter-
    national Law*, 17 (1923), 309–13
Revista Lotería, 368 (September–October 1987), 157–88: Porras to Polk and Lansing,
    8, 9, and 15.8.19, 10 and 16.9.19
Rippy, J. Fred, 'Political issues in Panama today', *Current History*, 28 (1928), 226–7
Roosevelt, Elliott (ed.), *The Roosevelt letters*, vol. 2 (London, 1950)
Roosevelt, Theodore, 'The Panama blackmail treaty', *Metropolitan*, 41 (1915), 8–10, 69–72

Salter, R. W. A., 'The Panama Rail Road', *Railway Magazine*, 41 (1917), 77–84

Scott, James Brown, 'The treaty between Colombia and the United States', *American Journal of International Law*, 15 (1921), 430–9

'The slippery slope of imperialism', *Spectator*, 138 (1927), 69–70

Stevens, John, 'Is a second canal necessary?' *Foreign Affairs*, 8 (1929–30), 417–29

'The Panama Canal', *Transactions of the American Society of Civil Engineers*, 91 (1927), 946–67

Stewart, Watt, 'The ratification of the Thomson–Urrutia treaty', *Southwestern Political and Social Science Quarterly*, 10 (1930), 416–28

Strout, Richard Lee, 'The League and the Panama treaty', *Independent*, 118 (1927), 95–6, 111

Thompson, A. Blanchfield, *Résumé of the Silver employees' strike on the Canal Zone* (Panamá, 1920)

Tulchin, Joseph, *The aftermath of war: World War One and United States policy toward Latin America* (New York, 1971)

United States, Department of State, *Papers relating to the foreign relations of the United States*:

>   *1914* (1922)
>   *1915* (1924)
>   *1916* (1925)
>   *1917* (1926)
>   *1918* (1930)
>   *1919*, vol. 2 (1934)
>   *1920*, vol. 3 (1936)
>   *1921*, vol. 2 (1936)
>   *1922*, vol. 2 (1938)
>   *1923*, vol. 2 (1938)
>   *1924*, vol. 2 (1939)
>   *1925*, vol. 2 (1940)
>   *1926*, vol. 2 (1941)
>   *1927*, vol. 3 (1942)
>   *1928*, vol. 3 (1943)
>   *1929*, vol. 3 (1944)

United States, Navy, *Code of Navy regulations* (Washington, D.C., 1920 edn)

United States, Panama Canal, *Annual report* [of the governor of the Panama Canal for the fiscal years 1915 to 1929 inclusive] (Washington, D.C., 1915–29)

United States, President, *Executive Orders relating to the Panama Canal (March 8, 1904, to December 31 1921)* (Mount Hope, CZ, 1922)

United States, President, Special Panama Canal Commission, *Report* [September 15, 1921] ... *with letter from the governor of the Panama Canal to the secretary of war dated September 17, 1921 and letter from the secretary of war to the governor of the Panama Canal dated October 18, 1921* (Washington, D.C., 1922)

Velarde, Fabian, *Análisis del nuevo tratado* (Panamá, 1927)

Wheeler, Gerald, *Admiral William Veazie Pratt, U.S. Navy: A sailor's life* (Washington, D.C., 1974)

Woolsey, L. H., 'The sovereignty of the Panama Canal Zone', *American Journal of International Law*, 20 (1926), 117–24

Zuñiga Guardia, Carlos Iván, *El desarme de la Policia Nacional en 1916* (Panamá, 1973)

1930–1949

Acosta, David, *La influenza decisiva de la opinión publica en el rechazo del Convenio Filós– Hines de 1947* (Panamá, 1981)

Alfaro, Olmedo, *El canal de Panamá en las guerras futuras* (Guayaquil, 1930)

Alfaro, Ricardo, *Los acuerdos entre Panamá y los Estados Unidos* (Panamá, 1943)
  'Conferencia relativa la Articulo III del tratado del Canal', *Revista de la Camera de Comercio de Panamá*, nos. 44–5 (1948)

Blanchard, William, 'The Panama Canal', in William Haas (ed.), *The American empire: A study of the outlying territory of the United States* (Chicago, Ill., 1940), 123–50

Blanshard, Paul, *Democracy and empire in the Caribbean* (New York, 1947)

Braden, Spruille, *Diplomats and demagogues: The memoirs of Spruille Braden* (New Rochelle, N.Y., 1971)

Briggs, Herbert, 'Treaties, executive agreements, and the Joint Panama Resolution of 1943', *American Political Science Review*, 37 (1943), 686–91

Bryan, G. S., 'Geography and the defense of the Caribbean and the Panama Canal', *Annals of the Association of American Geographers*, 31 (1941), 83–94

Buell, Raymond, 'Panama and the United States', *Foreign Policy Reports*, 7 (20 January 1932), 409–26

Burke, Céspedes, *The forgotten silver workers* (Panamá, 1950)

Colby, Elbridge, 'The safety of the Panama Canal', *Military Engineering*, 31 (1939), 247–53

Congressional Record (Senate), 19 January 1932, 2311; 24 July 1939, 9833–45; 25 July 1939, 9903–4

Conn, Stetson, and Fairchild, Byron, *The framework of hemisphere defense* (volume of *The U.S. Army in World War II: The Western Hemisphere*) (Washington, D.C., 1960)

Conn, Stetson, and Fairchild, Byron, *Guarding the United States and its outposts*, (volume of *the U.S. Army in World War II: The Western Hemisphere*) (Washington, D.C., 1964)

Conte-Porras, Jorge, *Arnulfo Arias Madrid* (Panamá, 1980)
  'Octavio Méndez Pereira y el ciclo generacional de 1931', *Revista Lotería*, 270–1 (August–September 1978), 29–45

Coombs, G. M., 'The Panama Canal and its defence', *Contemporary Review*, 161 (July–December 1942), 178–80

DeToledano, Ralph, 'Stalin's hand in the Panama Canal', *Plain Talk*, November 1946, 31–9

DuBois, Jules, *Danger over Panama* (Indianapolis, Ind., 1964)

Eliot, George Fielding, *The ramparts we watch: A study of the problems of American national defense* (New York, 1938)

Escobar, Felipe, *Arnulfo Arias, o el credo panameñista, 1930–1940: Ensayo psico-patológico de la política panameña* (Panamá, 1946)

Fujita, Shin-Ishiro, 'Japan's position in Manchuria compared to the U.S. role in Panama', *Trans-Pacific*, 20 (8 September 1932), 5

Galambos, Louis (ed.), *The papers of Dwight David Eisenhower*, vols. 7–9, *The chief of staff* (Baltimore, Md., 1979)

Garay, Narciso, *Panamá y las guerras de los Estados Unidos* (Panamá, 1930)

Garciá-Mora, Manuel, 'International law applicable to the defense of the Panama Canal', *University of Detroit Law Journal*, 12 (1949), 63–73

Haglund, David, *Latin America and the transformation of U.S. strategic thought, 1936–1940* (Albuquerque, N.M., 1984)

Hooper, Ofelia, 'Rural Panama: Its needs and prospects', *Rural Sociology*, 8 (1943), 247–53

Hoskins, Halford, 'The Suez Canal and the outlook for Egypt', *American Political Science Review*, 38 (1944), 110–19
   'The Suez Canal as an international waterway', *American Journal of International Law*, 37 (1943), 373–85

The Imperial Japanese Navy, vol. 12, *Submarines* (Tokyo, 1990) [in Japanese]

Johnson, Emory, 'The Panama Canal tolls problem and its solution', *Proceedings of the American Philosophical Society*, 78 (July–December 1938), 671–84

Langer, William, and Gleason, S. Everett, *The world crisis and American foreign policy*, vol. 2, *The undeclared war 1940–1941* (London, 1953).

Langley, Lester, 'Negotiating new treaties with Panama: 1936', *Hispanic American Historical Review*, 48 (1968), 220–33
   'The United States and Panama, 1933–1941: A study in strategy and diplomacy' (doctoral diss., University of Kansas, 1965)
   'The world crisis and the Good Neighbor policy in Panama, 1936–1941', *The Americas*, 24 (1967), 137–52

Lawyers' Co-operative Publishing Company, *Cases argued and decided in the Supreme Court of the United States*, 79 (Rochester, N.Y., 1935), 885–933

Leonard, Thomas, 'United States perception of Panamanian politics, 1944–1949', *Journal of Third World Studies*, 5 (1988), 112–38

Long, E. John, 'Japan's "underseas carriers" ', *U.S. Naval Institute Proceedings*, 76 (1950), 607–13

Major, John, 'F.D.R. and Panama', *Historical Journal*, 28 (1985), 357–77
   ' "Pro mundi beneficio"? The Panama Canal as an international issue, 1943–8', *Review of International Studies*, 9 (1983), 17–34
   'Wasting asset: The U.S. re-assessment of the Panama Canal, 1945–1949', *Journal of Strategic Studies*, 3 (1980), 123–46

Mansfield, Mike, *The Panama bases* (Washington, D.C., 1948)

Nixon, Edgar (ed.), *Franklin D. Roosevelt and foreign affairs*, 3 vols. (Cambridge, Mass., 1969)

Orita, Zenji, and Harrington, Joseph, *I-Boat captain* (Canoga Park, Calif., 1976)

Pérez, V. M., *El movimiento de Acción Comunal en Panamá* (Panamá, 1964)

Pippin, Larry LaRae, *The Remón era: An analysis of the decade of events in Panama, 1947–1957* (Stanford, Calif., 1964)

Porras, Demetrio, 'El movimiento inquilinario', *Revista Lotería*, 212–13 (October–November 1973), 169–98

Railey, Hilton, *Touched with madness* (New York, 1938)

Revista Lotería, 200 (July 1972), 35–45: 'Historia de la Compañia Panameña de Fuerza y Luz'

Roberts, George, *Investigación económica de la República de Panamá* (Panamá, 1933)

Romualdi, Serafino, *Presidents and peons: Recollections of a labor ambassador in Latin America* (New York, 1967)

[Roosevelt, Franklin], *Complete presidential press conferences of Franklin D. Roosevelt*, vols. 2 and 15 (New York, 1972)

Rounsevell, Nelson, *The life story of 'N.R.'; or, 40 years of rambling, gambling and publishing* (Panamá, 1933)

Schnabel, James, *The Joint Chiefs of Staff and national policy* (vol. 1 of *The history of the Joint Chiefs of Staff*) (Wilmington, Del., 1979)

Sepulveda, Melinda, *Harmodio Arias Madrid: El hombre, el estadista y el periodista* (Panamá, 1983)

Shalett, Sidney, 'Can we defend the Panama Canal?' *Saturday Evening Post*, 9 October 1948, 15–17, 158, 161–3

Sherry, Michael, *Preparing for the next war: American plans for postwar defense, 1941–45* (New Haven, Conn., 1977)

Sociedad Panameña de Acción Internacional, *Panama–United States relations: A situation that must be changed for the welfare of Panama and the honor of the United States. True history of the Panama Canal treaty, born from fraud, perfidy, inequity, dishonor, coercion, chicanery, menace, disloyalty and injustice. Panama's rights on the Canal Zone voiced by distinguished American officials and statesmen* (Panamá, 1934)

Stimson, Henry, and Bundy, McGeorge, *On active service in peace and war* (New York, 1948)

Thomas, J. Parnell, 'Reds in the Panama Canal Zone', *Liberty*, 25 (1948), 14–15, 47, 54

United States, Department of State, *Papers relating to the foreign relations of the United States*:
    1930, vol. 3 (1945)
    1931, vol. 2 (1946)
Foreign relations of the United States: Diplomatic papers:
    1932, vol. 5 (1948)
    1933, vol. 5 (1952)
    1934, vol. 5 (1952)
    1935, vol. 4 (1953)
    1936, vol. 5 (1954)
    1937, vol. 5 (1954)
    1938, vol. 5 (1956)
    1939, vol. 5 (1957)
    1940, vol. 5 (1961)
    1941, vol. 7 (1962)
    1942, vol. 6 (1963)
    1943, vol. 6 (1965)
    1944, vol. 7 (1967)
    1945, vol. 9 (1969)

Foreign relations of the United States:
    1946, vol. 11 (1969)
    1947, vol. 8 (1972)
    1948, vol. 9 (1972)
    1949, vol. 2 (1975)
United States, Navy, Fifteenth Naval District, *Administrative history, Fifteenth Naval District and Panama sea frontier*, 2 vols. (Balboa, CZ, 1947)
United States, Panama Canal, *Annual report* [of the governor of the Panama Canal for the fiscal years 1930 to 1949 inclusive] (Washington, D.C., 1930–49)
United States, President, *Title 3 (The President) Code of Federal Regulations Compilation, 1936–65* (1968)
Van Olst, H. Rijken, *The national income and national accounts of the Republic of Panama 1944–1952* (New York, 1953)
Watson, Mark, *Chief of staff: Prewar plans and preparations* (The U.S. Army in World War II: The War Department) (Washington, D.C., 1950)
Welles, Sumner, *Seven major decisions* (London, 1951)
Westerman, George, 'Gold vs. Silver workers in the Canal Zone', *Common Ground*, 8 (1948), 92–5
Williams, Kathleen, *Air defense of the Panama Canal, 1 January 1939 – 7 December 1941*, Army Air Forces Historical Studies, no. 42 (Washington, D.C., 1946)
Woolsey, L. H., 'Executive agreements relating to Panama', *American Journal of International Law*, 37 (1943), 482–9
    [Comment on the 1936 treaty], ibid., 31 (1937), 297–300
Wright, Almon, 'Defense site negotiations between the United States and Panama, 1936–1948', *Department of State Bulletin*, 27 (11 August 1952), 212–19
    'German interest in Panama's Piñas Bay, 1910–1938', *Journal of Modern History*, 27 (1955), 61–6
    The United States and Panama, 1933–1949, U.S. Department of State, Bureau of Public Affairs, Research Project no. 499 (August 1952)

1950–1979

'America's troubled canal', *Fortune*, 55 (January–June, 1957), 129–32, 160, 162, 167, 168
Armbrister, Trevor, 'Panama: Why they hate us – More than one torn flag', *Saturday Evening Post*, 237 (7 March 1964)
Baldwin, Hanson, 'Con: The Panama Canal – Sovereignty and security', *AEI Defense Review*, no. 4 (1977), 12–34
Bendahmane, Diane, and McDonald, John (eds.), *Perspectives on negotiation: Four case studies and interpretations* (Washington, D.C., 1986), 3–50 [the Panama Canal treaties]
Brzezinski, Zbigniew, *Power and principle: Memoirs of the national security adviser 1977–1981* (New York, 1983)
Buckley, William, 'On the right', *National Review*, 12 and 26.11.76
Busey, James, *Political aspects of the Panama Canal: The problem of location* (Tucson, Ariz., 1974)

Carter, Jimmy, *Keeping faith: Memoirs of a president* (London, 1982)
Chuang, Richard, 'The enactment of the implementation legislation of the Panama
    Canal treaty of 1977', *Revue de Droit International de Sciences Diplomatiques et
    Politiques*, 58 (October–December 1980), 197–216
    'The process and politics of the ratification of the Panama Canal treaties in the United
    States', ibid., 56 (April–June 1978), 95–113
    'The ratification of the Panama Canal treaty: A sequel to the ratification of the
    neutrality treaty by the United States', ibid., 57 (July–September 1979), 153–65
Congressional Quarterly, Inc., *Congress and the nation*, vol. 5, *1977–1980* (Washington,
    D.C., 1981)
Congressional Record (House), 6 October 1975, 31874–6
Conte-Porras, Jorge, *Arnulfo Arias Madrid* (Panamá, 1980)
Cox, Robert, 'Choices for partnership or bloodshed in Panama', in Kalman Silvert (ed.),
    *The Americas in a changing world: A report of the Commission on United States – Latin
    American – relations* (New York, 1975)
Crane, Philip, *Surrender in Panama: The case against the treaty* (New York, 1978)
Declassified documents reference system, various years (Arlington, Va., 1976–81, and
    Woodbridge, Conn., 1982–)
Destler, I. M., 'Treaty troubles: Versailles in reverse', *Foreign Policy*, no. 33 (Winter 1978–
    9), 45–65
Dozer, Donald, *The Panama Canal in perspective* (Washington, D.C., 1978)
    'The economic development of Panama', *Economic Bulletin for Latin America*, 2 (1959),
    48–59
Eisenhower, Dwight D., *Mandate for change, 1953–1956* (London, 1963)
    Waging peace, 1956–1961 (London, 1966)
Eisenhower, Milton, *The wine is bitter: The United States and Latin America* (New York,
    1963)
Enelow, James, and Koehler, David, 'Amendment in legislative strategy: Sophisticated
    voting in the U.S. Congress', *Journal of Politics*, 42 (1980), 396–413
EPICA Task Force, *Panama: Sovereignty for a land divided* (Washington, D.C., 1976)
Escobar Bethancourt, Rómulo, *Torrijos: Colonia americana, no!* (Bogotá, 1981)
Fábrega, Octavio, Sucre, Carlos, and Huertematte, Roberto, 'Informe completo de la
    misión especial negociadora de Panamá', *Anuario de Derecho*, 1 (1956), 113ff
Falk, R. A., 'Panama treaty trap', *Foreign Policy*, no. 30 (Spring 1978), 68–82
Fenwick, Charles, 'Legal aspects of the Panama case', *American Journal of International
    Law*, 58 (1964), 436–41
    'Treaty of 1955 between the United States and Panama', ibid., 49 (1955), 543–7
Finer, Herman, *Dulles over Suez: The theory and practice of his diplomacy* (London, 1964)
Flood, Daniel, *Isthmian canal policy questions: Canal Zone–Panama Canal sovereignty;
    Panama Canal modernization; new canal* (Washington, D.C., 1966)
    'Panama Canal Zone: Constitutional domain of the United States', *World Affairs*, 131
    (1958), 74–7
Foy, H. M., 'The president, the Congress, and the Panama Canal: An essay on the
    powers of the executive and legislative branches in the field of foreign affairs',
    Georgia Journal of International and Comparative Law, 16 (1986), 607–54

Franck, Thomas, and Weisband, Edward, 'Panama paralysis', *Foreign Policy*, no. 21 (Winter 1975–6), 168–87

Fulbright, J. William, *Old myths and new realities* (New York, 1964)

Furlong, William, and Scranton, Margaret, *The dynamics of foreign policymaking: The president, the Congress, and the Panama Canal treaties* (Boulder, Colo., 1984)

García-Mora, Manuel, 'The Panama Canal controversy: A sixty-year unresolved problem', *Vital Speeches of the Day*, 30 (1964), 412–16

Georgetown University, Center for Strategic Studies, *Panama Canal: Issues and treaty talks* (Washington, D.C., 1967)

Geyelin, Philip, *Lyndon Johnson and the world* (New York, 1966)

Goldman, Eric, *The tragedy of Lyndon Johnson* (New York, 1969)

Goldrich, Daniel, 'Requisites for political legitimacy in Panama', *Public Opinion Quarterly*, 36 (1962), 664–8

Sons of the Establishment: Élite youth in Panama (Chicago, Ill., 1966)

Greene, Graham, *Getting to know the general: The story of an involvement* (London, 1984)

Hamlin, Wilbur, 'Panama Canal: Legal issues involved in the transfer of the Canal to Panama', *Harvard International Law Journal*, 19 (1978–9), 279–328

Herrera, Luis, *The Panama Canal: An exercise in international relations* (Tampere, Finland, 1978)

Hogan, J. Michael, *The Panama Canal in American politics: Domestic advocacy and the evolution of policy* (Carbondale, Ill., 1986)

Hughes, Thomas, 'Carter and the management of contradictions', *Foreign Policy*, no. 31 (Summer 1978), 34–55

Illueca, Jorge, in U.S. Department of Commerce, *Foreign Broadcast Information Service*, 6 (13.12.72), M1–M12, and ibid., 6 (14.12.72), M1–M4 [speech of 12 December 1972 at University of Panama]

Johnson, Lyndon, *The vantage-point: Perspectives of the presidency 1963–1969* (London, 1972)

Jorden, William, *Panama odyssey* (Austin, Tex., 1984)

Kitchel, Denison, *The truth about the Panama Canal* (New Rochelle, N.Y., 1978)

LaFeber, Walter, 'Latin American Policy', in Robert Divine (ed.), *Exploring the Johnson years* (Austin, Tex., 1981), 63–90

Langley, Lester, 'U.S.–Panama relations since 1941', *Journal of Inter-American Studies and World Affairs*, 12 (1970), 339–66

Leonard, Thomas, 'The 1977 Panama Canal treaties in historical perspective', *Journal of Caribbean Studies*, 2 (1981), 190–209

Levine, Isaac Don, *Hands off the Panama Canal!* (Washington, D.C., 1976)

Linowitz, Sol, *The making of a public man: A memoir* (Boston, 1985)

López-Guevara, Carlos, 'Negotiating a peaceful solution to the Panama Canal question', *New York University Journal of International Law and Politics*, 9 (1976), 3–14

'Panama tiene derecho a denunciar la convención del canal istmico por violación a la misma por parte de los Estados Unidos', *Revista Lotería*, 196 (March 1972), 97–117

Lowenthal, Abraham, and Charlton, Milton, 'Pro: The United States and Panama – Confrontation or cooperation?' *AEI Defense Review*, no. 4 (1977), 2–11

McGee, Gale, 'After Panama: Some lessons and opportunities in the aftermath of the canal treaties debate', *South Atlantic Quarterly*, 78 (1979), 1–16

Maier, H. G., 'United States' defense rights in the Panama Canal treaties: The need for clarification of a studied ambiguity', *Virginia Journal of International Law*, 24 (1984), 287–322

Minor, Kent, 'United States – Panamanian relations, 1958–1973' (doctoral diss., Case Western Reserve University, 1974)

Moffett, George, *The limits of victory: The ratification of the Panama Canal treaties, 1977–1978* (Ithaca, N.Y., 1985)

Morris, Jan, 'Panama, an imperial specimen', in *Destinations: Essays from 'Rolling Stone'* (Oxford, 1980), 55–79

Opperman, John, 'The Panama Canal treaties', in Hoyt Purvis and Steven Baker (eds.), *Legislating foreign policy* (Boulder, Colo., 1984), 77–105

Padelford, Norman, 'The Panama Canal and the Suez crisis', *Proceedings of the American Society of International Law* (51st annual meeting, 25–7 April 1957), 10–19

Pippin, Larry LaRae, *The Remón era: An analysis of a decade of events in Panama, 1947–1957* (Stanford, Calif., 1964)

Pruessen, Ronald, *John Foster Dulles: The road to power* (New York, 1982)

Revista Lotería, 191 (October 1971) [issue on the 1964 crisis]
    266–7 (April–May 1978 [treaty negotiation documents, 1970–5]

Rippy, J. Fred, 'The United States and Panama: The high cost of appeasement', *Inter-American Economic Affairs*, 17 (1964), 87–94

Rode, Zvonko, 'The International Claims Commission of the United States', *American Journal of International Law*, 47 (1953), 615–37

Ropp, Steve, 'Negotiating the 1978 Panama Canal treaties: Contending theoretical perspectives', in John Martz (ed.), *United States policy in Latin America: A quarter century of crisis and challenge, 1961–1986* (Lincoln, Nebr., 1988), 175–201
    'Panama and the Canal', in Jan Knippers Black (ed.), *Latin America: Its problems and promises* (Boulder, Colo., 1984), 329–42

Rosenfeld, Stephen, 'The Panama Canal negotiations: A close-run thing', *Foreign Affairs*, 54 (1975–6), 1–13

Royo, Arístides, *Las negociaciones con los Estados Unidos sobre el canal de Panamá* (Panamá, 1979)

Rubin, Barry, 'Panama Canal retrospective', *Contemporary Review*, 234 (January–June 1979), 80–4

Ryan, Paul, 'Canal diplomacy and U.S. interests', *U.S. Naval Institute Proceedings*, 103 (1977), 43–53
    The Panama Canal controversy: United States diplomatic and defense interests (Stanford, Calif., 1977)

Scranton, Margaret, 'Changing United States foreign policy: Negotiating new Panama Canal treaties, 1958–1978' (doctoral diss., University of Pittsburgh, 1980)

Simpson, Michael, 'Panama: The proposed transfer of the Canal and Canal Zone by treaty', *Georgia Journal of International and Comparative Law*, 5 (1975), 195–215

Smit, Hans, 'The Panama Canal: A national or an international waterway?' *Columbia Law Review*, 76 (1976), 965–88

'The proposed Panama Canal treaties: A triple failure', *Columbia Journal of Transnational Law*, 17 (1978), 1–32

Smith, T. J., and Hogan, J. Michael, 'Public opinion and the Panama Canal treaties of 1977', *Public Opinion Quarterly*, 51 (1987), 5–30

Speller, Jon, *The Panama Canal: Heart of America's security* (New York, 1972)

Strong, Robert, 'Jimmy Carter and the Panama Canal treaties', *Presidential Studies Quarterly*, 21 (1991), 269–86

Stuart, Graham, 'Should the Panama Canal be internationalized?' in Alva Wilgus (ed.), *The Caribbean: Contemporary international relations* (Gainesville, Fla., 1957), 39–50

Sulzberger, Cyrus, *The last of the giants* (London, 1970)

Summ, G. Harvey, and Kelly, Tom (eds.), *The Good Neighbors: America, Panama and the 1977 canal treaties* (Athens, Ohio, 1988)

Tack, Juan Antonio, 'La lucha de Omar Torrijos por la recuperación de la integridad nacional', *Revista Lotería*, 305–9 (August–December 1981), pt. 1, 219–34

Tate, Mercer, 'The Panama Canal and political partnership', *Journal of Politics*, 25 (1963), 119–38

Tate, Mercer, and Allen, Edward, 'The proposed new treaties for the Panama Canal', *International Affairs*, 45 (1969), 269–78

Tondel, Lyman (ed.), *The Panama Canal: Background papers and proceedings of the Sixth Hammarskjöld Forum* (Dobbs Ferry, N.Y., 1965)

'Transfer of the Panama Canal by treaty without House approval: *Edwards* v. *Carter*', *Harvard Law Review*, 92 (1978–79), 524–35

Travis, Martin, and Watkins, James, 'Control of the Panama Canal: An obsolete shibboleth?' *Foreign Affairs*, 37 (1958–9), 407–18

Turner, Domingo, 'Foster Dulles y el Canal de Panamá', *Humanisimo*, 5 (1957), 21–35

United States, Congress, House of Representatives, *Communication from the President of the United States transmitting the report and recommendations of the Bureau of the Budget with respect to the organization and operations of the Panama Canal and Panama Railroad Company, pursuant to House Report No. 1304, eighty-first Congress, 31 January 1950*, 81st Cong., 2d sess. (1950)

House of Representatives, Committee on Foreign Affairs, Subcommittee on Inter-American Affairs, *Hearings on United States relations with Panama* and *Report on United States relations with Panama*, 86th Cong., 2d sess. (1960)

House of Representatives, Committee on International Relations, *Hearings on proposed Panama Canal treaties*, 95th Cong., 1st sess. (1978)

House of Representatives, Committee on Merchant Marine and Fisheries, *Hearings on the agreement in principle with respect to the proposed Panama Canal treaties of 1977*, 95th Cong., 1st sess. (1977)

House of Representatives, Committee on Merchant Marine and Fisheries, Subcommittee on the Panama Canal, *Hearings on authorization and provision for the maintenance and operation of the Panama Canal by the present corporate adjunct of the Panama Canal, as renamed*, 81st Cong., 2d sess. (1950)

Senate, Committee on Armed Services, *Hearings on defense, maintenance and operation of the Panama Canal, including administration and government of the Canal Zone*, 95th Cong., 1st sess. (1978)

Senate, Committee on Foreign Relations, *Hearings on Executive F, the treaty of mutual understanding and cooperation with the Republic of Panama*, 84th Cong., 1st sess. (1955)

Senate, Committee on Foreign Relations, *Executive sessions of the Senate Foreign Relations Committee: Historical series*, vol. 7, *1955* (95th Cong., 2d sess.) (1978)

Senate, Committee on Foreign Relations, *Hearings on Executive N . . . the Panama Canal treaty and the treaty concerning the permanent neutrality and operation of the Panama Canal, signed on behalf of the United States at the headquarters of the Organization of American States on September 7, 1977*, 4 vols., 95th Cong., 1st sess. (1978)

Senate, Committee on the Judiciary, Subcommittee on Separation of Powers, *Panama Canal treaties [United States Senate debate] 1977–78*, 3 vols., 95th Cong., 2d sess. (1978)

Senate, Committee on the Judiciary, Subcommittee on Separation of Powers, *The Panama Canal treaty – Consitutional and legal aspects. of the ratification process: Hearing*, 98th Cong., 2d sess. (1984)

United States, Department of State, *Foreign Relations of the United States*:

> *1950*, vol. 2 (1976)
>
> *1951*, vol. 2 (1979)
>
> *1952–1954*, vol. 4 (1983)
>
> *1955–1957*, vol. 7 (1987); vol. 16 (1990)
>
> *1958–1960*, vol. 5, *Microform supplement* (1991)

United States treaties and other international agreements, vol. 33, pt 1 (1981), TIAS 10029–32 [texts of 1977 canal treaties and agreements]

United States, General Accounting Office, *Report on audit of the Panama Canal Company and the Canal Zone Government for the fiscal year ended June 30, 1952, by the comptroller-general of the United States* (1953)

Report on audit of the Panama Canal Company and the Canal Zone Government for the fiscal year ended June 30, 1953, by the comptroller-general of the United States (1954)

United States, Panama Canal, *Annual report* [of the governor of the Panama Canal for the fiscal years 1950 and 1951] (1950–1)

United States, Panama Canal Company/Canal Zone Government, *Annual report* [for the fiscal years, 1952 to 1979 inclusive] (1952–79)

United States Code, *Congressional and administrative news: 96th Congress, 1st session, 1979*, vol. 2, *Legislative history of the Panama Canal Act of 27 September 1979* (1980)

'United States defense rights in the Panama Canal', *Brooklyn Journal of International Law*, 16 (1990), 647–74

United States statutes at large, *Public Law 81–841 of 26 September 1950: An act to authorize and provide for the maintenance and operation of the Panama Canal by the present corporate adjunct of the Panama Canal, as renamed; to reconstitute the agency charged with the civil government of the Canal Zone, and for other purposes*, 64 (1950), 1032–7

Public Law 96–70 of 27 September 1979: The Panama Canal Act of 1979, 93 (1979), 452–500

Van Alstyne, Richard, 'The Panama Canal: A classical case of an imperial hangover', *Journal of Contemporary History*, 15 (1980), 299–316

Vance, Cyrus, *Hard choices: Four critical years in managing America's foreign policy* (New York, 1983)

Vaughn, Jack Hood, 'A Latin-American Vietnam', *Washington Monthly*, October 1973, 30–4

1987–1989

Arias Calderón, Ricardo, 'Panama: Disaster or democracy?' *Foreign Affairs*, 66 (1987–8), 328–47

Berman, A., 'In mitigation of illegality: The United States invasion of Panama', *Kentucky Law Journal*, 79 (1990–1), 735–800

D'Amato, Anthony, 'The invasion of Panama was a lawful response to tyranny', *American Journal of International Law*, 84 (1990), 516–24

Dinges, John, *Our man in Panama* (New York, 1990)

Farer, Tom, 'Panama: Beyond the Charter paradigm', *American Journal of International Law*, 84 (1990), 503–15

Henkin, Louis, 'The invasion of Panama under international law: A gross violation', *Columbia Journal of Transnational Law*, 29 (1991), 293–317

Independent Commission of Inquiry on the U.S. Invasion of Panama, *The U.S. invasion of Panama: The truth behind Operation 'Just Cause'* (Boston, 1991)

James, Joy, 'US policy in Panama', *Race and Class*, 32 (1990), 17–32

Kempe, Frederick, *Divorcing the dictator: America's bungled affair with Noriega* (New York, 1990)

Lombard, Joseph, 'The survival of Noriega: Lessons from the U.S. sanctions against Panama', *Stanford Journal of International Law*, 26 (1989), 269–323

Maechling, Charles, 'Washington's illegal invasion', *Foreign Policy*, no. 79 (Summer 1990), 113–31

Miller, Jennifer, 'International intervention – The United States invasion of Panama', *Harvard International Law Journal*, 31 (1990), 633–46

Millett, Richard, 'The aftermath of intervention: Panama 1990', *Journal of Inter-American Studies and World Affairs*, 32 (1990), 1–15

'Looking beyond Noriega', *Foreign Policy*, no. 71 (Summer 1988), 46–63

Moss, Ambler, 'A policy dilemma: The future of United States interests in Panama' [typescript of lecture delivered in October 1988 at Bridgewater College]

Nanda, Ved, 'The validity of United States intervention in Panama', *American Journal of International Law*, 84 (1990), 494–503

Public papers of the presidents of the United States: George Bush: 1989, vol. 2 (Washington, D.C., 1990)

Quigley, John, 'The legality of the United States invasion of Panama', *Yale Journal of International Law*, 15 (1990), 276–315

Scranton, Margaret, *The Noriega years: US–Panamanian relations, 1981–1990* (Little Rock, Ark., 1991)

Sherman, Mark, 'An inquiry regarding the international and domestic legal problems presented in *United States* v. *Noriega*', *University of Miami Inter-American Law Review*, 20 (1989), 393–428

Sofaer, Abraham, 'The legality of the United States action in Panama', *Columbia Journal of Transnational Law*, 29 (1991), 281–92

Terry, J. P., 'The Panama intervention: Law in support of policy', *Naval Law Review*, 39 (1990), 5–13

United States, Congress, House of Representatives, Committee on Foreign Affairs, Subcommittee on Western Hemisphere Affairs, *The political situation in Panama and options for U.S. policy: Hearing*, 100th Cong., 2d sess. (1988)

Watson, Bruce, and Tsouras, Peter (eds.), *Operation JUST CAUSE: The U.S. intervention in Panama* (Boulder, Colo., 1991)

Wedgwood, Ruth, 'The use of armed force in international affairs: Self-defense and the Panama invasion', *Columbia Journal of Transnational Law*, 29 (1991), 609–28

Weeks, John, 'Panama: The roots of current political instability', *Third World Quarterly*, 9 (1987), 763–87

Weeks, John, and Gunson, Phil, *Panama: Made in the USA* (London, 1991)

Zimbalist, Andrew, 'The failure of intervention in Panama: Humiliation in the back yard', *Third World Quarterly*, 11 (1989), 1–27

Zimbalist, Andrew, and Weeks, John, *Panama at the Crossroads: Economic development and political change in the twentieth century* (Berkeley, Calif., 1991)

Index

Index

Commissary, 5, 86, 101–7, 110, 112, 230–1, 236–9, 243, 245–6, 248; 'Dingley Tariff', 98, 101; entrepôt, Canal Zone as, 104–5, 107; luxuries, sale of, 102, 112, 230–1; manufacturing in Canal Zone, 238, 243, 245; 'necessary and convenient' imports, 97–8, 100–1, 232, 243; Panama and, 97–115, 230–49; post exchanges, U.S. Army, 239–40, 243, 246, 248; Prohibition, 108, 231, 233; ships, sales to, 104, 106, 110, 230–2, 234–5, 237, 240, 245, 248; smuggling from Canal Zone to Panama, 102, 113, 231, 239–40; 'Taft Agreement' of 1904, 100–2, 104–5, 106–11, 114; tariffs, 97–101
Commissary, see commercial policy in Canal Zone, Commissary
Company-Government, see Panama Canal Company-Canal Zone Government
Concha, José Vicente, 28–30, 35
Constantinople convention of 1888, 25–6, 155, 362, 364, 375
control of canal, U.S., 4, 19–22, 24–7, 29, 33, 43–4, 49, 63, 361–2, 364, 369–70, 373, 375, 377
construction of canal, see Panama canal (waterway), construction of
convention of 1849, U.S.-Nicaragua, 14, 361
convention of 1850, U.S.-U.K.; 14–16, 21, 25–6, 29, 36, 155, 361
convention of 1900, U.S.-U.K., 25–6, 155–6
convention of 1903, U.S.-Colombia, 27–34, 37, 42–6, 49–50, 60, 97–8
convention of 1903, U.S.-Panama (see also revision of 1903 convention): abrogation of, 5, 339; cited in period 1956–79, 330, 335–6, 339–40; and commercial policy in Canal Zone, 98–101, 106–7, 109, 111–12, 114, 230, 233, 236, 243, 245–7; and defence of canal, 157, 160, 162, 164–5, 182, 184, 285–6, 291, 317; framing of, 42–51; and mandate concept, 362, 367, 373–5; and Panama, 117, 119, 122, 124–5, 132, 134, 136, 142, 251, 255
Crittenberger, Willis, 195, 310–11, 314–15, 317–21
Cromwell, William Nelson: and events of 1902–3, 27–32, 37–8; as fiscal agent of Panama, 133–4, 258–9, 279
Cronkhite, Adalbert, 169
Cuba (see also Guantánamo), 4, 13, 25, 54–5, 62, 116, 119, 121, 123, 130–1, 133, 150, 157, 190, 233–4, 266, 331
Culebra Cut, see Panama canal (waterway) Gaillard Cut
Cullom, Shelby, 31–2, 35, 56

Daniels, Jonathan, 214–17
Daniels, Josephus, 73, 162, 168, 174, 179
Davis, George, 58, 68–9, 80–2, 99, 101, 117–18, 157, 332
Davis, Roy Tasco, 205, 251–3, 255
Davis, Roy Tasco, Jr., 46
Dawson, William, 165–6, 262–6, 295, 300
DeConcini, Dennis, 351–3
defence of canal (see also Army, U.S.; Canal Zone (administration); Navy, U.S.; State Department, U.S.): agreement on defence sites of 1942, 262, 267, 299–301, 304–6, 310–12, 320; agreement on defence sites of 1947, 241–2, 310–12, 316–22; air attack, 170, 181, 189–90, 280–1, 284, 294, 302, 307; air defence, 173, 175–6, 181–2, 189–90, 280–1, 293–6, 298–9, 302–4, 310–11, 322; aliens, internment of, 172–3, 267, 298, 304; Atlantic approaches, 156–7, 162, 168, 294–5, 299, 301–2, 362; atomic bomb, 309–10, 313–15, 325, 334; bases, see Albrook Field, Cocos Island, Coco Solo, France Field, Galápagos Islands, Guantánamo, Guatemala City, Howard Field, Puerto Rico, Rio Hato, Trinidad; blockade, 155–6, 174; Brazil, 174; bridges, 183–4, Canal Zone, inadequacy of, 170, 186, 281, 295, 299, 308; closure of canal, 14, 18–22, 25–6, 302; Colombia and, 18, 28–9, 32, 44; 'Destroyers for Bases' agreement of 1940, 299, 301, 322; fortification, 14, 21–2, 25–6, 44, 155–8, 164, 188; Gatún dam, 166, 174, 176, 182, 190, 304; harbours, 174–5, 298; hydroplanes, 169–70, 176; jungle, 158–60, 171–2; land acquisition in Panama, 5, 170–1, 184, 281, 285–7, 290, 295–6, 299–301, 304–6, 340–1; long-range defence, 162, 177, 181, 190, 281, 294, 298–9, 303–4, 310–11; naval bombardment, 157, 164, 169, 180, 188; neutralisation, 155–8, 188, 363; neutrality, U.S. guarantee of, 11–12, 14, 18–19, 167–8, 170, 254, 346–7, 349–53, 377; overflights, 170, 182–3, 288, 307–8, 341–2; Pacific approaches, 158–9, 162–3, 168–9, 173–4, 177, 180, 281, 294, 298–9, 303–4, 362; Panama and, 136–7, 161, 170, 185–6, 285–9, 290–2, 339, 342, 346; radar, 299, 304, 329; raid, contingency of, 158; railways and 5, 165–7; roads and, 5, 171–2, 183, 260; sabotage, 156, 159, 172–3, 193, 282, 292–3, 296–7, 302, 322, 351, 354; sea-level canal project, 47, 163, 188–9, 284, 306–7, 312–16, 319, 323, 332–4, 336–9, 341–3, 348, 376;